Accountancy in Transition

Edited by Richard P. Brief, NEW YORK UNIVERSITY

A GARLAND SERIES

United States of America Before the Securities and Exchange Commission in the Matter of McKesson & Robbins, Inc.

Report on Investigation

Garland Publishing, Inc.
New York & London 1982

This facsimile has been made from a copy in the Yale University Library.

Library of Congress Cataloging in Publication Data

Main entry under title:

United States of America before the Securities and Exchange Commission in the matter of McKesson & Robbins, Inc.

(Accountancy in transition)

Reprint. Originally published: Washington : U.S. G.P.O., 1940.

1. McKesson and Robbins, inc. 2. Corporations—United States—Auditing—Case studies. I. United States. Securities and Exchange Commission. II. Series.

HD9666.9.M25U67 1982 364.1′63 82-48373

ISBN 0-8240-5330-3

The volumes in this series are printed on acid-free, 250-year-life paper.

Printed in the United States of America

UNITED STATES OF AMERICA

BEFORE THE

SECURITIES AND EXCHANGE COMMISSION

IN THE MATTER OF

McKESSON & ROBBINS, INC.

Pursuant to Section 21(a) of the
Securities Exchange Act of 1934

*

Report on Investigation

UNITED STATES
GOVERNMENT PRINTING OFFICE
WASHINGTON : 1940

For sale by the Superintendent of Documents, Washington, D. C. - - - - - - - - Price 60 cents

COMMISSIONERS

Jerome N. Frank, *Chairman*
Robert E. Healy
Edward C. Eicher
Leon Henderson
Sumner T. Pike
Francis P. Brassor, *Secretary*

George C. Mathews
Resigned April 15, 1940
William O. Douglas
Resigned April 16, 1939

FOREWORD

This is a report of the Securities and Exchange Commission based upon the Commission's order of December 29, 1938 which is reproduced herein as Appendix C. Public hearings held thereunder began on January 5, 1939 and ended on April 25, 1939, and were conducted for the Commission by Irving J. Galpeer of the New York Regional Office and William W. Werntz, Chief Accountant, before Adrian C. Humphreys, Trial Examiner.

The following counsel represented witnesses in these proceedings and were afforded an opportunity to examine all witnesses called by the Commission as well as to call their own witnesses:

Cravath, de Gersdorff, Swaine & Wood, by A. I. Henderson, Samuel B. Stewart, Jr., and Robert D. Blasier, for Price, Waterhouse & Co.;

Hodges, Reavis, Pantaleoni & Downey, by C. Frank Reavis, Francis Downey, and Martin D. Jacobs, for Joseph L. Bedsole, George V. Doerr, Henry D. Faxon, Charles F. Michaels, William J. Murray, Jr., and Julian F. Thompson;

Rand & French, by Robert C. Rand, for John H. McGloon;

Sullivan & Cromwell, by Edward H. Green and R. L. Lingelbach, for Wilbur L. Cummings, Richard G. Pettingill, and Sidney J. Weinberg; and

Winthrop, Stimson, Putnam & Roberts, by Hamilton Hadley, for William J. Wardall, Trustee of the Estate of McKesson & Robbins, Incorporated, Debtor, in connection with the appearance of Nicholas J. Mertens and Arthur Seal of S. D. Leidesdorf & Co., accountants for the Trustee.

Copies of the draft of this report were submitted to Price, Waterhouse & Co. and their counsel, and their criticism and brief thereon were considered by the Commission before issuing this report. In this, as well as in the Commission's supervision of the preparation of this report, the present Commissioners had the assistance of Commissioner Mathews whose resignation did not take effect until practically all of the substantive work on the report had been completed.

The draft of this report was prepared for the Commission under the active direction of the Chief Accountant, William W. Werntz, by Andrew Barr, Research Accountant, and Irving J. Galpeer, Senior Attorney. Important assistance was rendered by Earle C. King,

Assistant Chief Accountant; Robert F. Graham, Research Accountant; Richard J. Cornell, Accountant-Investigator; and Henry G. Fischer, of the Legal Division.

The investigation pursuant to the Commission's order of December 6, 1938, which resulted in securing the criminal indictments against the Musica brothers referred to in the report and which led up to and furnished valuable information for the auditing investigation reported in this volume, was conducted under the active direction of James J. Caffrey, Regional Administrator in charge of our New York office, and Robert E. Kline, Jr., Assistant General Counsel, by H. J. Dowd, former Chief Accountant-Investigator, and Irving J. Galpeer, Senior Attorney. Important parts of this investigation were carried out and assistance in the auditing hearings was rendered by numerous members of the New York Regional Office, among whom, principally, were John H. Kelly, Assistant General Counsel; Richard J. Cornell, Frederic H. Curran, James E. Cochran, Charles C. Ferrall, and John Shaw of the Investigation Division; and Sydney I. Harris, E. Allen MacDuffie, William J. Cogan, John Knox, and Philip Wagner of the Legal Division.

TABLE OF CONTENTS

Section I

Section II

Section III

Section IV

Section V

Appendix A

Appendix B

Appendix C

Appendix D

Appendix E

Section I

SUMMARY OF FINDINGS AND CONCLUSIONS

This is a report on a proceeding pursuant to our order of December 29, 1938 under Section 21 (a) of the Securities Exchange Act of 1934. The order was based upon evidence that the information set forth in the registration statement and annual reports of McKesson & Robbins, Incorporated, especially the financial statements and schedules included therein which were prepared and certified by Price, Waterhouse & Co., was materially false and misleading. We stated our purpose to be to determine:

(1) the character, detail and scope of the audit procedure followed by Price, Waterhouse & Co. in the preparation of the financial statements included in the said registration statement and reports;

(2) the extent to which prevailing and generally accepted standards and requirements of audit procedure were adhered to and applied by Price, Waterhouse & Co. in the preparation of the said financial statements; and

(3) the adequacy of the safeguards inhering in the said generally accepted practices and principles of audit procedure to assure reliability and accuracy of financial statements.

As directed, hearings commenced on January 5, 1939 and continued, with some necessary adjournments, through April 25, 1939. Throughout the hearings Price, Waterhouse & Co. were represented by counsel, as were all witnesses who desired counsel. Opportunity was accorded such counsel to examine witnesses called by the Commission and to call their own witnesses. In all, 46 witnesses were examined. Of these, 9 were partners and employees of Price, Waterhouse & Co.; 12 were accountants of other firms called to testify as experts; 1 represented the Controllers Institute of America and 1 the American Institute of Consulting Engineers; 2 were from S. D. Leidesdorf & Co., accountants for the Trustee of McKesson & Robbins; 1 was a person who prepared many of the fictitious documents; 8 were employees of McKesson & Robbins; 11 were McKesson directors; and the last was a Commission investigator, who was called to identify certain documents. Throughout, Price, Waterhouse & Co., the witnesses, and their counsel extended the fullest cooperation in facilitating the conduct of the proceedings. The record of the public hearings is contained in 4587 pages of testimony and 285 exhibits comprising in excess of 3000 pages.[1]

This report based upon the testimony and the exhibits and our study of recognized authoritative works on auditing consists of five sections in the text and five appendices as follows:

Section I. A summary of our findings and conclusions;

Section II. A brief statement reciting the manner in which the fraud came to the attention of the public and this Commission;

Section III. A description of the manner in which the manipulation of the accounts of McKesson & Robbins was carried out by Coster-Musica and his associates;

Section IV. A description of the audit conducted by Price, Waterhouse & Co.;

Section V. Our conclusions as to the Price, Waterhouse & Co. audit of McKesson & Robbins, Incorporated, and as to the adequacy of the safeguards inhering in generally accepted auditing practices;

Appendix A. A brief summary of action taken subsequent to the discovery of the fraud by accounting organizations and others interested in the work of independent public accountants;

Appendix B. A comparison of those sections of the English Companies Act of 1929 dealing with appointment of auditors and Horace B. Samuel's suggested amendments to those sections of that Act;

Appendix C. Our order for public hearings in this matter;

Appendix D. A list of all witnesses who testified, with the page numbers of their testimony;

Appendix E. A description of all exhibits introduced in the hearings.

---

[1] A list of all witnesses who testified, with the page numbers of their testimony, is appended to this report. The testimony of the accountants called as experts and statements by representatives of the Controllers Institute of America and the American Institute of Consulting Engineers have been printed and may be obtained from the Superintendent of Documents, United States Government Printing Office, Washington, D. C. (*In the Matter of McKesson & Robbins, Inc.*, Testimony of Expert Witnesses, Price 65 cents.) The remaining testimony, in mimeographed form, is available for public inspection at the Washington, New York, and Chicago Offices of the Commission. Transcripts of any portion thereof may be obtained from Smith & Hulse, Official Reporters, 1742 K Street, N. W., Washington, D. C., at 35 cents per page.

A list of all exhibits introduced in the hearings is also appended to this report. Photocopies of any of the exhibits may be obtained from the Securities and Exchange Commission, 1778 Pennsylvania Avenue, Washington, D. C. at the following rates per photocopy, whether several copies of a single original page or one or more copies of several original pages are ordered: 10 cents per photocopy of each page, for all copies up to and including 100 pages in a single order; 7 cents per photocopy of each page, for all copies over 100 in a single order.

In this report references to the testimony and exhibits will be abbreviated as follows: R. *followed by a numeral refers to pages of testimony in mimeographed form;* P. *followed by a numeral refers to pages of testimony in printed form;* Ex. *followed by a numeral refers to a Commission exhibit; and* Ex. *followed by a letter refers to a Price, Waterhouse & Co. exhibit.* ***Printed reproductions of exhibits or parts of exhibits follow the copy as exactly as type limitations permit, including reproduction of errors without indication of where these occur.***

A. SUMMARY OF PRINCIPAL FACTS

The securities of McKesson & Robbins, Incorporated (Maryland) were listed and traded on the New York Stock Exchange and registered under the Securities Exchange Act of 1934. Financial statements of the Corporation and its subsidiaries for the year ended December 31, 1937 (the last before the disclosure of the fraud hereinafter described) certified by Price, Waterhouse & Co., filed with this Commission and the New York Stock Exchange, and issued to stockholders reported total consolidated assets in excess of $87,000,000. Approximately $19,000,000 of these assets are now known to have been entirely fictitious. The fictitious items consisted of inventories, $10,000,000; accounts receivable, $9,000,000; and cash in bank, $75,000; and arose out of the operation at the Bridgeport offices of a wholly fictitious foreign crude drug business shown on the books of the Connecticut Division of McKesson & Robbins, Incorporated (Maryland) and McKesson & Robbins, Limited (Canada), one of its subsidiaries. For the year 1937, fictitious sales in these units amounted to $18,247,020.60 on which fictitious gross profit of $1,801,390.60 was recorded. At the time of the exposure of the fraud on or about December 5, 1938 the fictitious assets had increased to approximately $21,000,000.

The fraud was engineered by Frank Donald Coster, president of McKesson & Robbins since its merger with Girard & Co., Inc. in November 1926. In reality Coster was Philip M. Musica who, under the latter name, had been convicted of commercial frauds. In carrying out the fraud Coster, in the later years, was assisted principally by his three brothers: George E. Dietrich, assistant treasurer of the Corporation, who was in reality George Musica; Robert J Dietrich, head of the shipping, receiving, and warehousing department of McKesson & Robbins at Bridgeport, Connecticut, who was in reality Robert Musica; and George Vernard, who was in reality Arthur Musica and who managed the offices, mailing addresses, bank accounts and other activities of the dummy concerns with whom the McKesson Companies supposedly conducted the fictitious business.

To accomplish the deception, purchases were pretended to have been made by the McKesson Companies from five Canadian vendors, who thereafter purportedly retained the merchandise at their warehouses for the account of McKesson. Sales were pretended to have been made for McKesson's account by W. W. Smith & Company, Inc. and the goods shipped directly by the latter from the Canadian vendors to the customers. Payments for goods purchased and collections from customers for goods sold were pretended to have been made by the Montreal banking firm of Manning & Company also for the account of McKesson. W. W. Smith & Company, Inc.,

Manning & Company, and the five Canadian vendors are now known to have been either entirely fictitious or merely blinds used by Coster for the purpose of supporting the fictitious transactions.

Invoices, advices, and other documents prepared on printed forms in the names of these firms were used to give an appearance of reality to the fictitious transactions. In addition to this manufacture of documents, a series of contracts and guaranties with Smith and Manning and forged credit reports on Smith were also utilized. The foreign firms to whom the goods were supposed to have been sold were real but had done no business of the type indicated with McKesson.

The fictitious transactions originated early in the life of Girard & Co., Inc., Coster's predecessor concern, incorporated on January 31, 1923 and increased until they reached the proportions mentioned above. The manner of handling the transactions described above was the one in vogue since the middle of 1935. Prior to that time the fictitious goods were supposed to have been physically received at and reshipped from the Bridgeport plant of McKesson. And prior to 1931 McKesson made actual cash payments directly for the fictitious purchases, which at that time were supposed to have been made from a group of domestic vendors, but recovered a large part of this cash purportedly as collections on the fictitious sales. The change from using actual cash to the supposed clearance through Manning & Company was not effected abruptly but for some time after 1931 both systems were used. The Canadian vendors, however, were used only in connection with the Manning clearance system. From the report of the accountant for the Trustee in reorganization of McKesson & Robbins, Incorporated, it appears that out of an actual cash outgo from the McKesson Companies in connection with these fictitious transactions of $24,777,851.90 all but $2,869,482.95 came back to the McKesson Companies in collection of fictitious receivables or as cash transfers from the pretended bank of Manning & Company.

B. SUMMARY OF CONCLUSIONS AS TO INDIVIDUAL AUDITING PROCEDURES

Our conclusions as to the individual auditing procedures are developed in detail in section V of our report. The full discussion of each topic should be consulted for the basis and complete statement of the conclusions which we here summarize.

1. Appointment and Responsibility of Auditors; Determination of the Scope of the Engagement

All appointments of Price, Waterhouse & Co. as auditors for Girard & Co., Inc. and the successor McKesson Companies were made by letter from Coster or the comptroller, McGloon, near the close of the year to be audited. The testimony of the directors is that with rare exceptions members of the board had no part in arranging for the audit and did not know the content either of the letters of engagement or of the long form report addressed to Coster, in which the character of the work was set forth.

While the appointment of Price, Waterhouse & Co. and the method of determining the scope of the engagement in this case was in accord with generally accepted practice, we do not feel that it insures to the auditor, in all cases, that degree of independence which we deem necessary for the protection of investors. Adoption of the following program, we feel, would aid materially in correcting present conditions:

1. Election of the auditors for the current year by a vote of the stockholders at the annual meeting followed immediately by notice to the auditors of their appointment.

2. Establishment of a committee to be selected from non-officer members of the board of directors which shall make all company or management nominations of auditors and shall be charged with the duty of arranging the details of the engagement.

3. The certificate (sometimes called short-form report or opinion) should be addressed to the stockholders. All other reports should be addressed to the board of directors, and copies delivered by the auditors to each member of the board.

4. The auditors should be required to attend meetings of the stockholders at which their report is presented to answer questions thereon, to state whether or not they have been given all the information and access to all the books and records which they have required, and to have the right to make any statement or explanation they desire with respect to the accounts.

5. If for any reason the auditors do not complete the engagement and render a report thereon, they shall, nevertheless, render a report on the amount of work they have done and the reasons for noncompletion, which report should be sent by the company to all stockholders.

In approaching his work with respect to companies which file with us or in which there is a large public interest, the auditor must realize that, regardless of what his position and obligations might have been when reporting to managers or to owner-managers, he must now recognize fully his responsibility to public investors by including the activities of the management itself within the scope of his work and by reporting thereon to investors. The adoption of a program such as that outlined above should serve to secure recognition of these newly emphasized obligations of the auditor to public investors.

2. Organization and Training of Staff

We have found that there is great similarity among accounting firms in the organization of the staff and assignments to engagements. We deplore, as do accounting firms, the necessity for recruiting large numbers of temporary employees during a very short busy season. This condition and the lack of training in the firm's methods which it ordinarily entails are inimical to attaining the best results from the auditors' services. A major improvement in this condition could be made by the general adoption by corporations of the natural business year for accounting purposes. The recruiting of temporary employees was more aggravated in Price, Waterhouse & Co. than in other comparable firms whose representatives testified as experts. This situation, coupled with the fact that Price, Waterhouse & Co. had a higher ratio of both permanent and peak staff per partner than other firms, leads us to the conclusion that Price, Waterhouse & Co. partners could not have given adequate attention to the training, development, and supervision of their staff.

3. Investigation of New Clients

The facts of this case suggest that for new and unknown clients some independent investigation should be made of the company and of its principal officers prior to undertaking the work. Such an inquiry should provide a valuable background for interpreting conditions revealed during the audit or, in extreme cases, might lead to a refusal of the engagement.

4. Review of the Client's System of Internal Check and Control

We are convinced by the record that the review of the system of internal check and control at the Bridgeport offices of McKesson & Robbins was carried out in an unsatisfactory manner. The testimony of the experts leads us to the further conclusion that this vital and basic problem of all audits for the purpose of certifying financial statements has been treated in entirely too casual a manner by many accountants. Since in examinations of financial statements of corporations whose securities are publicly owned the procedures of testing and sampling are employed in most cases, it appears to us that the necessity for a comprehensive knowledge of the client's system of internal check and control cannot be overemphasized.

5. Cash

The record is clear that the cash work performed on this engagement by Price, Waterhouse & Co. conformed in scope to the then generally accepted standards of the profession. It is equally clear to us that prior to this case many independent public accountants depended entirely too much upon the verification of cash as the basis for the whole auditing program and hence as underlying proof of the authenticity of all transactions. Where, as here, during the final three years of the audit, physical contact with the operations of a major portion of the business was limited to examination of supposed documentary evidence of transactions carried on completely offstage through agents unknown to the auditors save in connection with the one engagement, it appears to us that the reliability of these agents must be established by completely independent methods. Confirmation of the bank balance under these circumstances was proven in this case to be an inadequate basis for concluding that all the transactions were authentic.

6. Accounts Receivable

Viewed as a whole the audit program for accounts receivable as used by Price, Waterhouse & Co. conformed to then generally accepted procedures for an examination of financial statements although confirmation of the accounts was not included in the program. The facts of this case, however, demonstrate the utility of circularization and the wisdom of the profession in subsequently adopting confirmation of accounts and notes receivable as a required procedure "* * * wherever practicable and reasonable, and where the aggregate amount of notes and accounts receivable represents a significant proportion of the current assets or of the total assets of a concern * * *"

7. Intercompany Accounts

The record indicates that it is not enough for auditors to reconcile intercompany balances and that valuable insight into the company's manner of doing business may be gained by a review of the transactions passed through such accounts during the year. Best practice we believe requires the latter procedure. In this case the recommended procedure, although employed to some extent, was not applied in a thoroughgoing and penetrating manner.

8. Inventories

Price, Waterhouse & Co.'s audit program for the verification of inventories was essentially that which was prescribed by generally accepted auditing practice for the period. However, we find that a substantial difference of opinion existed among accountants during this time as to the extent of the auditors' duties and responsibilities in connection with physical verification of quantities, quality, and condition. Price, Waterhouse & Co., in common with a substantial portion of the profession, took the position that the verification of quantities, quality, and condition of inventories should be confined to the records. There was, however, a substantial body of equally authoritative opinion which supported the view, which we endorse, that auditors should gain physical contact with the inventory either by test counts, by observation of the inventory taking, or by a combination of these methods. Meticulous verification of the inventory was not needed in this case to discover the fraud. We are not satisfied, therefore, that even under Price, Waterhouse & Co.'s views other accountants would condone their failure to make inquiries of the employees who actually took the inventory and to determine by inspection whether there was an inventory as represented by the client. We commend the action of the profession in subsequently adopting, as normal, procedures requiring physical contact with clients' inventories.

9. Other Balance Sheet Accounts

a. The testimony in respect to the auditing of plant accounts suggests that some accountants, including Price, Waterhouse & Co., could, with advantage, devote more attention to physical inspection than has been general practice with them in the past.

b. The work in respect to liabilities was in accord with generally accepted practice but suggests the desirability of independent inquiry when large purchases are made from a very few otherwise unknown suppliers.

c. The record demonstrates the necessity of a thorough understanding of the client's tax situation which apparently was not obtained by Price, Waterhouse & Co. in regard to the application of the Canadian law.

10. Profit and Loss Accounts

We are of the opinion that such analyses of profit and loss accounts as were made were applied to improper combinations of departments with the result that significant relationships were concealed. It is our conclusion that the independent accountant is derelict in his duty if he does not insist upon having proper analyses available for his review. It is our opinion that best practice supports this view.

11. The Wholesale Houses

It must be emphasized again that although the bulk of this report deals with the two units in which the fraud occurred, which were under the direct charge of the Company's principal officer, some material bearing on the work in the other units, mostly wholesale houses, was introduced at the hearings. As to this portion of the audit, which constituted the larger part of the Price, Waterhouse & Co. engagement, covering for 1937 approximately 70% of the reported assets and 85% of the net sales, and which occupied approximately 97% of the auditors' time, it appears that the work in these other units was carried out in a thorough fashion in accordance with generally accepted auditing practice prevailing during the periods involved, including limited inspections of inventories but no confirmation of accounts and notes receivable.

12. Review Procedure

The mechanics of the review procedure as carried out by Price, Waterhouse & Co. on this engagement were substantially the same as those of the majority of accounting firms. However, it is our opinion that the partner in charge in this case was not sufficiently familiar with the business practices of the industry in question and was not sufficiently concerned with the basic problems of internal check and control to make the searching review which an engagement requires

13. The Certificate

The form of certificate used by Price, Waterhouse & Co. conformed to generally accepted practice during the period of the Girard-McKesson engagement. We are of the opinion that the form of the accountant's certificate should be amended to include in addition to the description of the scope of the audit a clear certification that the audit performed was, or was not, adequate for the purpose of expressing an independent opinion in respect to the financial statements. If any generally accepted procedures are omitted these should be named together with the reasons for their omission. Exceptions to the scope of the audit or to the accounts must be clearly designated as "exceptions".

14. Circumstances Available for the Auditors' Observation in the Procedures and Records of the Girard-McKesson Companies Which Might Have Led to the Discovery of the Fraud

The firm of Price, Waterhouse & Co. for fourteen years served as independent public accountants for F. Donald Coster's enterprises. Within range of the procedures which they followed there were numerous circumstances which, if they had been recognized and carefully investigated by resourceful auditors, should have revealed the gross inflation in the accounts.

We can not and do not say that every one of the items should have been recognized by the auditors as significant and, if investigated, would have led to the exposure of the gross falsification of the financial statements. It is also quite conceivable that for a time many could have been and perhaps were explained away. We do believe, however, that the number of items and the period of time over which some of them repeated themselves gave ample opportunity for detection by alert and inquisitive auditors.

C. CONCLUSION

In conclusion we reproduce the summary from the last section of our report:

"Our conclusion based upon the facts revealed by the record, the testimony of the expert witnesses, and the writings of recognized authorities is that the audits performed by Price, Waterhouse & Co. substantially conformed, in form, as to the scope and procedures employed, to what was generally considered mandatory during the period of the Girard-McKesson engagements. Their failure to discover the gross overstatement of assets and of earnings is attributable to the manner in which the audit work was done. In carrying out the work they failed to employ that degree of vigilance, inquisitiveness, and analysis of the evidence available that is necessary in a professional undertaking and is recommended in all well-known and authoritative works on auditing. In addition, the overstatement should have been disclosed if the auditors had corroborated the Company's records by actual observation and independent confirmation through procedures involving regular inspection of inventories and confirmation of accounts receivable, audit steps which, although considered better practice and used by many accountants, were not considered mandatory by the profession prior to our hearings.

"Price, Waterhouse & Co. maintain that a balance sheet examination is not intended and cannot be expected to detect a falsification of records concealing an inflation of assets and of earnings if accomplished by a widespread conspiracy carried on by the president of a corporation, aided by others within and without the recognized ranks of a corporation's operating personnel, and that no practical system of internal check can be devised the effectiveness of which cannot be nullified by criminal collusion on the part of a chief executive and key employees. Such cases are so rare, in their opinion, that there is no economic justification for the amount of auditing work which would be required to increase materially the protection against it.

"The inference to be drawn from this position and from statements made by others in connection with this case is that a detailed audit of all transactions as distinguished from an examination based on tests and samples would have been necessary to reveal the falsification. However, as we view the situation in this case, a detailed audit of all transactions carried out by the same staff would merely have covered a larger volume of the same kinds of fictitious documents and transactions. While this might have brought under review more instances of what we have listed as circumstances suggesting further investigation, there is little ground for believing that this alone would have raised any greater question as to the authenticity of the transactions.

"Moreover, we believe that, even in balance sheet examinations for corporations whose securities are held by the public, accountants can be expected to detect gross overstatements of assets and profits whether resulting from collusive fraud or otherwise. We believe that alertness on the part of the entire staff, coupled with intelligent analysis by experienced accountants of the manner of doing business, should detect overstatements in the accounts, regardless of their cause, long before they assume the magnitude reached in this case. Furthermore, an examination of this kind should not, in our opinion, exclude the highest officers of the corporation from its appraisal of the manner in which the business under review is conducted. Without underestimating the important service rendered by independent public accountants in their review of the accounting principles employed in the preparation of financial statements filed with us and issued to stockholders, we feel that the discovery of gross overstatements in the accounts is a major purpose of such an audit even though it be conceded that it might not disclose every minor defalcation. In short, Price, Waterhouse & Co.'s failure to uncover the gross overstatement of assets and of earnings in this case should not, in our opinion, lead to general condemnation of recognized procedures for the examination of financial statements by means of tests and samples.

"We do feel, however, that there should be a material advance in the development of auditing procedures whereby the facts disclosed by the records and documents of the firm being examined are to a greater extent checked by the auditors through physical inspection or independent confirmation. The time has long passed, if it ever existed, when the basis of an audit was restricted to the material appearing in the books and records. For many years accountants have in regularly applied procedures gone outside the records to establish the actual existence of assets and liabilities by physical inspection or independent confirmation. As pointed out repeatedly in this report, there are many ways in which this can be extended. Particularly, it is our opinion that auditing procedures relating to the inspection of inventories and confirmation of receivables, which, prior to our hearings, had been considered optional steps, should, in accordance with the resolutions already adopted by the various accounting societies, be accepted as normal auditing procedures in connection with the presentation of comprehensive and dependable financial statements to investors.

"We have carefully considered the desirability of specific rules and regulations governing the auditing steps to be performed by accountants in certifying financial statements to be filed with us. Action has already been taken by the accounting profession adopting certain of the auditing procedures considered in this case. We have no reason to believe at this time that these extensions will not be maintained or that further extensions of auditing procedures along the lines suggested in this report will not be made. Further, the adoption of the specific recommendations made in this report as to the type of disclosure to be made in the accountant's certificate and as to the election of accountants by stockholders should insure that acceptable standards of auditing procedure will be observed, that specific deviations therefrom may be considered in the particular instances in which they arise, and that accountants will be more independent of management. Until experience should prove the contrary, we feel that this program is preferable to its alternative—the detailed prescription of the scope of and procedures to be followed in the audit for the various types of issuers of securities who file statements with us—and will allow for further consideration of varying audit procedures and for the development of different treatment for specific types of issuers."

Section II

THE DISCLOSURE OF THE FRAUD

The first public intimation of the inflation in assets on the books and statements of McKesson & Robbins was contained in a complaint which sought the appointment of a receiver for the Corporation. The complaint was filed in the United States District Court at Hartford, Conn., on Monday afternoon, December 5, 1938, by Vincent W. Dennis, Corporation Counsel of that city, as a stockholder "* * * suing on behalf of himself and on behalf of all other stockholders of McKesson & Robbins, Incorporated * * *." It alleged merely that the Corporation "* * * through its officers and directors, for a long time prior to the date hereof had fraudulently represented its assets to be of a substantial character and in its statement to stockholders, security holders and to the general public has included in its inventory and accounts receivable, inventories which do not and have not existed and accounts receivable which do not and have not existed." The complaint further stated that the fictitious inventories and accounts receivable aggregated in excess of $10,000,000 and "* * * that the affairs of the defendant corporation have been and are now, by its officers and directors, being negligently and carelessly conducted and mismanaged * * * ."[2]

Immediately upon filing of this complaint, Judge Edwin S. Thomas appointed Thomas J. Spellacy, Mayor of Hartford, and Abram S. Weissman, a New Haven attorney, as Temporary Receivers for the Corporation.

It is interesting now to be able to trace the origin of this suit. The complaint as filed by Corporation Counsel Dennis, in addition to the allegations concerning the shortages in inventories and accounts receivable, stated that the complainant, a stockholder, held 2,000 shares of the common stock of McKesson & Robbins. Dennis first was told of the shortages and received the shares in question from Mayor Spellacy early Monday morning just before Spellacy presented the complaint to him for signature.[3]

Mayor Spellacy had obtained his information concerning the existence of shortages in inventories and accounts receivable and the 2,000 shares of stock on the preceding Saturday afternoon from

[2] *Dennis* v. *McKesson & Robbins, Incorporated,* U. S. D. C. Dist. of Conn. Civil Action No. 66.

[3] Before the Att'y. Gen'l. of the State of N. Y., *In the Matter of McKesson & Robbins, Inc.* Testimony of Vincent W. Dennis, January 4, 1939.

Benjamin Slade, a New Haven attorney, who said he represented an undisclosed officer of the company. In addition, Mayor Spellacy had his information concerning the existence of shortages corroborated by Judge Thomas during a conference in the Judge's chambers early Monday morning, where it was finally decided that application for receivership should be made. The selection of Corporation Counsel Dennis as the plaintiff in the action was not made by Mayor Spellacy until after this talk with Judge Thomas.[4]

It would appear that Judge Thomas had been advised previously of the existence of shortages by Abram S. Weissman. On Sunday, Weissman, whom the Judge thereafter appointed Co-receiver with Mayor Spellacy, consulted with the Judge about a conference he had had with George E. Dietrich, assistant treasurer of the Corporation.

The certificates for the 2,000 shares of common stock [5] given Mayor Spellacy by Benjamin Slade on Saturday afternoon had been delivered that same morning by a New York Stock Exchange firm from the account of Mrs. F. Donald Coster to Robert J. Dietrich, the head of the shipping, receiving, and warehousing department of McKesson at Bridgeport.[6]

Later it was disclosed that George E. Dietrich and Robert J. Dietrich were George and Robert Musica, respectively, brothers of Philip M. Musica, who was masquerading as F. Donald Coster, the head of the drug concern.[7]

The origin of the suit and relationship of the parties were, of course, not publicly known when news of the receivership reached New York City on Monday evening, December 5.

When informed of the receivership action, over the telephone, by Wilbur L. Cummings, who was a director of the Corporation as well as a partner of Sullivan & Cromwell, counsel for the Corporation, Sidney Weinberg, partner of Goldman Sachs & Co. and also a director of McKesson & Robbins, suggested an immediate meeting of the executive officers. Weinberg, who was, in addition, a governor of the New York Stock Exchange, where the McKesson securities were traded, reported at once what he knew to John M. Hancock, chairman of the Committee on Stock List, who happened to be attending a dinner at the Waldorf Astoria which Weinberg also was attending when he received Cummings' call.

---

[4] Before the Att'y. Gen'l. of the State of N. Y., *In the Matter of McKesson & Robbins, Inc.* Testimony of Thomas J. Spellacy, January 5, 1939.

[5] Registered in "street names."

[6] Ascertained by comparison of certificate numbers.

[7] For the sake of clarity, the brothers Musica will be referred to hereinafter under their assumed names which, in the order of their ages, are:

Frank Donald Coster	—Philip M. Musica
George Vernard	—Arthur Musica
George E. Dietrich	—George Musica
Robert J. Dietrich	—Robert Musica

A meeting at Weinberg's apartment that evening was attended by Charles F. Michaels, executive vice-president of the Corporation, William J. Murray, Jr., first vice-president of the Corporation, Julian F. Thompson, treasurer of the Corporation, Cummings and Weinberg. Except for Coster, who was not present, and aside from Thompson, who was not then a member, these men composed the Executive Committee of the Board of Directors of the Corporation. Weinberg described the meeting in part, as follows:

"* * * During one stage of the discussion at the meeting I suggested that as Price, Waterhouse & Company were the accountants for the company I thought this was an important and startling enough matter to get hold of Mr. May, the Senior Partner of the firm and have him come down, and they all agreed, and I did that. I called him up at his home in New York City and he came down immediately.

* * * * * * *

"None present knew why the Receivership had taken place, and it was agreed that I try to get Mr. Coster on the telephone at his home in Bridgeport, as they were not able to get him. I put in a call for him and, strange to those who had been trying to get him all afternoon, he got on immediately, and I said to him, 'This is a frightful thing that has happened. What is it all about?' He said, 'I know nothing about it. Here I am, living in Connecticut. Surely some one would have told me.' 'Well', I said to him, 'It is a very serious matter, and I think you ought to come down to New York immediately, tomorrow morning, and have a meeting with the Executive Committee', and he said, 'I have got to go to the Bridgeport office to get my mail, and I will come down, and I'll be there at 10 o'clock.'

"Mr. Thompson during the course of the evening outlined certain suspicions that he had as to what appeared to him to be fraudulent transactions in the crude drug department,[8] and after a long discussion, in which Mr. May agreed to come to the meeting the following morning at the Company's office with one of his partners and the man in charge of the work at McKesson & Robbins, we adjourned.

* * * * * * *

"Now the next morning we met informally, the Members of the Executive Committee of the Company met informally at the offices of the Company, hoping that Mr. Coster would be present, but as I got into the office he called me on the telephone and said that it was impossible for him to be there due to the fact that a Receiver of the Company had just shown up at the Bridgeport office and ordered him to stay there * * *."[9]

Meanwhile, at the opening of the market on Tuesday morning December 6, the New York Stock Exchange held up trading in McKesson securities. At the time there were listed on the Exchange $15,834,000 principal amount 20-year 5½% convertible debentures, due May 1, 1950; 605,964 shares preference stock $3 series, cumulative, convertible, no par value; and 1,282,983 shares common stock, $5 par value. At 11:30 a. m. the Board of Governors met and voted an indefinite suspension, emphasizing "* * * that they had ordered

[8] See pages 128 ff. *infra.*

[9] Before Committee on Stock List, New York Stock Exchange. Testimony of Sidney J. Weinberg, December 7, 1938.

the indefinite suspension, not because of things that they knew but because of things which they did not know."[10]

Later the same day Cummings called the then Chairman of the Securities and Exchange Commission, William O. Douglas, "* * * and told him we'd welcome an investigation * * *. They [the SEC] have much more power than the auditors or even Receivers, definitely, and I think it would considerably expedite clearing up the situation." [11]

It was at this point, and with this background, that the Securities and Exchange Commission instituted proceedings. Finding reasonable grounds to believe that the financial statements contained in the most recent annual report filed by McKesson & Robbins with the Commission and the New York Stock Exchange as required by Section 13 of the Securities Exchange Act of 1934 "* * * did not fairly present the financial position of the company and its subsidiaries as of the date of such statements, and were false and misleading with respect to various items whereby the assets of the company and its subsidiaries were made to appear substantially greater than was actually the fact * * *," the Commission, on Tuesday afternoon, entered an order for investigation.[12] Representatives were sent at once from the Commission's New York Regional Office to Fairfield, just outside of Bridgeport, Conn., where the head office and manufacturing plant of McKesson were located.

Wednesday and Thursday they interrogated officers and employees at the plant and examined the books and records and accounting system. Although it was impossible to track down all the ramifications in that short period, they reported a sufficient outline of the situation to impel the Commission on Friday morning, December 9, to refer the matter to the Department of Justice for necessary criminal proceedings.

Commission representatives then conferred with agents of the Department of Justice in Washington, with the result that about noon of the same day it was announced that the case would be con-

---

[10] New York Times, December 7, 1938. The securities (less $109,000 debentures held in treasury at December 31, 1938) were restored to trading at the opening of business, March 29, 1940.

" 'These securities still remain subject to the changes which will undoubtedly be made in the Company's financial and corporate structure as the result of the reorganization proceedings now pending. All that is being done at this time is to restore to McKesson security holders the broad national market which the New York Stock Exchange affords and which was lost to them through the automatic suspension by the Exchange of trading privileges when the Company's difficulties arose in December, 1938.

" 'This restoration of trading privileges has been dependent not only upon providing the S. E. C. with acceptable data as to current operations of the Company, but also upon correcting annual reports and registrations filed during the period of the Coster-Musica manipulations of the Company's financial affairs. This has taken time'. " New York Stock Exchange, Supplement to Listing Application, McKesson & Robbins, Incorporated, March 22, 1940, Exhibit A.

[11] Before Committee on Stock List, New York Stock Exchange. Testimony of Wilbur L. Cummings, December 7, 1938.

[12] Before the Securities and Exchange Commission, *In the Matter of McKesson & Robbins, Incorporated*, December 6, 1938.

sidered by a Federal Grand Jury under the direction of the United States Attorney's Office in New York.

In the interim the Executive Committee of McKesson & Robbins held a meeting (which Coster did not attend) at which it was decided that a petition be filed in the United States District Court for the Southern District of New York for permission to reorganize the corporation under Chapter X of the Chandler Act. On Thursday, December 8, Judge Alfred C. Coxe in New York approved the petition and appointed William J. Wardall and Charles F. Michaels as Trustees for the Corporation. On the same day, Judge Coxe signed an order allowing the Securities and Exchange Commission to intervene and take part in the reorganization proceeding. The Trustees appointed by Judge Coxe immediately took charge of the business superseding the Receivers previously appointed by Judge Thomas.[13]

Following the reference to the Department of Justice, the Commission broadened its criminal investigation. In addition to continuing its inquiries in and around Bridgeport and developing the parts played by Coster and the two Dietrichs in operating the fictitious foreign crude drug business at the plant, investigators from the New York Regional Office were sent to Brooklyn, N. Y., to check on George Vernard (later disclosed as Arthur Musica, the fourth brother) and the Brooklyn offices and bank accounts kept in the names of W. W. Smith & Co., W. W. Smith & Co., Ltd. and W. W. Smith & Company, Inc., pretended sales agencies, and Manning & Company, pretended Montreal bankers, which he handled in connection with the fictitious transactions. Investigators also were sent to Mt. Vernon, N. Y. to check Coster's antecedents and dealings in connection with his original firm of Girard & Co., Inc.; to Montreal, Canada, to check the Montreal offices and bank accounts kept in the names of Smith and Manning, and to check the Canadian concerns (disclosed as mere mailing addresses) which supposedly were warehousing the crude drugs in question; and to Stamford, Conn., where they located an abandoned office, which the Musicas had used as headquarters for preparing their fictitious documents. There a discarded piece of wrapping paper, addressed to George Vernard in Brooklyn, gave the clue to the location of the source of the printing of all the letterheads, statement forms, bill heads, and other stationery of Smith, Manning, and the Canadian vendors which had been used to report the fictitious transactions. In New York City investigation of the past history of Coster resulted in a Commission representative obtaining from a Brooklyn attorney an unwitting disclosure that F. Donald Coster was known to him as Philip Musica.

[13] *In the Matter of McKesson & Robbins, Incorporated*, Debtor, U. S. D. C. So. Dist. of N. Y. In proceedings for the reorganization of a corporation No. 72697.

In addition confirmation of the non-existence of the inventories and accounts receivable of the foreign crude drug business as recorded on the books of McKesson was speedily obtained, by cable and telephone, through the cooperation of Adolphe Routhier, Registrar, Securities Act, Province of Quebec, Canada; of Edouard Asselin, Deputy Attorney General for the Province of Quebec, Canada; of John E. Crankshaw, Crown Prosecutor at Montreal, Canada; and of the Commissioners of Police of the Metropolis and for the City of London, England.

As the results of this widespread investigation began to accumulate, evidence of criminal responsibility in connection with the false financial statements contained in the application for registration and annual reports filed by McKesson & Robbins, Incorporated, with this Commission and the New York Stock Exchange [14] became increasingly clear. On Tuesday, December 13, a complaint was sworn out by the Securities and Exchange Commission's Chief Accountant-Investigator for the arrest of F. Donald Coster, George E. Dietrich, and George Vernard on the charge of conspiring to violate Section 32 of the Securities Exchange Act of 1934.[15] The complaint was approved by the office of the United States Attorney, and Commissioner Garrett W. Cotter of the Southern District of New York issued orders for the arrest of the defendants.

The arrests of Coster and George Dietrich were made on the next day, Wednesday, December 14,[16] when for the first time Coster's picture and, more important, fingerprints were obtained. It was not until the next evening, however, that a copy of Philip Musica's fingerprints were finally located in the old files of the Sheriff Street Police Station in New York City and Inspector Joseph J. Donovan, in charge of the Bureau of Criminal Identification, was able to announce that the comparison proved that F. Donald Coster was Philip M. Musica, notorious swindler who had twice before pleaded guilty to commercial frauds. In 1909 he pleaded guilty to having bribed a customs official to mark down weights on cheese imports. And in 1913 he pleaded guilty to having committed grand larceny in connection with the affairs of the United States Hair Company, in which faked shipments and documents on human hair are estimated to have involved 22 banks in a loss of over $1,000,000. In the first case, Philip Musica was sentenced to 1 year in prison and fined $5,000, but in less than 6 months he received a Presidential pardon. In the

[14] The original application for registration on Form 10 was filed on May 21, 1935 and annual reports on Form 10-K for the fiscal years ending December 31, 1935, 1936, and 1937 were filed on June 29, 1936, May 19, 1937, and April 29, 1938, respectively, File No. 1-1435.

[15] "* * * any person who wilfully and knowingly makes, or causes to be made, any statement in any application, report, or document required to be filed under this title * * * which statement was false or misleading with respect to any material fact, shall upon conviction be fined not more than $10,000, or imprisoned not more than two years or both * * *"

[16] George Vernard was arrested on December 15.

second case, after the Musica family had been apprehended on a boat leaving New Orleans for Honduras (where they could have avoided extradition), Philip Musica took the entire blame upon himself but had his sentence delayed for 3 years and then suspended,[16a] apparently in return for aiding the authorities in investigatory work. Later, he was employed as a private investigator until indicted for subornation of perjury in 1920 in connection with the Barnett Baff "chicken murder" case. It was not until 1929, after he had been well launched on his new career as F. Donald Coster, president of McKesson & Robbins, that bail was discharged and the indictment of Philip Musica on this last charge was dismissed.[17]

Earlier in the day on which the identity of F. Donald Coster as Philip Musica was established by comparison of fingerprints, the United States Grand Jury at New York, acting on the evidence already assembled, indicted F. Donald Coster, George E. Dietrich, George Vernard, and McKesson & Robbins, Incorporated for violating Sections 13 and 32 of the Securities Exchange Act of 1934 in connection with the annual reports of McKesson & Robbins, Incorporated filed with the Commission and the New York Stock Exchange, and for conspiring to violate those sections. It was at noon of the following day, Friday, December 16, after his past career had been exposed and just as the United States Marshal reached his home to rearrest him under this indictment, that Philip Musica, alias F. Donald Coster committed suicide. The three remaining Musica brothers, known as George Dietrich, George Vernard, and Robert Dietrich [18] were taken into custody.

Having been occupied theretofore solely with the criminal investigation, the Securities and Exchange Commission, on Monday, December 19, turned its attention to investigating the auditing practices and procedures which, for a period of 14 years, failed to disclose the gross inflation of assets on the books of McKesson & Robbins and Coster's earlier concern, Girard & Co., Inc. A preliminary survey was undertaken immediately with a view to determining the best way to study and present this matter for consideration.

On the same day, Monday, December 19, Charles F. Michaels resigned as Co-trustee [19] but was immediately thereafter elected by the Board of Directors as president of the Corporation, to replace Coster.[20]

[16a] Two of his brothers, George Dietrich and George Vernard, also pleaded guilty and received suspended sentences.

[17] From records and news clippings in files of New York City Police Department, Bureau of Criminal Identification.

[18] A complaint had meanwhile been sworn out against Robert Dietrich.

[19] In the latter part of October and November 1938, about a month prior to the receivership, Michaels sold 15,600 shares of McKesson common stock for himself and his family. As to the reasons for this sale, see footnote 466 *infra*.

[20] New York Times, December 20, 1938.

Also on Monday, December 19, the three surviving Musica brothers were indicted by the New York County Grand Jury on charges of grand larceny and forgery.

The United States Grand Jury on Thursday, December 22, re-indicted George Dietrich, George Vernard, and Robert Dietrich. The indictment charged the same offenses as did the first Federal indictment returned on December 15, 1938, but cited the brothers as George Musica, Arthur Musica, and Robert Musica, respectively, with their assumed names as aliases. All three have since pleaded guilty to this indictment.

On March 30, 1939, the United States Grand Jury returned its third indictment in this matter, naming, in addition to the three surviving Musica brothers, Benjamin Simon, John Jenkins, Leonard Jenkins, John H. McGloon, Horace B. Merwin, and Rowley W. Phillips. The indictment charged violations of the mail fraud statute, of Sections 13 and 32 of the Securities Exchange Act of 1934,[21] and a conspiracy to violate the foregoing statutes. The Musica brothers pleaded guilty before trial. So did Benjamin Simon. In so far as the fictitious crude drug transactions were concerned, it appears that at an early date he performed some of the functions later carried on by George Vernard. John Jenkins and Leonard Jenkins, brothers-in-law of Coster, both pleaded guilty during the trial, the latter only to the conspiracy count. It appears that they signed contracts, checks, and so forth, in the names of persons supposedly connected with the fictitious concerns used to carry on the fraud.

Horace B. Merwin and Rowley W. Phillips, who were directors of McKesson & Robbins, Incorporated (Maryland) and of its predecessors and subsidiaries, McKesson & Robbins, Incorporated (Connecticut), McKesson & Robbins, Limited, and Girard & Co., Inc., were acquitted by the jury on all counts. John H. McGloon, comptroller of McKesson & Robbins since 1928, was acquitted of being a party to the conspiracy, of mail fraud, and of violating Sections 13 and 32 of the Securities Exchange Act of 1934 in connection with the 1935 and 1936 annual reports filed by McKesson & Robbins, Incorporated, but was found guilty on the count charging violation of Sections 13 and 32 of the Securities Exchange Act of 1934 in connection with the filing of the 1937 annual report, the last prior to the disclosure of the fraud.[22] An appeal by McGloon is now pending.[23]

---

[21] See footnote 15 *supra*.

[22] Cf. pages 128 ff. *infra*.

[23] *U. S. of America* v. *George Musica, et al.*, U. S. D. C., So. Dist. of N. Y. No. 80995. The sentences imposed by Judge Grover M. Moscowitz at the conclusion of the trial on May 22, 1940, were as follows: George Dietrich, two years and six months; George Vernard, three years; Robert Dietrich, one year and six months; Benjamin Simon, three years; and John Jenkins, one year and one day; all on one count of the indictment, sentences on other counts being suspended with periods of probation imposed to start after imprisonment. John H. McGloon was sentenced to one year and one day and was fined $5,000.00. Sentence as to Leonard Jenkins was suspended and he was placed on immediate probation.

Meanwhile, in view of the false and misleading information set forth in the financial statements prepared and certified by Price, Waterhouse & Co., which were contained in the application for registration and annual reports filed by McKesson & Robbins with the Commission and the New York Stock Exchange,[24] and on the basis of its preliminary investigation into the auditing phases, the Commission, on December 29, 1938, entered an order [25] directing that public hearings be held for the purposes mentioned at the outset of this report. The facts developed in the course of these hearings, together with the conclusions of the Commission with respect thereto, are contained in the sections of this report which follow.

---

[24] See footnote 14 *supra*.

[25] Before the Securities and Exchange Commission, *In the Matter of McKesson & Robbins, Inc.*, December 29, 1938. A copy of the order is appended to this report, as Appendix C.

Section III

THE FICTITIOUS CRUDE DRUG BUSINESS

McKesson & Robbins, Incorporated (Maryland) when it was petitioned into receivership on December 5, 1938, had reported assets of approximately $90,000,000 and was the result of a merger or consolidation of more than 50 separate corporations. The fictitious crude drug business accounted for approximately $21,000,000 of these assets, represented by fictitious inventories, accounts receivable, and cash in bank carried on the books of the Connecticut Division of McKesson & Robbins, Incorporated (Maryland) and by one of its subsidiaries, McKesson & Robbins, Limited (Canada).[26] Prior to October 31, 1934, all of the business of the Connecticut Division was conducted by a separate subsidiary, McKesson & Robbins, Incorporated (Connecticut). At the time of the formation of McKesson & Robbins, Incorporated (Maryland), as a holding company in August 1928, when McKesson started acquiring numerous wholesale drug houses throughout the country, McKesson & Robbins, Incorporated (Connecticut) and McKesson & Robbins, Limited (Canada) were already in existence. The latter had been formed as a new enterprise in October 1927, and the former to give effect to the merger of the old McKesson & Robbins, Incorporated (New York) and Coster's Girard & Co., Inc. in October 1926.

In order properly to appraise the procedures followed in auditing the fictitious crude drug business, it is necessary first to understand the relationship between this business and the concern as a whole.

---

[26] See the following table:

Fictitious assets as at Dec. 31, 1938	McKesson & Robbins, Incorporated, (Maryland) (Connecticut Division)	McKesson & Robbins, Limited (Canada)	Together
Cash in bank	$ 361,472.86	$ 51,095.70	$ 412,568.56
Accounts receivable	8,472,630.10	1,564,688.00	10,037,318.10
Inventories	9,503,025.00	1,072,746.50	10,575,771.50
	$18,337,127.96	$2,688,530.20	$21,025,658.16

Second Report of William J. Wardall, Trustee, *In the Matter of McKesson & Robbins, Incorporated*, Debtor, at p. 25.

The fictitious assets comprised in excess of 75% of total reported assets of the Connecticut Division and in excess of 85% of total reported assets of the Canadian Company. See pages 43–45 *infra*.

205078—40——3

Since, as above indicated, the corporate structure was constantly changing, this relationship can best be set forth by first tracing chronologically the various corporate steps by which the present McKesson concern was assembled, with Coster at its head, and then showing the exact place in the corporate structure occupied by the fictitious crude drug business.

A. BRIEF CORPORATE HISTORY

1. Girard & Co., Inc.

Frank Donald Coster's rise to the head of the $90,000,000 drug concern had its start in the incorporation of Girard & Co., Inc. under the laws of the State of New York on January 31, 1923. The authorized capital stock of this company consisted of 2,000 shares of common stock of $100 par value. However, only 1,250 shares originally were outstanding. The consideration reported to have been received by Girard & Co., Inc., for these shares was cash, merchandise, and other working assets with which the Company began operations on March 31, 1923, in leased premises at 209 Washington Street, Mount Vernon, N. Y. At the beginning of 1925 these shares were reputedly owned by the following persons:

Frank D. Coster, president and treasurer	850 shares.
P. Horace Girard,[27] vice-president	350 shares.
George Dietrich, bookkeeper	50 shares.[28]

The firm was reputed to have been engaged in business as manufacturing chemists of products most of which contained alcohol.[29] Its books were first audited by Price, Waterhouse & Co. as of December 31, 1924 and covered operations for the 9 months preceding that date.[30] Speaking of the balance sheet prepared at this time Jaureguy, a partner of Price, Waterhouse & Co., testified:

"Q. [By Mr. GALPEER.] Now, as far as you know, this is the first published statement of Girard and Company, that I showed you before?

A. To the best of my knowledge and belief it is.

Q. And this statement, as far as your certification goes, contains no qualifications at all?

A. No, sir.

---

[27] Horace B. Merwin, who early became a director of Girard & Co., Inc. and continued his association when it was succeeded by McKesson & Robbins, testified concerning P. Horace Girard as follows:

> "Q [By Mr. GALPEER.] Who is Mr. P. Horace Girard, or who was Mr. P. Horace Girard?
>
> A. If you will look at the first page of Mr. Thompson's report in 1925 [Ex. 177] you will find that he was one of the first three stockholders of Girard & Co. I never saw him. I do not know of anybody else who ever did. I remember inquiring about him from Mr. Coster, and if my memory serves me correctly, he told me that he was ill; had tuberculosis and I believe was in Saranac or some where up in that vicinity, as I remember. He apparently eventually died off soon after that." R. 2291-2292. See also R. 66-67.

It seems that P. Horace Girard was another alias used by Philip Musica (Frank Donald Coster) up to the time of his suicide. See Second Report of William J. Wardall, Trustee, *In the Matter of McKesson & Robbins, Incorporated*, Debtor, at p. 14.

[28] Ex. 138, 177.

[29] Ex. 177.

[30] Ex. 2, 138.

Q. So you might really say that this was the start of Girard and Company on your name?

A. I think that is true." [31]

All subsequent regular audits of Girard & Co., Inc. and of McKesson when it succeeded Girard were performed by Price, Waterhouse & Co.[32]

A short time prior to December 31, 1924, the Company entered into a contract to purchase from the First National Bank of Bridgeport the plant of the Hawthorne Company at Fairfield (near Bridgeport), Conn.,[33] which had been taken over by the bank. The terms were $25,000 cash and the balance of $100,000 was to be paid in 10 annual installments of $10,000 each, all repairs to be made by the bank. Title passed on March 2, 1925, and Girard & Co., Inc. moved from Mt. Vernon to Fairfield in April 1925.[34]

In May 1925 the firm borrowed $80,000 from The Bridgeport Trust Company, and at the same time C. Barnum Seeley, then president of the bank, purchased 275 shares of Girard's authorized but unissued common stock, at par, for $27,500. Seeley allowed two of his associates at the bank, Horace B. Merwin, later president of the bank, and Egbert Marsh, later also president and then chairman of the Board of Directors of the bank, to take a small portion of this stock.[35]

In the first quarter of 1926 a 25% dividend in cash was paid on the outstanding stock.[36] In the second quarter the certificate of incorporation of Girard & Co., Inc. was amended, changing the authorized capital stock to 5,000 shares of 7% cumulative participating preferred of $100 par and 50,000 shares of no par common. On June 10, 1926, the Company issued the full 50,000 shares of no par common in exchange for the then outstanding 1,525 shares of $100 par value common. At the same time 3,000 shares of the preferred stock were sold by The Bridgeport Trust Company and The

31 R. 55.

32 Ex. 169.

33 Because of its close proximity, this plant is sometimes referred to as being in Bridgeport.

34 Ex. 138, 177.

35 Ex 139 R. 2241-2242. In this connection Merwin testified:

"Well, Mr. Seeley looked at their statement which, incidentally was, I think, at that time, it was a statement prepared by Price, Waterhouse and dated December 31, 1924. My files do not seem to have any May statement. That would be the one, I think, that was brought in to us at that time. At that time Mr. Seeley discussed with them the matter of the loan and noticed or got the information in the conversation with Mr. Carpenter, who came in at the time, that they had some capital stock that was unissued. He suggested that possibly they might sell a part of that stock and they would not then have to borrow quite so much money and that would strengthen up their financial statement.

After some conversation, he agreed to buy $27,500 of that stock and about that time, we loaned them as our records show—I think it was during the month of May; probably the latter part of that month—$80,000. That loan was paid off so that on December of that year, they owed us nothing.

* * * * * * *

He bought that [stock] for himself and later on spoke to me about it and asked me if I would like to buy part of it. He also spoke to Mr. Marsh, who was another officer of the institution and both of us bought a small part of it." R. 2241-2242.

36 Ex. 140.

R. F. Griggs Company of Waterbury, Conn. After the deduction of a selling commission of $30,000 the sale netted Girard & Co., Inc. $270,000 in cash.[37] At this time Horace B. Merwin and Rowley W. Phillips, respectively representing the two firms above mentioned, became directors of the drug concern.[38]

The purported growth of Girard & Co., Inc., is reflected in the following figures certified by Price, Waterhouse & Co.: [39]

Date	Total assets	Capital and surplus	Net sales	
December 31, 1924	$ 295, 028	$ 161, 561	$ 251, 977	(9 mos. to 12–31–24.)
December 31, 1925	584, 050	334, 392	1, 129, 302	(Calendar year 1925.)
November 30, 1926	1, 306, 338	863, 601	2, 215, 811	(11 mos. to 11–30–26.)

2. McKesson & Robbins, Incorporated (Connecticut)

McKesson & Robbins, Incorporated (Connecticut) was organized on October 28, 1926 to effect the merger of McKesson & Robbins, Incorporated (New York) and Girard & Co., Inc., a project on which Coster had been working at least since the previous January.[40] A prospectus issued in connection with the financing at this time gives the following description of the merger and of the concerns involved:

---

[37] Ex. 141; R. 2245–2246, 2302–2304. For present purposes in this and subsequent stock offerings referred to herein, we treat only the shares sold by the corporate issuer. Sale of privately owned shares or use thereof as bonus stock in connection with the sale of corporate shares or resale or syndicate activities of the bankers are not included.

[38] R. 2306, 2263.

[39] R. 56–57; Ex. 2, 141, 142, 170.

[40] In a letter to Horace B. Merwin, then vice-president of The Bridgeport Trust Company, dated January 18, 1926, Coster said of the old McKesson:

> "After a very careful investigation of the facts and circumstances surrounding this property, I am convinced that it is from the view point of standing and prestige in the international drug trade the leader, it having been before the public ninety-three years, their record with every retail and wholesale druggist in the United States is of the highest, and in determining the value of the good will the name alone aside from the valuable asset of the specialty trade names should be given careful consideration.
>
> * * * * * * *
>
> "I shall be glad to furnish you with any further information you might desire. What is essential this situation is action at the earliest possible moment." Ex. 174.

In the President's Report to Stockholders and Directors of Girard & Co., Inc. dated January 25, 1926, Coster said:

> "I also recommend for careful consideration the possibilities of amalgamating with an old established firm such as McKesson & Robbins. While I look upon with a great deal of satisfaction to the advancement of Girard & Co., I cannot lose sight of the fact that even by making a sacrifice at the present time in any such amalgamation, the ultimate result would undoubtedly be to the advantage of the present stock holders of Girard & Co. in that they would secure an element of good will and a method of high class distribution which takes years and incalculable expenses to acquire." Ex. 176.

Replying to Coster's proposal concerning McKesson, Merwin wrote to him on January 27, 1926:

> "Our brief investigation seems to disclose the fact that such information as we have been able to get through trade, banking and other channels indicates that their expenses are entirely out of proportion to their profits and that they have been losing ground, and furthermore that their chances for future development do not look too bright.
>
> "We cannot help but feel for the best interest of Girard & Company it might be better to drop any further consideration of this matter and look about for something else which would be much sounder from a banking point of view." Ex. 175.

"McKesson & Robbins, Inc. (A Connecticut Corporation)

A Merger of McKesson & Robbins, Inc. of N. Y. with Girard & Co., Inc. of N. Y.

* * * * * * *

"CAPITAL STRUCTURE (UPON COMPLETION OF THIS FINANCING)

	Authorized and outstanding
"Preferred Stock—par value $100	$1, 650, 000
Common Stock—without par value	100, 000 shares

"History and Business.—McKesson & Robbins, Inc. of New York was established in 1833 and during its ninety-three years of existence developed and maintained a high national and international reputation with the public, the medical profession and the trade as a purveyor of fine drugs and rare chemicals. Its sales were effected through branches in London, Paris and South America and through more than one hundred distributors selected from the oldest and most prominent druggists and jobbers throughout the United States. In addition to its standard line of fine drugs, chemical and pharmaceutical products it also manufactured and distributed such nationally known specialties as 'Calox' tooth powder, 'Liquid Alborlene', 'Analax', McK & R Milk of Magnesia and McK & R Asperin.

"Girard & Co., Inc. was for a number of years engaged in procuring from original sources of supply the basic raw materials essential to the manufacture of fine drugs, chemical and pharmaceutical products and converting them by mass low cost production into such finished products as McKesson & Robbins distributed.

"Thus the consolidation of McKesson & Robbins with Girard & Co. is an ideal one as, besides effecting the usual economies attendant upon centralization of production and management, it combines a most formidable sales organization of ninety-three years experience and standing with a modern and aggressive plant of almost unlimited capacity having direct established contact throughout the world with original sources of its basic raw materials." [41]

The prospectus also states that "* * * Mr. Frank D. Coster, for the past four years President of Girard & Co., Inc., has been chosen President of the new company and will be in active charge of operations. * * *"

All of the new common stock (100,000 shares) was issued in exchange for the 50,000 shares of Girard common outstanding. Of the new preferred stock, 3,000 shares were issued in exchange for the 3,000 shares of Girard preferred outstanding and 13,500 shares were sold for cash by a group composed of The Bridgeport Trust Company, The R. F. Griggs Company of Waterbury, Conn., H. C. Warren & Co., Inc., of New Haven, Conn., and Fuller, Richter, Aldrich & Co., of Hartford, Conn. From the proceeds of the sale $1,000,000 went to pay off Messrs. Saunders Norvell and Herbert D. Robbins, the then owners of McKesson & Robbins, Incorporated (New York). The remainder apparently was made available to the new Corporation as additional working capital. After the deduction of a payment to the bankers of $135,000 this amounted to $215,000.[42]

---

[41] Ex. 259.

[42] Ex. 144; R. 2246–2248, 2303–2304.

The old McKesson firm was moved from Brooklyn, N. Y., to the plant at Fairfield, where an addition was built in order to house the combined concerns.[43] Another office was established at 79 Cliff Street, New York City, to which the bulk or trading department of the old McKesson firm was transferred.[44]

In order to finance the new construction at Fairfield, as well as to provide additional working capital, on or about May 1, 1927, rights were issued to common stockholders of the new McKesson & Robbins, Incorporated (Connecticut) to purchase additional common stock at $20 a share. Apparently, the full 15,000-share offering was subscribed for, the Corporation receiving $300,000 [45] less $15,000 commission paid to the underwriters.[46]

3. McKesson & Robbins, Limited (Canada)

The reasons for the formation of this new Company in October 1927 were stated in a prospectus covering the initial offering of 10,000 shares of its preference stock as follows:

"NATURE OF BUSINESS.—We quote the following excerpts from a letter written to us by Mr. Frank D. Coster, President of the Company:

"'McKesson & Robbins, Limited, is to be organized for the purpose of expanding the trade of McKesson & Robbins, Inc., of Connecticut, not only in the Dominion of Canada, but throughout the British Empire, Colonies and possessions.

"'McKesson & Robbins, Inc., for the past 40 years under its former management has enjoyed an appreciable amount of business within this territory; however, this business has been limited mostly to raw materials where the barrier of tariff could be overcome and to not more than two or three specialties that were not highly competitive with specialties manufactured under British dominion.

"'Under the present management liberal national advertising has brought us to the point where we must either manufacture our most profitable and successful items within the British confines or else renounce this not only attractive but profitable trade.

"'In order to keep abreast with the leading competitors in our line, we have determined that it is for the best interests of McKesson & Robbins of Connecticut to manufacture such preparations now in their line that are suitable for British trade in Canada, and that by doing so McKesson & Robbins Limited of Canada will be enabled to expand its trade as successfully in the Dominion of Canada and in other British possessions.

"'In addition to the actual manufacturing of present preparations, fine chemicals, pharmaceuticals and surgical dressings, McKesson & Robbins of Canada will also be able to handle direct importations into Canada of basic raw materials in which McKesson & Robbins of Connecticut is now a large factor.'" [47]

---

[43] Ex. 128; R. 2253.

[44] R. 2596, 2615.

[45] Ex. 146; R. 2305, 2258.

[46] R. 2306.

[47] Ex. 260.

In respect to the management of the new Company, the prospectus stated:

"MANAGEMENT.—The President, Frank D. Coster, is also President and active manager of McKesson & Robbins of Connecticut, and will be assisted by the full personnel of the organization of the latter company, which company has a ninety-four year record of success and prosperity.

"The officers and directors of this company will be practically identical with those of the Connecticut Company." [48]

The details of the organization of McKesson & Robbins, Limited (Canada), and its relationship to McKesson & Robbins, Incorporated (Connecticut) were summarized in one of the Price, Waterhouse & Co. reports as follows:

"A new company, McKesson & Robbins, Limited, was organized on October 17, 1927 under the laws of the Dominion of Canada with an authorized capital of 10,000 shares of 7% cumulative convertible preference stock having a par value of $100.00 each, and 80,000 common shares without nominal or par value. All of the preference stock and 52,000 of the common shares were purchased by McKesson & Robbins, Incorporated, the consideration being $900,000.00 in cash and the goodwill of McKesson & Robbins, Incorporated, in Canada, the British Empire and British Colonies and possessions with the use in those countries of this company's trade names, copyrights, inventions, improvements, processes and franchises.

"Subsequently all of the preference stock and 10,000 common shares were resold [by McKesson & Robbins, Incorporated] to The Bridgeport Trust Company and The R. F. Griggs Company for $900,000.00 in cash. In accordance with a vote of the board of directors, the remaining 42,000 common shares retained by the company [McKesson & Robbins, Incorporated] as an investment, have been taken up on the books [of McKesson & Robbins, Incorporated] at a valuation of $420,000.00.

"Under the terms of the charter of the Canadian company, the preference stock is convertible before November 1, 1932 into common shares at the rate of two common shares for each share of preference stock; and 20,000 of its unissued common shares have been accordingly reserved for that purpose.

"In connection with the purchase and sale referred to above of the capital stock of the Canadian company, McKesson & Robbins, Incorporated, have guaranteed to McKesson & Robbins, Limited, gross sales of not less than $1,000,000.00 per annum and annual net profits available for dividends of not less than $100,000.00 so long as any of its preference stock is outstanding. In consideration of this guarantee, the Connecticut company has the first right to subscribe for the remaining 8,000 common shares of the authorized issue of the Canadian company which have not been reserved for the conversion of preference stock." [49]

The reasons for this guaranty arrangement are indicated in the testimony of Horace B. Merwin, who stated:

"Well, Mr. Coster advanced the idea that he would like to form a foreign corporation, indicating that he had a large volume of foreign business that could be handled better through a foreign corporation and the matter was quite a difficult one to finance, as you might suspect. We were talking about a brand new corporation which had no past experience of earnings and we wondered how

[48] Ex. 260.
[49] Ex. 146.

we could wrap up a package like that and make it saleable so that an investor would put his money in it. So that, the matter was talked about for a long time. * * * And then, the Connecticut corporation stated its willingness to guarantee * * * that it could and would allocate to the British corporation, a volume of business not to be less than a million dollars a year and at a profit not to be less than $100,000 a year. After our attorneys had convinced themselves that those guarantees had been drawn up to suit them and they felt they were good and valuable and protected the stockholders, we then offered that to the public * * *." [50]

Although the prospectus above quoted only makes reference to the public offering of $1,000,000 preference stock, it appears that the 10,000 shares of common stock purchased by the bankers along with the preference stock, were also resold by them.[51] The stock was offered by the same Connecticut group that theretofore had handled the financing of McKesson & Robbins, Incorporated (Connecticut), namely The Bridgeport Trust Company, The R. F. Griggs Company, Edward M. Bradley & Co., Inc.,[52] and Fuller, Richter, Aldrich & Co.[53] As above stated, the net amount paid by the bankers to McKesson & Robbins, Incorporated for 10,000 shares of preference stock, and 10,000 shares of common stock was $900,000, the same amount as the cash paid by McKesson & Robbins, Incorporated to McKesson & Robbins, Limited for the 10,000 shares of preference stock and 52,000 shares of common.

In 1931, McKesson & Robbins, Limited (Canada) established a small branch in London, England,[54] which, in 1933, was incorporated as a separate subsidiary, also called McKesson & Robbins, Limited.[55] Aside from the London unit, the business of McKesson & Robbins, Limited (Canada) since its inception, and despite the statements made in the prospectus above referred to, has consisted solely of the purported purchase and resale of crude drugs as distinguished from the sale of products already manufactured and ready for the retail drug trade, such as the "McKesson Line", or the manufacturing of such products. The business conducted by the London Company was negligible in amount in comparison with the purported sales of its parent.[56]

McKesson & Robbins, Limited (Canada) established offices at the Fairfield plant of McKesson, and its operations, besides being reflected in the consolidated McKesson accounts, were also separately certified by Price, Waterhouse & Co. for annual release to its own stockholders.[57]

---

[50] R. 2255–2256.
[51] R. 2257.
[52] Successors to H. C. Warren & Co., Inc., R. 2304.
[53] Ex. 260.
[54] Ex. 154.
[55] Ex. 74.
[56] R. 108 ff., 2262.
[57] Ex. 161–167.

4. McKesson & Robbins, Incorporated (Maryland)

The next corporate move is described in the following testimony of Horace B. Merwin, who at this time, in addition to being a director of the drug concern and an officer of The Bridgeport Trust Company, became treasurer of McKesson & Robbins, Incorporated (Maryland) until succeeded by Julian F. Thompson in February 1930.[58]

"By Mr. GALPEER:

Q. Let us take up the financial picture from that point, after the financing of the Limited Company, what was the next step?

A. Well, things moved pretty fast. We were impressed by the tremendous dynamic power behind this man Coster. He could think up a new idea about as fast as anybody I have ever met. He began then talking about a great idea that would make a lot of money. He said he had this fine name now, there was none better; we thought it was pretty good ourselves. He was now all set to develop the thing properly. He came to us with the idea that he wanted to get the drug distributor, the drug wholesaler, throughout the country, of which there were a good many, who was not doing as well as he should, and his idea would be to combine them into one huge national distributing organization under the name of McKesson.

He completely took our breath away. We country boys figured that we better let go the tail of the bear about then. We then tried to persuade him to make a test. I remember suggesting to him that he take something like the Eastern Drug of Boston and Whittlesey and Company of New Haven and possibly Gibson and Snow, who had offices in Rochester, Syracuse and up there through that way, making a little group, and see if the thing would work. It sounded logical, it sounded splendid. He claimed the salesmen overlapped each other's territory and they were in competition and all that sort of stuff.

It was obviously going to involve a lot of money; it was getting out of our class entirely. He said it wouldn't do any good to make a test, somebody else would swipe his idea. The only thing to do was to make a national job of it, so finally, in order to hold him down, I think we agreed on 17 or 18 distributors who were kind of hand picked and particularly good.

I was very much impressed that when these men were approached they were very much impressed with the idea, which made me believe there was a lot in it. After some conferences in New York, Mr. Coster himself, I believe, went to, I think, I am not sure, Goldman, Sachs who sort of turned him over to Bond & Goodwin with whom they had some pretty intimate association, and the developments and negotiations began.

That was the forerunner of the move which enlarged McKesson into quite a large outfit. In fact, I think it was then that they became McKesson & Robbins of Maryland, which is a holding corporation, which in turn purchased all these distributors. They were first held, I believe, as separate corporations.

* * * * * * *

The way that financing was done, it was done primarily under the auspices of Goldman, Sachs, Bond & Goodwin and we Connecticut bankers, the old originals, sort of tagged along and took small participation in the financing at the time."[59]

As testified by Merwin, a new McKesson & Robbins was organized in Maryland on August 4, 1928 as a holding company for the purpose

[58] R. 2263, 2296–2297.

[59] R. 2263–2265.

of acquiring, either directly or through subsidiaries, the stock of such wholesale drug companies as might be approved by the Corporation as well as the stock of McKesson & Robbins, Incorporated (Connecticut).[60] The Maryland Company had an authorized capitalization of 500,000 shares of preference stock (par value $50) and 5,000,000 shares of common stock (no par value).[61]

F. Donald Coster, president of the new Company, gives the following description of its purpose in a prospectus, dated September 8, 1928, covering an offering of 193,907 shares of 7% cumulative convertible preference stock at $51 per share:

> "The purpose of this consolidation is to combine under one ownership a group of old, well-established wholesale drug houses, widely distributed geographically, and a manufacturing unit producing a nationally known line of merchandise and capable of handling, in addition, all of the supplementary manufacturing activities ordinarily conducted separately by the wholesale distributors themselves." [62]

The offering was made by Goldman, Sachs & Co., Bond & Goodwin, Inc., The Bridgeport Trust Company, and The R. F. Griggs Company. Actually, the underwriters took down and paid for 177,774 shares of the preference stock at $51 per share, netting the Corporation $7,999,830 in cash after deducting $6 per share, or $1,066,644, as underwriting commission.

The balance of the originally outstanding 320,000 shares of preference stock and all of the originally outstanding 664,409 shares of common, together with the cash proceeds of the public offering of preference stock, above referred to, were used to acquire, on September 28, 1928, all of the outstanding common stocks of 15 wholesale drug concerns [63] and of McKesson & Robbins, Incorporated (Connecticut).[64]

[60] Ex. 148. For the sake of clarity and convenience, the following McKesson concerns are sometimes herein briefly referred to as follows:

McKesson & Robbins, Incorporated (Maryland), as the Maryland Company;
McKesson & Robbins, Incorporated (Connecticut), as the Connecticut Company;
McKesson & Robbins, Limited (Canada), as the Canadian Company; and
McKesson & Robbins, Limited (London), as the London Company.

[61] Ex. 152.

[62] Ex. 178.

[63]

Bedsole-Colvin Drug Company, Inc	Mobile, Ala.
Churchill Drug Companies	Cedar Rapids, Iowa Burlington, Iowa Peoria, Ill. Omaha, Nebr.
Eastern Drug Company	Boston, Mass.
Farrand, Williams & Clark	Detroit, Mich.
Fuller-Morrisson Company	Chicago, Ill.
Faxon & Gallagher Drug Company	Kansas City, Mo.

Meanwhile, in preparation for these developments, McKesson & Robbins, Incorporated (Connecticut), on September 1, 1928, offered to its common stockholders the right to subscribe, at $75 per share, to an additional share of its common for each two held. 57,500 additional shares of common were thus issued, netting the Connecticut Company $3,881,250, after deducting an underwriting fee of $7.50 per share or $431,250. This money was used by the Connecticut Company to redeem its own outstanding preferred stock and to acquire preferred stock and notes of certain of the wholesale drug distributors whose common stocks were to be acquired by the Maryland Company as above stated. Thereafter, on September 28, 1928, at the time of the acquisition by the Maryland Company of the wholesale drug subsidiaries, the total outstanding common stock of the Connecticut Company, 172,500 shares, was acquired by the Maryland Company in exchange for twice that number, or 345,000 shares, of its own common stock.[65]

In November 1928, the originally outstanding shares of the Maryland Company were admitted to trading on the New York Stock Exchange as were all subsequent securities issued by this Company.[66]

Besides the 664,409 shares of common and 320,000 shares of preference stock originally issued by the Maryland Company in September of 1928, before the close of that year an additional 10,079 shares of common and 1,507 shares of preference stock were issued in connection with the acquisition of another wholesale drug com-

---

Gibson-Snow Co., Inc.	Troy, N. Y.; Buffalo, N. Y.; Albany, N. Y.; Syracuse, N. Y.; Rochester, N. Y.
The Hall-Van Gorder Company	Cleveland, Ohio
Kirk, Geary & Co.	Sacramento, Calif.
Langley and Michaels Company	San Francisco, Calif.
Minneapolis Drug Company	Minneapolis, Minn.
The Murray Drug Company	Columbia, S. C.
Roeber & Kuebler Company	Newark, N. J.
Southern Drug Company	Houston, Tex.
Western Wholesale Drug Company	Los Angeles, Calif.

[64] Ex. 152. Includes an appreciable amount of stock and cash issued to the bankers in this connection. McKesson & Robbins, Incorporated (Connecticut) was acquired on an earnings basis, while the wholesale houses came into the merger on an asset basis. R. 4270.

[65] Ex. 148, 152, 178.

[66] New York Stock Exchange Listing Applications, McKesson & Robbins, Incorporated (a holding corporation organized under the laws of Maryland, August 4, 1928). For securities outstanding and admitted to trading at the time of the receivership see page 15 *supra*.

pany,[67] 5,237 shares of common in connection with employee stock subscription plans and 2,389 shares of common in connection with retailer stock subscription plans; making the total issued stock of the Maryland Company at December 31, 1928, 682,114 shares of common and 321,507 shares of preference stock.[68]

Concerning activities in 1929, Merwin further testified:

"By Mr. GALPEER:

Q. Now, I understand that in addition to the merger of these group 1 houses in 1928 there was a further merger by McKesson of a group of houses known as the group 2 houses in the following year, is that correct?

A. Yes. In spite of all we conservative individuals could do to try to hold Mr. Coster back, he seemed to feel that he wanted to go further and he plunged ahead and added quite a good many other houses, most all of them practically very good ones. I think possibly many of them invited themselves in, in a way."[69]

As indicated by Merwin, in 1929 the Maryland Company acquired 28 additional wholesale drug houses, the consideration given again being part stock of the Maryland Company and part cash. The first 17 of these houses were acquired in March and April 1929.[70] The rest were absorbed from time to time during the balance of the year.[71] Also in 1929 the Maryland Company acquired Isdahl & Co., A/S, of Bergen, Norway, to engage in the business of selling cod liver oil.[72]

---

[67] The Groover-Stewart Drug Company, Jacksonville, Fla.

[68] Ex. 152.

[69] R. 2266-2267.

[70]	H. & J. Brewer Co.	Springfield, Mass.
	The Bronx Drug Co.	Borough of Bronx, N. Y.
	The J. W. Crowdus Drug Company	Dallas, Tex.
	Doster-Northington, Incorporated	Birmingham, Ala.
	L. Eisen & Co. Inc.	Yonkers, N. Y.
	C. S. Littell & Co., Inc.	Borough of Manhattan, N. Y.
	J. S. Merrell Drug Company	St. Louis, Mo.
	Ogden Wholesale Drug Company	Ogden, Utah.
	Peter-Neat-Richardson Co.	Louisville, Ky.
	Rhode Island Wholesale Drug Company	Providence, R. I.
	J. B. Riley Drug Company	Macon, Ga.
	Roanoke Drug Company, Inc.	Roanoke, Va.
	The Schuh Drug Company of Cairo, Ill.	Cairo, Ill.
	Charles E. Schumacher Co.	Borough of Brooklyn, N. Y.
	Spokane Drug Company	Spokane, Wash.
	Spurlock-Neal Company	Nashville, Tenn. Florence, Ala.
	The Alfred Vogeler Drug Company	Cincinnati, Ohio.
[71]	Hornick, More & Porterfield	Sioux City, Iowa.
	Huntington Drug Company	Huntington, W. Va.
	The Parker-Blake Drug Company, Limited	New Orleans, La.
	Noyes Bros. & Cutler Incorporated	St. Paul, Minn.
	C. E. Potts Drug Company	Wichita, Kans.
	C. J. Lincoln Company	Little Rock, Ark.
	The Colorado Wholesale Drug Company	Denver, Colo.
	Stewart and Holmes Drug Company	Seattle, Wash.
	Berry, DeMoville and Company	Nashville, Tenn.
	Duff Drug Company	Chattanooga, Tenn.
	The Charles W. Whittlesey Company	New Haven, Conn.

[72] Ex. 152.

During the year 1929, the Maryland Company issued 336,936 additional shares of common stock and 104,283 shares of preference stock.[73] Of these, 208,743 shares of common and 54,283 shares of preference stock were issued in connection with the acquisition of stocks of the companies mentioned above.[74] 100,000 shares of common and 50,000 shares of preference stock were sold to bankers for cash, netting the corporation $6,350,000.[75] In addition, 5,219 shares of common were issued in connection with employee stock subscription plans, 22,964 shares of common in connection with retailer stock subscription plans, and 10 shares of common on the conversion of an equal number of shares of preference stock. The total number of shares issued on December 31, 1929 was 1,019,050 common and 425,780 preference stock.[76]

On January 31, 1930, another wholesale drug house was acquired [77] and, in connection therewith, the Maryland Company issued an additional 28,517 shares of common and 2,476 shares of preference stock. About the same time, 36,648 shares of common were taken down for cash at 32 by bankers under an option netting the corporation $1,172,736, which furnished part of the consideration for the purchase of two drug chains. The only other stock issued during the year was 305 shares of common in conversion of rights previously issued to retailers. On December 31, 1930 the total issued stock was 1,082,542 shares of common and 428,256 shares of preference stock.[78]

As above stated, the securities of the subsidiary wholesale houses were acquired by the Maryland Company, partially in exchange for its own securities and partially for cash. In addition, some small wholesale drug houses were acquired wholly for cash and absorbed as branches of existing subsidiaries. However, the proceeds from the sale by the Maryland Company of its preference and common stocks to and through its bankers did not keep pace with the considerable amount of cash expended in this manner. On December 31, 1928, notes and acceptances payable amounted to $4,538,993.71. By December 31, 1929 they had risen to $16,753,904.97, and, in the first quarter of 1930, they increased still further.[79]

Despite the 1929 crash, the company was able to fund this indebtedness by an additional public offering of its securities in April 1930. On

---

[73] Including 11,314 shares of common and 3,881 shares of preference to be issued in 1930 in connection with companies already acquired. Ex. 130, 152, 153.

[74] See footnote 73 *supra*.

[75] 25,000 shares of preference were sold at 51, less a commission of $5 per share. The remaining shares were taken down under options, as follows: 25,000 shares of preference at 50, 20,000 shares of common at 37½, and 80,000 shares of common at 40.

[76] See footnote 73 *supra*.

[77] Van Vleet-Ellis Corporation, Memphis, Tenn.

[78] Ex. 153. As stated in footnote 73 *supra*, the number of shares of stock reported issued on December 31, 1929 included 11,314 shares of common to be issued during 1930 in connection with companies already acquired. Instead of issuing new shares in this amount, 1,978 of these shares were taken from treasury shares, thereby decreasing by this amount the number of new shares actually issued.

[79] Ex. 129, 130, 152, 153.

the twenty-first of that month, the Maryland Company entered into an agreement, under the terms of which $22,000,000 of 20-year 5½% convertible debentures (out of a total of $25,000,000 authorized) were issued and sold to an underwriting syndicate composed of Chatham Phenix Corp., Edward B. Smith & Co., Halsey, Stuart & Co., Inc., Stone & Webster and Blodget Incorporated, and Chase Securities Corporation. The debentures were dated as of May 1, 1930, to mature May 1, 1950, and provision was made for a sinking fund for this issue. The public offering was at 96 and the corporation received 90½ from the underwriters. The proceeds of the sale of these debentures were used principally to retire obligations of the Maryland Company and its subsidiary companies, amounting in all to $19,275,266.53.[80]

After acquiring the capital stocks or the assets and business of the various wholesale drug companies above referred to, the Maryland Company caused their businesses to be taken over by new subsidiaries in which the name McKesson preceded the name of the old concern. For example: The Murray Drug Company became the "McKesson-Murray Drug Company." In some instances several subsidiaries were grouped. For example: the McKesson-Murray Drug Company included not only The Murray Drug Company of Columbia, S. C., but also the Augusta Drug Co., of Augusta, Ga. At the end of 1930, there were 43 such McKesson wholesale subsidiaries located in 67 different cities in the United States. In many instances members of the family who owned and managed the original wholesale houses which bore their names remained as presidents of the new McKesson subsidiaries and became vice-presidents and, in some cases, directors of the Maryland Company as well.[81]

In succeeding years the grouping of these wholesale subsidiaries changed somewhat. In addition, other subsidiary corporations were formed to handle such trade investments as drug chains, sales agencies, and other miscellaneous activities that were engaged in from time to time.[82]

In 1931 the only change in capital stock resulted from the issuance of 13 shares of common on conversion of rights held by retailers.[83]

---

[80] Ex. 153, 184. In connection with the execution of the underwriting agreement, an option expiring May 1, 1931 was granted to the bankers, to purchase 300,000 shares of common stock of the Maryland Company, which, however, was never exercised. Ex. 153, 154.

[81] Ex. 131. On the Board of Directors of the Maryland Company at the time of receivership were:
J. L. Bedsole—formerly Bedsole-Colvin Drug Company, Inc. acquired by McKesson 1928;
George V. Doerr—formerly Minneapolis Drug Company acquired by McKesson 1928;
T. O. Duff—formerly Duff Drug Company acquired by McKesson 1929;
Henry D. Faxon—formerly Faxon & Gallagher Drug Company acquired by McKesson 1928;
B. B. Gilmer—formerly Southern Drug Company acquired by McKesson 1928;
Charles F. Michaels—formerly Langley and Michaels Company acquired by McKesson 1928;
W. J. Murray, Jr.—formerly the Murray Drug Company acquired by McKesson 1928;
A. H. Van Gorder—formerly The Hall-Van Gorder Company acquired by McKesson 1928;
McKay Van Vleet—formerly Van Vleet-Ellis Corporation acquired by McKesson 1930.

[82] E. g. Ex. 154.

[83] Ex. 154.

There were no further changes in the number of shares of preference and common stocks issued until a plan of recapitalization was adopted in the latter part of 1935.

Meanwhile in 1932 the Maryland Company organized two wholly owned subsidiary holding companies, McKesson Wholesalers, Inc. and McKesson Development Corporation. To the former the Maryland Company transferred all of its interest in the McKesson wholesale houses and to the latter all of its trade and miscellaneous investments.

As a result of the transfers to McKesson Wholesalers, Inc., and McKesson Development Corporation, the Maryland Company's investment as at December 31, 1932, consisted of only three companies: (1) McKesson & Robbins, Incorporated (Connecticut), the manufacturing unit, (2) McKesson Wholesalers, Inc., the holding company for the wholesale houses, and (3) McKesson Development Corporation, which held various small wholly owned companies and trade and miscellaneous investments. As to the foreign subsidiary companies, McKesson & Robbins, Incorporated (Connecticut) retained its interest of approximately 80% in McKesson & Robbins, Limited (Canada) and McKesson Development Corporation held the capital stock of Isdahl & Co., A/S, Bergen, Norway.[84]

Also in 1932, the common stock of the Maryland Company was changed from shares without nominal or par value to shares having a par value of $5 each. The stated value of the common stock prior thereto had been $15 per share. The reduction to a par value of $5 per share on the 1,082,555 common shares issued resulted in a credit of $10,825,550 to capital surplus, against which there were charges in the same year of $5,033,125.34 resulting from revaluation of fixed assets of subsidiary companies as at December 31, 1932, and $4,889,-263.19 operating deficit[85] as at December 31, 1932.[86]

For the first time since its organization in 1928, the Maryland Company, in 1932, reported an operating loss[87] and paid no dividends on either its preference or common stocks. At December 15, 1932, four quarterly dividend payments on the preference stock were in arrears, and, pursuant to the certificate of incorporation, voting rights thereupon became vested exclusively in the holders of the preference stock.[88]

In 1933 the Maryland Company again paid no dividends on either its preference or common stocks, although the Company reported net

---

84 Ex. 155.

85 After providing for a general reserve of $3,000,000 against non current receivables and $1,000,000 against trade investments. Ex. 155.

86 Ex. 155, 133, 134.

87 After provision for debenture interest (over $1,000,000), adjustment of inventory values and other charges, including a provision for doubtful notes and accounts in the amount of $2,639.053.09. ($1,109.754.80 in excess of a similar charge the year before) the operating loss reported for the year ending December 31, 1932, was $921,641.62. The two general reserves of $3,000,000 and $1,000,000 each (see footnote 85 *supra*) were charged directly to earned surplus. Ex. 133, 155.

88 Ex. 155.

earnings for the year of $936,700.09. The annual report to stockholders stated that,

> "During the year a new wholly-owned subsidiary was organized under the name of Spirits Import Company, Inc., for the purpose of giving adequate service to our distributing houses for their requirements of both foreign and domestic wines and liquors made possible through the Repeal of the Eighteenth Amendment. * * *" [89]

In 1934 the management decided to discontinue the operations of as many subsidiary companies as possible and to operate the various units of the business as divisions of the Maryland Company. Prior to this the Maryland Company had been exclusively a holding company. With this end in view, the two sub-holding companies, McKesson Wholesalers, Inc., and McKesson Development Corporation, were dissolved and their "net assets" taken over by the Maryland Company as of October 30, 1934. The Maryland Company then held directly the capital stocks of its operating subsidiary companies and thereupon the "net assets" of these companies, with minor exceptions, were transferred to the Maryland Company as of October 31, 1934, in the form of liquidating dividends. In the case of four companies which operated both a wholesale drug and liquor business, only the "net assets" relating to the wholesale drug business were transferred, and these companies continued to operate a wholesale liquor or alcohol business. After October 31, 1934, all of the manufacturing and wholesale drug units were operated as divisions of the Maryland Company and there were only nine operating subsidiary companies, exclusive of miscellaneous small and inactive companies.[90]

As part of this simplification procedure, McKesson & Robbins, Incorporated (Connecticut) whose stock was wholly owned by the Maryland Company was liquidated on October 31, 1934, and the Maryland Company acquired all the assets of the Connecticut Company, including the shares of McKesson & Robbins, Limited (Canada) theretofore held by the Connecticut Company. In this connection, the Maryland Company assumed "* * * the liability of the Connecticut Company under its agreement with McKesson & Robbins, Limited [Canada] to guarantee sales yielding profits available for dividends of not less than One Hundred Thousand Dollars ($100,000.00) per annum as long as any of the Preference shares of McKesson & Robbins, Limited [Canada] should be outstanding." [91] The business of the Connecticut Company was thereafter carried on as the Connecticut Division of the Maryland Company.

Although the Maryland Company in 1934 again reported net earnings which for the year amounted to $1,720,259.78, no dividends were

[89] Ex. 134.

[90] Ex. 157. In subsequent years there were some additional changes in the number of active subsidiary companies maintained, principally in connection with the wine and liquor division. Ex. 158, 159, 160.

[91] Ex. 164.

paid on either its preference or common stocks, allegedly because of the appreciable additional working capital required by the development and expansion of the wine and liquor business.[92]

On November 1, 1935, the Board of Directors of McKesson & Robbins, Incorporated (Maryland) recommended to its stockholders a plan of recapitalization for the purpose of liquidating the dividends accrued on the 7% preference stock which, at December 15, 1935, amounted to $5,969,600, or $14 per share, on the 426,400 preference shares then outstanding.[93] In lieu of the theretofore authorized 500,000 shares of $50 par preference stock, the Company recapitalized with 750,000 shares of no par preference stock (entitled to $55 on voluntary liquidation). There was no change in the authorized common of 5,000,000 shares of $5 par value.[94]

Holders of the then outstanding 7% preference stock of $50 par received 1¼ shares of the new preference stock $3 series,[95] ½ share of common stock and 50 cents in cash for each share of old preference stock. The plan was approved and carried into effect, with the result that the Maryland Company had issued and outstanding on December 31, 1935, after giving effect to the exchange, 1,282,983 shares of common and 533,000 shares of $3 preference stock.[96] Dividends were regularly paid on the new preference stock up to the time of the receivership.[97] For his advice and work in connection with this recapitalization, which cured the default in the preference stock, Sidney Weinberg, who became a director of the Maryland Company in 1934, received $15,000, which he turned over to his firm, Goldman, Sachs & Co.[98]

In 1936 the wine and liquor activities of the Corporation were increased through the formation of the Hunter Baltimore Rye Distillery, Inc., and the acquisition by it of the Gwynn Falls Distilling Corporation for the distilling, blending, rectifying, and bottling of whiskies, gins, cordials, and so forth.[99] Although earnings applicable to common stock of the Maryland Company were reported at $1.32 per share on the 1,282,983 shares issued and outstanding, no dividends were paid on these shares, because, as stated by F. Donald Coster in the annual report for 1936,

"* * * it is a fact that the soundest and strongest businesses have been built on the policy of ploughing a substantial part of the earnings back into the business. It has never been considered sound business management to withdraw and dis-

92 Ex. 135.

93 428,256 shares issued less shares held in treasury.

94 Ex. 158.

95 Recorded at a stated value of $50 per share when issued. Ex. 136.

96 Ex. 158, 136. 1,856 old preference shares and 12,772 common shares held in the treasury had been retired on November 14, 1935.

97 Ex. 136, 137, 106.

98 R. 2408.

99 Ex. 159.

tribute profits from a business having substantial debt obligations; and in the case of this company increased sales of $21,000,000.00 necessitated a resort to bank borrowing to carry increased inventories and accounts receivable." [100]

In 1937 three more established wholesale drug houses were acquired by the Maryland Company.[101] 21,654 shares of preference stock $3 series were issued as partial consideration for two of these acquisitions.[102] Earnings for the year were reported at $1.47 per share on common stock. 51,310 shares of preference stock $3 series were issued on December 15, 1937, as a stock dividend on the common, the payment being in the ratio of 1/25 share of preference for each share of common held.[103] Including the above, the total stock issued by the Maryland Company prior to the receivership amounted to 605,964 shares of preference stock $3 series and 1,282,983 shares of common.

Notes and acceptances payable which, on December 31, 1930 (after the debenture issue had been floated), amounted to $2,710,594.59, again rose and by December 31, 1937, the date of the last annual report prior to the receivership, amounted to $11,954,076.32. In the same period $5,494,000 principal amount of debentures were retired through operation of the sinking fund leaving $16,192,000 outstanding as at December 31, 1937.[104]

At the date of the receivership there was pending a proposed private sale by the Maryland Company to the Equitable Life Assurance Society of the remaining authorized but unissued $3,000,000 5½% 20-year convertible debentures at 103. Goldman, Sachs & Co. were to have received ½% for their services in negotiating this placement. Apparently, all that remained to be done to conclude the sale was the certification of figures by Company officials [104a] and the approval and execution of a formal contract, but the receivership intervened.[105]

This completes the brief outline of the story of the corporate expansion of the companies under the direction of F. Donald Coster from the organization of Girard & Co., Inc., on January 31, 1923, to the filing of the petition for receivership of the Maryland Company on December 5, 1938; from the first balance sheet certified by Price, Waterhouse & Co. dated December 31, 1924, which stated capital and surplus at $161,560.52, and total assets at $295,028.12 [106] to the last, dated December 31, 1937, which stated capital and surplus at

[100] Ex. 137.

[101]

Milwaukee Drug Company	Milwaukee, Wis.
W. A. Hover & Company	Denver, Colo.
Blumauer-Frank Drug Company	Portland, Oreg.; Seattle, Wash.; Spokane, Wash.

[102] 14,269 of these shares were not delivered until the early part of 1938 and were therefore not carried as issued on the December 31, 1937 balance sheet.

[103] Ex. 106.

[104] Ex. 131, 106.

[104a] See page 132 *infra*.

[105] Ex. 182, 183; R. 2409 ff.

[106] Ex. 2.

$46,118,734.14, and consolidated total assets at $87,182,765.74;[107] and from reported sales of $251,977 for the 9 months ended December 31, 1924 [108] to reported sales of $174,572,229 for the year 1937.[109]

B. THE AMOUNT AND LOCATION OF THE INFLATION IN ASSETS, SALES, AND GROSS PROFITS

Although the petition for receivership filed on December 5, 1938, alleged only generally that the published statements of McKesson & Robbins, Incorporated, included fictitious inventories and accounts receivable aggregating in excess of $10,000,000, investigations thereupon instituted quickly disclosed that the false items were those arising in connection with the wholly fictitious foreign purchase and sale of "crude drugs." [110] As previously stated, this fictitious foreign crude drug business was conducted by both the Connecticut Division (formerly Company) and the Canadian Company.[111]

The exact amount of inflation in assets, sales, and gross profits arising from this fictitious business, and the relation which this bore to the real business of the Connecticut Division (formerly Company), the Canadian Company, and the Maryland Company as a whole, will be the subject of this subsection. The manner in which the fictitious transactions were handled and recorded on the books of McKesson, and the nature of the documents involved, will be described in the following subsection.

At the outset of the present hearings, Albert B. Ritts, Price, Waterhouse & Co.'s senior in charge at Bridgeport since 1932 and assistant to Ralph E. Thorn, manager of the McKesson engagement, testified that the operations of the Connecticut Division (formerly Company) consisted of both the manufacture and sale of McKesson products and the purchase and sale of crude drugs and essential oils. Included in the latter, however, was the domestic business done out of the Cliff Street, New York City office, but Ritts stated that the proportion this (real) Cliff Street business bore to the (fictitious) foreign business

107 Ex. 106.

108 R. 56–57.

109 Ex. 106.

110 In their testimony at the very outset of the present hearings the auditors (following their practice in their various memoranda and reports) referred to the items in question as "crude drugs" and sometimes as "crude drugs and essential oils." R. 108 ff. Later, Charles Hermann, an employee of the old McKesson & Robbins, Incorporated (New York) since 1903, who continued working for the firm after it was acquired by Coster and who, at the Cliff Street office, actually dealt in the kind of bulk drugs and chemicals that were listed on the foreign "crude drug" inventory (R. 2595–2596), testified that "crude drugs" was an incorrect name for them (R. 2624). However, the term "crude drugs" had already so permeated the testimony that, for the sake of consistency therewith, they will hereinafter also be referred to by that name.

111 See *infra* this and following subsections.

handled at Bridgeport was not substantial.[112] In the Connecticut Division in 1937, this foreign crude drug business accounted for in excess of 60% of total net sales and gave rise to approximately 88% of the total current assets.[113]

As for the Canadian Company, Ritts testified that the total sales of the London subsidiary were negligible and that, except for this (real) business, all the business of the Canadian Company consisted of the (fictitious) foreign purchase and sale of crude drugs. Of the total foreign crude drug business supposedly carried on by McKesson in 1937, approximately 83% was put through the books of the Connecticut Division and 17% was allotted to the Canadian Company.[114]

After the institution of the reorganization proceedings, S. D. Leidesdorf & Co., certified public accountants, were engaged by the Trustee, with the approval of the Court, to conduct an examination of the affairs of the debtor, McKesson & Robbins, Incorporated (Maryland). Such examination has shown that the inventories, accounts receivable, cash, sales, purchases, and gross profits, as carried on the books and records of McKesson and as stated in the annual reports, were materially overstated as the result of the non-existence of the inventories, receivables, and cash reportedly carried and the falsity of the purchases and sales reportedly effected in connection with this foreign crude drug business.[115]

Specifically, at December 31, 1937,[116] inventories, accounts receivable, and cash of the Connecticut Division and Canadian Company combined were found to include fictitious items in the sum of $19,249,100.64, and for the year 1937 consolidated net sales were found to include $18,247,020.60 in fictitious transactions, on which a fictitious gross profit of $1,801,390.60 was recorded. In detail, the amount of the inflation in assets, in sales, and in profits arising from this fictitious foreign crude drug business in the Connecticut Division and in the Canadian Company and as reflected on the consolidated accounts of the Maryland Company and its subsidiaries, compares, as follows, with the previous reports for that period:

[112] This domestic business was managed by Charles Hermann assisted by Simon Baum. Also at the Cliff Street office, there was conducted a Spanish-American or export business in McKesson products, crude drugs, and other merchandise under John T. Stebe. *When used in this report and in the testimony, the term "foreign" refers to the fictitious crude drug business of the type purportedly done through Smith* and does not include Stebe's "Spanish-American" or "export" business or imports made in connection with production or for domestic resale through Hermann's department or otherwise.

[113] R. 110–113 and tables on pages 43–44 *infra*.

[114] R. 109–110 and tables on pages 43–44 *infra*.

[115] R. 4547 ff.

[116] The end of the last full fiscal year prior to the receivership on December 5, 1938.

Comparison of Assets

Connecticut Division	Reported as at December 31, 1937 [a]	Fictitious [b]	Reported Less Fictitious [c]
Cash in banks and on hand	$ 498, 762. 66	$ [d] 44, 041. 06	$ 454, 721. 60
Notes and accounts receivable, less reserves	7, 774, 541. 95	[e] 7, 505, 730. 50	268, 811. 45
Inventories of merchandise	10, 634, 943. 94	[f] 9, 097, 115. 00	1, 537, 828. 94
Total current assets	$18, 908, 248. 55	$16, 646, 886. 56	$ 2, 261, 361. 99
Interbranch and intercompany accounts receivable	1, 268, 435. 97	—	1, 268, 435. 97
Investment in common stock of McKesson & Robbins, Limited	420, 000. 00	—	420, 000. 00
Other assets, less reserves	1, 089, 448. 48	—	1, 089, 448. 48
Total Assets	$21, 686, 133. 00	$16, 646, 886. 56	$ 5, 039, 246. 44
Canadian Company and Subsidiary			
Cash in banks	$ 60, 778. 94	$ [d] 32, 486. 08	$ 28, 292. 86
Accounts receivable	1, 582, 703. 39	[e] 1, 579, 143. 00	3, 560. 39
Inventories of raw materials	1, 002, 321. 60	[f] 990, 585. 00	11, 736. 60
Total current assets	$ 2, 645, 803. 93	$ 2, 602, 214. 08	$ 43, 589. 85
Goodwill, tradenames, franchises, etc. (Valued by directors as of October 28, 1927)	420, 000. 00	—	420, 000. 00
Other assets, less reserves	1, 627. 64	—	1, 627. 64
Total assets	$ 3, 067, 431. 57	$ 2, 602, 214. 08	$ 465, 217. 49
Maryland Company and Subsidiaries Consolidated			
Cash in banks and on hand	$ 3, 358, 571. 39	$ [d] 76, 527. 14	$ 3, 282, 044. 25
Notes and accounts receivable, less reserves	28, 405, 495. 05	[e] 9, 084, 873. 50	19, 320, 621. 55
Inventories of merchandise, materials, and supplies	44, 254, 735. 70	[f] 10, 087, 700. 00	34, 167, 035. 70
Total current assets	$76, 018, 802. 14	$19, 249, 100. 64	$56, 769, 701. 50
Other assets, less reserves	11, 163, 963. 60	—	11, 163, 963. 60
Total assets	$87, 182, 765. 74	$19, 249, 100. 64	$67, 933, 665. 10

[a] Ex. 261, 167, 106.

[b] Ex. 255.

[c] In computing assets as at Dec. 31, 1937, allowance should also be made for adjustments in intercompany items, possible recoveries in connection with these fictitious transactions, including tax adjustments, and other relevant items. For corrected statement of assets of Maryland Company as at Dec. 31, 1938, see Second Report of William J. Wardall, Trustee, *In the Matter of McKesson & Robbins, Incorporated*, Debtor, Exhibit B, in which the Canadian Company and its subsidiary are not consolidated with the Maryland accounts and in which the Maryland Company's advance of $1,000,000.00 to the Canadian Company and the Maryland Company's investment (represented by 42,000 of the 52,000 common shares outstanding) in the Canadian Company were charged off because such investment and advances were believed to be worthless.

[d] Balances carried as due from Manning & Company.

[e] Balances carried as due from approximately 650 foreign accounts (Connecticut Division) and 115 foreign accounts (Canadian Company). Cf. Ex. 255; R. 935, 4436.

[f] Supposedly held by the 5 Canadian vendors for the account of the McKesson Companies.

Comparison of Operations

Connecticut Division	Reported for the year 1937 [a]	Fictitious [b]	Reported less Fictitious [c]
Net sales	$ 24, 210, 714. 41	$ 15, 126, 825. 20	$ 9,083,889.21
Cost of sales	20, 290, 170. 14	[d] 13, 610, 355. 00	6,679,815.14
Gross profit on sales	$ 3, 920, 544. 27	$ 1, 516, 470. 20	$ 2,404,074.07
Expenses, other income, and other deductions (net)	1, 980, 486. 23	—	1,980,486.23
Net profit	$ 1, 940, 058. 04	$ 1, 516, 470. 20	$ 423,587.84
Canadian Company and Subsidiary			
Net sales	$ 3, 811, 422. 45	$ 3, 365, 070. 40	$ 446,352.05
Cost of sales	3, 500, 211. 48	[d] 3, 080, 150. 00	420,061.48
Gross profit on sales	$ 311, 210. 97	$ 284, 920. 40	$ 26,290.57
Expenses, other income, and other deductions (net)	132, 938. 05	—	132,938.05
Net profit or (loss)	$ 178, 272. 92	$ 284, 920. 40	$ (106,647.48)
Maryland Company and Subsidiaries Consolidated			
Net sales	$174, 572, 229. 57	$ [e] 18, 247, 020. 60	$156,325,208.97
Cost of sales	147, 634, 438. 71	[d] 16, 445, 630. 00	131,188,808.71
Gross profit on sales	$ 26, 937, 790. 86	$ 1, 801, 390. 60	$ 25,136,400.26
Expenses, other income, and other deductions (net)	23, 270, 466. 11	—	23,270,466.11
Net profit	$ 3, 667, 324. 75	$ 1, 801, 390. 60	$ 1,865,934.15

[a] Ex. 261, 167, 106.

[b] Ex. 255.

[c] A number of expenses actually paid for in connection with the fictitious transactions, such as the Smith fees, clerical and administrative overhead, taxes, and other relevant items, should also be deducted if it be desired to establish the past results of operations of the real business alone. (However, expenses in connection with these transactions do not appear to be substantial in relation to the totals shown. See pages 311-313 *infra.*) And to the extent that the Trustee may recover any such items they should also be deducted to establish the final results of past operations. For a reconstructed comparative consolidated statement of income and profit and loss of the Maryland Company, for the years ended Dec. 31, 1936, 1937, and 1938, see Second Report of William J. Wardall, Trustee, *In the Matter of McKesson & Robbins, Incorporated,* Debtor, Exhibit E, in which the Canadian Company and its subsidiary are not consolidated with the Maryland accounts because the Maryland Company's investment in the Canadian Company was believed to be worthless, and in which, pending the treatment by the Court of such claims as may be filed, no provision was made for possible claims by the Canadian Company, pursuant to the agreement whereby the Maryland Company, as successor to the Connecticut Company, was obligated, in the event the net profits of the Canadian Company available for dividends were less than $100,000.00 in any year, to pay in Canadian currency to the Canadian Company such difference.

[d] Computed by adding or subtracting difference between opening and closing inventories to or from purchases.

[e] After elimination of purported intercompany sales of foreign crude drugs by Canadian Company to Connecticut Division of $244,875.00.

As indicated in the foregoing tables, the fictitious items comprised approximately 88% of the total reported current assets of the Connecticut Division as at December 31, 1937; approximately 98% of the total reported current assets of the Canadian Company and subsidiary; and approximately 25% of the total reported current assets of the Maryland Company and subsidiaries consolidated.

Since total current assets in all three units comprised a very substantial part of total assets,[117] the fictitious items were found to comprise approximately 77% of total reported assets in the Connecticut Division as at December 31, 1937; approximately 85% of total reported assets in the Canadian Company and subsidiary; and approximately 22% of total reported assets of the Maryland Company and subsidiaries consolidated.

Also, as indicated by the foregoing tables, the fictitious transactions comprised approximately 62% of reported net sales of the Connecticut Division for the year 1937; approximately 88% of reported net sales of the Canadian Company and subsidiary; and approximately 10% of reported net sales of the Maryland Company and subsidiaries consolidated.

Finally, as shown by the foregoing tables, the fictitious gross profit arising from these items comprised approximately 39% of reported gross profit of the Connecticut Division for the year 1937; approximately 92% of reported gross profit of the Canadian Company and subsidiary; and approximately 7% of reported gross profit of the Maryland Company and subsidiaries consolidated. But, since expenses in connection with the fictitious business when compared to the real business were not large; it should be noted that the elimination of fictitious items had a far greater proportional effect on reported net profit.[118] And, since in earlier years total reported net profit of the Maryland Company and subsidiaries consolidated was not as large as it was in 1937, the elimination of these fictitious transactions would have had an even greater effect on net profits in those years.

For the 6 years 1932–1937, gross profit on the fictitious sales purportedly effected through Smith for both the Connecticut Company (later Division) and Canadian Company combined amounted to approximately $8,800,000,[119] while combined inventories and accounts receivable purportedly carried by the two units in connection with

[117] Ex. 28. See also tables on pages 43-44 *supra* and page 250 *infra*.

[118] For amounts involved see tables on page 44 *supra*.

[119] The Canadian Company accounted for approximately $1,500,000. Ex. 43, Q. The Connecticut Company (later Division) accounted for approximately $7,300,000, Ex. 124, 267, N. The latter figure includes for 1932 "Special Finished Stock," apparently comprising part of "Export sales of crude drugs and finished stock through W. W. Smith & Co." Ex. 81, 82. For "Special Finished Stock," see section IV, subsection I *infra*.

these foreign crude drug transactions increased during the same period approximately $9,600,000.[120]

The situation in the Connecticut Division was summarized by Julian F. Thompson, treasurer of McKesson, who stated, in a memorandum to F. D. Coster dated April 18, 1938, copies of which were sent to Charles F. Michaels and William J. Murray, Jr., that

> "It will be observed [121] that the inventory and receivables of the Bulk Department [122] increase annually and approximately the amount of the profit of the department, and that the Connecticut Division has not contributed a net balance to the [Maryland] Corporation for the purposes of bond interest, dividends or bank debt reduction during the past three years. In mentioning this fact, however, it would not be fair to fail to point out that through the use of the capital in the Connecticut Division there is contributed approximately two-fifths of the profits [of the Maryland Company] available for interest, dividends, taxes, etc." [123]

As to the period prior to 1932, there are references in the Price, Waterhouse & Co. papers indicating that the inventories and accounts receivable in question were large in amount (though smaller in each preceding year).[124] Some idea of the amount of the transactions can be obtained from the report by S. D. Leidesdorf & Co. to William J. Wardall, Trustee of McKesson & Robbins, Incorporated, relating to the crude drug fraud. In considering the figures mentioned in this report, it should be remembered that the great bulk of the actual cash payments referred to therein occurred prior to 1932, after which more and more of the transactions were purportedly cleared through the pretended bank, Manning & Company, until, with the exception of the Smith service and guaranty fees, all transactions were so handled. Speaking of the Leidesdorf report, the Trustee in his report dated July 1, 1939 says:

> "The report in summary shows that cash disbursements, all in connection with payments for purchase of fictitious drugs or for non-existent services in connection with the operation of the Crude Drug Department, aggregated $24,777,851.90. Of this total cash outgo, $17,571,546.46 was paid out in the first instance by the Company, [125] and $7,206,305.44 by McKesson & Robbins, Limited, a Canadian

[120] The combined inventories and accounts receivable of the Canadian Company remained fairly constant, the increase taking place in the Connecticut Company (later Division). In some years the increase was in either inventories or accounts receivable, with a slight decrease in the other. Ex. 43, Q.

[121] The paragraph here quoted follows a table of figures for the years 1935, 1936, and 1937.

[122] Included real domestic crude business, as well as fictitious foreign. However, the figures for the former comprised by a minor portion of the total. R. 110-113 and tables on pages 43-44 *supra*.

[123] Ex. 114. See also R. 1388-1389; Ex. 115.

[124] For notations during this period as to increases in inventories of crude drugs of the type later purportedly sold through Smith, see Ex. 154 at p. 19, Ex. 153 at p. 20, Ex. 151 at p. 6, Ex. 148 at p. 11, and Ex. 147 at p. 7. On accounts receivable of the type later purportedly resulting from sales through Smith, see Ex. 83 at p. 1 and Ex. 151 at p. 2. Gross profit on "Export sales of crude drugs and finished stock through W. W. Smith & Co." for the Connecticut Company in 1931 are stated in the memorandum of accounts for that year at $1,413,889.25, Ex. 82. (An interesting breakdown of this latter figure as between "Resale Stock" and "Finished Stock," and by months, is contained in Ex. 105, prepared by a McKesson employee.) On the Canadian Company, see Ex. 149, 150, 161. Finally, a number of the concerns in the fictitious chain, e. g., W. W. Smith & Co., J. P. Meyer & Co., George Vernard & Co., appear among the early accounts receivable of Girard & Co., Inc., indicating that fictitious transactions most probably existed even then, although possibly not with foreign accounts. Ex. 170; R. 4580-4581.

[125] When used in this quotation, "Company" refers to Connecticut Company, a subsidiary of the Maryland Company and after October 31, 1934, a division of the Maryland Company.

subsidiary. These payments were principally made to George Vernard, a brother of F. Donald Coster, whose real name was Arthur Musica, who received $9,316,-770.76; Simon Brothers, who received $5,877,942.22; W. W. Smith & Company; J. P. Meyer & Company; The Woodtone Co., Inc.; Liberty Drug & Chemical Company; United Chemical & Drug Corporation; and Ramse's, Inc. The figure given above of $24,777,851.90 consists only of initial payments made by the Company and its Canadian subsidiary and does not include deposits on subsequent transfers of these funds. The aggregate of all deposits in bank accounts other than accounts of the Company and its Canadian subsidiary, involved in the circle of funds in the crude drug fraud was $43,764,585.00.

"Of the total cash outgo mentioned above, by far the greater part was traced back by Messrs. S. D. Leidesdorf & Co. into the Company or its Canadian subsidiary. The amount of these refunds so traced and identified amounted to $19,674,858.66, of which $12,719,503.14 was returned to the Company and $6,955,355.52 to McKesson & Robbins, Limited. The bulk of these refunds was made through cash payments against fictitious accounts receivable. The bank account most actively used as a medium for making these refunds was that of The Woodtone Co., Inc., through the medium of which repayments of $9,744,477.70 were made, and the second most active account used as a medium for making these refunds was that of Liberty Drug & Chemical Company, through the medium of which repayments of $2,481,982.44 were made.

"From the foregoing it appears that of the approximate $24,000,000 of cash outgo from the Company and its Canadian subsidiary in connection with fictitious transactions, approximately $19,000,000 was actually traced dollar for dollar through the course of various bank accounts and shown to have been eventually refunded. The net cash loss, however, is not as great as the difference between these two figures as there was also paid in and credited on the accounts receivable cards of fictitious customers an additional amount of $2,203,544.20. Of this amount, $397,410 was paid in from sources indirectly involved in the circle of funds. The detail records are not sufficient actually to identify the transactions relating to the balance of $1,806,134.20 paid in against fictitious accounts receivable; but the transactions were similar to those which were reconciled with the detail records in the amount of $19,674,858.66, above mentioned. Accordingly, the balance of $1,806,134.20 has been assumed to have been returned in the same manner as the $19,674,858.66 actually traced.

"It appears that the amount definitely lost by virtue of the crude drug fraud is now set at a figure of $2,869,482.95, of which the largest items were $958,323.79 traced to bank or brokerage accounts of F. Donald Coster, payments of $715,676.12 made by McKesson & Robbins, Limited to William T. Truxtun & Company and not traced to any bank account, payments to Simon Brothers of $278,453.65 also not traced to a bank account, and $30,749.29 traced to a bank account of Benjamin Simon.

"Following the adoption of the fiscal agency of Manning & Company in 1931, the amount of cash in the circle of funds described above steadily diminished. At the commencement of this proceeding on December 8, 1938, the cash circle of funds had substantially disappeared, and the mechanism which was then being used was that described in the First Report of the Trustee, consisting of fictitious purchases of crude drugs purportedly stored in Montreal and then purportedly shipped to purchasers abroad, the payments to the sellers and the collections from the purchasers being purportedly made through the fiscal agents, Manning & Company. In connection with this mechanism, the principal outgo was the payment of commissions and a guaranty fee to W. W. Smith & Company. The amount of such payments to W. W. Smith & Company over the period 1931 to 1938 was $886,999.26, of which $206,290.22 was paid by McKesson & Robbins,

Limited. These figures are included in the aggregate figures given above for the outgo in connection with the fictitious operations of the Crude Drug Department." [126]

Leidesdorf's examination further indicates that the fictitious transactions in crude drugs go back at least to early in 1927, the first year of the Connecticut and Canadian Companies.[127] The inclusion of accounts of this type on the Connecticut Company's books in a category known as "Special foreign (Girard division),"[128] and the inclusion of W. W. Smith & Co. as an account receivable at the time of the first Price, Waterhouse & Co. audit of Girard & Co., Inc. as at December 31, 1924,[129] indicate that fictitious entries probably go back to the inception of that concern also.

C. THE MANNER IN WHICH THE FICTITIOUS ACCOUNTS WERE HANDLED

Since the middle of 1935, the fictitious foreign crude drug purchases were pretended to have been made from five Canadian vendors, who thereafter purportedly retained the merchandise at their warehouses for the account of McKesson. Sales were pretended to have been made for McKesson's account by W. W. Smith & Company, Inc. and the goods shipped directly by the latter from the Canadian vendors to the customers. Payments for goods purchased and collections from customers for goods sold were pretended to have been made by the Montreal banking firm of Manning & Company also for the account of McKesson. W. W. Smith & Company, Inc., Manning & Company, and the five Canadian vendors are now known to have been either entirely fictitious or merely blinds used by Coster for the purpose of supporting the fictitious transactions.

Invoices, advices, and other documents prepared on printed forms in the names of these firms were used to give an appearance of reality to the fictitious transactions. In addition to this manufacture of documents, a series of contracts and guaranties with Smith and Manning, and forged credit reports on Smith were also utilized. The foreign firms to whom the goods were supposed to have been sold were real but had done no business of the type indicated with McKesson.

Prior to 1935 the fictitious goods were supposed to have been physically received at and reshipped from the Bridgeport plant of McKesson. And prior to 1931 McKesson made actual cash payments directly for the fictitious purchases, which at that time were supposed to have been made from a group of domestic vendors, but recovered a large

[126] Second Report of William J. Wardall, Trustee, *In the Matter of McKesson & Robbins, Incorporated*, Debtor, at pp. 11–12. Figures introduced by S. D. Leidesdorf & Co. in the present hearing, R. 4573–4574, were preliminary and therefore differ somewhat from the final figures above quoted.

[127] R. 4554 ff.

[128] Ex. 146.

[129] Ex. 170.

part of this cash purportedly as collections on the fictitious sales. The change from using actual cash to the supposed clearance through Manning & Company was not effected abruptly but for some time after 1931 both systems were used. The Canadian vendors, however, were used only in connection with the Manning clearance system. For about a year prior to August 1, 1931, the date of the first purported sales agency arrangement with W. W. Smith & Company, Inc., the sales supposedly were made for the account of McKesson by the purported sales agency of Charles Manning & Company, Limited.

A detailed account of the manner in which the fictitious accounts were handled will be described in the following subsections:

1. The Office at Bridgeport

All of McKesson's records pertaining to the foreign crude drug transactions both for the Connecticut Division (formerly Company) and for the Canadian Company were kept in offices at the Bridgeport plant. The relationship of these offices and the people who ran them is important to a consideration of the manner in which the transactions themselves were handled.

As previously stated, F. Donald Coster was president of the Maryland, Connecticut, and Canadian Companies. He also acted as the treasurer of the Connecticut and Canadian Companies in which the foreign crude drug transactions were centered. The office of treasurer in the top Maryland Company was held by Horace B. Merwin until February 19, 1930, when he was succeeded by Julian F. Thompson. Throughout the whole period George Dietrich was the assistant treasurer of all three companies, the Maryland, Connecticut, and Canadian, and, after the Maryland Company absorbed the Connecticut in October 1934, continued in charge of the detailed financial transactions of that Division. Thompson, the treasurer of the Maryland Company, spent most of his time in New York and took no part in the routine functioning of the Connecticut Division business but rather concerned himself with the financial problems of the Maryland Company as a whole.[130]

Speaking of the personal relationship between Coster and George Dietrich, as well as of the physical location of their offices, Thorn, of Price, Waterhouse & Co., testified:

> "* * * George Dietrich's office adjoined Mr. Coster and there was a connecting door, of course, and that door was always open except when Mr. Coster was in conference and the two men worked together almost the same as if their desks were side by side, and anyone seeing the two men, watching them for a short time could have no question about who gave the orders and who did the clerical work." [131]

[130] R. 1593, 2064–2065.
[131] R. 1166.

Referring further to the relationship of the two men, McGloon, the comptroller, said:

"If you look at the organization chart, dated September 1, 1937 [Ex. 97] it appears that Mr. George Dietrich was responsible to Mr. Dewell, but in practice, Mr. George Dietrich was very close to Mr. Coster and many of us considered Mr. George Dietrich as Coster's right hand man or confidential secretary." [132]

And Thompson, the treasurer, speaking of Coster and George Dietrich, the assistant treasurer, said:

"He [George Dietrich] was scarcely my assistant at all and was very definitely Mr. Coster's agent.

* * * * * * *

"I don't think I ever mentioned any subject to Mr. George Dietrich that wasn't mentioned [by him] to Mr. Coster in our entire relationship." [133]

As stated by Thorn, on one side George Dietrich's office had a door leading into Coster's room and on the other side adjoined the cashier's office, where three girls worked under George Dietrich's supervision, recording remittances and disbursements and preparing deposits, outgoing checks, bank reconciliations, and so forth.[134] George Dietrich, as assistant treasurer, also signed practically all the checks of the Connecticut Company (later Division),[135] at first alone, later with the co-signature of one of the girls who worked under him.[136] He also routed incoming remittances to the cashiers [137] and was custodian of petty cash funds.[138]

In addition to the foregoing, George Dietrich, under Coster, ran the foreign crude drug business for both the Connecticut Division (formerly Company) and Canadian Company, which, as previously stated, comprised well over two-thirds of the total business done at Bridgeport. While the exact assumption of initiative between Coster and George Dietrich in the supposed running of this business is not clear, it was George Dietrich's initials or verbal clearance, at any rate, that furnished the internal authority for all foreign crude drug purchases and sales orders.[139]

Besides, George Dietrich also exercised control over all incoming mail. Ritts, of Price, Waterhouse & Co., stated:

"All incoming mail would be received by George Dietrich, which would not necessarily mean that he opened all incoming mail. In fact, a number of these mailing boys opened the mail and laid it on his desk; in other words, he was the

[132] R. 1590. See also R. 1158, 1360.

[133] R. 2096, 2079.

[134] R. 118, 1172, 1358, 1381, 1590, 2642, 2659. Although the actual cashier's work was under the supervision of George Dietrich, Johnson, the office manager, planned their office hours and routine. R. 1401.

[135] R. 1159, 1432.

[136] R. 1639.

[137] R. 1158–1159 and footnote 140 *infra*.

[138] Ex. 17.

[139] R. 772–773, 1347, 1413–1414, 1617, 1661–1662, 2068, 4528 and see subsections 3 ff. *infra*. Ritts and Thorn, of Price, Waterhouse & Co., testified that it was their impression that Coster made the decisions and told George Dietrich what to do. R. 697, 736–738, 1133, 1163–1168; Ex. 83.

first person in the organization, apart from those mailing boys, that saw the mail. He would sort it for classification * * *." [140]

After the mail was sorted it was placed in a rack in George Dietrich's office, in pigeon-holes for the different departments. The same procedure would be followed as to mail marked for personal attention as well as to mail addressed to the firm.[141] As hereinafter pointed out, George Dietrich also controlled outgoing mail on foreign crude drug transactions, particularly customers' sales invoices and monthly statements.[142]

As previously stated, on one side Coster's room had a door leading into George Dietrich's office, which, in turn, adjoined the cashier's office. On the other side of Coster's room there was a door leading into the Board of Directors' room.[143] Next to this was the office occupied by Margaret Walsh, the sole employee of the Canadian Company,[144] who kept all of its books and who also received all of her instructions from George Dietrich.[145] Neither the cashier's office, referred to above, nor the main accounting office, referred to hereinafter, handled any of the detailed transactions of the Canadian Company.[146]

All of the offices previously described were on the side of the building. Across a hallway in the center were the main accounting offices, which included the billing, bookkeeping, and cost departments.[147] Then there was "* * * the comptroller's office, of course, that was separate from everything else." [148] And, finally, there were the offices of Robert J. Dietrich on the same floor as the other offices but in the back part of the building.[149] He had charge of shipping, receiving, plant purchasing,[150] and warehousing.[151]

---

140 R. 715. See also R. 1361, 1427, 1588.

141 R. 1427.

142 See page 86 *infra*.

143 R. 236.

144 Besides Miss Walsh, at one time there appear to have been two watchmen and another man on the pay-roll of the Canadian Company for a short while. R. 4392. The watchmen were employed in connection with a building the company leased but did not occupy in Canada. R. 4401 ff. Concernng the other man, Miss Walsh testified that she did not think he did anything for the Canadian Company, that she paid him on George Dietrich's instructions and that the only time she saw him was in George Dietrich's office, not working, but talking. R. 4402–4404. In addition to the work done by Miss Walsh, certain other work was done for the Canadian Company, e. g., tax work by the tax department; shipping, receiving, and duplicate inventory records by Robert J. Dietrich's department; and billing. See testimony of Walsh at R. 4383, 4389, 4394–4395, quoted in part at pages 93 ff. *infra*.

145 Ex. 19 (A3, A3a); R. 4391–4392.

146 R. 2692, 1371.

147 R. 4391, 1358.

148 Testimony of Johnson, R. 1358.

149 R. 1500.

150 "* * * Mr. Robert Dietrich purchased materials for the factory. Mr. McGloon purchased office supplies and machinery and equipment for the office, and George Dietrich purchased raw materials and crude drugs." Testimony of Johnson, R. 1359.

"* * * I think of Mr. Robert Dietrich as the purchasing agent for items other than these crude drugs, and in general in charge generally of the shipping and receiving. * * *" Testimony of Thorn, R. 1161.

151 R. 1358.

Concerning the responsibility of Robert Dietrich, Johnson, the office manager, testified:

"Q. [By Mr. GALPEER.] And whom would you say Mr. Robert Dietrich was responsible to?
A. Mr. Coster and Mr. Dietrich.
Q. That is, Mr. George Dietrich?
A. George Dietrich.
Q. Now, there is a number of clerks and employees in Mr. R. Dietrich's division?
A. Yes, sir.
Q. Are they all responsible to Mr. Robert Dietrich?
A. Every one of them.
Q. Are any of them under your orders or Mr. McGloon's orders?
A. No, sir." [152]

On the same subject McGloon testified:

"Q. [By Mr. GALPEER.] How about Mr. Robert Dietrich, to whom was he responsible?
A. According to the charts of September 1, 1937 [Ex. 97], he too was responsible to Mr. Dewell.
Q. But in practice?
A. Well, I guess in practice he was responsible to Mr. Dewell, but he is a very difficult man to control and he formulated his own rules and regulations and always had access to Mr. Coster's office.
Q. Do you know of Mr. Dewell having given him any orders?
A. Oh, at times, yes; I have often seen in the last two years, Mr. Robert Dietrich in Mr. Dewell's office with others.
Q. Did others have the same access to Mr. Coster's office as Mr. Robert Dietrich had?
A. No, not the same as Mr. Robert Dietrich, no." [153]

Regardless of what control Dewell could or could not exercise over Robert Dietrich in the other branches of the business, in respect to the foreign crude drug transactions, in any event, there was no connection between them,[154] and on this phase, therefore, Johnson's testimony would appear wholly applicable.

Somewhat the same idea as that expressed by McGloon concerning Robert Dietrich's access to Coster's office was perhaps differently stated by Harry W. Osterhout, an employee in the cost department at Bridgeport since November 1925,[155] who testified:

"Q. [By Mr. STEWART.] Did you know of any relationship between Mr. Coster and the Dietrichs?
A. No, sir, although it was rumored—we heard all sorts of rumors. I did hear a rumor that they were cousins, or something like that, but nothing definite."[156]

Moreover, it was well established that neither of the Dietrichs took any vacations. With one exception,[156a] the longest George Dietrich

[152] R. 1360.
[153] R. 1590–1591.
[154] R. 1162.
[155] R. 4523–4524.
[156] R. 4525. Osterhout stated that this did not make him suspicious and that he never communicated this rumor to Price, Waterhouse & Co. See page 269 *infra*.
[156a] In *U. S. of America* v. *George Musica, et al.* (footnote 23 *supra*), George Dietrich testified that during the whole ten years he was only away from the plant because of sickness for one period of five weeks.

was away from the plant while it was in operation, including time off for sickness, was a half day. Similarly, the longest Robert Dietrich stayed away was 2 or 3 days. Whenever George Dietrich did leave, even for a few hours, Robert Dietrich would move up and occupy his office, next to Coster's, but while occupying George's office would never do any of his work.[157]

2. Smith and Manning

At the time of the 1937 audit, all of the sales of foreign crude drugs, both by the Connecticut Division and Canadian Company, were purportedly made for their account under a contract with the pretended sales agency, W. W. Smith & Company, Inc., while payment for goods purchased and collections on goods sold were purportedly made direct by the assumed bankers, Manning & Company, also for the account of the respective McKesson Companies. The goods themselves were supposedly retained by the five Canadian vendors previously mentioned until sold and shipped by W. W. Smith & Company, Inc., under the contract referred to above.[158] The contract also contained collection guaranty provisions. As previously stated, Smith and Manning would now appear to have been either entirely fictitious or, to the extent that they had any reality, were blinds used by Coster for his fictitious transactions. In order properly to appreciate the various documents and methods of handling the fictitious transactions it is necessary first to know the purported relationship of Smith and Manning to the McKesson Companies and the predecessor, Girard & Co., Inc., and the details of the contracts under which they were supposed to have been operating.

In 1925, while still with Bond & Goodwin, Inc., investment bankers, Julian Thompson prepared a report on Girard & Co., Inc.,[159] in which he gave the following description of the purported origin of that concern and the prior connection of its personnel with W. W. Smith & Co.:

> "Frank D. Coster and P. Horace Girard were for many years associated together in the employ of W. W. Smith & Company, importers, exporters and brokers of chemicals under the Senior Mr. Smith, now deceased. A few years ago W. W. Smith & Company found themselves owed a substantial amount of money by the Adelphi Pharmaceutical Mfg. Company and Mr. Coster was sent over there by W. W. Smith & Company as General Manager to try and assist them in their difficulties and incidentally to try and get W. W. Smith & Company's money.
>
> *　　*　　*　　*　　*　　*　　*
>
> "At about the time he [Coster] withdrew [from Adelphi Pharmaceutical Mfg. Company], the Senior Mr. Smith died and Mr. Girard had decided to go into busi-

[157] R. 1361-1362, 1430-1433, 1472, 1489-1493, 1591, 1701-1704, 4431-4432, 4435-4436. However, Price, Waterhouse & Co. representatives who testified at the hearings stated they were not aware of the situation mentioned in this paragraph.

[158] See page 48 *supra* and page 68 *infra*.

[159] Ex. 177; R. 2242-2243. A copy of the report was given to Horace B. Merwin but nothing in the record ndicates that Price, Waterhouse & Co. saw this report or knew iits contents.

ness for himself, having already applied for a corporate charter under the name of Girard & Company. Mr. Coster therefore joined forces with Mr. Girard, put in a larger amount of capital and they started business, securing Mr. George A. Dietrich, who is a practical experienced accountant, to handle the billing and bookkeeping end."[160]

In Thompson's report there is also set forth the following answer he received from W. W. Smith & Co., in response to a trade inquiry on Girard & Co., Inc.:

"In reply to your inquiry on Girard & Co., Inc., Mount Vernon, New York, we have sold them both for account of ourselves and for foreign accounts that we represent on a basis of 10 days less 1 or 2% or 30–60 days net, the range of billings has been from $200 low to $50,000 highest. They have at all times taken advantage of discounts.

"We consider them a very desirable account and fully reliable and responsible for their engagements.

Very truly yours,

W. W. SMITH & Co.,
(signed) by WILLIAM W. SMITH."[161]

From the work sheets of Price, Waterhouse & Co., it appears that W. W. Smith & Co. was also an important account receivable on the books of Girard & Co., Inc. So, too, was the Charles Manning Chemical Company.[162] The amounts owing by these firms, and the percentage this bore to the total reported accounts receivable of Girard & Co., Inc., are indicated in the following table:[163]

Audit date	W. W. Smith & Co.	Charles Manning Chemical Company	Percentage of the two accounts combined to total accounts receivable
Dec. 31, 1924	$ 9, 305. 05	$ —	27%
Dec. 31, 1925	22, 750. 00	—	13%
Mar. 31, 1926	32, 246. 00	31, 025. 00	29%
June 30, 1926	20, 025. 00	21, 875. 00	18%
Sept. 30, 1926	31, 650. 00	24, 100. 00	13%
Nov. 30, 1926	18, 925. 00	24, 700. 00	11%

An additional relationship with Manning is indicated in the Price, Waterhouse & Co. report on the operations of the Connecticut Company for the 4 months ended March 31, 1927, where reference is made to the receivable owing by:

"Estate of Charles Manning for improvements at 79 Cliff Street, New York chargeable to owners .... $20, 995. 54"[164]

[160] Ex. 177. See also R. 2119. P. Horace Girard appears to be another of the Musica-Coster aliases. See footnote 27 *supra*.

[161] Ex. 177.

[162] R. 48.

[163] Ex. 170.

[164] Ex. 145. The premises referred to, 79 Cliff Street, New York City, were then being occupied by the Connecticut Company and were still being used by McKesson at the time of the present hearings. R. 2611 and footnote 44 *supra*.

The first of the series of sales agency contracts with McKesson appears to have been entered into on March 12, 1930, with Charles Manning & Company, Limited. In view of the reliance placed by the auditors upon these contracts as explaining the basis for the differences in the manner of handling all the fictitious foreign crude drug transactions they must be considered in some detail. The first contract with Charles Manning & Company, Limited was summarized in one of Price, Waterhouse & Co.'s papers as follows:

"McKesson & Robbins, Incorporated (Connecticut)—
Extracts From Manning Agreement

* * * * *

Dated: March 12, 1930.

Parties: Charles Manning & Company, Limited, 1396 St. Catherine St., West, Montreal, Canada, 1st party. McKesson & Robbins, Incorporated, McKesson & Robbins, Limited, 2nd parties.

Compensation: 2nd party to pay 1st party $12,000.00 for services during 1930.

Service: 1st party agrees to give 2nd party preference on all purchase inquiries in their line, and whenever requested to handle shipping and forwarding.

Credits and guaranty. The acceptance or rejection of an order to be at discretion of 2nd party but 1st party unconditionally guarantees the full payment of all orders booked through them, in case of any default, upon 30 days notice from 2nd party in writing of such default, said liability to be limited to $150,000.00. This guaranty to remain in full force and effect at all times that any sales made through 1st party remain outstanding and unpaid.

Term: One year from date.

Signed by Chas. Manning, *President.*

Note.—Balance sheet of the Manning Co. certified by the president shows net worth at Dec. 31, 1929 of $582,404.65." [165]

In a supplement to the memorandum on accounts of the Connecticut Company for 1930, Thorn described the arrangement as follows:

"The orders covering the sales of bulk crude drugs are received from Manning & Co., Ltd., Montreal. Manning is the purchasing agent for several hundred retailers and jobbers throughout the British Empire. Manning's clients place all their foreign buying orders with him and he in turn places the order with a seller with whom he has a contract. He does not charge either party any commission. The buyer and seller each pay him a flat fee annually. In the case of McKesson & Robbins, they pay a fee of $12,000.00 per year." [166]

On or about August 1, 1931, there was a shift in the reputed sales agency arrangement from Manning to Smith and, in this connection, there were three separate documents in the contract file at Bridgeport.[167]

The first was an unsigned copy of an agreement dated August 1, 1931, between Manning & Company, a co-partnership of Montreal, Canada, and McKesson & Robbins, Incorporated (of Connecticut) and McKesson & Robbins, Limited (of Canada) to which was attached an unsigned copy of an agreement also dated August 1, 1931 between W. W. Smith & Company, Inc., and McKesson & Robbins, Incor-

[165] Ex. 89.

[166] Ex. 83.

[167] Ex. 206, 215, 216; R. 4348, 4459–4461.

porated (of Connecticut) and McKesson & Robbins, Limited (of Canada).[168]

The second was a separate copy of the agreement dated August 1, 1931, between W. W. Smith & Company, Inc., and McKesson & Robbins, Incorporated (of Connecticut) and McKesson & Robbins, Limited (of Canada) referred to above but signed by James Lamont as president of W. W. Smith & Company, Inc.[169]

The third was a digest of an agreement also dated August 1, 1931, which stated that—

> "W. W. Smith & Co., a co-partnership of Liverpool, England unconditionally guarantees the performance of the contract entered into on August 1, 1931, by W. W. Smith & Co., Inc., * * * insofar as the performance of W. W. Smith & Co., Inc., is concerned."

The digest had been stamped "cancelled." [170]

The first document, the copy of the agreement with Manning & Company dated August 1, 1931 first stated that—

> "WHEREAS, the Connecticut Company for the joint and several benefit of itself and the Canadian Company did on March 12, 1930, enter into a contract with Charles Manning & Company, Limited, a Canadian corporation and whereby the latter agreed for the considerations therein set forth to render certain services in promoting the foreign trade of the Connecticut and of the Canadian Company and said contract has since been renewed for a period extending to March 12, 1932, and
>
> "WHEREAS, the assets and business of the said Charles Manning & Company, Limited, have been acquired by said Manning & Company, which has assumed all of the liabilities of said Charles Manning & Company, Limited, and which has caused all the foreign and domestic buying and selling offices and agencies formerly owned and conducted by said Charles Manning & Company, Limited, to be transferred to W. W. Smith & Company, Inc., a New York corporation which it has caused to be organized for the purpose of acquiring the same and the said Manning & Company have requested the Connecticut Company and the Canadian Company to execute a new agreement with said W. W. Smith & Company, Inc., in lieu of said contract of March 12, 1930, as renewed and extended, all being in furtherance of the plans of said Manning & Company to conserve, for the benefit of said W. W. Smith & Company, Inc. (one hundred per cent (100%), of the stock of which it owns), and indirectly for its own benefit the business and good will of said Charles Manning & Company, Limited;" [171]

and then provided in part that—

> "3. Manning & Company expressly represent that it has acquired all of the foreign exchange and banking business formerly conducted by said Charles Manning & Company, Limited, and that hereafter such business will be conducted by it under its own name.
>
> "4. Manning & Company hereby unconditionally guarantees the complete and prompt performance by W. W. Smith & Company, Inc., of all of the obligations

---

168 Ex. 216.

169 Ex. 206.

170 Ex. 215. The auditors were apparently unaware of the first of the three documents just mentioned but assumed the third to be in force during its term. See pages 63, 203–204 *infra*.

171 Ex. 216.

and undertakings of the latter under and by virtue of the contract entered into between W. W. Smith & Company, Inc., with the Connecticut Company and the Canadian Company, a copy of which is hereto attached * * *.

"5. The guarantee of Manning & Company of the said contract between the McKesson Companies and W. W. Smith & Company, Inc., extends to and includes the agreements of W. W. Smith & Company, Inc., with respect to the guaranteeing to the McKesson Companies the accounts of purchasers of goods under said contract * * *.

"6. Manning & Company hereby further agree that they will at the request of the McKesson Companies, or either of them, at any time during the period of this contract, place at the disposal of the Connecticut Company, and/or the Canadian Company, credit accommodations on commercial credits not to exceed in the aggregate at any one time the sum of one million dollars ($1,000,000) United States dollars, or the equivalent thereof in the currency of Great Britain, France, Germany, Italy, Austria, Sweden or Norway, said commercial letters and credits to be issued against shipments of merchandise and to be made available by bills of exchange payable at sight, or with maturities not to exceed one hundred eighty (180) days sight.

"The rates of commission to be charged by Manning & Company for the granting of such credits to be as follows:

Sight Credits	1/20 of 1%
30 days sight	1/10 of 1%
60 " "	1/8 of 1%
90 " "	1/4 of 1%
120 " "	1/2 of 1%
180 " "	3/4 of 1%

"It is understood and agreed that the above rates shall be subject to change from time to time to conform to the lowest schedule and prevailing market rates established from time to time by recognized commercial banks and bankers, and it is further understood and agreed that the proportion of said total of one million dollars ($1,000,000) to be outstanding at one time shall be made available to the two McKesson Companies in such proportions as to each as the Connecticut Company may from time to time direct.

"7. The term of this agreement shall be for a period of two years beginning August 1, 1931 * * *.'' [172]

The second document, a copy of which was attached to the Manning agreement, was a contract between W. W. Smith & Company, Inc. (New York), and McKesson & Robbins, Incorporated (Connecticut), and McKesson & Robbins, Limited (Canada), and was also dated August 1, 1931.

First, it recited the same two "Whereas" clauses above quoted in the Manning & Company agreement which referred to the prior contract with Charles Manning & Company, Limited, the acquisition of that firm by Manning & Company, and the formation by Manning & Company of W. W. Smith & Company, Inc., the New York Company, as a wholly owned subsidiary, and then provided: [173]

"Now, Therefore, it is agreed between the parties hereto as follows:

"1. The New York Company expressly represents that it has acquired and now owns and controls all of the domestic and foreign buying and selling offices,

[172] Ex. 216.

[173] In view of the basic nature of this contract, its remaining provisions are set forth in full.

agencies and facilities formerly owned by Charles Manning & Company, Limited, and located in Canada, New York City, Australia, London (England), Hamburg (Germany), Hong Kong (China), Ceylon (India), Yokohama (Japan), Genoa (Italy), Bergen (Norway), and Marseilles (France), and that it will continue to conduct such offices and agencies under the corporate name of W. W. Smith & Company, Inc.

"2. All purchase inquiries received by the New York Company for drugs, chemicals and any other commodities dealt in by the McKesson Companies, or either of them, will be submitted to either or both of said McKesson Companies to enable them to submit prices and quotations on the same and in the event that the prices, quality, terms and conditions of sale quoted by the Connecticut and/or Canadian Company are as favorable as others received by the New York Company in the open market, the latter will grant a preference to the McKesson Company which has quoted such price and will place all such business with it.

"3. Whenever requested so to do by either of the McKesson Companies the New York Company will as forwarding agents and at its own expense, attend to and assume responsibility for the proper shipping, storing, forwarding, withdrawal, weighing, handling and insuring of all such goods and the securing of consular invoices or other documents convenient or necessary to expedite or insure the delivery thereof, all expense thereby incurred by the New York Company to be for the account of and billed to the purchaser by the New York Company as forwarding agents' charges, it being the intent hereof that delivery by the McKesson Companies shall consist of delivery f. o. b. New York.

"4. Neither the Connecticut Company, nor the Canadian Company shall be obligated hereby to submit bids or prices in response to inquiries of the New York Company and either of them shall have the option to accept or reject, with or without cause, any order which the New York Company may seek to place with it.

"5. In consideration of a premium of one-half of one per cent (in addition to the service charge hereinafter provided for) of the total amount of any order placed under the provisions hereof, the New York Company will, if requested so to do in writing, unconditionally guaranty the full and prompt payment therefor by the purchaser in dollars, it being understood that the liability under this guaranty will become absolute thirty (30) days after written notice to the New York Company that such purchaser has defaulted payment in whole or in part, provided, however, that the total of accounts so guaranteed shall not at any time exceed the sum of $350,000. The liability of the New York Company hereunder shall not be affected by the fact that the guaranty premium shall not have been actually paid in advance, it being the intention of the parties that such premium items shall be billed monthly to the McKesson Companies. In the event the New York Company is required to and does re-imburse either of the McKesson Companies as herein provided, then it shall be entitled to an assignment in its favor of the claim of such company against the defaulting purchaser.

"6. It is understood that the New York Company will transact business in other commodities than those dealt in by the McKesson Companies and with respect thereto may have occasion to make guaranties similar to those above referred to, but the New York Company hereby agrees that at no time while this contract is in effect will the total amount so guaranteed by it, under this contract and otherwise, exceed the sum of $500,000.

"7. Inasmuch as the New York Company in its capacity as purchasing agent for foreign principals is precluded from collecting directly or indirectly any brokerage or commission from any seller, it hereby agrees that it will charge no brokerage or commission to either of the McKesson Companies on orders placed by it with such companies but that the latter will bill to the purchaser at the actual net price such orders as are accepted.

"8. The McKesson Companies in full consideration of the services to be rendered by the New York Company hereunder (except the guaranty of accounts) will jointly pay to the New York Company a service charge at the rate of $18,000. a year, the same to be payable in equal monthly installments of $1,500. each, the first of such installments to become due thirty days after the date hereof, it being understood that the aforesaid service charge shall be payable regardless of the amount of business that shall accrue to the McKesson Companies hereunder. The McKesson Companies shall divide said total service charge of $1,500. a month between them in such manner as they deem proper.

"9. The McKesson Companies will bill all purchasers in terms of dollars and wherever herein the term 'dollar' or its symbol is used the United States dollar is thereby intended.

"10. All sales made by the McKesson Companies hereunder shall be made direct to the purchaser and in no case to the New York Company (unless this be varied by written instructions to the contrary) and all documents representing the proceeds of such sales shall be in the name of either the Connecticut Company or the Canadian Company, provided, however, that nothing contained in this paragraph shall be construed to alter the liability assumed by the New York Company under Paragraph 3 hereof with respect to the forwarding, delivery and insuring of the shipments.

"11. The McKesson Companies agree that they or neither of them will while this contract is in effect solicit orders from any other brokers or commission merchants in any country where the New York Company maintains offices or agencies except in the United States and that they or either of them will not accept or execute orders from customers in any such country (other than the United States) and whose orders have at any time been referred by the New York Company to either of the McKesson Companies.

"12. This agreement shall remain in force for a period of two years from the date hereof, but the same may be cancelled by either party on ninety (90) days notice in writing, provided, however, that the termination hereof, either by expiration or cancellation, shall not alter the liability of the New York Company for outstanding commitments.

"13. The New York Company hereby assumes all of the outstanding liability of Charles Manning & Company under said contract of March 12, 1930, as renewed and extended and agrees to hold the McKesson Companies harmless on account of any future liability of the McKesson Companies or either of them thereunder." [174]

The third document, the digest of agreement with W. W. Smith & Co. also dated August 1, 1931, read as follows:

"DIGEST OF CONTRACT

"1. W. W. Smith & Co., a co-partnership of Liverpool, England, unconditionally guarantees the performance of contract entered into on August 1, 1931 by W. W. Smith & Co., Inc., and McKesson & Robbins, Inc. (Conn.) and/or McKesson & Robbins, Limited, insofar as the performance of W. W. Smith & Co. Inc. is concerned.

"2. McKesson & Robbins, Inc. (Conn.) and/or McKesson & Robbins, Ltd., have the right to enforce guarantee by an action against the co-partnership,

---

[174] Ex. 206.

without first proceeding against or having execution returned unsatisfied against said W. W. Smith & Co. Inc." [175]

In this connection, the minutes of a special meeting of the Board of Directors of McKesson & Robbins, Incorporated (Connecticut) held on September 3, 1931, recited that:

"The President stated to the meeting that the experience of the Company in its foreign business had demonstrated that it was inadvisable to maintain extensive branch offices or selling organizations in such countries and that such business could be more efficiently and cheaply handled by enlisting the services of reputable foreign buying commissionnaires and brokers and that this was the practice with a number of large American companies which had extensive foreign business. He pointed out that the Company thereby obtained the best informed advice as to foreign accounts and credits which it would be impossible for the Company to obtain directly in view of the practice in foreign countries in this respect. He added that this Company had used this method in the past with excellent results, especially with respect to the avoidance of credit losses, and that the expense represented by the commissions of such foreign commissionnaires, including their charges for the guaranteeing of accounts was fully justified and a great benefit to the Company. He stated that the officers of this Company had, therefore, negotiated a contract with Manning & Co. a co-partnership of Montreal, Canada and a subsidiary contract with W. W. Smith, Inc. a New York corporation, for the purpose of obtaining foreign representation of the kind hereinabove described. The President exhibited copies of said contracts to the meeting and explained that the amount to be paid to Manning & Co. was somewhat higher than that formerly paid but that in his opinion the charge was entirely reasonable and proper.

"On motion duly made and seconded and by the affirmative vote of all present the following resolution was adopted:

"RESOLVED, That the system of foreign representation as explained to the meeting by the President has the entire approval of this Board of Directors and that the action of the President and of the other executive officers of this Company in negotiating, executing and delivering, in the name of this Company, a contract with Manning Co., a co-partnership of Montreal, Canada, and of a subsidiary contract with W. W. Smith, Inc., a New York corporation, dated as of the first day of August, 1931 and in the form submitted to this meeting be, and the same hereby is approved, ratified and confirmed." [176]

The minutes of a directors' meeting of the Canadian Company, also held on September 3, 1931, contained an identical recital.[177] These resolutions would appear clearly to refer to the first and second documents set forth above, the agreement with Manning & Company

[175] Ex. 215.

[176] Ex. 180.

[177] Ex. 179. Cf.

"You will probably recall that at the last meeting of the directors of McKesson & Robbins Ltd., which was preceded by a meeting of the directors of McKesson & Robbins Inc., the two meetings overlapped in such a way that it was hard to tell when the first was over and the second had begun, with the result that Mr. Coster did not know whether the directors of the Limited Company understood that he intended the resolution having to do with foreign representation by foreign commissionnaires to be passed by the Boards of both companies. I am writing to see if you so understood, and if you have any objection to the inclusion of the same resolution in the minutes of both companies. I have reached the other directors by telephone and they have all agreed." Ex. 204, letter of Jonathan Grout to Rowley W. Phillips, Sept. 16, 1931. With one exception at this time, the same men served on the board of both companies. Pages 119–120 *infra*.

and the agreement with W. W. Smith & Company, Inc., "* * * a New York corporation which it [Manning & Company] has caused to be organized * * * one hundred percent (100%) of the stock of which it owns * * *," and offer no explanation for the purported guaranty by the Liverpool partnership of W. W. Smith & Co.[178]

A Bradstreet's report, dated October 14, 1931, was obtained from McKesson by Price, Waterhouse & Co. in connection with the 1931 audit.[179] This report was reputedly on W. W. Smith & Co. and stated that this firm was "Established originally in 1857 * * * at London * * *" and "* * * that in July 1931 this firm organized a corporation under the laws of the State of New York as W. W. Smith & Co., Inc. * * *." [180] A reproduction of this report is set forth on the following page.[181]

In later years, succeeding credit reports were also obtained on W. W. Smith & Co. These reports were similar to the first, reproduced herein, except that no reference was made to W. W. Smith & Company, Inc. and that the alleged financial resources of W. W. Smith & Co. increased appreciably.

Report	Date	Alleged resources of W. W. Smith & Co.
Ex. 207	Oct. 14, 1931	over $ 2,000,000
Ex. 217	Jan. 30, 1934	between $3–5,000,000
Ex. 218	Jan. 31, 1935	over $ 5,300,000
Ex. 219	Jan. 30, 1936	over $ 5,000,000
Ex. 52	Jan. 28, 1937	over $ 6,000,000
Ex. 51	Jan. 29, 1938	almost $ 7,000,000

The first two reports indicated an investigation at the W. W. Smith & Co. branch office, 191 Montague Street, Brooklyn, N. Y. and later reports indicated an investigation at the branch office at 1405 Bishop Street, Montreal, Canada. The first report was headed "Bradstreet's", the next three "Consolidated Report, Foreign Departments, Dun & Bradstreet, Inc. National Credit Office", and the last two "Dun & Bradstreet of Canada, Limited, Continuous Service." All of these reports were forgeries.[182]

According to an abstract in the files of Price, Waterhouse & Co., the agreement "* * * between W. W. Smith & Co. Inc. (N. Y.) and McKesson & Robbins, Inc. (Conn.) and McKesson & Robbins, Ltd. (Canada)" was extended for 2 years from August 1, 1933 to July 31, 1935, with the following changes: The guaranty premium was fixed at ¾ of 1% instead of ½ of 1%. "The total of accounts of the McKesson Companies permitted to be guaranteed by the New York Company shall be $700,000 instead of $350,000." Provision

[178] Ex. 216, 206.
[179] R. 568.
[180] Ex. 207.
[181] Ex. 207.
[182] R. 2081–2082, 4462.

BRADSTREET'S

296- 9--23--31
W.W.SMITH & CO.
William W.Smith
Howard C.Smith
George A. Smith
James Lamont
Walter C.Brown PARTNERS
Oscar Smith (Special Partner)

COMMISSION MERCHANTS
PURCHASING,FORWARDING
STEAMSHIP AGENTS.

(Branch Office)
191 Montague Street
Also Brooklyn N.Y.
Montreal,Hamburg,Genoa,
Liverlool,Marseilles,
Melbourne,Ceylon,Bombay
Honkong.

Established originally in 1857 as traders and guaranty brokers in general merchandise at London,the firm are in an important way operating also at Lloyds as brokers in general Insurance,maintain a general forwarding and shipping service for clients located at the principal centers on the Continent as well as the Orient South and Central America the major part of their operations it is said by authorities consulted is with British Colonies and Possessions.

Their principal business being to act as purchasing agents and forwarders for a large number of important firms located in the vicinity of their branch offices. Employ at present a staff of about 900 which includes some 600 salesmen and special representatives.

While a defenite estimate of resourses is not obtained those consulted in the trade express the opinion that the financial responsibility of this firm would run well over Two Million Dollars.Nothing is being done involving commercial credit in a general sense,however the ability to successfully meet its contracts and engagments is conceeded without hesitation.

The individual partners are favorably regarded,considered able and reliable intheir field and reputed to be individualy wealthy outside of their business investment.The record shows that in July 1931 this firm organized a corporation under the Laws of the State of New York as W.W.Smith & Co.Inc. with a nominal capital of $10,000.-L.C.Wilson Chief Clerk stated to our reporter that this had been done as a matter of convenience to facilatate important trade in the United States heretofore handled through brokers,and special agents,that it was not the policy of the firm to issue financial statements and that no credit accomodations were sought.In August 1931 the firm is known to have acquired the business of Chas.Manning Ltd.of Montreal engaged in a general merchandise brokerage business no details of the acquisition are available.Are authorized Lloyds Agents.

FIRE RECORD No Fires Reported

TRADE OPINIONS

Favorably,--Regarded reliable and responsible for their engagements not known to seek credit accomodations.

56--g.--63 G,Aa Oct. 14,1931

$1,000,000. Highest credit

EXHIBIT 207.—A purported Bradstreet's Report on W. W. Smith & Co. (Size 7¾" x 9¾".)

was also made that "W. W. Smith [were] to maintain such records in Montreal as McKesson's may request at a cost not to exceed $40 per week for clerical hire. Any additional clerks or bookkeepers, shall be authorized by McKesson's and the expense thereof shall be borne by them." The abstract also noted that "No mention is made with respect to the flat fee of $18,000 but Mr. G. Dietrich advises that upon advice of counsel, they have continued to make same." [183]

Attached to this abstract there was also an "Abstract of Guaranty Agreement by W. W. Smith & Co. (co-partnership) to McKesson Robbins, Inc. et al. Date July 31, 1933" which read:

"W. W. Smith & Co. by its duly authorized partner James Lamont, unconditionally guarantees the complete and prompt performance of all of the obligations and undertakings of W. W. Smith & Co. Inc. under and by virtue of an agreement between it and the McKesson Co.'s dated 7/31/33. Nothing contained in guaranty agreement dated 8/1/31 shall be altered or effected by this new agreement.

W. W. SMITH & CO.
(Signed) (by) JAMES LAMONT
Resident Partner and Authorized Agent

"In the presence of—
MAE L. ERLAND (JOHNSON) (Signed)
WILLIAM BROWN (Signed)

Signature Guaranteed:
The CHASE NATL. BANK
OF THE CITY OF N. Y.
HAMILTON TRUST BRANCH
(Signed) By T. D.?
Vice President." [184]

In connection with the absorption of the business of the Connecticut Company by the Maryland Company in October 1934, Marsh, Stoddard & Day, Bridgeport attorneys, whose name appeared on the covers of the various Manning and Smith contracts referred to herein, advised Sullivan & Cromwell, New York attorneys for the Maryland company, that, in their opinion, the "* * * agreement and guaranty between the [Connecticut] company and W. W. Smith & Company, Inc., and W. W. Smith & Co., and to which McKesson & Robbins, Limited is a party" has "* * * been validly assigned and transferred to McKesson & Robbins, Incorporated, a Maryland Corporation." [185]

Under date of August 1, 1935, a new agreemxnt was entered into between W. W. Smith & Company, Inc. (New York), and McKesson & Robbins, Incorporated (Maryland), and McKesson & Robbins, Limited (Canada). First the agreement provided that:

"WHEREAS, W. W. SMITH & Co. a co-partnership of Liverpool, England has a substantial financial interest in the New York Company and has requested the McKesson Companies to enter into this agreement because said partnership

[183] Ex. 56.
[184] Ex. 56.
[185] Ex. 173.

will derive some share of the profits accruing to the New York Company therefrom; and

"WHEREAS, the McKesson Companies desire to secure the services of the New York Company in promoting the foreign trade of the McKesson Companies and the New York Company is willing to render such services upon the terms and conditions and for the consideration hereinafter set forth;

"NOW THEREFORE, it is mutually agreed as follows:

"1. The New York Company expressly represents that W. W. SMITH & Co., a co-partnership of Liverpool, England, by reason of a substantial interest in the New York Company will directly benefit from any profits realized by the New York Company under this agreement and the New York Company further represents that it has acquired and now owns and controls all of the foreign and domestic buying and selling offices and agencies formerly owned and controlled by Charles Manning & Company, Limited, a Canadian corporation and that it now owns, controls and operates the selling offices and facilities located in Canada, New York City, Australia, London (England), Hamburg (Germany), Hong Kong (China), Ceylon (India), Yokohama (Japan), Genoa (Italy), Bergen (Norway), and Marseilles (France).

"2. The New York Company agrees that it will continue to conduct the aforesaid offices but that this agreement shall apply with like effect to offices and facilities now or hereafter operated or provided by the New York Company in other foreign countries." [186]

Then followed provisions like those contained in the 1931 agreement with W. W. Smith & Company, Inc., above quoted, as amended by the 1933 extension above referred to, except that the Maryland Company was substituted for the Connecticut Company, the limit of accounts guaranteed at any time was raised to $900,000, the provision in respect to the limit of guaranties by the New York Company to other than the McKesson Companies was dropped, and it was provided that the agreement was to remain in force for 5 years. The agreement concluded:

"14. It is mutually agreed that the execution of this agreement shall in no respect alter the rights of the parties hereto under a previous agreement between them dated August 1, 1931, and which has been extended and will expire at midnight on July 31, 1935, at which time this present agreement shall become effective.

"IN WITNESS WHEREOF, the parties hereto have caused this agreement and three counterparts hereof to be executed and their corporate seals affixed.

W. W. SMITH & COMPANY, INC.
By (s) JAMES LAMONT
Its President
MCKESSON & ROBBINS, INCORPORATED
By (s) F. D. COSTER
Its President
MCKESSON & ROBBINS, LIMITED
By (s) F. D. COSTER
Its ~~Vice~~ President" [187]

Attached to this agreement there was a "Guaranty of Agreement" by W. W. Smith & Co., which read as follows:

186 Ex. 50.

187 Ex. 50.

"WHEREAS under date of August 1, 1935, a certain agreement, duplicate original copy of which is attached hereto, was entered into between W. W. SMITH & COMPANY, INC., a corporation organized under the laws of the State of New York, (hereinafter sometimes referred to as the 'New York Company'); McKESSON & ROBBINS, INCORPORATED, a corporation organized and existing under the laws of the State of Maryland (hereinafter sometimes referred to as the 'Maryland Company') and McKESSON & ROBBINS, LIMITED, a corporation organized and existing under the laws of the Dominion of Canada, (hereinafter sometimes referred to as the 'Canadian Company'), (The said Maryland Company and the said Canadian Company being sometimes referred to jointly as the 'McKesson Companies'); and

"WHEREAS, W. W. SMITH & Co. is a co-partnership having its principal office at Liverpool, England and composed of GEORGE A. SMITH, HOWARD C. SMITH, WILLIAM W. SMITH, JAMES LAMONT and WALTER C. BROWN as General Partners, and OSCAR SMITH as a Special Partner, and the said JAMES LAMONT as such General Partner is duly authorized on behalf of said partnership to execute this agreement; and

"WHEREAS, said co-partnership of W. W. SMITH & Co. has a substantial financial interest in the New York Company and will share directly or indirectly in any profits derived by the New York Company under said agreement and on that account the said Guarantor has specially requested the McKesson Companies to enter into such agreement, but the latter were unwilling to do so unless such agreement was supported by the written guarantee of the said co-partnership of W. W. SMITH & Co.

"NOW THEREFORE, in consideration of the execution by the McKesson Companies of said contract of even date herewith between the McKesson Companies and the New York Company, the undersigned partnership of W. W. SMITH & Co. does hereby unconditionally guarantee the complete and prompt performance by the said New York Company of all of its obligations and undertakings under and by virtue of said contract hereto attached and in view of the close relationship which exists between the New York Company and the undersigned co-partnership, the undersigned hereby agrees that its liability under this guarantee shall not be altered or affected in any way by reason of any modification or waiver of any of the provisions of said agreement without notice to the undersigned Guarantor, or by reason of the fact that the McKesson Companies or either of them shall fail to promptly assert and notify the undersigned Guarantor of any breach of any of the provisions of said contract and the undersigned Guarantor further agrees that this guarantee shall be deemed to be an absolute one so that the McKesson Companies or either of them shall have the right to enforce the same by an action or actions directed against such Guarantor and without the necessity of any legal proceedings of any description against the said New York Company, it being further agreed by the Guarantor that this contract, both as to its construction and legal remedies, shall be governed by the laws of the State of Connecticut, and that nothing herein contained shall alter or affect in any way the liability of the undersigned as Guarantor of a certain similar agreement between the McKesson Companies and the New York Company dated August 1, 1933, and which by its terms terminates at midnight on the 31st day of July, 1935.

W. W. SMITH & Co.
By (s) JAMES LAMONT

Its Resident Partner and Authorized Agent."[188]

[188] Ex. 50.

The last agreement and guaranty above referred to had until July 31, 1939 to run and were believed to be in effect at the time of the appointment of the receivers.[189]

Despite the agreements with W. W. Smith & Company, Inc. referred to above, whereby the latter was supposed to act as sales agent for the McKesson Companies, the McKesson Companies also purportedly continued to purchase goods from W. W. Smith & Co. at least through 1934. Price, Waterhouse & Co.'s memorandum on accounts of the Connecticut Company for 1932 stated that "Practically all of the Company's sales of crude drugs and heavy chemicals are made * * * through the firm of W. W. Smith & Co. * * *" and also referred to W. W. Smith & Co. as the concern "* * * from whom the bulk of their [Connecticut Company's] crude stocks are purchased * * *."[190] A supplement to the 1933 memorandum on the Canadian Company stated "Negotiations for the purchases are made principally through agents, one of which is Smith & Company * * *. Sales are negotiated through the same agents as arrange for the purchases."[191] The inventory price test schedules for 1934 showed W. W. Smith & Co. as the vendor on three of the invoices included in the inventory at the year end.[192]

Another vendor from whom fictitious purchases were made, both immediately before and after the August 1, 1931 sales agency contract with W. W. Smith & Company, Inc., was J. P. Meyer & Co., Inc.[193] Referring to the inventory of the Canadian Company on December 31, 1931, the memorandum on accounts stated:

> "All the merchandise was purchased from J. P. Meyer & Co., Inc., of Brooklyn whose address is the same as that of Smith & Co., mentioned above."[194]

This would appear to be the same J. P. Meyer who appeared as an account receivable on the books of Girard & Co., Inc.,[195] and to whom, in 1925, the Girard plant at Mt. Vernon was "* * * finally disposed of for $20,000 cash * * *."[196]

The August 1, 1931 contracts, previously quoted, referred to the acquisition of Charles Manning & Company, Limited by Manning & Company and to the transfer by the latter of "* * * all the foreign

[189] R. 362. Although the auditors and others were unaware of its existence (R. 844, 2072; Ex. 26), there was introduced at the trial, *U. S. of America* v. *George Musica, et al.* (footnote 23 *supra*), a signed copy of an agreement dated January 3, 1936 which stated that W. W. Smith & Company, Ltd. had assumed the contract of W. W. Smith & Company, Inc. dated August 1, 1935 with the approval of W. W. Smith & Co. which was stated to have a similar substantial financial interest in W. W. Smith & Company, Ltd. as it had in W. W. Smith & Company, Inc., all of whose assets had been acquired by W. W. Smith & Company, Ltd. At the trial there were also introduced signed copies of all of he agreements hereinabove referred to, based on Ex. 89, 216, 206, 215, 56, 50.

[190] Ex. 81. See also R. 1239.

[191] Ex. 75.

[192] Ex. 42 (D 34, D 37).

[193] R. 4581.

[194] Ex. 76. See also Ex. F.

[195] Ex. 170.

[196] Ex. 176.

and domestic buying and selling offices and agencies formerly owned and conducted by said Charles Manning & Company, Limited * * * to W. W. Smith & Company, Inc., a New York corporation, which it has caused to be organized for the purpose of acquiring the same * * * (one hundred per cent (100%) of the stock of which it owns) * * *." [197] Price, Waterhouse & Co., in their memorandum on accounts of the Connecticut Company for 1931, stated that "* * * Manning Co. during the year * * * went into the private banking business exclusively and sold its export business to W. W. Smith & Co., whose main office is in Liverpool * * *." [198] It appears that it was at this time that the McKesson accounts with the pretended bank of Manning & Company were established. Manning & Company purported to effect payment for purchases and to receive remittances for goods sold for the account of the respective McKesson Companies. After the establishment of Manning & Company in this capacity, the use of actual cash in payment for fictitious purchases and in receipt of fictitious receivables steadily diminished until at the time of the receivership it had disappeared and all purchases and sales of foreign crude drugs were being cleared through Manning & Company.[199]

Concerning the nature of McKesson's account with Manning & Company, there is a note in the Price, Waterhouse & Co. work papers in 1931, the year the account was opened, stating:

> "We satisfied ourselves that this account is payable in U. S. dollars. This is a collection account rather than a deposit account. Bills and accounts payable in U. S. dollars as collected through Manning who remits in U. S. dollar. Manning does not remit as collected, but when requested to by the company. Checks are not drawn on this account. We investigated a transfer of $50,000 to a New York bank in November and found that Manning charged that amount to the account." [200]

In addition, the usual bank confirmation requested by the auditors from Manning & Company on the Connecticut Company, as at December 31, 1931, recited a "Commercial Letter of Credit–B–2830–$250,000. Revolving, dated August 5th, 1931 expiring August 5, 1932. No unpaid acceptances outstanding thereunder." [201] Thorn, however, testified that this was a sight draft letter of credit.[202] There was also a similar letter of credit for $150,000 confirmed to

[197] Ex. 216, 206.

[198] Ex. 82.

[199] See pages 46 ff. *supra*.

[200] "* * * and in December there was a cash transfer of $120,000 to a New York bank." R. 691–692. See also R. 951–952, 1176. There were also similar transfers to bank accounts of the Canadian Company. R. 4404, 4423. In all $2,260,800 was deposited in McKesson bank accounts as coming from Manning & Company, the greatest part between December 1931 and December 1933, inclusive. The last cash received was in 1933 for the Connecticut Company and in 1936 for the Canadian Company. As to the source of these funds see footnote 407 *infra*.

[201] Ex. O; R. 691.

[202] R. 1138.

the Canadian Company.[203] These are the only references to letters of credit, all other transactions apparently being effected by Manning & Company debiting the accounts of the respective McKesson Companies on drafts drawn by the five Canadian vendors pursuant to McKesson authorization.[204] No checks were drawn on Manning [205] and it was not included in the list of banks on the daily cash report.[206]

However, at a meeting of the Board of Directors of the Canadian Company, held on April 4, 1935, it was resolved:

> "That Manning & Co. of Montreal, Canada and branch of Manning & Co. in New York be and they hereby are appointed bank depositaries for McKesson & Robbins, Limited, et cetera," and "* * * that the foregoing resolution shall from this day on supersede so much of the resolution adopted at the meeting of the Board of Directors held September 3, 1931 with respect to the appointment of Manning & Company in Montreal, Canada as a bank depositary for this company as is inconsistent therewith." [207]

3. Purchases of Foreign Crude Drugs by the Connecticut Division at the Time of the 1937 Audit, and How They Were Handled

The first document apparently involved in a purchase of foreign crude drugs at the time of the 1937 audit was a letter requesting quotations on five different products. Similar letters were supposedly sent to all five Canadian vendors, A. H. Raymond & Company, D. C. Reynolds & Company, P. Pierson & Company, B. Miller & Company and H. Monroe & Company, and, upon receipt of replies from them,[208] the prices offered were scheduled, with underscoring to indicate the lowest bid on each product.[209] A copy of a purported request for quotations, a supposed reply thereto, and the applicable schedule are reproduced herein; the request and reply on the following pages and the schedule as an insert.[210]

The existence of this purported practice was apparently not generally known prior to the receivership, for McGloon, the comptroller, testified that he was not aware of it prior to December 10, 1938, when the carbon copies of requests for quotations, original replies and schedules were first discovered in the files of Robert Dietrich.[211]

---

203 Ex. P.

204 R. 734-735, 1139.

205 R. 951, 4407.

206 R. 1642-1643; Ex. 228.

207 R. 695. For resolution of September 3, 1931, see page 60 *supra*.

208 As previously stated, the five Canadian vendors, Smith, and Manning would now appear to be entirely fictitious or to the extent that they had any reality were mere blinds used by Coster for his fictitious transactions. After the 1937 audit was completed, three new fictitious Canadian vendors appeared: R. D. Backer & Company, J. C. Conway & Company, and C. H. Williams & Company. Ex. 30. For the manner in which the documents referred to in this and in the following subsections which purportedly emanated from these pretended concerns were prepared under the direction of George Vernard (in reality Coster's brother) see subsection D *infra*.

209 Ex. 238.

210 Ex. 238 A. The present record does not contain a complete set of documents pertaining to a single transaction and, therefore, in this and succeeding subsections, the documents exhibited are to be taken as typical of the kind used rather than as arising from the same transaction. For an illustration of the letterheads of all five Canadian vendors, see pages 102-103 *infra*.

211 R. 1587-1588, 1669-1670, 4496. Cf.: R. 1346.

R.J. DIETRICH:BMP

April 26, 1938

B. Miller & Company,
Southam Bldg.,
Montreal, Canada

Gentlemen:

Kindly quote on the following items:

320 Cases Procain
Packed 25 - 1 lb. tins to a case

500 Kegs Salol Powder U.S.P.
Packed 200 lbs. to a keg

400 Drums Amidopyrine
Packed 50 lbs. net to a drum

260 Cases Santonine Crystals
Packed 17 lbs. to a case

460 Cases Antipyrine Crystals
Packed 100 lbs. net to a case

Trusting in an early reply and with kindest regards, we remain,

Very truly yours,

McKESSON & ROBBINS, INCORPORATED

Purchasing Agent

EXHIBIT 238A.—Copy of a purported request for quotations on foreign crude drugs. (Size 8½" x 11".)

B. MILLER & COMPANY

IMPORTERS AND BROKERS

Telephone LANCASTER 4298 — SOUTHAM BUILDING, MONTREAL, CANADA

April 30, 1938

McKesson & Robbins, Inc.
Bridgeport,
Connecticut

Gentlemen:

We are glad to offer the following items:

Procain	$ 12.60 lb.
Salol Powder U.S.P.	.87 lb.
Amidopyrine	3.40 lb.
Santonine Crystals	20.00 lb.
Antipyrine Crystals	1.91 lb.

in reply to your quotation of April 26th, 1938.

Hoping we will be favored with your orders, we remain,

Truly yours,

B. MILLER & COMPANY

C Read

RC

EXHIBIT 238A.—A purported letter of quotations on foreign crude drugs. (Size 8½" x 11".)

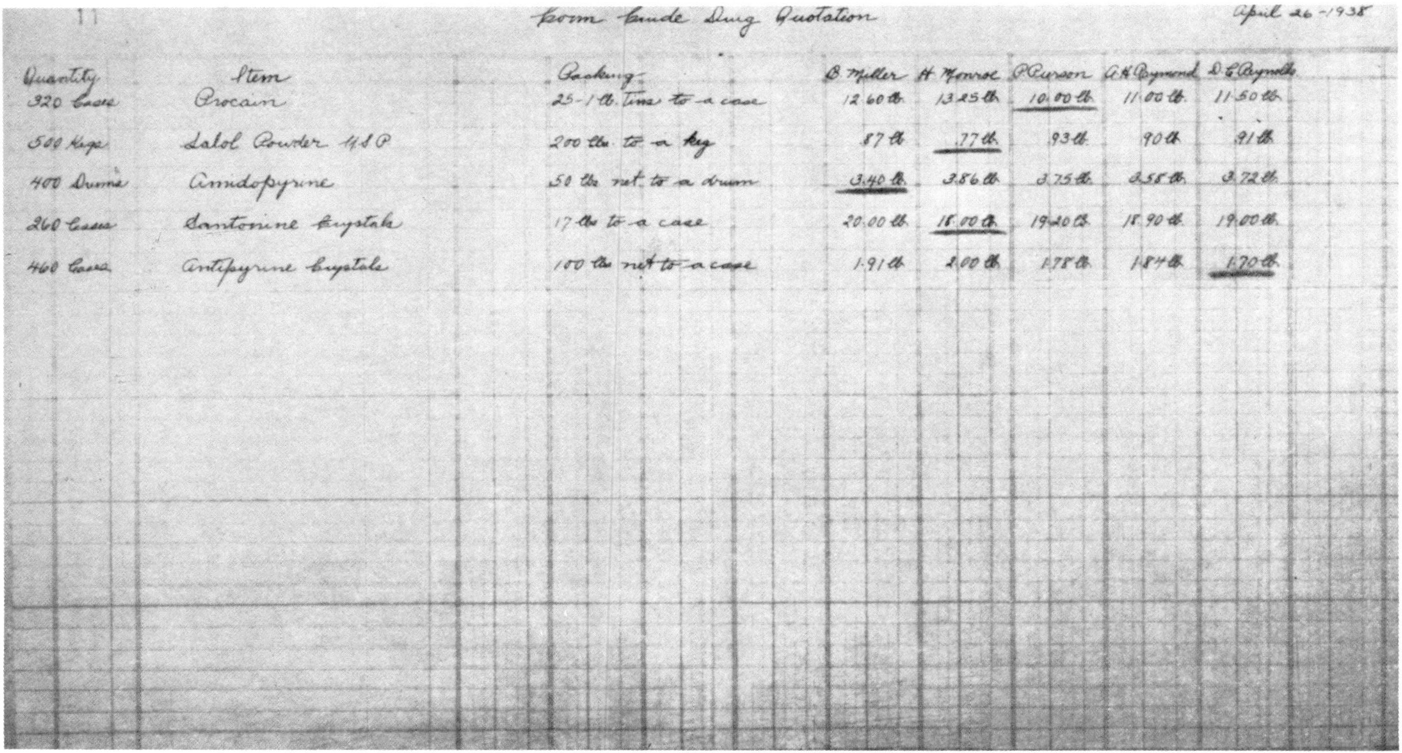

Form Crude Drug Quotation — April 26-1938

Quantity	Item	Packing	B. Miller	H. Monroe	P. Pierson	A.H. Raymond	D.E. Reynolds
320 Cases	Procain	25-1 lb. tins to a case	12.60 lb.	13.25 lb.	10.00 lb.	11.00 lb.	11.50 lb.
500 Kegs	Salol Powder U.S.P.	200 lbs. to a keg	.87 lb.	.77 lb.	.93 lb.	.90 lb.	.91 lb.
400 Drums	Amidopyrine	50 lbs. net to a drum	3.40 lb.	3.86 lb.	3.75 lb.	3.58 lb.	3.72 lb.
260 Cases	Santonine Crystals	17 lbs. to a case	20.00 lb.	18.00 lb.	19.20 lb.	18.90 lb.	19.00 lb.
460 Cases	Antipyrine Crystals	100 lbs. net to a case	1.91 lb.	2.00 lb.	1.78 lb.	1.84 lb.	1.70 lb.

EXHIBIT 238F.—Summary of foreign crude drug quotations. (Size 14″ x 8½″.)

The purported variation in the prices quoted, as summarized on the schedules, presents an interesting comparison with the relative stability of prices on purchases actually consummated, as indicated by the inventory price test schedules.[212] Also in view of such variation in the quotations, the length of time purportedly taken in consummating these purchases through this exchange of letters presents an interesting comparison with the way Charles Hermann, of the Cliff Street office, did his business.

"He will call up four or five brokers [on the telephone] and get a bid on the items that he is considering buying and he will make his purchase that afternoon or he will give up the idea and wait until some other date." [213]

Supposedly upon the basis of the foregoing quotations, a McKesson purchase order would be initialed and released by George Dietrich.[214] Each purchase order would cover only one product and would be addressed to one of the five Canadian vendors. The terms were stated as "Cash against Documents Net No Discount U. S. Cy. F. O. B. Bridgeport or New York, U. S. A." [215] A reproduction of an accounting department copy of such a purchase order follows:[216]

1-37 500 Pads

ACCOUNTING DEPT.

McKESSON & ROBBINS
INCORPORATED
BRIDGEPORT CONNECTICUT
U. S. A.

Date DECEMBER 27, 1937 Nº 5634

M D.C. REYNOLDS & COMPANY,
192 BANK STREET,
OTTAWA, CANADA

FOR DEPT.

Kindly enter our order for the following and ship to
Marked: Via

Mail Invoices, B/L and all Shipping Documents to McKesson & Robbins, Incorporated, Bridgeport, Conn.

QUANTITY	DESCRIPTION	PRICE	UNIT
310 CADYS	MUSK PODS		
	20 ozs. net to each cady @	12.00	per oz.
	Delivery on this order to be made as follows:		

Terms CASH AGAINST DOCUMENTS NET NO DISCOUNT U.S. CY. F.O.B. BRIDGEPORT
Remarks OR NEW YORK U.S.A.

McKESSON & ROBBINS
Incorporated

PER G.E. DIETRICH

EXHIBIT 12B.—Accounting department copy of a purported purchase order for foreign crude drugs. (Size 8½" x 7¼.")

[212] See pages 104–105 *infra*.
[213] Testimony of John H. McGloon, R. 1672.
[214] R. 1588, 1347. For part played by Coster in this connection see footnote 139 *supra*.
[215] Ex. 12B.
[216] Ex. 12B.

Eugene A. Johnson, Jr., office manager for McKesson at Bridgeport, testified, as follows, concerning the number of copies of McKesson purchase orders prepared and their distribution:

"Q. [By Mr. Galpeer.] Do you know how many copies of those purchase orders were prepared?

A. Four.

Q. Do you know where they went?

A. The Accounting Division received one copy for the accounts payable; the other three copies I would not know where they went. The original was to be mailed. The third copy was to go to the receiving department. The fourth copy should be retained by the man making out the purchase order." [217]

A covering letter was then supposedly dictated by George Dietrich forwarding the original McKesson purchase order to the vendor and authorizing draft on Manning & Company for the amount of the charge.[218] A copy of one of these purported letters is reproduced on the opposite page.[219]

At the same time George Dietrich also supposedly dictated a letter to Manning & Company instructing them to honor the draft.[220] A copy of one of these purported letters is reproduced on page 74.[221]

Carbon copies of the foregoing letters were found in George Dietrich's files.[222] Johnson, the office manager, testified that he had never seen or heard of them even after the receivership, when he looked for all documents pertaining to the Manning account.[223]

A few days after the McKesson purchase order was purportedly sent out the purchase invoice from the vendor was supposedly received [224] with other incoming mail all of which, as previously stated, first went to the desk of George Dietrich.[225] The terms were stated the same as on the purchase order "Cash against documents Net No Discount—U. S. Cy. F. O. B.—Bridgeport or New York, U. S. A." [226] A reproduction of one of these purchase invoices is inserted opposite page 75.[227]

Concerning the disposition of the invoice, Johnson testified:

"Q. [By Mr. Galpeer.] From where would the invoice come to the accounts payable department?

A. Well, it would be in the mail rack; in the accounts payable [box], which was in George Dietrich's office.

Q. These invoices, were they marked 'hold, do not pay'?

---

[217] R. 1347.

[218] Ex. 230.

[219] Ex. 230.

[220] Ex. 231.

[221] Ex. 231.

[222] R. 4469–4471.

[223] R. 1351–1353, 1402–1403.

[224] R. 1588.

[225] See footnote 140 *supra.*

[226] Ex. 12A.

[227] Ex. 12A.

December 27, 1937

Messrs. D. C. Reynolds & Company,
192 Bank Street,
Ottawa, Canada

Gentlemen:

Enclosed you will find purchase order for 310 cadys of Musk Pods, 20 ozs. net to each cady at $12.00 per oz.

We hereby authorize you to draw a sight draft on Manning & Company, Montreal, Canada for the full amount of your charge.

Yours truly,

McKESSON & ROBBINS, INC.

GED'ck
ENC.

Exhibit 230.—Copy of a purported letter of authority to draw on Manning & Company. (Size 8½" x 11".)

December 27, 1937

Messrs. Manning & Company
Montreal, Canada

Gentlemen:

We have instructed Messrs. D.C. Reynolds & Company to draw against our a/c sight draft in amount of $74,400.00.

Will you please honor same and charge our current account with you, under advice to our Bridgeport Office.

Yours truly,

McKESSON & ROBBINS, INC.

GED'ck

EXHIBIT 231.—Copy of a purported letter authorizing payment of a vendor's draft. (Size 8½" x 11".)

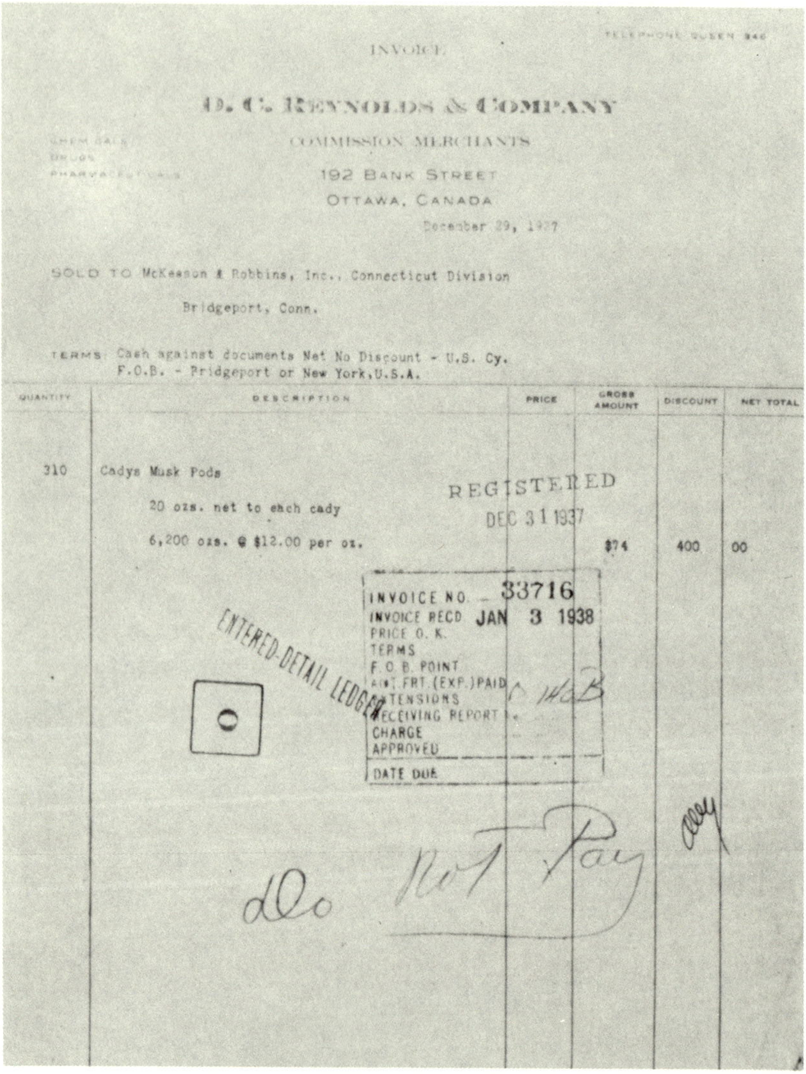

INVOICE

D. C. REYNOLDS & COMPANY

COMMISSION MERCHANTS

192 BANK STREET
OTTAWA, CANADA

December 29, 1937

SOLD TO McKesson & Robbins, Inc., Connecticut Division

Bridgeport, Conn.

TERMS Cash against documents Net No Discount - U.S. Cy.
F.O.B. - Bridgeport or New York, U.S.A.

QUANTITY	DESCRIPTION	PRICE	GROSS AMOUNT	DISCOUNT	NET TOTAL
310	Cadys Musk Pods				
	20 ozs. net to each cady				
	6,200 ozs. @ $12.00 per oz.		$74	400	00

REGISTERED
DEC 31 1937

INVOICE NO. 33716
INVOICE RECD JAN 3 1938
PRICE O. K.
TERMS
F. O. B. POINT
AMT. FRT. (EXP.) PAID
EXTENSIONS
RECEIVING REPORT
CHARGE
APPROVED
DATE DUE

ENTERED-DETAIL LEDGER

Do Not Pay

EXHIBIT 12A.—A purported purchase invoice for foreign crude drugs. (Size 8½″ x 11″.)

A. No, the accounts payable clerk would put that on when they matched them with the purchase order.

* * * * * * *

The EXAMINER. Would it be customary for the accounts payable clerk to mark all invoices that were against documents, 'hold, do not pay'?

A. Yes.

* * * * * * *

Q. [By Mr. GALPEER.] You just said that the invoice recited, 'cash against document'; did your department ever see the documents referred to in such an invoice?

A. No.

Q. Do you know what those documents were supposed to be?

A. No.

* * * * * * *

Q. What would the next step be in connection with those purchases?

A. Well, the invoices would go to accounts payable; they would register it and it would be posted to the accounts payable ledger." [228]

In this connection an accounts payable voucher also was prepared.[229] A reproduction of one of these vouchers follows.[230]

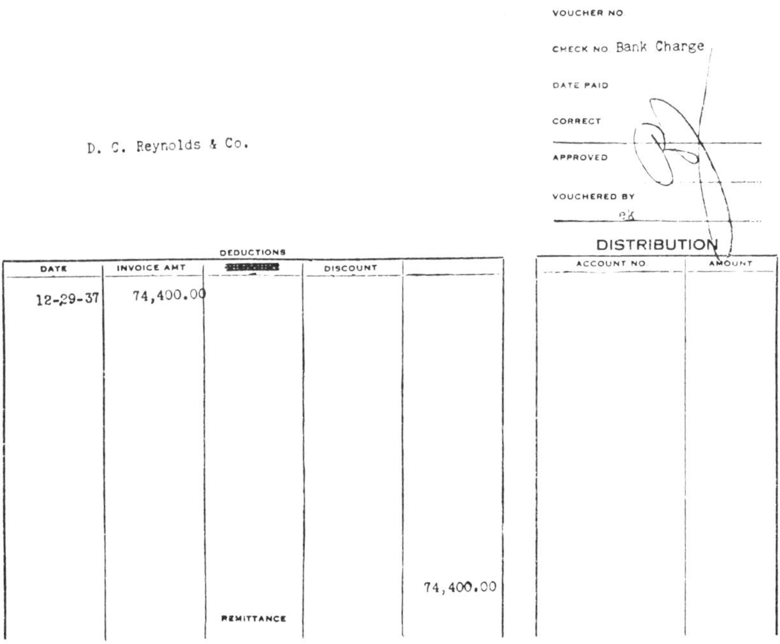

VOUCHER NO

CHECK NO Bank Charge

DATE PAID

CORRECT

APPROVED

VOUCHERED BY

D. C. Reynolds & Co.

DATE	INVOICE AMT	DEDUCTIONS	DISCOUNT	
12-29-37	74,400.00			
		REMITTANCE		74,400.00

DISTRIBUTION

ACCOUNT NO	AMOUNT

EXHIBIT 12C.—Accounts payable voucher. (Size 8¼" x 6¾".)

It will be noted that nothing on any of these three documents, the McKesson purchase order, the purchase invoice, or the voucher

[228] R. 1348–1350.

[229] Ex. 12C.

[230] Ex. 12C.

gives any indication that the goods were not to be shipped to McKesson but were to be held by the suppliers.[231]

However, in connection with each purported purchase, there was prepared a receiving ticket.[232] A reproduction of one of these is inserted facing page 77.[233]

The receiving tickets which were stamped "Held at Suppliers, No Other Charges," were prepared in Robert Dietrich's department and were then sent to the accounting office.[234] The initials like "J. W." [235] were put on merely to make the tickets conform with those covering non-foreign crude drug transactions.[236] The tickets themselves could have been prepared from copies of the McKesson purchase orders which were sent regularly to the receiving department on all goods.[237]

About the same time as the purported receipt of the purchase invoice from the vendor, an "Advice of Debit" was also supposedly received from Manning & Company informing McKesson that its account had been charged for a draft drawn by the vendor under McKesson's letter of authority.[238] A reproduction of one of these is inserted facing this page.[239]

The advice of debit would purportedly be received with other mail in George Dietrich's office [240] and would be routed by him to the cashier's office where, before being entered as a cash disbursement, it would be checked with the previous record in the accounts payable department.[241] At the end of the month the main accounting office would receive from the cashier's office the cash disbursement book, which would furnish the basis of canceling the liability set up on the accounts payable ledger. The advice of debit itself would apparently be retained by the cashier's department.[242]

Apparently, no documents came with or were attached to the advice of debit.[243] Thorn thought that the word "documents" referred to in the phrase "cash against documents" as used in the McKesson purchase order and purchase invoice meant the purchase order itself which the vendor upon receipt from McKesson would attach to the draft drawn on Manning & Company.[244]

---

231 R. 159.
232 Ex. 20.
233 Ex. 20.
234 R. 1348, 1710.
235 Ex. 20. John White, who testified in this proceeding. R. 1471–1564. See also pages 108–113 *infra*.
236 R. 1561 ff.
237 Ex. 17, p. 10, item 4; R. 1241. Apparently each purchase order was filled as a single transaction. Cf. Ex. 20 and Ex. 265.
238 Ex. 33.
239 Ex. 33.
240 R. 1589.
241 R. 696, 722–723, 12.
242 R. 1350–1351. See also Ex. M–27.
243 R. 457, 739.
244 R. 1187.

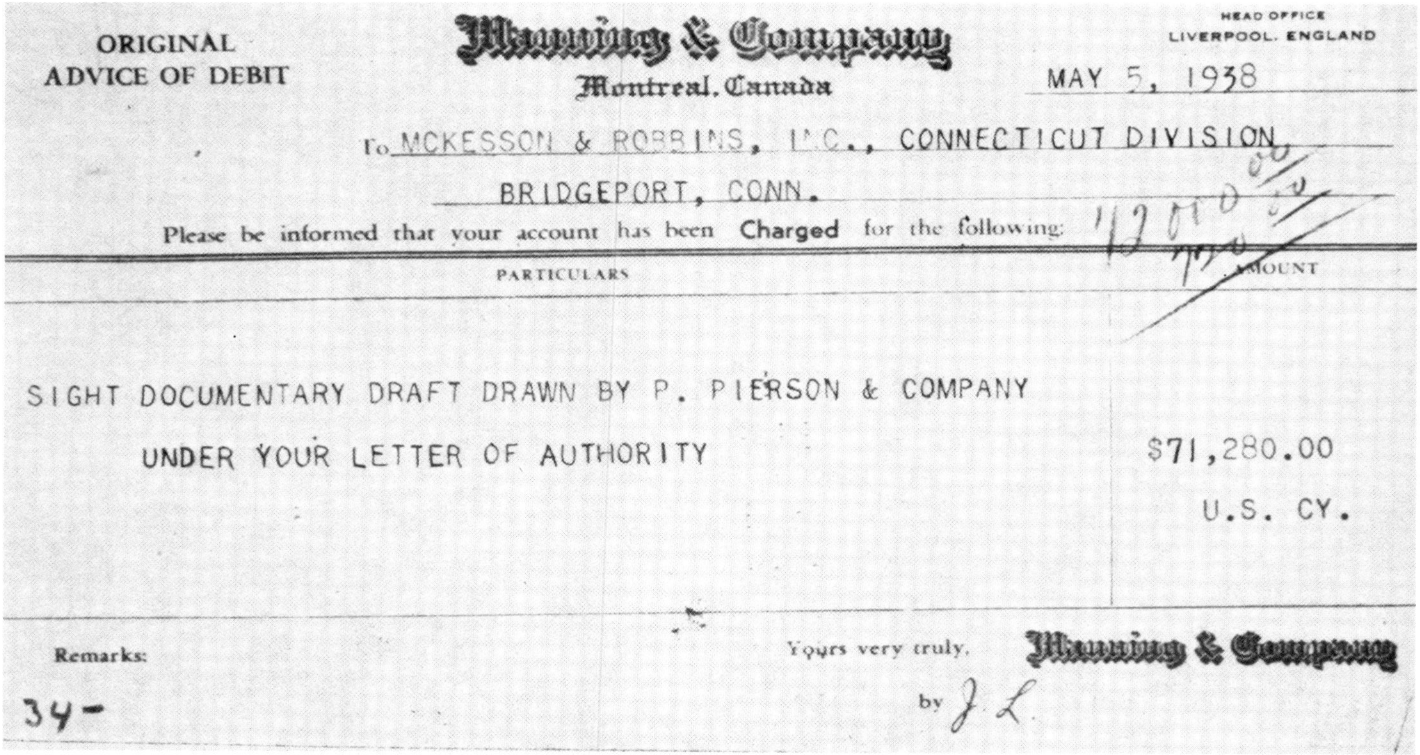

ORIGINAL
ADVICE OF DEBIT

Manning & Company
Montreal, Canada

HEAD OFFICE
LIVERPOOL, ENGLAND

MAY 5, 1938

To MCKESSON & ROBBINS, INC., CONNECTICUT DIVISION
BRIDGEPORT, CONN.

Please be informed that your account has been **Charged** for the following:

PARTICULARS	AMOUNT
SIGHT DOCUMENTARY DRAFT DRAWN BY P. PIERSON & COMPANY UNDER YOUR LETTER OF AUTHORITY	$71,280.00 U.S. CY.

Remarks:

34-

Yours very truly,
Manning & Company
by J. L.

EXHIBIT 33.—Manning & Company advice of debit. (Size 8⅜″ x 4⅝″.)

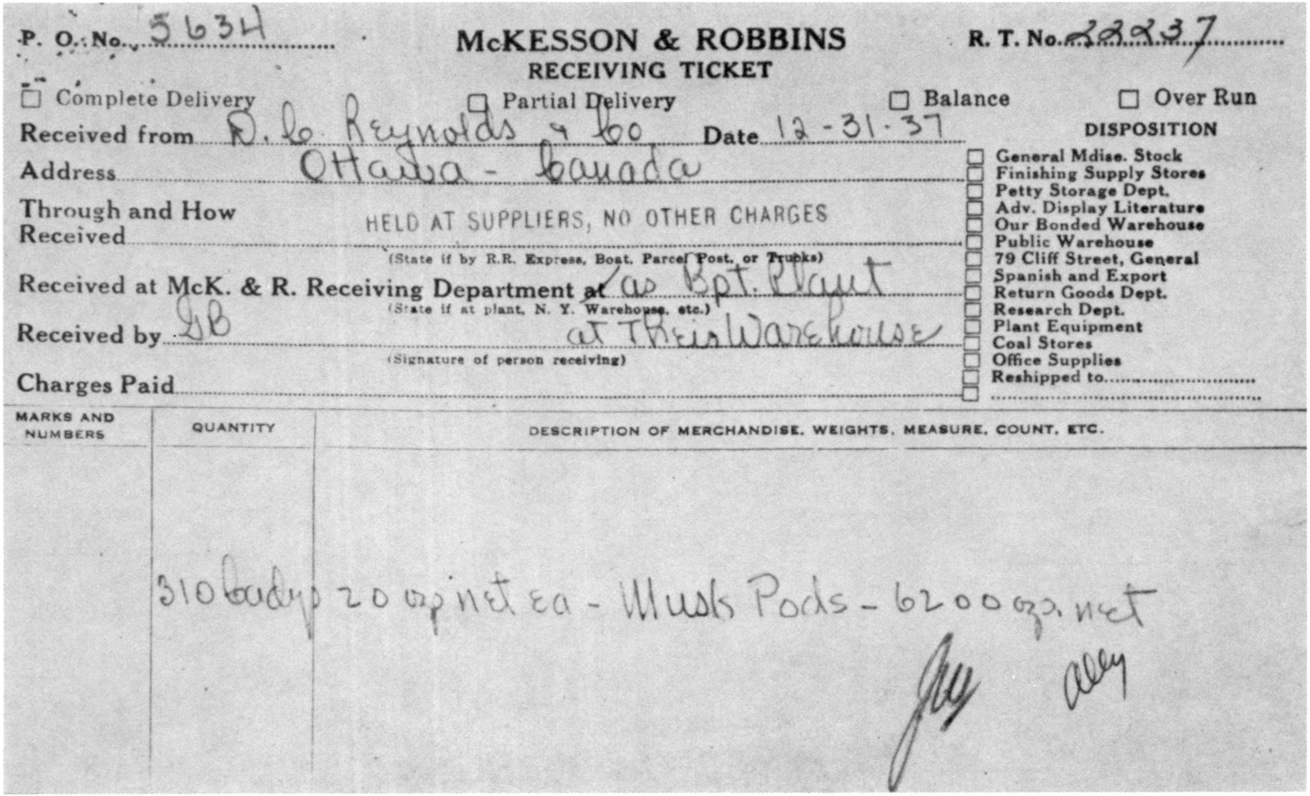

P. O. No. 5634

McKESSON & ROBBINS
RECEIVING TICKET

R. T. No. 22237

☐ Complete Delivery ☐ Partial Delivery ☐ Balance ☐ Over Run

Received from D. C. Reynolds & Co Date 12-31-37

Address Ottawa - Canada

Through and How Received HELD AT SUPPLIERS, NO OTHER CHARGES
(State if by R.R. Express, Boat, Parcel Post, or Trucks)

Received at McK. & R. Receiving Department at as Bpt. Plant
(State if at plant, N. Y. Warehouse, etc.)

Received by GB at Their Warehouse
(Signature of person receiving)

Charges Paid

DISPOSITION
☐ General Mdise. Stock
☐ Finishing Supply Stores
☐ Petty Storage Dept.
☐ Adv. Display Literature
☐ Our Bonded Warehouse
☐ Public Warehouse
☐ 79 Cliff Street, General
☐ Spanish and Export
☐ Return Goods Dept.
☐ Research Dept.
☐ Plant Equipment
☐ Coal Stores
☐ Office Supplies
☐ Reshipped to

MARKS AND NUMBERS	QUANTITY	DESCRIPTION OF MERCHANDISE, WEIGHTS, MEASURE, COUNT, ETC.
	310 bags	20 oz net ea - Musk Pods - 6200 ozs net

EXHIBIT 20.—Receiving ticket for a purported purchase of foreign crude drugs. (Size 8⅝″ x 5⅝″.)

In connection with the foreign crude drug items, two sets of perpetual inventory cards were maintained; one in Robert Dietrich's office and the other in the cost department in the general accounting office.[245] The receiving ticket was the source for the entry of acquisitions on the cost department cards [246] and, presumably, either the receiving ticket or the source of the receiving ticket [247] furnished the basis of the entry on Robert Dietrich's set.

4. Sales of Foreign Crude Drugs by the Connecticut Division at the Time of the 1937 Audit, and How They Were Handled

The first document apparently involved in a sale of foreign crude drugs at the time of the 1937 audit was a "Purchase Order" headed "W. W. Smith & Co., * * * Liverpool, 3, England," reading, "Kindly enter the order listed below sold by us for your account." [248] One of these is reproduced on the following page.[249]

McKesson next purportedly received a "Notice of Shipment" also headed "W. W. Smith & Co., * * * Liverpool, 3, England," dated 3 days later than the purchase order, reading: "We beg to advise having shipped for your account and risk and in accordance with your instructions * * * the merchandise listed below for which enclosed please find Documents as noted." [250] One of these is reproduced on the second page following.[251]

The notice of shipment, like the purchase order from W. W. Smith & Co., was supposed to have been received through the mail and routed by George Dietrich in the regular way.[252] No evidence was developed however, showing any tangible means by which the price quoted or the sale itself purported to be made by W. W. Smith & Co. for McKesson was accepted or approved by the latter, nor how the former knew or was advised from which of the various Canadian vendors, who were thought to be holding the inventories in question, the goods were supposed to have been shipped. Neither the W. W. Smith & Co. notice of shipment nor any of the subsequent documents prepared by McKesson as set forth herein indicated from which vendor the goods were supposed to have been taken or from what point they were supposed to have been shipped.

In the lower left-hand corner of the notice of shipment there is printed "Documents enclosed," underneath which there is a box in

---

245 R. 1368, 1421–1422. The cards in Robert Dietrich's office would, in form, appear to be like Ex. 107 and Ex. A. R. 724, 1478, 1509. For a description of the cost department cards, in relation to Ex. 107 and Ex. A, see R. 4531–4533.

246 R. 1423. The initials "A. U. G." also appearing on Ex. 20 would appear to be those of the cost clerk who did the posting. R. 4530.

247 The documents in evidence would indicate either the purchase order or the purchase invoice.

248 Ex. 7, 8B, 11C.

249 Ex. 11C.

250 Ex. 8C, 11B.

251 Ex. 11B.

252 R. 1588–1589.

W. W. Smith & Co.
Commission Merchants
Purchasing, Forwarding & Shipping Agents
Liverpool 3. England

Purchase Order
No. 17738

JANUARY 28, 1938

To McKESSON & ROBBINS, INC., CONNECTICUT DIVISION, BRIDGEPORT, CONN.

Kindly enter the order listed below sold by us for your account *Terms* 180 DAYS DATE

Quantity	*Description*	*Price*
331	CASES GUM CAMPHOR, SLABS 100 LBS. TO A CASE 33,100 LBS. NET @	.44
	Sold to SILVERTON TANNERY LTD. PRETORIA, SO. AFRICA	

Please render invoice in Duplicate
Brokerage ______ %
Guarantee 3/4 of 1% %

W. W. Smith & Co.

EXHIBIT 11C.—W. W. Smith & Co. purchase order. (Size 9¼″ x 6½″.)

Notice of Shipment

W. W. Smith & Co.
Commission Merchants
Purchasing Forwarding & Shipping Agents
Liverpool, 3, England

JANUARY 31, 1938

To McKESSON & ROBBINS, INC., CONNECTICUT DIVISION
BRIDGEPORT, CONN.

Dear Sirs

We beg to advise having shipped for your account and risk and in accordance with your instructions to

SILVERTON TANNERY LTD.
PRETORIA, SO. AFRICA

the merchandise listed below for which enclosed please find Documents as noted.

Very truly yours
W. W. Smith & Co.
By J. M. Cook Agent

Documents enclosed

- [x] Bill of Lading
- [x] Consular Invoice
- [x] Invoice
- [ ] Warehouse Receipt
- [x] Insurance Certificate

Merchandise

331 CASES GUM CAMPHOR, SLABS

EXHIBIT 11B.—W. W. Smith & Co. notice of shipment. (Size 7¼″ x 10¼″.)

front of each of the following: "Bill of Lading," "Consular Invoice," "Invoice," "Warehouse Receipt," and "Insurance Certificate." All the boxes except the one in front of "Warehouse Receipt" were checked.[253] Neither the comptroller, office manager, assistant head of the billing department, or anyone else who testified in the present hearings remembered ever having seen any of the documents checked as enclosed.[254]

The next step in the purported transaction apparently rested on a regular McKesson "Factory Order." [255] A reproduction of one of these is inserted facing page 83.[256]

This factory order was the source of the preparation of a regular McKesson sales invoice. As typed, the terms on the sales invoice would be stated as 180 or 120 days from date,[257] but the "F. O. B." and "VIA" spaces would be left blank. The designations "FROM" and "SALESMAN" would be filled in "BPT" (Bridgeport) and "WWS" (W. W. Smith), respectively.[258] A copy of one of these invoices is reproduced on the opposite page.[259]

In addition to the notations appearing on the copy of the invoice reproduced, the original was stamped by a checker in the billing department, "Payment for this invoice must be made in U. S. currency." [260]

Helen Freer, assistant to the head of the billing department, gave the following comparison between the handling of factory orders and invoices on regular orders and on foreign crude drug orders:

"Q. [By Mr. GALPEER.] Now, will you please tell me in detail, * * * what the routine of the billing department was in handling regular bills on shipments made?

* * * * * * *

A. Well, when an original customer's order would come into the department, Mr. Bonsby would note the terms, the f. o. b. points, the salesman, and the price on the order. He would then give it to me, and I in turn would type it, on an order form, which consisted of three copies.

Q. Was that a factory order form?

A. Yes, that was a pink, a blue, and a white. The pink, blue, and white would be numbered and then they would be separated. The pink and blue would go out to Mr. Robert Dietrich's department for shipping. The customer's order would be attached to the white copy, and then filed in the billing department.

After the order was shipped, the pink copy [of the factory order] would come back into the billing department, and * * * the corresponding white copy would be pulled out of the file, and then it would be put through for billing.

The weights and the quantities shipped and everything would [already] be noted [on the pink copy of the factory order] * * * and then an invoice

[253] Ex. 8C, 11B.

[254] R. 1354, 1411-1413, 1696-1697, 4360, 4372.

[255] Ex. 7, 8A, 9, 10, 11A.

[256] Ex. 11A.

[257] R. 1589.

[258] Ex. 7, 8D, 11D.

[259] Ex. 11D.

[260] Ex. 229; R. 4361, 4469.

CHECKED BY

FOR CUSTOMER'S USE ONLY

Connecticut Division of

McKESSON & ROBBINS

Incorporated

BRIDGEPORT, CONN., U. S. A.

Established 1833

YOUR ORDER

INVOICE NO. 131239
DATE 1-31-38

Sold To

SILVERTON TANNERY LTD.
PRETONIA, SO. AFRICA

SHIPPED TO

PREPAID OR COLLECT

TERMS 180 DAYS
F. O. B. FROM DATE
VIA FROM BPT SALESMAN WWS

QUANTITY	DESCRIPTION	PRICE	GROSS AMOUNT	DISCOUNT	NET TOTAL
	OUR ORDER 2993				
331 CASES	GUM CAMPHOR, SLABS				
	100 LBS TO A CASE 33,100 LBS NET	44	14 564 00		14 564 00

IMPORTANT:—Bills not paid when due will be subject to draft with exchange on New York. After obtaining a receipt for merchandise, as "Shipped in Good Order," we are not responsible for any damage or loss that may occur in transportation. All claims must be made within five days after receipt of merchandise.

WE GUARANTEE THE MERCHANDISE ENTERED HEREON, MANUFACTURED BY McKESSON & ROBBINS, TO COMPLY WITH THE FEDERAL FOOD AND DRUGS ACT AND AMENDMENTS THERETO, AND THAT THEY WERE PRODUCED OR MANUFACTURED, IN ACCORDANCE WITH THE FEDERAL CHILD LABOR ACT OF SEPT. 1, 1916.

EXHIBIT 11D.—Duplicate copy of an invoice for a purported sale of foreign crude drugs. (Size 8½" x 11".)

number would be put on. That would be given to the billing clerk, and she in turn would bill the order.

*   *   *   *   *   *   *

* * * the invoice form consisted of three whites, a pink, a blue, and a yellow. They would be separated. [The proper number of white copies together with the bill of lading if the bill of lading was attached to the factory order when it came back from Robert Dietrich's department would be mailed to the customer by the checking girl.] The pinks would be totaled and handed to the inventory department. The blues would be made up into ledgers, and they would be given to the bookkeeping department and the yellows we used to keep for posting records.

*   *   *   *   *   *   *

* * * at the end of the day all the orders that were billed would be given to me * * * and I would take out the orders that applied on contract, making the withdrawals against the different contracts, and then I in turn would give all the orders to another girl, who used to put the invoice number opposite the order number in the order register book, and she in turn would send them out to file.

Q. Now, when you prepared the factory orders, in pink, blue and white, you said that you put a number on that, or that a number was put on in your department. Would that be the order number, so-called?

A. That is right, yes sir.

Q. Now, when the pink copy of the factory order came back to you, from what department did that come back? I think you stated that you sent it out to Robert Dietrich's department originally?

A. Yes.

Q. Did it come back from that department?

A. No, I think it came in to Mr. Osterhout. He was in charge of the inventory department. He used to separate the orders. I meant to tell you that.

He used to separate the orders, separate [regular] crude drug orders from health helps. The health helps used to be sent in to Mr. Borchers, who used to enter them, and the [regular] crude drugs used to be entered in our own department, and then Mr. Borchers, after he reviewed them, would send them in to our department to be billed.

Q. I see. So that they would come through Mr. Osterhout, and through Mr. Borchers from Robert Dietrich?

A. That is right.

Q. Now, when the pink factory orders came back to you, were they in the same form, with the same notations as when you originally sent them out?

A. No, we sent them out typed up, with all the necessary information on them, and just the order number on them.

Q. When they came back, what additional appeared on them?

A. The weights, and the bill of lading was attached, and if the quantity was changed or increased or decreased, they would always make that notation.

Q. Would there be a stamp of the shipping department on it?

A. Oh, yes.

Q. What sort of a stamp would that be?

A. It was just a square stamp put on the order in the upper right hand corner. It said, 'Shipped,' and the date, and 'per R. J. D.'

Q. Then, these factory orders already contained the order number, and it was after the factory order came back, when the bill was prepared, that you would give it additionally an invoice number?

A. Yes.

*   *   *   *   *   *   *

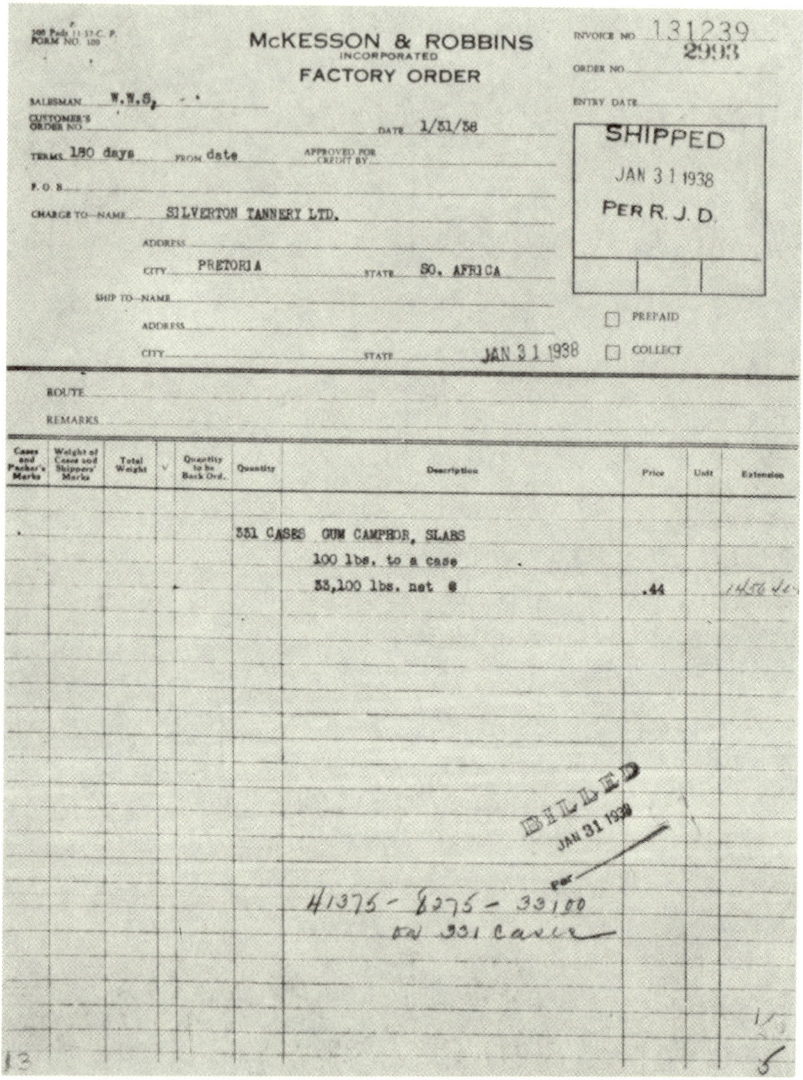

100 Pads 11-37-C. P.
FORM NO. 109

McKESSON & ROBBINS
INCORPORATED
FACTORY ORDER

INVOICE NO. 131239
2993
ORDER NO.
ENTRY DATE

SALESMAN W.W.S.
CUSTOMER'S ORDER NO.
DATE 1/31/38
TERMS 180 days FROM date
APPROVED FOR CREDIT BY
F. O. B.
CHARGE TO—NAME SILVERTON TANNERY LTD.
ADDRESS
CITY PRETORIA STATE SO. AFRICA
SHIP TO—NAME
ADDRESS
CITY STATE JAN 31 1938

SHIPPED
JAN 31 1938
PER R. J. D.

☐ PREPAID
☐ COLLECT

ROUTE
REMARKS

Cases and Packer's Marks	Weight of Cases and Shippers' Marks	Total Weight	√	Quantity to be Back Ord.	Quantity	Description	Price	Unit	Extension
					331 CASES	GUM CAMPHOR, SLABS			
						100 lbs. to a case			
						33,100 lbs. net @	.44		14564.00

BILLED
JAN 31 1938
per

41375 – 8275 – 33100
on 331 cases

13 15 5

Exhibit 11A.—Factory order for a purported shipment of foreign crude drugs. (Size $8\frac{1}{2}'' \times 11''$.)

Q. And how would the mailing of those [invoices] that went to the customers be handled? Would your department put them in envelopes?

A. Generally, we did. With affiliated houses, we didn't because the boys, always, at the end of the day, put them—put all the mail for affiliated houses in one envelope.

Q. I see, but you would give them to the mail boys; in case of affiliated houses you would give the mail boys the open invoices; in the case of others, you would give them the invoices already put in envelopes?

A. That's right.

Q. Now, was there another class of orders covering large shipments of what was known as [foreign] crude drugs, handled in a slightly different fashion?

A. Yes, there were.

Q. Will you tell us now how those orders were handled?

A. The telephone would ring and it would be Mr. George Dietrich calling. He would request that Mr. Bonsby—he would request that either he or I get the orders.

Q. You are referring to—what did you mean by orders?

A. They were what we called 'pet' orders.

Mr. STEWART. What was that word?

The WITNESS. Pet orders.

Mr. STEWART. Pet?

The WITNESS. That's right.

Mr. STEWART. All right.

The WITNESS. When we went in to get them all he would hand us was pink copies [of factory orders]. They were all typed up.

* * * * * * *

* * * They would be brought into the order department and given to an order register clerk. She would put an order number on them and in turn give them to a girl who would put the invoice number on and then return them to the order register clerk, and she would extend them and give them to the billing clerk.

The billing clerk would bill them and give them to the checker. The checker would give the two white copies [of the invoices] * * * to George Dietrich.

* * * [The third] white copy of the invoice, together with the pink copy [of the factory order] would be sent in to Robert Dietrich and then the three other copies [of the invoices], the pink, blue and yellow, would be separated and put through in the usual manner.

* * * * * * *

Q. [By Mr. GALPEER.] Now, this pink copy of the factory order, was that similar in form when you received it from Mr. George Dietrich as to those which you yourself typed on the regular orders?

A. No, because all we received was the pink [copy] no bill of lading, no [gross, tare, and net] weights [in pencil on bottom], no other markings.

Q. I see. In other words, it had no stampings on it, [like] where shipped, with the date, R. J. D., that did not appear on the pink factory order?

A. That's right.

Q. In other words, it was just plain typing on it with no supporting evidence of shipment, you would say?

A. No.

Q. And after you sent this pink copy of the factory order, together with the white copy of the invoice to Mr. Robert Dietrich, did you receive them back again?

A. I don't know.

Q. But the invoices were already made out and were handed to Mr. George Dietrich simultaneously with sending the pink factory and white invoice to Mr. Robert Dietrich's department?

A. That's right.

* * * * * * *

Q. [By Mr. STEWART.] Now, whose pets were these orders?

A. I couldn't say.

Q. Where did they get that designation?

A. I don't know. It is a name I found out when I first entered the department.

Q. In 1929?

A. Yes.

Q. Who told you that they were called pet orders?

A. I don't know.

Q. You don't happen to remember?

A. I just happened to hear somebody mention the name I guess. Because when anybody mentioned pet orders, we just had to drop everything and devote all our time to the pet orders.

* * * * * * *

Q. In other words, so far as you were concerned, 'pet' was just a name but didn't have any particular significance before last December. Is that right?

A. That's right.

Q. When you said that you had not seen exhibits 8–B [W. W. Smith & Co. purchase order] and 8–C [notice of shipment], did you mean to say that you never had seen any like those or you had just not seen those particular documents?

A. I never had seen any like those.

Q. Did you ever see any documents involving W. W. Smith & Company?

A. No sir, all I saw were the pink copies [of the factory orders].

Q. Were these initials 'W. W. S.' up in the left-hand corner following the word 'salesman' on there when you saw it?

A. Yes, we used to type that on our invoice.

Q. Did you know who 'W. W. S.' was?

A. No, we didn't, at least I didn't.

Q. Do you know what became of the pink copy of the factory order after it left your hands?

A. It went out to Bob Dietrich together with the white copy of the invoice.

* * * * * * *

Q. Did you ever have occasion to refer to the files where these pink copies [of the factory orders], such as 8–A would be filed?

A. No, sir.

Q. So you don't know whether the documents such as 8–B and 8–C or any other documents were filed with them in the files?

A. I don't know.

* * * * * * *

Mr. GALPEER. Well, now, is it not true that in the case of the pet orders the invoice number and the bills were already prepared before the pink factory order was sent out to Mr. Robert Dietrich's department?

The WITNESS. The invoice was prepared, yes.

Mr. GALPEER. And was already given invoice number?

The WITNESS. Yes.

The EXAMINER. Do I understand, Mr. Galpeer, that in the regular business, the customer's order was attached to the filed copy of the factory order, and remained with it, but in the case of the pet orders, this order of W. W. Smith was not in the accounting department or not in the billing department?

Mr. GALPEER. No. This is the point, as I understand it, your Honor: In the case of the regular orders, they would be broken into two stages; After the customer's order was received by the billing department, a series of manifold or factory orders would be made up, and an order number would be given.

Then there would be a break in procedure. The pink copy of the factory order would be sent down to the shipping department, and they would await the return of that pink copy of the factory order, with evidence of shipment, before the actual bills were prepared.

In the case of the pet orders, however, they would receive in the first instance one copy of the pink factory order and would go right through the billing process, giving it an invoice number, and preparing the bills, and then send the factory order out, without having received any evidence or notation on the pink factory order, or any supporting documents evidencing shipment.

Is that correct, Mrs. Freer?

The WITNESS. That is correct.

The EXAMINER. The point I made was this: The customer's order was attached to the billing department's copy, as I understand, but in these pet orders, they never saw the customer's order?

The WITNESS. That's right.

The EXAMINER. That is what I wanted to get." [261]

The factory orders themselves on the foreign crude drug transactions were typed by Robert Dietrich's department.[262] The blue and a yellow copy were found in his files.[263] Apparently, some time after the invoices had been prepared and two white copies thereof sent to George Dietrich for mailing and the pink copy of the factory order with one white copy of the invoice sent to Robert Dietrich (as testified to above by Helen Freer), the respective W. W. Smith & Co. purchase orders and notices of shipment and the pink copy of the factory order were pinned together and filed in the accounting department.[264]

From the testimony of Helen Freer, it would appear that, in the case of the foreign crude drug transactions, the stamp "SHIPPED [date] PER RJD" and the pencil notations of gross, tare, and net weights appearing on the bottom of all three factory orders (the pink, blue, and yellow)[265] must have been put on after the invoices were prepared. In fact, John White testified that the blue factory orders were given to him by Robert Dietrich once, twice, or three times a month, together with a weight sheet that showed the gross, tare, and net weight of one case or one container. Just as a matter of multiplication, he would find the total gross, tare, and net weight corresponding to the number of containers shown on the order and he would write the total on the bottom of the blue copy of the factory order.[266] Apparently, they would then be copied on to the pink and yellow copies

261 R. 4352–4372.

262 R. 1355, 1406, 1409–1410, 1589.

263 R. 1381; Ex. 9, 10.

264 R. 1459.

265 Ex. 7, 8A, 9, 10, 11.

266 R. 1482–1483.

of the factory order.[267] A possible explanation for this procedure can be found in the testimony of John White:

"* * * that it has always been driven in to us that all transactions had to conform to the same procedure irrespective of whether it was direct shipping or not." [268]

The space on the factory order following "APPROVED FOR CREDIT BY" was left blank. This would not seem peculiar to the foreign crude drug transactions, however, for Johnson testified:

"The EXAMINER. Then it is a fair statement to say that as a standing rule you had no regular system of approval of the credit manager on the shipments that went out?

The WITNESS. That is correct." [269]

Although the Company ostensibly employed a credit man, by the name of Blakeman, for the foreign crude drug business, George Dietrich, in addition to all of his other duties, acted as the executive in charge of credits for this business and it was the latter, not Blakeman, to whom all the invoices and monthly statements on foreign crude drugs were sent after having been prepared by the billing and bookkeeping departments, respectively.[270]

Although the f. o. b. data was also left blank on the factory order and invoice, the contract for the sale of goods through W. W. Smith & Company, Inc., provided "* * * that delivery by the McKesson Companies shall consist of delivery F. O. B. New York." [271] As noted in the previous section, the terms on which the goods were bought were also "* * * F. O. B. Bridgeport or New York, U. S. A." [272] While the goods were supposed to have been held in Canada and shipped direct from there to England, Scotland, Ireland, Wales, and other places, there is no evidence of any adjustments having been made as a result of using a more direct route of shipment than through New York, and thus effecting a saving in expense, assumed by the supplier, of transporting the goods to New York and by the customer of transporting the goods from that point.[273]

The goods were purportedly sold principally to customers in the British Empire. The distribution of accounts receivable of the Connecticut Division arising out of foreign crude drug sales as at December 31, 1937, as compared with the prior year, was as follows: [274]

---

[267] Ex. 9, 10, 11A.

[268] R. 1561.

[269] R. 1464.

[270] R. 1427–1428, 1462, 1646–1651, 1698–1699. For the part Price, Waterhouse & Co. thought Coster played in passing on credits see page 222 *infra*.

[271] Ex. 50.

[272] Ex. 12A, 12B.

[273] R. 159–161, 790–794.

[274] Ex. 49. For earlier years see Ex. 78, 79, 268, 80.

	December 31, 1936	December 31, 1937
"British Empire:		
England	$2, 948, 089. 75	$3, 788, 437. 65
Scotland	1, 427, 104. 50	1, 458, 314. 10
Ireland	891, 510. 60	1, 019, 446. 40
Wales	99, 026. 60	130, 109. 80
Australia	896, 073. 90	743, 718. 95
New Zealand	134, 822. 95	109, 575. 60
South Africa	239, 200. 10	193, 498. 00
India	27, 642. 00	54, 980. 00
	$6, 663, 470. 40	$7, 498, 080. 50
Other foreign countries:		
Holland	40, 294. 00	7, 650. 00
Denmark	53, 116. 60	
Belgium	12, 341. 00	
Switzerland	11, 446. 00	
Sweden	11, 904. 00	
Asia	10, 670. 00	
Total foreign	$6, 803, 242. 00	$7, 505, 730. 50"

Of the 651 foreign crude drug accounts of the Connecticut Division for which requests for confirmation were sent by S. D. Leidesdorf & Co., [275] 536 apparently were with existing concerns, who replied that the amounts were not owing. In 90 instances no replies were received, and the remaining 25 requests were returned because of incorrect addresses.[276]

On each sale "Uniform Straight Bill of Lading" forms were prepared. The forms read, "RECEIVED * * * at BRIDGEPORT, CONN. [date] from McKESSON & ROBBINS INCORPORATED * * * Consigned to" a foreign purchaser, "Route THEIR TRUCK" and was stamped "SHIPPED [date] PER R. J. D." and "RECEIVED [date] W. W. SMITH & COMPANY, INC. FORWARDING DEPARTMENT BY ----------." The forms apparently were prepared under Robert J. Dietrich's supervision.[277] One of these is reproduced on the following page.[278]

Similar documents were prepared for the full 3-year period during which the goods were purportedly held by the Canadian suppliers and shipped direct from there.[279] Like the W. W. Smith & Co. notice of shipment, the bill of lading forms did not indicate to which of the five Canadian vendors the goods in question should be allocated.[280]

The first, third, and fourth copies of these bill of lading forms, all stamped as above, were found in the files of Robert Dietrich attached

275 Those purportedly outstanding as at Dec. 7, 1938.

276 Ex. 255.

277 Ex. 9, 10.

278 Ex. 9.

279 R. 1383. For the auditors' interpretation of these documents see pages 234 ff. *infra.*

280 R. 198.

(Uniform Domestic Straight Bill of Lading, adopted by Carriers in Official, Southern, Western and Illinois Classification territories, March 15, 1922, as amended August 1, 1930.)

UNIFORM STRAIGHT BILL OF LADING
ORIGINAL—NOT NEGOTIABLE

Shipper's No. 2993

______________________________ Company

Agent's No.

RECEIVED, subject to the classifications and tariffs in effect on the date of the issue of this Bill of Lading.

at BRIDGEPORT, CONN., JANUARY 31, 193 8

from **McKESSON & ROBBINS, Incorporated**

the property described below, in apparent good order, except as noted (contents and condition of contents of packages unknown), marked, consigned, and destined as indicated below, which said company (the word company being understood throughout this contract as meaning any person or corporation in possession of the property under the contract) agrees to carry to its usual place of delivery at said destination, if on its own road or its own water line, otherwise to deliver to another carrier on the route to said destination. It is mutually agreed, as to each carrier of all or any of said property over all or any portion of said route to destination, and as to each party at any time interested in all or any of said property, that every service to be performed hereunder shall be subject to all the conditions not prohibited by law, whether printed or written, herein contained, including the conditions on back hereof, which are hereby agreed to by the shipper and accepted for himself and his assigns.

(Mail or street address of consignee—For purposes of notification only.)

Consigned to SILVERTON TANNERY LTD.

Destination PRETORIA State of SO. AFRICA County of

Route THEIR TRUCK

Delivering Carrier Car Initial Car No.

No. Packages	Description of Articles, Special Marks and Exceptions	*WEIGHT (Subject to Correction)	Class or Rate	Check Column
331	CASES OF GUM CAMPHOR, SLABS'	41375#		
	41375 - 8275 - 33100.			
		SHIPPED JAN 31 1938 PER R. J. D.		

Subject to Section 7 of conditions, if this shipment is to be delivered to the consignee without recourse on the consignor, the consignor shall sign the following statement:
The carrier shall not make delivery of this shipment without payment of freight and all other lawful charges.

____
(Signature of Consignor)

If charges are to be prepaid, write or stamp here, "To be Prepaid."

Received $________
to apply in prepayment of the charges on the property described hereon.

____
Agent or Cashier

Per________________________
(The signature here acknowledges only the amount prepaid.)

Charges Advanced: $________

†The fibre boxes used for this shipment conform to the specifications set forth in the box maker's certificate thereon, and all other requirements of Rule 41 of the Consolidated Freight Classification.
†This is to certify that the above articles are properly described by name and are packed and marked and are in proper condition for transportation according to the regulations prescribed by the Interstate Commerce Commission.
†Shipper's imprint in lieu of stamp; not a part of bill of lading approved by the Interstate Commerce Commission.

* If the shipment moves between two ports by a carrier by water, the law requires that the bill of lading shall state whether it is "carrier's or shipper's weight."
NOTE—Where the rate is dependent on value, shippers are required to state specifically in writing the agreed or declared value of the property.
The agreed or declared value of the property is hereby specifically stated by the shipper to be not exceeding

________________ per ________________

RECEIVED JAN 31 1938 W. W. SMITH & COMPANY, Inc. FORWARDING DEPARTMENT By ____________

McKESSON & ROBBINS, Incorporated, Shipper. ________________ Agent,

Per ROBERT J. DIETRICH MEH. Per ________________

Permanent post-office address of shipper, BRIDGEPORT, CONN.

1

EXHIBIT 9.—Original bill of lading form for a purported shipment of foreign crude drugs. (Size 8½" x 11".)

to the blue and yellow copies of the respective factory orders.[281] The gross, tare, and net weights mathematically computed by John White from a standard weight chart given him by Robert Dietrich, and transcribed by him on to the blue copy of the factory order,[282] also appear typed on these bill of lading forms.

On the sample set of documents reproduced herein covering the purported shipment of 331 cases of gum camphor slabs to Silverton Tannery, Ltd., Pretoria, So. Africa, the W. W. Smith & Co. purchase order was dated January 28, 1938, the W. W. Smith & Co. notice of shipment, the factory order, the sales invoice, the bill of lading form, the R. J. D. "Shipped" stamp on the factory order and on the bill of lading form, and the W. W. Smith & Company, Inc. "Received" stamp on the bill of lading form were all dated January 31, 1938,[283] the same day as the sales invoice was typed at the McKesson offices.[284]

The next document in the apparent chain consisted of a letter purportedly dictated by George Dietrich, addressed to the foreign customer, enclosing documents covering goods "* * * shipped you on order received from your purchasing agents, W. W. Smith & Co. Ltd. of New York, for which we would appreciate receiving New York U. S. Dollars exchange 180 days after date of shipment." [285] One of these purported letters is reproduced on the following page.[286]

These letters, located in George Dietrich's office, were all of original typing on plain paper. Whatever purpose they were intended to serve, it appears that no carbons or originals on McKesson letterheads were prepared, only originals on plain paper.[287] While three variations in language were used, the substance of all was the same as the exhibit reproduced.[288]

Like the purchases, the sales of foreign crude drugs were entered on perpetual inventory cards both in Robert Dietrich's office and in the cost department in the general accounting office.[289] The latter were kept on a first-in first-out basis.[290] The foreign crude drug sales were also recorded by the cost department in a separate register, giving, on each transaction, the date, customer, invoice number, item, quantity, unit sales price, total sales value, unit cost price, total cost value, and profit.[291] No transaction was ever recorded thereon at a

281 Ex. 9, 10; R. 1381.

282 R. 1482–1483.

283 Ex. 9, 11A, 11B, 11D.

284 Date after "State" Ex. 11A. See R. 4363 and cf. Ex. 7 where invoice physically billed 4 days after invoice date.

285 Ex. 232, 233.

286 Ex. 233.

287 R. 4471–4472; cf. R. 4490.

288 Ex. 232, 233; cf. R. 4490.

289 R. 1368, 1421–1422.

290 R. 1424.

291 Ex. 40 (D13, D14), 84; R. 1371, 1372

March 11, 1938

African Soap & Chemical Works
Johannesburg, So. Africa

Gentlemen:

Enclosed you will find documents covering

15 Cases Oil of Lemon Sequiterpeneless, 1,500 lbs., shipped you on order received from your purchasing agents, W.W. Smith &Co., Ltd. of New York, for which we would appreciate receiving New York U.S. Dollars exchange 180 days after date of shipment.

Trusting you will find everything in order and assuring you of our appreciation of your favoring us with this business.

Very truly yours,

MCKESSON & ROBBINS, INC.
CONNECTICUT DIVISION

GED/GH

Exhibit 233.—Letter purportedly transmitting documents covering a shipment of foreign crude drugs.
(Size 8½" x 10¾".)

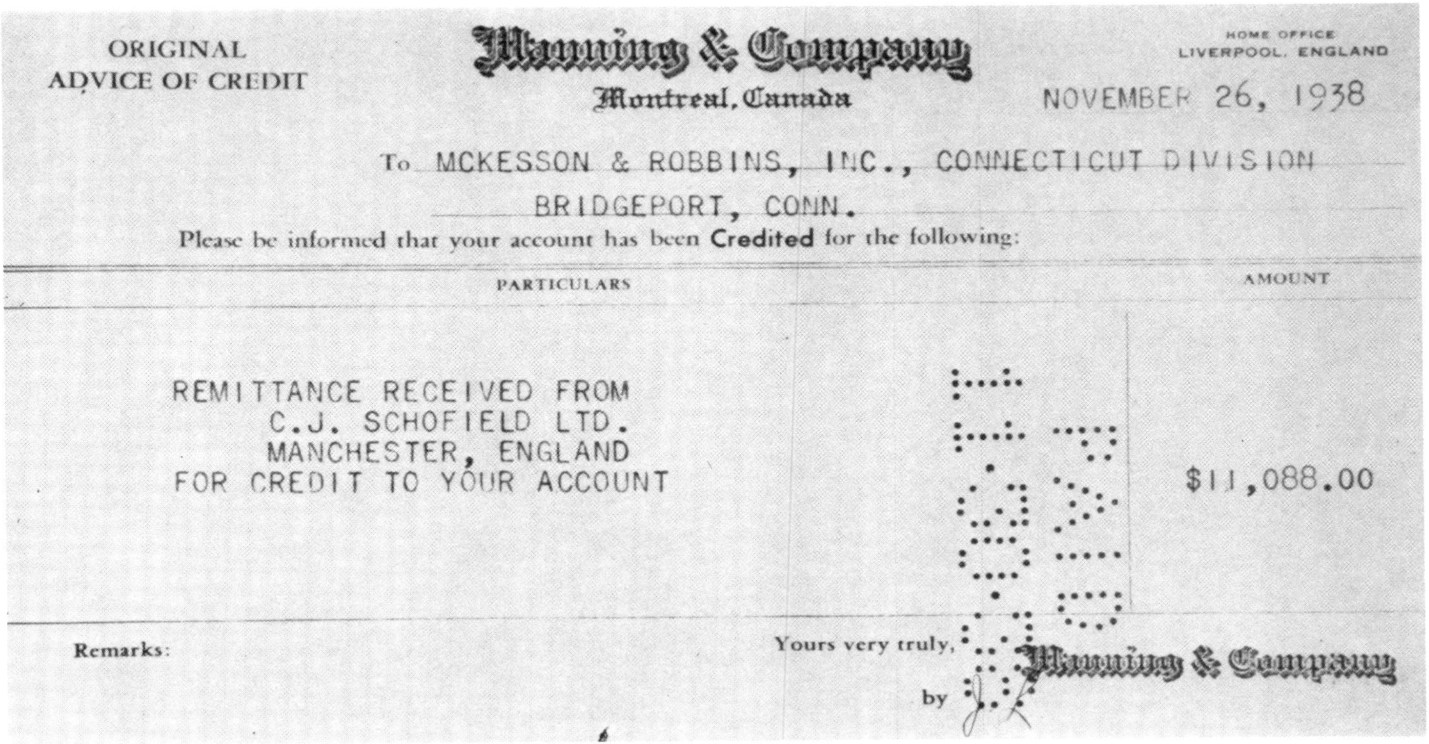

ORIGINAL
ADVICE OF CREDIT

Manning & Company
Montreal, Canada

HOME OFFICE
LIVERPOOL, ENGLAND

NOVEMBER 26, 1938

To MCKESSON & ROBBINS, INC., CONNECTICUT DIVISION
BRIDGEPORT, CONN.

Please be informed that your account has been **Credited** for the following:

PARTICULARS	AMOUNT
REMITTANCE RECEIVED FROM C.J. SCHOFIELD LTD. MANCHESTER, ENGLAND FOR CREDIT TO YOUR ACCOUNT	$11,088.00

Remarks:

Yours very truly,
Manning & Company
by

EXHIBIT 34.—Manning & Company advice of credit. (Size 8⅜" x 4⅝".)

loss.[292] And this despite the fact that in some instances the regular market for these products declined materially.[293]

In this connection, the Price, Waterhouse & Co. memorandum on accounts for the Connecticut Division as at December 31, 1937, stated:

"A number of items were priced at lower values than at December 31, 1936, but the company did not, so far as we have been able to determine, sustain any loss on these stocks during the year due to the depreciation in market value." [294]

Another illustration is furnished by the foreign crude drug product santonine crystals which purportedly cost McKesson $107.332 per lb. in 1931, $52 and $49 a lb. in 1933, $20 a lb. in 1934, $30 a lb. in 1935 and 1936, and $18 a lb. in 1937.[295]

Payment for goods sold would be evidenced when due by the purported receipt from Manning & Company of an "Advice of Credit" informing McKesson that its "* * * account has been credited for the following remittance received from * * *" a foreign customer.[296] A reproduction of one of these is inserted facing this page.[297]

These advices of credit would be received in the first instance by George Dietrich,[298] who would send them to the cashier's office.[299] They were not numbered and, aside from the name and address of the customer and amount of remittance, did not contain any description or indication of the type of remittance received by Manning. Nor was any definite evidence developed showing the exact means by which the customers were supposedly advised to remit to Manning & Company at Montreal on account of these McKesson invoices.[300] Thorn thought George Dietrich put a sticker to this effect on the invoices before he mailed them.[301] Concerning the form of these advices of credit, Miss Bakos, one of the cashiers who handled them, testified:

"Q. [By Mr. STEWART.] You simply got a credit advice from Manning & Company which looked similar to the credit advices you had seen from other banks?

A. I wouldn't say they looked similar, because they were different from any other bank advice I had, but it was supposed to be a credit advice from Manning & Company.

Q. Did it strike you that there was anything irregular about its form? Were you suspicious at the time you saw them?

A. Well, I didn't particularly note it, but it didn't have the general printing that the other advices have.

---

292 R. 1373. See also R. 798–799, 924, 1010.
293 Ex. 38, 40, 41, 42, 82; R. 799.
294 Ex. 49.
295 Ex. E, 42, 41, 40, 38.
296 Ex. 34.
297 Ex. 34.
298 R. 1589–1590.
299 R. 2686.
300 R. 143, 1141, 1357
301 R. 1141.

Q. But were you suspicious of it?

A. At that time, I would say no.

Q. Well, if there was anything on it that was suspicious looking, you would have been suspicious, would you not?

A. Well, it was a very clean looking advice; just had Manning & Company and the necessary data showing the account to be credited and the amount. That was all.[302]

* * * * * * *

Q. I mean, was that a thing which struck you as being irregular?

A. No, the irregularity was the size of the advices. Banks ordinarily had narrow, elongated sized advices, whereas this one was unusually large. I had never seen any advices of that type coming from any bank, but I couldn't truly say I was suspicious on account of the size of the paper, or the cleanliness." [303]

On the basis of the credit advice which they would receive from George Dietrich, the cashiers would prepare a cash ticket.[304] A copy of one of these follows: [305]

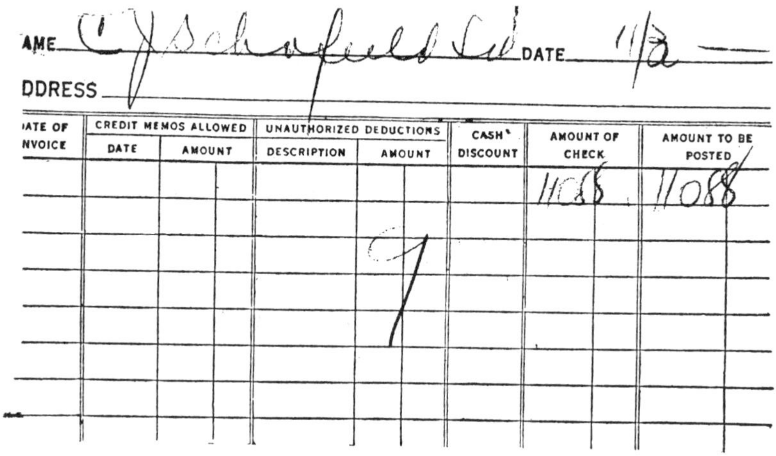

AME C J Schofield Co DATE 11/2

DDRESS

ATE OF NVOICE	CREDIT MEMOS ALLOWED — DATE	CREDIT MEMOS ALLOWED — AMOUNT	UNAUTHORIZED DEDUCTIONS — DESCRIPTION	UNAUTHORIZED DEDUCTIONS — AMOUNT	CASH DISCOUNT	AMOUNT OF CHECK	AMOUNT TO BE POSTED
						11088	11088

EXHIBIT 264.—Posting ticket for cash purportedly received from a foreign crude drug customer. (Size 6" x 3½".)

Miss Bakos testified that after preparing the cash ticket she would put a dated entry in pencil against the amount to be credited on the accounts receivable ledger so that if anyone wanted to check before the tickets were posted that pencil entry would disclose whether or not the item had been paid.[306] The cash tickets, which then went to the accounting department, presumably furnished the basis for the actual postings by machine operators on to the accounts receivable ledger canceling the amount due thereon as entered from the sales invoices.[307]

---

302 R. 2686.

303 R. 2694–2695.

304 Ex. 264; R. 2674, 2686.

305 Ex. 264.

306 R. 2669–2670, 2692A.

307 R. 1357, 2669–2670, 2674, 2689.

Concerning her observations in comparing the amount of the purported remittances with the accounts receivable record, Miss Bakos also testified that these used to be called "nice accounts" and that, while not suspicious, she could not remember ever having had any difficulty at any time of reporting a shortage or anything concerning any of these accounts, although in other departments she would come across little irregularities from time to time.[308]

No credits were ever given to customers by McKesson for returns, discounts or allowances in connection with sales of these goods,[309] and, according to the Price, Waterhouse & Co. memoranda on accounts of the Connecticut Division, all these receivables, regardless of foreign currency conditions, were usually paid promptly at maturity, in United States dollars, short delays in settlement usually being attributed to the time element in transmitting remittances; no losses were ever sustained on these accounts nor were any balances ever charged back to W. W. Smith & Co.[310]

5. Purchases and Sales of Foreign Crude Drugs by the Canadian Company at the Time of the 1937 Audit, and How They Were Handled

The manner in which the purchases and sales of foreign crude drugs were handled by the Canadian Company at the time of the 1937 audit can best be explained in the language of Margaret Walsh, its bookkeeper and sole employee.[311]

"Q. [By Mr. GALPEER.] Would you tell us in detail, starting in on each transaction with the purchase, going through the payment for the purchase, the inventory and then the sale; would you tell us how that was handled and specifically what you did in connection with each of those items, recording them on the books of McKesson & Robbins, Ltd.?

A. Well, when the purchase came in, when we purchased merchandise from one of the vendors up in Canada, I would receive the original purchase order and the [purchase] invoice would be in my box in Mr. [George] Dietrich's office and attached to that would be the Manning charge—Manning Company charge.

Q. That is, the debit advice?

A. The debit advice and two or three days later I would receive a receiving ticket showing that the merchandise had been received and I would voucher that and enter it on the inventory cards from the purchase order. That would be all on that.

Q. From whom, or where did you receive the receiving ticket?

A. That would come from Mr. Robert Dietrich's department.

* * * * * * *

Q. Now, how would the sales be handled, as far as you were concerned?

A. Well, on the sales, I would get the bookkeeper's copy, which was a yellow

---

[308] R. 2693–2694.

[309] Ex. 120, 124, 267, N; R. 1378–1379.

[310] Ex. 49, 78, 79, 268, 80, 81, 82. The same situation appears to have prevailed from the inception of this business even prior to the adoption of the Smith sales agency—guaranty arrangement, for the Price, Waterhouse & Co. report for 1929 stated: "* * * No credit losses have been sustained by the company thus far in this department of the business." Ex. 151. See also Ex. 83.

[311] Ex. 19 (A3, A3a); R. 4391–4392.

duplicate copy of the sale. That would be in my box. I would get that from Mr. George Dietrich.

Q. What do you mean by copy of the sale? Would that be a factory order or an invoice?

A. That was a copy of the [sales] invoice that went to the customer, carbon copy of the [sales] invoice, and then, the supporting papers for that, which would be the Smith, W. W. Smith documents, and the pink [factory] order copy, would come from Bob Dietrich's department.

* * * * * * *

Q. Would they come about the same time?

A. No, I always got them later than the bookkeeper's yellow copy [of the sales invoice].

Q. You would enter those on the books of the Limited Company?

A. On the inventory cards, and on the sales register.

Q. How would you receive notice of payment?

A. They would come at various times through the month, just separately.

* * * * * * *

Q. Credit advices from Manning & Company?

A. Yes.

* * * * * * *

The EXAMINER. Mr. Galpeer, do I understand there that all of the transactions in the Limited Company were by debits and credits through Manning & Company, or was there actually cash transactions with other customers?

Q. [By Mr. GALPEER.] Excluding the small branch of the Limited Company which operated in London, with which I assume you did not have anything to do, ——

A. No, I didn't.

Q. Were all the transactions of the Limited Company during the period that you were the bookkeeper from 1931 on, handled by debit and credit advices from Manning & Company?

A. That's right.

The EXAMINER. No cash in it at all?

The WITNESS. Not on the Manning account. We did have cash accounts.

Q. [By Mr. GALPEER.] Well, now, did those cash accounts—were they used in connection with purchases or sales, or were they in the nature of dividend accounts?

A. Well, either that, or transfers from one bank to another, or to pay small expenses.

Q. I see, but the purchase and sales transactions were handled solely by the debit and credit advices?

A. That's right.

* * * * * * *

Q. * * * There was no crude drug business done through the Limited Company that was not tied into these Manning transactions and W. W. Smith?

A. Not since 1931.

The EXAMINER. That clears it up.

* * * * * * *

Q. [By Mr. GALPEER.] You stated that in connection with the sales that you received * * * [a yellow] copy of the [sales] invoice. Who prepared those [sales] invoices * * *?

A. I don't know.

Q. Did you keep the accounts receivable ledgers?

A. Yes, sir.

Q. And you made your entries there from this yellow copy of the [sales] invoice?

A. Yes, sir.

* * * * * * *

Q. Now, you received the purchase orders and the [purchase] invoice and debit advice from this box in George Dietrich's office?

A. That's right.

Q. And you received the yellow copies of the [sales] invoice from the box in George Dietrich's office?

A. Yes, sir.

Q. And you received the credit advice also in the box in George Dietrich's office?

A. Yes, sir.

Q. And the accounts payable and accounts receivable ledgers which you maintained and the inventory cards, the entries which you made on those, were made from those documents?

A. Yes, sir.

Q. Now, were you part of the general accounting office of McKesson & Robbins?

A. No.

Q. Under whose supervision did you act?

A. Mr. George Dietrich.

Q. And you were responsible to him?

A. Yes.

* * * * * * *

Q. Was there any one else in your office?

A. No.

Q. The office that you occupied had all the books of the Limited Company?

A. Yes.

* * * * * * *

Q. Did Mr. McGloon ever give you any orders or make any comment as to your work?

A. No, sir.

Q. You received all those instructions from Mr. George Dietrich?

A. Yes.

* * * * * * *

The EXAMINER. Were those debit advices and other papers that came in to you from Mr. Dietrich folded and otherwise have the appearance of coming in through the mail?

The WITNESS. Yes, sir.

By Mr. GALPEER:

Q. Miss Walsh, in connection with the debit advices that were issued by Manning & Company, which apparently were in payment of the purchase invoices, do you know in what manner those debit advices were authorized. In other words, how Manning & Company was advised to make the payment to the purchaser?

A. No, I never had anything to do with that.

Q. And similarly, on the sales, do you know in what manner the customer was advised to make the payment to Manning as distinguished from McKesson?

A. No.

* * * * * * *

Q. [By Mr. STEWART.] Was this box from which you obtained the various papers in Mr. George Dietrich's office a regular mail box where mail for you was deposited?

A. Yes, sir.

Q. You got other mail out of that box in addition to those papers?

A. Yes, sir.

Q. Now, did you take care of the billing of the transactions in the Limited Company?

A. No, I did not.

Q. That was handled by another department?

A. Yes, I imagine so. I never saw any one working on it.

Q. Did you spend your entire time on the work of the Limited Company, or did you spend some time on other work?

A. Well, at various times I helped out in the main office. I did personal work for Mr. George Dietrich, balancing check books and so forth.

Q. And what was the nature of the work you did in the main office?

A. I helped out in the cashier's office when any one was ill.

At one time I helped out in the bookkeeping machine room when one of the operators was out.

Q. Now, do you know what other work, other than billing, was done for the Limited Company by the Connecticut Company employees?

What I have in mind is, I understand there was a 7,500 dollar a year charge, something like that, made by the Connecticut Company for services, and I was wondering whether you could tell us what that charge was made for other than the billing service?

A. Well, I don't know whether the billing service was done out in the main office or not. I don't know where that was done.

Q. I see.

A. But Mr. Ettershank, he made up the income tax reports on the Limited Company and took care of all tax matters.

Q. And Mr. Robert Dietrich did some work on the inventory records, did he?

A. Well, I did have to check the inventories out there with the duplicate set of cards that they had.

* * * * * * *

Q. Did you prepare a regular statement, monthly or at regular periods, of the affairs of the Limited Company?

A. You mean customers' statements, or financial statements?

Q. No, financial statements.

A. Yes.

Q. To whom were those submitted?

A. To the accounting department of the main office.

Q. That is, Mr. McGloon's department?

A. Yes. Mr. Kollar took care of it.

Q. Do you know for what purpose those were submitted to Mr. Kollar?

A. They were consolidated with the other statements.

Q. And were they reviewed out there by Mr. Kollar?

A. Just as a matter of consolidation.

Q. Did he ever talk to you about them?

A. No.

Q. Never asked you any questions about them?

A. Just when they were ready, when he expected them.

Q. Did you ever ask him any questions about what he wanted, any information on them?

A. No, it was a regular form. I knew how to fill it out.

* * * * * * *

Q. Do you recall whether the accounts receivable of the Limited Company were also paid when they were due, or did you sometimes have some past due?

A. Well, if they were past due it was just a few days of the next month that they ran over, not any longer period.

Q. They were pretty good, but they did sometimes go over a little bit, is that right?

A. Yes, sir.

* * * * * * *

Q. Now, where did you get your information as to the location of the merchandise which is set out on that [inventory] card?

A. From Mr. [George] Dietrich.

* * * * * * *

Q. In what form did you get that information?

A. He just told me what to write on the inventory cards.

Q. And that's the only evidence you have of it?

A. That's where I got my instructions from that I wrote down.

* * * * * * *

Q. Now, during the period since the inventories had been stored in Canada, did you get from somewhere a receiving ticket when the merchandise would be received?

A. Yes.

Q. Would that receiving ticket be similar in form to exhibit No. 20?

A. Yes.

Q. Would it have all the information on it which is indicated on exhibit 20?

A. Yes, I would say it did.

Q. Including the language, 'held at suppliers, no other charges'?

A. Yes, I think that was stamped on.

* * * * * * *

Q. So that would be an additional source of information that you had as to where it was held in addition to Mr. George Dietrich telling you where it was held?

A. Yes.

* * * * * * *

Q. [By Mr. GALPEER.] Now, when you received the purchase orders, the suppliers' invoices and the debit memorandums in this mail rack, or box, in Mr. George Dietrich's office, was there any evidence of mailing to those? In other words, were they ever in envelopes or anything that would show they came through the mail?

A. No, they never were in envelopes.

* * * * * * *

Q. Did you have, or see, or file, or handle, or type any letters, correspondence, with the customers, in reference to any matters at all, in reference to time of shipment, payment?

A. No, never.

Q. Returns or anything of that sort?

A. Never.

Q. Did you ever type any letters to W. W. Smith & Company in reference to any matters which might come up in connection with these transactions?

A. No. * * *" [312]

Like the Connecticut Division, the sales were purportedly made principally to customers in the British Empire, and the accounts were

[312] R. 4382–4424.

supposed to be payable in U. S. dollars.[313] A geographical summary of the foreign crude drug accounts receivable at December 31, 1937, as compared with the year before shows the following distribution:[314]

"Country	December 31, 1936	December 31, 1937
England	$ 909, 673. 05	$ 870, 387. 90
Scotland	226, 470. 00	238, 053. 45
Wales	74, 222. 00	56, 665. 00
Ireland	101, 136. 85	122, 244. 60
Australia	69, 120. 60	142, 701. 45
British Guiana	6, 732. 00	—
New Zealand	12, 980. 00	13, 588. 00
India	33, 560. 50	43, 743. 00
South Africa	25, 780. 00	67, 662. 60
Sweden	11, 594. 00	11, 305. 00
Holland	12, 635. 00	12, 792. 00
	$1, 483, 904. 00	$1, 579, 143. 00"

Of the 116 accounts for which requests for confirmation were sent by S. D. Leidesdorf & Co.,[315] 96 apparently were with existing concerns who replied that the amounts were not owing. In 13 instances no replies were received and the remaining 7 requests were returned because of incorrect addresses.[316]

Like the Connecticut Division, too, the books of the Canadian Company did not disclose any allowances or adjustments to customers or any bad debts resulting from these transactions.[317] According to the Price, Waterhouse & Co. memoranda on accounts of the Canadian Company, all of these receivables were paid when due, minor exceptions being attributed to certain customers computing the credit period from the date the merchandise was received rather than invoiced. The Company consistently realized a profit on all transactions throughout the year. No losses were ever sustained on these accounts, nor were any of them charged back under the guaranty contract because of failure to collect.[318]

In addition to the foreign crude drug sales discussed above, the Canadian Company also purported to sell foreign crude drugs to the Connecticut Division. The Connecticut Division made payment by check which would be deposited by the Canadian Company in either its Bridgeport or New York bank account.[319] In 1937, these sales amounted to $244,875[320] and certain of them coincided with the

313 Ex. 26.
314 Ex. 26. For earlier years see Ex. 72, 73, 74, 75, 77, 205.
315 Those purportedly outstanding as at December 7, 1938.
316 Ex. 255.
317 R. 4424–4426; Ex. 19 (Limited, C. 4, Item 2).
318 Ex. 26, 72, 73, 74, 75, 205, 76. See also Ex. 77, H.
319 R. 4423.
320 Ex. 26, 255.

dividend payment dates on the preferred stock of the Canadian Company. Without the transfer of these funds, the Canadian Company would not have had sufficient balance in the bank to pay the dividends in question.[321]

6. Periodic Accounting in Connection With the Foreign Crude Drug Transactions at the Time of the 1937 Audit

a. MONTHLY STATEMENTS FROM MANNING & COMPANY

In addition to the individual debit and credit advices on each purchase and sale Manning & Company also purportedly issued regular monthly statements of account to both "McKesson & Robbins, Inc. Connecticut Division" and "McKesson & Robbins, Ltd." [322] One of these is reproduced on the following page.[323]

As previously stated all incoming mail first went to the desk of George Dietrich.[324] Ultimately, the Manning & Company statement of account with the Connecticut Division went to the cashiers for reconciliation,[325] and the statement of account with the Canadian Company to Miss Walsh.[326] Miss Walsh testified that no drafts, duplicate advices of debit or credit, or other material were enclosed with the statements when they were received by her.[327] Although as indicated by the statements the volume of transactions purportedly going through the accounts was large [328] at the year ends, at least, the balances carried were comparatively small.[329] Also, at least at the year ends, in 1935, 1936, and 1937, there were no outstanding payables to the vendors, advices of debit having apparently been issued before the close of the year to cover all invoices dated prior thereto.[330]

b. MONTHLY STATEMENTS FOR GUARANTY AND SERVICE CHARGES

Apparently pursuant to Articles 6 and 9 of the 1935 agreement between McKesson & Robbins, Incorporated and McKesson & Robbins, Limited and W. W. Smith & Company, Inc. (the New York company) [331] separate statements, which were the only invoices rendered for such charges, were purportedly received monthly by the Connecticut Division and Canadian Company "To Service Charge for the month * * *" in the sum of $750 each and "To Charge of ¾ of

---

321 Ex. 258; R. 4586. See pages 241–242 *infra*. The particular situation described in the last two sentences apparently existed also in 1935 and in 1938 which was subsequent to the last audit.

322 Ex. 30.

323 Ex. 30. While the statement for the Canadian Company reproduced on the following page occupies only the upper half of one sheet of the statement form, the statements for the Connecticut Company (later Division) usually filled one sheet and part of another.

324 R. 715, 1361, 1427, 1588.

325 Ex. 17 (p. 2), 18 (A4).

326 R. 4384–4385.

327 R. 4385.

328 Ex. 30.

329 R. 954.

330 R. 544, 635, 1328–1329.

331 Ex. 50. Like Articles 5 and 8 of the 1931 contract quoted on pages 58–59 *supra* with changes mentioned on pages 61 and 64 *supra*.

MANNING & COMPANY
FOREIGN DEPARTMENT
MONTREAL, CANADA

MAIN OFFICE
143-163 LONDON ROAD
LIVERPOOL, 3, ENGLAND

STATEMENT OF A/C WITH

MCKESSON & ROBBINS, LTD.
BRIDGEPORT, CONN.

DECEMBER 31, 1937

DATE		ITEMS	DEBITS	CREDITS	BALANCE	VALUE DATE	DAYS	AGGREGATE	ADJUSTMENTS DR. RED CR. BLACK
Dec.	1				$37,445.33				
	1			10,285.00					
	2			12,240.00					
	4			12,250.00					
	6			13,943.00					
	7			15,001.50					
	7	H. Monroe & Company	58,800.00						
	9			14,691.25					
	11			12,410.00					
	13			11,900.00					
	14			11,800.00					
	16			12,580.00					
	18			14,782.50					
	18	A.H. Raymond & Company	51,480.00						
	20			5,600.00					
	21			12,000.00					
	23			12,050.00					
	27			17,358.25					
	28			11,985.00					
	29	P. Pierson & Company	54,697.50						
	30			14,581.75					
	31	H. Monroe & Company	55,440.00						
	31				$32,486.08				

EXHIBIT 30.—Manning & Company statement of account, upper half of sheet. (Full size, 12½″ x 17½″.)

Branch Account
Statement

December 1, 1937

McKesson & Robbins, Ltd.

Bridgeport, Conn.

To W. W. Smith & Co. Dr.
Commission Merchants
Purchasing Forwarding & Shipping Agents
Liverpool 3 England

Terms

To Service Charge for the month of November, 1937	$750 00

This statement is due and payable at our NEW YORK office
in U.S. currency Address all enquiries there

W. W. Smith & Co.

EXHIBIT 224.—W. W. Smith & Co. statement for service charge. (Size 6½" x 10".)

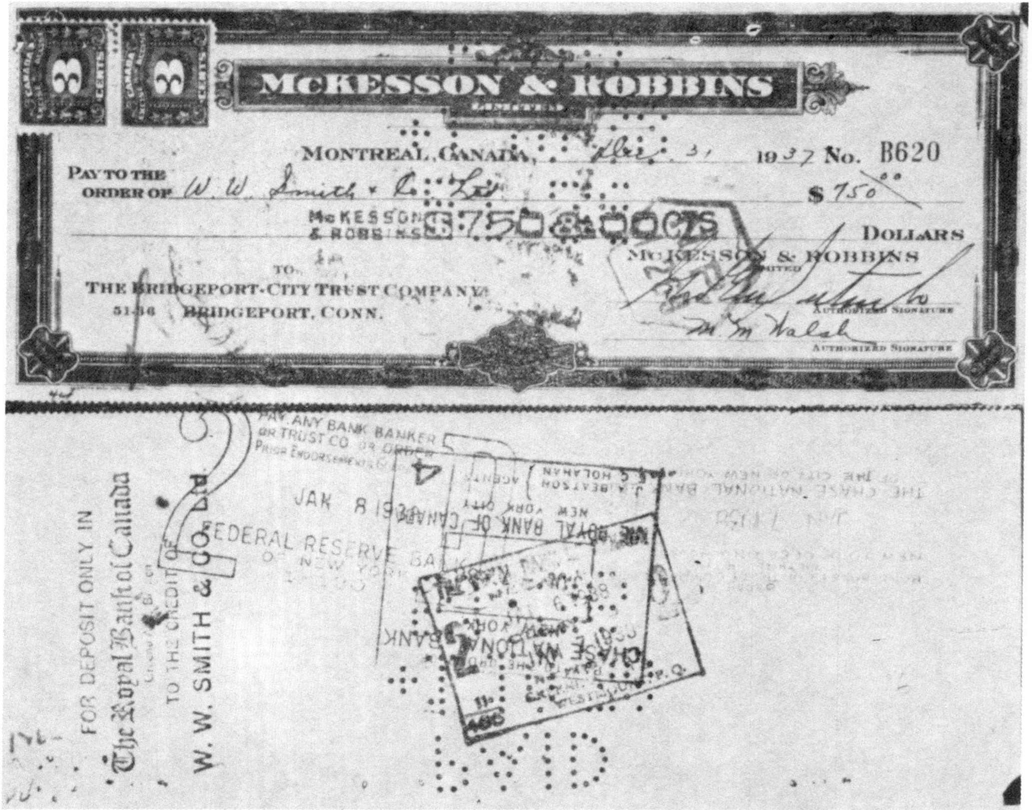

EXHIBIT 224.—Check in payment of service charge. (Size 8½" x 3½".)

Branch Account

Statement

McKesson & Robbins, Ltd. December 1, 1937

Bridgeport, Conn.

To W. W. Smith & Co. Dr.

Commission Merchants

Purchasing, Forwarding & Shipping Agents

Liverpool, 3, England

Terms

To Charge of 3/4 of 1% on total of $241,588.50 on orders for the month of November, 1937	$1 811	91

This statement is due and payable at our NEW YORK *office in* U.S. *currency. Address all inquiries there.*

W. W. Smith & Co.

EXHIBIT 225.—W. W. Smith & Co. statement for guaranty fees. (Size 6½" x 10".)

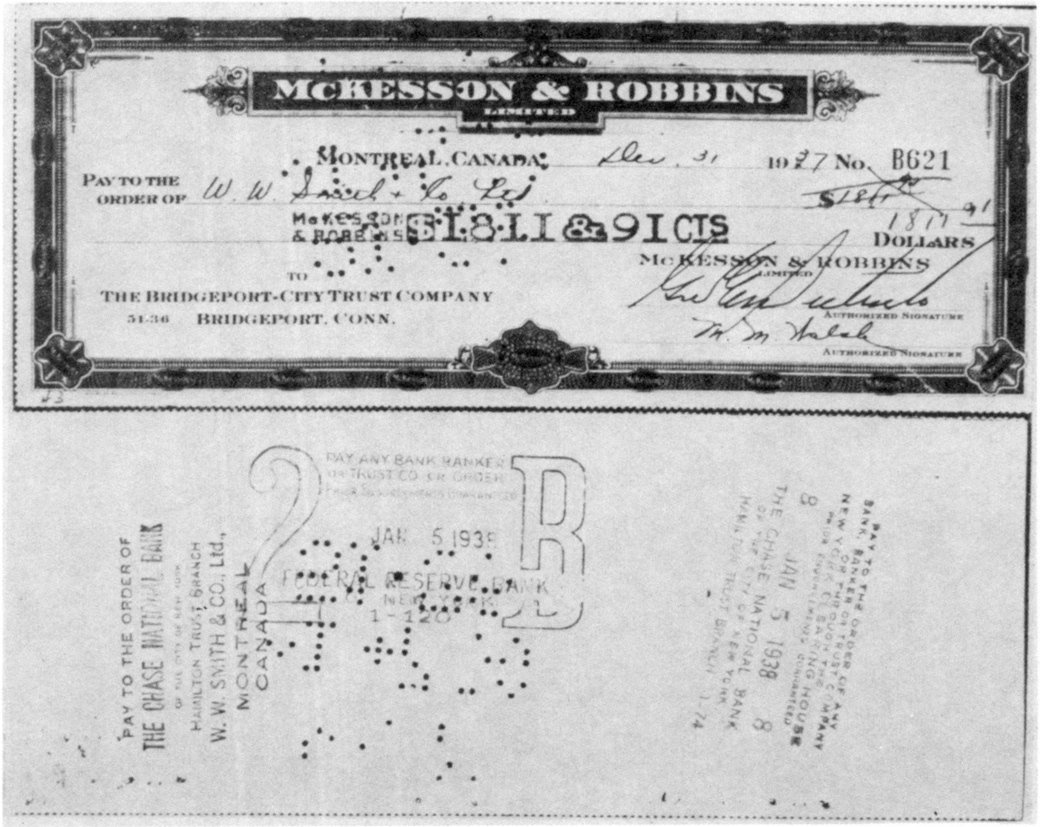

McKESSON & ROBBINS
LIMITED

MONTREAL, CANADA Dec. 31 1937 No. B621

PAY TO THE ORDER OF W. W. Smith + Co. Ltd. $1811.91

McKESSON & ROBBINS $1811 & 91 CTS DOLLARS

TO THE BRIDGEPORT-CITY TRUST COMPANY
51-36 BRIDGEPORT, CONN.

McKESSON & ROBBINS LIMITED
AUTHORIZED SIGNATURE
AUTHORIZED SIGNATURE

PAY TO THE ORDER OF
THE CHASE NATIONAL BANK
OF THE CITY OF NEW YORK
HAMILTON TRUST BRANCH
W. W. SMITH & CO., Ltd.,
MONTREAL
CANADA

PAY ANY BANK BANKER OR TRUST CO. OR ORDER
PRIOR ENDORSEMENTS GUARANTEED
JAN 5 1938
FEDERAL RESERVE BANK
NEW YORK
1-120

PAY TO THE ORDER OF ANY BANK, BANKER OR TRUST COMPANY OR THROUGH THE NEW YORK CLEARING HOUSE
PRIOR ENDORSEMENTS GUARANTEED
8 JAN 5 1938 8
THE CHASE NATIONAL BANK
OF THE CITY OF NEW YORK
HAMILTON TRUST BRANCH 1-74

EXHIBIT 225.—Check in payment of guaranty fees. (Size 8½" x 3½".)

1% on total of * * * orders for the month * * *." [332] Reproductions of both types of these statements are inserted at this point.[333]

The statement heads are those of W. W. Smith & Co., Liverpool, England, Branch Account, and on the bottom there is printed "This statement is due and payable at our NEW YORK office in U. S. currency. Address all inquiries there. W. W. Smith & Co." The "New York" and "U. S." are stamped and typed respectively.[334]

The Connecticut Division statements were checked in the accounting department against the sales that had been made.[335] The Canadian Company statements were checked by Miss Walsh.[336] The respective checks were prepared by the cashiers' department and Miss Walsh and after the one was signed by Miss Danis, a cashier, and the other by Miss Walsh, they were both given to George Dietrich whose signature also appeared thereon.[337] The checks issued about the time of the 1937 audit were made payable to W. W. Smith & Co., Ltd.[338] Reproductions of the checks corresponding to the statements are also inserted at this point.[339]

The contract provided that—

"In consideration of a premium of three-quarters of one percent (in addition to the service charge * * *) of the total amount of any order placed under the provisions hereof, the New York Company will, if requested so to do in writing, unconditionally guaranty the full and prompt payment therefor * * * provided, however, that the total of accounts so guaranteed shall not at any time exceed the sum of $900,000 * * *." [340]

The W. W. Smith & Co. purchase orders stated "Guarantee ¾ of 1%" on each transaction,[341] the monthly statements charged "* * * ¾ of 1% on total * * * orders for the month * * *" [342] and the total accounts outstanding at any one time on which the guaranty fee had been paid approximated nine million dollars.[343]

The total amount paid to Smith during 1937 for these charges amounted to $154,811.16. Of this sum, which includes the $18,000 service fee, $122,409.71 was paid by the Connecticut Division and $32,401.45 by the Canadian Company.[344]

---

332 Ex. 224–227.

333 Ex. 224, 225.

334 Ex. 224–227.

335 R. 1641.

336 R. 4424.

337 R. 1625, 1639, 4399; Ex. 86, 224–227.

338 Ex. 86, 224–227. When introduced Ritts testified that Price, Waterhouse & Co. would not ordinarily examine such statements and that he had no recollection of having seen them. R. 4467–4468. Previously, however, Price, Waterhouse & Co. had introduced from their work papers a schedule of Accounts Payable of the Canadian Company as of December 31, 1937, which had been marked by someone else, probably Wyman, "Invoice seen" in referring to the statements in question. Ex. L; R. 365 ff.

339 Ex. 224, 225.

340 Ex. 50.

341 Ex. 7, 8B, 11C.

342 Ex. 224–227.

343 Ex. 26, 49.

344 Ex. 255.

Telephone Queen 982

B. MILLER & COMPANY

Importers and Brokers

45 QUEEN STREET, OTTAWA, CANADA

January 13, 1938.

TELEPHONE ELGIN 2686

H. MONROE & COMPANY

BROKERS & AGENTS

27 WELLINGTON STREET, EAST
TORONTO, CANADA

January 11, 1938.

TELEPHONE LANCASTER 7975

P. PIERSON & COMPANY

FOREIGN REPRESENTATIVES

UNIVERSITY TOWER
MONTREAL, CANADA

January 12, 1938.

Telephone Plateau 6844

A. H. RAYMOND & COMPANY

Importers

504 DOMINION SQUARE BUILDING
MONTREAL, CANADA

January 13, 1938.

EXHIBIT 53.—Letterheads from purported confirmations of inventory of foreign crude drugs held by four of the five Canadian vendors. (Size 8½" x 11".)

TELEPHONE QUEEN 846

D

D. C. REYNOLDS & COMPANY

COMMISSION MERCHANTS

CHEMICALS
DRUGS
PHARMACEUTICALS

192 BANK STREET
OTTAWA, CANADA

January 12, 1938.

Messrs. Price Waterhouse & Co.,
56 Pine Street,
New York City, New York.

Dear Sirs:

At the request of McKesson & Robbins, Incorporated, Bridgeport, Conn. dated December 31, 1937, we are listing below description of merchandise carried by us for their account at close of business December 31, 1937; said merchandise being free of all charges and subject to their withdrawal.

Antipyrine Crystals U.S.P.	100 lbs. net to a case	94,000 lbs. ✓
Bismuth Subnitrate	50 lbs. to a box	220,000 lbs. ✓
Hexylresorcinol	50 lbs. to a can	17,500 lbs. ✓
Musk Pods	20 ozs.net to each cady	12,800 ozs. ✓
Oil of Cinnamon Ceylon Pure	50-1 lb. bottles to a case	8,700 lbs. ✓
Oil of Coriander Terpeneless-	100-1 lb. bottles to a case-	12,400 lbs. ✓
Potassium Iodide	100 lbs. net to a case	200,000 lbs. ✓
Pyrogallic Acid Resublimed Crystals	100 lbs. net to a tin	117,000 lbs. ✓
Sacharine Powder U.S.P.	4-25 lb. tins to a case	175,000 lbs. ✓

Faithfully yours,

M. A. O'Donnell

D.C. REYNOLDS & COMPANY

EF/MAOD

Agreed with Inventory
C. H

EXHIBIT 53.—Purported confirmation of inventory of foreign crude drugs held by one of the five Canadian vendors. (Size 8½" x 11".)

c. SEMI-ANNUAL REQUESTS FOR CONFIRMATIONS OF INVENTORIES

Semi-annually McKesson would prepare letters requesting statements of inventories not held by themselves or in their own warehouses. The letters did not describe the merchandise of which a confirmation was requested but merely requested "* * * a statement certifying to the amount of merchandise you hold in storage for our account * * *."[345] Although prepared by the Company, on the year-end the requests were mailed by Price, Waterhouse & Co., when the original confirmations were returned directly to them and carbon copies to McKesson. On June 30th, the request presumably was mailed by McKesson directly and the confirmation sent only to it.[346]

Among others, these requests went to the five pretended vendors who, as previously stated, were supposedly holding the foreign crude drugs after their purchase by the McKesson Companies until their sale under the contract with W. W. Smith & Company, Inc. The replies received from these assumed suppliers were all on different colored stationery and varied in language used but none stated the exact location of the goods or gave any markings which might identify particular stocks.[347] As at December 31, 1937, the combined inventories of the Connecticut Division and Canadian Company purportedly held by these five Canadian vendors and covered by these replies amounted to approximately $10,000,000.[348] The pretended confirmation of one of these vendors is reproduced on the preceding page and samples of the letterheads of the other four are reproduced on the second page preceding.[349]

Johnson, the office manager who handled all of these confirmations, did not remember any that did not balance with the inventory cards with which they were compared, although on one year end a request for confirmation came back because incorrectly addressed to 48 rather than to 45 Queen Street, Ottawa, Canada.[350]

Further, the surprising regularity of the foreign crude drug transactions as recorded on McKesson's books is illustrated by the data contained in the Price, Waterhouse & Co. year-end inventory price test schedules for 1934, 1935, 1936, and 1937 which were introduced in evidence at the hearings. While the goods were turned over on an average of less than twice a year [351] an examination of the schedules

---

345 Ex. D.

346 R. 1662–1663, 1659; Ex. 40 (1–3), 41 (D85–90), D.

347 Ex. 40 (5, 16, 18, 20, 22, 23), 41 (D91–96), 53, 54. Cf. Ex. 49, 73, 78; R. 595.

348 See page 43 *supra* and footnote 982 *infra*.

349 Ex. 53.

350 R. 1364–1366, 1433–1434.

351 Ex. Q.

for the Connecticut Division indicates that none of the goods in question were ever held over from one year end to the next.[352] Also, while purchases of each commodity were supposedly made in comparatively large units, for example, aloin U. S. P. purchase 84,000 lbs., and sales in much smaller units, e. g., aloin U. S. P. 11,340, 12,460, 12,040, 12,880, 12,320, 11,060, and 11,900 lbs.,[353] it was only in rare instances that the inventory at the year end did not exactly equal in quantity a particular purchase or purchases.[354] Further, although the sales were made in smaller than purchase units, the total sales for January in any one product almost always exactly equalled a single purchase of that product.[355] Finally, only rarely were different purchases of the same goods carried in the closing inventory made at different prices.[356] The foregoing facts may be summarized in the following table:[357]

Connecticut Division

Foreign Crude Drug Inventory	No. of Items	No. of Items with Broken Purchase Quantities at Year End	No. of Items sold Following Jan.	No. of Items for which Jan. Sales did not Equal Purchase Quantity	Earliest purchase of goods in Inventory at Year End	No. of Items with Purchases at Varying Prices
Dec. 31, 1937	40	[a] 1	17	[a] 2	Mar. 22, 1937	0
Dec. 31, 1936	44	[a] 3	15	[a] 5	Apr. 29, 1936	0
Dec. 31, 1935	45	[a] 1	12	[a] 2	July 3, 1935	0
Dec. 31, 1934	50	0	9	1	Apr. 17, 1934	1

[a] 1 of the 2 items and 3 of the 5 items in which January sales did not equal a purchase quantity were the items with broken purchase quantities at end of year and the January sales exactly equalled such broken purchase quantity at the end of the year.

Concerning the foreign crude drug inventory as set forth on the price test schedules and as confirmed by the pretended Canadian vendors, Charles Hermann, an employee of McKesson for 36 years and their buyer of bulk drugs and chemicals at the Cliff Street, New York City office, testified that in practically all of the items the quantities expressed were greater than the amounts traded in the United States in those particular items during the course of a year either

[352] Ex. 38, 40, 41, 42.

[353] Ex. 40.

[354] Ex. 38, 40, 41, 42. See also Ex. 61.

[355] Ex. 38, 40, 41, 42, 84.

[356] Ex. 38, 40, 41, 42. See also Ex. 61 and memorandum on accounts of Canadian Company as at Dec. 31, 1937 (Ex. 26) "* * * the stock records of the company do not disclose any price changes in any of the commodities traded in since April 21, 1937" and memorandum on accounts of Connecticut Division as at Dec. 31, 1937 (Ex. 49) "* * * In most cases the purchase cost of these stocks has remained fairly constant notwithstanding the generally depressed commodity market * * *." But cf. Ex. 42 and Ex. 61. Eight items in the Canadian Company inventory on Dec. 31, 1934 were also in the Connecticut Company inventory on the same date. Uniform prices were paid by each Company for each commodity. On seven items, however, the purchase price paid by one Company differed from that paid by the other even though the purchases for identical commodities were sometimes made by one Company both before and after those of the other Company.

[357] Ex. 38, 40, 41, 42, 84.

domestically or for export [358] and continued to point out other impossibilities in the manner in which the business was supposedly conducted.

"Q. [By Mr. GALPEER.] Will you please look also, Mr. Hermann, at the description of the containers in which these goods were carried, and tell me in which cases, in which instances, to your experience and knowledge, the goods are not handled in the manner as stated on that exhibit.

* * * * * * *

A. Amidopyrine is in hundred pound drums, not fifties. Coumarin is in 25 pound tins and not hundreds. Thymol Iodide is in hundred pound barrels, not 75's. Salol is in hundred pound kegs, not in two hundred. Santonine crystals are in 25 one kilo cans, not in 17 pound cases. A kilo is 2.2 pounds. * * * oil of peppermint natural, * * * would be in drums, although it is ditto marked cases [on the exhibit]. Mexican Vanilla beans are not packed in two hundred pound bags; they must be packed in tins, usually four to a case. Bismuth subnitrate is packed in hundred pounds [not fifty]. That is all.

* * * * * * *

Q. Mr. Herman, why would Mexican vanilla beans be packed in tins rather than bags?

A. Due to the nature of the item. They are very perishable; loss of weight. The cost of the item itself.[359]

* * * * * * *

Q. * * * could any one purchase this crude iodine for re-shipment into another country other than Chile, and make a profit and meet the competition of the syndicate itself?

A. In my experience with the house, we have never been able to do it.

* * * * * * *

The EXAMINER. * * * if you were selling iodine to England, for example, would you be competing with the group, or the cartel?

The WITNESS. Yes, sir.

By Mr. GALPEER:

Q. Does that cartel condition exist in the case of any of the other products you have read off? Not the same cartel, but other cartels.

A. Quinine.

Q. How about gum camphor slabs from Japan?

A. There is none on that.

Q. Could anybody buy camphor in Japan?

A. Yes, sir.

Q. How is the world distribution of that carried out, by the Japanese interests?

A. By the Japanese interests.

Q. So would it be possible for any one to buy camphor themselves in Japan and compete with, or undersell, the Japanese interests in world distribution?

A. Not in my experience.

* * * * * * *

Q. Now, are there any other products on this exhibit which are subject to price regulation, either through cartel or some similar arrangement other than those you have already mentioned in this connection?

A. Well, Santonine is quite well controlled by the Russians. The others—most of the others look like domestic—some of these are domestic manufactured chemicals here.[360]

* * * * * * *

[358] R. 2597, 2600. See also figures reported in "Trade of Canada" Ex. 191 discussed in pages 270–271 *infra.*

[359] R. 2598–2599.

[360] R. 2607–2609.

Q. [By Mr. STEWART.] How long would you say that it took you to acquire the detailed knowledge of the various products about which you have been testifying this morning, as to their sources and the markets and the extent to which they were traded and the extent of control over their prices and so on?

A. I don't know how long it took. I know I came there in 1902. What year I acquired to know it, I couldn't tell you. I have been handling them for 36 years.

Q. And your testimony this morning is based upon 36 years of training and experience in that field?

A. Yes sir." [361]

Finally, on this subject it was noted that although since 1934 the goods were supposed to have been stored in Canada at the suppliers, there were attached to copies of the Canadian Company's Connecticut State income tax return for the period ended Dec. 31, 1935 (taken from the files of the tax department of McKesson) confirmations from the five Canadian vendors (apparently additional to the regular semi-annual), stating that as at Dec. 31, 1935 the goods were all being held in the State of New Jersey.[362]

d. MONTHLY REPORTS TO MANAGEMENT

Each month the comptroller's office would issue financial statements addressed "To Messrs. F. Donald Coster, C. F. Michaels, W. J. Murray, Jr., J. F. Thompson, Divisional Vice Presidents and Assistants to Divisional Vice Presidents." [363] The report also went to directors not included in the above.[364]

The Connecticut Division statement of profit and loss was broken down into the following classifications: General Sales, Cosmetics, McKesson Products, Spanish American, Angostura Bitters, and Spice. The foreign crude drug business was not separately set forth but was combined with Hermann's domestic business in General Sales.[365]

---

[361] R. 2614–2615.

[362] R. 518, 599, 939, 946, 4472–4475; Ex. 234. Ritts testified that Price, Waterhouse & Co. did not see such confirmations or have any knowledge of them prior to their introduction ot the hearings. R. 4473–4475.

[363] Ex. 185.

[364] R. 2223, 2272–2273, 2394, 2437.

[365] Ex. 185 (esp. Connecticut Division); R. 2440, 2491, 2553, 4265. For the Canadian Company only the figures for net sales and estimated net profits were given. Ex. 185 (Form 1002, p. 3). Although the reports like Ex. 185 came out over the name of J. H. McGloon, his discretion in matters of this kind may perhaps be illustrated by the following sentence from a memorandum dated June 7, 1938, addressed to "Dear Mr. McGloon," from F. D. Coster: "Remind me at the first opportunity to rearrange the names of the different accounts containing subscriptions and dues, to obtain a more accurate and intelligent distribution." Ex. 110. See also R. 1706–1707:

"Q. [By Mr. GALPEER.] Mr. McGloon, how would you describe briefly the influence, direction, policy making which Mr. Coster exerted over the general accounting and bookkeeping of McKesson & Robbins. Would you say that he took an interest in the detail and directed the detail at many points?

A. Yes, I would.

By Mr. STEWART:

Q. Did you regard that as creditable zeal on the part of the chief executive of the company prior to a few weeks ago?

A. No.

Q. How did you regard it, as a suspicious circumstance?

A. No, I didn't.

Q. Just the sort of thing you would expect.

A. No, I don't think it was the sort of thing that I would expect but Mr. Coster had his fingers on the pulse of the business; he knew what was going on in every department of the business.

Q. And you thought that that was just another phase of that?

A. Yes."

In any event the directors could not tell from these reports and did not have any idea of the amount of foreign crude drug business supposedly carried on through Smith and Manning.[366] And even the auditors could not tell at the hearings exactly how much of the sales and gross profits were attributable to the foreign crude drug business.[367]

7. The Manner in Which the Foreign Crude Drug Transactions Were Handled Prior to 1935

Prior to 1935 [368] the foreign crude drug inventories were supposedly kept at Bridgeport.[369] Robert Dietrich supervised the taking of the crude drug inventories.[370] Comparing the method of preparing the regular and foreign crude drug inventory count sheets at this time, John White, who for 11 years worked under Robert Dietrich,[371] testified:

"Q. [By Mr. GALPEER.] Now, Mr. White, I call your attention to Commission's exhibit No. 57 [inventory count sheets for 1934], and ask you to what goods the sheets composing this exhibit pertain? In other words, do they pertain to the regular crude or the foreign resale crude?

A. The regular crude, the sheets here.

Q. Do you know whether the merchandise covered by these sheets, part of exhibit No. 57, was actually counted?

A. Yes, sir.

Q. Was it counted under your supervision?

A. Yes, sir.

Q. Now, will you explain the system or significance of the various initials and names that appear on those count sheets?

* * * * * * *

A. Well, we were given four sheets of a set, four copies of a set, three of which were used by each of three men or one each by three men, or in cases where stock demanded the services of an adding machine, we had two men working to a sheet. The fourth copy was kept by myself or whoever might happen to be in charge of a crew of three, four or six, or whatever the number of men were as the case may be, as a control copy. Each man took a copy of the set, not the same set, a different set, so that no two men would be in the same part of the building counting the same stock at the same time, and when they had completed their count, they returned it to the man in charge of the crew who assembled them, and when the three counts agreed, it was attached to the control copy, which was his own copy, showing the names of the counters, and he either took them into the office or sent them into the office as they were completed.

Q. And by 'office,' you mean Mr. Robert Dietrich's office?

A. Yes.

---

366 R. 2157–2158, 2223, 2274, 2317, 2423, 2440, 2491–2492, 2495–2496, 2518, 4265–4266.

367 Ex. 43; R. 527–528, 889, 1082. But cf. Ex. 120, 124, 267, N, Q.

368 While not as much is known of the manner in which the transactions were handled prior to the 1937 audit as at that time, certain important differentiations have been developed and will be pointed out in this and succeeding subsections. It is not to be assumed, however, that where no differentiation is noted the practice was necessarily the same as at the 1937 audit.

369 R. 420, 603, 1681. While all of the inventories in question were supposedly at Bridgeport on December 31, 1934 (R. 420) and 1933 (R. 1223), prior to that time some of the foreign crude drugs were purportedly stored in outside warehouses. Ex. 76, 83, 104.

370 R. 658, 1467.

371 R. 1471–1472.

Q. And then the pencil writing appearing on those count sheets, comprising part of exhibit 57, were put on by the men as they were counting the goods?

A. Yes, those pencil notations are [those of] the man that actually counted that merchandise.

Q. The signatures of the man appearing on each of the sheets were the men who actually counted the goods?

A. That is right.

Q. And the names of the men appearing on the fourth sheet were put in by the man who was in charge of that crew?

A. That is right, two, four, six, as the case may be.

Q. Now, I call your attention to Commission's exhibit No. 58 [inventory count sheets for 1934] and ask you whether the merchandise there set forth pertains to the foreign resale crude, or the general crude?

A. Well, it belongs to what we understood to be the export crude, or which would be foreign crude.

Q. Will you tell me, as far as you know, the manner in which those sheets were filled out?

A. These sheets were handed to me together with the record [inventory] cards——

* * * * * * *

And [I was] asked or directed to transfer the balances shown on those cards to these sheets and originally, probably the first time that he [Robert Dietrich] asked me to do this particular job, he explained about showing the number of containers by dividing the size of any individual container into the net weight shown on the card balances.

Q. In other words, this count sheet which was handed to you already had typed on it the item and the size——

A. That is right.

Q. And you copied, in pencil, the quantity from the inventory cards?

A. That is right.

Q. And then divided the size as shown into the quantity to fill in the other column entitled 'Number of barrels, drums, etc.'

A. That is right.

Q. The handwriting appearing on this first count sheet is your handwriting?

A. Yes, sir.

Q. The handwriting appearing on the second and third count sheets, which are carbon copies of this same merchandise appearing on the first one, is that your handwriting also?

A. No, sir.

Q. Do you know whose handwriting that is?

A. I don't.

Q. But the handwriting appearing on the original copy of page 2, is that your handwriting?

A. It is.

Q. And the handwriting appearing on the carbon copies on page 2, is that your handwriting?

A. No.

Q. Do you know whose handwriting it is?

A. No.

Q. Do you know whether the typing, 'Building No. 2, first floor,' appearing on the top of the page underneath crude drug inventory, and above item size, number of barrels, drums, et cetera, quantity, was on this sheet at the time you filled it in in pencil?

A. I don't recall having seen it there.

Mr. GALPEER. I would like to have the record show that from looking at the carbon copy, where 'Building No. 2, first floor' appears in original typing, although the rest of the typing on the page appears to be carbon copy, I would like to have the record show that fact in connection with Mr. White's testimony as to whether or not that appeared on these sheets at the time he filled it in in pencil?

The EXAMINER. Do I understand that Mr. White simply copied these from cards, that there was no actual count of this merchandise?

The WITNESS. That is right.

The EXAMINER. There was no such merchandise in building 2 on the first floor as of December 31, 1934?

The WITNESS. No, sir.[372]

* * * * * * *

Q. [By Mr. STEWART.] And would you say these sheets, like Exhibit 58, were made up in the same way every year from 1931 or 1932, when you started making them up?

A. I cannot say just when these sheets started, this particular set-up, I can't place for sure; it was probably around 1931 or 1932, though.

Q. Well, whenever it was the first time that you made them up, you made them up in exactly the same way in which you described as the way in which Exhibit 58 was made up?

A. Oh, yes, it has been the same operation from the time he first asked me to do this all along.

Q. It was always a case of copying quantities off the cards rather than a case of physical counting?

A. That is right." [373]

In accordance with this testimony it may be noted that the count sheets, Exhibit 58, covering the foreign crude drugs were not initialed and were more regular in writing than those of Exhibit 57 covering the regular goods which were actually taken around in the count.[374] Commenting further on the impossibility of the foreign crude inventory having been stored where indicated, John White testified:

"Q. [By Mr. GALPEER.] Let me ask you, Mr. White, in view of your familiarity with the plant at Bridgeport, with building No. 2 on the first floor and with your familiarity in handling such crude drugs that would come into Bridgeport, whether building No. 2 could have contained the quantities of merchandise as set forth on those count sheets?

A. No, sir, it would be impossible.[375]

* * * * * * *

Q. [By Mr. STEWART.] Let us see if we can start at the beginning now. Are you able to say, under oath right now, that the merchandise listed on these two sheets, Exhibit 58, was not in the warehouse at Bridgeport at the time these sheets were prepared?

A. Right, I did say they were not there.

Q. How do you know that?

A. Well, on this particular stock it had always been outlined to us that there was an outside warehouse and there had never been any stock in Bridgeport. It was always direct shipping, and therefore we would not have stock.

---

[372] R. 1475–1480.

[373] R. 1500–1501. White also filled out count sheets for the Canadian Company. R. 1532–1536.

[374] R. 1494. Similarly the count sheets of the Canadian Company. Ex. 60.

[375] R. 1480–1481.

Q. Are you sure that was always so, or only in the last three years?

A. Well, as far as I was concerned, it was always right from the beginning, from the first time he told me about this particular stock, that it was direct shipments from the warehouses. I always believed it to be the same.

Q. And the man who outlined that to you was Robert Dietrich?

A. Yes.[376]

* * * * * * *

Q. Now, let us come back to the question we were on a moment ago. If you did not know this merchandise when you saw it, how did you know it was not in that warehouse in 1934 and in prior years?

A. If I didn't know the merchandise when I saw it?

Q. Yes.

A. You refer to what, please?

Q. Exhibit 58, the thing from which I read you several items a few moments ago which you said you would not know if you saw them.

A. Well, looking over this stock here, looking over this list here, there are certain items on here that I do know what they are and it would be impossible to get these other items in the space that we had in the particular building up there.

* * * * * * *

Q. All right. Which item are you talking about in your last answer?

A. Well, here, for instance, gum camphor slabs, 2,000 cases, with the space that we have in that particular building it would be almost an impossibility to get that one item in it.[377]

* * * * * * *

Q. [By Mr. GALPEER.] And from that indication showing that all the space was taken up by certain commodities [you knew were there], you were sure that there was no space left for the resale crude commodities as set forth on Commission's Exhibit 58?

A. That is right." [378]

Either the foreign crude drug count sheets as prepared by White or the new inventory cards made up from the count sheets, furnished the basis for the entries on the inventory book sheets.[379] Spaces on the book sheets [380] were provided for initialing to indicate who the inventory was "Counted by" (physically), "Recounted by" (physically), "Entered by" (on perpetual inventory cards), "Count checked by" (for accuracy of entering), "Priced by" (on basis of cost), "Extended by" (comptometer operator who checked clerical accuracy) and "Verified by" (second check of clerical accuracy).[381]

On none of the 1934 inventory book sheets for "Book No. 7" which included foreign crude drugs, do any initials appear over "Counted by" or "Recounted by." [382] On the 1931 inventory book sheets the initials of John White and Howard Cone appear over "Counted by" and "Recounted by," respectively.[383] Concerning the manner in

376 R. 1522–1523.

377 R. 1526–1527.

378 R. 1545.

379 R. 1515–1516.

380 Ex. 59, E.

381 R. 1678–1681.

382 Ex. 59.

383 Ex. E; R. 1678–1679.

which these initials were customarily inserted before the inventory books were sent to the accounting department, White testified:

"* * * I will tell you just how I used to initial these and in that way it is quite possible that there was something on there that we wouldn't see. When the inventory was completed, Robert Dietrich would call me and get somebody else.

" 'Here, I have got to rush these out to the main office as soon as I can. Initial these sheets,' he would say, and he would give us all these sheets. We used to take them down and line them up on the desk with just enough room for some one to initial them, to the next man who was initialing them. It saved time and we did it that way for that purpose." [384]

With such procedures, it is understandable that there never were any quantity adjustments between the purported physical inventory on foreign crude drugs and the book figures.[385]

Despite the fact that the goods were supposed to have been in Bridgeport at this time,[386] the Connecticut State income tax return filed by the Maryland Company for the calendar year 1934 on its face showed only $689,697.68 average monthly fair cash value of real estate and tangible personal property within Connecticut as against $10,302,-539.09 in "various locations throughout the United States and in foreign countries." [387] Attached to the copy of this return (in the files of McKesson's tax department) was a schedule signed by Robert J. Dietrich which stated "* * * we are holding in our New Jersey Warehouse the following merchandise as of December 31, 1934," following which was itemized the foreign crude drug inventory of the Connecticut Division in the amount of $6,389,125.00.[388]

Finally, in view of White's testimony as to the mechanical way in which he initialed receiving tickets [389] and inventory book sheets [390] and in which he prepared the inventory count sheets on foreign crude drugs,[391] and in view of the fact that Robert Dietrich's employees, to whom he was known as "the terror" [392] apparently did anything he asked them to,[393] there would not seem to have been any difficulty in securing initials for the receiving tickets which were issued prior to 1935 covering purported receipt of foreign crude drugs at Bridge-

---

384 R. 1512.

385 R. 650–652, 726–727, 1369, 1418–1421. Apparently after 1934 there were not even adjustments for market price.

"Q. [By Mr. GALPEER.] You mean, after 1934 whenever items cost more than what the market price appeared, that those items would be closed out before the end of the year?

A. [By JOHNSON.] That is what it appeared to be." R. 1370.

386 R. 939.

387 Ex. 235.

388 Ex. 235; R. 4473.

389 R. 1561 ff.

390 R. 1512 ff.

391 R. 1477 ff.

392 R. 1490.

393 R. 1541.

port [394] especially since, as evidenced by White's testimony, Robert Dietrich had told him in 1928 or 1929 that this kind of merchandise did not have to be handled "it was all direct shipping-export" [395] and since to White the significance of his initials on these transactions did not mean "* * * anything at all outside of the fact that it has always been driven into us that all transactions had to conform to the same procedure irrespective of whether it was direct shipping or not." [396]

8. The Manner in Which the Foreign Crude Drug Transactions Were Handled Prior to 1931

Miss Bakos, since 1929 cashier of the Connecticut Company (later Division), gave the following comparison of the manner of handling remittances on regular accounts with the manner of handling remittances on foreign crude drug accounts during the period prior to the adoption of Manning & Company as a purported bank [397] (to whom subsequently remittances on account of foreign crude drug sales were supposedly made):

"Q. [By Mr. GALPEER.] Now, did you ever make up cash tickets from any other source of information than the actual checks or credit advices from banks?

A. Yes, I did. I would get a copy of a number of credit advices from Mr. Dietrich and he would advise me which bank they were to be picked up in, and I would do as advised.

Q. What was the form of Mr. Dietrich's advice to you?

A. As I can remember, at that time there would be just a pencil notation listing the accounts to be credited * * * [and] the bank, in which they were credited.

Q. In those cases you saw no checks?

A. No.

Q. Nor did you see any credit advice?

A. No actual credit advices.

Q. Now, in other cases you stated that you would either actually see the check or see the credit advice itself?

A. Yes, from the bank.

Q. From the bank, but in these cases, where Mr. George Dietrich gave you this list, he would just tell you to make up the cash tickets and credit the accounts, and tell you against which bank the debit was to be made?

A. Yes, that is right.

* * * * * * *

Q. Now, Miss Bakos, from what notations on this exhibit No. 195 or from what other information can you tell that these particular cash tickets were prepared from lists submitted to you by Mr. George Dietrich as distinguished from actual bank checks or credit advices [received] directly from the bank?

* * * * * * *

A. Well, I really cannot say other than those large amounts always stayed in my memory as having come from him. They did not represent actual cash

[394] Ex. F; R. 4417.

[395] R. 1500.

[396] R. 1561.

[397] See footnote 368 *supra*.

[that I saw as cash] [398] and I would mark it in this manner to distinguish it from other larger checks had I had one at that date.

* * * * * * *

Q. In other words, you mean that this group of accounts which subsequently—which, in 1931 were handled through Manning & Company prior to that date, were distinguishable in your mind——

A. Yes.

Q. And in your records as having been handled in this manner from Mr. George Dietrich?

A. That is right.

Q. And this was a regular flow or manner in which those accounts were handled?

A. Yes, sir.

Q. Not merely on the dates on which these particular cash slips were made out but currently through the year at that time?

A. At that time, that is the way I distinguished them from the actual cash checks that we received.

* * * * * * *

Q. Now, I show you a photostatic copy of a bank deposit slip dated December 30, 1930, in the amount of $18,077.23. Would that bank deposit slip be prepared by you or under your direction?

A. This particular one was prepared under my direction.

Q. All right. And how was that bank deposit slip prepared? From what records?

A. They were prepared from the actual checks received that day.

* * * * * * *

Q. And you would send these checks, together with the bank deposit slip to the bank?

A. That is right.

* * * * * * *

Q. Now, you will notice that the net cash deposited on that day, December 30, in the Bridgeport Trust Company * * * was $52,301.23. Now, the deposit slip I have shown you only accounts for $18,077.23. How do you account for the difference?

A. Well, the difference would represent the items given me by Mr. Dietrich to be credited in the Bridgeport Trust Company.

Q. I see. And on that difference you did not handle the checks. As a matter of fact, did you have any knowledge as to how the credit was made in the Bridgeport Trust Company?

A. No.

Q. Exactly what did you know in reference to that part of the deposit?

A. I inferred—I would have been told by Mr. Dietrich that the credit was in the Trust Company, and that we were to pick those up and record it in the day's work.

Q. Now, I show you another deposit slip on the same bank, the Bridgeport Trust Company, dated the same day, December 30, 1930, [for $34,224.00—making up the difference] and ask you in whose handwriting the written part of that deposit appears?

A. That is Mr. Dietrich's handwriting.

[A statement was then made for the record by Mr. Galpeer that the photo-

---

[398] R. 2672.

static copies of the deposit slips shown the witness were obtained directly from The Bridgeport–City Trust Company.]

* * * * * * *

The EXAMINER. I believe the witness stated that it was not the custom of the company to keep the deposit slips.

Mr. GALPEER. That is correct.

The EXAMINER. Does that apply to all times, or just during this period?

Mr. GALPEER. Let us ask the witness.

The WITNESS. That applied at all times.

* * * * * * *

Q. [By Mr. GALPEER]. Now, this system of receiving the list from Mr. Dietrich was the system in vogue prior to the establishment of the Manning account [sometime in June 1931]?

A. That's right.

Q. Now, how far back did that go, to your knowledge? Was that system used as long as you were cashier?

A. As far back as I can remember, I would say, yes.

Q. So that you do not know—in fact, you never did know what funds were used to pay these accounts?

A. No, I never knew.

Q. Now, can you tell from examining Commission's exhibit 193, which is the cash record for December 30 [1930], Commission's exhibit 195, which contains two cash tickets for December 30 and Commission's exhibit 197, which is the deposit slip in the handwriting of Mr. George Dietrich for December 30, how many accounts receivable this one item of deposit, appearing on exhibit 197, being in the amount of $34,224.00 represents?

A. I would say it represented two cash tickets, totaling that figure [indicating].

Q. In other words, this one item of deposit represented two accounts receivable?

A. That's right.

Q. And looking at exhibit 195, which two accounts receivable do you refer to?

A. I refer to R. Darne and Company, $17,732; and Cowe and Company, Limited for $16,492." [399]

Miss Bakos also identified a deposit slip of the Canadian Company for December 30, 1930 in which a single item of deposit in the sum of $33,279.75 covered two accounts receivable.[400] The deposit slip was also in the handwriting of George Dietrich.[401] At this time, all of the daily transactions in the books of the Canadian Company were entered by George Dietrich.[402]

Prior to the adoption of Manning & Company as a sort of fiscal agent which purportedly made payment for and effected collections on the foreign crude drug transactions, the Connecticut and Canadian Companies actually issued their checks in payment of fictitious purchases.[403] The checks could be signed by either Coster or George Dietrich without counter-signature.[404] As previously stated, most

399 R. 2647–2656.

400 Ex. 201; R. 2664, 2671.

401 R. 2663.

402 R. 2666–2668, 4408, 4414–4415, 4420.

403 R. 4560. For a while after the adoption of Manning & Company as a purported bank both systems were used in establishing payment for fictitious purchases and sales of foreign crude drugs, i. e., Manning debit-credit advices and actual cash outgo and income. R. 4562 and page 47 *supra*.

404 Ex. 17.

of the money paid out on such purchases actually came back to McKesson purportedly in payment for the fictitious sales.[405]

An illustration of the manner in which this was done, based upon the deposit slips previously identified by Miss Bakos, was supplied by the testimony of Arthur Seal, accountant in charge for S. D. Leidesdorf & Co., who conducted the fraud investigation for the Trustee.

Seal testified that on December 24 and 26, 1930, the Canadian Company drew two checks to the order of George Vernard for $64,300.50 each, on account of fictitious purchases of crude drugs. These checks were deposited in George Vernard's bank account with the Chase National Bank on December 26 and 27. On the same days the same amounts of money were drawn out from that account and deposited in the account of Woodtone Company, Inc., also at the Chase National Bank.

Then the Woodtone Company, Inc. drew one check on its account with the Chase National Bank to the order of the Canadian Company for $33,279.25. This was recorded on the Canadian Company's books in payment of the accounts of A. P. Miller & Company, whose address was given as 420 Liverpool Street, Tasmania, Australia, in the sum of $19,380.00, and James Dixon, Limited, 94 Oxford Street, Sydney, Australia, in the sum of $13,899.75. The check of the Woodtone Company, Inc. was deposited by the Canadian Company on December 30 (see Ex. 201 deposit slip in George Dietrich's handwriting identified by Miss Bakos) and was debited against Woodtone's Chase National Bank account on December 31.

At the same time as the Woodtone Company, Inc. drew the check for $33,279.25 to the order of the Canadian Company, it also drew a check to the order of the Connecticut Company for $34,224.00 which was recorded on the Connecticut Company's books in payment of the accounts of R. Darne & Co., whose address was given as Mauritius, Togoland, Africa, in the sum of $17,732.00, and F. Cowe & Co., Limited, whose address was also given as Mauritius, Togoland, Africa, in the sum of $16,492.00 covering purported shipments on August 7 and 8, 1930 of that amount of virgin mercury. The check of the Woodtone Company, Inc. was deposited by the Connecticut Company on December 30 (see Ex. 197 deposit slip in George Dietrich's handwriting identified by Miss Bakos) and was debited against Woodtone's Chase National Bank account on December 31.[406]

This transaction was an example. With one exception hereinafter noted, all of the actual cash received on account of foreign crude drug receivables came in a similar "ring-a-round" from payments made on

[405] See pages 46 ff. *supra*.

[406] Ex. 197, 201, 256; R. 4562–4565.

fictitious purchases.[407] The exception concerns a deposit of $397,410 on April 27, 1928 which came from sources other than those which directly received McKesson funds on account of fictitious purchases.[408] Three days later, April 30, 1928, was the date as of which the Connecticut Company was audited and on the basis of which it and the Group One wholesale houses were acquired by the Maryland Company.[409]

D. THE MANNER IN WHICH THE OUTSIDE DOCUMENTS ON THE FICTITIOUS TRANSACTIONS WERE PREPARED

As previously stated, Smith, Manning, and the five Canadian vendors would now appear to have been either entirely fictitious or to the extent that they had any reality, were mere blinds used by Coster for his fictitious transactions, and the documents purportedly emanating from these concerns were prepared under the direction of George Vernard, Coster's brother. Rose Otting, employed by George Vernard since August 1931, first at 189 Montague Street, then 185 Montague Street, Brooklyn, N. Y., and since April 1937 at Room 711, 300 Main Street, Stamford, Conn., testified at the hearings as to the manner in which she prepared the documents on George Vernard's instructions.[410]

Once a month she received a batch of McKesson & Robbins purchase orders [411] from which she typed corresponding purchase invoices on the billheads of the respective Canadian vendors [412] and Manning & Company advices of debit [413] covering each transaction. Once a month she also received a batch of McKesson & Robbins factory orders [414] from which she typed corresponding Smith purchase orders,[415] Smith notices of shipments,[416] and letters from McKesson to the customers [417] covering each transaction. The latter letters were in three different styles, all substantially the same, and were always typed on blank sheets of paper, originals without any carbon copies.

---

407 Pages 46-48 *supra*. After the adoption of W. W. Smith & Company, Inc. as a purported sales agency and the adoption of Manning & Company as a purported bank in 1931, the actual cash outgo and income circle described above was not eliminated immediately but was superseded gradually by the system of Manning debit and credit advices. In addition to the payments which were continued to be made on fictitious purchases, there was then added to the actual cash outgo in connection with these operations, the payments made for guaranty and service charges under the Smith contracts. The money transferred by Manning & Company into McKesson New York and Bridgeport bank accounts (footnote 200 *supra*) had its source in and became part of this remaining actual cash outgo and income circle. R. 4581-4583 and pages 47-48 *supra*.

408 R. 4574-4576.

409 Ex. 1; R. 2175. Accounts receivable as of this date showed a decrease from the previous year end of $349,823.62. Ex. 147.

410 R. 4484-4514.

411 Similar to Ex. 12-B.

412 Similar to Ex. 12-A.

413 Similar to Ex. 33.

414 Similar to Ex. 8-A, 11-A.

415 Similar to Ex. 8-B, 11-C.

416 Similar to Ex. 8-C, 11-B.

417 Similar to Ex. 232, 233.

From copies of McKesson & Robbins sales invoices,[418] which she also received, Miss Otting typed Manning & Company advices of credit [419] corresponding with each sales invoice.

In dating the documents she prepared from the McKesson & Robbins purchase orders, Miss Otting would follow the notations on an attached slip of paper; on the documents prepared from the McKesson & Robbins factory orders she would follow a fixed schedule based upon the date of the factory order.

As Miss Otting typed the Manning & Company advices of debit and advices of credit she would list them in a black book and from the list she would prepare each month a Manning & Company statement of account.[420] Also each month she would type two Smith statements,[421] one for $750 and the other for a percentage of the sales as added from the factory orders received that month.

Twice a year, Miss Otting typed inventory confirmations [422] on the letterheads of the five Canadian vendors and she also typed the quotations [423] which purportedly emanated from those concerns.

All of the documents described above she typed in two groups, one for the Connecticut Company (later Division) and one for the Canadian Company.

Miss Otting had in her office five portable typewriters of different makes and two standard typewriters, one large carriage and one small. She testified that she consistently used specific machines for each of the five Canadian vendors, Smith, and Manning.

Miss Otting also testified that for a few months in 1935, she used to stamp the bill of lading forms with the Smith "RECEIVED" stamp [424] but that subsequently the stamp was taken up to Bridgeport. In the earlier years she had also worked on J. P. Meyer and Woodtone documents.

As to the manner of receiving and transmitting the documents she stated:

> "Well, when I first started to work for Mr. Vernard, I received them by mail. They came by mail from McKesson & Robbins, and then, when I finished the typing, I would send them back to McKesson & Robbins in care of Mr. George Dietrich.
>
> "Then, when I went up to Stamford, Mr. Robert Dietrich would bring them in, or else I would find it in the file. Who brought it in I wouldn't know then.
>
> "Then, when I had finished it, Mr. Robert Dietrich would call for it, or else, during the night, somebody else would call for it." [425]

---

[418] Similar to Ex. 8-D, 11-D.
[419] Similar to Ex. 34.
[420] Similar to Ex. 30.
[421] Similar to Ex. 222, 224, 225.
[422] Similar to Ex. 53, 54.
[423] Similar to Ex. 238.
[424] Similar to stamp on Ex. 9.
[425] R. 4496.

E. CONTROL EXERCISED BY DIRECTORS OVER THE FOREIGN CRUDE DRUG BUSINESS

At the time the fraud was made public the Board of Directors of the Maryland Company was composed of the following:

J. L. Bedsole (1928),[426] divisional vice-president, formerly Bedsole-Colvin Drug Company, Inc. acquired by McKesson in 1928.

F. Donald Coster (1928), president.

W. L. Cummings (1936), Sullivan & Cromwell, counsel for McKesson.

George V. Doerr (1928), divisional vice-president, formerly Minneapolis Drug Company acquired by McKesson in 1928.

T. O. Duff (1935), vice-president, formerly Duff Drug Company acquired by McKesson in 1929.

Henry D. Faxon (1928), secretary and divisional vice-president, formerly Faxon & Gallagher Drug Company acquired by McKesson in 1928.

B. B. Gilmer (1928), divisional vice-president, formerly Southern Drug Company acquired by McKesson in 1928.

L. A. Lanigan (1938), vice-president, formerly Fuller-Morrison Company acquired by McKesson in 1928.

Horace B. Merwin (1928), The Bridgeport-City Trust Company.

Charles F. Michaels (1928), executive vice-president, formerly Langley and Michaels Company acquired by McKesson in 1928.

William J. Murray, Jr. (1928), first vice-president, formerly The Murray Drug Company acquired by McKesson in 1928.

R. G. Pettingill (1937), Sullivan & Cromwell, counsel for McKesson.

Rowley W. Phillips (1928), The R. F. Griggs Company, Waterbury, Connecticut.

C. Barnum Seeley (1928), formerly The Bridgeport-City Trust Company.

Julian F. Thompson (1928), treasurer,[427] formerly Bond & Goodwin, Inc.

A. H. Van Gorder (1928), vice-president, formerly The Hall-Van Gorder Company acquired by McKesson in 1928.

McKay Van Vleet (1931), vice-president, formerly Van Vleet-Ellis Corporation acquired by McKesson in 1930.

Sidney J. Weinberg (1934), Goldman, Sachs & Co.

In the Canadian Company, the Board of Directors remained the same since its inception until the public disclosure of the fraud. It consisted of:

F. Donald Coster, president and treasurer.

George E. Dietrich, secretary and assistant treasurer.

Jonathan Grout, Boardman, Grout, Swain & McCarthy, attorneys.

Horace B. Merwin,
Rowley W. Phillips, } See Maryland Company above.
C. Barnum Seeley,

The Board of Directors, president and treasurer, and secretary and assistant treasurer of the Connecticut Company from its inception until it ceased being an active operating subsidiary and its business was taken over directly by the Maryland Company in October 1934 were exactly the same as that of the Canadian Company listed above,

[426] Indicates year became Director.

[427] Prior to February 1930, Horace B. Merwin acted as treasurer.

except that Herbert D. Robbins and Saunders Norvell, who owned the old McKesson & Robbins, Incorporated (New York), were on the board of the Connecticut Company until the latter part of 1932 and the middle of 1928, respectively, and that Jonathan Grout did not come on the board of the Connecticut Company until Herbert D. Robbins left it.

The directors of the Maryland, Connecticut, and Canadian Companies, who testified in the present proceedings, knew little about the operations of the foreign crude drug business, except that it was under the direct supervision of Coster and that crude drug trading, as a whole, appeared to be showing consistent profits. As previously pointed out, however, the directors had no idea of the proportion attributable to Hermann's business at Cliff Street, as distinguished from the foreign business purportedly done through Smith.[428]

Charles F. Michaels, director of the Maryland Company, executive vice-president in charge of all wholesale operations, both drugs (other than crude drugs) and liquors, and a member of both the Management and Executive Committees, testified:

"Q. [By Mr. GALPEER.] * * * what was your understanding as to the nature of the business, the type of customers sold, how it was handled, who directed the business?

A. The business was supposed to come in from McKesson & Robbins of Connecticut, which was the prior organization, and Mr. Coster explained that the business was an export and import one and had to be handled differently from any other business, and subsequently a few years ago he claimed that it was being transferred to Canada largely for ease of operation, but like any new account, it was not my particular job, and when it showed profits I didn't ask him any questions about it.

Q. Did he elaborate at all, or did you ask any questions concerning the type of ease he had in mind in transferring it to Canada?

A. No, he only said it was, in doing this type of export service, it was more convenient to do it through Canada.

Q. What was your understanding, or knowledge, concerning McKesson & Robbins, Ltd.?

A. That company was part of the Connecticut Company before we came into it and I have always been told it was conducting a certain amount of business in Canada for ease in operation.

Q. Well, now, what was the difference, or your understanding of the difference between the Limited Company and the crude drug operations?

A. Well, not knowing the details of the operations of either, it would be pretty hard to answer that question.[429]

* * * * * * *

Q. * * * How would you compare the nature of the business done by the limited company with the nature of the export-import general crude business that was done by the Connecticut Division directly?

A. The information I had was very much the same type of business. I want to add to that and say that I never knew where the distinction came in between the two.

---

[428] Footnote 366 *supra*.

[429] R. 4263-4264.

Q. Well, now, what determined the differentiation as to who did which if it was so similar?

A. I couldn't answer that. I haven't the slightest idea.[430]

* * * * * * *

Mr. REAVIS. And you wouldn't pretend to have any special knowledge at all about crude drugs, Mr. Michaels?

The WITNESS. No.

By Mr. GALPEER:

Q. In other words, you wouldn't deal in such things that have been mentioned here, for example, as oil of lavender, santonin crystals, or things of that sort?

A. Only minute quantities.

Mr. REAVIS. If at all, did you ever deal in those particular things at all?

The WITNESS. I couldn't say we did not, because I know we always have a few ounces of oil left in the house, small quantities of that kind.[431]

* * * * * * *

Q. [By Mr. GALPEER.] What did you understand was the source of supply on these crude drugs that were subsequently sold on orders received from W. W. Smith and Company?

A. I had no knowledge of that.[432]

* * * * * * *

Mr. GALPEER. Did you ever see a list of the inventory by items, with quantities, of what was supposed to make up this division?

The WITNESS. No, I never did." [433]

William J. Murray, Jr., director of the Maryland Company, first vice-president, assistant to Michaels in charge of wholesale operations,

---

[430] R. 4268–4269.

[431] R. 4277.

[432] R. 4278–4279.

[433] R. 4343. In explanation of this lack of familiarity with the activities of the foreign crude drug business, Michaels, on cross examination by his own counsel, testified:

"Q. [By Mr. REAVIS.] Now, on the question of the responsibility of Directors respecting the accounts of the company, you had quite a lot to do, did you not, in your running of the wholesale houses?

A. Yes, I had a great deal to do.

Q. How many branches has the company today of the wholesale houses?

A. Around 70.

Q. And you also operate a wholesale liquor division, do you not?

A. Yes, partly the same houses and partly independent houses.

Q. Well, bunching them together, how many branches have you?

A. At least 80.

Q. And you are, and have been for some years, generally chief responsible officer for the operation of that string of houses?

A. That's right.

Q. And that's a full time job, I take it?

A. I find it so.

* * * * * * *

Q. And daily you have had charge of and taken care of the many problems that arise in connection with the 80 branches that you now have?

A. Yes.

Q. And it is to that that your particular attention has been spent?

A. Correct.

Q. And it would be impossible, would it not, for any one man to have a detailed contact with or charge of all of the detailed operations of all of the different branches of the company's business?

A. It is a physical impossibility, yes.

Q. And you assumed those matters, of which you didn't have charge, were being taken care of by the people responsible for them?

A. Yes.

Mr. REAVIS. That is all." R. 4329–4331.

and a member of both the Management and Executive Committees, testified:

"Q. [By Mr. GALPEER.] Did you have any knowledge prior to December 6th of the way the foreign crude drug department operated, the one at Bridgeport?

A. Only a very general knowledge.

Q. Tell us what you understood.

A. I understood that there was a bank firm who had offices all over the world and who sold these goods on commission and guaranteed the receivables, that they were really our selling agents and that we carried these inventories in order to be able to supply promptly their sales.

Q. Had you any idea as to where the inventories were physically carried?

A. No, I didn't. I just understood that they were carried in warehouses. I understood that one was in Montreal and that they were in strategic shipping points around the world.

Q. Did you ever understand that the goods were supposed to be physically kept at Bridgeport at certain periods?

A. Early in the organization, in going up to Bridgeport, we passed additional buildings on the railroad. You could see them from the railroad there and they had our name McKesson & Robbins on them, and we were told that those warehouses had crude drugs in them.

Q. Had you ever heard of Manning & Company prior to December 6th?

A. Prior to December 6th I had never heard of it at all.

Q. Had you understood that the name of this international firm who were your selling agents was W. W. Smith?

A. It is rather hard to know now what I knew before then, but I know it now so well, but I will have to say of the crude department, and that whole Bridgeport affair, we were so busy with our wholesale drug business down here and it was under the direction and supervision of the president of the company. It was in there when we came. I knew very little about it and I was so darn busy with other things that I didn't give it a great deal of attention.[434]

* * * * * * *

Q. As a drug man, Mr. Murray, and not specifically of any knowledge gained of the situation in Bridgeport, are you generally familiar with crude drugs?

A. No, sir. I am a wholesale drug man entirely. Crude drugs were—you know that is a very large classification, * * * We had in the wholesale houses, not in the ones I worked in, but we had chemical departments in some of them that sold, what some people designate, as crude drugs. That is, fertilizer material and acids and those sort of things. But in the wholesale houses we sold packaged material practically entirely." [435]

Joseph L. Bedsole, director of the Maryland Company, divisional vice-president in charge of a group of wholesale houses, vice-president in charge of all trade investments, and a member of the Management Committee, testified:

"Q. [By Mr. GALPEER.] And you saw that the profits appeared high?

A. Yes, sir.

Q. But aside from that there was no consideration as to the manner in which the business was done, the type of markets, or anything of that sort?

A. No.[436]

* * * * * * *

[434] R. 2158–2160.

[435] R. 2174.

[436] R. 2480.

Q. Had you, prior to December 6, 1938, any idea as to how the crude drug division operated? That is, whether it sold goods through McKesson employees or through a selling agent?

A. No, I didn't know that.[437]

* * * * * * *

Q. Now, Mr. Coster was quite active in the wholesale divisions. In other words, he concerned himself with your problems with the things that were concerning you?

A. I'd say so.

Q. Did anybody aside from Mr. Coster, himself, concern themselves with the crude drug division? In other words, was that a sort of a sawed-off division there?

A. That was a model.[438]

* * * * * * *

Q. So that you would say that the reason the other directors didn't give consideration to that division was because it seemed to be going along all right?

A. Correct. And the regularity of it, too. I looked at the profits lots of times and they were splendid. In fact, looking back now I am sure that the regularity of the profits was the most satisfying thing we had all along." [439]

Henry D. Faxon, director and secretary of the Maryland Company, divisional vice-president, in charge of a group of wholesale houses, and a member of the Management Committee, testified:

"Q. [By Mr. Galpeer.] Now, Mr. Faxon, in any of the meetings that you attended, either the management committee or the Board of Directors, or as secretary or in any other way, did you consider the crude drug department?

A. That never came to our attention for consideration, no.

Q. Prior to December 5, 1938, what, if anything, did you understand concerning the method or manner in which this deprtment was operated?

A. Well, I understood nothing of it. I took the word it was a very profitable department and was the one successful feature of the company.[440]

* * * * * * *

Q. Have you ever heard of McKesson & Robbins, Ltd.?

A. Yes.

Q. What was your understanding concerning that corporation?

A. I was pretty misty about that." [441]

George V. Doerr, director of the Maryland Company, divisional vice-president, in charge of a group of wholesale houses, and member of the Management Committee, testified:

"Q. [By Mr. Galpeer.] Now, did you at any of these committees, either the management or the executive committee or the Board of Directors itself, did you ever have any occasion to go into the crude drug business?

A. No.

Q. Will you explain that?

A. Well, my first understanding of the crude drug department was at the time I went in the consolidation. I might say I was one of the first ones that went on the dotted line. When I went up to Bridgeport to look over Bridgeport to see what they had put in, I was shown invoices of trading internationally. camphor,

[437] R. 2481.

[438] R. 2488A.

[439] R. 2439.

[440] R. 2524–2525.

[441] R. 2525–2525A

china-wood oil and various other things. And also shown the balance sheet of '27; earning statements. I have always had an understanding that, from the inception, the industrial chemical division was profitable. One of my own friends used to tell me, 'I am quite a good customer of yours, I buy china-wood oil [real domestic] in tank cars.' I said, 'Fine, that's where we are making some of our profits.'

So, I have always considered that that activity was profitable although I have never had anything to do with it; never had any occasion to have anything to do with it.

Q. Had you ever heard of W. W. Smith & Company before December 5th, 1938?

A. No; I hadn't.

Q. The same would be true as to Manning & Company?

A. Yes, sir.[442]

* * * * * * *

Q. Have you ever heard of McKesson & Robbins, Limited?

A. Yes.[443]

* * * * * * *

Q. And your impression, at least, prior to December 5, 1938, was that it was engaged in the sale of drugs of the type that you sell in your wholesale house?

A. That is right—well, no—to tell you the truth I didn't know much about it." [444]

Horace B. Merwin, of The Bridgeport-City Trust Company, who in addition to being a director of the Maryland Company, was also a director of the Canadian Company and of the Connecticut Company until its active business was taken over by the Maryland Company in October 1934, testified:

"Q. [By Mr. Galpeer.] Have you any idea as to this foreign crude drug business as to how much of it was put through the Limited Company and how much of it was retained by the Connecticut company?

A. No; I never did. I could tell by the reports of the Canadian Corporation what presumably went through it, but how—what remained for the other corporation, I do not know; no.[445]

* * * * * * *

* * * He [Coster] ran that department as far as I could see with the help of one or two of his close associates. It seemed to be his baby and his pet which nobody else paid much attention to." [446]

Rowley W. Phillips, then of The R. F. Griggs Company, Waterbury, Connecticut,[446a] a director of the Maryland and Canadian Companies, as well as of the Connecticut Company until its active business was taken over by the Maryland Company in October 1934, testified:

"Q. [By Mr. Galpeer.] * * * what, if anything did you know, prior to December 6, 1938 about this foreign crude drug business?

[442] R. 2551–2552.
[443] R. 2554.
[444] R. 2554.
[445] R. 2274–2275.
[446] R. 2276.
[446a] Until January 1, 1940.

A. I knew there was a crude drug department and I knew that it did a considerable amount of business. I didn't know how much business it did. The reason I knew there was a crude drug department was that I had on two or three occasions been in the crude drug department in Cliff Street and knew some of the men who were running that department. I did not ever have broken down figures of that thing because they were contained in reports of the Connecticut Division.[447]

* * * * * * *

Q. Prior to December 6, 1938, what was your understanding as to how this foreign crude drug business was handled?

A. By Coster and a few men under him such as Stebe and Herman.

Q. Had you heard of W. W. Smith & Company?

A. Not to my recollection and the first time that I remembered that I had heard of it was about a week ago when I saw a minute book of the Canadian Company—the minutes of some meeting in 1931. Those minutes [Ex. 179] took up three or four pages. They were—they contained a great many resolutions such as the appointment of a bank in Yokahama and another one in India and so on and so forth and at the very end there was a notation to the effect that the president had read a memorandum on the subject of the appointment of two agents and that he recommended that they be employed as agents.

Q. Who were the two agents, do you know?

A. And the two were Manning & Company and W. W. Smith, but I state this: That that is the only time I ever heard of them because I now understand there was a McKesson of Connecticut meeting held the same day and it was all passed at that time. [Ex. 180, 204]. Those names meant nothing to me and until last week I had absolutely no knowledge of them and I still do not remember anything about voting for their appointment. However, in voting to appoint them as agents and so forth, I undoubtedly would have done it on the recommendation of the president.

Q. Had you ever heard anything else of Manning & Company aside from the minutes of those meetings you referred to?

A. No; never a thing until I began to read mention of them in the papers.

Q. Did you understand before you read about it in the papers; that is, prior to December 6th, 1938, that Manning and Company was a bank?

A. No, I had no knowledge that they were a bank. I did not know what they were." [448]

Sidney J. Weinberg, of Goldman, Sachs & Co., director of the Maryland Company and a member of the Executive Committee, testified:

"Q. [By Mr. GALPEER.] Prior to December 5th, 1938, did you know how the sales and handling of the crude drugs were made, whether the goods were sold and purchased by McKesson's employees or by outsiders?

A. I did not, sir.

Q. Did you know whether they employed selling agents or made the sales through their own employees?

A. I did not, sir.

Q. Had you ever heard of W. W. Smith?

A. No, the name had never come up. Nor did I hear of it prior to December 5th.

Q. Now, how can you explain the fact, Mr. Weinberg, that in the last annual report filed with this Commission by McKesson & Robbins, that's for the year

---

[447] R. 2316-2317.

[448] R. 2329-2330.

ending December 31, 1937, in answer to item 11, which in effect requires a disclosure of all payments made to persons in excess of $20,000 under any sales or management contracts, I think the language is,—it is under contracts of a certain type, there are three firms listed, Sullivan & Cromwell, Price, Waterhouse & Company, and W. W. Smith. Don't you think, as a director, you would be interested in knowing who was receiving that money?

A. I never saw the report. I never saw the report that mentioned them.

Q. Had you ever heard of Manning & Company?

A. No, sir, I did not.

Q. Well, what did you know about Crude drugs?

A. All I knew is that they were in the import and export business.

Q. Well, does that mean that they didn't do any of it domestically?

A. I didn't know whether they did it domestically or foreign. It had never come up at any time that I was present. The only knowledge I had was that we were importing crude drugs and chemicals of all kinds." [449]

Wilbur L. Cummings, partner of Sullivan & Cromwell, director of the Maryland Company and a member of the Executive Committee, testified:

"Q. [By Mr. Galpeer.] Well, was it your impression that * * * what we have been calling crude drugs—was sold through your various branch houses?

A. No; I supposed they were sold out of Cliff Street and out of Connecticut.

Q. Now, did you know the manner in which they were sold?

A. I did not know the manner in which they were sold.

Q. Had you ever heard of W. W. Smith before?

A. I never heard of W. W. Smith before.

Q. And I presume you had not seen that registration statement, either?

A. I did not. It was supervised in our office, but I did not see it.

Q. Had you ever heard of Manning & Company prior to December 5th?

A. You say prior to December 5th. I heard of both Smith and Manning & Company a week or ten days before December 5th.[450] Until that time, I had never heard their names mentioned." [451]

Richard G. Pettingill, with Sullivan & Cromwell, director of the Maryland Company, testified:

"Q. [By Mr. Galpeer.] Mr. Pettingill, were there any discussions at any of these Board meetings concerning the operations of the foreign crude drug division?

A. Not of that particular division. I am speaking, of course, of only the period that I was on the Board.

Q. Did you know anything about this division during the period that you were a director?

A. I knew that the company had a foreign crude drug department. I knew it was operated in part from Bridgeport and in part from Cliff Street in New York City and I had been in the Cliff Street Office. I can't say, however, that I knew anything concerning the details of the operation of the department.[452]

* * * * * * *

Q. Had you ever heard of W. W. Smith & Company prior to December 5, 1938?

A. Yes, sir.

---

[449] R. 2423–2425. Cf. Ex. 181. Letter from Weinberg to Coster, April 4, 1934, and attached memorandum with respect to the responsibility of directors.

[450] See pages 131 ff. *infra*.

[451] R. 2441–2442.

[452] R. 2222–2223.

Q. Will you tell us when you heard about it, in what connection, and what you understood its connection was with McKesson?

A. The first time I came across the name of the company was in December of 1934; in October of that year McKesson had liquidated practically all of its operating subsidiaries, a task that I had been engaged upon in part and local counsel had been employed by McKesson to complete the transfer of specific assets in all of the states in which former subsidiaries had been located.

Among those states was Connecticut and a law firm of that state had been retained to handle the specific assignments of the Connecticut Company to the Maryland Company; in December of 1934 that counsel wrote to me [Ex. 173] and advised me that they had completed the transfer entrusted to them and that among other things they had assigned a contract made by W. W. Smith & Co. to the Maryland Company which had previously been with the Connecticut Company.[453]

*   *   *   *   *   *   *

Q. When is the next you heard of W. W. Smith as well as you can remember?

A. April 12, 1938. At that time I received a letter from Mr. McGloon [Ex. 171] dealing with the form of the annual 10–K report of McKesson that was required to be filed under the Securities Exchange Act of 1934.

In this letter he refers to a contract with W. W. Smith & Company and asked whether the remuneration paid to W. W. Smith & Company under that contract was required to be reported on the 10–K report.

*   *   *   *   *   *   *

Q. And you advised that the amount paid should be reported under this item that you referred to?

A. I did [Ex. 172].

Q. Is that the last contact you have had with the question of W. W. Smith prior to December 5, 1938?

A. It was." [454]

Julian F. Thompson, director and treasurer of the Maryland Company, testified:

"Q. [By Mr. GALPEER.] When is the first time that Manning & Company came to your attention?

A. I can't tell you. I really don't know. I knew that Manning & Company were involved in the transaction but I can't tell you when I first heard about it.

Q. In what capacity were they involved when you first found out?

A. Of course, I know now, but I don't think I had a clear picture in my own mind as to how they were involved at the time.[455]

*   *   *   *   *   *   *

Q. On the question of insurance, Mr. Thompson, the insurance department, whatever it was, was that nominally under your direction as treasurer?

A. Yes, it was.

*   *   *   *   *   *   *

* * * Mr. Robinson, * * * handles the entire details and I was simply a superior officer to him * * *.

Q. Did you or he ever consider the question of whether the total assets of the corporation were covered by insurance?

A. Not until April of 1938.

---

[453] R. 2223–2224.
[454] R. 2225, 2226.
[455] R. 2068.

Q. And at that time, are you referring to your own check or his, or both?

A. I am referring to our conversation together, which developed the knowledge to me for the first time that the two items didn't balance and that I had not known that he had previously been instructed that he need not insure that particular inventory that was in Canada.

Q. Who had instructed him?

A. Mr. Dietrich, so he tells me. That is hearsay.

Q. And that was the first that you knew about it, was this conversation in April?

A. Yes, and at that time I happened to compare the balance sheet inventory with his total inventory fire schedule.

* * * * * * *

* * * I asked him what the discrepancy was and he, at first, couldn't remember. He was really surprised to see the discrepancy as I showed to him. Then he went back to check up and came back and said I remember I have checked it and I have found out why there is that discrepancy between those two figures. Naturally, he didn't handle balance sheets very much and didn't have it in his routine very much, and he apparently didn't have that type of comparison." [456]

The crude drug operations as such were never discussed at any meeting of the Board of Directors or Executive or Management Committees.[457] However, as a result of growing bank debt, the decision was reached in April 1937 to reduce inventories by $4,000,000 in the subsequent 4 months; $1,000,000 of this was to come out of the Connecticut Division, $2,000,000 out of the liquor inventory, and $1,000,000 out of the wholesale drug inventory.[458] It was following up on this decision that finally made Thompson suspicious. He testified: [459]

"Q. [By Mr. Galpeer.] Now, with those few remarks do you want to pick up the story where you left it in April, '37, at this meeting of the operating committee which resolved to try to reduce inventories $4,000,000 in four months?

A. Yes, we undertook that plan and we had had as one of our control schedules a monthly inventory report and so that I was watching that with interest in connection with this program. As the months passed, I observed that the crude drug department was going up steadily in inventory instead of coming down. There was a reduction made in other departments.

I don't think we quite accomplished the $4,000,000, it was something like two and a half—three million.

I called it to Mr. Coster's attention after the four months were over, or five months, somewhere along there, and he said that he would get it down, that it hadn't been done, but it would come down. I think I must have called it to his attention in November or December with the same comment.

Q. That was in 1937?

A. '37. And it was in our conversation after the year '37 had been completed, which was either January or February when I again showed him that the entire year was—the trend was in the wrong way.

Q. January and February, 1938?

---

[456] R. 2096–2098.

[457] R. 2155, 2222–2223, 2479, 2524, 2551, 4259.

[458] R. 2067, 2156, 2396, 2479, 4259.

[459] See also Ex. 221 (Time Schedule of Julian F. Thompson's Activities in Investigating Foreign Crude Drug Department).

A. 1938, yes. That he told me that he had depended, or rather he said that Herman and Stebe had over-bought and were not selling and were not keeping the thing in control, that he would give them hell and get after them. That, I knew was a lie because I knew they did not have anything to do with that department.[460]

* * * * * * *

* * * I decided after he had—after I was sure that he lied to me that something must be seriously wrong or he wouldn't have lied, and I thought to myself that I better not ask him any more questions about that because unless I had some idea that I know the answer and that the only way to really know the answer was to know something about the details of the way the accounting and records were kept.[461]

* * * * * * *

* * * So I asked for information from Mr. McGloon, asked him to bring me some of the details so I could look at it, study the machinery. I took down the names of the warehouses in Canada, their addresses. I again looked at the Smith contract. I made careful notes that the contract was really with W. W. Smith & Company, a New York corporation, guaranteed by the Liverpool firm, and I think the first thing I did was to go to Grand Central and get a telephone book of Montreal and look for W. W. Smith & Company, look for these warehouses in these Canadian telephone books. I found them there. Although, what I found was W. W. Smith and Company, Limited, I think, in Canada, which was not the company that was tied in with the contract.

Mr. Reavis. You mean not the company that made the contract?

The Witness. Neither of the companies that made the contract. So then I went to this old friend of mine whom I had roomed with in college, and who was a lawyer and who was president of a varnish company over in Long Island City, Edward Smith & Company, I asked him to get me Dun reports. I didn't want to ask for them through our company. He got Dun reports on Smith and on these warehouses.

The Examiner. When was that?

The Witness. The Dun report on Smith is dated, I think, the 28th of February, 1938, and the—some of the others are about that time or March and then others came in in April. They indicated, of course, that there apparently was no business done at those addresses that amounted to anything.[462]

* * * * * * *

* * * Mr. Prentice [partner of Thompson's attorney] also made an investigation on the New York corporation of W. W. Smith and found that it had been dissolved, I think in 1936, although our contract was a five-year contract dated 1935.

So far as I could tell at that stage of the investigation there was no office of W. W. Smith in the United States.[463]

* * * * * * *

* * * I tried—my attorneys tried to get further information on the business over there. There was correspondence back and forth with England which resulted in very little. We couldn't get anything very positive. A lot of time went by with this correspondence and with discussing what to do.

Sometime during the summer Mr. Prentice, very properly, said to me, 'Now,

[460] R. 2069–2070.
[461] R. 2071.
[462] R. 2072–2073.
[463] R. 2074.

you got to do something about this, you are trying to think of things to do and you are trying to think of ways. You got to make a decision as to what to do.' He said, 'I think the thing to do is to take it up with Mr. Michaels and tell him the story and proceed from there.'

Mr. Michaels was on the Pacific Coast, as he normally was in the summer. I said, 'So much time has gone on now, I think we ought to wait until he gets back.'

In the meantime we tried other things, various types, and didn't get any really important information one way or the other.

When Mr. Michaels came back in the Fall, or shortly before he came back, Prentice discovered that W. W. Smith were in the Brooklyn telephone book. I don't know how he happened to run on that; we didn't know that before that time. He then sent someone over there to check it and discovered the office of Vernard and then discovered that some of these other companies [Canadian vendors] on the bulletin board at the same place were tied in there with this Vernard name. We had found before he was in the real estate business. I then asked for, on one of my trips to Bridgeport, asked for all the documents again and——

* * * * * * *

* * * Yes, I think it was McGloon. And I went over them again. This time there was brought to me what I hadn't seen before, the voucher showing the commission check that was paid W. W. Smith & Company.

I don't know why I hadn't thought of that before but I suppose it just occurred to me that it was paid off, the same account.

Q. [By Mr. GALPEER.] That is the Manning account?

A. That it was paid out of the Smith-Manning account in some way and I discovered then that it was paid off the manufacturing company funds and here was a possibility of looking up the check that was issued to find out what bank it went into. I found out that the cancelled checks of that division were all kept in Mr. George Dietrich's office so I didn't want to go and ask for them to arouse suspicion, so I went to Guaranty Trust and asked them to permit me to see the cancelled checks before they were sent to Bridgeport, which they did semi-monthly.[464]

* * * * * * *

* * * Well, I got the cancelled checks but there was no check to W. W. Smith, on my first two visits I think to the Guaranty Trust, which were two weeks apart. In the meantime Mr. Michaels returned and I told him the story.

Q. That would be about what date, sir?

A. I think it was about the 16th of October.

Mr. REAVIS. Do you mind if I ask a question?

Mr. Thompson, that was the first time you had spoken of this to anybody in the company excepting your talk with Mr. McGloon?

The WITNESS. That's right. I want to amend that to say that I had inquired about this W. W. Smith account casually in attempting not to arouse any suspicion with various other people during my investigation. I asked Herman, for example, whether he did any business with Smith at one time. I asked Stebe what he knew. Just threw it out casually to see if they knew anything about it. I was using every method of inquiring through various people in the organization whether they had any relationship with the various departments.

By Mr. GALPEER:

Q. What information did you get?

A. They didn't know anything about it.

---

[464] R. 2077–2079.

Mr. REAVIS. I might ask my question a little more intelligently. October 16 is the first time you stated to anybody in the company anything concerning your suspicions or the facts you had found?

The WITNESS. That's correct.

Mr. REAVIS. Other than the talk you had with Mr. McGloon getting information from him?

The WITNESS. That's correct.

Mr. STEWART. Perhaps that would be a good point to ask one other question along the same line. I take it you had not, up to that time, spoken with anybody connected with Price, Waterhouse & Company about your suspicions?

The WITNESS. No, not at all. I left out completely the forged Dun reports which I also got hold of early in the Spring from our files so that I knew about them.

* * * * * * *

Mr. REAVIS. I don't think—you said forged. Did you know they were forged then? You knew they disagreed.

The WITNESS. I suspected they were forged. Mr. Michaels concurred in the feeling that I had that the important thing was to get something tangible, that this was all negative information and not positive, and that we didn't know where these assets were and that we ought to find out something definitely about that. I was absolutely convinced that there were assets somewhere that he had set up a screen to hide and that he was doing some other sort of business. I didn't know what.

Mr. REAVIS. You mean Coster?

The WITNESS. I just couldn't believe that there weren't assets based on my knowledge of the man's ability and efficiency and intelligence. And I knew I was going to have to put this thing up to him and I wanted just as much knowledge as I could have before I did it.

By Mr. GALPEER:

Q. That is, put it up to Coster?

A. Yes, and I told Mr. Michaels that I was working on trying to find this check and he said that is one of the things that certainly should be done and it would be very helpful and he had to go right back to the Coast and he told me to keep right on working on that and see if I could get any additional information on that, and he would be prepared to come back at any time when I got something tangible.

Mr. REAVIS. Did you talk to him about employment of counsel at that time?

A. Yes, he suggested at that time that he would like to engage Mr. Downey, who is Mr. Reavis' partner, to advise him in the matter, as Mr. Downey had been formerly with Sullivan & Cromwell and was familiar with the personalities involved. Mr. Downey was in Bermuda and I wasn't able to engage him in Mr. Michaels' behalf until after he had gone back to the Coast.[465]

* * * * * * *

---

[465] "Q. [By Mr. REAVIS.] Did you talk about who would pay the counsel fees?

A. [By THOMPSON.] I believe that was discussed.

Q. My point is, did Mr. Michaels make any statement about that?

A. Yes, he said he would pay for Mr. Downey.

Q. He was independently going to bear the cost of an independent investigation?

A. Yes." R. 2084.

But cf.

"Q. [By Mr. GALPEER.] And you said you would assume the expense. You meant that you would see that the corporation bore the expense, or that you would pay it personally?

A. [By MICHAELS.] I would pay it personally. If the thing did not pan out as we suspected it might, I would.

Q. In other words, you would underwrite the expense?

A. That is correct." R. 4299.

* * * Mr. Downey, on his return, reviewed the whole subject with me and recommended right away, I think, that we should talk to Mr. Cummings, of Sullivan & Cromwell.

By Mr. GALPEER:

Q. About what day did Mr. Downey get back, about a week or ten days after Mr. Michaels left?

A. I should think about November 1st.

Q. And Mr. Michaels left about the 16th or 17th of October?

A. Yes, and some time about that time I succeeded in seeing a check drawn to W. W. Smith & Co., Ltd. for something over $10,000, and another for, I think, $750, and the large one had been deposited in the Hamilton Trust branch of the Chase National Bank in Brooklyn and the smaller one had been deposited in the Greene Avenue branch of the Royal Bank of Canada in Montreal.

Q. You saw these at the Guaranty Trust Company in New York?

A. Yes, so I immediately checked with the Chase Bank and found that they did have such an account and on a mere chance I asked them whether they also had the account of Manning & Co., and they told me they did, and that both accounts were in the Hamilton Trust branch of the Chase.

I checked those accounts, hoping that I would find that Manning & Co. had large funds flowing in from foreign creditors, but there were about 16 checks went through in the entire month as against one and a half million dollar sales that was being done by the department monthly, and that was the first tangible piece of evidence that I had which appeared to indicate clearly that something very wrong was going on in that account.

Q. What was the date that you saw this Manning account, as well as you can remember?

A. I don't recall. I guess that is pretty well recorded in some other spot.

Q. It was some time during the month of November, at any rate, of 1938?

A. Yes, and that gave me information that I felt I would have to go on rapidly, and there was also developing another situation which made it equally necessary to move rapidly in that we were negotiating for the sale of three million dollars additional authorized, but unissued bonds which involved a listing application and various other certifications of figures.

I went to Mr. Cummings before Mr. Michaels got back from the Coast.

Q. This trip that Mr. Michaels made to the Coast, had he planned to make that trip—it was one of the regular business trips?

A. Yes, it was a regular business trip and, as a matter of fact, he would not normally have come back at that time. I would say the date on seeing Mr. Cummings would be about the middle of November. He felt that there was nothing to do but immediately take it up with Mr. Coster, and after some discussion and seeking of proper opportunity, etc., I finally did that on November 27th, which was before Mr. Michaels got back.

Q. Had you been in touch with Mr. Michaels at all during this period?

A. Yes, I got in touch with him and told him of Mr. Cummings' reaction and belief that it should be taken up right away with Mr. Coster, and he said that he was planning to come back and would be back within a few days, would start back.

Q. This was a telephone call?

A. Yes.[466]

Q. You spoke to Mr. Coster on the 27th; when did Mr. Michaels get back?

A. I think the 27th was a Sunday and I think he got back the following Tuesday, the 29th.

Q. Briefly, what was the outcome of your discussions with Mr. Coster during this week?

A. He at no time admitted anything being wrong with the account. He said that he would supply me with warehouse receipts. He said that another question that I had asked was as to the insurance and he stated that it was insured with Lloyds, and that he would give me evidence of insurance.

Q. Did he give you to believe that McKesson were doing the insuring or that somebody else was?

A. That the bankers who were handling and supervising the inventory for him were handling the insurance.

Q. Meaning Manning & Co., or wasn't he specific?

A. He wasn't specific. He told me that the Smith statements of sales were being mailed from Liverpool.

Q. Which statements of sales are those?

A. Where they reported their sales.

Q. You mean the purchase orders or notices of shipment?

A. No, first came the notice that they had made the sale. He, of course, was very bitter with me, accused me of not being frank with him or telling him what I was doing and accused me of disloyalty and we had a very difficult time.

Q. Was there any final ultimatum or final show-down?

---

[466] According to Michaels' testimony, while on the Coast he received two telephone calls from Thompson, one on October 29th, the other shortly before Thanksgiving. R. 4301-4302. In the first call, on October 29th, Thompson reported "* * * that the investigation was proceeding and that they apparently were developing quite a lot of material and it looked very bad." R. 4301. On November 2nd, Michaels entered an order to sell on the New York Stock Exchange, at market, but gradually, approximately 15,000 shares of McKesson common stock, his entire common holdings. R. 4305. Sales by Michaels for his own account were as follows: November 2, 300 shares; November 4, 2,500 shares; November 5, 200 shares; November 7, 1,000 shares; November 9, 3,000 shares; November 10, 2,200 shares; November 12, 4,561 shares; total 13,761 shares (Securities and Exchange Commission official summary of securities transactions and holdings, Vol. 4, No. 23, p. 33). In this connection, Michaels testified:

(*a*) While he and his family sold common stock which included his entire common holdings, for the sum of approximately $100,000, he and his family owned at the time over 35,000 shares of the preferred stock having a market value of over $1,268,000, none of which was sold;

(*b*) The common stock owned by him and his family had been received by them as a dividend on the preferred stock, and his policy had been to hold preferred but not common stock of McKesson & Robbins; and

(*c*) He would have sold his common stock prior to 1938 excepting for the large tax which would have resulted because of a capital gain. Because of a change in the 1937 tax law, his income tax advisers told him as early as February, 1938, that he could sell his common stock without suffering a large tax, made out schedules for him respecting the tax which would result, and he then made up his mind to sell all of this common stock during the year 1938. In addition, he had a large debt of approximately $265,000 to a California bank secured by, among other securities, his common stock (approximately 14,000 shares), which debt he wanted to liquidate. He returned to California from New York, arriving in California about October 23, 1938, and immediately upon his arrival his tax advisers came to see him and urged him to sell the stock promptly because, they said, as the year-end approached the market would soften because of year-end selling. He thereupon instructed his brokers to sell his common stock, but told them there was no rush about it. At the same time he instructed them to sell other securities. The first sale was made on November 2, nine days after his arrival in California and four days after Thompson's telephone call referred to above. R. 4306-4307, 4311-4317

A. Yes, I finally told him on either Friday or Saturday of that same week that if he didn't give me the information by Monday—I don't know but what it was the following Monday that I gave him the ultimatum, that if he didn't give me the information the following day, that I would report it to the Executive Committee.

Q. Was it that evening that the announcement of the receivership became public?

A. Yes." [467]

---

[467] R. 2080-2088.

Section IV

DESCRIPTION OF THE AUDIT CONDUCTED BY PRICE, WATERHOUSE & CO.

A. PRICE, WATERHOUSE & CO.

1. The Firm

Price, Waterhouse & Co. was founded in London, England, in 1865.[468] The firm was represented for the first time in the United States by two chartered accountants sent over in 1890 to act as agents of the firm. These men were not partners of Price, Waterhouse & Co. but formed the firm known as Jones, Caesar & Co. which practiced on its own account as well as in behalf of their London employers. When one of these men died and the other retired, the English firm of Price, Waterhouse & Co. took over the business. In 1901 a separate partnership under the same name of Price, Waterhouse & Co. was organized in the United States.[469]

On January 1, 1939, Price, Waterhouse & Co. was, in effect, a group of interrelated partnerships with offices in many of the principal cities of the world. The American (or United States) firm consisted of 24 partners and had 17 offices [470] in the United States and one in Havana, Cuba. The executive office of the firm was in New York and had 10 partners in residence. The other 14 partners were in residence singly at 5 offices, 2 in each of 3 offices and 3 at 1 office (Chicago).[471] The offices at which no partner was in residence were operated by managers.

The English firm was a separate partnership with 11 partners in London. Two partners of the United States firm were partners individually in the English firm but none of the London partners were members of the United States firm. Neither the American nor the English firm was a partner in the other, but both of these firms were partners in the continental firm of Price, Waterhouse & Co. which

468 It is interesting to note in this connection that the first step toward the formation of a Society of Accountants was taken in Edinburgh, Scotland, January 17, 1853 and a Royal warrant was granted October 23, 1854. Similar societies were organized in Liverpool in January, and in London in November 1870. The London city directory listed 11 accountants in 1799 and 310 in 1860. See Richard Brown, Ed., *A History of Accounting and Accountants*, T. C. & E. C. Jack, Edinburgh, 1905.

469 R. 14, supplemented by information supplied by Price, Waterhouse & Co.

470 New York; Boston; Buffalo; Chicago; Cleveland; Detroit; Houston; Los Angeles; Milwaukee; Philadelphia; Pittsburgh; Portland, Oregon; Providence; St. Louis; San Francisco; Seattle; and Washington, D. C. R. 17.

471 R. 18.

had its head office in Paris, France.[472] The South American firm of Price, Waterhouse & Co. had as partners the American and English firms of Price, Waterhouse & Co.; Peat, Marwick, Mitchell & Co.; and "* * * perhaps five resident partners * * *."[473]

There was also the Mexican firm of Price, Waterhouse & Co., in which the resident Mexican partner was joined by four partners, individually, from the New York office. And, finally, the American firm was a partner in the Canadian firm of Price, Waterhouse & Co., which had five offices in that country.

The loosely knit organization which we have described is perhaps the largest organization of public accountants in the world and the United States firm, the largest in this country. The next largest in this country, based on size of staff and scope of operations, would appear to be the firm of Haskins & Sells,[474] of American origin, with 28 offices here, 3 in Europe, 2 in the Far East. As a partner in Deloitte, Plender, Haskins & Sells, they also have offices in Canada, Cuba, Mexico, South America, and South Africa. The only other firms in the United States comparable to these two in size of organization are Ernst & Ernst,[475] with 45 offices here and 1 in Canada; and Lybrand, Ross Bros. & Montgomery,[476] which has 19 offices throughout the United States and 2 in Europe. While there are other accounting firms with foreign affiliations and many offices in this country, none appear to be comparable in size of organization with these four.

The number of employees on the staff of a large accounting firm varies widely during the year. Comparable figures for the peak staff, permanent staff, number of partners, and offices of the United States firm of Price, Waterhouse & Co. (which is the organization referred to hereinafter when the name is used) with those of other accounting firms whose partners were called as expert witnesses in this case are given below.[477]

---

[472] R. 15-16.

[473] R. 15.

[474] P. 172.

[475] P. 538.

[476] P. 222.

[477] P. 3, 64, 120, 172, 222, 272, 316, 378, 478, 538, 586.

Size of Accounting Organizations Represented by Partners Called as Expert Witnesses, Compared with the Price, Waterhouse & Co. Organization

[Arranged in order of appearance of partner as a witness]

Firm	Number of offices in the United States	Number of partners	Number of staff [a] Peak	Number of staff [a] Permanent
Price, Waterhouse & Co.	17	24	1,465	750
Peat, Marwick, Mitchell & Co.	29	25	([b])	([b])
Scovell, Wellington & Co.	11	11	175	125
Touche, Niven & Co.	8	17	230	150
Haskins & Sells	28	57	1,120	720
Lybrand, Ross Bros. & Montgomery	19	32	[c] 815+	[c] 590
Mathieson, Aitken & Co.	1	4	40	40
Webster, Horne & Blanchard	2	4	25	25
Barrow, Wade, Guthrie & Co.	17	17	350	260
Klein, Hinds & Finke	1	6	100	50
Ernst & Ernst	45	27	950	650
Arthur Andersen & Co.	10	15	([d])	([d])

[a] Staff figures are for accountants only. In addition the four large firms reported corresponding figures for office employees as follows:

	Peak	Permanent
Price, Waterhouse & Co.	201	176
Haskins & Sells	240	240
Lybrand, Ross Bros. & Montgomery	[c] 185	[c] 160
Ernst & Ernst	250	200

[b] Several hundred employees, ratio of permanent to peak staff not given.

[c] "In recent years the [total] number of employees has not gone below 750 and has exceeded a thousand at the peak." P. 222.

[d] Several hundred employees, 35% of peak staff being temporary.

Some measure of the professional work performed by firms of public accountants is gained from an analysis of registration statements and annual reports filed with this Commission under the Securities Act of 1933 and the Securities Exchange Act of 1934. The table below gives some indication of the activity of accountants in connection with security offerings under the Securities Act of 1933 during the 2½ year period from July 1, 1936 to December 31, 1938 in issues of one million dollars or over.[478]

[478] Material in this table was prepared in the Capital Market Subsection, Research and Statistics Section, Trading and Exchange Division of the Commission.

Employment of Accountants in the Flotation of Stock and Bond Issues of $1,000,000 or Over Registered Under the Securities Act of 1933 and Offered for Sale From July 1, 1936, to December 31, 1938.

	Number of registrants by which expert was employed	Percent of total	Gross proceeds of issues in which expert was employed ($000)	Percent of total
Price, Waterhouse & Co.	54	16. 12	959, 984	20. 35
Arthur Andersen & Co.	53	15. 82	889, 207	18. 85
Haskins & Sells	47	14. 03	571, 158	12. 11
Lybrand, Ross Bros. & Montgomery	40	11. 94	871, 049	18. 46
Total, 4 experts	194	57. 91	3, 291, 398	69. 77
Arthur Young & Company	16	4. 77	171, 462	3. 63
Peat, Marwick, Mitchell & Co.	15	4. 48	55, 829	1. 18
Barrow, Wade, Guthrie & Co.	14	4. 18	87, 239	1. 85
Total, 7 experts	239	71. 34	3, 605, 928	76. 43
S. D. Leidesdorf & Co.	8	2. 39	24, 387	. 52
Touche, Niven & Co.	6	1. 79	63, 160	1. 34
Allen R. Smart & Co.	5	1. 49	30, 556	. 65
Total, 10 experts	258	77. 01	3, 724, 031	78. 94
2 experts, 4 each	8	2. 39	310, 985	6. 60
2 experts, 3 each	6	1. 79	151, 761	3. 21
7 experts, 2 each	14	4. 18	248, 515	5. 27
49 experts, 1 each	49	14. 63	282, 214	5. 98
Total, 70 experts	335	100. 00	4, 717, 506	100. 00

This table should be compared with the one which follows which shows the number of firms of accountants which certified to financial statements contained in annual reports for 1937 filed with the Commission in accordance with the provisions of the Securities Exchange Act of 1934. While the preceding table may be irregular in amount and incidence both in time and as to accountants involved the following table may be some indication of regularly recurring auditing work.[479]

[479] Material in this table was taken from the records of The Survey of American Listed Corporations, a Works Progress Administration project sponsored by the Securities and Exchange Commission. The limitations of the table are expressed in the following paragraphs from Report No. 1 of the survey:

> "The study as now constituted, therefore, includes about 2,100 companies which is about 79% of the 2,651 companies fully or provisionally registered or exempt from registration under the Securities Exchange Act of 1934 at June 30, 1938. The total number of companies with securities admitted to listed and unlisted trading on national securities exchanges at June 30, 1938 was 3,356, of which total the present study covers about 63%.
>
> "Registration is not required of companies with securities admitted to unlisted trading privileges or of companies with securities traded on exempt exchanges, and these were not included in the study. Other types of enterprises with securities traded on stock exchanges but which were not covered are: Railroads and other carriers reporting to the Interstate Commerce Commission; communication companies reporting to the Federal Communications Commission; insurance companies; banks and trust companies; bank holding companies; bondholders' protective committees; and foreign issuers other than Canadian and Cuban."

For IMMEDIATE Release Friday, February 21, 1941

SECURITIES AND EXCHANGE COMMISSION
Washington

In the Matter of McKESSON & ROBBINS, Inc. File No. 1–1435 Securities Exchange Act of 1934 Section 21 (a)	NOTICE OF CORRECTION

There is presented on the inside pages herewith a correction of pages 138 and 139 of the Report on Investigation In the Matter of McKesson & Robbins, Inc. The correction concerns the table on page 138. The following pages amend the table on page 138 and the reference thereto in the text on the bottom of page 139 and are intended to replace those pages. Additional copies of this release for insertion in copies of the Report may be obtained by writing the Securities and Exchange Commission, 1778 Pennsylvania Avenue, Washington, D. C. Copies of the Report may be obtained from the Superintendent of Documents, United States Government Printing Office, Washington, D. C. (*In the Matter of McKesson & Robbins, Inc.* Report on Investigation, Price 60 cents.)

293541°—41

Employment of Accountants in the Flotation of Underwritten Stock and Bond Issues of $1,000,000 or Over Registered Under the Securities Act of 1933 and Offered for Cash Sale From July 1, 1936, to December 31, 1938.

	Registrants by which expert was employed		Gross proceeds of issues in which expert was employed	
	Number	Percent of total	($000)	Percent of total
Price, Waterhouse & Co.	54	15. 43	959, 984	20. 36
Arthur Andersen & Co.	51	14. 57	889, 207	18. 85
Haskins & Sells	46	13. 14	571, 158	12. 11
Lybrand, Ross Bros. & Montgomery	41	11. 71	871, 049	18. 47
Total, 4 experts	192	54. 85	3, 291, 398	69. 79
Ernst & Ernst	22	6. 29	129, 516	2. 75
Arthur Young & Company	16	4. 57	171, 462	3. 64
Peat, Marwick, Mitchell & Co.	15	4. 29	55, 829	1. 18
Total, 7 experts	245	70. 00	3, 648, 205	77. 36
Barrow, Wade, Guthrie & Co.	14	4. 00	87, 239	1. 85
S. D. Leidesdorf & Co.	8	2. 29	24, 387	0. 52
Touche, Niven & Co.	6	1. 71	63, 160	1. 34
Total, 10 experts	273	78. 00	3, 822, 991	81. 07
2 experts, 4 and 5 respectively	9	2. 57	210, 528	4. 46
2 experts, 3 each	6	1. 71	151, 761	3. 22
6 experts, 2 each	12	3. 43	107, 877	2. 29
50 experts, 1 each	50	14. 29	422, 852	8. 96
Total, 70 experts	350	100. 00	4, 716, 009	100. 00

This table should be compared with the one which follows which shows the number of firms of accountants which certified to financial statements contained in annual reports for 1937 filed with the Commission in accordance with the provisions of the Securities Exchange Act of 1934. While the preceding table may be irregular in amount and incidence both in time and as to accountants involved the following table may be some indication of regularly recurring auditing work.[479]

[479] Material in this table was taken from the records of The Survey of American Listed Corporations, a Works Progress Administration project sponsored by the Securities and Exchange Commission. The limitations of the table are expressed in the following paragraphs from Report No. 1 of the survey:

> "The study as now constituted, therefore, includes about 2,100 companies which is about 79% of the 2,651 companies fully or provisionally registered or exempt from registration under the Securities Exchange Act of 1934 at June 30, 1938. The total number of companies with securities admitted to listed and unlisted trading on national securities exchanges at June 30, 1938, was 3,356, of which total the present study covers about 63%.
>
> "Registration is not required of companies with securities admitted to unlisted trading privileges or of companies with securities traded on exempt exchanges, and these were not included in the study. Other types of enterprises with securities traded on stock exchanges but which were not covered are: Railroads and other carriers reporting to the Interstate Commerce Commission; communication companies reporting to the Federal Communications Commission; insurance companies; banks and trust companies; bank holding companies; bondholders' protective committees; and foreign issuers other than Canadian and Cuban."

Statements Filed for the Fiscal Year 1937
Under the Securities Exchange Act of 1934

Accountants certifying	Number of statements		Percent of total: Firms	Percent of total: Statements
Price, Waterhouse & Co.	238		.25—	11.91
Ernst & Ernst	204		.25—	10.21
2 firms		442	.49—	22.12
Lybrand, Ross Bros. & Montgomery	162		.25—	8.11
Haskins & Sells	157		.25—	7.86
Arthur Andersen & Co.	127		.25—	6.36
Peat, Marwick, Mitchell & Co.	103		.25—	5.15
Arthur Young & Company	67		.25—	3.35
7 firms		1,058	1.72	52.95
S. D. Leidesdorf & Co.	39		.25—	1.96
Touche, Niven & Co.	36		.25—	1.80
Barrow, Wade, Guthrie & Co.	35		.25—	1.75
10 firms		1,168	2.46—	58.46
5 firms, 13, 15, 18, 21, 29 respectively	96		1.23—	4.80
10 firms, 10–13 each	116		2.46—	5.81
25 firms		1,380	6.14	69.07
18 firms, 5–9 each	122		4.42	6.11
12 firms, 4 each	48		2.95	2.40
55 firms		1,550	13.51	77.58
19 firms, 3 each	57		4.67	2.85
58 firms, 2 each	116		14.25	5.81
132 firms		1,723	32.43	86.24
275 firms, 1 each	275		67.57	13.76
407 firms		1,998	100.00	100.00

It is interesting to note that the same accounting firms, although with some shifting in position, occupy the first 10 places in the 2 tables set forth above.

U. S. GOVERNMENT PRINTING OFFICE: 1941

Statements Filed for the Fiscal Year 1937
Under the Securities Exchange Act of 1934

Accountants certifying	Number of statements		Percent of total: Firms	Percent of total: Statements
Price, Waterhouse & Co.	238		.25—	11.91
Ernst & Ernst	204		.25—	10.21
2 firms		442	.49—	22.12
Lybrand, Ross Bros. & Montgomery	162		.25—	8.11
Haskins & Sells	157		.25—	7.86
Arthur Andersen & Co.	127		.25—	6.36
Peat, Marwick, Mitchell & Co.	103		.25—	5.15
Arthur Young & Company	67		.25—	3.35
7 firms		1,058	1.72	52.95
S. D. Leidesdorf & Co.	39		.25—	1.96
Touche, Niven & Co.	36		.25—	1.80
Barrow, Wade, Guthrie & Co.	35		.25—	1.75
10 firms		1,168	2.46—	58.46
5 firms, 13, 15, 18, 21, 29 respectively	96		1.23—	4.80
10 firms, 10–13 each	116		2.46—	5.81
25 firms		1,380	6.14	69.07
18 firms, 5–9 each	122		4.42	6.11
12 firms, 4 each	48		2.95	2.40
55 firms		1,550	13.51	77.58
19 firms, 3 each	57		4.67	2.85
58 firms, 2 each	116		14.25	5.81
132 firms		1,723	32.43	86.24
275 firms, 1 each	275		67.57	13.76
407 firms		1,998	100.00	100.00

It is interesting to note that there is only one difference in the names of the first 10 accountants in the two tables set forth above: Ernst & Ernst, with the second largest number of annual reports, does not appear in the first 10 accountants employed by registrants of new security offerings during the period shown, whereas Allen R. Smart & Co., with the tenth largest number of registrants of new security offerings, does not come in the first 10 for annual reports.[480]

[480] Ernst & Ernst certified registration statements for 4 registrants in the period covered, while Allen R. Smart & Co. certified 6 annual reports for 1937.

Price, Waterhouse & Co. occupies a closely contested first place in both lists.

A less tangible way of appraising the position of Price, Waterhouse & Co. in the accounting world, but basically more important than mere size of staff or volume of business to a professional organization, is the reputation it enjoys. The importance of this factor alone is significant in the history of this case. It is well expressed in Julian F. Thompson's report on Girard & Co., Inc., which he submitted to Horace B. Merwin of The Bridgeport Trust Company in the spring of 1925. Thompson in speaking of Coster's management policies said, "When he decided to have an audit, he inquired as to who the finest in the country were and finally chose Price, Waterhouse & Company. * * *"[481] Anthony Jaureguy (now partner of Price, Waterhouse & Co.) agreed that the first audit report by his firm referred to here was the start of Girard & Co., Inc. on the Price, Waterhouse & Co. name.[482] That Coster secured the audit report for credit purposes is evident from the fact that the report was submitted to The Bridgeport Trust Company when a loan of $80,000 was secured in May 1925.[483] At the same time three officers of that bank bought stock in the Company, while two of them later became and continued to be directors in Coster's Companies.

That this reliance on the Price, Waterhouse & Co. name was generally recognized practice in financial circles is well demonstrated by the colorful language in which it is expressed by other directors of McKesson & Robbins, Incorporated. Henry D. Faxon, for example, when asked what he considered to be the purpose of having an audit, answered:

> "You know I never considered that. I just took it that when you put Price, Waterhouse on the bottom of the statement, it was Sterling Silver, and every thing went." [484]

Other directors[485] referred to the auditors as "the Blue Ribbon firm

---

[481] R. 2243, 2252; Ex. 177. It should be noted that this report was written before Thompson became connected with Coster's Company. The engagement to which we refer is the first audit of Girard & Co., Inc. by Price, Waterhouse & Co. which covered the audit of the last 9 months of 1924 and a report to include a summary of sales contracts entered into in 1924 but applicable to 1925.

[482] R. 55; pages 24-25 *supra*.

[483] R. 2241-2242; footnote 35 *supra*.

[484] R. 2529.

[485] The following testimony of Rowley W. Phillips illustrates the unquestioned public reliance on the mere fact that statements have been audited:

> "* * * In 99 cases out of 100, I never see the certificate of it. I look in Moody's Manual. I am not the investment banker of more than a very few corporations. If you, as an individual, asked me to tell you the condition, say of du Pont and asked me for my advice as to whether it is a good stock for you to buy or sell, I would look in, say, Moody's Manual; that is the first thing I will do. We will look together to see who audited it. There is no qualifying statement of any nature, it gives those figures. The balance sheet and earning statement, I assume, and I have assumed, and will continue to assume that those are all right because there is no possible way that I can check up on the thing. I have no intention of making a personal investigation of du Pont, nor can I very well ask you to wait for a couple of weeks while I send for a statement and see whether the audit was complete or merely a verification of columns of figures, or what it was." R. 2354-2355

of America", "they were tops", "one of the outstanding firms in America; if not the most outstanding firm",[486] and Wilbur L. Cummings, a partner in one of New York City's leading law firms specializing in corporation law, in his testimony as a director of McKesson summed up his opinion of the auditors in two sentences:

"I have had implicit faith in Price, Waterhouse, and I still have. Absolutely nothing that has occurred here changes my faith in Price, Waterhouse." [487]

The firm of Price, Waterhouse & Co. has not been insensible to the prominent place it holds in the ranks of the profession. The influence of members of the firm and staff on accounting thought in the last 25 years has been outstanding. Perhaps no one has been more prominent in this regard than the senior partner, George O. May, whose extensive writings were collected by his associates a few years ago and published under the title, "Twenty-Five Years of Accounting Responsibility." [488] May's influence has been felt also in his capacity as lecturer in accounting on the A. Lowes Dickinson Foundation [489] at the Harvard Graduate School of Business Administration and in his participation in the affairs of the American Institute of Accountants and of the New York Stock Exchange over a long period.

Members of the firm have taken part in the preparation of the widely accepted and authoritative series of bulletins, which was initiated in 1917 by the publication under the auspices of the Federal Reserve Board of the pamphlet, entitled, "Approved Methods for the Preparation of Balance Sheet Statements." This pamphlet was revised by the American Institute of Accountants and reissued in 1929 by the Federal Reserve Board under the title, "Verification of Financial Statements", and was addressed to bankers, merchants, manufacturers, auditors, and accountants. The most recent revision of this document was prepared by a committee, of which P. F. Brundage, of Price, Waterhouse & Co., was a member, and was published by the American Institute of Accountants in January 1936 under the name, "Examination of Financial Statements by Independent Public Accountants." [490] As we shall show later, this Bulletin has been considered to be an authoritative statement of present day auditing procedures.

Members of the staff, also, have written widely accepted books dealing with auditing practice and procedure. F. W. Thornton, for many years on the staff of Price, Waterhouse & Co., wrote by request of the publishers, American Institute Publishing Co., Inc., "Financial

---

[486] R. 2210, 2403. See also R. 4269–4270.

[487] R. 2450.

[488] May, George Oliver, Twenty-five Years of Accounting Responsibility—1911-1936; American Institut Publishing Co., Inc. New York, 1936.

[489] Named after Sir A. Lowes Dickinson who died February 28, 1935, having been a partner in the English firm of Price, Waterhouse & Co. from 1913 until he retired in 1932 and previously senior partner in the New York office from 1901 to 1913.

[490] Ex. 117; R. 1766–1767.

Examinations", as an interpretation of the bulletin "Verification of Financial Statements." He also wrote, "Duties of a Senior Accountant." "Duties of the Junior Accountant" was written originally by Thornton and W. B. Reynolds, also with Price, Waterhouse & Co., and was revised by A. B. Cipriani, with the Price, Waterhouse & Co. Pittsburgh office.[491] D. L. Trouant, with the firm's Philadelphia office, wrote "Financial Audits",[492] an interpretation of the last of the series of bulletins referred to above. These books and "Audit Working Papers", by J. Hugh Jackson,[493] now of Stanford University, formerly of Harvard University Graduate School of Business, and for a time on the staff of Price, Waterhouse & Co., have made known in a very effective manner what may be assumed to be methods advocated by that firm. Except for the last mentioned book, however, the firm connection of the authors is not given in the books themselves.

The importance of maintaining a high code of ethics within the profession, and more especially in his own firm, could not be told in a more convincing manner than is done by R. O. Berger, a partner in the firm's Chicago office, in a booklet "Organization Ethics and Team Work" [494] written by him for the benefit of the staff and privately published in 1925. While now out of print, it is the first of five items listed in the firm's "Office Manual" as recommended reading,[495] and is available in the firm's library, although in the last few years classroom training has largely replaced this less direct method of instruction for new members of the staff. Berger, at page 5 of his booklet concludes a list of six points to be covered with the following:

> " * * * the cultivation and retention of the Goodwill of our clientele is practically the only means we have for development. Advertising is not looked upon with favor in the profession and we must leave the spreading of our name and reputation into new channels, first, to those having had experience with us who were well satisfied and, second, to the cumulative prestige following the successful carrying out of our practice and obligations as a whole and the Goodwill inherent in such prestige."

This leads him to conclude that:

> "We have been in business in this country for a number of decades and cherish

[491] R. 1761–1765.

[492] R. 1771.

[493] The first important book on the subject. Published by The American Institute of Accountants Foundation in 1923.

[494] Ex. 168; R. 2030–2031.

[495] The "Office Manual" which was published in 1931 is somewhat out of date, and no doubt would include additional or different references if revised. See footnote 550 *infra*. However, it is interesting to note that in addition to Berger's booklet, four books are recommended as sources from which the principles and standards upheld by the firm may be obtained. These four are:

> "The Duties of a Junior Accountant," by W. B. Reynolds and F. W. Thornton; "Verification of Financial Statements" (Federal Reserve Bulletin); "Audit Working Papers," by J. Hugh Jackson; and "Accounting Practice and Procedure," by A. Lowes Dickinson.

W. B. Reynolds, F. W. Thornton, and J. Hugh Jackson were associated with Price, Waterhouse & Co. when their books were written; Sir A. Lowes Dickinson was a partner. See footnote 489 *supra*.

the hope and belief that we shall continue indefinitely to be important factors in the profession and in the financial structure so that our policy should be that once we establish a new connection we should endeavor to make it a permanent one."

The general tenor of the 32 pages of the pamphlet is indicated in the second from the last paragraph, where reference is made to the staff's responsibility to the firm and the firm's responsibility directly, as well as indirectly through the professional societies, to the client and the public.

"But greater than the responsibility to any such institutions or individuals is the moral responsibility that every one should do his full share according to the best of his ability and knowledge of the requirements in placing the profession on a higher footing so that it may in fact as well as in theory be entitled to the fullest respect from the financial and business public. Likewise, it is the duty of each of us to seize any opportunities to correct unfavorable impressions which may exist in the minds of the public as to the profession or any individual or firm in practice when we know that the charge on which such impression is based is a false one."[496]

In the foregoing paragraphs, we have given some indication of the size, prestige, and attitude of the firm of Price, Waterhouse & Co. in their professional work. In anticipation of a detailed review of their methods of procedure, it seems desirable to consider the composition of the firm's staff and the training methods employed.

For the fiscal year ended June 30, 1938, the staff ranged from a low of 940 members in July 1937 to a peak of 1,666 in January 1938 and back to a low of 926 in June 1938.[497] Minor additions to the staff were made in October and November of 1937, while an increase of approximately 20% was made in December over the November figures, and in January 1938 a 25% increase was made over December's roster. Unimportant losses took place in February; while approximately one-fifth and one-fourth of the declining numbers were dismissed in March and April, respectively; one-tenth in May; and half as many in June to reach the low point for the period. In short, eliminating minor additions and dismissals, the increased staff was carried only from December through March with the bulk of these only in January and February.

On July 1, 1938, the staff, in addition to the 24 partners mentioned above, consisted of 112 contract managers,[498] 227 seniors, 207 first assistants, 173 second assistants, and 176 on the office staff for a total of 895 persons.[499] In expanding this basic staff to meet the demands of the busy season, most of the additions are made in the junior ranks,

---

[496] Ex. 168; R. 2030-2031.

[497] Ex. 122.

[498] Contract managers correspond to managing accountants or supervisors as the terms are used in other offices. In Price, Waterhouse & Co. the title recognizes the terms of employment whereby the members of this group are given a contract for a definite term and specifying a given number of shares in the bonus fund, whereas the seniors do not have a contract. "Seniors" is a universal term. First assistants and second assistants may be better known as semi-seniors and juniors respectively. R. 22, 30.

[499] R. 30.

although some experienced applicants are employed as seniors.[500] Rating above juniors, however, is attained generally by promotion.

Additions to the staff in the junior ranks in recent years were from two classes. These were college men who wanted to go into accounting work and applicants who had had experience of a clerical or accounting nature. All applicants were interviewed by one man, who is a contract manager, and who estimated their adaptability to the work and gave them a practical examination (no theory questions) to test their capabilities. Three references were required in each case.[501]

Berger said that "After engaging men one of the important responsibilities of the firm and of the profession is to provide adequate facilities for the **training of the staff** in order to equip the members thereof for meeting the demands of accountancy work." [502] Price, Waterhouse & Co. attempted to meet their responsibility in this regard by means of classes during the fall months and by encouraging the staff to keep abreast of current literature in the field and to attend meetings of the professional societies. In the practical application of accounting knowledge, supervision while on the engagement was considered perhaps the most essential phase of the training. Berger, for example, after outlining a course for personal advancement, said:

> "In the preceding remarks I have dealt with what may be termed the Educational side of the training of the staff, but, important as this may be, substantial development rests more particularly on the practical work on assignments, as after all experience is the best teacher. Therefore, anyone wishing to attain the maximum progress should make the most of his opportunities daily throughout the year while engaged on the work for the firm. He should endeavor to understand fully the objects of the work which he is requested to take up and to avoid carrying out instructions in a purely mechanical way. When in doubt he should ask those in charge, who will gladly extend a helping hand such as they received when they were in a similar position."[503]

Geoffrey G. Rowbotham, the partner in charge of the McKesson audit since 1928, in speaking of the manager in charge under him, said that Thorn received—

> "* * * from Jaureguy a very thorough training in a personal way in which it always seems to me an accountant should be trained.
>
> "I am, perhaps, a product of the apprenticeship system myself and am impressed with personal training more than classroom training. That is merely a personal prejudice on my part." [504]

Success in the training program was measured by results obtained in the field. Contract managers and seniors reported currently on the qualifications and personality of the men working under them. These reports were analyzed to form the basis for a periodical review of the

500 R. 31.
501 R. 19–20; Ex. 212.
502 Ex. 168 (pp. 7–8).
503 Idem (p. 10).
504 R. 2053.

status and salary of each member of the organization.[505] To reach the status of contract manager, substantial experience with the firm was required.[506]

Of the 112 contract managers as of July 1, 1938, 66 entered the group since 1930 and 46 prior to that date. Their average age in February 1939 was 41.6 years, and average period of service with Price, Waterhouse & Co. was 16.1 years. Their average service when first awarded a contract was 8.4 years. The 66 managers appointed since 1930 remain from a group of 71 (five resigned) who were offered contracts after an average of 9.4 years of service at an average age of 33.8 years. Of this group, only four were under 30, while 17 were over 35.

The average compensation, including overtime and bonus in the several ranks for the year ended June 30, 1938 was as follows:[507]

Contract managers	$10, 106. 00
Seniors	3, 924. 00
First assistants	2, 493. 00
Second assistants	1, 837. 00

Junior assistants and office staff (in general, employees paid less than $200 per month[508]) are paid overtime

"* * * at the equivalent hourly rate for all overtime worked after 6 P. M., but no overtime is expected to be charged if the time worked does not exceed one hour. * * * In any one month in which available time, holidays or sickness are charged as well as overtime, the latter, if not considerable, should in most cases be offset against the non-chargeable time as shown. Payment for overtime will be made annually at June 30, or at the time of release or resignation.

* * * * * * *

"Supper allowances of $1.50 per night will be made when overtime is worked, provided it is necessary to return to the office, or when the time so worked exceeds two hours."[509]

Employees at a salary of $200 per month or more are paid a bonus, which is at least equal to overtime.[510]

2. The Origin and Terms of the Engagement

a. LETTERS OF ENGAGEMENT

(1) Girard & Co., Inc.

In the preceding section we have sketched very briefly a picture of the firm of Price, Waterhouse & Co. and indicated that it would appear that they were sought out by Girard & Co., Inc. because of their outstanding position in the profession. In this section it is important

505 Ex. 168 (pp. 6–7).
506 R. 2054–2055.
507 R. 31–32.
508 R. 29.
509 Ex. 121 (pp. 2–3).
510 R. 29.

that we show the manner in which F. D. Coster's new enterprise was accepted as a client by the firm of Price, Waterhouse & Co. and the development of the contract or understanding between the parties as expressed in annual exchanges of letters preceding each engagement.

Geoffrey G. Rowbotham testified that an official of First National Pictures met their W. B. Reynolds one day and said an acquaintance of his, named Coster, in Mount Vernon, wanted some accounting work done and that he, Harwood, had given Coster the name of Price, Waterhouse & Co. and Harwood thought the firm might hear from him in a few days. This single personal contact seems to have been the only information obtained by Price, Waterhouse & Co. about the prospective client except what came to them in the correspondence with the client which we will review. Entire reliance for information about the client was placed upon an examination of the books after taking the engagement.[511] Whether independent inquiry in other quarters would have cast any doubts on Coster's reputation seems impossible to say at this late date.[512] In any event the negotiations proceeded as we will recite and the audit was carried out apparently without any suspicions arising as to the reliability of the client.

The outstanding features of the negotiations for the first engagement was a conflict between Coster's insistence for service from a large accounting firm in the midst of a busy season and that firm's attempt to postpone the work until a more convenient time. Correspondence in respect to the engagement opened with a letter from

---

[511] R. 35–37, especially the following passage:

"Q. [By Mr. GALPEER.] What examination did you make of Mr. Coster, or what examination did you make of this account to determine whether you would take it and sign your name to it on its certification?

A. [By ROWBOTHAM.] The only examination we make is the actual examination of the company's accounts themselves. I mean, we don't make a preliminary examination of a president of a company in order to see whether he is a desirable man.

Q. You don't make any examination of your clients at all to determine whether they are desirable so that you would handle their account?

A. That is not quite so. Most of them, of course, we have known for years, 30 years' time, but if a man comes in who is president of an apparently reputable company, and we go in and look at his accounts and he seems to be a reputable man, we don't have anything, I don't know how to describe it, any detective service. We don't have any.

Q. You don't make any independent check?

A. We don't make any independent check. Usually he comes to us with some kind of a recommendation.

Mr. STEWART: As in this case, Mr. Coster came to you from Mr. Harwood?

The WITNESS: Yes.

Q. [By Mr. GALPEER.] Would you say that Mr. Harwood recommended Mr. Coster or merely said that he had recommended you to Mr. Coster?

A. I think the facts are that he had recommended us to Coster and I think it was assumed at the time that had he known anything detrimental to Coster he wouldn't have sent him on to us.

Q. But yet in summary, it is not your practice to make any independent check of people or firms whose work you undertake?

A. No, if a man comes in and he is president of the company, we go around to his company. He is president, he has a treasurer, he has a plant, we don't go into his past history.

Q. Did anyone in your firm meet the man who represented himself to be P. Horace Girard, who sent you the first letter?

A. I can't answer that." R. 36–37.

[512] Cf. Ex. 177.

Girard & Co., Inc., dated December 17, 1924, signed by P. Horace Girard, vice-president.[513] This first letter was a two-sentence inquiry as to charges for auditing the books for 1 year and advice on the installation of a new bookkeeping system. It carried no information as to the size of the company except to say that they expected to branch out into a different field and for that reason felt that their present bookkeeping could be greatly improved.[514] As this inquiry came in at the start of the busy season, it was acknowledged by stating that the regular charges would be $30 per day for a senior accountant, $20 per day for an assistant, and $50 per day for such time as might be required of a manager. The letter closed by stating that the firm was extremely busy and would be glad to have as much notice as possible if the work was to be entrusted to them.[515]

This exchange of letters was followed by one from the prospective client, this time signed by F. D. Coster, President, and dated December 26, 1924, in which the writer said that they were in no particular hurry—sometime in January would do very well if the auditors would not be so busy at that time. The letter asked how much notice would be required but this point was avoided in the acknowledgment on December 30, wherein the responsibility for further negotiations was placed on Coster.

Two weeks later, Coster wrote again to the attention of Reynolds, with whom he had had some conversations over the telephone. This letter gives a brief description of the business and plans for the future. The last paragraph is so full of significance in giving Coster's conception of the functions of auditors in checking employees as distinguished from officers that we quote it in full:

"Our book entries up to December 31st while running into fairly large figures are comparatively few on account of the character of our business, and as there is no particular investigation that we have in mind to be pursued for the reason that stocks and merchandise, cash, etc. have been under the constant scrutiny of one of our officers; the work to be done in that respect, is comparatively light as our trial balances agree to date; but what we are extremely anxious to have accomplished at the earliest possible date, is to plan and install the most economical and efficient system that you can plan for us in our new operations and thereafter arrange with you to check up on the system on a monthly or quarterly basis, whichever you prefer, in other words, make some arrangement whereby we can rest assured that we have someone in our confidence who can check up and control the operations of our employees so that the officers who have been devoting part

[513] P. Horace Girard seems to be another alias of Philip Musica—Frank D. Coster. Footnote 27 *supra*. The examiner asked Jaureguy if he had ever met the man. The reply was that he had never met Girard, who had died before he came on the audit for the first time soon after November 30, 1926. His recollection was that he was told that Girard's widow lived in the country near Bridgeport. He had never heard of any family relationship existing between Girard and Coster. R. 46, 66–67. In the early part of 1925 P. Horace Girard was represented to Thompson (subsequently treasurer of McKesson & Robbins) as being in charge of production. Ex. 177.

[514] Ex. 116.

[515] Ex. 116. Letter dated December 18, 1924.

of their time in the keeping of our records, will be able to devote their entire time to more important matters."[516]

Girard & Co., Inc., soon became impatient for action as the next letter, signed P. Horace Girard, was dated January 19, 1925 and pleaded for at least one man to get them started as they had made no entries since January 1, which was rather "confusing" to them. Receiving no answer, Coster wrote 1 week later, asking for immediate attention to the system installation. This letter also was not answered. On February 3, Coster wrote again, asking for at least "one or two ordinary checkers" to get the audit out of the way if it was impossible to send one of "your best experts to plan our new books." Letters of February 6 and 11 followed which referred to ineffectual efforts to reach Reynolds by telephone, the last letter raising a new problem—the necessity of filing a tax report. Finally, this persistence was rewarded by a letter, dated February 13, 1925, saying "This letter will introduce our representative, Mr. C. R. Hartzell, who will proceed with the audit of your company if you will furnish him the necessary facilities."

The engagement was renewed the following year with much less difficulty than was encountered in getting under way the first year. A conversation confirmed by an exchange of letters dated December 28 and 29, 1925 in which Coster expressed his satisfaction with the report on the previous year's work and asked that the same procedure be followed again, the details to be discussed with the auditor's representative on the work, was all that was necessary.

On April 14, 1926, Price, Waterhouse & Co. wrote a letter to Girard & Co., Inc., introducing their representative, J. H. McGloon, who was to be the senior in charge of a first quarterly audit for 1926 under D. F. Morland, who had been in charge for the annual audit for 1925, and was now manager. The audit for the second quarter was requested in a letter dated June 25, 1926 in which Coster stated that he preferred "* * * if possible, someone that has had previous experience on our accounts * * *" In accordance with this request McGloon returned for this and the audit for the third quarter of 1926.[517]

(2) Merger of Girard & Co., Inc. and McKesson & Robbins, Incorporated (New York)

Events moved rapidly during the latter part of 1926 for at the close of October the merger of Girard & Co., Inc. and McKesson & Robbins, Incorporated (New York) to form the new McKesson & Robbins, Incorporated (Connecticut) required extra work by the auditors, who were instructed to do this in a long letter from Coster, addressed to

[516] Ex. 116. Letter dated January 14, 1925. Plans for expansion contemplated transactions ranging from $10 to $500 with fifteen hundred to five thousand accounts. The system to be installed was to provide for control over district managers, receipts of merchandise, conversions of manufactured products, and aid in reducing cost of production and overhead.

[517] Ex. 116.

the attention of Morland. This letter covered the final closing of Girard's books and an audit of McKesson & Robbins, Incorporated (New York) since the date of the last audit which had been done by Price, Waterhouse & Co. as of December 31, 1925.

The letter instructs Price, Waterhouse & Co. to coordinate the accounting departments of the two companies at Bridgeport and to make the audit, even though other auditors had done certain work for the bankers in connection with the financing. The audit instructions are very briefly summarized in this paragraph from the letter:

> "4. The books and records of McKesson & Robbins of New York have been very thoroughly investigated by Messrs. R. G. Rankin & Co., who have acted for the bankers, who are effecting the financing of the transaction. In the course of said investigation, we have had members of our staff co-operate with Messrs. R. G. Rankin & Co., and we have satisfied ourselves on the matters of inventories and accounts receivable, both foreign and domestic; therefore, it will be unnecessary to take up any physical inventories or verification of accounts receivable, and your investigation may be confined to the usual verification of these assets, and you may proceed in the same manner that you have done for Girard & Co., Inc." [518]

On effecting the merger, resignations were accepted from certain employees of McKesson & Robbins, Incorporated (New York) and J. H. McGloon of Price, Waterhouse & Co., in a letter dated November 10, 1926, was instructed to take charge of all books of account and complete records of the Company at 1:00 o'clock, p. m. of that day "* * * and assume full supervision and direction of all accounting or record keeping of any nature and description." [519] The work apparently kept McGloon busy until August of the following year. Under this arrangement McGloon's salary was billed to McKesson monthly but Price, Waterhouse & Co. had no other connection with the work.[520]

(3) McKesson & Robbins, Incorporated (Connecticut)

Instructions for the 1927 audit were issued by Coster under date of November 28, 1927. The auditors were requested to pursue the same procedure as in the past, to supply 10 signed copies of the report, 10 copies of signed certified balance sheets, and under separate cover for his personal information certain schedules of expenses in connection with the merger and moving and so forth. The letter requested that the report be ready as soon after January 10 as possible as plans were under consideration for the absorption of other companies about the middle of January. A perfunctory acknowledgment to the effect that these instructions would receive attention in due course completed the formal arrangements. It may be noted that the resulting report is dated January 31, 1928.[521]

---

[518] Ex. 116. Letter of October 30, 1926.

[519] Ex. 116.

[520] R. 60–65.

[521] Ex. 146.

(4) McKesson & Robbins, Incorporated (Maryland) and Subsidiaries

The year 1928 saw the formation of McKesson & Robbins, Incorporated (Maryland) and opened with a request dated April 14, 1928 for balance sheet audits, similar to those conducted for McKesson & Robbins, of drug houses at 17 locations. These audits were to include the years 1925, 1926, and 1927 and the first 4 months of 1928 and special reports as required by the bankers in connection with their acquisition. Fixed assets were to be appraised by the American Appraisal Company and inventories were to be taken under the supervision of R. G. Rankin & Co. with responsibility for proper pricing on Price, Waterhouse & Co., but for quantities and quality on Rankin. Coster requested of Morland, manager in charge, that Jaureguy, Harvey, and McGloon be assigned to the work with a special request that McGloon be intrusted with the investigation of receivables of the retail druggists as he had done an especially good job during the preceding year in connection with the accounts of McKesson & Robbins, Incorporated (New York).[522]

This letter was acknowledged by Geoffrey G. Rowbotham, a partner of the firm, who about this time had made a specialty of refinancing work. This special work on McKesson was assigned to him and led to his permanent assignment on all of their work. The acknowledgment was longer than those of other years which we have noted in that it recognized the various points made in Coster's letter and in addition suggested that the management of the various companies to be examined be instructed to prepare aging schedules of accounts, notes, and acceptances receivable in accordance with a classification indicated. This suggestion was accepted by Coster in an acknowledgment which contained instructions to be prepared to make a similar audit of a number of additional companies on the same basis. This letter also asked Price, Waterhouse & Co. to disregard the work that R. G. Rankin & Co. and McKesson's own staff would do on inventories and to get the customary certificates from the managements of the several wholesale houses covering the correctness of their inventories. Beyond this no specific instructions were given to Price, Waterhouse & Co. on this subject.[523] Concurrent with these audits of wholesale houses destined to become parts of the McKesson organization, Price, Waterhouse & Co. also made an examination of the Connecticut Company which "* * * consisted principally of a verification of the assets and liabilities of the company as at April 30, 1928 and of a general review of the profit and loss account for the four months ending April 30, 1928. * * *"[523a]

[522] Ex. 116.

[523] Ex. 116. Letter of April 27, 1928.

[523a] Ex. 147.

In May 1928, J. H. McGloon resigned from Price, Waterhouse & Co. to become comptroller of McKesson. Instructions for the regular annual audit for 1928 were sent to Price, Waterhouse & Co. over McGloon's signature as comptroller. The examination for this year was to be along the lines of a balance sheet audit with the following reports:

"(1) Report and accounts for each Company.
(2) Certified balance sheet and profit and loss for each Company.
(3) Consolidated certified balance sheet and profit and loss statement.
(4) Consolidated Federal Income Tax Return." [524]

The letter listed 16 subsidiaries of the Maryland Company and a supplementary letter listed McKesson & Robbins, Incorporated, of Connecticut, and McKesson & Robbins, Limited, of Canada. Neither letter nor Rowbotham's acceptance of the work for Price, Waterhouse & Co. mentioned any details of the auditing work other than the general requirements above.

McGloon's letter of the following year was in much the same form but reduced the requirements to "a. Reports and Accounts; b. Certified Balance Sheet" with instructions "* * * that the Balance Sheet and the Profit and Loss Statement be prepared in accordance with our usual forms, copies of which will be mailed to you within the next few days." [525]

The Price, Waterhouse & Co. acceptance this year dated December 19, 1929 (the file copy is initialed by Rowbotham and Jaureguy) closed with a paragraph explaining that the examination would be along the lines of a balance sheet audit and would not include a detailed check of all transactions for the year.[526] The engagement for the following year consisted of a written acceptance of oral instructions, the acceptance opening with a new wording of the preceding year's description of the scope of the work stating that the detailed checking would not be "* * * such as might disclose a misappropriation of funds or manipulation of the accounts." [527] For 1931 the letter of acceptance followed a conversation covering the work to be done and was couched in language similar to the preceding year with the addition of two

---

[524] Ex. 116. Letter of November 3, 1928.

[525] Ex. 116. Letter dated December 14, 1929.

[526] "In accordance with your instructions our examinations will be made along the lines of balance sheet audits and, in that connection, you will of course understand that we will not attempt to check all the cash and other detailed transactions during the year under review but that our work will be restricted principally to the verification of the assets and liabilities as at December 31, 1929 and to incidental tests. As requested, we will prepare reports and accounts and certified accounts and will submit either two or three copies of each to Mr. Coster and one copy to the presidents of the respective subsidiary companies." Ex. 116. Letter dated December 19, 1929.

[527] "We thank you for your oral instructions to audit the books and accounts of McKesson & Robbins, Incorporated (Maryland) and subsidiary companies for the year ending December 31, 1930. We confirm our understanding that our audits are to be conducted, as heretofore, along the lines of our usual balance sheet or financial audit which would consist of a verification of the assets and liabilities as at December 31, 1930 and a general review of the profit and loss accounts for the year ending on that date, but would not include a detailed check of the cash and other bookkeeping transactions such as might disclose a misappropriation of funds or manipulation of the accounts." Ex. 116. Letter dated September 9, 1930.

significant sentences. This is the first year that the letter accepting the engagement stated that "As requested, our audits will not include an examination of bank deposit slips or any circularization of receivables." It also stated that separate certified accounts would not be furnished for "* * * the very small subsidiary companies which maintain an inadequate system of internal accounting check * * *."[528]

The next year similar references to deposit slips and circularization of receivables were retained in the letter. No mention was made, however, as to supplying certified accounts on the subsidiaries. In compliance with an oral request two copies of the Price, Waterhouse & Co.'s mimeographed memorandum of instructions prepared for the guidance of their representatives in connection with the examination of the McKesson subsidiaries [529] were enclosed with the letter.

Subsequent letters accepting the work through the 1937 audit were substantially the same, varying slightly in the description of the engagement.[530] The statement respecting examination of bank deposit slips and the circularization of receivables referred to above was retained. From 1934 on the circularization of payables was also included in the statement of work not to be done. The letter of December 5, 1934 closed with the reminder that the regulations of the Securities and Exchange Commission must be observed by the Company in preparing the accounts.[531] The former policy of furnishing separate certified reports on the subsidiaries was changed to one of supplying unsigned statements with a covering letter including comments on the audits and calling attention to deficiencies in internal check and control. The policy of supplying copies of the instructions was continued and was accompanied by conferences between Ralph E. Thorn, manager in charge of the work for Price, Waterhouse & Co. and McGloon, McKesson's comptroller, in order to coordinate the Company's closing instructions to the divisions and the Price, Waterhouse & Co. instructions to their representatives.

---

528 Ex. 116. Letter dated October 14, 1931.

529 The character of these instructions are explained at pages 165–166 *infra*.

530 E. g. "In accordance with your instructions, our work will be conducted, as heretofore, along the lines of a financial or balance sheet examination consisting of an examination of the balance sheets of McKesson & Robbins, Incorporated and its subsidiary companies as at December 31, 1937 and a general review of the profit and loss accounts for the year ending on that date, but will not include a detailed check of the cash and other bookkeeping transactions such as might disclose a misappropriation of funds or manipulation of the accounts, should any exist. It is our understanding that the examination will not include an inspection of bank deposit slips or any circularization of debtors or creditors in verification of receivables and payables." Ex. 116. Letter dated December 17, 1937. See also Ex. 100.

531 "As you know, the accounts of your company as at December 31, 1934 will have to be presented in accordance with the accounting regulations of the new Securities and Exchange Commission. These regulations have not yet been issued, but we do not anticipate that they will require any substantial changes in the scope of the examinations of your companies. It is, however, we think, fairly certain that the responsibilities which the Act and Regulations will place on directors and officers will be considerable and we believe that it would be inadvisable for you to issue your accounts without thorough consideration on your part and, possibly, after consultation with your counsel. It seems to us, therefore, that it will not be feasible to issue your accounts so promptly as you have done in past years and we suggest this to your consideration." Ex. 116.

b. AUDIT REPORTS

As previously stated the first warning, in a letter of acceptance of the work, as to the limitations of a balance sheet audit in respect to manipulation of the accounts and disclosure of defalcations was incorporated after the expansion of the organization in 1928 and 1929 when part of the records were kept at points away from the head office. With the recurring appointment of the auditors, however, it seems proper to consider the paragraph in each audit report [532] in respect to the scope of the audit as part of these annual renewals of the contract. A reference to scope appeared in the first report on Girard & Co., Inc. for the 9 months ended December 31, 1924 in the following language:

"Our examination was conducted along the lines of a balance sheet audit and was directed primarily to the verification of the financial position of the company as of December 31, 1924 and the results from operations for the nine months ending that date. It will therefore be understood that we have not attempted to check all the cash transactions during the period under review but have limited our examination in this respect to tests of periods selected at random and we are pleased to report that, so far as our examination extended, the accounts were found in order." [533]

This paragraph was used without important variation in the reports on Girard & Co., Inc., the Canadian Company, and on the Connecticut Company after the first quarter of 1927. A corresponding paragraph in the first (1929) and all subsequent reports on the Maryland Company and subsidiaries consolidated omitted the reference to the condition of the accounts.[534] In the report on the 1930 accounts of the Maryland Company the phrase "* * * nor did we circularize the debtors in verification of the receivables" appeared for the first time [535] and continued without other change until the report for 1934 when the language of the American Institute of Accountant's form of certificate, adopted after conferences with the New York Stock Exchange—

"In connection with our examinations, we examined or tested accounting records of the companies and other supporting evidence and obtained information and explanations from officers and employees of the companies; we also made a general review of the accounting methods and of the operating and income accounts for the year, but we did not make a detailed audit of the transactions * * *"

was used with the addition of the phrase "* * * nor did we circularize the debtors in verification of receivables." [536] This was expanded slightly in the 1935 report to cover the non-circularization

[532] The report referred to here is Price, Waterhouse & Co.'s report addressed to F. D. Coster and is to be distinguished from the certificate published in the Company's report to stockholders and from the annual reports filed with the Securities and Exchange Commission. See pages 344 ff. *infra*.

[533] Ex. 138.

[534] Ex. 139, 140, 141, 142, 143, 146, 147, 148, 149, 150, 151, 152.

[535] Ex. 153.

[536] Ex. 157.

of creditors in verification of payables.[537] This last form also was used for 1936 and 1937.[538]

c. GENERAL

It seems to have been understood from the beginning that the auditors would not make physical tests of inventories or supervise their taking, but would secure certificates from management as to quality, quantity, and condition. This fact was not mentioned in any of the letters of engagement except in the references to the work of R. G. Rankin & Co. in connection with the mergers.[539] The reports and the published balance sheets, however, contain statements to the effect that inventories were "* * * certified by responsible officials" [540] and the last letter enclosing the accounts of the Canadian Company stated "* * * The merchandise carried in the inventories of McKesson & Robbins, Limited at December 31, 1937 was confirmed to us by the vendors who held this merchandise at that date, but we have not attempted to otherwise verify the amount of merchandise so held." [541]

The statement that original bank deposit slips were not examined appeared in the letters of engagement for the 1931 audit and thereafter. Jaureguy had taken up the question with Coster during the 1930 engagement suggesting to him the desirability of making this test but after a few days consideration by the client, Price, Waterhouse & Co. were instructed not to do this.[542] Jaureguy's draft of the first report on the Maryland Company made no reference to the condition of the accounts, and in subsequent reports the statement that receivables had not been verified by circularization of debtors was included. That this was in recognition of the unsatisfactory conditions existing in the subsidiary companies of the organization[543] and consequently the increased difficulties encountered in making a satisfactory audit seems to be indicated by a letter written by him for transmission to Coster. Two paragraphs of this letter warrant quoting below in support of this observation.[544] And finally soon after the merger of

---

[537] Ex. 158.

[538] Ex. 159, 160.

[539] Footnote 518 *supra*.

[540] E. g. Ex. 128, 106.

[541] Ex. 100.

[542] Ex. 83.

[543] Representatives of Price, Waterhouse & Co. testified that all of their comments in this connection applied only to the wholesale houses and not to the Bridgeport companies.

[544] "In submitting the December 31, 1932 financial statements which we have sent you to date, we have called your attention, in the case of a number of companies, to the fact that there is not an adequate system of internal check to protect them against irregularities and misappropriations of funds. We believe that this condition exists in a majority of the subsidiary companies. It occurs to us, however, that since we have advised you in considerable detail in previous years regarding the situation in the various houses, you may perhaps consider it unnecessary for us to write you again this year regarding each individual company whose system of internal check is inadequate. Unless you advise us that you wish to have us report to you again

Girard & Co., Inc. and McKesson & Robbins, Incorporated of New York and McGloon's appointment as the first comptroller of the Company there was an increasing amount of pressure brought to bear on the auditors to reduce work and an attempt to exercise some influence over the kind of work to be done as evidenced by Coster's request for copies of Price, Waterhouse & Co.'s instructions to their representatives.[545]

The term "balance sheet audit" was used repeatedly in the correspondence and reports in defining the character of work to be done on this engagement. We have noted that Hartzell was introduced to Girard & Co., Inc. as the person who would "proceed with the audit" of the Company. The work was referred to as an "audit" in all of the letters accepting the engagement until that covering the work as of April 30, 1928 when the phrase "examination of the accounts" was used for the first time. The terms "audit" and "examination" were used indiscriminately thereafter with the McKesson letters requesting an "audit of our books and accounts" and Price, Waterhouse & Co. letters stating that "our examinations" would be "on the basis of balance sheet audits" and since 1932 "along the lines of a balance sheet examination," although even in these letters reference was made to the "audited" accounts or statements of minor subsidiaries and branches prepared by other accountants. The last letter of acceptance, December 17, 1937, was the only one to avoid the term "audit" entirely.[546] Somewhat similarly in the letters covering the audit for the year 1931 and prior thereto reference was made to a "verification of the assets and liabilities", for 1932 to an "examination of the assets and liabilities" and for 1933 and thereafter to an "examination of the balance sheet."

"Q. [By Mr. GALPEER.] And therefore you would say that the actual work you did at first in Bridgeport, and in later years was the same, and it was merely a change in description?

A. [By ROWBOTHAM.] I would say it was merely a change in description, that the work we have done on this has been the same from beginning to end." [547]

We have referred to the series of bulletins prepared by the American Institute of Accountants and Price, Waterhouse & Co.'s participation in their preparation. Although the last two of the series refer in their titles to "verification" and "examination" of financial statements, both use the term "audit" and "auditors" as well as "verification" and "examination." The predecessor of the latest of these bulletins

---

this year regarding the individual houses which do not maintain an adequate system of internal check, we shall accordingly not write you concerning them.

"While a great many of the houses do not have a satisfactory check on collections from cash sales and C. O. D. sales, and this is one of the principal weaknesses among the subsidiary companies, there is also the possibility of misappropriation of funds through manipulation of the customers' accounts, which is serious, and we believe that you should give careful consideration to the advisability of having a surprise circularization some time in the future of the larger balances carried in the notes and accounts receivable." Ex. 88.

[545] See pages 167 ff. *infra*.

[546] Ex. 116.

[547] R. 1750. See also R. 1747–1751 and footnote 1293 *infra*.

was recommended reading for the Price, Waterhouse & Co. staff and we shall see that the firm also referred their clients to it as a source of information as to the work of public accountants.[548] Rowbotham was questioned as to the extent to which these bulletins were followed in his practice. He stated that the latest bulletin applied to small and moderate-sized companies but agreed that insofar as it was applicable his firm "* * * would follow something generally along those lines."[549] He felt that section three "Modifications of Program for Larger or Smaller Companies" was so general in nature that it would not be very helpful on a large job. Nevertheless this bulletin was given to all staff members as a general guide.[550]

However, as applied to McKesson, the size of the engagement insofar as the detailed work of the audit was concerned was dictated by the size of the individual branches which were treated as separate engagements until the consolidating stage was reached.[551] Another major difference between the affiliated group and separate corporations was in the degree of head office control. Rowbotham felt that Coster exercised some control over the branches but the audit was not relaxed at any point because of this.[552] After some discussion similar to that quoted below, the following question and answer were recorded:

---

[548] Footnote 590, *infra.*

[549] R. 1766–1771.

[550] "Q. [By Mr. STEWART.] At pages 1904 and 1905, Mr. Galpeer asked you some questions about the office manual which has been introduced into evidence as Exhibit 121, and he followed that by asking: 'Is there any other booklet which more particularly describes the work on an actual job,' to which you answered: 'Why, that would be done, I think, from the working papers.' Now, did you mean by that, that there is no other booklet published by Price, Waterhouse & Co., or that there is no other booklet?

A. [By ROWBOTHAM.] Well, I don't understand what the answer in the record means, but there is no other booklet published by Price, Waterhouse & Co. beyond this blue booklet, whatever it is.

Q. Office manual?

A. Office manual, but we do, of course, hand out this pamphlet, 'Examination of Financial Statements' to our men and we do expect them to thoroughly master it and follow it in their general work.

Q. That is the pamphlet published by the American Institute of Accountants of which the most recent edition has been marked Exhibit 117. And would you say that that booklet is constantly used as a general guide book by Price, Waterhouse men conducting examinations?

A. Yes, undoubtedly." R. 2049–2050.

Cf. Ex. 118 in which Rowbotham on April 11, 1933 in a Price, Waterhouse & Co. letter to Coster said, "Our examination of your accounts for the year 1932 was, in our judgment as extensive as that contemplated in the bulletin, 'Verification of Financial Statements', issued by the Federal Reserve Board." See also footnote 590 and page 350 *infra.*

[551] See section III, A *supra* for a description of the McKesson organization and section IV, M *infra* for a discussion of the fee.

[552] "Q. [By Mr. GALPEER.] That is what I am trying to get at. Actually in the McKesson case, what sort of a control was there? I mean, wherein would that control make your work less arduous or less detailed, let us say, in the branch.

A. [By ROWBOTHAM.] The control that came in here, as I saw it, I cannot tell you so much about accounting, but as I saw it, Coster was continually on the necks of these divisional vice presidents trying to get their accounts in order, trying to get their receivables in order the whole way down the line and that seemed to me at the time to exercise a very salutary influence on those divisional vice presidents and on their accounting. Now, in an individual company, had the company been a—wait a minute—in the case of a separate company, they would not have that control and check from some, shall we say, outside source; it is not an outside source but some other source.

Q. Now, this influence of Mr. Coster, if we can call it that, referring to what you are speaking of, while that might have been salutary in your opinion, do you think that it was of such a nature that you could have legitimately relied thereon to do less detailed audit work in a branch than if that influence was not exerted?

A. No, I think we did quite as much detailed audit work in the branch. As I tried to express it on Friday, I am sorry that it is repetition, but cash is cash, and you verify cash in the branch as you would in an indi-

"Q. [By Mr. GALPEER.] In view of that, Mr. Rowbotham, wouldn't you say that except for the consolidating work that the actual auditing work on each of these branch houses would be the audit of a small or medium sized corporation as referred to in the bulletin.

A. I would say probably yes sir. It is very hard for me to divorce my mind from the fact that a branch; I think the answer is yes."[553]

Although the expression "these branch houses" used in this quotation refers to wholesale houses specifically, we will see later that the general audit program was uniform for all divisions of the company. As we have shown earlier in this report the records audited at Bridgeport included those of the home office (the Maryland Company) and likewise those of the Canadian Company and the Connecticut Division (prior to 1934 a separate subsidiary corporation). The Connecticut Division was the largest subsidiary unit of the Maryland Company and included in its books the records covering manufacturing of drugs for the wholesale houses and the resale operations in crude drugs. Rowbotham's testimony as a whole indicates that the American Institute of Accountants' Bulletin is a fair guide to the procedures followed in examining the books of all of the divisions.[554] Detailed comparison of procedures recommended in the Bulletin and procedures actually followed by Price, Waterhouse & Co. will be made hereinafter.[555]

3. Assignments of Price, Waterhouse & Co. Staff to the Engagement

The quality of the work done on an audit is governed necessarily by the ability of those assigned to the task. Therefore, before taking up a detailed study of the audit program and of the manner in which it was carried out by those assigned to the job, it seems appropriate to consider briefly the type of men employed, their training prior to the engagement, and the manner in which the firm of Price, Waterhouse & Co. made assignments to the work. The engagement falls naturally into two periods. Prior to the early part of 1928, when the audit was confined to a small business operating primarily at one location, the work required the services of only a small staff of auditors. With the formation of the Maryland Company and the acquisition of wholesale houses throughout the United States, the engagement required the attention of most, and at times, all of the branch offices of Price, Waterhouse & Co. For the purposes of this inquiry we limit our

---

vidual company, but you do have a feeling, undoubtedly, that in a branch there are other checks than the one you are making yourself. In this case, I do not think we relaxed in our work anywhere along the line

* * * * * * *

Q. Now, I meant actually as you went into your audit work of a branch, you would audit that branch as if it stood on its own feet.

A. I don't think, sir, we made any change in our audit from the time those branches were separate corporations up to 1934, I think the date was, and then they merged and became branches and I do not think we relaxed our work in any way, because they ceased to be corporations and became branches." R. 1836-1838.

[553] R. 1839-1840.

[554] R. 1834-1840.

[555] Subsections C. ff. *infra.*

appraisal of the auditors' staff to the men assigned to the work at Mt. Vernon and Bridgeport, and to the control of the engagement by the New York office of the auditors.

C. R. Hartzell was the first man assigned to the work.[556] He enjoyed senior status with Price, Waterhouse & Co., having been in their employ since January 19, 1920. His experience prior to that time consisted of 2 years in business college and 1 year of university work coupled with 2 years in the army, 6 months with Standard Oil Co. and another half year of sundry business experience. He passed the New York State C. P. A. examinations several years after leaving Price, Waterhouse & Co. Hartzell did this first work for 1924 under the nominal supervision of J. C. Scobie, a partner, who charged 1 hour to the job and E. Christensen, manager, who charged 4 hours to the audit and 3½ hours to supervision of the other work done during the spring of 1925 as requested in Coster's letters. The assignment was practically a one-man job for the senior's time was 126 hours and the time of two juniors totaled 23 hours. The other work mentioned occupied Hartzell's time for 58 hours and led to his resignation from Price, Waterhouse & Co. to become the accountant for Girard & Co., Inc. His subsequent treatment is told in Coster's own words in his report to the stockholders and directors of Girard & Co., Inc. for 1925 in which he set forth certain expenses of 1925 which he anticipated would not recur in 1926.[557]

The work on the 1925 audit was performed under the direction of D. F. Morland, a manager who remained in a supervisory capacity for all of the audits of Girard & Co., Inc. and for the audits of McKesson & Robbins, Incorporated (Connecticut) through 1927 and who with one exception drafted all of the reports during this period. Morland had attended London University, is a chartered accountant (England) and had had 4 years of varied public accounting experience prior to January 8, 1913, when he joined Price, Waterhouse & Co., by whom he is still employed as a manager.[558] Partners Scobie, J. H. Bowman, and Rowbotham were in charge over Morland during his connection with the work. Partner's time chargeable to the work during this period was: 1 hour for 1925 (Scobie); ½ hour for first quarter 1926 (Bowman); 5 hours for second quarter 1926 (Rowbotham-McGloon drafted the report); 1 hour for third quarter 1926 (Scobie); 2 hours for October and

---

556 Page 148 *supra*.

557 "$2991.62 Represents officers salary paid to C. R. Hartzell. Mr. Hartzell was taken on from Price, Waterhouse & Co. at a salary of $6,000 per year believing that he would actually work himself and be useful in installing cost systems and generally improve our bookkeeping. Instead it worked out that he surrounded himself with an elaborate staff and his work became more of a supervising and consulting nature. After consultation with the partners of Price, Waterhouse & Co. an able local bookkeeper that was an assistant to Mr. Hartzell was placed in charge at a salary of $2400 a year, the staff cut down and the consulting and supervision placed in the hands of Price, Waterhouse & Co. at not over $1,000 per year. This change means a saving of at least $4,000 per year and more and this department is geared to handle three times over present volume if necessary." Ex. 176 (p. 5).

558 Ex. 212.

November 1926, the merger period, (Scobie); 14½ hours for 1927, McKesson & Robbins, Incorporated (Connecticut), (Bowman).

The field work of the audit for 1925 was done by Morland with the assistance of a man classed as a junior and in the employ of the firm only on a temporary basis during that season and the preceding season (resigned end of second season). This junior had had over 11 years' experience as an internal bank auditor and clerk prior to this time. Morland spent 29 hours and his assistant 102 hours on the work.

We have referred to McGloon who served under Morland during 1926 and made a favorable impression on Coster. McGloon himself did practically all of the field work of the first quarter and about half of the chargeable time applicable to the next two quarters when he had the assistance of juniors for a substantial part of the work. McGloon had a high school education supplemented by a course at New York University (the record does not indicate that any degree was received), and had worked a half year with another accounting firm and a year and three-quarters as clerk and bookkeeper with sundry concerns prior to joining Price, Waterhouse & Co. on February 2, 1920. He had not acquired a C. P. A. certificate before he left the firm in May of 1928 after nearly 8½ years with them. When McGloon was loaned to Coster for special work incidental to the merger at the close of 1926, Anthony Jaureguy [559] took over the work and continued as senior in charge through the 1927 audit.

The personnel on the engagement from its inception to the close of the work for 1926 may be summed up briefly. Other than partners, 18 names are associated with the work: Christensen, the first manager, is now a partner in the Chicago office; Morland, the second manager, is still a manager in New York. Of the seniors in charge, Hartzell and McGloon resigned to work for the client, Jaureguy became a manager, and in 1934 a partner in charge of the Boston office. Of the remainder of the group, four are still with the firm, seven resigned, and two were temporary employees, one during nine seasons.[560] The educational and experience level of the group was relatively high, four having college degrees and all having had some college work or accounting school courses. Seven had passed their C. P. A. examinations or were chartered accountants at the time they were associated with this engagement and four others passed C. P. A. examinations later. Hartzell and McGloon of this group seem to have had the weakest record of progressive educational and business experience prior to their engagement by Price, Waterhouse & Co.

---

[559] Partner in the Boston office, B. S. University of Oregon, 1915; 1 year accounting department, Western Electric Co.; 1¼ years U. S. Army; 2½ years High School instructor; M. B. A., Harvard Graduate School of Business Administration; employed by Price, Waterhouse & Co., October 3, 1921. Ex. 212.

[560] Ex. 212. Exhibit does not include information for men employed on audits of the Connecticut Company as at March 31, 1927, December 31, 1927 and April 30, 1928 being the period between the merger of Girard & Co., Inc. with McKesson & Robbins, Incorporated (New York) when the Connecticut Company was formed, and the formation of the Maryland Company. See pages 26 ff. *supra*.

The year 1928 was the turning point in McKesson & Robbins, Incorporated and likewise, on that account, in the character of Price, Waterhouse & Co.'s engagement to audit the books of the Company. With this year the engagement developed into an audit of wholesale houses under contract to join the expanding McKesson & Robbins organization and the regular annual engagement was broadened from a two-man audit at one location to a nationwide engagement requiring the services of nearly every office of the firm with the directing and consolidating work being done in New York under the supervision of Geoffrey G. Rowbotham [561] whose assignment to the work at this juncture we have noted.[562]

At the hearings Rowbotham explained the procedure for organizing a staff for a job of this magnitude. As in this case, where the client dealt with the New York office, a manager in that office directed the work. Below him managers in key positions throughout the country were assigned from branch offices of the firm. Each of these managers then organized a unit, consisting of a senior, possibly a manager on difficult work, and as many first and second assistants (semi-seniors and juniors) as were necessary to conduct the audit in the allotted time. In addition, the New York manager organized similar units for the divisions examined directly by the New York office.

To sum up, on the 1937 examination conducted by the Price, Waterhouse & Co. staff in the United States, 15 offices participated and in the respective offices there were employed from one to five managers for a total of 24 managers; from no seniors to eléven, totaling 48; and from one to 39 assistants, 145 in total; making a grand total engaged for that audit of 217 staff men in addition to the partner in charge. Of the total of 21,620 hours spent on the entire engagement, 86 represented partners' time, 1,769 managers', 3,714 seniors' and 16,051 assistants'.

We do not have the personnel records of each of the 217 staff men mentioned above and the many other engaged on all of the annual audits for the 10 years 1928 to 1937, inclusive, but an appraisal of the staff engaged on the work at Bridgeport where the fraudulent transactions were recorded may be of interest. Six or seven men were used each year, 37 different names appearing on the roster throughout the period. Of the 37 men in this group eight were, at the time of the hearings, still on the permanent staff and one was employed annually on a temporary basis. Two resigned after serving for some time on a permanent basis. Twenty-six were only employed for temporary periods during the peak seasons, seven resigning after

---

561 Rowbotham secured his training during 5 years' apprenticeship with chartered accountants in Glasgow, Scotland, passed the several examinations required and was elected a member of the Institute of Accountants and Actuaries in Glasgow. He came to the United States in 1908 and joined Price, Waterhouse & Co. as a junior and, after promotion through the ranks, was made a partner in 1926.

562 Page 150 *supra*.

such employment and the remaining nineteen being released although four of these had previously enjoyed continuous employment for several years.

Of the group of 37, 13 possessed college degrees (three held master's degrees). Of the rest, 13 had done some accredited college work, seven had attended business colleges or night school, three possessed only a high school education, and for one, Price, Waterhouse & Co.'s record in this regard was blank. Except for two college graduates (still on the staff), all of the 37 men had had some accounting or business experience, ranging from 5 months (in the case of another college graduate) to 23 years, prior to their employment by Price, Waterhouse & Co. Of the eight survivors on the permanent staff, four were from those holding college degrees, three had had some college work and one was from the high school group. All of these men who were retained on a permament basis passed C. P. A. examinations after joining the firm.

Of the group of 37 men employed on the engagement at Bridgeport under Rowbotham's direction for the annual examinations of 1928 through 1937, Jauregny served as manager for 5 years; Thorn served as a senior 4 years and as manager 5 years; and Ritts, who served as a semi-senior for his first 2 years, continued as senior in charge at Bridgeport the last 6 years. Three of the other five permanent staff men served on the McKesson work as juniors in the first year of their employment, one going back once after missing a year. The other two permanent men were seniors, each serving 1 year only at Bridgeport but several years at other locations. Of the remaining 29 men, 28 may be described as temporary juniors and one a permanent senior when they were assigned to Bridgeport for the first time. One was assigned 4 years, one 3 years, and two 2 years in succession as juniors, and one returned after an interval of a year as a senior assistant. Seventeen of the entire group of 37 were assigned to Bridgeport as juniors in the first or only year of their employment by Price, Waterhouse & Co.[563]

Of these 37 men who, from 1928 through 1937, at various times worked on the engagement at Bridgeport, there was one certified public accountant (Jauregny) and one chartered accountant (of Scotland) on the 1928 audit, and thereafter, except for the New York manager in charge of the entire engagement, no certified public accountants or chartered accountants were employed at Bridgeport until the audit for 1937 (the last) when Ritts had his certificate. In addition, it should be mentioned that Thorn, Ritts, and three others received their certificates after a particular year's engagement at Bridge-

[563] The educational and business records of six of the 37 men indicate that they came to the United States from Great Britain, Ireland, and Canada. Of these, two served one season; three several seasons on a term porary basis (two resigning); and the sixth, a chartered accountant of Scotland, resigned after 5 years.

port, based on examinations taken (each in a different year—1928, 1931, 1935, 1936, 1937) before such engagement. In only one case (1928), however, would it appear that the results of the examination were known at the time of the assignment to the engagement.[564]

With the exception of Thorn (junior 1 year), Jaureguy appears to be the only one of those employed prior to the 1928 audit who was included in the 37 men who carried on after that time. Jaureguy continued as manager through the 1932 audit after which he was transferred to Boston in anticipation of his promotion to partner.[565] Ralph E. Thorn was then made manager in charge of the work on the entire audit and Albert B. Ritts retained the senior assignment at the Bridgeport office of the client.

Prior to his employment by Price, Waterhouse & Co. on January 9, 1928, Thorn had had over 10 years experience in banking, broken by a period of 2¼ years in the army.[566] He worked through various positions in the Clarinda National Bank in Iowa, leaving that bank as assistant cashier to become cashier of the Commercial Savings Bank of Farragut, Iowa. This work in the country banks required him to supplement his high school education and 2 years at the University of Chicago with a LaSalle Correspondence Course in accounting and law so that he could advise depositors of the bank on accounting, income taxes, insurance and other matters.

When his health failed during this work, he was advised to leave banking. He moved to New York and took a position as auditor in the stock transfer department of the Bankers Trust Company. There he stayed for 2 years until he was successful in getting a position in public accounting, which had been his intention on moving to New York.[567]

Thorn's first experience in public accounting was as a junior in January 1928 under Jaureguy on the McKesson audit for 1927 at Bridgeport. During most of 1928 and a substantial part of 1929, he assisted Jaureguy in New York on the work in connection with the acquisition of the Group One and Group Two companies [568] which launched McKesson as a nationwide wholesale distributor of drugs. At the end of 1928, he made the examination of the Bronx Drug Company, one of the Group Two companies, and at the end of 1929 he examined subsidiary companies in New Haven, Conn. and Scranton, Pa. Early in 1930 after 2 years experience in public accounting a majority of which was gained on the McKesson work, he went to Bridgeport as the senior nominally in charge of the 1929 audit under Jaureguy. On the audits for 1930 and 1931, Thorn was in full charge

---

[564] Foregoing two paragraphs based on Ex. 212. Price, Waterhouse & Co.'s records also indicate that six (juniors) passed the examination after the elapse of various periods following their work at Bridgeport (two after leaving Price, Waterhouse & Co.) but do not indicate the subsequent history of the remaining 24.

[565] R. 2053.

[566] Ex. 212; R. 90–91.

[567] R. 857–861.

[568] See pages 33–34 *supra*.

at Bridgeport. On the examination for 1932, Thorn worked with Jauregny in New York, as it was known that Jauregny was to go to Boston and that Thorn, having impressed Rowbotham with his work, was to be in charge of the entire job throughout the country. Thorn thereupon was given a contract as manager at the end of 5½ years [569] with Price, Waterhouse & Co., as contrasted with the average of 9.4 years service of men appointed from 1930 to 1938, inclusive, and remained in charge of the McKesson work from 1933 on, in recent years devoting about half of his time to it. In addition to McKesson, Thorn had a varied experience as a senior and was regularly in charge, as manager, of examinations of a fertilizer company, a corset and box manufacturing company, an electrical specialty company, and banks.[570] He became a New York certified public accountant in the spring of 1932 after passing the examination given in the fall of 1931.[571]

Albert B. Ritts became a New York certified public accountant in the spring of 1937 after passing the examination given the preceding October. He started work for National Biscuit Company in Altoona, Pa. during summers while still in high school. From Altoona he was transferred to the Pittsburgh sales office of the company, where he was bookkeeper and then in charge of accounts. He left this company in August 1928, after 9½ years employment, to do accounting work on his own in Altoona. This he abandoned in December of that year when he went to New York and was employed by Price, Waterhouse & Co.[572]

Ritts had never taken a course of instruction in accounting or auditing until he joined Price, Waterhouse & Co., when he took the required staff training, which consisted of classes and required reading. When questioned by counsel for Price, Waterhouse & Co. as to his study of standard textbooks and authorities on audit procedure, Ritts testified:[573]

> "Q. [By Mr. Stewart.] And you have made studies of the books that would customarily be studied by anybody taking a regular accounting course in college?
>
> A. I think I have read and studied every recognized book on accounting and audit procedure, yes, sir."

Ritts' first contact with the McKesson work was as a semi-senior when he made an examination of the New Haven subsidiary for 1930 (2 years after he came with Price, Waterhouse & Co.) and then assisted Thorn in the work at the Bridgeport office. He was Thorn's first assistant on the work at Bridgeport for 1931 and took charge for 1932 when Thorn, preparatory to taking over the entire engagement

---

569 R. 2053-2054.
570 R. 891.
571 Ex. 212; R. 102.
572 Ex. 212; R. 828-829.
573 R. 851.

the following year, was kept in New York to assist in the consolidating work. Ritts continued in charge at Bridgeport through the 1937 audit and in recent years also assisted Thorn on the consolidating work in New York. On the 1937 work particularly he was not on duty at Bridgeport for the entire audit as George F. Wyman, who had had experience on audits for 1932 through 1936 at various branches of McKesson, had been assigned to Bridgeport that year as his understudy,[574] Ritts having been promoted to a manager's status.[575]

As he had for Thorn, Rowbotham, the partner in charge, also had a high regard for Ritts, an opinion which he stated he reached after a period of close association on a difficult consolidation assignment in Chile where Ritts was given one of three posts of considerable responsibility on one of the most troublesome points in the engagement.[576]

B. BEGINNING THE EXAMINATION

To carry out a balance sheet examination requires a mutual understanding between the client and the auditors of the scope of the work to be performed and a definite agreement as to the place and time of doing the work and the preparations that must be made by the client to insure that the books are ready so that no delays or needless work will fall on the auditors.

The first step in organizing an audit of this magnitude was for the manager in charge to arrange with the client for a uniform method of closing the books of all of the associated companies or divisions involved in the audit. In the interests of economy to the client, these plans included specifications for sundry schedules and analyses to be prepared by the client's clerical staff for the use of the auditors. Having made these arrangements with the client, the next step was to draft a uniform set of instructions for each examination which were sent to the cooperating managers in other offices. These general instructions were supplemented by each manager with an audit program going into considerable detail on the major points in the examination. The firm's "Office Manual" covers this point quite clearly under the caption "Responsibility for Work," at page 14:

"4. On all regular audits, programs should be made up and periodically revised, notations being made explaining any deviation therefrom.

"Programs in general are for guidance of seniors in charge of audits, and omission of work called for by a program (except on the approval of a partner) will be regarded as evidence of neglect on the part of the senior; omission from the program of work which should be done will not, however, be regarded as relieving the

[574] R. 306–308; footnote 690 *infra*.

[575] R. 105.

[576] "One of these was the man who is now the manager in our Valparaiso office. One of the others was Ritts. For weeks he worked in the next room to me, and I had a personal chance of seeing his work from personal and direct observation and I formed then a very high opinion of his ability, intelligence, and energy which I have not lost since." R. 2056.

senior of responsibility for the failure to perform such work. Seniors should bear in mind the importance of eliminating any unnecessary work and take up with a partner any requirements in a program which seem to them superfluous or ineffective." [577]

In carrying out the engagement in this case, the arrangements were worked out through McGloon, who became comptroller in 1928. One of his first duties was to secure some uniformity in accounting procedure in the branch houses. He issued accounting instructions in 1928 and a chart of accounts effective as of January 1, 1929.[578] In preparation for the annual audit, mimeographed instructions for closing the books were prepared by the company after consultation with the auditors as to their requirements. Price, Waterhouse & Co., in turn, prepared "Private and Confidential" instructions to their representatives in charge of the several audits, which for 1937 totaled 84 different examinations.[579]

The practice of regularly submitting to McKesson in advance of the audit, copies of Price, Waterhouse & Co.'s instructions to their representatives was started by the auditors with the preparations being made for the 1930 audit, and was continued to the end, the draft copy of instructions for the 1938 audit bearing a date of November 22, 1938, having been submitted to McGloon for review. These instructions opened with a brief statement as to the scope of the audit and a warning that "The extent of the work should be kept on a practical basis consistent with sound procedure for a balance sheet examination of a branch office." [580] There followed advice to study the client's closing instructions as they contained an outline of work to be done in anticipation of the audit such as detailed descriptions of schedules to be prepared in advance.

The next section listed statements and papers to be sent to the New York office and the character of the report to be made on the branch. One paragraph at this point warrants quotation in view of the stress to be laid on the subject later in this report:

"In view of the importance of the system of internal check, the questionnaire on this subject included in your working papers should be brought up to date and your memorandum to us should state your opinion of the effectiveness of the system and specify the particulars of any points of weakness." [581]

Succeeding paragraphs dealt with general procedures to be followed in respect to the various accounts and outlined in a broad way the amount of work to be done. In those cases in which arrangements with the client had resulted in an understanding that certain audit steps would not be used, these were called to the attention of the staff. Two items of this character appeared in appropriate places in the following lan-

---

577 Ex. 121.

578 R. 1736.

579 R. 92–96.

580 Identical in 1937 and 1938 instructions, Ex. 13, 92.

581 Ex. 13 (p. 3), 92 (p. 4).

guage: "At the request of the company, we have agreed not to ask the banks for copies of deposit tickets for deposits made near the end of the year", and "We have been requested by the company not to circularize customers for confirmations of the receivables, but you should obtain confirmations of the balances due from officers, directors and employees." [582]

The text of the instructions closed with this paragraph:

> "Everything possible, consistent with the scope of a branch examination, should be done to reduce to a minimum the time required for the work. As previously mentioned, the head office has instructed the branches to assist you in every way possible and you should avail yourself of their help in preparing schedules or with any other work that will save your time."

The McKesson & Robbins closing instructions for December 31, 1937, consisted of a mimeographed pamphlet of 68 pages, of which 24 pages were descriptive text of instructions and the remainder model forms of schedules and exhibits and lists which were to be prepared for the Bridgeport office and for the auditors. The text constituted a head office order to the branches to be ready for the auditors by not later than January 20, not to close the books until the auditors had finished their work, and to make sure that their figures were in agreement with those of the auditors before mailing them to Bridgeport.

The body of the instructions followed in general the same order as the Price, Waterhouse & Co. instructions to their representatives with a similar detailed treatment of the major balance sheet items. One of the most troublesome points, for example, was covered by seven pages of instructions for preparing trial balances of notes and accounts receivable and the analysis of these accounts and the treatment of related reserves.

One of McKesson's two concluding paragraphs may be compared with Price, Waterhouse & Co.'s concluding paragraph quoted above:

> "It is obviously to our own interest to cooperate with the auditors in every way possible in order to keep down the time spent on the audit to a minimum. Should you feel that your audit is not being conducted properly, please advise us so that we can discuss all such matters with the New York office of Price, Waterhouse & Co., for we are anxious to have the audits of all our houses conducted as efficiently as possible and with the minimum of friction. This request to be advised does not, of course, mean that you, yourself, should not, at the same time, endeavor to clear up any points of contention or complaints as to the conduct of the audit directly with the senior in charge." [583]

Whether because of, or in spite of, the fact that McGloon was a Price, Waterhouse & Co. man, the history of the engagement since he took office as comptroller of the client in 1928 was not one of complete harmony. Some of the early differences of opinion and the origin of the practice of consultation on, and exchange of, instructions are re-

---

[582] Ex. 13, 92.

[583] Ex. 15.

vealed, from McGloon's point of view, in a memorandum prepared in his office in anticipation of a conference with the auditors in regard to the 1930 audit. Reproduction of that document gives at least an indication of the atmosphere in which the audit was conducted from this period down through the last year.[584]

"MEMORANDUM OF POINTS TO BE DISCUSSED WITH MR. CAMPBELL AND MR. JAUREGUY IN CONNECTION WITH THE ANNUAL AUDIT OF DECEMBER 31, 1930.

"Heretofore we have been denied the privilege of reviewing instructions to representatives of Price, Waterhouse & Co. We did, however, examine the instructions covering the audit of December 31, 1929, but not until June 4th, 1930, the date Mr. Coster requested the information.

"The following items, in my opinion, should be discussed in detail with the partners of Price, Waterhouse & Co.

"1. Their remarks regarding the re-organization of wholesale houses. On Page 30 in their closing instructions, they mention the fact that our houses were incorporated under the State of Delaware and other States having lenient laws.

"2. In my opinion Price, Waterhouse should not convey to their assistants that we are likely to do a little 'window dressing' at December 31st of each year.

"3. Price, Waterhouse & Co. have warned their assistants to see to it that manipulations as between accounts and notes receivables are not resorted to in order to have old accounts appear to be of current dating. We should explain our views in detail to Price, Waterhouse & Co.

"LISTS OF NOTES RECEIVABLE

"A. If the date of the original transaction is not easily ascertained, Price, Waterhouse & Co. should not demand the information or spend time ascertaining the information.

"B. Price, Waterhouse & Co. should be instructed to accept our schedules on notes receivable.

"C. Trade Notes, Contract Notes, and Acceptances should be classified in the Balance Sheet as follows:

"Current Assets

"a. Trade notes falling due in 1931.

"b. Trade notes past due at December 31, 1930.

"c. Instalment notes falling due in Dec. 1931.

"d. Instalment notes past due at Dec. 31, 1930.

"e. Serial notes falling due in 1931.

"f. Serial notes past due at December 31, 1930.

"g. All other notes including past due time loans and demand loans which are likely to be paid prior to December 31, 1931.

---

[584] Ex. 111; R 1714–1727.

"The EXAMINER. Do you know whether or not it was prepared under your direction?

The WITNESS [MCGLOON]. If I didn't prepare it, it was prepared under my direction.

Mr. GALPEER. Well, Mr. Examiner, I would like to state now, perhaps we can end it this way, that this document is being offered with the entire understanding that this was an internal memorandum of McKesson's, there is no claim here that any facts appearing in this document were communicated to Price, Waterhouse & Co. It was merely offered for what it is, namely, an inter-office memorandum taken out of McKesson's files.

Mr. STEWART. On the understanding that it is not to be taken as an indication that any of the statements therein were communicated to Price, Waterhouse, or that Price, Waterhouse & Co. knew anything about the statements therein made, I have no objection to it." R. 1726–1727.

"Non-Current Assets

"a. Trade notes falling due subsequent to Dec. 31, 1931.

"b. Instalment notes falling due subsequent to December 31, 1931.

"c. Serial notes falling due subsequent to December 31, 1931.

"d. All other notes including time loans and demand loans which are not likely to be paid prior to December 31, 1931.

"e. Price, Waterhouse & Co. should be instructed not to age notes receivables.

"f. If we prepare detailed schedules of all notes receivable, Price, Waterhouse & Co. should not trace individual notes to both our schedules and the notes receivable ledger.

"ACCOUNTS RECEIVABLE

"A. Heretofore, Price, Waterhouse & Co. have prepared detail lists of accounts receivable showing the following information:

"1. Customer's name.

"2. Amount owing on the date of their examination.

"3. Balances classified under four general headings. Our executives are of the opinion that Price, Waterhouse & Co. should be satisfied with an adding-machine tape of all open accounts, together with a schedule of past due accounts.

"4. Past due accounts are to be aged and classified as follows:

"a. Amounts resulting from sales made during October and November 1930.

"b. Amounts resulting from sales made during July, August and September 1930.

"c. Amounts resulting from sales made prior to July 1, 1930.

"In addition, our accountants will furnish Price, Waterhouse & Co. with a summary sheet which will show one amount for sales made during December 1930 and sales made prior to that date if the amount is not due at December 31, 1930. This schedule will also show a total for columns a, b, and c mentioned above.

"Last year Price, Waterhouse & Co. devoted a great deal of unnecessary time summarizing amounts due from customers for sales made prior to December 31, 1929, the amount of which was not due at December 31, 1929.

"According to Price, Waterhouse & Co. closing instructions of December 31, 1929, we could not close our books and prepare our financial statements until we were advised what figure we should provide for doubtful accounts.

"We should either adopt Price, Waterhouse & Co.'s formula for providing reserves for doubtful account, or have them adopt our formula.

"Our formula calls for less detail work and we believe the final results are about the same.

"Our method of satisfying ourselves that the reserve for doubtful accounts is adequate is briefly outlined hereunder:

"1. All notes and accounts on which there is no hope of recovery should be written off to the reserve for doubtful accounts.

"2. Provide a reserve in whole or in part for the remaining notes and accounts.

"3. A sum added, equal to a blank percentage of the net sales for the four months ending December 31, 1930. This provision is for the portion of the receivables which, by reason of their recent dating, appear at the date of the audit to be good and collectible, but which will become uncollectible at a later date.

"4. Ascertain the amount of detail posting Price, Waterhouse & Co. intend to do December 31, 1930.

"5. Under ordinary circumstances, the reserve for cash discounts should not exceed the average monthly allowance. The practice of analyzing each customer's account in order to ascertain the amount of discount which will be taken, should be discontinued. The Chief Executive of each house will, at our request, furnish the representatives of Price, Waterhouse & Co. with a list of customers who are entitled to special discount rates.

"6. The reserve for allowances should be based upon the gross profit on the amount of merchandise returned. In a few instances we have been compelled to provide a reserve equal to an average month's charge for allowances.

"7. All open accounts should be classified under Current Assets, unless the item represents an advance of a more or less permanent nature which is not likely to be paid prior to December 31st.

"8. Amounts due from officers and employees for merchandise sales should be treated as 'Amounts Due from Customers.'

"INVENTORIES

"a. Price, Waterhouse & Co. should use standard price books in verifying prices. According to our accountants, Price, Waterhouse & Co. are required to spend hours tracing small items from such suppliers as Eli Lilly, Merck, McKesson & Robbins, Conn., etc.

"b. Arrange for outside machine operators to verify footings of inventory sheets.

"c. Owing to the fact that Price, Waterhouse & Co.'s closing instructions refer to the matter of slow-moving and obsolete merchandise, their representatives are likely to spend a great deal of time on this phase of work unless we work out a satisfactory arrangement with Mr. Campbell.

"d. Intercompany profits on merchandise will, as heretofore, be eliminated from the records in the Bridgeport office. It should be understood, however, that we will not be required to eliminate intercompany profit on the sale of general and bulk items sold thru the Maryland Company on which there is a small profit.

"e. Price, Waterhouse & Co. should not attempt to verify quantities of merchandise listed in the physical inventory.

"f. Price, Waterhouse & Co. should not attempt to ascertain the amount of rebates due each subsidiary. This information will be handled in Bridgeport.

"FIXED ASSETS

"1. Price, Waterhouse & Co. have gone on record that all additions to fixed property in excess of $50.00 are to be vouched. If practical, the amount should be changed to $100.00.

"2. During the year 1930 our houses did not follow a standard method of adjusting depreciation on fixed assets. In the majority of the cases, the provision for depreciation was based upon the balance in the property account at the close of business each month, but several of our houses followed the practice of adjusting depreciation at the end of each three months and others at the end of each six months. Price, Waterhouse & Co. should accept the method used in each house.

"ACCOUNTS PAYABLE

"1. Price, Waterhouse & Co. should agree to accept an adding machine tape for the open items at December 31, 1930. Heretofore, we have been compelled to furnish them with a detailed list of the items which were open, showing the names and amounts due.

"INTERCOMPANY ACCOUNTS

"1. Price, Waterhouse & Co. should be asked to confirm intercompany balances by correspondence. Telegrams and telephone calls are too expensive and should not be restored to except in emergency cases.

"GENERAL NOTES

"1. Ascertain how many nominal accounts Price, Waterhouse & Co. intend to analyze.

"2. Price, Waterhouse & Co. should be asked to use our classification for nominal accounts or inform us where our Chart of Accounts are wrong.

"3. The method of handling the following accounts should be discussed with Mr. Campbell:

"a. Cash discounts allowed customers

"b. Provision for doubtful accounts

"4. According to our accountants, Price, Waterhouse & Co. frequently send Junior accountants on the job who are not qualified to conduct an audit and in the opinion of our men, a great deal of time is wasted by the Junior accountants until the Senior accountant arrives. Our accountants have also notified us that in many cases the Senior Accountant is dissatisfied with the schedules prepared by the Junior accountant and it is necessary for the Senior to verify the account for the second time.

"5. In several instances according to our own accountants, Price, Waterhouse & Co.'s, representatives have had many important and elaborate schedules prepared for them but have refused to use the schedules as part of their working papers. In other words, they have prepared their own schedules. According to our Chief Executives and Accountants, Price, Waterhouse & Co. are in the habit of adjusting our books and accounts without discussing the items with our Manager.

"6. Our accountants have been instructed not to release their December financial reports until after Price, Waterhouse & Co. have completed their examination and all adjustments taken up on the books. This practice was followed last year except in a few cases where Price, Waterhouse & Co. made adjustments without discussing the item with our accountant. Last year it was also noted that several adjustments effective the net profits were adjusted by the partners and no notice was given to our executives and accountants.

"7. Instructions should be issued to Price, Waterhouse & Co. that they are not to verify the collections of guaranteed receivables.

"8. Price, Waterhouse & Co. have agreed to employ outside auditors to audit the books of the following companies:

"McKesson-Kelly & Pollard Co.

"McKesson-Midwest Drug Co.

"Arrangements should be made to have outside auditors verify the records of McKesson-Langley-Michaels Co. Ltd. Honolulu. Discuss with Mr. Campbell accounts of Doster-Northington and secure their permission to re-value the accounts as of the date of acquisition and charge all adjustments to 'Paid-in-Surplus.'

"9. Unless special arrangements are made with regard to the treatment of laboratory equipment of our wholesale houses, Price, Waterhouse & Co. will insist upon adjusting the accounts to give effect to the loss on machinery which is no longer actively engaged in the manufacturing of merchandise.

"10. Inasmuch as Price, Waterhouse & Co. are not to furnish us with a report or prepare the Federal Tax Return, they should refer to these points in their closing instructions and inform their own auditors that the work should be governed accordingly. If the assistants on the job will follow this suggestion it will be possible for them to eliminate several unimportant schedules.

"11. The Federal Income Tax Return is to be prepared in the Bridgeport office but we will be greatly indebted to Price, Waterhouse & Co. if they will request their branches to forward the working papers on each audit to the New York office where they can be held after we complete the consolidated Federal Tax Return.

"12. Price, Waterhouse & Co. should be requested to accept the audit with the view of reducing the fee 50% or more. 10/27/30"

McGloon was questioned at some length about this memorandum. He explained that it was prepared as a guide for a conference in which the parties were to try to get together and reach a clear understanding as to the work to be performed and what the client could do to expedite it and thus reduce the expense.[585] His memory was inadequate to the task of recalling the results of the conference or the significance of many of the points in the memorandum. He was quite clear on the point of manipulation of notes and accounts receivable, however, for he explained that he was trying to convince the auditors that it was not necessary to know the date of the original transaction with the customer where a note had taken the place of an account. His memory was fresh on this point because the auditors insisted upon getting the information and as late as the 1937 audit the client had prepared it as regular routine preliminary to the audit.

Other conferences resulted in an agreement as to the method of checking prices on inventory items purchased from certain suppliers with price lists rather than by the laborious process of tracing many small items to invoices.[586]

Much of the friction on the work developed in the wholesale houses which were in many cases being subjected to an audit for the first time. McKesson files examined in the preparation of this case revealed a number of letters from heads of the various branch houses complaining about the methods employed by the auditors and the time consumed in various phases of the work. For example, the San Francisco branch wrote a memorandum following the 1932 audit. The gist of this was that the auditors' instructions to their representatives were not specific enough. Too much latitude as to the checking on inventory work was left to the senior on the job. This memorandum also suggested that expense could be reduced by employing a calculating agency to check all inventory computations.[587] A similar complaint was registered with McGloon by G. V. Doerr, executive vice president, in respect to audits of the Akron and Cleveland units, where he felt that excessive checking was done on inventories. Price, Waterhouse & Co.'s reply to McGloon indicated that Doerr was not accurately informed as to what was done on the audit and gave an analysis of the time in support of their opinion.[588]

585 R. 1722.
586 R. 1733.
587 Ex. 112.
588 Ex. 186, 187.

These criticisms resulting in pressure on McGloon, which he in turn passed on to the auditors, seem, in these cases and in others we will cite elsewhere, to be based partly upon a hardheaded business-man's desire to keep down the cost and partly upon an inadequate knowledge of necessary auditing procedure, extending even to McGloon on some points, although he had had over 8 years experience in public accounting work with Price, Waterhouse & Co.[589] However, the arrangement for the audit was renewed each year even though the fee was not reduced 50% in 1930, the goal set in the memorandum quoted above.[590] The policy of year-end discussions and exchange of closing and audit instructions established in that year may have aided in removing, to some extent at least, the conception that too much work or unnecessary work was being done. The propriety of giving the client a copy of the audit instructions was discussed at some length throughout the testimony in the hearings as it appeared at least possible that Coster's interest in the instructions may have been due to ulterior motives. Whether or not this was so, it seems that some

---

[589] R. 1583-1586.

"Q. [By Mr. GALPEER.] Mr. McGloon, would you say that it was your effort to keep these fees at a minimum?

A. Yes.

Q. Would you say, Mr. McGloon, that your familiarity with the procedure followed by Price, Waterhouse & Company gained while you were employed by them, aided you in this undertaking, in other words, of knowing whether the auditors were doing more than necessary or less than necessary?

A. No, I don't think so.

Q. Well, in the various discussions that came up, would you judge what they did by what you thought necessary, gained from the experience while you were employed by them?

A. No, when I discussed the point with Price, Waterhouse & Company I tried to find a yardstick so that we could measure the fee of one house against the other, and I remember one year preparing a schedule to show the total assets involved, broken down to show cash and receivables and inventory, and I listed the figures according to size and then I compared the fee and that was the only yardstick that I ever used in discussing reduction of fee with Price, Waterhouse & Company.

Q. Did you follow the type of work they did each year based upon your experience?

A. No, I didn't follow what they did except through these closing instructions we would check with Price, Waterhouse & Company before they were engaged or immediately after they were engaged and we would see what schedules we could prepare for them but I never made any attempt at any time to find out what they were doing on their assignment.

Q. Who would you say exerted the pressure so far as McKesson & Robbins was concerned as to keeping these fees down to a minimum, who was interested in that, who took an active part?

A. I think it can be said that all the members of the operating committee of McKesson & Robbins including myself." R. 1585-1586.

[590] A letter from Jaureguy of the New York office to the Seattle office followed a criticism from that source and indicates one method of dealing with the problem:

"While we feel that on the whole your recent examinations were probably conducted intelligently and without waste of time, and this letter is not intended as a criticism of your work, we feel that, coming through Mr. Coster, Mr. Ballinger's latest complaints are of sufficient importance to warrant our calling them to your attention. We believe that some time after formal instructions for the December 31st audit are received by us from Mr. Coster, Mr. White should call on Mr. Ballinger to discuss the points he has mentioned and that a special effort should be made, both in planning the work and in assigning assistants, to have the next audit conducted to Mr. Ballinger's entire satisfaction, if possible. We are, of course, quite aware that clients frequently have an inadequate idea of what is required in an audit and it might be well for you to furnish him with a copy of the Federal Reserve Bulletin and tell him that, in a general way, we follow the procedure outlined therein.

"McKesson & Robbins, Incorporated has become a large organization and we consider the connection of sufficient importance to warrant our making every effort to clear up without delay any sore spots which may develop among the executives. Since Mr. White is to be in New York within the next few days to attend the meeting of partners and managers, we shall be glad to discuss the above matter with him at that time." Ex. 119.

arrangement was necessary to insure harmonious preparation for the actual work of the audit which now will be considered.[591] In the detailed description of the audit which is to follow, the principal emphasis must be placed on the work done on the Connecticut Division and its predecessor companies, McKesson & Robbins, Incorporated (Connecticut) and Girard & Co., Inc.; and on McKesson & Robbins, Limited (Canada) as the fraudulent transactions discussed herein were confined to these units.[592] To give a proper conception of the size of the engagement, the nature of the problems arising on the entire audit, and the relationship of the two units in which principal interest lies to the entire work directed from the New York office of Price, Waterhouse & Co., it is necessary to point out deviations in the conduct of the work at Bridgeport from that in the other units and to describe to some extent at least the nature of the work done in those units.

C. INTERNAL CHECK AND CONTROL

In the preceding pages the negotiations with F. Donald Coster surrounding the origin and continuance of the series of audits have been set forth in sufficient detail to establish that the work was in the nature of a so-called balance sheet audit or examination and that as a general guide for this type of work Price, Waterhouse & Co. accepted the series of bulletins which culminated in the one published in January 1936 by the American Institute of Accountants under the title "Examination of Financial Statements by Independent Public Accountants."

In introducing the outline for the audit this Bulletin states:

"In determining the nature and extent of his examination the accountant will necessarily take into consideration, among other things, (a) the purpose of the examination, (b) the amount of detail included in the statements to be covered by his report, (c) the type of business the accounts of which are to be examined, and (d) the system of internal check and control." [593]

Each of the first three points in the quoted paragraph are given a short paragraph of explanation in the Bulletin but the fourth on "internal check and control" is given a relatively extended discussion. This, in view of the importance of the subject generally and particularly in this case, is reproduced here:

"An important factor to be considered by an accountant in formulating his program is the nature and extent of the internal check and control in the organization under examination. The more extensive a company's system of accounting and internal control the less extensive will be the detailed checking necessary.

---

[591] R. 1724, 1586, 674–676, 965–969, 981–991, 1973–1975.

[592] At December 31, 1934, inventories of crude drugs, since proven to be non-existent, were supposed to have been stored in the plant at Bridgeport, whereas at December 31, 1937, such inventories were supposed to have been in the hands of the suppliers in Canada. On December 31, 1930, payments on purchases and sales since proven to have been fictitious were made directly by and to McKesson, whereas subsequently they were purportedly made by and to Manning & Company, the pretended bank. By selecting these three dates for detailed study, the major differences in the conditions existing throughout the period were covered.

[593] Ex. 117 (p. 7).

For example, a plant addition in a large-sized company may be limited to the amount of a specific appropriation made by the administration; the work may be undertaken by a construction department, the funds be disbursed by the treasurer's department and the whole be subject to review in the controller's department when the necessary entries are made. In such a case the accountant is obviously warranted in making a much less extensive check of the details than in a small company where the manager orders the expenditure and the bookkeeper makes the entries.

"The term 'internal check and control' is used to describe those measures and methods adopted within the organization itself to safeguard the cash and other assets of the company as well as to check the clerical accuracy of the bookkeeping. The safeguards will cover such matters as the handling of incoming mail and remittances, the proceeds of cash sales, the preparation and payment of payrolls and the disbursement of funds generally, and the receipt and shipment of goods. These safeguards will frequently take the form of a definite segregation of duties or the utilization of mechanical devices. For example, the cashier will have no part in the entering of customers' accounts or the preparation of their statements, and neither he nor the ledger keeper will have authority to issue or approve credits to customers; the clerk recording the labor time and preparing the payroll will not be permitted to handle the funds; approval and entry of vouchers will be made by others than the disbursing officer; and stock records and inventory control will be kept independent of both the shipping and receiving departments. The extent to which these and other measures are practicable will naturally vary with the size of the organization and the personnel employed.

"The detailed scrutiny and check of cash transactions of large companies can be performed more economically by permanent company employees. Where such a check is provided, the accountant will modify his program accordingly. Where the internal check and control are necessarily limited or severely restricted the examination to be made will be more comprehensive in character but no examination should be regarded as taking the place of sound measures of internal check and control, except in cases where the organization is so small as to make adequate internal check impracticable. Except in the case of a small business, the cost of a detailed audit would be prohibitive, and the problem is to develop a general system of examination under which reasonably adequate safeguards may be secured at a cost that will be within the limits of a prudent economy. In the large majority of cases a detailed audit is not justified and the accountant relies on various test-checks of the records. The extent of the examination and of these test-checks is essentially a matter of judgment which must be exercised by the accountant, based on his experience, on his knowledge of the individual situation and on the extent of the internal check and control." [594]

The third point of the four set forth in the Bulletin indicates that the accountant should consider the type of business of the client in determining the character of the work to be done. Berger said that with a new client inquiry as to the principal characteristics of the business should be made when arranging for the work.[595] This preliminary knowledge, or in a continuing engagement knowledge gained

[594] Ex. 117 (pp. 8–9).

[595] "When receiving instructions from new clients it is also desirable to have a brief discussion as to the nature of the business, the manner of conducting it, the condition of the records, whether the Company sells direct to customers, or to jobbers, whether any branches are maintained, etc., and whether there are any peculiarities in the business. Information of this kind is useful in instructing our representatives assigned to the work and a bare outline is frequently sufficient to enable a principal to direct attention to special features which should be stressed or pitfalls which should be guarded against." Ex. 168 (p. 12).

by seniors in charge, can be supplemented by more detailed discussions with officials during the course of the work.

Of the Price, Waterhouse & Co. staff who testified in these proceedings, Thorn seems to have been the only member, at least since the 1928 audit, who inspected the plant.[596] When he was placed in charge in 1929, he wanted to familiarize himself with the business and with that in mind made a trip through the manufacturing sections, because he felt that some cost accounting problems might develop there. Thorn also testified that during the same year he had a long discussion with Coster about the crude drug operations and visited the Cliff Street office in New York to discuss the operations there in crude drugs (real).[597]

However, as a junior on the audit for 1927, Thorn (under Jaureguy) had not been through the plant nor did he (Thorn) take any of his juniors through when he took charge.[598] Ritts had been through a portion of one of the units of the building not as a part of his audit work but because when leaving at night the main entrance was closed and he and his crew had to use the employee's exit.[599] Ritts testified that he did not take his staff on inspection tours and that he had never been on one himself. Contact with various divisions of the office was limited to that gained in carrying out various audit steps. When any staff member started a new phase of the work, Ritts escorted his assistant to the proper division and introduced him to the persons in charge of the records.[600] Headquarters for the auditors, where most

---

596 The plant at Fairfield (near Bridgeport) consisted of one large building housing storage, manufacturing, and office activities of the business.

597 R. 866, 954, 1134.

598 R. 866–867.

599 R. 649. See also R. 390, 1337, 1343.

600 "Q. [By Mr. GALPEER.] When you get up there with your staff, Mr. Ritts, you would sometimes have men who were on the job for the first time with you?

A. Yes, that is true. That is their first assignment on the McKesson job.

Q. Do you take men who have this first assignment, take them into the plant, acquaint them with the physical layout, warehouses, accounting offices, et cetera?

A. No, we don't do that. Each man, however, is introduced to the various people whom he will come in contact with later on throughout his examination, but we make no physical inspection of the plant or the offices and such.

Q. Where does he meet these people? Do you make your headquarters in a certain room and these people come in and meet you?

A. In recent years, we have done most of our work in the director's room in the company's office in Bridgeport, and when a man, say, was assigned to the verification of cash he would be taken into the cashier's office and introduced to the various people with whom he would deal in order to obtain the records and necessary information he needed.

Another one would be assigned to do accounts receivable and would be taken out into the company's general accounting office and introduced to the office manager and the various people he would come in contact with in the Accounts Receivable Department et cetera, throughout the entire job.

Q. In other words, you do take them and introduce them to specific people where there were specific jobs to be done, but there would be no general inspection?

A. No.

Q. When you first came on the job yourself, if you can take your mind back to that time, when Mr. Thorn, I believe was there in charge, was that correct?

A. Yes.

Q. Was the same procedure followed then?

A. Yes.

Q. In other words, you were taken through no general inspection tour of the plant?

A. No, I was not." R. 234–235.

of their work was done, was established in the directors' room which was next to Coster's office. In short, in recent years, with the exception of Thorn, no member of the auditors' staff who testified in the hearings seems to have had more than a limited knowledge of the plant in which he worked.[601]

Rowbotham, when asked generally if the paragraphs on internal control quoted above indicated "* * * that the accountant in charge should have a complete and thorough knowledge of the extent of the internal control in the particular house on which he is doing the audit * * *" replied, "Yes, I should say he should understand it." [602]

Various methods are employed by accountants in ascertaining and appraising the effectiveness of the client's system. Price, Waterhouse & Co. for a number of years have used questionnaires as an aid in developing the necessary information as to the adequacy of their client's system of internal check and control. The cover page of their general questionnaire contained instructions for the completion of the questionnaire and is of sufficient importance to warrant its reproduction here:

"QUESTIONNAIRE RE SYSTEM OF INTERNAL CHECK
(FOR USE ON BALANCE SHEET AUDITS)

"The scope of a balance sheet audit as defined in the Federal Reserve Bulletin of April 1917, comprises a verification of the Assets and Liabilities as of a certain date, a general examination of the Profit and Loss Account for a period ending on that date, and incidental thereto *an examination into essential features of the accounting, i. e., the system of internal check.* There is reason for believing that the latter requirement has not always received the attention it deserves and the following questions have been prepared partially to correct this weakness. It should be borne in mind, however, that the questions are more suggestive than exhaustive and are, of course, not precisely applicable to every balance sheet audit.

"The majority of the questions will be found to be answerable from observations actually made during the course of the work **and should be answered by the assistant doing the particular section of the work to which the questions apply.** If the assistant is unable to answer the questions on the work assigned to him it is evident that a careful and thorough verification has not been made.

"In cases where the direct method of interrogation is used, the questions should be taken up with the Comptroller or other responsible officials of the Company and a note made as to the source of the replies.

"The questions under each section should be answered during the progress of that part of the work and while the matter is fresh in the mind of the assistant.

"If this method is adopted it will be found that the questionnaire is not at all burdensome, and that it requires comparatively little time.

"In cases where the name of an employee is asked, his position (when not evident from the question) should also be stated.

"In filling out questionnaire you should not only ascertain that the necessary

[601] Footnotes 598, 599, 600 *supra* and R. 1115–1117, 1339, 1317–1318 with which cf. R. 1365–1368.
[602] R. 1840.

safeguards for purposes of internal control are provided, but you should also be able to say definitely from observation, inquiry and tests during the course of the examination that the prescribed procedure is being observed." [Emphasis in original.][603]

The first questionnaire used on this engagement at Bridgeport was the printed one from which we have reproduced above the instructions for its use. Ritts testified that this general questionnaire was prepared with the Connecticut Company in mind but that it was "* * * fair to say that it also * * * [applied] in general to the Canadian Company." [604] It was filled in for the first time on the 1932 audit in conference with McGloon who, in Ritts' presence, wrote all of the answers to the printed questions. Ritts stated that in subsequent years the accounting procedures were reviewed with some responsible accounting officer and by observation.[605] "I don't know that we would sit down and actually review it, but if any major changes came to our attention, I believe we would examine the questionnaire to see what was reported for the prior year, make such changes wherever necessary." [606] McGloon, however, testified that if he had again been asked the answers to some of these questions, for example, "Do employees in position of trust take regular annual vacations?" he would have changed the answer from "Yes," stating, "* * * I would have said that the Dietrichs didn't take vacations, and I don't know yet why I didn't say it in that particular memorandum because everybody knew that the Dietrichs didn't take vacations." [607] Rowbotham testified in respect to this question that he would have asked it again each year but not necessarily of the same person.[608]

On the audits for 1936 and 1937 supplementary questionnaires for the Canadian Company and Connecticut Division dealing with cash, receivables and inventories were prepared in mimeographed form and filled in anew in both of these years by the assistants handling each part of the work.[609] In addition to the questionnaire in 1937 there were also handwritten memoranda on accounts payable and cash receipts. Likewise on the 1932 audit the working papers contained a handwritten supplement to the cash questions in which a junior described the disbursing and payroll system and Ritts recorded

---

603 Ex. 17.

604 R. 260. In fact major differences prevailed between them. See section III *supra* and page 187 *infra*.

605 R. 214, 1154–1155.

606 R. 262–263. The questionnaire was amended as to two questions. One of these, were creditors' statements compared with balances shown in accounts payable record, as amended to "No" is not entirely consistent with the accounts payable work program "(5) Test check open balances at December 31st by reference to creditors' monthly statements." Ex. 47.

607 R. 1700–1701.

"Mr. Stewart. You don't intend to testify that the representatives of Price, Waterhouse & Company knew it, do you, Mr. McGloon?

The Witness. No, I am speaking of employees of McKesson here." R. 1702.

608 R. 1852–1853.

609 R. 257–268.

answers to sundry questions in regard to cash receipts and disbursements. In 1933 there was another memorandum on the payroll system and in 1934 there was a note on the Company's physical count of inventories. A junior, who prepared the inventory supplementary questionnaires in 1936 and 1937, was the only assistant who signed or initialed the supplementary questionnaires.[610]

Rowbotham was questioned as to the propriety of Ritts' method of procedure in having McGloon fill in the questionnaire completely when the instructions we reproduced above indicated that assistants were to supply some of the information and the last page of the form had spaces for indicating the pages filled up by the different assistants but in this case signed only by Ritts. Rowbotham's interpretation was that Ritts must have verified McGloon's answers in consultation with his assistants or by his own observation but that in any event McGloon's answers were "basic compliance." He felt that the main responsibility for the questionnaire laid with the man in charge of the job.[611]

Testimony of a junior [612] on the 1937 audit, indicates the manner in which the answering of one of the questionnaires was approached by one of the assistants on the audit. This junior did certain work on receivables and was asked by Ritts to get answers to some of the questions in connection with that work. He sought out Johnson, the office manager of McKesson & Robbins, as the best source of the information he wanted. The following extract is significant:

"Q. [By Mr. GALPEER] Did Mr. Johnson give you a detailed explanation?

A. Well, as I recall it, on the first question he was going to go into detail, but I explained to him that I just wanted the question answered in as brief a way and as accurate a way as possible, and just wanted to get the answers down in here, that is all I recall on that.

Q. And you gave that back to Mr. Ritts?

A. I gave that back to Mr. Ritts and told him that I had filled that out as per his instructions." [613]

Rowbotham stated that he thought Price, Waterhouse & Co. "would have a look at" internal control every year and that while knowledge of the system of internal control should be current at least in the minds of the men on the job, he did not think it necessary that the questionnaire be changed or rewritten yearly. When confronted, apparently for the first time, with the fact that the questionnaires, especially the more recent ones, contained several unanswered questions and others

---

610 Ex. 18, 19, M-3, M-16, M-21, M-26.

611 R. 1773-1780.

612 Graduated from a large southern university, with an A. B. degree in 1936, where he had studied accounting and assisted in the accounting department during his senior year. Following graduation he worked for a year as an investigator for the Household Finance Corporation. He joined the staff of Price, Waterhouse & Co. December 16, 1937, through the aid of an employment agency. He worked that winter until February 15 and again the next season from November 28 to December 28 when he resigned to take a State Civil Service position in New Jersey.

613 R.1112-1113.

incorrectly or incompletely answered his reaction was that the purpose of the procedure was to provide information for the senior on the job, and that the senior would not be misled by minor errors and omissions, and although the answers should be corrected as a matter of routine,[614] that Ritts "* * * simply taking the job in his stride doesn't bother correcting the questionnaire in what has seemed to him probably at the time as detail." As a practical matter, Rowbotham felt that the manager in charge of the work would learn of changes in the client's procedure by questioning the senior on the engagement, and therefore the deficiencies were merely "a matter of paper work."[615]

Rowbotham was asked to characterize certain of the conditions reported in the questionnaires as to whether they indicated points of strength or weakness in the system. "Does the cashier have access to any of the ledgers?" was asked in 1932, 1936, and 1937, and resulted in apparently conflicting answers. McGloon's answer for 1932—"Yes, customers ledgers"—was correct as far as it went. "No" in 1936 revealed a possible failure to discover all the facts. This was remedied by a more comprehensive answer in 1937: "Not under conditions which would permit of entries being made—Sometimes consults ledger cards to determine applicability of a cash item received." Rowbotham felt that the condition which seemed to be indicated by the 1932 answer would not be a point of strength.[616]

The questionnaire in 1932 indicated that the president, F. D. Coster (he was also treasurer of the Connecticut and Canadian Companies), and assistant treasurer, George E. Dietrich, each had authority to sign checks without countersignature. Although not so indicated on the questionnaire this procedure was changed later to require countersignatures, which Rowbotham approved as the better procedure.[617] In the Canadian Company, however, the countersigner was Margaret Walsh, the only bookkeeper, who worked solely under George E. Dietrich's direction; while in the Connecticut Division the countersigner could be one of George E. Dietrich's women cashiers.

To the question "Who reconciles the bank accounts and does employee preparing or approving checks effect or have supervision over bank reconciliations?" McGloon answered "Bank accounts reconciled by cashiers who prepare checks." Rowbotham's opinion of this situation was that it "was not strong."[618] In 1936 and 1937 this question was changed to read "If employee keeping part or all of cash book(s) also reconciles bank accounts—how often, by whom and to

[614] R. 1933–1934. Rowbotham remarked with respect to paper work:

"Well, sir, if I ever saw a perfect set of working papers I would want to fire the man because I would think he was paying too much attention to the questionnaire and that he was not attending to the job." R. 1907.

[615] R. 1781–1782, 1829–1832.

[616] R. 1780–1781; Ex. 19.

[617] Ex. 17; R. 1781.

[618] R. 1785.

what extent are reconciliations verified (other than P. W. & Co. examinations)?" The answer for 1936 was "Yes—semi-monthly—None," and for 1937 no answer appeared.

The general questionnaire was supplemented in 1932 by another work paper in Ritts' handwriting which contained a few pertinent questions on cash disbursements and by a memorandum on "Cash System" prepared by a junior. These stated that vouchers for cash disbursements were prepared by a woman employee and approved for payment by George E. Dietrich although he usually neglected to indicate this in writing for his signature rarely appeared on the voucher. A special form was used for all disbursements such as advances, transfers, and sundry items for which no vouchers were prepared in advance. These disbursements could originate in several departments including that of George Dietrich, who approved all of them. In these cases the payment was made before the liability was recorded in the accounting department.[619] It should be recalled that George Dietrich, as assistant treasurer, not only approved these vouchers, but also signed the checks with a counter-signature by a person under his control.[620]

The fact that the assistant treasurer opened the mail Rowbotham thought was "definitely a point of strength" for he felt that some responsible person should do this work. The fact that George Dietrich in addition to his other duties also handled foreign crude drug purchases and sales for Coster did not alter his opinion on this point so long as he did not have access to the general books, specifically the accounts receivable ledgers which he understood were controlled by McGloon and thus served as a check on Dietrich.[621]

As for the question, "Is an independent record of incoming remittances prepared for comparison later with the collections recorded by the cashier and, if so, is the comparison made, and by whom?" which was answered "No," Rowbotham stated that although lists were frequently made, this was not much of a point either way; failure to do it "would not necessarily be a point of weakness."[622] A point closely related to this was covered by Ritts in the short supplementary questionnaire for 1932, mentioned above, in which he asked "Are duplicate certified deposit slips retained?" The answer being "No," it followed that no answer appeared for his next question "Can they be checked out in detail with cash books receipts?" The memorandum on the cash system referred to above likewise stated that "No duplicate deposit slips are received. The deposits are made up by Miss

[619] Ex. M-3; R. 1624–1642.

[620] R. 1639.

[621] R. 1786–1788.

[622] Compare this point of view with letters to McKesson-Whittlesey Company and Milwaukee Drug Division reproduced at pages 321–322 and 324 *infra*.

Bohus."[623] It seems that this refers to Miss Bakos who testified that prior to the use of Manning & Company as a bank, she made up deposits of actual cash and checks received from real customers but not the deposits purporting to cover receipts from foreign crude drug customers, since shown to be false, for which memoranda were given to her by George Dietrich.[624] At the time the receipts on the latter accounts which amounted to approximately 65% of the Connecticut Company's receipts on sales were reported on Manning & Company credit advices and were not covered in the memorandum.

Questions on receivables included two dealing with circularization which Rowbotham felt were out of place in a questionnaire as that subject was covered in arranging for the audit. These were followed by two questions dealing with regular monthly statements sent to customers and a third which asked "Who mails them?" to which the answer was given simply "Asst. Treas.," referring to George Dietrich. Rowbotham, when asked about this, first questioned whether it was in fact done by the particular person as stated in the questionnaire but limiting his reply to the answer as made, said that it was not a point of strength. Three other questions dealing with the credit limit of customers he felt were inapplicable to this audit. The first "Does ledger sheet show credit limit or what record is kept of it?" was answered "No." The next two questions asked about accounts receivable in excess of credit limits and unusually large balances. These were merely checked. A question similar to the first of the three was answered in 1936 and 1937 by stating that the credit manager did set limits and that they were followed.[625] In the 1932 questionnaire in addition to Titus, a credit manager, George Dietrich and F. D. Coster were listed as passing on credit terms. Rowbotham stated that he could not remember seeing a credit limit shown on a ledger sheet of a large industry as distinguished from a department store, so he could not see the purpose of the questions when applied to the Connecticut Company.[626]

George E. Dietrich was custodian of securities at Bridgeport. Rowbotham felt that all purchases of securities should be authorized by the Board of Directors which was not the case here at least at the time the 1932 questionnaire was prepared. It may be noted that the same questionnaire stated that George Dietrich was also the custodian of all notes receivable and related collateral and that he also retained control of all notes which had been written off as uncollectible.

G. E. Dietrich and F. D. Coster, with only one signature required, were listed by McGloon as the only ones authorized to sign notes

[623] Ex. M-3.

[624] R. 2649-2654, quoted in part at pages **113 ff.** *supra.*

[625] The answers do not distinguish foreign crude drug and other business. See pages **232** ***infra.***

[626] R. 1795-1798.

payable and acceptances while the same officers and McGloon were authorized to approve loans to officials and employees. Rowbotham was surprised at this latter point, for he supposed that only Coster had that power.[627]

Rowbotham agreed that the answers to questions dealing with shipments were not informative although Ritts had previously referred to the questionnaires in explanation of this subject.[628] Shipments it seemed were made on regular "order forms" which went to the production and shipping departments. What happened after that was left with a question mark, and whether the tick mark after a question about back orders meant there were none was left to conjecture. These answers were all in McGloon's handwriting.

The question, "Do employees in position of trust take regular annual vacations?" was answered "Yes," although the testimony in these proceedings indicated that the answer was incorrect when applied to the brothers Dietrich. Rowbotham's attitude toward this point may be considered in connection with his attitude on the desirability of outlining the Company's organization to show each department and to whom it is responsible, a step required by the questionnaire. Both points to Rowbotham were more or less textbook matters rather than the concern of practical working accountants; neither one would come to a partner's attention.[629]

The last point worthy of comment in connection with Rowbotham's review of the questionnaires are his observations on a question and

---

[627] R. 1803–1804.

[628] R. 214.

[629] "Q. [By Mr. GALPEER]: Mr. Rowbotham, on page 14 of the questionnaire under the category of General, question No. 7: 'Do employees in position of trust take regular annual vacations?' The answer to that is 'Yes.' If the answer had been recorded as 'No,' what would your reactions have been?

A. Well, as a matter of fact, my reaction would have been this: That I am afraid I am approaching it not from the accounting end. My reaction was that it was a bad policy for the corporation not to give its employees vacations because in our place I think officials absolutely need vacations.

I know that is not the answer you want, but that is the way I would have approached the thing.

In the same thing in this, if there had been some fairly high placed employee who hadn't taken it for several years, I might have taken it up with, let us say, the president of the company and asked him why this was so. I might have gotten some satisfactory explanation. I would have gone back or had the men go back and check that man's book a little more carefully than previously, but beyond that, if the president, the executive officer, had been satisfied I don't think that it would have concerned me very greatly.

* * * * * * *

Q. On the next page, item 16: 'Outline the company's organization, showing each department and to whom it is responsible.' Would you say that that would be a useful thing to do in connection with your audit and check, or your check of the internal check?

A. I think the man ought to have the outline of the thing pretty clearly in his head. I mean, we don't as a rule insist upon a man going out and coming back with a chart. Is there a place here where they speak of a chart?

Mr. GALPEER: Not that I know of. I don't know.

The WITNESS: That simply isn't the way we work. I think the man ought to have the outline of the organization in his head and know what he is doing. And I think he should take it up with his particular superior, Ritts, let us say here, with Thorn.

Q. Would that come to your attention, or would that end with Thorn?

A. That would end with Thorn.

Q. Shouldn't there be some list of officials with titles, duties, perhaps, somewhere in your papers?

A. That is,—I don't want to be misunderstood,—a text book requirement, it is not done in real life." R. 1812–1815.

answer on the Canadian Company supplemental questionnaire for 1937, which brought out the fact that one person kept all the books. This one person was at first George Dietrich, and since 1931 Margaret Walsh, a bookkeeper, who worked solely for him on the Canadian Company as bookkeeper and stenographer. This situation, Rowbotham agreed, would require more detailed auditing than a situation in which a greater subdivision of work could be obtained.[630]

Rowbotham's attitude toward the details of auditing mechanics is clearly evident from many of the answers given to the questions in the part of his testimony reviewed above. With regard to the adequacy of the client's system of internal control he testified:

"No, I did not specifically review the questionnaire, and on the question of internal control all that I would say to Mr. Thorn was:—I do not remember any precise form of words,—but what kind of internal control have they got up there and he would tell me whatever it was that he told me which, in this case, was that they had a good control and I would not sit down with him and go into the internal control specifically for this reason,—I may be giving you an individual opinion here,—but it is this, that I do not think an accountant can go into a system of internal control unless he actually goes up and sees it himself. In other words, sir, I think if Thorn here went into the system, I mean, if he is the man on the job, he has to go up and look into it and satifsy himself * * *."[631]

Thorn, in this case, had been close to the work as junior and senior and since confining himself to managerial duties had received reports currently from Ritts. If Thorn had brought any weaknesses to his attention, Rowbotham stated he would have gone into the matter more thoroughly.

"Q. [By Mr. STEWART.] Just one other question on that. Did you regard Mr. Thorn, during the time he was manager of the McKesson job as being a perfectly competent man to pass on the adequacy of the system of internal control?

A. Yes, I most undoubtedly did."[632]

---

[630] "Q. [By Mr. GALPEER.] Now, on question 9 of the cash questionnaire of the Limited Company for 1937, reading: 'Does the cashier have access to any of the ledgers?' The answer is: 'One employee keeps all the books,' would you say that that condition would require a more careful audit than otherwise, Mr. Rowbotham?

A. I think it would, and I think it does.

Q. Would you say in view of that that the audit of the Limited Company was the audit of a large or a small company?

A. It is an audit of an actually—legally, it does happen to be a separate corporation, but it does form part of this whole McKesson picture. I don't think that you can quite call it a small company. In quite the sense—I do agree and I think this is the point you have in mind, I do agree that more care should be exercised where one man has control of the books, as I think was true in this case.

Q. As a matter of fact, just to clear the record and see if we can come to a common view: In a situation like this, where the Limited Company's books were all kept by one man, in what respect would the audit of that company be any different for being a subsidiary of McKesson than if you had just gone in and, let us say, had been retained solely to do these books for the Limited Company?

A. If you had been retained solely to do these books for the Limited Company and one man had access to everything, I think you would make a pretty well detailed audit. If it fits into part of a larger picture, I think you can lessen the amount of detail, but I think you do more detail than you do on the ordinary financial or balance sheet examination." R. 1825–1827.

[631] R. 1932.

[632] R. 1933–1934.

The foregoing review of the questionnaires indicates that Rowbotham held Thorn, the manager in charge, responsible for a correct appraisal of the adequacy of McKesson's system of internal check and control. Thorn's appraisal of the system is summarized in the following paragraphs.

The fact that George Dietrich combined the office of assistant treasurer (in which capacity he controlled all receipts and disbursements) and his duties in buying and selling foreign crude drugs, did not seem to Thorn to have any bearing on internal check, even though these foreign transactions were approximately 65% of the Connecticut Division's business and approximately 90% of the Canadian Company's business.[633] As Thorn understood the system as it applied to foreign crude drugs, Dietrich was merely a clerk executing orders for Coster who made the decisions. Thorn had talked with Coster in 1929, and at various times since then, and had the definite impression that Coster had been in that business for many years and continued to decide all questions of purchase and sale of crude drugs himself. While theoretically Thorn thought there might be a minor weakness in this system, nevertheless he felt that Coster's control over Dietrich was so close, that Coster would have caught the first attempt to put through a fictitious order. Observation convinced him as to who gave the orders and who did the clerical work.[634]

Thorn testified that all incoming mail came to George Dietrich's office, that no list of remittances was prepared, and that he could not recall ever having suggested that it be done nor could he récall having discussed the problem with Ritts.[635] Thorn also related that until recent years, all customers' statements went over George Dietrich's desk for approval before mailing, but that W. E. Titus, credit manager for receivables of the Connecticut Division other than crude drugs complained of the delay in mailing statements, so that thereafter only foreign crude drug statements were sent to Dietrich prior to mailing.[636] McGloon testified that Titus, whose office was in New York, then made it a practice to go to Bridgeport the first of each month to review the statements of the other customers.[637]

The cashier's office was under George Dietrich and bank accounts were reconciled by the women in this office. Thorn did not know to whom they were responsible, whether McGloon or Dietrich.[638] McGloon, whose department received duplicates of checks as prepared, testified that bank statements and cancelled checks themselves were kept in the vault in Dietrich's office, to which he did not have

[633] Page 45 *supra*.
[634] R. 1163–1169.
[635] R. 1171.
[636] R. 1169–1170.
[637] R. 1646–1650.
[638] R. 1172.

access, although he did not remember having been refused any documents he requested from Dietrich.[639]

Although purchase orders went to the receiving department and while it was better for the receiving clerk not to know what had been ordered, Thorn was of the opinion that the men actually preparing the receiving tickets would not have the orders, even though Robert Dietrich, who controlled their work, would have them. The fact that Robert Dietrich was in control of warehousing, as well as head of the receiving and shipping departments, Thorn thought was only a minor weakness. During the last 3 years when the foreign crude drugs presumably were held at suppliers Robert Dietrich's clerks made out memoranda indicating this, using the regular receiving ticket forms. On the basis of the documents in evidence it would appear that these memoranda must have been prepared either from a copy of the McKesson purchase order or from the vendor's invoice.

The effect of the series of transactions as Thorn understood them was that he relied on the purchase order originating with Coster and initialed by George Dietrich, a purchase invoice from outside and a debit advice from Manning & Company.[640] For sales he relied on an order from outside, "W. W. Smith & Co.", an approval by Coster passed along by George Dietrich, shipment from an outside source, "Smith acting as shipping agent" and, finally, on actual receipts of cash. However, the apparent actual collection of the cash was to him the most positive evidence of the transactions.[641] But Thorn did not know that soon after the pretended establishment of Manning & Company as a bank all of the foreign crude drug customers supposedly paid through it.[642]

The question was raised with Thorn as to whether George Dietrich could have authorized credits to customers' accounts to cover up abstraction of receipts from customers. He thought that if this had been attempted the transactions would have come to the attention of Johnson (office manager) or McGloon, but that it was probable that Dietrich's authority to order the credits would have been recognized by these men, although Thorn thought that Dietrich "* * * couldn't have done that consistently at least."[643]

Thorn got the impression from conversations with George Dietrich that he went on hunting trips. Thorn was not sure now what he would have done but said that if he had known that George Dietrich

---

639 R. 1590, 1663–1665.

640 R. 1175.

641 "You first have the order coming in from the outside, in this case the order would be offered by W. W. Smith & Co., you have the approval by Mr. Coster passed along by George Dietrich. You have later the advice of shipment from the outside source, in this case, Smith, acting as shipping agent, and you have later on the actual cash coming in paying for that sale, the cash actually coming in, I say, and that is, it seems to me, the most positive evidence that you can have of these tranactions." R. 1175–1176. See also R. 1128–1129 quoted at page 226 *infra*.

642 "No, I had not understood that all these collections did go into Manning & Company." R. 1177. See also R. 910–911. Ritts testified to the same effect. R. 558–559, 140.

643 R. 1180.

never took regular vacations, he thought he would have gone to Thompson, the treasurer, rather than to Coster just as a matter of diplomacy, for Coster might have resented any implication he might take from the inquiry. Furthermore, George Dietrich was acting under Thompson as assistant treasurer of the Maryland Company.[644] As a last resort Thorn said he would have gone to Coster from whom there would have been no appeal.[645]

As for the Canadian Company, Thorn did not know what Miss Walsh's duties were, whether she could co-sign checks or that she kept a cash book separate from those maintained by the cashiers under Dietrich's direction.[646]

Thorn's general approach to the use of questionnaires is indicated by the fact that he did not enforce their preparation on all divisions of the McKesson work for he said that a senior could omit revising or preparing a questionnaire:

> "In cases where the senior thought that it was not necessary, I might say, if it will clarify this matter any, that that question of questionnaires is something that is in a continual state of revision, you might say. In fact, I believe new forms, new ideas are being applied to that almost every year, and there are some seniors that either because they think that particular examination does not require a questionnaire or because possibly in some cases that they do not believe in questionnaires, wouldn't make one out."[647]

Thus it appears that Thorn, as manager, delegated the decision as to the manner of securing such information to the men under him.[648] On the Bridgeport work in recent years Ritts then was responsible for developing the facts with respect to the system of internal check and control.[649] How thorough was his knowledge and how did he appraise his findings in reporting to his superiors?

Ritts is on record in only one place in the working papers, as to his opinion of the client's system of internal check and control. At the close of each engagement, a form, known as a condensed examination summary, was prepared and filed with the working papers. Although this practice was abandoned prior to the completion of the 1937 audit, Ritts for that year, as he had done for prior years, prepared and signed one of these summaries for the Canadian Company and one for the Maryland Company and subsidiaries.[650] The report for the Maryland Company and subsidiaries for 1934 (approved by Thorn)[651] described the internal check as "fairly satisfactory." The first report of this type for the Canadian Company was prepared by Ritts

---

644 R. 1183.
645 R. 1238.
646 R. 1181.
647 R. 1153. But cf. page 165 *supra*.
648 Page 183 *supra*. Cf. R. 1123.
649 R. 1121.
650 R. 4449–4453.
651 Ex. 211 (not prepared by Ritts).

for the 1935 audit. It described the internal check as "satisfactory." [652] For 1937, Ritts called the internal check of the Canadian Company "satisfactory" and that of the Maryland Company and subsidiaries "fairly satisfactory." [653]

The form carried brief specimen comments for matters on which a rating was requested. Under internal check were suggested "excellent," "fairly satisfactory," "should be strengthened," and "organization too small to permit adequate check." The Canadian Company's system of internal check, by this scale, was just short of excellent according to Ritts' judgment, yet the working papers indicated what has been shown above, that all the books were kept in the beginning by George Dietrich and in recent years by one bookkeeper under his supervision and Rowbotham testified that under such circumstances " * * * you do more detail than you do on the ordinary financial or balance sheet examination." [654]

Although the instructions to representatives of the firm required that comments on the system of internal check and control be included in the report to the New York office on each branch audit, Ritts never included such comments in his memorandum to Thorn on the work done at Bridgeport, although Thorn stated that such matters were discussed with him.[655 656] Thorn testified that while he gave Ritts a copy of these instructions, they applied only to the wholesale houses and not to the divisions at Bridgeport, and it was his opinion that Ritts never read them.[657]

Ritts, whom Thorn considered competent and understood what to do, stated that he made a survey of the system and was sure he was satisfied that the system was satisfactory.[658] In respect to the foreign crude drug transactions, Ritts relied upon the fact that all the transactions went through the general office staff on both purchases and sales at at least one point and that they were not a segregated division of the office routine. There seemed to him to be enough people required in the receiving and shipping office to prepare the receiving tickets besides Robert Dietrich to preclude their being forged. He also relied upon the fact that there was an outside invoice in addition to George Dietrich's approval of the purchase order, and that it was matched in the comptroller's office with the order and receiving ticket.[659] This was the same system that applied to other purchases.

652 Ex. 209.

653 Ex. 208, 210. The rating for the latter would appear to be lower than the former because of the influence of unsatisfactory conditions in the wholesale houses which will be discussed in a subsequent subsection, pages 315 ff. *infra*.

654 R. 1826 quoted at footnote 630 *supra*. See also pages 51 and 182–183 *supra*.

655 656 R. 1121.

657 R. 614, 985, 1120.

658 R. 209, 615, 969–971, 1120.

659 R. 619–621.

On sales, Ritts explained that the billing was done on the basis of a factory order, which in turn was based upon a W. W. Smith & Co. shipping notice (from an outside source) but he gave conflicting testimony as to how these transactions were handled for he could not recollect the details. He did not recall seeing any bills of lading, consular invoices or insurance certificates covering these shipments, and explained that these must have been sent to the customer with the invoice. He could not state definitely from recollection how the system worked but he agreed that all the documents involved, insofar as the general accounting office was concerned with these sales transactions, came from or went back to George Dietrich's office.[660] In short, as will be shown more fully hereinafter in connection with the discussion of the audit of cash, accounts receivable, intercompany accounts, inventories, accounts payable, sales, and other profit and loss accounts, Ritts although on the job at Bridgeport for 8 years could not state with precision the manner in which the foreign crude drug transactions were handled at the Bridgeport offices. In particular it should be observed that important differences in the manner of handling the foreign crude drug accounts and the other accounts receivable seem to have been overlooked by Ritts and his staff.[661]

Ritts' conception of the reliance to be placed upon officers and the extent to which he would determine by independent checking whether the answers as given to him by McGloon, were, in fact, a correct statement of the conditions actually prevailing in the office is indicated by the following quotation from his testimony:

"Q. [By Mr. Galpeer.] And if you had known, as a matter of fact that Mr. Robert Dietrich and George Dietrich had never taken an annual vacation, would that have made a difference to you?

A. It may or may not have.

Q. What is the purpose of asking this question if the answer does not make any difference to you?

A. If the question there had been no, they do not, or if you had inquired specifically regarding any one particular employee and you were told no, then, you might inquire as to why, or call it to the attention of the company and place the responsibility direct with them.

Q. Well, isn't it the auditor's responsibility—what is the purpose of asking these questions if you are not to assume some responsibility for their answers?

A. Well, I think when we answered the question yes, that they did, that that was as far as we need go.

Q. And you took Mr. McGloon's word for that and you didn't make any independent check aside from that to determine whether the two men in fact did take or did not take annual vacations?

A. I did not inquire specifically of anyone, that is a question directed to any and all responsible employees, and when the vice-president and comptroller of the company tells you something, there is no need to question it that I could see.

Q. Without arguing about this further, will you just follow me here. Assuming you had independently checked, and assuming that you did find out that these two

---

660 R. 625-627

661 E. g. pages 231–239 *infra*.

men in these two key positions never took any annual vacations, and assuming you did find out that whenever Mr. George Dietrich was away on account of illness, Mr. Robert Dietrich took his position, would that have had any effect on you?

A. That is a hypothetical question. I don't know. That would depend on the circumstances.

Q. What circumstances would help you determine?

A. I really couldn't say. It depends on a great many things, I suppose. I mean, isn't that rather hypothetical?

Q. I mean it as such. After all, one of our purposes here is to examine what safeguards exist and whether these things can be detected.

A. I suppose you might inquire as to why they didn't take annual vacations. If you got a reasonable explanation from them and had no further reason to inquire into that question, you may be inclined to drop it or if you felt you should follow or rather follow the question further on you would. You might discuss it with the treasurer of the company, you might discuss it with the president of the company——

Q. But at any rate, if you had run down some of these items, such as we have discussed this morning in regard to mail and in regard to vacations, you might have gotten some key to the situation that we are here trying to look into.

A. You may have. I don't know. My belief is that they would have probably given you some reasonable explanation that you would have been willing to accept in the absence of any information such as we have now.

Q. Well, isn't it the auditor's job also to be, perhaps, * * * a little suspicious of these things, not just take things at their say-so?

A. I don't think any auditor is ever instructed or told to be suspicious. I think the average auditor is inclined to be somewhat skeptical, but, on the other hand, when you are dealing with what appear to be responsible and reputable people, and they make a statement of fact to you, I don't think that I possess the tact to contradict them in such a way as not to offend them and imply that I do not believe what they are telling me.

Q. Do you believe it to be part of your job that if you are told by a comptroller or an assistant treasurer that a certain fact is the case, that so and so mailed letters, or that so and so does take a vacation, that you owe no further duty to make any further independent check?

A. I think so, yes.

Q. That would apply to any job you would do, not particularly McKesson & Robbins?

A. That's right.

Q. And, here, if such check had been made to a further degree, you might have discovered things that led to this entire situation?

A. I don't think I would subscribe to that statement. Actually I don't know what might happen. My belief is that I might have received some reasonable explanation from someone, which I might have been willing to accept.

Mr. HENDERSON. May I just ask one question there?

Mr. GALPEER. Certainly.

Mr. HENDERSON. To whom would you have next gone to get an explanation?

The WITNESS. Mr. Coster." [662]

The foregoing review of the Price, Waterhouse & Co. approach to the important question of internal check and control may be summarized by recalling that the questionnaires used by the firm directed

[662] R. 294B–297.

attention to the importance of making sure that the procedures described by officials of the client were actually followed in practice and were adequate protection; that Rowbotham, the partner, did not read the questionnaires but relied instead on Thorn, the manager, to report any significant discoveries; that Thorn in turn felt that minor weaknesses in internal check and control as reflected in the questionnaires were not important enough to report to a partner, and furthermore that he left the manner of using the questionnaires to the discretion of the senior on the job; and that Ritts, upon whom Thorn relied to gather the facts at Bridgeport, felt that in making balance sheet examinations, the "* * * accountant is only charged with making general inquiries with regard to the internal control exercised by the company."[663]

It may also be recalled that Rowbotham thought that the unanswered requirement on the questionnaire to outline the Company's organization to show each department and lines of responsibility was a textbook requirement not carried out by practical accountants, although he thought the man on the job ought to have the outline of the organization in his head and take it up with his immediate superior.[664]

It is interesting to observe in this connection that although the McKesson & Robbins organization was set forth in a printed chart and was accompanied by a bulletin of instructions in the form of a letter by F. Donald Coster to all executives and heads of departments in the Company, both effective September 1, 1937, no member of the auditors' staff who was questioned about it could recall having seen either chart or bulletin. Ritts when asked about the bulletin said that other bulletins issued by Coster from time to time were sent to his office but that he had never seen this one and that in so far as he knew it was not in their permanent file for the engagement.[665]

The style of this bulletin was marked by repeated emphasis on the direct responsibility of all departmental executives, including the secretary, treasurer, and vice-president in charge of auditing and accounting (the comptroller), to the president of the corporation.[666] Although the organization chart indicated that the president was responsible to the Executive Committee and it in turn to the Board of Directors, no reference to this control was made in the bulletin except that the bulletin mentioned that the chart was adopted and approved by the Executive Committee. Coster said in the bulletin, however, that "At all times it is to be made clear that every one in the company is responsible, directly or indirectly, to the President of the corporation. The President, however, in his general super-

[663] R. 218.

[664] Footnote 629 *supra*.

[665] Ex. 14, 97; R. 240.

[666] Cf. footnote 365 *supra*. Cf. also R. 4279–4280; Ex. 203.

vision of the business shall act through the men of proper responsibility as indicated in the chart attached hereto."

"Mr. Geo. E. Dietrich" was shown on the chart as the senior of three officers of the "Drugs & Chemicals Trading & Buying" department. Shown as associated with him were "Mr. Chas. Hermann" and "Mr. Simon Baum." Testimony of Hermann indicated that he and Baum operated the real trading of this department and that they were not subject to Dietrich in their work. The department was shown on the chart as a part of the Connecticut Division under "Mr. Wilbur Dewell", vice-president in charge. All foreign subsidiaries and all foreign departments were shown as under the direct and exclusive supervision of Coster.

Thorn was asked if the chart seemed to him to be an accurate presentation of the organization as he knew it. Looking at it generally he could not point out any inaccuracies. Thorn's opinion of George Dietrich's position was that in respect to crude drug operations he acted only in a clerical capacity and did not have any executive position in the foreign department. When questioned specifically, however, Thorn agreed that in this capacity George Dietrich received instructions from Coster direct and not from Dewell as indicated on the chart. Thorn also agreed that the chart was in error in omitting any reference to George Dietrich as assistant treasurer, in which capacity he routed all routine receipts and signed the checks for most disbursements.[667]

Thorn understood that Robert Dietrich's purchasing activities were confined to items other than crude drugs, and that he was in general charge of shipping and receiving and of inventories located at Bridgeport. In so far as these activities involved transactions in foreign crude drugs, Robert Dietrich also was not in fact subordinate to Dewell as shown on the chart.[668]

Thorn was quite certain that neither the bulletin nor chart were in the permanent files for the engagement as he reviewed those each year himself. When he was asked what he would have done if he had seen a reference to them in minutes of the Executive Committee, he testified that he might have looked at them and would have asked for copies had he thought them important.[669]

In closing this general survey of the auditors' knowledge of the McKesson system of internal check and control it may be appropriate to quote a question asked of both Ritts and Thorn by counsel for Price, Waterhouse & Co..

"Summarizing the net effect of all of the controls that you have described and the number of people who had to handle each transaction in the crude drug de-

[667] R. 1157–1162.
[668] R. 1162.
[669] R. 1162–1163.

partment in the way it was handled, is it fair to say that it would have been impossible for the fraud which is now indicated in this situation to have been carried out without collusion between the president of the corporation, the assistant treasurer of the corporation, the head of the stock department of the corporation, and somebody on the outside to take care of sending in invoices from suppliers, bank statements, bank debit advices and other papers?"

Ritts answered, "I think that is quite obvious." Thorn's answer was, "It would have been absolutely impossible without very extensive collusion from the president of the company right on down" through all the people mentioned in the question.[670]

Then followed another question by counsel for Price, Waterhouse & Co.:

"* * * have you, in your study of accounting and in your experience as a public accountant prior to the present case ever read or come in contact with or heard of any situation in which there existed such widespread collusion between high officials, subordinates and outsiders?"

Both answered that they had not,[671] although Price, Waterhouse & Co. in an examination some years ago uncovered the clue to the gigantic fraud perpetrated by Ivar Kreuger.[672] While there may be points of dissimilarity between the fraud perpetrated by Ivar Kreuger and that perpetrated by Coster, the following excerpts from the Price, Waterhouse & Co.[673] report in the earlier case seem particularly appropriate in view of the specific question asked of Ritts and Thorn.

"The perpetration of frauds on so large a scale and over so long a period would have been impossible but for * * * (4) the loyalty or unquestioning obedience of officials, who were evidently selected with great care (some for their ability and honesty, others for their weaknesses), having regard to the parts which Kreuger intended them to take in the execution of his plans.

* * * * * * *

"The frauds could not have been consummated without assistance—witting or unwitting—of some of his associates, including some of the officers of the holding and financial companies * * * It is apparent that * * * subserviency if not complicity on the part of some of the employees * * * and forgery of documents in order to meet demands for evidence confirmatory of book entries, all contributed to prevent such audits as were made from resulting in exposure."[674]

D. CASH IN BANKS AND ON HAND

The preceding subsection dealing with internal check and control indicated the importance of that subject in relation to the audit program and a subsequent section will demonstrate Price, Water-

[670] R. 724, 724A, 1232. (For Rowbotham's opinion. see his testimony quoted as the conclusion of this section, page 358 *infra*.)

[671] R. 724A, 1233.

[672] P. 495.

[673] Continental firm.

[674] "A. B. Kreuger & Toll Group of Companies—Final Report dated November 28, 1932—Price, Waterhouse & Co., Stockholm" printed in Hearings before a Sub-Committee of the Committee on Banking and Currency of the United States Senate on Stock Exchange Practices, Part 4, January 11–12, 1933. Thorn stated he had read about the report but of course had nothing to do with the work on it. R. 1246. See also P. 495–496 and Ivar Kreuger II, "Fortune," June 1933.

house & Co.'s recognition of the inadequacy of such control in some of the units of McKesson & Robbins subject to their examination.[675] Further recognition of the internal control feature of the work is found in the firm's instructions to the staff in connection with the examination of cash transactions. Testimony reviewed in the previous section, in this, and in sections to follow on receivables and inventories indicate that a proper verification of the cash transactions was considered an important step in establishing the authenticity of transactions with customers and creditors, as well as in verifying the balances of cash on hand and in bank. The following quotation is from the cover page of a two page Price, Waterhouse & Co. memorandum regarding verification of cash and bank balances in connection with so-called balance sheet audits and appears beneath the comment that "this is a supplement to, and not a substitute for, the Federal Reserve Bulletin." [676]

"TO THE MEMBERS OF THE STAFF:

We think it well to call the attention of our staff to the fact that, in organizations where an adequate system of internal check cannot be maintained by reason of the smallness of the organization, our examination into the cash transactions, particularly the verification of the cash and bank balances at the close of the period under audit, should be conducted in a careful and painstaking manner and that the limited verification as outlined in the Federal Reserve Bulletin of April, 1917, should be extended. We have, accordingly, prepared and are attaching hereto a memorandum outlining the procedure to be followed in connection with the verification of the cash and bank balances and it is requested that the schedules containing particulars thereof should show clearly the extent of the verification effected. Where bank practice does not permit of an exact adherence to the methods outlined (as in New York), the verifications should be of a character substantially equivalent.

PRICE, WATERHOUSE & CO."

The memorandum itself, because of its importance in relation to the work of the audit, is reproduced in full:

"MEMORANDUM REGARDING VERIFICATION OF CASH AND BANK BALANCES IN CONNECTION WITH SO-CALLED BALANCE SHEET AUDITS

"In verifying the cash the following procedure should be adopted, viz:

"(1) The cash on hand in so far as circumstances permit should be counted promptly at the close of business on the last day of the month of the period covered by the audit.

"(2) In the event that the cash is not counted at that time it may be necessary when it is actually counted to make a supplementary and simultaneous verification of the bank balances.

"NOTE.—This applies particularly to companies not having a petty cash fund under the imprest system.

---

[675] Pages 186-187 *supra* and 318 ff. *infra*.

[676] Ex. 17.

"(3) Items other than currency and coin must be listed in detail and the nature thereof properly described in the working schedules.

"(4) Checks and vouchers supporting disbursements and held in lieu of cash must be listed and full particulars regarding the date of the check and voucher and names of payee and payer embodied in the schedules.

"(5) Receipts from employees for advances or any other items should be listed in detail with dates.

"NOTE.—The items listed under (4) and (5) should be presented to a responsible official of the company for his approval.

"(6) The cancelled checks returned by the bank during the last month of the period should be compared with the entries in the cash book, i. e., name of payee and amount of check, while checks dated prior to the closing month should be compared with the previous reconciliation prepared by the client. The endorsements on the checks must be scrutinized; and where endorsements exist other than those of banks and the payee, inquiries should be made to determine whether or not irregularities exist in connection with such unusual or irregular endorsements. Before the completion of the audit the outstanding checks which form part of the bank reconciliation should be obtained from the bank direct and compared with entries in the cash book.

"(7) Outstanding checks not examined at previous audit on account of not being cancelled and returned by the bank before completion of work should be inspected and traced to the cash book entries.

"(8) In cases where the system of internal check in force is weak the cancelled checks for some other month than the last month of the year should also be examined and compared with the disbursements recorded in the cash book.

"(9) Currency checks for other than petty cash disbursements should be inquired into and tested by examination of supporting documents. A list of such checks and the account to which expenditure has been charged should be prepared for official's approval.

"(10) Any erasures on a check, indistinct endorsements or other suspicious features should be carefully inquired into.

"(11) Securities or negotiable instruments should be examined simultaneously with cash count.

"(12) Cash receipts (daily) for at least the last month of the period should be traced to the bank statement.

"(13) In cases where the internal check is weak a comparison of the collections recorded in the cash book should be made with the original deposit slips on file at the bank or with copies thereof obtained direct from the bank for a period of at least ten days prior or subsequent to the close of the period.

"NOTE.—If any suspicious circumstances develop during the course of the examination they should immediately be called to the attention of a principal of the firm or to the manager in charge of the work. This should be done by the assistant before the matter is discussed with the client."

The actual cash work program prepared for use on the McKesson engagement adhered closely to the requirements laid down in the memorandum. The program [677] reproduced below was prepared in mimeographed form by Thorn for use on all units of McKesson & Robbins under examination by Price, Waterhouse & Co.'s New York staff. A similar program of work was followed in the other offices of the firm.[678]

[677] Ex. 21, 29; R. 970.

[678] R. 439–441, 970–971.

"Cash—Work Program

"(1) Prepare and mail requests for confirmations, enclosing self-addressed return envelope.

"(2) Obtain and foot company's bank reconciliation as at November 30th. Check company's balance to the books and check bank balance to the opening balance shown on the December bank statement.

"(3) Obtain the December bank statement and the checks paid by the bank during December. Compare these checks dated in December with the December entries in the cash disbursements book as to date, payee and amount. Compare checks dated prior to December 1st with the company's reconciliation at November 30th. In connection with this work, examine the checks as to signatures, endorsements, and date of the bank's paid perforation and list for approval checks bearing the second endorsements of employees. List for further inquiry any checks for substantial amounts drawn to 'Cash' and any checks representing large and unusual payments to officers or employees.

"(4) Compare checks left open in the company's November 30th reconciliation and in the December cash disbursements book with the outstanding checks shown on the December 31st reconciliation prepared for us by the company.

"(5) Trace all receipts shown in the December cash receipts book and receipts shown on the company's November 30th reconciliation to the credits shown on the December bank statement and to the December 31st reconciliation. Note whether there were any unreasonable delays in depositing cash receipts as indicated by the cash-book dates and the bank statement dates. Check the details of the last three deposits in December and first three deposits in January from the cash receipts book to company's duplicate deposit tickets. The company has requested us not to confirm deposit tickets with the banks. If receipts are not deposited intact, this fact should be mentioned in your memorandum.

"(6) Foot the December 31st reconciliation and make sure that there are no open items thereon.

"(7) Foot the cash receipts and disbursement books for December and trace the totals to the general ledger.

"(8) Reconcile the total disbursements per the cash-book for December with the total charges per the December bank statement.

"(9) Reconcile total receipts per the cash-book for December with total credits per the bank statement for December.

"(10) Reconcile total disbursements and receipts per the cash-book with the total charges and credits per the bank statement for the month of July and check company's reconciliation at July 31st as outlined in the foregoing items (2), (3) and (4). Foot the cash receipts and disbursements books for July and trace the totals to the general ledger.

"(11) Prepare schedules of interbranch, intercompany, and inter-bank cash transfers for the period from December 20th to January 10th.

"(12) Examine checks outstanding at the time of our previous examination which were not examined by us at that time.

"(13) At a convenient date in January, obtain directly from the bank the bank statement and checks paid to date. If this statement is not obtained from the bank unopened, compare the checks with the bank statement to see that none is missing. Trace all paid checks dated December 31st or prior to the checks shown outstanding on the December 31st reconciliation and, in addition, scrutinize very carefully the dates of endorsements and paid perforations to determine that checks dated in January had not been actually issued in December. This phase of the work is of the utmost importance. Trace deposits in transit per the December 31st reconciliation to the January bank statement.

"(14) With reference to the petty cash fund, this fund should be counted and the notes receivable examined at the close of business on December 31st, if this work can be done without incurring traveling expenses; otherwise, these assets may be examined at the beginning of the examination without concurrently reconciling the bank accounts.

"(15) The foregoing is a general program outlining the minimum work to be done on cash. This program should of course, be modified and added to in order to meet the requirements of each particular examination. The additional work done should be described below."

It will be noted that this specific work program varied in at least one respect from the foregoing general memorandum. Where internal control is weak, the memorandum required that original deposit slips or copies obtained from the bank be compared with the cash book for 10 days before and 10 days after the closing date. The specific work program, however, required a comparison for 3 days before and 3 days after closing date with the Company's duplicate deposit slips as the client requested that the deposit slips not be confirmed at the banks.

In our hearings, this specific work program was compared item by item by Rowbotham with the suggested program laid down in the American Institute of Accountants' bulletin "Examination of Financial Statement by Independent Public Accountants." The comparison showed that the programs were substantially the same except for inapplicable items and the omission of the optional procedure as to checking receipts with deposit slips obtained from the bank [679] which was covered in the Bulletin by this sentence: "In certain instances such comparison may be extended to include a check of original deposit slips or authenticated copies thereof." [680]

The procedure laid down by Thorn in the specific cash work program reproduced above was changed in two significant respects on the work at Bridgeport. The first of these was that part of item five which required the comparison of duplicate deposit slips for the last 3 days of December and the first 3 days of January with the cash book entries. Ritts testified that no duplicate deposit tickets were available at Bridgeport as the Company never followed the practice of keeping them in that office. He could not recall whether he had ever suggested a change in this system although he personally preferred having duplicates of all deposit slips. Instead of checking with duplicate deposit slips, the deposits as shown on the bank statement were compared with the detail in the cash books.[681] The comparison with the Company's duplicate deposit slips was made in the wholesale houses but originals or copies authenticated by the banks were not obtained anywhere because in arranging for the work Coster requested

---

[679] R. 1858-1860. "* * * that was omitted because the problem there seemed to be one of catching minor defalcations of cashiers around those 48 houses * * *." Testimony of Rowbotham, R. 1860.

[680] Ex. 117 (p. 12).

[681] R. 437-443.

that this step be omitted,[682] and Price, Waterhouse & Co., although recommending it, did not consider this step necessary as part of their balance sheet examinations in this case.[683]

In connection with this variation of the audit program to adjust it to conditions found at Bridgeport and to comply with Coster's request not to ask the banks for original or authenticated copies of deposit slips, it should be recalled that at the time this audit step was recommended by Price, Waterhouse & Co. and rejected by Coster, there was no Manning & Company and receipts purportedly from the foreign crude drug customers were deposited separately from the other receipts. The deposit slips on the latter were prepared by Miss Bakos, a cashier in George Dietrich's office. However, she never saw the remittances from the foreign crude drug customers but for her records was advised of them and the bank in which they were deposited by George Dietrich.[684] McKesson deposit slips covering these transactions, secured from the bank for the hearings, disclosed single items of deposit covering credits to more than one account and were identified as having been written by George Dietrich. It will also be recalled that Seal of S. D. Leidesdorf & Co., in explaining the manner in which the fraudulent transactions were handled at this time, testified that single checks from accounts controlled by Coster and his brothers were deposited (deposits not made by Miss Bakos) and recorded on the books of the McKesson Companies at Bridgeport as receipts frequently from two or more foreign crude drug customers located in different cities.[685]

The other requirement omitted at Bridgeport (with Thorn's approval) was the reconciliation of the bank accounts at July 31. It was stated that this work was done in the wholesale houses as an extra precaution to catch minor defalcations of cashiers where all the cash records were handled by one person.[686] In lieu of this procedure at Bridgeport, Ritts required the vouching of all items returned with the January bank statements.[687]

At this point a somewhat detailed consideration of the cash work done at Bridgeport is especially necessary because Price, Waterhouse & Co.'s representatives testified that they relied heavily on apparent

---

682 "I also said that we would like to have Mr. Coster consider whether we should examine a few days' original bank deposit slips in connection with our cash verification and that, unless he instructed us to the contrary, we would in future check original bank deposit slips for a few days in December and January, to the cash receipts book. After considering the point for a few days, Mr. Coster instructed us not to do this. This is referred to in a subsequent letter we later wrote to Mr. Coster confirming our understanding of the matter." Ex. 83, Memorandum regarding 1930 accounts of the Connecticut Company, signed by A. Jaureguy.

683 R. 439.

684 R. 2643–2658; pages 113–115 *supra*.

685 R. 4562–4567; pages 116–117 *supra*.

686 R. 442. Wyman understood that the step was added to satisfy officials at Bridgeport as to the handling of cash at the branches. R. 328.

687 R. 442.

collection as the best evidence of the authenticity of the foreign crude business.[688] If suspicion had pointed to Manning & Company, through whom all of the collections were supposedly effected in later years, as being fraudulent, it is probable that the entire scheme would have been uncovered.

All of the staff who took part in the work on this cash program on the 1937 audit at Bridgeport were questioned at the hearings concerning the manner of its execution. Thorn in that year counted the cash there and mailed the requests for confirmation of bank balances on December 31.[689] Wyman [690] completed the program for the Canadian Company and two juniors,[691, 692] under Ritts' or Wyman's supervision completed the work on the Connecticut Division.

The bank accounts examined for the Canadian Company included two in the same bank in Bridgeport, two in Montreal banks, one in a branch of a New York bank, and Manning & Company of Montreal. For the Connecticut Division four accounts were carried in Bridgeport, three in New York, one in Paris, France, and Manning & Company in Montreal.[693] The head office of the Maryland Company at Bridgeport and other units of the Company throughout the country carried bank accounts in various cities in the United States and in foreign countries.

Wyman, who had progressed from junior to senior status in 6 years work with Price, Waterhouse & Co. was in charge at Bridgeport in 1937 during the time the cash work was in progress, as Ritts was in New York assisting Thorn much of the time. Wyman testified that he received no oral instructions from Ritts but merely followed the

---

[688] See testimony of Rowbotham at R. 2008:

> "Now, as for accounts receivable, it has always seemed to me that the best verification you could get on the accounts receivable is the fact of the collection of it and that seemed to me proof of the existence of these accounts, but as to whether Robert Dietrich had a warehouse full of crude drugs ultimately some time or other we had to rely on the officials of the company as to that quantity and quality and condition. I mean, I could go out there and look at those crude drugs and then be none the wiser."

See also testimony of Thorn at footnote 641 *supra*.

[689] R. 878–879.

[690] *George F. Wyman* (Harvard AB, 1927), Ritts' understudy in 1937, was employed by Price, Waterhouse & Co. through the placement bureau of the American Institute of Accountants, December 1, 1931, after 2 years with a newspaper concern and a year and a half as a clerk in the mortgage department of the Guardian Life Insurance Company of America. He first worked on the McKesson engagement as a junior in the 1932 and 1933 examinations at Jacksonville, in charge at Chattanooga for 1934 and 1935, and Birmingham in 1936. He secured his certificate as a certified public accountant in New York in April 1938. (R. 305–307, 386; Ex. 212.)

[691] One of these, who graduated from a prominent eastern university in 1924 and attended a metropolitan university for 1 year, was employed by Price, Waterhouse & Co. from January 4 to February 18, 1932, and again from January 17 to 29, 1938. He hoped the first employment would be permanent but took the second on a temporary basis and resigned on the date stated. He had done investment analysis work for 5 years and was a special investigator for 2 years for one concern and an accountant for 2 years for another. He was not a C. P. A. (R. 1323–1324, 1340; Ex. 212.)

[692] The other, who took about 2½ years' work in a metropolitan university, was employed by Price, Waterhouse & Co. on December 27, 1937, on his own application. He had had a varied experience as bookkeeper and accountant with several business firms over a period of 5 years before deciding to apply for a position in public accounting work. He had passed the New York C. P. A. examination and was entitled to his certificate on completion of the experience requirement (R. 386–387, 402; Ex. 212).

[693] Ex. 21, 29, 29A.

typed work program by comparing it with what had been done the previous year as shown by that year's work papers for the Canadian Company.[694] One junior carried out most of the cash work on the Connecticut Company in one of the two weeks he was employed by Price, Waterhouse & Co. On his resignation another junior completed the work. The junior who began the work testified that Ritts was not in Bridgeport during the week while he was at Bridgeport and presumed that he received instructions from Wyman although he could not recall any special instructions.[695]

This junior remembered very little about his week's work and had difficulty in explaining why some of the steps in the program were required. When he took up the work the bank statements and canceled checks were handed to him in a box. He did his work in the directors' room, and put the papers away in a safe at night, but he could not remember where the safe was. The Manning & Company account did not then appear unusual to him,[696] nor did he recollect having asked any questions about the account but presumed that he did ask Wyman if Manning & Company was a bank. He never asked any employee of McKesson & Robbins about it. Counsel for Price, Waterhouse & Co. asked him if the papers from Manning & Company appeared "* * * to be such papers as would come from a bank." His answer was: "Not a bank, but a banking firm, possibly."

"Mr. STEWART. A private bank?
The WITNESS. Yes."[697]

He could not recall seeing any Manning & Company canceled checks or debit and credit advices such as were used by Manning & Company. He remembered nothing but the statements and one item.[698] He did not recall comparing entries in the cash book or looking for signatures, endorsements, or perforations. He "frankly" did not remember any positive step he took in connection with Manning & Company. He did not know whether duplicate deposit slips were kept at Bridgeport. When asked what purpose would be served by comparing them with the cash book entries he replied:

"A. I can say that it is just added, just an added check on the mechanism of the system of depositing receipts in the bank.
Q. [By Mr. GALPEER.] Specifically, what would that check, if you know?
A. It is a little vague. I find it a little hard to say exactly what it imports."[699]

---

[694] R. 314.
[695] All references to this testimony are included in R. 1326–1344.
[696] "Q. [By Mr. GALPEER.] Did the fact that there were no open items on those dates strike you in any way unusual with an active bank account?
A. Without a knowledge of Manning & Company's bank account I would say no." R. 1329.
[697] R. 1330.
[698] R. 1330–1331.
[699] R. 1334–1335.

It appears from the following answer to a question as to why he should look at bank perforations that he also was not sure on that point.

"A. I would say that that was to show that there was no substitution in any way of checks that went through the bank, also the proper date; in other words, the amount being checked.

Q. Why would that be significant?

A. The substitution, you mean, or the checking?

Q. The substitution.

A. Well, it just assures that everything is going through in a proper flow, I would say.

Q. Do you know of any other reason for watching perforations on bank checks?

A. I don't think of one at the moment." [700]

The same junior testified that he supposed he learned who had custody of the canceled checks and bank statements, but that he could not remember whether it was the comptroller's office or assistant treasurer's office. Neither did he know who made the regular monthly reconciliation.[701]

In response to further questions this junior said that he felt quite free at all times to ask questions of the senior in charge, Wyman.

"Q. [By Mr. STEWART.] Did you, from the work that you did on cash, see any occasion to ask any more questions about the Manning & Company account than any of the other banking accounts you examined?

A. Except that it was a different form and it was a private banking firm, not a national bank or trust company.

Q. But beyond that difference in form, did you see any more occasion to question the fact as to whether it was, in fact, a bank?

A. No." [702]

The foregoing quotation suggests that a description of the Manning & Company statement may be helpful here. The Manning & Company statements were printed in black on white paper, ruled in blue ink and measured 12½ inches in width by 17½ inches deep. Aside from its size, the Manning statement also differed from those of ordinary commercial banks [703] in its columnar headings and in other details. The Manning & Company December 1937 statement for the Canadian Company reproduced in section III is typical of these statements except that the entries occupy only one-half the sheet whereas the statements for the Connecticut Company and Division usually filled one sheet and part of another.[704] Except for Manning & Company, the eight banks represented in the accounts of the Canadian Company and the Connecticut Division were well known commercial banks, the form of whose statements and documents would be familiar to any junior.

---

[700] R. 1335–1336. Cf. Item (13) page 195 *supra*.

[701] R. 1338.

[702] R. 1341–1342.

[703] E. g. Ex. 198, 199, 239.

[704] Ex. 30; page 100 *supra*.

The erroneous acceptance of Manning & Company by Price, Waterhouse & Co. as a real bank goes back to its pretended inception in 1931. Thorn was in charge of the work in Bridgeport for this year.

Price, Waterhouse & Co.'s permanent file contained a memorandum regarding accounts receivable arising from crude drug exports prepared the year before during the 1930 audit in which Thorn described a sales contract with "Manning & Co., Ltd.," of Montreal in which Manning was referred to as a purchasing agent for several hundred retailers and jobbers throughout the British Empire.[705] The Charles Manning & Company, Limited contract with the Connecticut and Canadian (McKesson) Companies to which the foregoing referred was dated March 12, 1930 and had a 1-year term from that date. An abstract of this contract was included by Thorn in the Price, Waterhouse & Co. working papers.[706] An alleged balance sheet of Charles Manning & Company, Limited, which Thorn examined showed that Company's net worth at December 31, 1929, to be approximately $600,000.00.[707]

Jaureguy's memorandum to Rowbotham on the 1931 accounts devoted one page to an explanation of a new sales contract with "W. W. Smith & Co." replacing the previous year's arrangement with "Manning & Co." and related that "* * * Manning & Co., Montreal * * * during the year * * * went into the private banking business exclusively and sold its export business to W. W. Smith & Co. whose main office is in Liverpool and who are said to have 600 or so representatives all over the world * * *."[708] This new contract dated August 1, 1931, was between the Connecticut and Canadian (McKesson) Companies and W. W. Smith & Company, Inc., of New York (referred to therein as the New York Company) and was represented in the working papers by a two-page abstract.[709]

The second paragraph is the part of this abstract of interest in connection with Manning & Company's identity:

"Since the Connecticut Company on March 12, 1930 entered into a contract with Charles Manning & Co. Limited, a Canadian Corporation, for the latter to render certain services in promoting foreign trade of the McKesson Companies and contract has been renewed since to March 12, 1932. Also since Charles Manning and Co. Limited, have been acquired by Manning and Co. a co-partnership of Montreal, and which has caused all domestic and foreign buying and selling offices formerly owned by Charles Manning and Co. Limited to be transferred to the New York Company, which it has caused to be organized, and the said Manning and Co. have requested the Connecticut and Canadian Companys to

[705] Ex. 83, R. 811–12. Quoted in part at page 55 *supra*.

[706] Ex. 89, R. 956. Quoted at page 55 *supra*.

[707] Ex. 83, 89.

[708] Ex. 82.

[709] Ex. 55, R. 958–959. Price, Waterhouse & Co. reported through their counsel that this abstract was prepared by an assistant,—a temporary employee when on this engagement but previously employed for two periods of 2½ years each interrupted by resignations to enter private accounting work. Thorn when asked at the hearings to read the second paragraph said he could not read it.

execute a new agreement with the New York Company in lieu of contract of March 12, 1930."

The actual contract between the McKesson Companies and the New York Company (W. W. Smith & Company, Inc.),[710] referred to the formation of W. W. Smith & Company, Inc. by Manning & Company in the following words: "* * * which it caused to be organized * * * (one hundred per cent (100%) of the stock of which it owns) * * *." As appears, the assistant to whom Thorn delegated this important work did not abstract the reference to the 100% ownership of W. W. Smith & Company, Inc. by Manning & Company and thus either overlooked or did not know that according to other documents equally relied upon, the ownership of W. W. Smith & Company, Inc. was supposed to be in W. W. Smith & Co. of Liverpool.[711]

The new arrangement as made at August 1, 1931, was approved by the directors of the Connecticut and Canadian Companies at meetings recorded as having been held on September 3, 1931, the former at 3 o'clock in the afternoon and the latter at 3:45 p. m. Coster presided over both meetings and George E. Dietrich acted as secretary.[712]

According to the minutes [713] Coster explained the need for making the contracts which he exhibited to the meeting and "* * * explained that the amount to be paid Manning & Co. was somewhat higher than that formerly paid but that in his opinion the charge was entirely reasonable and proper." Then

"On motion duly made and seconded and by the affirmative vote of all present the following resolution was adopted:

"*Resolved*, That the system of foreign representation as explained to the meeting by the President has the entire approval of this Board of Directors and that the action of the President and of the other executive officers of this Company in negotiating, executing and delivering, in the name of this Company, a contract with Manning & Co., a co-partnership of Montreal, Canada, and of a subsidiary contract with W. W. Smith, Inc., a New York corporation, dated as of the first day of August, 1931 and in the form submitted to this meeting be, and the same hereby is approved, ratified and confirmed." [714]

Similar procedure was reported in identical language in the Canadian Company meeting.[715]

Thorn included abstracts of these minutes in his working papers and was questioned at some length about them. He insisted that he knew of only one contract—the signed one with W. W. Smith &

[710] Ex. 206. Quoted in part at pages 57-59 *supra*.

[711] Ex. 207. See also Ex. 82, 215.

[712] The minutes of the Connecticut Company meeting recite that F. Donald Coster, C. Barnum Seeley, Horace B. Merwin, Rowley W. Phillips, and George E. Dietrich (being the entire board except Herbert D. Robbins) were present. The minutes of the Canadian Company meeting recite that "All of the directors were present" (being those present at the Connecticut Company meeting plus Jonathan Grout). Ex. 179, 180 and pages 119-120 *supra*.

[713] Quoted at page 60 *supra*.

[714] Ex. 180.

[715] Ex. 179.

Company, Inc., and none with Manning & Company although the abstract opened with the phrase, "Re contract with Manning & Company and subsidiary contract with W. W. Smith, Inc."

"Q. [By Mr. GALPEER.] So that it is your idea that the present abstract covers both contracts referred to in the Board of Directors' minutes?

A. [By THORN.] My idea really is that there is really only one contract referred to in the minutes.

Mr. STEWART. Is it your inference, then, Mr. Thorn, that the reference to subsidiary contract with W. W. Smith & Company refers to the fact that the Smith Contract was a successor contract to the Manning contract, of the preceding year which is mentioned in that abstract?

The WITNESS. Yes." [716]

Although Price, Waterhouse & Co. was thus apparently unaware of its existence, there was introduced at the hearings a nine page agreement between Manning & Company and the McKesson Companies, dated August 1, 1931,[717] taken from the contract files of McKesson & Robbins [718] to which was attached a copy of the W. W. Smith & Company, Inc. contract previously referred to. Although the copy introduced was unsigned it appears to be the one referred to in the minutes.

The Manning & Company agreement recited that the assets and business of Charles Manning & Company, Limited had been acquired by said Manning & Company which had caused all the foreign and domestic buying and selling offices and agencies formerly owned and conducted by said Charles Manning & Company, Limited to be transferred to W. W. Smith & Company, Inc., a New York corporation which it had caused to be organized for that purpose, and 100% of the stock of which it owned. It also stated that Manning & Company had requested the McKesson Companies to execute a new agreement with said W. W. Smith & Company, Inc. in lieu of the contract of March 12, 1930 with Charles Manning & Company, Limited, as renewed and extended and that Manning & Company which as above stated owned 100% of the stock of W. W. Smith & Company, Inc. unconditionally guaranteed complete and prompt performance of said new agreement between W. W. Smith & Company, Inc. and the McKesson Companies, a copy of which was annexed to the Manning contract.

Paragraph three of the contract stated:

"Manning & Company expressly represent that it has acquired all of the foreign exchange and banking business formerly conducted by said Charles Manning & Company, Limited, and that hereafter such business will be conducted by it under its own name."

Paragraph six of the contract covered the banking service contracted for between the co-partnership of Manning & Company and

---

716 R. 960. See also R. 957–960.

717 Ex. 216. Quoted in part at pages 56–57 *supra*.

718 R. 4460.

the McKesson Companies. Briefly, the partnership was prepared to handle letters of credit to finance shipments of merchandise up to one million dollars at any one time, at varying rates of commission, depending on the length of the credit.[719]

Here then was the origin of Manning & Company as a bank which opened with two letters of credit, one with the Connecticut Company for $250,000, and the other for $150,000 with the Canadian Company, both dated August 5, 1931, and expiring August 5, 1932 after which this method of apparently doing business was abandoned supposedly in favor of individual letters of authority covering each sight draft.[720]

In addition to the W. W. Smith & Company, Inc. contract and the Manning & Company contract, both dated August 1, 1931, which referred to the 100% ownership of W. W. Smith & Company, Inc. by Manning & Company, there was also a guaranty of the W. W. Smith & Company, Inc. contract by a co-partnership, W. W. Smith & Co. of Liverpool, England. This third contract, also dated August 1, 1931, is represented in evidence by a digest taken from the files of McKesson & Robbins, Incorporated [721] and by a note added to the Price, Waterhouse & Co. abstract of the W. W. Smith & Company, Inc., contract.[722] The Liverpool partnership's interest in guaranteeing performance by a corporation stated to be 100% owned by the Montreal partnership of Manning & Company is not apparent.

Had Thorn been familiar with both the W. W. Smith & Company, Inc. and Manning & Company contracts of August 1, 1931, it would appear that he might have questioned not only the guaranty by the Liverpool partnership also dated August 1, 1931 but the purported Bradstreet's report dated October 14, 1931, which described W. W. Smith & Co. as the parent of "W. W. Smith & Co. Inc." W. W. Smith & Co. was described by this report as being Commission Merchants, purchasing, forwarding, and steamship agents with offices at 191 Montague Street, Brooklyn, New York, also Montreal, Hamburg, Genoa, Liverpool, Marseilles, Melbourne, Ceylon, Bombay, Hongkong. The report stated that the firm was established at London in 1857 and that the partnership W. W. Smith & Co. in July 1931, as a convenience in handling United States business, organized a corporation, "W. W. Smith & Co., Inc." in the State of New York, with a nominal capital of $10,000. It also was reported to have acquired in August 1931, the business of "Chas. Manning Ltd." of Montreal engaged in a general merchandise brokerage business.[723]

An important factor in the conflicting interests of Manning & Company and W. W. Smith & Co. in W. W. Smith & Company, Inc.

719 Ex. 216. Quoted in part at pages 56–57 *supra*.

720 Ex. O, P; and pages 117 ff. *infra*.

721 Ex. 215. Quoted at pages 59–60 *supra*.

722 Ex. 55.

723 Ex. 207 reproduced at page. 62 *supra*.

is that in one version the New York Corporation acquired a worldwide organization of buying and selling offices from Manning & Company, whereas under another interpretation the New York Corporation was merely the United States office for the old established partnership of W. W. Smith & Co. which had 600 representatives throughout the world.[724] Further inconsistency develops when the practice of Manning & Company in its purported banking business is examined to see in what manner the business might have yielded a profit to Manning & Company. Article 6 of the Manning & Company agreement provided a schedule of rates of commission to be charged for the granting of credits and further provided that the rates were to be subject to change from time to time to conform to the lowest prevailing market rates established by recognized commercial banks and bankers. But, as we have seen, letters of credit were only issued thereunder covering the first year's operations of the McKesson Companies under this arrangement and thereafter no credit was extended. The Manning & Company bank statements and samples of debit and credit advices from which such statements were prepared do not indicate that any charge was made by the bank for service in connection with either collections or payments.[725] In addition, since it was the opinion of Thorn that because the McKesson balance with Manning & Company was carried in United States dollars and that Manning & Company would have to carry this with New York banks,[726] and, since the year end balances indicated that the deposit carried with Manning & Company was comparatively small in any event, it is hard to conceive that a bank profit ordinarily available from deposits would have been available to Manning & Company at least in an amount to compensate for the purported services rendered.

The 1933 extensions of the W. W. Smith & Company, Inc. contract and W. W. Smith & Co. contract of guaranty as abstracted by Price, Waterhouse & Co. [727] made no mention of Manning & Company. The new W. W. Smith & Company, Inc. contract and W. W. Smith & Co. contract of guaranty of August 1, 1935 made no reference to Manning & Company either, but stated that W. W. Smith & Co. had a substantial financial interest in W. W. Smith & Company, Inc. and would derive some share of the profits accruing to W. W. Smith & Company, Inc. from the McKesson agreements.[728]

The foregoing paragraphs cover the pretended establishment of Manning & Company as a bank. Some aspects of its purported operations must be examined. For example, at our hearings a question was raised with Thorn, who had been cashier of a country bank

---

[724] Ex. 207.
[725] Ex. 30, 33, 34.
[726] R. 951, quoted in part at page 206 *infra*.
[727] Ex. 56. Quoted in part at page 63 *supra*.
[728] Ex. 50. Quoted in part at pages 63–65 *supra*.

and had worked in a New York bank, as to the practice of Manning & Company (a Canadian bank) of carrying the McKesson accounts in United States dollars. In the case of other dollar balances difficulties were encountered as reflected in the Price, Waterhouse & Co. memorandum on the Canadian Company accounts for 1931 where it was stated that McGloon did not give his reasons for maintaining that no adjustment for exchange between Canadian and United States dollars should be made in the balances carried with two Canadian banks. Thorn explained that the two banks must have been the Royal Bank of Canada and the Canadian Bank of Commerce and that McGloon probably thought the adjustment of $601.68 was too small an amount to bother with, that it was a minor matter and might well have been left out of the memorandum. The foreign exchange situation was reviewed again the next year, for the first item in the memorandum on the 1932 accounts stated "Two of the bank accounts with Canadian banks were stated in Canadian currency but the balances have been adjusted to U. S. dollars." [729]

But as for Manning & Company, Thorn made sure it carried McKesson's balances in U. S. dollars (no adjustments therefore being necessary). Thorn's understanding of the situation was summarized in his testimony at page 951:

> "Q. [By Mr. Galpeer.] If I understand you correctly, you assumed that Manning & Company would have covering commitments with New York banks for the amount of the balance that McKesson had with it?
>
> A. They would simply have an account in the New York banks. I have a note in my papers there in the year that account was opened which states that this account was to be carried in United States dollars. The collection would be made in United States dollars and deposited by Manning in their New York Account. This note also states that it is a collection account and not a deposit account and that checks will not be drawn on the account [730] and that remittances will be made to Bridgeport as requested."

He felt justified in including the balance of this account under cash in banks because the amount was available on demand and he had seen deposits in New York bank accounts of McKesson coming from Manning & Company.[731] Thorn never discussed the classification of the Manning & Company account balance with Rowbotham.[732] On this point of classification it may be noted here that George Dietrich's department prepared a daily cash report,[733] copies of which went to the treasurer and comptroller of the Company. There is no evidence

[729] Ex. 205; R. 949.

[730] On the 1931 Manning & Company confirmation, however, there is no answer to the request, "State if balance is not subject to withdrawal by check." Ex. O. P.

[731] Page 67, footnote 200 *supra* and pages 212-213 *infra*.

[732] "Q. [By Mr. Galpeer]. Did you discuss this with Mr. Rowbotham or anybody else, I mean the sort of point we are discussing now?

A. [By Thorn.] No, in the first place I have no recollection of discussing it with him and I think I wouldn't discuss any matter like a bank account with him." R. 952.

[733] Ex. 228.

that this type of report which was an internal memorandum of the Company, was ever examined by the auditors. The report showed seven bank accounts with names of the banks in print and others were written in as required. Balances were shown for "Maryland Account," "Wholesalers' Division Account," "Connecticut Division Account" and "Totals." This report did not cover the Canadian Company and never included Manning & Company. Why it did not include Manning & Company, McGloon, the comptroller of the Company, was unable to say. On this point he referred us to Thompson, the treasurer, who, when he first learned of Manning & Company, did not have a clear picture of how it functioned but later got the impression it was not a true bank account.[734]

Pursuing still further Thorn's knowledge of how the Manning & Company account operated more confusion develops. Despite the fact that all invoices to foreign crude drug customers were stamped "Payment for this invoice must be made in U. S. currency" [735] and the printed invoices stated "Important:—Bills not paid when due will be subject to draft with exchange on New York" [736] Thorn testified that Manning & Company, a collection receiver,[737] might receive drafts on London or Montreal as well as on New York, but all collections would be deposited in New York and hence the former converted into U. S. dollars.[738] Although all debit memoranda for sight drafts drawn by vendors against Manning & Company indicated that the amount was in U. S. currency, the credit memoranda on payments purportedly received by Manning & Company for McKesson did not specify whether in Canadian or United States dollars.[739] When asked why, if the payments were to be in U. S. dollars and balances were to be carried by it in New York bank accounts, Manning & Company of Montreal was employed to handle this business Thorn said he

---

[734] R. 1643, 2068, 2117.

[735] Ex. 229.

[736] Ex. 8D.

[737] "Q. [By Mr. Galpeer.] In the particular situation here, how would these customers spread all over the world be notified to pay Manning and not McKesson?

A. [By Thorn] As I understood it, they used the regular McKesson billhead, but attached a notice of some kind to it, I thought in sticker form.

Q. Who attached that notice?

A. I thought it was George Dietrich.

Q. Did you ever ask him, did you ever see that sticker?

A. No, I never did, and I might say and in general at that point, I might say that I am not particularly concerned with forms, as to just what the particular form of any of these items is, from my standpoint." R. 1141.

[738] "Q. [By Mr. Galpeer.] So that it was your conception that Manning & Company would receive United States funds and would deposit it in some account which it had in the United States?

A. Well, I shouldn't say they would receive United States funds, but they would receive funds which they would convert into United States funds. That is, if they didn't receive a draft drawn on New York they received a draft on London or Montreal, they would deposit that in New York for conversion into United States dollars." R. 952.

[739] Ex. 33, 34.

could not tell but he probably got an explanation "right from the source"—Coster.

"A. The explanation I imagine I got from him would be the matter of goodwill, to have those funds collected within the British Empire,—the funds held within the British Empire, to put it another way, than to have them collected in Bridgeport.

Q. [By Mr. GALPEER.] The contract itself, as you know, provided,—and the bills themselves that went out to the customers provided that the payment was to be made in U. S. Dollars?

A. Yes, sir.

Q. So that to that extent, at any rate, it would not be a question of paying in Empire currency, I mean it was apparent on the face that it would have to be U. S. dollars?

A. Yes, sir." [740]

While Thorn considered the Manning balance to be available on demand he admitted that he saw no evidence that such transfers as were made [741] might not have been made after notice. This did not disturb him, however, for he felt the amounts involved were insignificant, being only $75,000, approximately, at December 31, 1937 in a total of $3,358,571.39 cash in banks and on hand as reported in the consolidated balance sheet on that date. Other years the balance, Thorn testified, was more nearly $5,000. The real significance of the account then lies in the millions of dollars of transactions which were supposed to have gone through it rather than in the year end balance.[742] Thorn testified that it was not customary and it did not occur to him to ask the Montreal office of the Canadian firm of Price, Waterhouse & Co. to make such inquiries as would have revealed that Manning & Company was merely a mailing address and not a bank, although he had conducted correspondence with that office in respect to work they did on some wholesale drug houses which McKesson sought to acquire in Canada but never did.[743]

A final point in connection with Manning & Company on which Thorn, on the basis of his banking experience might have had special knowledge, was the documentary evidence which should accompany a bank debit advice. He got the impression from reports on a Norwegian subsidiary that foreign countries did not return checks or other documents but he did not know about Canadian practice although he did think that the Royal Bank of Canada and the Canadian Bank of Commerce did return checks. Thorn only professed to have a general knowledge of United States practice, he did not consider that he was an authority, although he thought it was customary here for banks to return drafts drawn against its depositors. In any event, he was

740 R. 954–955.

741 See pages 212–213 *infra*.

742 R. 953–954.

743 R 1204–1205.

satisfied in this case with receipt from the bank of a debit advice unsupported by any documents other than the monthly statements and the year end confirmation.[744]

Thorn apparently was reassured on all of these Manning transactions by explanations obtained from Coster and George Dietrich and the apparent similarity to him of the transactions with those carried on with New York banks prior to the transfer of the business to Manning in 1931. Thorn stated that had he been in Bridgeport after 1931 he would not have learned about letters of authority to draw on Manning & Company or other documents in connection with purchases for it was his understanding that Bridgeport was not to get documents other than the debit advice and vendor's invoice. Thorn's recollection was that these suppliers were authorized to draw on Manning by presenting a copy of McKesson's original purchase order and that no other documents were required.

"Since that document, of course, didn't carry title to the goods that was not sent to Bridgeport. Manning & Company would charge McKesson's account and remit to the supplier and simply advise McKesson of the amount of the charge." [745]

Thorn was asked whether he should not have been interested in these mechanical details in connection with his review of the client's system of internal check and control. His answer indicated his reliance on the fact that the Manning transactions appeared to him to be similar to those of other banks and his belief that the mechanics of internal control were unimportant so long as available evidence indicated to him that adequate control existed:

"Q. [By Mr. GALPEER.] Would you have said that the manner in which Manning & Company was advised to meet the draft of the suppliers or the manner in which the suppliers were advised to draw on Manning was or was not within the realm of things that you would have checked or cared about in this connection?

A. I think the exact manner was not. I think what was important there from the standpoint of internal control, what authorization we had for that payment, whether it was independently supported, and as I understood these transactions, there was the purchase order from McKesson, there was the purchase invoice from the supplier, there was the debit advice from the bank, and that was satisfactory to me.

It seemed to me that McKesson was protected there as much as they are protected on any revolving letter of credit, and it seemed to me that their payments were well controlled.

Q. In connection with the question of internal control, would it have been pertinent to you to find out who prepared the purchase orders, who received the purchase invoices and who received the Manning debit advices, that is, who at McKesson?

A. I think I would want to know who prepared the purchase order. I am not sure that I have the other questions in mind now. What was the next?

---

[744] R. 1127–1131.

[745] R. 1138–1139.

Q. Generally speaking, I mean the mechanics in which these three instruments that you speak of that you would have been satisfied with were handled at McKesson; in other words, the sources from which they emanated and how they were subsequently handled.

A. No, I don't believe I would be particularly concerned with that." [746]

In respect to collections from customers Thorn's opinion was very much the same for he pointed out that the entire selling and collecting routine were related in such a way that seeing the cash collected was evidence of the authenticity of the series of transactions culminating in the collection:

"Q. [By Mr. GALPEER.] As a matter of fact, when you say that you see all the cash received from the customer, again just a definition of terms, what we have in mind is the credit advice from Manning stating that they had credited McKesson's account on account of a remittance from a certain customer.

A. I think it should always be borne in mind that that was to me the same as a credit advice from Guaranty Trust Company which, prior to 1931, we had.

Q. When somebody paid the Guaranty Trust Company and you received a credit advice of that, there would have been some notice or notification by McKesson to that party to pay the Guaranty Trust Company?

A. No doubt." [747]

Although Thorn assumed that McKesson must have advised its customers to pay the Guaranty Trust Company he saw no documents to that effect—in fact no more evidence than he saw in connection with Manning & Company. In both cases the money was assumed to have come from customers who paid it directly to the banks.[748] As in the case of payments for purchases, Thorn was not much concerned with the manner in which transactions were handled. "* * * from an auditing standpoint I have no concern with the exact mechanics down to the last particular with which they are able to do it. The main thing with me; after all, is that it works." Thorn summed up the receipts side of the Manning transactions as follows:

"* * * Similarly, I don't think the manner in which the customer is advised to remit direct to McKesson or to remit to a certain bank—I don't think that is a part of the internal control, and I don't think I would have inquired into it if I had been on the job at all. I don't think I would care." [749]

The 1931 memorandum on the Canadian Company written by Thorn seems to have been followed by Ritts in covering the Canadian Company for 1932 as he repeated material from the 1931 memorandum in respect to the Bradstreet report, recited the terms of the Smith

[746] R. 1150–1151.

[747] R. 1141.

[748] "Mr. STEWART. To sum it up, in the days when the Guaranty Trust Company was used, the system was the same as far as you can tell as it was in the days when Manning & Company was used except in one case, it was Manning and in the other it was the Guaranty.

The WITNESS. We shouldn't restrict it entirely to Guaranty Trust Company because I don't know what banks were used in addition to the Guaranty Trust Company. That is, I don't want to say that all of this business was handled through the Guaranty Trust Company. I don't know." R. 1144.

[749] R. 1149. "If I had been on the job" refers to the last 3 years when Ritts was in charge at Bridgeport.

contract, and did not mention Manning & Company.[750] The same holds true for the 1932 memorandum on the Connecticut Company.[751] Any possibility of a doubt as to Manning & Company's authentic character seems to have passed by the time Ritts took charge of the engagement at Bridgeport on the 1932 examination which was the second year of Manning & Company's treatment as a bank. Ritts had been an assistant on the work the preceding two years.

When questioned as to how he knew that Manning & Company was a bank, Ritts replied, "Well, actually the only knowledge we had that any of these institutions really existed was the documentary evidence that we had received from them in response to our requests." [752] He had, however, seen the offices of some of the other banks in the United States with which McKesson did business [753] such as The Bridgeport-City Trust Company and branch offices of Guaranty Trust Company of New York, Manufacturers Trust Company, and National City Bank. But there were other banks with which McKesson dealt that he knew no more about than Manning. He recalled that the latter included the Crocker State Bank of San Francisco; Chicago and foreign banks; and William Brandt and Son and William Bingham and Company (he did not recall the exact names), which did not include the words "bank" or "bankers" in their titles. It never occurred to Ritts to look in a bank directory to check on Manning & Company nor to ask the Montreal office of the Canadian firm of Price, Waterhouse & Co. to make an inquiry.[754]

Ritts referred to the minutes of a Board of Directors meeting of the Canadian Company held on April 4, 1935 which he had read and copies of which were retained in his working papers. He felt that he was entitled to rely on these minutes for there were two commercial bankers, H. B. Merwin and C. B. Seeley, and an investment banker, R. W. Phillips, among the directors present at the meeting at which Manning & Company was approved as a bank depositary for the Canadian Company.[755] Ritts understood that Manning & Company were fiscal agents for the McKesson Companies rather than factors, but he could not say from whom he got that impression.[756] And Ritts did not know that since 1932 all foreign crude drug accounts throughout the year were supposedly collected through Manning & Company.[757] He did not recall ever having discussed the condition of any of the

---

750 Ex. 205; R. 4347–4348.

751 Ex. 81.

752 R. 447; cf. R. 143-144.

753 R. 446–447.

754 R. 453.

755 R. 694–695. Quoted at page 68 *supra*. See also R. 144, 455, 693-696, 726. The minutes of April 4, 1935 also refer, in connection with Manning & Company, to the minutes of the meeting held on September 3, 1931 (quoted at page 60 *supra*) which approved the August 1, 1931 contract with Manning & Company of which Price, Waterhouse & Co. were unaware. See page 202 *supra*.

756 R. 455.

757 R. 558–559, 140.

banks with Thompson, the treasurer of the Corporation, nor for that matter any other phase of the audit, although he agreed it would be the treasurer's duty to be familiar with such matters.[758]

Documentary evidence Ritts had seen which indicated that Manning & Company was a bank included the bank's statement and debit and credit memoranda which Price, Waterhouse & Co. representatives inspected each year and a confirmation of the balance which was filled in on a standard form supplied by Price, Waterhouse & Co. He had seen no checks nor check books nor record of acceptances payable or any other record dealing exclusively with Manning & Company. The Manning account was carried in the general cash book and written up from the debit and credit advices which Ritts understood were received by the McKesson Companies throughout the month. Ritts said duplicates were included in the statements which appeared unopened when they were given to the auditors at January 31.[759] Miss Walsh, bookkeeper for the Canadian Company, testified that no documents of any kind were received by her with the monthly statements from Manning & Company.[760]

The bank confirmations referred to were on standard forms copyrighted by the American Institute Publishing Co., Inc., and for 1937 reported balances of $44,041.06 and $32,486.08 respectively for the Connecticut Division and Canadian Company at December 31. The balances were labelled in each case "U. S. A. Dollar Account, No Interest", and there was no answer to the request "State if balance is not subject to withdrawal by check * * *."[761] The answer was "None" to questions relating to liabilities on loans, acceptances, endorsements, and other contingent liabilities. The signatures in type were "Per Pro. Manning & Co." with identical illegible signatures below in the space provided for the name and title of the officer. The corresponding bank statements and credit advices did not indicate that the account was in U. S. A. dollars but the debit advices did. Ritts never questioned whether the account could have been carried in U. S. A. dollars in a Canadian bank for he thought it could have been.[762]

The strongest indication Ritts had, which convinced him beyond doubt that Manning & Company was a bank, was that he actually saw evidence of cash transfers to New York bank accounts of McKesson which indicated to him, as he had been told, that whenever cash

---

758 R. 446. See also page 207 of this report referring to testimony of Thompson at R. 2116–2117 to the effect that he did not know when the account with Manning was opened and did not consider it to be a bank.

759 R. 146, 151, 742–744. But compare a junior's testimony, page 199 *supra*.

760 "Q. [By Mr. GALPEER.] And when you received the statement of Manning & Company, did that statement contain any supporting vouchers, documents, duplicate copies of advices, or anything of that sort. A. No, just the statement." R. 4385.

761 Cf. Ex. M–17, confirmation at December 31, 1934 which stated: "Balance subject to withdrawal by drafts;" and Ex. O and P, confirmations at December 31, 1931, which did not mention a restriction on withdrawal by check.

762 R. 432, 451; Ex. 30A, 30B, 31A, 31B, 33.

was needed these funds were drawn from Manning & Company. The audit working papers for 1931 indicated a transfer of $50,000 to a New York bank in November and another of $120,000 in December of that year.[763] Seal of S. D. Leidesdorf & Co. explained how these transfers were effected. The item of $120,000 was drawn on the account in the name of Manning & Company in the Chase National Bank, Hamilton Branch, in favor of McKesson & Robbins, Incorporated, and deposited in their account at the Guaranty Trust Company. The funds drawn against came from various members of the chain explained in detail earlier in this report.[764]

This transfer of funds coupled with the fact that at December 31, 1931, the close of the first year of Manning & Company as a bank, the confirmations from Manning listed two revolving commercial letters of credit, one with the Connecticut Company for $250,000, and one with the Canadian Company for $150,000, both dated August 5, 1931, expiring August 5, 1932, made Manning & Company appear like other banks. To Ritts these Manning letters of credit were similar to letters of credit with the National City Bank of New York and the Guaranty Trust Company.[765] While the other banks reported such letters of credit in recent years, Manning & Company did not indicate on their confirmations that there were "any letters of credit except in the year 1931 when the account was first opened."[766]

Knowledge of this situation led to the questioning of Ritts as to the authority by which Manning & Company issued debit memoranda covering payment of invoices from the several Canadian vendors. On direct examination Ritts was not certain how Manning was authorized to make the payments but assumed that the suppliers were authorized to draw on Manning & Company. These assumptions seem to have been based on what he was told,[767] rather than on documentary evidence which it now appears might have been available to

---

763 R. 145, 692.

764 The last of these transfers in the Connecticut Company was in 1933 and in the Canadian Company in 1936. Thereafter the Manning & Company accounts on the McKesson Companies' books, included only entries based on debit and credit advices pretending to reflect payments and receipts by Manning for the account of McKesson. See footnotes 200 and 407 *supra*.

765 R. 688–691.

766 R. 734–735.

767 R. 120–122.

"Q. [By Mr. GALPEER.] But, just to summarize this one point,—you have no knowledge of how Manning & Company was advised to meet these drafts supposed to be drawn by the Canadian vendors?

A. [By RITTS.] I don't think it is entirely fair to say I have no knowledge. You are asking me to testify that I actually saw authorizations. No, I did not, but in conducting my examination and making inquiries of the various people that handle such transactions, that is what I was told.

Q. Told what, sir?

A. That this was the way these purchases were made and that is the way they were paid for.

Q. You were told that Manning was advised how to meet these drafts by what method?

A. That the purchase order submitted to the various suppliers, these suppliers were authorized to draw on Manning, and Manning, in turn, I believe, was authorized to honor such drafts.

Q. How was Manning authorized to honor such drafts?

A. I couldn't state specifically how. I never saw such authorizations." R. 128.

him.[768] The purchase orders and vendors' invoices which led to these debits at Manning & Company quoted terms, "CASH AGAINST DOCUMENTS NET NO DISCOUNT U.S. CY. F. O. B. BRIDGEPORT OR NEW YORK U. S. A." Ritts had never seen the "documents" referred to but assumed that they would be submitted to Manning & Company but he did not know this as a matter of fact and he saw no necessity for asking such a question. He supposed though that Manning & Company would demand some evidence before paying out cash.[769] He did not think it his duty as an auditor to go beyond the debit advice as authority for the disbursement entry in the McKesson cash records.[770] The debit advices said on their face "Per your letter of authority", so he assumed that it meant exactly that, but he saw no purpose in looking up the letters to see if any were in existence for these letters would merely authorize the discharge of a liability rather than the creation of one,[771] and the books showed that the liabilities were in fact properly discharged.

The letters of authority referred to above Ritts thought might have been general in form and similar in effect to the revolving letter of credit with which he was familiar or they might have been specific letters similar to letters of credit for millions of dollars by which purchases were handled through other banks. In these other cases McKesson kept a credit register and an acceptances payable register in which all letter of credit transactions were recorded. The original revolving letter of credit on Manning & Company was included in the register but no other transaction described as a letter of credit with Manning & Company appeared.[772]

No drafts came back with the debit advices as far as Ritts knew but he assumed that bills of lading were attached for otherwise McKesson could not have claimed the shipment. The bill of lading he thought would have been released to the carrier so it would not have been available, hence it seemed to him to follow that he was justified in assuming that all was in order when he had a vendor's invoice and a Manning debit memorandum which matched.[773] This practice was similar in all respects to McKesson's method of handling payments under letters of credit with New York banks.

Summarizing the foregoing, so far as Ritts was concerned, his knowledge of Manning & Company appears to be based on what he was told, reenforced by what seemed to him to be a record of transactions supported by genuine documentary evidence and similar in many respects to those carried on under letters of credit with well

---

[768] Ex. 230, 231; pages 73–74 *supra*.
[769] R. 719.
[770] R. 224–228.
[771] R. 699, 753.
[772] R. 687, 746–748.
[773] R. 722, 739–741.

known New York banks. The principal concern Ritts had with Manning & Company was to determine that the balances of McKesson's accounts with them were the right amounts. This he did by reconciling the accounts with the bank statements and confirming direct with Manning & Company. The accounts themselves Ritts testified were entirely written up from documents submitted in the first instance by the bank, as no transactions with Manning & Company since the debit and credit advice procedure was established were recorded originally on McKesson's books. The accounts therefore could not fail to reconcile except for a possible arithmetical error or for an item in transit from Manning & Company at the end of a month. On this latter possibility Ritts testified that he did not think there were many, if any, outstanding items as at the audit dates.[774]

Wyman, who followed the audit program and prior year's papers as his guide, had heard of the banks involved in the Canadian Company and the Connecticut Division work except for Manning & Company. The manner in which the Manning transactions were conducted did not seem unusual to him although he had never seen a situation in which all of the business was conducted in that manner.

"Q. [By Mr. GALPEER.] * * * the moneys came in directly to Manning & Company, apparently?

A. [By WYMAN.] That was the arrangement.

Q. How did you know that was the arrangement?

A. From the evidence offered.

* * * * * * *

Q. What evidence?

A. From the fact that I knew that it could be the case and it was presented to me as the case.

Q. Who presented it to you as the case?

A. There was no discussion of it at any length that would have involved that, just simple explanation of this is the way it works with this thing. I don't know who gave it to me or when, but it was to no great extent." [775]

A junior, who it may be recalled performed most of the cash work during the 1 week he was on the job, relied upon Wyman for guidance in the work he did.

Material reviewed in the foregoing pages indicates the reliance placed upon the bank transactions as proof of the authenticity of the customers' accounts. The next subsection will be devoted to a more thorough study of the audit of receivables.

E. ACCOUNTS RECEIVABLE

The work on accounts receivable on the 1937 audit of the Connecticut Division and Canadian Company followed the same mimeographed program prepared by Thorn for all work done on McKesson Divisions

774 R. 129–130.

775 R. 323–324.

by the New York office. Work under this program was carried out on the Canadian Company by Wyman with a few points covered by Ritts and by a junior. The work on the Connecticut Division was done by Ritts and the junior with one point covered by Wyman.

The work program was as follows:

"(1) Obtain the adding machine trial balances of the accounts receivable ledgers at the close of the period. Verify footings and summarize totals; agree grand total with general ledger control.

(2) Obtain aging schedules from the company and make a brief test check of the footing.

(3) Summarize aging schedules and compute the percentage of past-due accounts for the several periods to the total outstanding balances.

(4) Check the accounts receivable ledger balances to the adding machine trial balance and see that no past-due balance of a substantial amount is omitted from the aging schedules. Make a brief test check of the aging.

(5) Note on the aging schedule all pertinent information that will assist the senior in charge in discussing the collectibility of the accounts, including payments received since December 31st.

(6) Examine credit memorandums issued after the close of the period for credits applicable to the period under review.

(7) Scrutinize accounts for balances due from affiliated houses, officers, and employees.

(8) Obtain confirmations direct from officers, directors, and employees for open balances at close of the period.

(9) Transfer credit balances to accounts payable.

(10) Make inquiries as to whether balances represent either merchandise consigned to customers or charges for merchandise to be delivered subsequent to the close of the period.

(11) Analyze accounts receivable control account for the month of December and reconcile approximately the charges to this account with the credits to sales.

(12) Analyze the reserve for doubtful accounts.

(13) Check the branch's schedule of bad debts written off and see that these items are properly approved.

(14) Discuss collectibility of substantial balances with responsible officials, review available credit information and consider small doubtful accounts in total. Determine amounts of specific and general reserves required.

(15) Segregate receivables and reserves applicable thereto between current and non-current and give branch a copy of reclassification entry.

(16) Ascertain whether any differences existed between the accounts receivable ledgers and the general ledger control during the period, and state what disposition was made of these differences, if any.

(17) Prepare receivable certificate and obtain signatures of responsible officials." [776]

This was followed by an item 18 which was similar to the last item on the cash program stating that the work outlined was a minimum and might be added to or modified and that such changes should be noted. Wyman added one point on the Canadian Company—the preparation of a geographical summary of accounts receivable balances. This last point was added by Wyman because he noted that it had been done the previous year. He presumed Ritts told him that the purpose

[776] Ex. 22, 32.

of this analysis was to determine whether any amounts were due from customers in countries where there were blocked currencies or other regulations which might impede collection.[777]

The foreign accounts receivable in the Connecticut Division amounting to $7,505,730.50 as at December 31, 1937 were found to be large in individual amounts and none past due. Ritts had told his assistant when putting him to work on these accounts "* * * that they would probably be in good order."[778] Wyman found conditions in the Canadian Company "unusually good" at the same date in respect to $1,579,143.00 then due. Of this total only three items, $14,520.00, $10,788.00, and $13,485.00, were past due. On inquiring of George E. Dietrich, Wyman was told "* * * that the customers had probably taken the date of his receipt of the goods to figure his time allowed for payment." These accounts were paid soon after the due date. This good record struck Wyman "as a little unusual" but if he discussed it with anyone it would merely have been to check with the preceding year's working papers in which he found a similar situation with no question of impropriety apparently raised. Rather than to increase his skepticism this, and a discussion as to the nature of the accounts generally, convinced him that they reflected a normal condition.[779]

The accounts were also remarkable in that they contained no credits for returns, allowances, discounts, or bad debts charged off.[780] This unusual condition also does not appear to have aroused the suspicions of the junior or of Wyman who worked on the accounts.[781] Wyman, who considered these "* * * an unusually good set of accounts," was questioned at some length in regard to the fact that the books he examined for 1937 reflected no bad debt losses and no credits for damaged goods or other allowances in shipments to England, Scotland, Wales, Ireland, Australia, British Guiana, New Zealand, India, South Africa, Sweden, and Holland. Wyman knew of some other companies with exceptional collection records but did not know of any with no bad debts and no allowances of any kind. He never discussed these matters with anyone for he had read the W. W. Smith & Company, Inc. contract and conceived it to be "* * * possible that such claims might have been made and satisfied against W. W. Smith & Co. without anybody knowing of it."[782] When questioned on this conclusion, Wyman testified:

---

[777] R. 355.

[778] R. 1109.

[779] R. 336-338, 343. In his memorandum to Thorn and Rowbotham covering his work Wyman wrote, "So far as we have been able to determine no losses have ever been sustained on these accounts in the past, nor have any of the accounts been charged back to W. W. Smith & Company, Inc. because of McKesson's failure to collect." Ex. 26.

[780] R. 4425.

[781] R. 339-340, 1110.

[782] R. 343-347, 351.

"Q. [By Mr. GALPEER.] The goods that were sold or purportedly sold by W. W. Smith and Company were for the account of McKesson and Robbins; were they not?

A. Yes.

Q. So that, if there were any deteriorations or if there were any losses and so forth, it would really be McKesson's loss, wouldn't it? How did you reach the conclusion?

A. Not necessarily. I was aware that the contract stated $900,000 guarantee.

Q. That was on collectibility, wasn't it?

A. It was on collectibility, but I think it is a fair inference that it might take care of small items in related categories.

Q. Well, you mean that someone——

A. Damaged goods——

Q. You mean that someone who guarantees the collectibility of accounts might be intended to include in that the losses arising from deterioration in freight?

A. I am saying that because you asked me to visualize the circumstances in which losses, allowances or adjustments might be made, not because I have any knowledge that adjustments were made." [783]

The unusual character of the accounts did not disturb him because they were being collected and the only thing he was interested in was the worth of the accounts.[784]

A primary factor in the entire audit was the reliance placed on the contract with the New York firm, W. W. Smith & Company, Inc., and the supporting guaranty of the Liverpool firm, W. W. Smith & Co., which in turn was supported by Dun & Bradstreet reports on the latter firm's credit rating. Wyman referred to this in his memorandum on the Canadian Company's accounts which he said was a copy of Ritts' for the preceding year except for necessary changes in the figures.[785] The credit reports were not obtained directly from the credit agency but from George E. Dietrich who produced the last one 3 or 4 days after the request was made.

"Q. [By Mr. GALPEER.] Was it an independent check of the responsibility or not?

A. [By RITTS.] No, it was not an independent check." [786]

These forged reports from the first one dated October 14, 1931, through successive renewals, dealt with the credit rating of the pretended sales agency W. W. Smith & Co., a co-partnership of Liverpool, with branches in Brooklyn, N. Y., Montreal, and other cities. All of these reports told much the same story about the partnership and noted its phenomenal growth through the depression years.[787]

---

783 R. 348–349.

784 R. 352.

785 R. 380.

"As in the past, we have obtained a credit report from the foreign department of Dun & Bradstreet, Inc. on W. W. Smith & Company, Inc., guarantor of these obligations under the agreement previously referred to. It states that W. W. Smith & Co. is an old and well-established concern with branch offices and resident agents in the principal world markets * * *." Ex. 26.

786 R. 576.

787 Page 61 *supra*.

Wyman testified that he had secured credit reports from the client on other audits and that he had been told that Price, Waterhouse & Co. did not have a contract with Dun & Bradstreet. Ritts supported Wyman as to this practice and explained that there would be no point in getting a report on the New York firm when the Liverpool partnership would be the party ultimately responsible for any losses sustained under the contract. The report was obtained by Dietrich at Ritts' specific request but Ritts was not sure whether it was handed to him in the original envelope unopened, although he thought the usual practice would be to receive it without a cover.[788]

If the Dun & Bradstreet report in 1936 had been obtained direct from the agency in response to a request for information on W. W. Smith & Company, Inc., the report probably would at least have disclosed that the dummy New York firm, W. W. Smith & Company, Inc., such as it was, had been dissolved during that year (1936) [789] while the guaranty contract apparently still had 4 years to run. Ritts felt that in reality under these circumstances the partnership might still have been liable on their guaranty but that the situation would have been serious enough to warrant calling it to the attention of his superiors and possibly getting a legal opinion. All of this was speculation on Ritts' part for he had no knowledge that the corporation had been dissolved.[790] It should be noted here also that Ritts had never before heard of a forged Dun & Bradstreet report and he stated that he could not tell the difference between the forgery and a genuine report.[791]

Item 14 of the audit program, among other things, required the review of available credit information on accounts receivable. In complying with this requirement on the 1932 audit, the first year he was in charge, Ritts asked George Dietrich for credit reports on the customers as well as on W. W. Smith & Co. These reports indicated that the customers were all responsible people. He called for a great many of these reports in the earlier years, but not so many in recent years.[792] In addition to all this was the assurance from the president, Coster, that he looked into these matters himself—as Rowbotham put it—"Coster sat on the job."[793]

Further discussion of the audit of receivables was pursued with Ritts beginning with the matter of credit memoranda, item 6 on the program. This had to do with establishing that proper allowances for discounts, returns, and allowances had been made. Ritts noted none on the Canadian Company but stated that there was no segre-

---

788 R. 566–576.
789 R. 2074.
790 R. 587–592.
791 R. 832.
792 R. 474; Ex. M-1.
793 R. 1947.

gation on the books of the Connecticut Division that indicated whether there were any applicable to the foreign crude drug accounts. A schedule from the working papers introduced in evidence tabulated "Returns and Allowances", "Samples & Free Goods", "Discounts", and "Excise Tax" for 1937 by months but did not indicate the departments to which they were applicable.[794] Subsequently, however, other schedules prepared by the Company and accepted by Price, Waterhouse & Co. without verification were discovered in their work papers showing a tabulation of gross sales, returns and allowances, samples and free goods, cost of sales, and gross profit by departments for the Connecticut Division for the years 1932, 1934, 1935, 1936, 1937, and for the month of December 1937 in which "Special Resale Crude" (the foreign crude drug sales) did not reflect any "Returns and Allowances" or "Samples and Free Goods" charged against the Company's operations.[795]

Ritts testified that a junior with his eyes open during the checking of accounts receivable should notice any large credits for returns and allowances but stated that small credits might not be noticed nor would a complete absence of such credits be noticed. Ritts felt that if any claims for inferior or damaged merchandise had been made by the customers handled through W. W. Smith & Company, Inc., McKesson would recover such amounts from the suppliers and/or W. W. Smith & Company, Inc., the shipping agent, respectively. This was pure speculation for Ritts did not recall any such transactions and was sure that no notice would have been taken of them in his working papers. He agreed, however, that it would be impossible to run a business the size of the foreign crude drug division over a period of years without expecting some claims to arise.[796]

Ritts confirmed Wyman's reactions to the situation at all points. No reserve for bad debts was necessary for these accounts totaling some $9,000,000 because the record showed that all were collected promptly when due and there was the additional safeguard of the W. W. Smith & Co. guaranty. In the last 3 years, or the period covered by the last contract, foreign sales of crude drugs totaled approximately $50,000,000, $18,250,000 in the last year,[797] yet so far as the records examined under Ritts' direction were concerned no bad debts losses appeared. In fact, the memoranda on the accounts of both the Canadian and Connecticut Companies consistently stated that no losses were ever sustained on these accounts, nor were any of them ever charged back under the guaranty because of McKesson's failure to collect.[798] This did not appear unusual to Ritts for McKesson sold to a carefully selected class of customers. He was

[794] Ex. 36; R. 464.

[795] Ex. N, 124, 120. See also R. 1378–1379.

[796] R. 468–471.

[797] Individual orders averaged approximately $12,000 per customer. Ex. 30, 40.

[798] See footnotes 310, 318 *supra*.

told that not only did W. W. Smith & Co. verify the credit rating of these customers before guaranteeing the accounts, but McKesson made independent investigations of these people to decide if they were good credit risks, and as above stated, Ritts on the 1932 audit examined a great many credit reports on these customers which the Company had in its files.[799] Attempts made by the Commission and S. D. Leidesdorf & Co. (accountants for the Trustee) to confirm the accounts receivable established the existence of most of the customers as actual business firms but that none of them had done any business of this nature with McKesson.[800]

Ritts never questioned anyone as to why McKesson should pay a premium for a guaranty on accounts of this excellence, especially when they made their own investigation which as we have seen included the securing of Dun & Bradstreet reports. The language of paragraph six of the contract said that the premium was to be paid for the guaranty. When asked whether the premium was paid for a guaranty, Ritts said he thought so but that was a matter of legal definition. Yet without consulting counsel for a legal interpretation of the contract, he decided that the ¾ of 1% was not being paid specifically for the guaranty. He thought that the payment also covered the solicitation of the accounts.[801]

A similar confusion was revealed in the memoranda on the accounts of the Connecticut Company for 1931, 1932, and 1933 which linked the guaranty to the $18,000 fee provided in the contracts. The Smith contracts seem quite explicit as to the $18,000 fee for they say it is "* * * in full consideration of the services to be rendered by the New York Company [W. W. Smith & Company, Inc.] hereunder (*except the guaranty of accounts*) * * *"[802] [emphasis ours]. This and the section of the contract dealing with the guaranty[803] indicated that the premium of ¾ of 1% for the guaranty of accounts was not provided thereunder as a commission but solely for protection against bad debts that never materialized in 14 years.[803a]

Wyman, who read the Smith contract before going to Bridgeport, seemed unimpressed with the importance of correlating the terms of the contract with the recording of transactions under it. Purchase orders submitted by Smith to McKesson carried in the lower left hand corner the instruction "Please render invoice in Duplicate", below that, "Brokerage [blank] %", and still below that, "Guarantee

799 R. 474, 579–582, 1650–1651; Ex. M–1. Page 219 *supra*.

800 R. 4555; Ex. 255.

801 R. 583–586.

802 Page 59 *supra*. The confusion as to the interpretation of the $18,000 fee may have been due to the fact that a stated fee of $12,000 appears to have been the only payment required under the Charles Manning & Company, Limited contract of 1930 under which that company performed the services including the guaranty of accounts which W. W. Smith & Company, Inc. assumed as of August 1, 1931. Page 55 *supra*.

803 Quoted in part at page 224 *infra*.

803a See also section 7 "* * * New York Company * * * will charge no brokerage or commission to either of the McKesson Companies * * *." Page 58 *supra*.

¾ of 1 %%." [804] Wyman considered the premium of ¾ of 1 % to be a commission and not charged for the guaranty. Despite the notation on the purchase orders and despite the wording of the contract, when the latter was specifically called to his attention at the hearings, his conception of what W. W. Smith & Company, Inc. was being paid for was not altered.[805] He said he followed the Company's classification of the payment as a part of "selling salaries and commissions" [806] without questioning anyone about it. Whether for guaranty or commission, he felt the charge was selling expense, so the question never came up. His testimony seems to indicate that he did not give the contract particular attention because it seemed unnecessary for him to challenge what seemed to be a reasonable procedure established in prior years.[807]

To complete this topic of bad debts in relation to W. W. Smith & Company, Inc., Thorn was asked if he thought it possible for a firm to handle the business we have referred to with hundreds of customers in foreign trade from 1930 through 1937 without suffering a single bad debt loss. He thought it was possible and supported Ritts' position in the following answer:

> "The WITNESS. These representatives of W. W. Smith were right on the ground and making this sale, and knew that their firm bore the risk of those sales, and naturally would be very sure of those credit risks before they made the sale. Then, when the sale was offered to Bridgeport, Mr. Coster has told me that he investigated the credit of each of those customers, that is to say, a new customer would be investigated so far as possible through their New York banking connections and their foreign correspondents, and they also received credit reports from outside agencies such as Dun & Bradstreets and it does not seem, it never has seemed unreasonable to me that under those circumstances, dealing in relatively large quantities with large concerns, that there should not be bad debt losses here." [808]

Thorn also supported Ritts on the question of allowances by saying that claims for defective merchandise would have been made against the supplier, clearing through McKesson's books if they appeared

[804] Ex. 8–B; R. 587.

[805] "A. [By WYMAN.] No, sir, the fact of the wording of the contract wouldn't alter my general conception of what W. W. Smith & Co. was being paid for.

Q. [By Mr. GALPEER.] Who gave you this general conception contradictory to the terms of the contract in your permanent file which you read?

A. Nobody.

Q. Did you raise this question, discuss it with any one?

A. No, sir.

Q. Do you think you can take it upon yourself after you read a written contract stating that the three-fourths of one percent is to be a guarantee charge, to just yourself take it and put it in the commission charge without talking to any one about it?

A. The nature of an item—the classification of an item is guided by its nature. The contract has nothing to do with it.

Q. The contract has nothing to do with it?

A. The contract could have called that anything." R. 369–370.

[806] Operating accounts for the Connecticut Division seem to include the payment in "Miscellaneous selling expense." Ex. 185.

[807] R. 371–375.

[808] R .921.

there at all. The claims for losses in transit, if any, he thought would have been made against W. W. Smith & Company, Inc. directly or cleared through McKesson's books. Thorn's views on this question may be expressed in his own words:

"* * * Now, I have thought, in dealing with commodities of this kind, that it may be possible to run for many years without having those claims, but I quite agree with you that over an extended time there would be bound to be differences. I think I ought also add that those things, in the course of a balance sheet examination, would not come to our attention, that is to say the claims and allowances. We are concerned, however, at the end of the year with whether there were any claims or allowances affecting those receivables at that date so that they would not be collected in full, but if there appears a claim last March, I don't think it would come to our attention or that we would be concerned with it." [809]

In such work as was done on these accounts, no bad debts or claims ever were called to Thorn's attention.[809]

Thorn discussed the operations of the crude drug sales with Coster in 1929. He testified that he probably did not have very extensive discussions with Coster or anyone else after that date. He was certain that no one in Price, Waterhouse & Co. was consulted as to the actual mechanics of carrying out the Smith contract. He testified that he did not consider it necessary to obtain a legal opinion thereon.[810] There was one note in the papers made on the 1933 audit in connection with an abstract of the extension of the agreement in that year. This note, made by an assistant under Ritts, was referred to as evidence that Ritts had knowledge of the obtaining of a legal opinion although Thorn did not have such knowledge. The note merely said, "No mention is made with respect to the flat fee of $18,000, but Mr. G. Dietrich advises that upon advice of counsel, they have continued to make same." [811]

Rowbotham was questioned as to his knowledge of the bad debts, allowances, and returns situation on the crude drug sales through Smith, and he supported Thorn at all points. The matter of allowances and returns he explained had never been discussed with him and would not have been in ordinary course. Rowbotham said that he would not have expected Thorn to bring such matters to his attention, for in a balance sheet examination he would not go into such matters except to see if returns and allowances were excessive in relation to sales.[812]

On the matter of bad debts, Rowbotham felt that this business was with a chosen group of large and responsible customers and hence it was quite reasonable that there would be no losses on bad accounts. In this connection, on referring to the Smith guaranty

---

809 R. 923.
810 R. 1134–1135, 1190.
811 Ex. 56; R. 1196.
812 R. 1936–1939.

of the accounts, Rowbotham supported Ritts in the thought that the guaranty was insurance against losses and in that way the premium was money well spent if it resulted in a high class of customers on which no losses developed.[813] Such an impression was supported by the practice of the client in paying the guaranty fee on all sales through W. W. Smith & Company, Inc.

A review of the exhibits and testimony indicates that while a correct interpretation of the W. W. Smith & Company, Inc. contract was academic in so far as its guaranty of collection features were concerned, since no claims were ever made under it; the amounts paid in premiums were considerable,[813a] and the emphasis placed upon the contract in its bearing on all aspects of the foreign crude drug business was so great that one would assume a careful consideration of the applicable clauses by the auditors.

Article 6 of the 1935 contract provided:

"In consideration of a premium of three-quarters of one percent (in addition to the service charge hereinafter provided for) of the total amount of any order placed under the provisions hereof, the New York Company will, if requested so to do in writing, unconditionally guaranty the full and prompt payment therefor by the purchaser in dollars, it being understood that the liability under this guaranty will become absolute thirty (30) days after written notice to the New York Company that such purchaser has defaulted payment in whole or in part, provided, however, that the total of accounts so guaranteed shall not at any time exceed the sum of $900,000. The liability of the New York Company hereunder shall not be affected by the fact that the guaranty premium shall not have been actually paid in advance, it being the intention of the parties that such premium items shall be billed monthly to the McKesson Companies * * *."[814]

The 1933 and 1931 contracts used similar language. An abstract of the prior Manning agreement dated March 12, 1930 from the files

[813] "Q. [By Mr. GALPEEK.] * * * did it ever occur to you that it might be a useless expenditure of money to be paying this three-quarters of one percent, I mean where there was never one bad debt claim, did those two factors ever come together in your mind?

A. [By ROWBOTHAM.] Why, they did, sir, but I took exactly the opposite conclusion which you have, which apparently came to you, because it seemed to me this, that if these people could pay three-quarters of one percent to an international organization to look into their debt situation in such a way that they could have no bad debts, that that was an expenditure worth while having. In other words,—I am sorry, I cannot find the word, but the same words that you are using on the questionnaire, that it was a point of strength and not of weakness.

Q. [By Mr. STEWART.] Would another way of describing it be that you regarded it as cheap insurance against bad debts, Mr. Rowbotham?

A. Yes, sir. I thought it was an excellent arrangement." R. 1952.

The insuring of receivables was a practice adopted by Coster as early as 1925. Price, Waterhouse & Co. reports on the audits of Girard & Co., Inc. for the first three quarters of 1926 in referring to the status of accounts receivable said " * * * these were all considered good and collectible either from the customer or from the insurance company which has insured their collectibility." Ex. 140, 141, 142. Coster in his President's Report for 1925 listed a number of items of expense in that year which should not recur. One of these he commented upon as follows:

"$475.25. This amount represents premium for Credit Insurance. The policy does not expire until September 1926. On account of the terms and conditions of such insurance I do not recommend continuance of this form of insurance since in order to collect we must first suffer initial losses of $5,000. This added to $475 premium means that we are out $5475 before we start to collect. The class and character of the trade we sell is such that we would not incur such losses as warrant this insurance. We have had no bad debts in 1925." Ex. 176 (p. 6).

[813a] See pages 47–48 *supra*.

[814] Ex 50.

of Price, Waterhouse & Co.[815] interpreted that contract in the same way as the client and Price, Waterhouse & Co. interpreted the subsequent Smith contracts above mentioned to the effect that the premium was payable on total sales and that for these payments all outstanding accounts (which at all times were considerably in excess of the maximum sums mentioned in the applicable contracts) were guaranteed, provided, however, that W. W. Smith & Company, Inc.'s maximum liability for losses on the accounts in any one year would not exceed the amounts specified in the respective contracts. All of the memoranda written on the audits at Bridgeport assumed this interpretation. The language in the 1931 memoranda on the Connecticut and Canadian Companies stated that the combined accounts of the Companies were guaranteed by Smith against losses up to $350,000 in any one year, which in effect amounted to a reserve of $350,000 on these accounts.[816] Subsequent memoranda were similar except that commencing with the memoranda for 1933, the reference to the reserve was dropped.

The possible inconsistency between this interpretation and practice which treated all the accounts guaranteed, the amount specified in the contract being the limit of the guarantor's liability *during any one year*, and the express language of the 5-year contract which seems to restrict the amount of outstanding accounts that could be guaranteed *at any one time* to the amount specified in the contract, does not seem to have occurred to anyone on the auditors' staff at any time in the life of the engagement. Since the contract was never tested in practice by claims for losses, its ambiguous character in this respect is only interesting in that such ambiguity did not trouble the auditors despite the great reliance by them upon this and other provisions of the contract in explaining the many unusual features of the foreign crude drug business.

Another point in the contract which is not entirely clear when considered in the light of other facts in the record is the precise relationship existing between McKesson and Smith in regard to these foreign accounts. Article 2 of the 1931 contract under which this business was done stated that all purchase inquiries for drugs, chemicals, or any other commodities dealt in by McKesson would be submitted to McKesson for quotations. If such quotations were as favorable as others obtained by Smith in the open market, the business would be placed with McKesson.[817] According to the Price, Waterhouse & Co. memoranda of accounts, during 1932 and 1933 most of the crude drugs were reported to have been purchased from W. W. Smith & Co. which also served as McKesson's sales agent for the same merchandise much

---

[815] R. 956.
[816] Ex. 76, 82.
[817] Page 58 *supra*.

of which had its origin in foreign countries and was sold to customers in other foreign countries.[818] W. W. Smith & Co. was supposed to have had financial resources of several millions of dollars.[818a]

But, in the auditor's opinion, the real proof of the genuine character of the foreign crude drug accounts receivable was that the accounts were collected. If the sale was charged to the customer and there was evidence of the money having been received in payment of the goods, they felt that no question needed to be raised in regard to the genuineness of the transactions in the absence of suspicion.

The validity of this position is, of course, vitiated if the money was not received from the customer or his authorized agent. As to the situation prior to the use of Manning & Company as a bank Ritts testified, "* * * but I do know that prior to 1931, before Manning & Company were the fiscal agents of McKesson and Robbins, that actual cash was received in the various banks of the company, such as the Guaranty Trust Company, the New York Trust Company, the Manufacturers Trust Company and other banks that we knew did exist, so when you ask me whether I know that the actual money was received, I say, yes, definitely, we did know." [819] But there was no proof other than book entries that the money credited by the various banks came from the customers, which events have shown was not the case. After the transactions were concentrated in Manning & Company there was no investigation of that firm to establish that it was a bank, which, in fact, it was not. Reliance was placed on credit advices and monthly statements from Manning that collections had been received by Manning from the customers to whom shipments supposedly had been made through W. W. Smith & Company, Inc., thus supporting the authenticity of the accounts.

"Q. [By Mr. GALPEER.] Now, Mr. Thorn, on the McKesson sales side, when you say that you saw the cash for the payments, what you have reference to is the credit advice coming in from Manning & Company?

A. That is true during the period we examined.

Q. That is what I am speaking of now.

A. Yes, sir.

Q. And when you say you saw evidences of shipment, the only evidences you saw were again the letterheads of W. W. Smith & Company, containing advice of shipment.

A. Well, I think that is true, technically. Now, I may be making the same point Mr. Stewart just tried to, but the fact was, of course that seeing the collections in these receivables was also a support to that evidence of shipment, that is, when you see that the goods were paid for it would be the best possible evidence that they had been shipped." [820]

In the discussion of cash procedure it will be recalled that Thorn did not know how the customers were advised to pay Manning and did not consider it important to find out.[821] Rowbotham indicated his reliance on collection when questioned about this part of Thorn's testimony. He was asked if he agreed with Thorn's conclusions as to

[818] Ex. 75, 81. [818a] Page 61 *supra*. [819] R. 216-217. [820] R. 1128-1129. [821] Footnote 737 *supra*.

the non-necessity of being familiar with the forms used in handling transactions. His answer was, "Yes, sir, I do. If I were looking at this job and the money was being collected, I would not care whether they put a sticker on the bill or not." [822]

But there was one aspect of collection of these foreign accounts which did cause some concern, at least to Jaureguy, for he sent Thorn back to Bridgeport on the 1930 audit, after he had brought the papers to New York, to make an analysis of the foreign accounts, especially to determine the amount due from customers in Australia and New Zealand. The results of this analysis showed that of $4,180,000 customers' receivables on the Connecticut Company's books at December 31, 1930, probably $3,200,000 covered foreign sales, of which $2,433,-103.70 were Australian balances and $400,000 New Zealand. The Canadian Company at the same date had accounts totaling $795,660.25 outstanding in Australia and $303,718.75 in New Zealand out of a total of $1,316,623.50.[823] The investigation revealed that all of these accounts were current at the year end, none having been billed prior to August 1930. Besides, practically all the accounts due prior to the date of the inquiry, February 25, 1931, had been collected, proving that the foreign exchange situation in Australia whose pound was at a discount had not affected the collectibility of the accounts which were payable in U. S. dollars.[824]

During 1931 the accounts were still largely in Australia. Beginning with the 1932 memorandum on the accounts of the Canadian Company and with the 1933 memorandum on the accounts of the Connecticut Company, detailed geographical analyses were shown for the foreign accounts. The Canadian Company in 1932, for example, in addition to accounts in the British Empire, listed customers in France, Belgium,

---

[822] R. 1846.

[823] Ex. 83, 77; R. 916.

[824] "Q. [By Mr. GALPEER.] Was there a question there of exchange restrictions, or was it merely a question of the Australian pound going below par?

A. [By THORN.] I only remember the decline in the quotation of the Australian pound and through these years there have been questions of exchange restrictions, but I don't remember whether they apply here or not.

Q. The fact that you had this concern about the Australian balances, which totaled about two and a half million dollars, and I think you mentioned later on in this report that nevertheless the collections remained good and that there was no loss of any items; had that occurred to you as in any way strange or suspicious? Do you see my question, what I mean?

A. Yes. No, it did not. If there were restrictions there—we see cases right along of so-called bootleg exchange coming out and of course we verified the actual receipt of enough of this cash to know that it really was coming in.

Q. I understand that that was coming in to Manning & Company the same as we have described?

A. That was coming in to the Guaranty Trust Company mostly and possibly some to the Bridgeport City Trust Company.

Q. So the fact that there was this concern, but that despite this concern all these balances were paid in full did not strike you as unusual in any way?

A. No, not when they were actually being paid. We felt that the balances were collectible. We were not,—we were only concerned with how much they could realize on those accounts, that was our concern and we reached the conclusion that the fact that we actually saw this cash coming in that the balances were good and collectible." R. 916–918.

See also memorandum on accounts of Canadian Company for 1932: "The officials certified to us that the accounts are all payable in U. S. dollars and, although we believe some of the countries involved have exchange embargoes, Mr. Coster informed us that the debtors are able to 'bootleg' the exchange." Ex. 205.

Japan, Sweden, Norway, Denmark, and Rumania. New countries in 1933 were Italy, Holland, China, Spain, Germany, and Switzerland. By 1937 the only countries outside the British Empire were Holland and Sweden. These analyses were made to determine the balances due from customers in countries having exchange restrictions, but Thorn testified that he did not recall that any check was made as to depreciation in currency in the several countries.[825]

The history of these accounts reveals that sales were curtailed to customers in countries in which exchange restrictions were set up and that McKesson gradually worked out of such restricted countries. All of the accounts, however, were collected promptly in full as was also the case for accounts with customers in countries having depreciated currencies to which sales were not curtailed.

The withdrawal from restricted countries seemed to Thorn a reasonable thing to do and the fact that it was 100% successful did not disturb him in the least for he had heard that there were ways of "bootlegging" exchange "* * * and [he] saw that cash actually coming in".[826] Each year the situation in respect to exchange restrictions was checked by one of Thorn's assistants and on at least one occasion Thorn discussed the matter with either George Dietrich or Coster, who he says gave him a satisfactory explanation.[827]

---

[825] R. 1095.

[826] R. 1096–1098. "Q. [By Mr. GALPEER.] * * * I read you certain amounts owing from customers in Japan, Spain and Italy, and those amounts were owing, those sales have been undertaken at times when the restrictions were already in effect. My question is whether it didn't strike you, I know that you can get most of your money out despite restrictions, but didn't it strike you surprising that there was 100 percent compliance here again?

A. [By THORN.] No, it did not, because in the first instance we actually saw the cash coming in and we knew that it was perfectly possible for that situation to exist and we also knew that they were working out of those countries.

It might have appeared strange if there had been no change in the location of their business, but we noted from about, I think, about 1930 or 1931, along in there is when we first began to watch that, and we noted that their business worked out of those countries where there were restrictions, and it seemed perfectly natural to us." R. 1097–1098.

[827] "Q. [By Examiner HUMPHREYS.] Did you consider the difficulty with which McKesson & Robbins might get their money out of these countries?

A. [By THORN.] Yes, I did. I remember of talking to either George Dietrich or Mr. Coster personally about that once. It was probably when I was in Bridgeport reviewing the papers because I think it was after the period when I was senior on the work.

Q. Did you go into the question as to whether they might have to get their money out by barter?

A. Yes, I believe I did because I was just as a matter of human curiosity wondering how they did get their money out and as I recall that certain of these foreign customers, they said that these foreign customers being fairly large business men, with a large acquaintance among similar people would find someone in their country who had dollars, that is dollar balances here, that they would be able to make the exchange.

Q. Did you consider the question of expense in making such conversion?

A. That is, that it might be a very expensive process for the customer to have to get his dollars that way?

Q. Or McKesson & Robbins might have to take a discount in receivable, in cash, to get it out of the country?

A. No, that point seemed to be clear that they had to have their money in dollars. Every sale was made in dollars and the customer, of course, when he made this purchase, knew undoubtedly how he was going to be able to secure these dollars and how much this purchase was going to cost him in his own money which was naturally all that concerned him." R. 1101–1103.

See also R. 918–919. Likewise see Ex. 82 (Memorandum on 1931 Accounts) for a discussion of foreign exchange transactions in which the risk of foreign exchange fluctuations was borne by McKesson in connection with pepper transactions (Sterling) and in codliver oil (a loss of $28,000 incurred in the devaluation of the Norwegian Kroner).

The letters of engagement beginning with the 1931 audit, it will be recalled, specified that, in accordance with Coster's request, the customers' accounts would not be circularized. Circularization was again suggested to McKesson by the auditors in connection with the wholesale houses following the audit of 1932,[828] but Price, Waterhouse & Co. never considered it necessary in connection with the work at Bridgeport, although Thorn stated that they would have welcomed the opportunity to make this form of verification in either case. The relatively small accounts in the wholesale houses totaled approximately 90,000 divided over 80 to 85 different units of the Company while the foreign crude drug accounts numbered a little over 700. The reason given for suggesting the circularization of receivables in the wholesale houses was that there was less internal control there than at Bridgeport and collections were slower but in view of the distribution of the risk, this audit step was not considered necessary in order to express an opinion on the accounts.[829] It may be noted that when McKesson acquired the wholehouse houses in 1928 and in some cases in 1929 the accounts receivable taken over were guaranteed by the owners of those houses so that no independent confirmation was necessary in those cases in connection with the merger.[830] Thorn in reporting on the work at Bridgeport for 1933 wrote in his memorandum on the Canadian Company:

> "We have not confirmed any of the receivables with the debtors but, during the course of the examination, we did everything we could think of to satisfy ourselves that the accounts are authentic and that the balances outstanding at December 31, 1932 had been liquidated in cash when due." [831]

Similar notations to the effect that the receivables had not been confirmed but that comprehensive tests to establish the authenticity of these accounts had been made and liquidations in cash had been noted appear in all subsequent memoranda on the Canadian Company [832] and also since 1933 in all memoranda on the Connecticut Company, later Division.[833]

The omission of circularization was covered specifically in a certificate obtained at the close of the 1937 engagement (as well as in similar certificates obtained in connection with the 1934, 1935, and 1936 examinations). The 1937 certificate is reproduced in the footnote.[834]

---

[828] Ex. 88 quoted in part in footnote 544 *supra;* R. 934.

[829] R. 935–936.

[830] R. 876; Ex. 152 (pp. 14–16).

[831] Ex. 75.

[832] Ex. 74, 73, 72, 26.

[833] Ex. 80, 268, 79, 78, 49.

[834] Ex. 67:

"McKESSON & ROBBINS

Incorporated

Bridgeport, Conn., U. S. A.

CONNECTICUT DIVISION

MEMORANDUM TO PRICE, WATERHOUSE & CO. REGARDING NOTES AND ACCOUNTS RECEIVABLE AND RESERVES AS AT DECEMBER 31, 1937

SUMMARY OF RECEIVABLES AND RESERVES

DESCRIPTION:	AMOUNT		RESERVES
Current notes and accounts receivable:			
Bankers acceptances	$		
Other notes receivable	660.00		
Customers' accounts	7,800,287.87		68,202.20
Officers and employees	2,426.59		
Miscellaneous	35,849.35		
		$7,839,223.81	$ 68,202.20
Non-current notes and accounts receivable:			
Other notes			
Accounts	142,587.62		36,934.87
Total		$7,981,811.43	$105,137.07

1. The above receivables were all unencumbered assets of the branch at the above date and all receivables, other than interbranch and intercompany receivables, resulting from transactions of any kind entered into on or before December 31, 1937 are included, except such as have been written off as uncollectible.

2. No amounts are included in respect of sales made after December 31, 1937 of representing unsold goods shipped to others on consignment.

3. All receivables resulting from transactions outside the usual course of the branch's business are separately classified.

4. Segregation of receivables as between current and non-current has been made in accordance with the procedure set forth in the company's closing instructions.

5. In the light of our present information, the above-stated reserves are neither excessive nor deficient to cover:

Losses that may be sustained with respect to the above receivables

All rebates, allowances or other deductions that may be granted to the debtors

Any rebates and allowances that may be payable to customers as quantity discounts or otherwise, whether in respect of uncollected items or not.

Losses that may be sustained in collection of any receivables that have been discounted or sold with the branch's endorsement.

6. The debtors were not circularized, in accordance with our instructions, for confirmation of the unpaid balances at December 31, 1937.

7. The valuations of the collateral held against notes receivable as shown in the trial balances of the notes, in our opinion, represent the realizable value of the collateral.

Furthermore at the time of signing this memorandum we have no knowledge of any other information relating to the above, which would have any substantial effect on the branch's accounts, that is not referred to herein or that was not clearly disclosed in the branch's general books of account as at or before December 31, 1937.

(s) F. D. COSTER
President

(s) J. H. McGLOON
Comptroller

(s) GEO. E. DIETRICH
Assistant Treasurer

(s) E. A. JOHNSON
Office Manager

Date: February 23, 1938

(s) A. B. RITTS
Representative of Price, Waterhouse & Co."

It bears a notation in Thorn's handwriting, "Note for 12/31/38—Say payable in U. S. dollars."

In summing up the audit procedures followed in verifying accounts receivable, Rowbotham's comparison of the Price, Waterhouse & Co. program with that outlined in the Bulletin of the American Institute of Accountants revealed that these programs were substantially the same save for the important omission of the optional step of circularization of accounts and for the inclusion by Price, Waterhouse & Co. of some additional steps. The added steps were items 11, 16, and 17 of the work program quoted above.[835]

The Bulletin in referring to circularization says:

"The best verification of accounts receivable is to communicate directly with the debtor regarding the existence of the debt, and this course may be taken after arrangement with the client. While such confirmation is frequently considered unnecessary in the case of companies having an adequate system of internal check, it is one of the most effective means of disclosing irregularities."[836]

Rowbotham approved the omission of this step because in his judgment it was not necessary. He continued in his testimony:

"* * * In this case this seemed to me about the last type of case where a circularization would be applicable. You have, of course, as I have already testified, I think—no circularization is commenced nowadays until you get the consent of your client. You have to convince him that circularization is necessary. Now, in this case those receivables——

Q. [By Mr. STEWART.] Referring now to the crude drug department?

A. Yes, sir, these receivables were obtained by sales agents, W. W. Smith & Company, who made an extensive check or were supposed to have made an extensive check of their credit before submitting the bids to Coster. Smith also guaranteed these receivables to the extent of $900,000; they were supposed to be carefully checked up here and when I say here, I mean with a Dun & Bradstreet's report. Coster himself sat right on top of this thing and looked at those credits himself. On top of that there was an excellent record of collections and there was no reason at all that I could see, that I could ever see here for circularizing these receivables and I did not at any time raise the question and I did not think at any time that they should be circularized, and in the absence of suspicion, which I never did have, it would never have occurred to me that this was one place where circularization was necessary."[837]

Collection of the accounts coupled with what was considered to be good internal control was the auditors' basis for believing that the customers' accounts were authentic and were worth 100 cents on the dollar. Therefore a more detailed inquiry into internal control as it affected this question would appear to be appropriate at this point. Recording of sales is so closely associated with control of billing to and collection from customers that the two must be considered together.

In the review of the questionnaires it was found that on the 1937 audit a junior was sent to get answers to several questions on receiv-

[835] Page 216 *supra*.
[836] Ex. 117 (pp. 14–15).
[837] R. 1860–1861. See also R 2008–2009.

ables, and that he refused a detailed explanation which Johnson, the office manager, offered to give him requesting instead brief accurate answers for he "just wanted to get the answers down." [838] The first question called for a brief description of—

"safeguards in use to insure that (a) an invoice or record of charge to the customer is prepared for every shipment of merchandise leaving the warehouse; (b) every invoice, or record of charge to the customer, is entered in the accounts; (c) there is a charge to the customer for every direct shipment from supplier to customer."

The junior's answer was:

"(a–b) Shipping orders are controlled by billing dept.; invoicing is controlled thru separate invoice register independent of both billing & shipping dept. (c) Accounts Payable Register controls invoicing of customer thru billing dept."

Wyman's answer to the same question in respect to the Canadian Company was:

"All direct shipments from whse. to customer (a) [blank]; (b) shipping advices checked to sales reg.; (c) agreement whse. cerf. & stk. card."

Since Wyman's answer was correct for the Canadian Company, all of whose business since some time in 1935 was supposedly done through W. W. Smith & Company, Inc. by direct shipment from vendors' Canadian warehouses, it would appear that the junior failed to distinguish this type of business, which was handled in the same way in the Connecticut Division as in the Canadian Company, from the other business of the Connecticut Division.[839]

The junior's answer to question seven,

"(a) Who is responsible for the granting of credits? (b) Are credit limits established and followed?"

also revealed his failure to secure complete and accurate information for he wrote:

"(a) Mr. Titus, credit mgr., is responsible for granting credits. (b) Yes, as established by Mr. Titus."

This again applied to the real business which the junior apparently learned about but which was much the smaller part of the total business, although his superiors knew that Coster and George Dietrich performed these functions on what has been found to have been the larger fictitious business.[840] Wyman did not answer this question.[841]

In addition to his questionnaire on the Canadian Company and the work program on accounts receivable, Wyman prepared a sheet showing the work done on sales. Some of the items on this program

---

838 Pages 178 *supra*.

839 The junior's answer to "c" seems to apply to a small class of direct shipments for which McKesson received the vendor's invoice coincident with McKesson's billing to its customer. This latter type of direct shipment constituted an infinitesimal portion of total sales of the Connecticut Division, whereas the foreign crude drug sales supposedly shipped direct from vendors' warehouses some time after purchase was the major part of the Division's business.

840 Ex. 19; R. 1112.

841 Ex. 19.

referred to records dealing with shipments, which he examined. Item 2 stated that he traced duplicate invoices to December sales register and item 4 called for examining shipping advices on all December shipments. Item 5 required the tracing of quantities shown on invoices and shipping advices in December to perpetual inventory cards. Item 6 read "Examine all shipping advices for first ten days in January to see that charges have been made in proper period", and item 7 was, "Check postings for December from duplicate invoices to customer's ledger." Items 1 and 3 dealt only with sales and will be discussed later.[842]

Having done all of the above, the proof relied upon by the auditors for the authenticity of purchase and sale transactions throughout the rest of the year was the exact agreement of the inventory certificate quantities as reported by the vendors with the balances on the stock cards at the beginning and end of each year. Prior to 1935, the proof was the correspondence of the physical inventory count as certified by responsible officials with the book records. As for the internal paper work in the Canadian Company, there is nothing in the documents in evidence or in Wyman's testimony to show that he realized that all such documents supporting these transactions either originated in or came from George or Robert Dietrich's offices to the Canadian Company's one bookkeeper, Miss Walsh, who acted under George Dietrich's direct supervision.[843]

Wyman, although he checked the W. W. Smith & Co. notices of shipment, saw no evidence on them to indicate from which vendor's warehouse the order was filled nor did he ask the source of the merchandise. He did not see any bills of lading, consular invoices, invoices, or insurance certificates which were check-marked on the notices, as accompanying them. He did not ask to see any of these. The advice of shipment was on the letterhead of W. W. Smith & Co., of Liverpool, 3, England, but he did not notice that. He never inspected the copy of the McKesson factory order to which was attached copies 1, 3, and 4 of the McKesson uniform straight bill of lading form.[844] The work one junior did on the Connecticut Company did not require the examination of any shipping documents that he could recall, although he did examine sales invoices in connection with some inventory work.[845]

Wyman and this junior were on the McKesson audit only 1 year, but Ritts went on at Bridgeport as a junior on the 1930 examination and stayed with it through 1937, the last 6 years in charge of the work there. This is longer at Bridgeport than any other man as-

---

[842] Ex. 25; R. 376-378. See pages 300 ff. *infra.*

[843] R. 4382.

[844] R. 378-380.

[845] R. 1113-1114.

signed to the work and for this reason his understanding of the accounting procedures of McKesson is particularly significant.

A typical set of documents purportedly arising from a sale of crude drugs under the contract with W. W. Smith & Company, Inc. has been described and reproduced in an earlier section. Ritts in his first appearance at the present hearings testified that the sales procedure started on the receipt of a purchase order from "W. W. Smith & Company." These orders he said were sent to McKesson's billing department, where they would be transcribed onto their own forms, which he thought were of the fanfold type with the invoice on top, with several duplicates, and under them several order forms. When he was shown a copy of the factory order, however, he could not say where it was prepared, but he thought it went to the shipping department. He could not say whether the order was prepared before or after the invoice.[846]

Ritts continued his explanation by stating that one copy of the invoice went to the mailing department in George Dietrich's office, one copy to the clerks in charge of the sales records, one to the customers' ledger bookkeeper, and one to the department which kept the perpetual inventory. On the due date the customers paid through Manning & Company but Ritts had never seen any instructions for them to do so. He thought that possibly W. W. Smith & Co. told them.[847]

On the second day of the hearings, Ritts testified that when McKesson received an order from W. W. Smith & Co. to ship to certain customers, in recent years the Company prepared shipping instructions to the supplier holding the stock advising them to ship to designated customers. In due time, the supplier or custodian of the goods

> " * * * would advise McKesson by formal advice that this shipment had been made in accordance with their instructions and they would spell out all the details of the shipment, who the shipment was made to, and also accompanied these advices by bills of lading indicating actual shipments had been made to the various customers. From there on, McKesson and Robbins would use these advices as the basis of making the charge to the customer in their own account."

Continuing the discussion, Ritts said he had seen these advices from the suppliers and also bills of lading indicating that beginning in 1935 the shipments were made from Canada.[848]

At this point, Ritts was shown a W. W. Smith & Co. "Notice of Shipment." On seeing this document, Ritts changed his version of the system, for the documents indicated that notice of shipment reached McKesson through W. W. Smith & Co. rather than direct from the supplier. It now appeared to him that on receipt of the

---

846 R. 134–138.

847 R. 143. Cf. Thorn's version, footnote 737 *supra*.

848 R. 162–164.

W. W. Smith & Co. purchase order, McKesson must have issued an order to the supplier to deliver to W. W. Smith & Co. When that order was carried out, W. W. Smith & Co. would use the "Notice of Shipment" to advise McKesson that they, in turn, had made the shipment to the customer. He reiterated that McKesson issued orders to the suppliers to ship, although he could not say whether they went direct to the supplier or through Smith. He thought he had seen such orders, although employees of McKesson's accounting department testified that they had not seen them and none have been discovered.[849]

The samples of the two Smith documents reproduced, the "Purchase Order" dated January 28, 1938 and the corresponding "Notice of Shipment" dated January 31, 1938,[850] give only one address—Liverpool. Within the indicated three day interval it was necessary that the order be received, accepted, credit passed, a Canadian supplier be advised by McKesson, delivery made by the supplier to Smith, consular invoices and so forth be obtained, and actual shipment to the customer made by Smith. Ritts explained the Liverpool heading by saying it was not unusual that an affiliated company, in this case W. W. Smith & Company, Inc. of New York, would use stationery of the other affiliate.[851]

After an interval of ten days during which time Ritts made a careful study of all of the types of documents which had been produced in connection with the foreign crude drug sales he testified that these documents, the purchase order and shipping advice from W. W. Smith & Co. and the McKesson bill of lading form, indicated that W. W. Smith & Co. obtained the merchandise from the Canadian vendors by their truck and handled all the details in connection with the shipment to the customers. The advice of shipment, under this interpretation of the procedure by Ritts, was the only evidence of shipment necessary for the auditors as the bill of lading form was only an internal memorandum prepared in the McKesson shipping department and would not represent an outside proof of the transactions' authenticity. These so-called bills of lading were attached to the shipping department's duplicate invoice whereas the juniors under Ritts, in accordance with the audit program, used in their work the accounting department copy of the invoice to which the W. W. Smith & Co. purchase order and shipping advice were attached.[852]

In his first testimony concerning the documents used in connection with these transactions which are reproduced and described earlier in this report,[853] Ritts was positive that the auditors had seen bills of

[849] R. 165-169, 1355-1356.

[850] Ex. 11-C, 11-B. See pages 78-79 *supra*.

[851] R. 169-173, 195. Cf. Thompson's testimony at page 133 *supra* to the effect that Coster told him that the Smith advices were mailed from Liverpool.

[852] R. 716-717, 177-180.

[853] Pages 77 ff. *supra*.

lading covering a large number of these shipments [854] although in recent years, since he assumed senior status, he had delegated that examination to juniors under him.[855] At first he was sure that bill of lading forms similar to the ones shown to him and placed in evidence were examined as supporting these transactions [856] but then stated that it would not be such an examination as would disclose whether it was a genuine bill of lading—merely a cursory examination,[857] "Bills of lading were examined incidental to other documents that we examined. Our primary purpose is not directed to the genuineness of this bill of lading." After examining the bill of lading more carefully Ritts granted that it was not in order, but repeated that it was only one of many documents, which in the absence of suspicion would not be examined in detail for he relied primarily upon the other documents in support of the shipment.[858] Although Ritts stated that it would be part of his duty as senior on the job to know how and from where the goods were shipped,[859] he could not recall that he had examined any bills of lading since the goods had been stored in Canada.[860] He felt, however, that he had satisfied himself "* * * in a general way that there was a sufficient control to preclude any major defalcations in the accounts in the absence of any collusion or fraud."[861]

The development of Ritts' conception of the way these foreign crude drug sales were handled from his original ideas expressed on the second day of the hearings in this proceeding to his final version developed in testimony 10 days later throws some light on the extent of his familiarity with the client's accounting procedures.[862] Five days after his first testimony on the subject at the present hearings, Ritts testified that his recollection of the facts had not been too clear in his mind before but now that he had had time to examine all the documents, he believed the correct version could be given. The bill of lading, consular invoice, and insurance certificate checked as

[854] R. 174, 176–177.

[855] R. 177.

[856] R. 181–182.

[857] R. 185–190.

[858] R. 190–200. Ritts testified:

> "I will grant that subject to a scrutiny like we are giving it, it will be evident that this copy of the bill of lading is not in order, but if I may repeat myself, the bill of lading was only one of many documents. All work we did in this respect was merely a cursory examination. Unless we had some specific reason to believe that there was something wrong with this shipment, that we had reasons to believe that this shipment was not made, we wouldn't examine it in detail, we would rely principally on the other documents supporting the charge to the customer." R. 200.

[859] R. 214–215.

[860] R. 211.

[861] R. 209.

[862] In his testimony before the Attorney General of the State of New York on December 10, 1938, about a month before his testimony at the present hearings, Ritts gave still another version of that part of the procedure which concerned the warehousing of the goods after purchase. "The contract with Smith & Co. provided that they would store and insure and bear all necessary expenses applicable to these stocks of McKesson bought from Smith or Smith's agents." R. 514. At the present hearings Ritts stated that in giving the foregoing testimony he was the first witness to be questioned in connection with the McKesson case and spoke beyond his actual knowledge from memory without having the advantage of reviewing the working papers or collecting his thoughts. R. 515.

accompanying the W. W. Smith & Co. "Notice of Shipment", he thought would of necessity be forwarded to the customer with the sales invoice. That meant that the bill of lading in evidence did not purport to be the original bill of lading covering shipment to the customer. He assumed that the bill of lading, covering shipment by W. W. Smith & Company, Inc. as McKesson's forwarding agent, would have been made up in triplicate, one copy retained by the carrier, one by the shipping agent, and one sent to McKesson & Robbins to be forwarded to the customer so he could claim the goods. Under this interpretation no bill of lading would be in McKesson's files although it would appear that they should have been flowing through the office on current transactions while the audit was in progress. Ritts could not recall that he had ever seen any of these bills of lading, nor could he say definitely that his present version was correct.[863]

In further testimony another 5 days later, Ritts amplified the second explanation referred to briefly above. He now stated that he had no recollection of how bills of lading had been made out when he had last seen them 4 years before, except that they carried such identifying words on their face. During 1935, 1936, and 1937, there would have been no occasion for examining them, for during this period, the audit programs required an examination of shipping advices from W. W. Smith & Co. instead. If by chance one of his men had come across a bill of lading during the last 3 years, he would have looked at it only long enough "* * * to see that it was a document he was not interested in examining." Why this document was in the files may best be explained by the following extract from Mr. Stewart's examination of Ritts:

> "Q. [By Mr. STEWART.] Since your original examination by Mr. Galpeer, concerning bills of lading, have you for the first time had an opportunity to examine the document which you have there marked Commission's Exhibit 9 [Reproduced at page 88 *supra*] for the purpose of attempting to determine what it means and what its function was in the system of records of McKesson & Robbins?
>
> A. Yes, I have.
>
> Q. Now, from your knowledge of the way the McKesson & Robbins crude drug transactions were handled during the past three years, and your knowledge of the documents which were examined by you and your subordinates during that period, what is your present opinion as to the meaning of that document, Commission's Exhibit 9, and as to the function it performed in the records of McKesson & Robbins?
>
> A. I think it is clearly evident that it is intended to serve only as an office memorandum to indicate that this shipment was made, not by McKesson & Robbins, but by W. W. Smith & Co. as shipping agent.
>
> * * * * * * *
>
> Q. * * * Would you say that it is usual or unusual for printed forms to be used by a corporation or corporations for the purpose of keeping internal records and to be used for a purpose different from the purpose for which they were apparently used in the first place?

---

[863] R. 624-626.

A. There would be nothing unusual about it so long as it would serve the purpose it was intended for.

Q. Now, assuming that the document marked Commission's Exhibit 9 was intended to be merely an internal memorandum of the shipping department of McKesson & Robbins, will you point out what language in the document indicates to you the date of shipment that it intended to record?

A. Well, it is stamped on the face of it, "Shipped January 31, 1938, by R. J. D.," which is Robert J. Dietrich, which indicates that——

* * * * * * *

He merely noted on here that shipment had been made per the advice of the shipping agent.

Q. In other words, that he was willing to accept the responsibility for saying that he was satisfied that the shipment had been made?

A. Well, it is also stamped—this is on the copy of the bill of lading "Received W. W. Smith & Co., Inc., forwarding department."

Q. What do you understand that language to mean?

A. Well, I think that the purpose of this bill of lading—the stamps indicate thereon—merely mean this, that W. W. Smith & Co., has stated that it got the merchandise by their truck, from the supplier and made the shipment to the customer.

* * * * * * *

Q. And it was simply intended to be an internal memorandum of the corporation to record the disposition of the merchandise?

A. Yes, sir, that is my opinion after studying those documents.

Q. Is it your present understanding that that document, Commission's Exhibit 9, was intended to be a bill of lading or a copy of a bill of lading at any time?

A. No, I don't think so.

Q. Now, look at Exhibit 8–C, which you also have in your hand, that is the shipping advice from W. W. Smith & Co., and tell me whether it is your present understanding that the document which has been marked Commission's Exhibit 9 was intended to be the bill of lading referred to on the bottom of Commission's Exhibit 8–C?

A. No, I think not, as the bill of lading——

Q. Now, what do you understand that reference to the bill of lading on Commission's Exhibit 8–C to refer to?

A. Well, it would be a copy of the original bill of lading prepared by W. W. Smith & Co., I believe, who were acting as shipping agents. They would have to furnish McKesson with a copy of this bill of lading so that in billing the customer for this merchandise—they would also have to send the customer a copy of the bill of lading to enable him to receive the merchandise at the other end. In other words, when the shipment arrived, the customer would receive notice from the carrier that they held such and such merchandise there for his account. Now to enable him to claim that merchandise, the customer would have to present a copy of the original bill of lading.

Q. Would that copy of the original bill of lading sent by Smith & Co. to McKesson & Robbins and sent by McKesson & Robbins to the consignee of the merchandise be a paper you would expect to find in the files of McKesson & Robbins?

A. Certainly not.

Q. Why not?

A. Not unless they receive more than one copy of the bill of lading because if they received one it would have to be sent to the customer, otherwise the customer could not claim the merchandise at the other end." [864]

[864] R. 704–708.

As to the manner in which the billing was handled, Ritts now testified that when an order came in from Smith that it was sent to the billing department which prepared a factory order, or a combination order and bill. This was registered and given an order number and then sent to the shipping department which issued shipping instructions to Smith. In due course the Smith notice of shipment, together with the documents indicated thereon, would come back and be sent to Robert Dietrich. The factory order would then be stamped "Shipped such and such a date R. J. Dietrich" and accompanied by the notice of shipment and various underlying documents went back to the accounting office. Then it would be charged to the customer. The original invoice together with the documents that would accompany the notice of shipment would be sent through the mail to the customer. The copies of the invoice would be used internally.[865] On this point, Mrs. Freer, assistant to Bonsby—head of the billing department for most of the period under review, testified that while the regular orders were handled substantially in the manner as described by Ritts, on the foreign crude drug sales or "pet" orders, as they were called, her department received the factory orders from George Dietrich, one typed copy only, with no shipping stamps or documents attached, from which the invoice was prepared and sent back to George Dietrich for mailing, the factory order going to the shipping department after the invoice had been thus prepared.[866]

Thorn started his association with the McKesson audit under Jaureguy on the work for 1927 and naturally had only a vague recollection of detailed instructions given him at that time in respect to what was expected of him in connection with his examination of documents. He stated that as a general thing he was expected to be on the alert to notice anything that might be of interest to his superior. While the following passage refers to purchase invoices rather than sales invoices, it sums up the situation rather well:

"Q. [By Mr. GALPEER.] Let me ask you the question this way: When you were told to do a particular job which would, let us say, entail checking invoices against another sheet, as to amounts and dates and so forth, were you expected to do that or were you expected to spend a little time and perhaps analyze the process generally, examine the papers in more detail than perhaps was absolutely essential for the particular checking job you might have to do?

A. [By THORN.] No, I should say not in the absence of any irregularity in the work which I was told to do, but, of course, there would be no restrictions on me if I saw anything that I thought I should look a little deeper into, why I was perfectly free to do that.

* * * * * *

Q. What I mean was, when you went out to look at the invoices that you were to examine, would you look at the items of cost or would you look at other things, for example, the address of the vendor, the terms of sale and things like that which

[865] R. 766–767.

[866] R. 4352–4360, 4375–4377. Quoted in part at pages 80–85 *supra*.

were not immediately pertinent to the particular test check that you were told to do?

A. No, sir, I would say generally not, no." [867]

For the 1929 examination, Thorn served as senior in charge at Bridgeport. At this time shipments of foreign crude drugs were supposed to have been made from inventories carried there. The practice of keeping all of these inventories in Canada began in 1935 after Thorn assumed control of the entire audit and spent most of his time in New York. From this time on he had no first-hand knowledge of the procedure in Bridgeport but assumed from Ritts' explanations that the system provided good internal control. Although he assumed there were such, he had never seen a shipping instruction from McKesson to the supplier or to W. W. Smith & Co. and did not know what form they took or who received them.[868] It was his understanding, however, that the orders were signed by George Dietrich on instructions by Coster, so that insofar as the internal system at McKesson was concerned the signature of Dietrich would have been accepted as valid authority for the release of the merchandise.[869] Thorn testified that the only evidence, other than collection of the account, which his men saw relating to the shipment were the advices from W. W. Smith & Co.[870]

On examining the Smith advices, however, Thorn could find no indication from which of the five Canadian vendors the merchandise was supposed to have originated and furthermore was sure that he had never before seen documents like them. His testimony indicates clearly that he relied on collection rather than upon any

---

867 R. 868–869.

868 R. 1124 ff.

869 "Q. [By Mr. GALPEER.] Did you yourself review any of these documents? They must have changed somewhat in form, or did you ask Mr. Ritts to review them in connection with this change in 1935?

A. [By THORN.] You mean the shipping advices particularly?

Q. That is right.

A. No. As far as I know, I have never seen a shipping advice on those items. I, of course, was familiar with the Manning account, having been there after the account was opened.

Q. Now, you made some mention, I believe, before, of the shipping instructions sent by McKesson—you don't remember whether it was the supplier or W. W. Smith & Company?

A. Yes.

Q. Do you know what form they took?

A. No, I don't know.

Q. Who was supposed to have approved those shipping advices?

A. You mean the company, who sent those out?

Q. Who was responsible for their issuance?

Mr. STEWART. You mean shipping instructions. You say shipping advices.

Mr. GALPEER. Yes.

A. Mr. Coster handled the operations of that department and any sales, it is my understanding, would be approved by him. You want the man who made the decisions, I presume.

Q. The actual signatures on the orders, would that be Mr. Coster's, or someone else's?

A. The actual signatures on the orders, I think, would always be George Dietrich's, because he was Mr. Coster's handyman and did the clerical work, but Mr. Coster made the decision, told George what to do, and George did it.

Q. That is right. As far as the internal system of McKesson they would have recognized George's signatures as validating that document?

A. I should think so, absolutely." R. 1132–1133.

870 R. 1129.

documentary evidence surrounding the sale in support of the reality of the transactions. His attitude toward the mechanics of the procedure is revealed in the following passage from his testimony:

> "Q. [By Mr. GALPEER.] Let me put it this way: In referring to the documents that would have satisfied you that these shipments had been made, would you have accepted a set of this sort which didn't indicate the particular supply house or would you have insisted upon some evidence in these notices of shipment that the source or the supply from which the shipment had been made be indicated?
>
> A. I should have accepted those documents because I would not have been concerned with those operating details. I might have gone on, as a matter of curiosity to see how they were doing it but from an auditing standpoint I have no concern with the exact mechanics down to the last particular with which they are able to do it.
>
> The main thing with me, after all, is that it works.
>
> Q. I was thinking perhaps you used the word auditing in that connection, but I was thinking in connection with your check of the internal control, would this have satisfied you?
>
> A. That is the reason I used the word auditing, yes. No, I don't think that is an element of internal control." [871]

Rowbotham supported his staff's point of view as to forms by drawing a distinction between forms as forms (which would not require a meticulous study) and the method of procedure which he felt could be determined without checking the details of the forms used in carrying out that procedure.[872]

F. INTERCOMPANY ACCOUNTS

There are two aspects of the intercompany accounting which require attention. The first is the sale of foreign crude drugs by the Canadian Company to the Connecticut Division, which is definitely a working capital position question. The second, the plowing back of profits, on its face would appear to be an investment question rather than one of current position, but as will be shown later, this too is basically a matter of the allocation of working capital between the Maryland Company and the Connecticut Company (later Division) and wholesale houses.

The intercompany relations of the Canadian Company with the Connecticut Division were referred to by Wyman in his memorandum covering his work on the Canadian Company audit for 1937. In this memorandum he stated that:

> "With the exception of intercompany sales amounting to $244,875, the operations of McKesson & Robbins, Limited, have been confined, as in the past, to the sale abroad of crude drugs and essential oils. These sales have been made under a sales agreement with W. W. Smith & Company, Inc., New York, a firm having its head office in Liverpool, England, and conducting an international business as traders and guaranty brokers in general merchandise." [873]

[871] R. 1148–1149.

[872] R. 1846–1849.

[873] Ex. 26.

Ritts was asked to explain how the intercompany sales were handled by the affiliated companies. His examination of the December 31, 1937 balance sheet of the Canadian Company indicated no substantial intercompany account receivable at that date, the only item being $2,998.75 due from the London subsidiary. This led to the conclusion that the sales under discussion must have been cleared in some way during the year but he did not know how. Neither had he considered how the Canadian Company got funds for the payment of dividends and expenses.[874]

From the reputed establishment of Manning & Company as a bank in 1931 to the close of 1936 most of the Canadian Company's cash came from transfers from accounts maintained in the name of Manning & Company with recognized banks.[875] Miss Walsh testified, however, that most of the cash that came into the Canadian Company during the "last two years, or so", came from the sale of merchandise to the Connecticut Division.[876] Seal of S. D. Leidesdorf & Co. matched these sales and collections thereon from the parent company with the Canadian Company's need of funds for dividend purposes and testified that bank balances prior to such collections were inadequate to meet the dividend payments on the dates shown.[877] The following extract from a brief table prepared by him shows this relationship.

Evidence of Sale of Fictitious Drugs by the Canadian Company to the Maryland Company in Connection With the Payment of Dividends by the Canadian Company

Merchandise Sold		Cash Received	Dividends Paid	
Date	Amount	Date	Date	Amount
Apr. 21, 1937	$55,000	Apr. 29, 1937	May 1, 1937	$48,000
Oct. 13, 1937	50,400	Oct. 27, 1937	Nov. 1, 1937	48,000

In respect to transactions between the Maryland Company and the Connecticut Division and wholesale houses, it should be remembered that after 1934 most of the latter were operated as divisions. McGloon, during the last several years, caused to be prepared in his office a statement showing the changes in the branch control accounts and the employment of capital in the various divisions and subsidiary corporations. This document consisted of a covering letter addressed to Coster, Michaels, Murray, Thompson, and the "Divisional Vice Presidents"; and seven pages showing for each McKesson unit the balance

[874] R. 554–560, especially:

"Q. [By Mr. GALPEER.] Let me summarize it in one or two questions in connection with these intercompany sales which you refer to in Commission's Exhibit 26, which is Mr. Wyman's memorandum, in the amount of $244,875. Do you know how the Connecticut Division paid this sum to the Limited Company?

A. [By RITTS.] No, I do not.

Q. And the second question: Do you know from what source the Limited Company got the cash with which to pay the dividends on its securities and to pay the three-fourths of one per cent to Smith?

A. No, I do not." R. 559–560.

[875] Footnotes 200 and 407 *supra*.

[876] R. 4423.

[877] Ex. 258; R. 4585–4586.

in the branch control or, in the case of separately incorporated units, the Corporation's capital employed at the beginning and end of the year, the increase or decrease for the year, the net cash advanced to or from the home office, the net profit or loss of the unit for the year, and an analysis of other charges or credits to the account during the year.[878] This report for 1937 indicated that the majority of the units paid cash to the home office, a substantial number turning in amounts much in excess of the profit for the year. The total net profit attributed to the wholesale drug and liquor houses, was $3,233,571 and the net cash remitted to the home office from these units was $3,766,421. The liquor production divisions showed a profit of only $151,422 but paid to the home office $1,628,125 net. The Canadian Company, including its London subsidiary, made a profit of approximately $178,000 and paid the home office $43,500, of which $21,000 was a dividend paid the Connecticut Division which was its direct parent. The difference represented interest of $22,500. In addition, this Company paid dividends of $75,000 to the public.[879] The Connecticut Division, which included the manufacturing, import and export activities, real and fictitious, paid $236,889 to a foreign subsidiary, and drew $90,000 from the home office. However, the net result of all of this Division's transactions for the year, as revealed by this report, was that its profit of $1,940,058 remained in the Division plus an additional investment of approximately $100,000.

McGloon testified that reports of this type were never sent to Price, Waterhouse & Co. and he did not believe they knew they were in existence. If they had asked for them he would have produced them.[880] The report referred to above is dated March 10, 1938, while Ritts' memorandun covering his work at Bridgeport for the same year is dated in New York, February 24, 1938.

Other officers of the Company were questioned about this situation. Joseph L. Bedsole, vice-president and director, referred to the report we have just described as a source from which it appeared, after a little study, that the Connecticut Division profits were going back

---

[878] Ex. 115; R. 1740-1743.

[879] The manner in which funds for this and foregoing payments was made available was explained at pages 241-242 *supra*.

[880] "Q. [By Mr. GALPEER.] So that if Price, Waterhouse & Co. had not asked for, or seen, or had any connection with this particular report, they could have at any time obtained the facts therein set forth by referring to the books of the company?

A. [By McGLOON.] Yes.

Mr. STEWART. If it was any part of the scope of the examination they were conducting.

By Mr. GALPEER:

Q. You wouldn't have refused them access to any books, would you?

A. No.

Mr. STEWART. If they had been doing work they hadn't been employed to do, you would have been complaining about paying them for it, wouldn't you, Mr. McGloon?

A. Do you want an answer to that?

Q. I thought Mr. Galpeer might have some doubts about it. I don't. I think we had better have an answer.

A. Yes." R. 1740-1742.

into that Division, whereas other divisions were contributing cash to the home office. His own company at Mobile, for example, had returned $518,000 from May 1, 1928 through 1938 on an original investment of $413,000 by the Maryland Company. He accepted the situation as satisfactory because he thought the manufacturing department was growing and the heavy general sales required the reinvestment of the Connecticut Division profits where they were earned.[881]

The treasurer of the Corporation did not take this condition quite so calmly. Thompson prepared a memorandum on inventories in the early part of 1938 with the aid of McGloon's staff[882] and sent it to Coster, Michaels, and Murray under date of April 18, 1938. This report referred to the fact that a year before the treasurer had warned these officers that all inventories should be reduced and an agreement had been reached at that time to do so within the year. The report mentioned that since then liquor inventories had decreased, wholesale drug inventories were about the same, and Connecticut inventories had increased. A 3-year summary of sales, inventory, receivables, net profit, net worth, and net amount paid to Maryland Company was given for the Connecticut Division separating what he called the bulk department from other activities.[883]

Thompson's conclusions in his report on this particular subject were very concise:

> "It will be observed that the inventory and receivables of the Bulk Department increase annually and approximately the amount of the profit of the department, and that the Connecticut division has not contributed a net balance to the Corporation for the purposes of bond interest, dividends or bank debt reduction during the past three years. In mentioning this fact, however, it would not be fair to fail to point out that through the use of the capital in the Connecticut division there is contributed approximately two-fifths of the profits available for interest, dividends, taxes, etc."[884]

Thompson in his testimony stated that the first time he noticed this condition was early in 1936 and that he grew quite concerned about it when the bank debt began to go up, which led to a desire on his part to get cash up from the divisions in order to reduce the debt.[885] As pointed out heretofore it was Thompson's following up on this subject that led to the uncovering of the fraud.[886]

The auditors were questioned at the hearings as to whether the condition cited above was known to them and whether they had set forth the situation in any way. Ritts testified that during the last

---

881 R. 2489–2493.

882 R. 1737–1739.

883 Comparison of sales figures used in this summary with departmental statements (Ex. N, 124) indicates that the former included both the real and fictitious bulk business, of which the fictitious was much the larger.

884 Ex. 114.

885 R. 2065–2066.

886 Pages 128 ff. *supra*.

several years he prepared "* * * a 'Source and Application of Funds Statement', which would indicate the increase or decrease in both these accounts receivable and inventories * * *" for the Connecticut Division as a whole "* * * but there again it may be that such changes would be substantially changes in the crude drug stocks and crude drug receivables." [887] These statements indicated increases in inventories in some years and increases in receivables in some years, with a net increase in the sum of the two but not in each in every year. It never occurred to Ritts that apparently all of the earnings of this Division were being plowed "* * * back into one type of asset or another * * *"; consequently, he never set it forth in any of his reports. Even if he had noticed that fact, he thought it would be "* * * an operating question for the company rather than an accounting question." [888] In any event the increases in inventories and receivables by divisions were indicated in schedules included in the reports submitted to Coster, but Ritts never discussed the matter with anyone prior to the exposure.[889]

It should be noted that the financial statements for the Connecticut Division which were submitted to Coster, without comment by the auditors, included a "Statement of Branch Control Account" which displayed substantially the same information as that reflected in McGloon's report described above. The statement for 1937 is so brief that it may be reproduced here: [889a]

"Exhibit B

CONNECTICUT DIVISION

McKESSON & ROBBINS, INCORPORATED

STATEMENT OF BRANCH CONTROL ACCOUNT

FOR THE YEAR ENDING DECEMBER 31, 1937

* * * * *

Balance, December 31, 1936		$18, 405, 970. 77
Net profit for the year ending December 31, 1937 (Exhibit C)		1, 940, 058. 04
Advances received from the head office		455, 000. 00
Value of net assets transferred from Lucretia Vanderbilt, Incorporated, as shown by the books of that company		5, 090. 15
		$20, 806, 118. 96
Deduct:		
Payments made to the head office	$290, 000. 00	
Payment made to New Haven Division	75, 000. 00	365, 000. 00
Balance, December 31, 1937 (to Exhibit A)		$20, 441, 118. 96"

[887] R. 534. This was not a new idea, for such a statement was included in the audit report on Girard & Co., Inc., submitted to Coster under date of March 9, 1925, and each report thereafter on that Company and McKesson & Robbins, Incorporated (Connecticut) through 1929, when separate reports on the Connecticut Company were discontinued. See Ex. 138–148, 151. See also Ex. M–2, M–11.

[888] R. 536. [889] R. 538. [889a] Ex. 261.

After the fraud was exposed, Ritts collected his working papers and during the week of December 19 to 24, 1938, he prepared a schedule showing crude drug inventories, sales, and accounts receivable for the Connecticut Division and the Canadian Company for the years 1932 to 1937, inclusive.[890] This schedule included a comparatively small amount of real resale business in some years. Subject to the influence of this inaccuracy Ritts agreed that his schedule revealed that gross profit on foreign crude drugs over this period for the two units was substantially equal to the sum of the increases in accounts receivable and inventories, and that for each year that there was a close similarity in totals, but that inventories and receivables separately did not increase constantly each year.[891]

The following tables were condensed from a later more accurate schedule prepared from material in Price, Waterhouse & Co.'s working papers.[892]

---

[890] Ex. 43.

[891] R. 526-533.

[892] Ex. Q. The 1933 schedules in Price, Waterhouse & Co.'s papers do not segregate "Special Resale Stock" (fictitious foreign crude drugs). An adjustment to eliminate $131,000 gross profit for this year on real business of the Connecticut Division with which the fictitious was combined has therefore been made to arrive at the amount shown in the tables. Ex. 267. Other minor differences have been ignored as immaterial.

Statement of Foreign Crude Drug Gross Profits, Inventories, and Accounts Receivable for the Canadian Company, Connecticut Division, and the Two Units Combined

(000's omitted)

Year		Gross Profit	Increase or (Decrease) in Inventories and Accounts Receivable Combined	Increase or (Decrease) in Inventories	Increase or (Decrease) in Accounts Receivable
		Canadian Company			
1933		$ 237	$ (60)	$ (51)	$ (9)
1934		238	51	(37)	88
1935		256	78	(148)	226
1936		275	100	103	(3)
1937		285	32	(63)	95
	Total	$1, 291	$ 201	$ (196)	$ 397
		Connecticut Division			
1933		$ 994	$1, 679	$ 375	$1, 304
1934		922	1, 069	1, 168	(99)
1935		1, 437	1, 619	(236)	1, 855
1936		1, 513	1, 622	1, 775	(153)
1937		1, 516	1, 872	1, 169	703
	Total	$6, 382	$7, 861	$4, 251	$3, 610
		Canadian Company and Connecticut Division Combined			
1933		$1, 231	$1, 619	$ 324	$1, 295
1934		1, 160	1, 120	1, 131	(11)
1935		1, 693	1, 697	(384)	2, 081
1936		1, 788	1, 722	1, 878	(156)
1937		1, 801	1, 904	1, 106	798
	Total	$7, 673	$8, 062	$4, 055	$4, 007

The year 1932, included on the schedules, has been omitted from the above tables because the relation between gross profit and asset changes was obscured by the fact that in that year most of the change was made from an actual disbursement and receipt of cash to the device of Manning & Company debit and credit advices. For the entire period after 1932, the difference between the gross profit and the increase in accounts receivable and inventories for the Canadian Company and Connecticut Division combined is accounted for principally by fluctuations in the balance in the Manning & Company

205078—40——17

account (the third fictitious asset affected by the fictitious crude drug business) and by the fact that cash discounts recorded as taken on fictitious purchases from some of the purported vendors were included in "Other Income" in the profit and loss accounts rather than as an adjustment of purchases.

It will be noted that the fictitious assets of the Canadian Company did not rise with succeeding years' profits but that the fictitious items in the Connecticut Division rose in excess of the fictitious profits of that unit. The difference between the excess of approximately $1,500,000 of increase in fictitious assets over profits for the five-year period in the latter Division and the $1,100,000 excess of profits over the increase in fictitious assets in the former is approximately the amount of purchase discounts which should be included in determining the gross profits for this purpose. The shift in the growth of the assets from the Canadian Company to the Connecticut Division is accounted for by the fact that it was necessary to get actual cash into the Canadian Company so that actual disbursements could be made for expenses and dividends, since that unit, unlike the Connecticut Division, had no substantial real business which it could draw on directly for this purpose.

Thorn and Rowbotham echoed Ritts' views as to whether it was an auditor's duty to notice and bring matters such as those discussed above to the attention of the client's directors. Thorn did not see why the directors would be interested in knowing whether the increases mentioned were in the resale crude drug department or the manufacturing departments, the total was there if they wanted it, compared with the preceding year. In Thorn's discussion of the increases with Rowbotham the only question raised would be as to collectibility of the accounts and salability of the merchandise, both of which could be demonstrated to their entire satisfaction. In this connection, Thorn testified that he did not know, at the time, that all of these crude drug transactions handled through W. W. Smith & Company, Inc., were cleared through Manning & Company and that the cash for dividends and commission and expenses in connection with them, at least in later years, must have come from other departments of the business.[893] As a matter of fact, he felt that he would not have had any occasion to observe the movement of cash during the year. He had no idea as

[893] Ritts testified to the same effect. R. 554-560, 140. The last cash received as coming from Manning & Company was in 1933 for the Connecticut Company and 1936 for the Canadian Company. See footnote 200 *supra*.

to how much cash moved from the head office to the branch or the reverse.[894]

Rowbotham, as has been seen, was entirely convinced of the excellence of the accounts receivable, and, as will be shown in the next section, he also was satisfied with the inventory so that the plowing back of profits and the failure of the crude drug operations to contribute any cash toward the payment of dividends or reduction of debt never disturbed him. Rather, he felt that this was the way American business was done and it was highly commendable.[895]

In addition to the "Statement of Branch Control Account" reproduced above, there were occasional references in the audit reports to intercompany accounts and proration of expenses between Companies for one purpose or another, such as an analysis of intercompany accounts receivable appearing in the report on the 1929 audit [896], but it appears from the testimony of Rowbotham, Ritts, and Thorn that they attached no auditing significance to such analyses as were made year after year of the growing investment of the parent in the Connecticut Division as they considered the reinvestment of earnings in this unit to be an operating question rather than a problem for the auditors.

---

894 "A. [By THORN.] * * * Then beyond that point it becomes an operating problem because, after all, companies making money, having a profitable business, and able to expand that business—there is nothing we can say in the way of criticism even. In other words, that is an operating problem from then on out after we have satisfied ourselves.

Q. [By Mr. GALPEER.] Did you at that time discuss the connection of cash to these transactions: In other words, that as a result of this Manning clearance account, at least during the last three years or so that no cash was coming out of the transactions and that the actual payment to Smith of commission and the other expenses had to be borne in cash by the other branches of this business?

A. No, that I am sure hasn't been discussed because of the fact that I wasn't aware of that, as I didn't know at the time that all crude drug transactions were handled through Manning and I haven't known through the years exactly as to how much cash might have been paid over to the head office or the parent company or vice versa. As to that cash position, it is transactions that are occurring throughout the year and I wouldn't come in contact with those, so that I am sure that has not been discussed with the partners." R. 910–911.

895 "[By ROWBOTHAM.] * * * I think undoubtedly one of the points on this job is the fact that this crude drug business was expanding and that the profits on the crude drug business were being plowed back into it.

I didn't know that all the profits were being plowed and I don't understand that that is the fact. I believe money did come out of it. I am not certain of that, but I did know broadly that the profits of the crude drug business were being plowed back into that business.

Now, that is one of the points that would come up and would be discussed between Thorn and me, though I don't recollect for the moment that there is any specific sentence in any of those memoranda which says these words: 'The profits of this business are being plowed back' but that is one of the things that was discussed at the time that I knew about.

If I may say a word right there, it didn't seem to me at the time, it didn't cause me any discomfort, it didn't cause me any disquiet because it seemed to be just plain common sense that if a man has got a good business he ought to plow back his profits in there as long as that business is good. That is the way American business has been run in the past and it is only in very recent years that the other idea, that every cent of profit ought to be distributed to stockholders has come around and we have had, as you know, the undistributed profit tax and even then there has been quite a measure of opposition to that.

* * * * * * *

So that when this question of plowing back profits came up, to me it didn't seem anything unnatural and didn't seem to me out of the way and it just seemed to me just common sense if you had a business that could make profit." R. 1917–1919.

896 Ex. 151.

G. INVENTORIES

Inventories of merchandise constituted the largest single asset of the McKesson Companies, approximately 50% of total assets, and consequently required a substantial portion of the time spent on the audit. The following table [897] indicates clearly the heavy concentration of the assets of the Company as a whole, as well as of the Connecticut Division and Canadian Company, in inventories and in cash and customers' accounts receivable discussed above. Together these three categories comprised approximately 85% of the total assets of the three units.

Percentage of Certain Assets to Total per Balance Sheets as at December 31, 1937

	Maryland Company and Subsidiaries Consolidated	Connecticut Division	Canadian Company and Subsidiary
Total assets	$87, 182, 766	$21, 686, 133	$3, 067, 432
Cash	$ 3, 358, 571	$ 498, 763	$ 60, 779
Percent of division's assets	—	(2. 3)	(2. 0)
Percent of consolidated assets	(4. 0)	(. 6)	(. 1)
Customers' accounts	$25, 791, 604	$ 7, 803, 808	$1, 582, 703
Percent of division's assets	—	(35. 9)	(51. 0)
Percent of consolidated assets	(29. 5)	(8. 9)	(1. 8)
Inventories	$44, 254, 736	$10, 634, 944	$1, 002, 322
Percent of division's assets	—	(48. 8)	(33. 0)
Percent of consolidated assets	(51. 0)	(12. 2)	(1. 1)
Total	$73, 404, 911	$18, 937, 515	$2, 645, 804
Percent of division's assets	—	(87. 0)	(86. 0)
Percent of consolidated assets	(84. 5)	(21. 7)	(3. 0)

The Canadian Company and subsidiary total assets of $3,067,431.57 as stated on their own consolidated balance sheet included $420,000.00 for goodwill, trade names, franchises, etc., which was eliminated in consolidation with the Maryland Company. If the intangibles were eliminated from the total assets of the Canadian Company and subsidiary the three categories of assets set forth in the table above would constitute 99.9% of the total assets of that Company and subsidiary, there having been in addition only a negligible amount of furniture and fixtures and prepaid expenses. The distribution on this basis would have been: cash, 2.3%; customers' accounts, 59.8%; and inventories, 37.8% of the adjusted total.

Except for cash of the head office which amounted to approximately $1,000,000, the half million cash of the Connecticut Division was the largest balance in the 66 divisions and 14 subsidiary corporations at December 31, 1937. The other balances ranged from $75.00 to

[897] Adapted from Ex. 28 prepared by Price, Waterhouse & Co. R. 429-431.

$246,585.40.[898] The receivables in both the Connecticut Division and Canadian Company were each greater than in any of the other units of the Company. These other 80 units showed balances at that time ranging from $6,596.64 to $1,275,596.08.[899] The inventory balances were allocated to 78 units, some of the liquor divisions having been grouped to give them the second largest inventory total—$4,370,560.32 compared with the inventory in the Connecticut Division of $10,634,-943.94 and in the Canadian Company and subsidiary of $1,002,321.60. The other inventory balances ranged from $17,553.55 to $2,320,889.14 in the wholesale houses.[900]

The inventory on the books at Bridgeport in the Connecticut Division at December 31, 1937, as summarized by Ritts, consisted of 12 categories, the major items of which were listed as finished stock (manufactured products of the Company) $726,061.23, outside warehouses (other than Canadian vendors) $311,679.20, and book 7, general crude (stock listed as with the fictitious Canadian vendors and a small amount of real resale crude) $9,145,962.14.[901] The Canadian Company inventory of $990,585 at December 31, 1937 consisted entirely of merchandise listed as with the same Canadian vendors.[902]

Clifford H. Hill,[903] with the aid of two other juniors, carried out all of the work program as laid down for the audit of inventories of the Connecticut Division on the 1935, 1936, and 1937 engagements.[904] Wyman did all of the work on the Canadian Company for 1937 except one item investigated by Ritts.

At the outset it should be recalled that since some time in 1935, the inventories which were discovered to have been fictitious were supposed to have been in the warehouses of the vendors in Canada, but prior to that time these inventories were supposed to have been stored in some years (1933, 1934) entirely in the Company's plant at Bridgeport and in earlier years partly in outside public warehouses. Because of its relative simplicity and because it consisted entirely of the fictitious crude drugs and essential oils in question, the inventory work

---

898 Ex. 4; R. 100.

899 Ex. 5; R. 100.

900 Ex. 3; R. 98.

901 Ex. 6; R. 115.

902 Ex. 65. In addition, the Canadian Company consolidated balance sheet includes a small inventory of real products carried by its subsidiary, the London Company.

903 *Clifford H. Hill* was employed by Price, Waterhouse & Co. for the first time on January 6, 1936, and released on February 17, 1936. He was reemployed the following season from November 23, 1936, to April 8, 1937, and again from December 6, 1937, to April 20, 1938. He was further reemployed on December 9, 1938, and although a temporary employee, had not been released at April 20, 1939, when Exhibit 212 was placed in the record. In explaining his period of employment with Price, Waterhouse & Co., he testified on January 20, 1939, "In order not to lead you astray, I have had seven months vacation each year * * * ." He attended Nelson's Business College, Cincinnati, Ohio, for 10 months in 1909 following which he held several clerical positions there for 2 years; was bookkeeper for a coal company for 2 years; spent several years each with various insurance companies and agencies as cashier, bookkeeper, and accountant; and for eleven years prior to his engagement by Price, Waterhouse & Co. he was accountant for a firm of iron workers. He is not a certified public accountant. Ex. 212; R. 1255–1259.

904 Ex. 41, 40, 37.

program for the Canadian Company as carried out by Wyman in his examination for 1937, will be considered before reviewing the work in the Connecticut Division which also covered real merchandise.

In introducing the supplementary questionnaires on internal control it was mentioned that one of these covered inventories for the Connecticut Division. A separate questionnaire was not filled out for the Canadian Company for, Ritts explained, the problem was the same in the Canadian Company as in the Connecticut Division so there was no purpose in preparing a questionnaire on the Canadian procedure.[905] Wyman's work then was confined to the inventory work program itself which was a mimeographed sheet of instructions used for the Canadian Company and the wholesale houses audited by the New York office of Price, Waterhouse & Co.[906]

For reference later, the full work program is reproduced here:

"(1) Obtain the company's inventory sheets and discuss the method of taking the inventory with responsible officials.

"(2) If any inventories were stored in outside warehouses, obtain confirmations direct from the custodians and inspect warehouse receipts, if any.

"(3) Make inquiries relative to merchandise held on consignment or merchandise billed and not yet shipped to see that such items are not included in the inventories.

"(4) Make inquiries relative to merchandise shipped on consignment to see that it is included in the inventory and not in accounts receivable.

"(5) If the company has prepared price-test schedules, check particulars of schedules from the inventory sheets and add additional items considered necessary. If the company has not prepared such schedules, have them made up immediately so that invoices required for price verification may be assembled by the company while the other verification work is being done.

"(6) Foot inventory sheets from the $1 column. Foot only a representative number of sheets totaling less than $100 and scrutinize the others.

"(7) Summarize inventory page totals and agree grand total with general ledger control.

"(8) If company maintains stock cards, check a representative number of the larger items on the inventory sheets to the cards, note any substantial differences and see that the cards are adjusted to physical count; state what disposition is made of differences.

"(9) Verify extensions of items over a minimum amount determined by the assistant in charge and of enough smaller items to make a verification of two items on each other page.

"(10) Make an eye test of each extension not verified to determine that the decimal point is in the right place. In both this work and the verification of extensions, care should be taken to see that the same unit is used for quantities and pricing.

"(11) Schedule all differences for client's attention, and for any adjustments considered necessary.

"(12) Verify unit prices by reference to vendors' invoices and insert all pertinent information on price-test schedules. Price list may be used in some cases as specified in our instructions.

---

[905] R. 266.

[906] Ex. 23.

"(13) Insert last year's quantities and unit prices on price-test schedules in red for the more important items.

"(14) Obtain market quotations when available.

"(15) Schedule all items priced in excess of cost or market, whichever is lower, and adjust where necessary.

"(16) Scrutinize inventory records, especially stock cards, for slow and inactive goods.

"(17) Classify inventory in accordance with the company's instructions showing as many detailed classifications as possible.

"(18) Submit particulars of intercompany and interdivision inventories to New York office as instructed.

"(19) Take up all merchandise in transit at the close of the period, if it was billed or shipped F. O. B. on or before the closing date.

"(20) State the inventory value of any merchandise hypothecated or assigned, with particular reference to accepted drafts.

"(21) Show amount of taxes or duties payable on merchandise in bond or stored in foreign warehouses, if any.

"(22) Examine contracts for purchase commitments to see that quantities were neither in excess of normal requirements nor at prices in excess of current market prices at the date of the examination.

"(23) Prepare inventory certificate and obtain signatures of responsible officials.

"(24) The foregoing program should be modified and extended to meet the requirements of each particular examination. Additional work done may be described below."

The first point on the Canadian program required that the inventory sheets be obtained and the method of taking inventory be discussed with responsible officials. Wyman secured the inventory book sheets which had been prepared for him but did not compare them with the original count sheets nor did he discuss the method of taking the inventory with any official since the inventory was supposed to be in the warehouses of the vendors from whom, as the second requirement of his program, he was to get confirmations and inspect warehouse receipts, if any. Wyman secured confirmations which Price, Waterhouse & Co. obtained direct from the vendors but decided that it was unnecessary to ask for warehouse receipts as it had not been done before and the confirmations seemed sufficient.[907] As to this point he wrote in his memorandum that "The merchandise comprising the inventory at December 31, 1937 was all held by Canadian suppliers at that date and was confirmed by certificates received direct from the custodians thereof." [908] These false confirmations were received through the mail on letter-heads of the five fictitious Canadian vendors: B. Miller & Company, Importers and Brokers, 45 Queen Street, Ottawa; H. Monroe & Company, Brokers & Agents, 27 Wellington Street East, Toronto; P. Pierson & Company, Foreign Representatives, University Tower, Montreal; A. H. Raymond & Company, Importers, 504 Dominion Square Building, Montreal; and D. C. Reynolds & Company, Commission Merchants, 192 Bank Street, Ottawa. All of

[907] R. 357–361.

[908] Ex. 26.

them used a slightly different wording, such as, "holding for their account and subject to their disposition. * * * No charges are due," "held by us as their property," "held for their account," "holding * * * for account of," and "carried by us for their account * * * free of all charges and subject to their withdrawal." None of them stated the address at which the goods were held unless it be assumed to be at the letter-head address which, however, in some cases at least, appeared to be an office building. The number of items carried by each vendor varied from one to four, making a total at December 31, 1937 of 13 different items all of substantial quantities [909] easily checked against the inventory book sheets and verified as to purchase prices. Both of these steps were required, and done by Wyman.

The inventory was footed, extensions checked, purchase invoices examined for evidence of acquisition and unit prices, items compared with stock cards, quantities compared with prior years, and an inventory certificate was obtained signed by F. D. Coster as president and treasurer, Geo. E. Dietrich as secretary and assistant treasurer, J. H. McGloon as comptroller, and, for identification purposes only, by G. F. Wyman for Price, Waterhouse & Co. Since the inventory certificate obtained by Wyman from officials of the Canadian Company was the same as that on the Connecticut Division, except for two items in the latter referring to counting, a step not taken in the Canadian Company, a detailed consideration of certificates is deferred until that of the Connecticut Division is reached.

All of the 24 points on the work program for the Canadian Company were either covered, or crossed out as inapplicable. In addition, Wyman added three points not on the mimeographed work program. Sales subsequent to December 31 were listed and unit sales prices compared with the inventory prices; opening and closing inventories, both quantity and amount, were reconciled by commodities; and year-end purchases were traced to the purchase register to see that the proper liability was recorded.

Wyman was questioned in more detail on a few points of the work program. Item 12 required the verification of prices by reference to vendors' invoices, all of which quoted terms "Cash against documents." Although he recalled the form of these invoices, Wyman could not recall the terms and does not think he would have looked at the terms. He never asked anyone for documents and did not recall any discussions concerning them.

Item 21 of the program requested that the amount of taxes or duties payable on merchandise in bond or stored in foreign warehouses be shown, if any. It was marked "none." Wyman marked this but did not remember having done anything on it. He thought he might have

[909] Ex. 54. The total number of items for other years varied from two at December 31, 1928 to twenty at December 31, 1933. Ex. 149, 75; see also Ex. 72, 73, 74, 76, 205.

inquired of McGloon or possibly Dietrich but, if so, the answer was not important enough to record more fully than indicated. He did not recall how the taxes were handled but was sure they were taken care of—possibly W. W. Smith & Co. were required to take care of them under their contract.[910]

In his memorandum Wyman reported that "A dollar statement of the sales and cost of sales by commodities for the year, prepared in connection with the reconciliation of the quantities in the December 31, 1937 inventory, with those of the previous year, indicates that the company consistently realized a profit from its transactions throughout the year." That a profit was realized on all transactions was mentioned first by Ritts in his memorandum on the 1935 accounts when he said, "Because of the relatively small number of transactions during the year, we were able to reconcile the quantities in the opening and closing inventories by applying the purchases and sales of the several commodities. The dollar amounts of sales and cost of sales were also verified in connection with the above-mentioned reconciliation and it was noted that the company realized a profit on all their transactions throughout the year." [911]

Wyman also stated in the 1937 memorandum that the pricing was at cost, which appeared to be below current market quotations, although as they had been required to do in the past, they accepted quotations furnished by a vendor for several items not currently quoted. Wyman's only original contribution to the memorandum (he followed Ritts' 1936 memorandum closely) occurred at this point when he reported that the items for which quotations were not available were purchased in November or December, 1937, and that the stock records of the company did not disclose any price changes in any of the commodities traded in since April 21, 1937.[912]

The situation revealed above as to failure to find published quotations on some items in the inventory had prevailed since 1931, at least, for a similar comment to that referred to appears in the memorandum on the Canadian Company work of that year, the first reference to inventories. In that year Coster assured the auditors that the items in question "* * * could not have been bought at a lower price at December 31." Thorn, who wrote this memorandum, could not say at the hearings why he included his next remark in a document of this kind which was condensed and supposed to highlight important points on the job, but he said, "All the merchandise was purchased from J. P. Meyer & Co., Inc. of Brooklyn whose address is the same as that of Smith & Co., mentioned above" (in connection with the contract). He testified that "* * * there are inconse-

[910] R. 361–364 cover the discussion of items 12 and 21.

[911] Ex. 26, 73. See also Ex. 72.

[912] Ex. 26.

quential things that get into these memoranda because we can't always pick out what is important and what isn't" and that he presumed he was showing that these people being in the same class of business were in the same location or at the same addresses and that Jaureguy, who was then manager and had been on the work in some capacity since the audit at November 30, 1926, probably did not see any significance in it either but failed to take it out. Thorn saw no possibility that the similarity of addresses of J. P. Meyer (from whom all of the goods were supposedly purchased at this time) and of W. W. Smith (through whom they were all supposed to have been sold and shipped) might suggest some connection between the two concerns which would throw suspicion on the merchandise or the price or that the notation had been made for that reason.[913]

In the same memorandum Thorn stated that the inventory of the Canadian Company, which in former years had been in a public warehouse in Canada, was then in the Connecticut Company's warehouse in Bridgeport and that the goods were billed and shipped from Bridgeport. A warehouse in Montreal, to which the inventory was to have been transferred the following year, was rented in 1931 but at the next year-end the inventory was still in Bridgeport. Thorn's memorandum for 1933 had only one sentence in respect to inventories in which he said "The inventory consists of twenty items of crude drugs and we are satisfied as to the pricing." [914] The 1934 memorandum again stated definitely that the merchandise was stored in Bridgeport.

In 1935 the system was changed for the memorandum on the Canadian Company accounts that year stated that "The merchandise was all held by Canadian suppliers as at December 31, 1935 and was confirmed by certificates received direct from the vendors. The confirmations did not state the location of the stocks, but we were informed by the company that the merchandise is shipped from the vendors' various warehouses upon advices submitted from the company's Bridgeport office." [915]

The memorandum on the 1934 accounts commented on the small number of items in the Canadian Company inventory (18 in that year, 13 to 20 during the period 1931 to 1937), and noted that, "Because of the relatively small number of transactions during the year * * * ," it was possible to reconcile the beginning and ending inventory by taking purchases and sales into account.[916] The simplicity of these accounts is clearly demonstrated by reference to the copy of the inventory summary for December 31, 1934, included

---

913 Ex. 76; R. 962–965. See also page 66 *supra*; Ex. 170, 176.

914 Ex. 75.

915 Ex. 73.

"* * * the reference here to the location of the goods meant that I didn t know whether the office of this vendor was in his warehouse or whether he had warehouses some place else in the city or conceivably outside of Canada, * * *." Testimony of Thorn, R. 941.

916 Ex. 74.

in Price, Waterhouse & Co.'s working papers. Opposite each of the 18 items on the sheet the invoices of the vendors from whom the goods were purchased were shown. These invoices were all dated after July 1, 1934, and purchase quantities of one, or a combination of two or three, in 17 of the 18 items, exactly equaled the quantity and value shown for the inventory. The eighteenth item in the inventory is 2,000 pounds less than the invoice for 15,000 pounds of pure white vanillin with which it is matched.[917]

This merchandise was supposed to have been on hand and actually counted by the inventory crews at December 31, 1934. What purport to be inventory count sheets, an original and six carbons, with the name of the item and method of packing typed and the number of barrels, drums, etc., and quantity these represent written in with pencil on the original and two carbons, were discovered in McKesson's storage files. Each of the three sheets was in a different but regular handwriting with items not in stock crossed out in three cases on each sheet, but in a different manner. There were no erasures or corrections on any one of the three sheets, and none bore dates or initials to indicate when the goods were counted or by whom.[918] The caption on each sheet, typed was:

"LIMITED CRUDE DRUG INVENTORY
BUILDING #1—BASEMENT"

On the original, the first of these two lines is in heavy black type as from a new ribbon while the second line is in lighter type as from a ribbon half worn out. On all carbon copies the second line is not in carbon but in type apparently from the same ribbon as was used on the second line of the original indicating the possibility that the location was put on the sheets after the quantities were filled out in pencil.

John White, who worked in Robert Dietrich's department until a short time before the Commission's hearings were held, testified that, about 2 weeks before the hearings, he had marked the date and his initials "Dec. 1934 J. W." for identification purposes on the upper right hand corner of the top sheet when he took the sheets from the 1934 box of count sheets. He also testified that the writing on the first sheet was his but he could not identify the writing on the other two sheets. He could not remember whether the location was on the count sheets when he transcribed the quantities thereto, not from any actual count but from inventory cards.[919] The quantities shown on these sheets were the same as on the summary described above which appears to be a copy of the Canadian Company's inventory book

[917] Ex. 61.

[918] Ex. 60.

[919] R. 1532–1536. For White's description of the manner in which these sheets were prepared see pages 108–110 *supra*; R. 1478–1480.

sheets for that year. On these the spaces for the initials of those who counted and recounted the stock are likewise blank.[920]

Ritts was asked a few questions about the papers just described. He thought it would be better if the count sheets indicated by initials who had done the work. If they were missing, the sheets in some cases might be taken to the person who did the work and the initials obtained. But it would not necessarily be followed up. They might call the omission to the attention of some responsible person and be satisfied with that.[921]

Further consideration as to the existence of this merchandise and the authenticity of the documents just discussed will be given in connection with similar records of the Connecticut Division after reviewing the inventory work program followed in that unit. There are also other aspects of the inventory question which are common to both units and therefore may more clearly be treated together at that time.

The handwritten inventory work program carried out by Hill and his assistants in the Connecticut Division was identical in every respect during the last 2 years and these differed from 1935 only in the dropping of one item which related to the manufacturing operations. In that year the program carried a requirement to test check "* * * raw material costs method of applying overhead on production orders for work in process," but this does not appear in the later years.[922]

The first step for 1937 was to check the detail of price testing schedules to inventory books, after which these schedules were footed and extensions checked and a summary of the inventory books and price test schedules was spread across the work program and the percentage of inventory tested was calculated. The minimum amounts included in the tests varied by type of item. An item of $100.80 in the labels inventory was included while items under $1000 seemed to have been excluded in the larger departments. The total amounts tested ranged from 46.2% of book 10 (Cliff Street) to 99.9% of book 7 (general crude) which consisted almost entirely of foreign resale crude since proven to have been non-existent.

Items not on the price test schedules were sight checked for extension, noting particularly the placing of the decimal points. Page footings were checked to ten dollar amounts and totals traced to summaries which were footed. The balance of the work program was covered by the following steps, some of which will be discussed later.

"Examined latest invoices and/or production cards for all items on price testing schedules sufficient to account for quantity in the inventory

[920] Ex. 61; R. 653–654.

[921] R. 655–657.

[922] Ex. 41.

"Trace all large quantities and test check smaller items on price test schedules to stock cards or warehouse receipts

"Obtain market quotations where available, showing source

"Trace larger shipments at close of year per Shipping Dept. record to inventory cards to verify their removal

"Scheduled all items over $10,000.00 for special consideration

"Trace items on price testing schedules carried over from 12/31/36 to 12/31/37 inventory, noting prices, quantities, etc." [923]

In connection with this work Hill filled out the supplementary questionnaire on inventories. A comparison of the answers written for 1936 and 1937 indicates a new attack on the problem in 1937 for the answers that year in several instances were more complete and on the whole appear to be accurate. The questions dealt largely with the mechanics of inventory taking, personnel in charge, and precautions taken to insure correct pricing and a proper cut-off of purchases and sales.[924]

Hill testified that in 1937 he was given no instructions except to do the inventory work as he had done it the previous 2 years.[925] As has been seen, this required him to develop answers to the questionnaire and follow a very definite routine. Hill, however, did a number of things not definitely listed to be done, yet quite significant in inventory work. His first step was to check through the inventory books to make sure that he had the correct one for that year and that each page was initialed. This he thought was a simple matter of common sense and should be done even though not on the program.

"* * * where I found sheets where initials fail to appear, I had Mr. Geiger, the man in charge of the inventory, I had him take them out in the factory, I sent him out in the factory with the sheets, and if he came back with one initial I sent him back for the second initial * * *."

Spaces on the inventory book sheets were blank above the captions, "Counted by" and "Recounted by." Initials appear for "Entered by"; "Count checked by" (two sets here in same handwriting); "Priced by"; "1st Extension"; and "2nd Extension." "Count checked by" Hill believed indicated "* * * the men who counted and recounted the merchandise" in accordance with instructions. Concerning sheets covering inventory in outside warehouses (there were a different pair of initials over "Count checked by" than on the sheets representing stock at the plant) he testified:

"A. I don't know what the initials indicate in this particular case for this merchandise—that this merchandise, you say, was in warehouses?

Q. [By Mr. GALPEER.] Well, I was just reading what it said on top of the page.

A. They were, yes. I assumed they were the initials of the people that compiled this sheet." [926]

---

[923] Ex. 37.

[924] Ex. 19. See page 252 *supra*.

[925] R. 1300.

[926] R. 1266–1269; Ex. 85.

McGloon in his testimony explained that initials over "Count checked by" on McKesson inventory book sheets actually meant neither of the foregoing but that a second person had checked the accuracy of the posting of the inventory to new inventory cards.[927]

Another step not required by the program but generally considered essential is the checking of original count sheets or tickets against the final inventory sheets. Hill did this work to satisfy himself that the inventory had actually been taken. His method was indirect but effective, granting the authenticity of the count sheets which he saw were initialed although he could not say from a test inspection that they all were. His method was to check the count sheets to the perpetual inventory cards which, in turn, by the requirements of the program, were test checked against the price test schedules which then were checked to the inventory books.[928]

Hill's testimony indicated some familiarity with the mechanical aspects of inventory work but a reluctance to answer questions dealing with the relationship of his work to other phases of the audit. When questioned about various points in connection with accounting procedure surrounding inventory control, he was unable to see that the question was applicable. He thought, for example, that he could recognize a bill of lading but had never looked at any in connection with the McKesson inventory work and thought a question about the authenticity of the documents found in the files was irrelevant.[929] He did not make tests of the shipments to see which left the plant before and which after inventory taking. Someone else did this and he thought it "* * * better to confine the juniors to the work which they actually did rather than whether he knows the other man's job or not. We are supposed to know only our own job." [930] When asked if he would look at documents he handled to see if they were genuine, he said that he would not just out of curiosity, but if they did not look right he would verify the transaction in some other way.[931] If this could not be done to his satisfaction he would call the matter to the attention of a senior.[932]

Hill was familiar with purchases and the receiving of the merchandise but not with sales and shipping on which he did no work. His work included an examination of purchase invoices and receiving tickets to make sure that the proper liabilities were taken up and that receipts after the close of the year were excluded from the inven-

927 R. 1679.

928 R. 1317–1319; Ex. 37.

929 R. 1302.

930 R. 1305–1306. Work programs for 1935, 1936, 1937, and Hill's testimony indicate that he never worked on the sales cut-off feature of inventory work. Ex. 40, 41, 37.

931 In connection with the initials on the inventory sheets, however, he disclaimed sufficient familiarity with handwriting to note that the initials of two persons over the words "Count checked by" appear to have been written by one person. R. 1268.

932 R. 1308–1311.

tory and so forth. The receiving tickets covering merchandise in vendors' warehouses Hill was careful to describe as memorandum receiving tickets, "simply a record only" for he knew that this merchandise was held by the vendors and was not counted at the year end by employees of McKesson.[933]

Most of Hill's time seems to have been devoted to price testing which was quite thorough and covered practically 100% of the general crude inventory. This testing involved four distinct steps. First, sufficient recent purchase invoices were examined to account for the entire inventory.[934] The results of this test for 1937 were considered satisfactory for book 7, which combined general crude on hand in Bridgeport (real domestic) in the amount of $48,847.14 and $9,097,-115.00 (fictitious foreign) listed as in vendors' warehouses in Canada. As in the case of the Canadian Company, the invoice quantities (varying from one to four in number) exactly equalled the quantity on hand for each item of crude drugs in vendors' warehouses except that in one case the quantity on hand was slightly in excess of the sum of the last two invoices. This practically perfect correspondence of most recent purchase invoices with inventory quantities did not exist for a single item among 16 chosen for price testing out of 72 items in the lists of stock actually on hand at Bridgeport. It is also notable that in all cases in which two or more invoices were necessary to make up the total of an item in vendors' warehouses the prices were the same on invoices covering a period, in one case from March to October, and in others from April to December. On the price test schedule for this book only $3,915.00 represented goods carried over from the previous year. None of the goods carried over was from stock supposed to have been in Canada[935] although the inventory turn-over in 1937 in crude drugs was less than two times.

The second test of price was to compare each item with the price in the preceding year's inventory. This comparison revealed only six changes in price and two new items among the forty in the 1937 inventory. This comparison was not made for the small amount of general crude stock at Bridgeport.

The third test was to compare the inventory price with sales subsequent to the inventory taking but this was not done for the small amount of general crude stock actually carried at Bridgeport. Sale prices subsequent to the inventory date were available at the time the work was performed in 27 cases out of the 40 items listed at vendors' warehouses. This comparison revealed a uniform mark-up of approximately 10%.[935a] This test was made from duplicate copies of

---

[933] R. 1274, 1267.

[934] R. 1272.

[935] Ex. 38, 85.

[935a] See pages 304 ff. *infra* for a discussion of gross profit percentages in the Connecticut Division. See also Ex. Q in which the rates of gross profit on fictitious crude drug sales of this Division are shown to range from 8.03% in 1934 to 11.57% in 1935 (10.02% in 1937).

sales invoices for January and part of February which were checked to the Company's sales book and stock cards.[936]

Of the 27 products appearing on the price test schedule, of which sales were made after the year end, 17 appeared in January and 10 for the first time on the first 3 days in February. Of the 17 products sold in January, on 15 the quantities sold exactly equalled one or more purchase quantities.[937] The sales after the year end listed on the 1936, 1935, and 1934 price test schedules were apparently limited to the month of January and in any event coincided with purchase quantities as nicely as did those for January in connection with the 1937 price test schedule.[938]

The exceptional coincidence of sales quantities with purchase quantities as illustrated by unbroken year-end inventory quantities and January sales apparently existed since at least 1934, the earliest that Price, Waterhouse & Co. work papers are available in this record for such observation.[939] And such regularity apparently can not be explained by the nature of the business since sales were supposedly made in quantities that were irregular at least when compared to purchase quantities. For example a purchase of oil of patchouli—finest of 23,000 lbs. was purportedly sold out in units of 3,700 lbs., 3,300 lbs., 3,600 lbs., 2,900 lbs., 3,500 lbs., 3,200 lbs., and 2,800 lbs.[940]

Further examination reveals that the price test schedule for 1937 brought into close juxtaposition the cost and selling prices of items in the December 31, 1937 inventory which were sold subsequent to that date while the audit was still in progress. This showed that every sale during a period of 5 weeks was made at a gross profit.[941] This situation of every sale being made at a profit was reflected in the inventory papers for earlier years as well.[942] And Ritts in the 1934 memorandum on the Connecticut Division wrote "* * * our review of the sales subsequent to December 31, 1934 has shown that the company is realizing a comfortable profit on each sale * * *."[943] The same idea was conveyed in the memoranda for 1933 and 1935.[944] This information may also be obtained from McKesson's sales register for this

936 Ex. 38; R. 1113, 1283.

937 Ex. 38, 84.

938 Ex. 40, 41, 42.

939 See pages 104–105 *supra*.

940 Ex. 84.

941 Ex. 38, 84.

942 Ex. 40, 41, 42. Cf.

> "Q. [By Mr. Galpeer.] Will you please look now at your price test schedules in that connection and tell me whether in relation to the foreign crude drug division there was ever a sale made at a loss or at a price below the cost price of the merchandise?
>
> A. [By Ritts.] So far as I recall, sales made in January or February that we actually saw—no, I don't recall that they did have any losses." R. 798.

943 Ex. 268.

944 1933: "Sales of crude stocks made subsequent to December 31, 1933, amounting to approximately $700,000, have all realized a profit to the company." Ex. 80. 1935: "Crude drug sales since December 31, 1935 were all made at prices yielding a normal gross profit." Ex. 79.

business, copies of which, for the period while the audit was in progress, were included in the auditors' working papers for 1936 and 1937.[945] Although obvious from its face that it was limited to the foreign crude drug business, Hill apparently thought he had obtained the register on all crude drugs.[946] This sales register did not disclose a transaction at a loss at any time.[947] The auditors, however, disclaimed knowledge of the contents of the register for periods other than those included in their working papers.[948]

The fourth test on the price test schedule was to determine that the inventory price was under the market. This work presented some difficulties for published quotations were not available in all cases and even when they were it was difficult to be sure they were applicable for the quality of the merchandise was not indicated. In those cases in which prices were not quoted in the "Journal of Commerce" or the "Oil, Paint & Drug Reporter", prices were obtained from dealers. When Hill had difficulty in matching prices he sought enlightenment from Harry Osterhout, an old employee of McKesson who handled some of the inventory records and was understood by Hill to be an expert on prices.[949] Any unexplained discrepancies Hill would call to the attention of his superior, Ritts.[950]

Some of the trouble encountered in this work is reflected by a few samples from the 1937 inventory. Spanish saffron was quoted at $23 per pound in both of the journals named whereas the inventory and purchase invoice prices were both $12 per pound, and at December 31, 1936, the inventory had been priced at $8.10 per pound. Hill said Osterhout convinced him by explaining that this difference was due to the origin, quantity, and quality of the product; that McKesson dealt in such large quantities that quoted prices did not apply; and that in the case of some products the country of origin accounted for a great difference in quality. Hill noticed that the quoted prices of a drug originating in Spain would be different from the same product from China or South America, so the explanation he received seemed reasonable. In every case he either looked up invoices or had Osterhout convince him of the origin of the products, but he could not recall just

945 Ex. 84, 40 (D 13, D 14).

946 R. 1296–1300.

"Q. [By Mr. GALPEER.] Were you told to ask for it that way?

A. [By HILL.] I was told practically nothing. They told me to go ahead and do my job, those were my instructions.

I had been on the job two years consecutively and they told me to go ahead and do my job. They didn't give instructions unless I asked for them.

Mr. STEWART. That is, to do the same job as you did in the previous years about which you had been instructed before?

A. They told me I knew what I was supposed to do and to go ahead and do that.

Q. You knew that from the work you had done and the instructions you had in previous years?

A. I knew what I had to do as to that specific schedule at that time." R. 1300–1301.

947 R. 1373.

948 R. 814–820.

949 R. 1276.

950 R. 1277–1278.

how this was accomplished when most if not all of the products of foreign origin came in on invoices from a Canadian vendor rather than from the original shipper in the country of origin.[951] After the fraud had been disclosed Hill discovered from the Encyclopedia Britannica that many of the products came from the Far East.[952]

Another example was balsam of fir, Canada, priced at 60 cents per pound but quoted in both publications at $16 per gallon. The inventory sheet indicated a translation of this item at ten pounds to the gallon to reach a quoted price of $1.60 per pound. The weight of a gallon was obtained from Osterhout or Geiger (cost clerk in charge of inventories). But Osterhout testified that a gallon weighed eight pounds, which would give a per pound price of $2.[953] Hill thought Osterhout must have convinced him that the price was right but if he had had any doubt he would have checked with another employee.[954] The McKesson selling price was 67 cents per pound.

Mexican vanilla beans, 36,000 pounds at $2.25 per pound, were listed as packed in two hundred pound bags, whereas they were quoted at $4.25 per pound in tins. Hermann testified that these beans spoil quickly if not packed in air-tight containers.[955] Hill thought that difference in form of packing might have been a clerical error.[956]

As stated, Hill, on instructions from Ritts, relied to a great extent on Osterhout in his work on the price testing schedules. Osterhout, prior to joining Girard & Co., Inc. in November 1925 as an inventory clerk, had worked in a wholesale feed store and in a wholesale grocery store but had had no experience with drugs and chemicals.[957] His first duties were the keeping of inventory cards on manufactured products and for about a year and a half the cards on crude drugs, but after the merger of Girard with McKesson he was assigned in 1927 to keeping the inventories of Stebe's export department and Hermann's[958] crude drugs. In recent years his only contact with the records of the foreign crude drug inventories was during vacations of the clerks regularly assigned to the work.[959]

The extent of Osterhout's expert knowledge of crude drugs may be judged from the following extracts from his testimony:

"Q. [By Mr. Galpeer.] Mr. Osterhout, I show you a copy of Commission's exhibit 190, which is an extract of all the inventory sheets of McKesson and Robbins, December 31, 1937, in so far as it affects the crude drug department that was

[951] R. 1281–1283.

[952] R. 1279.

[953] R. 4519.

[954] "That is the way we usually do when there is any question in our minds—we approach two employees and get each one's version independently." R. 1285.

[955] R. 2598–2599.

[956] R. 1285–1286.

[957] R. 4516.

[958] See pages 268 ff. *infra* for further reference to Hermann.

[959] R. 4529–4530, 4516, 4522.

handled through W. W. Smith and Company. With the exception of such items as crude iodine and virgin mercury, which you might have handled also in Mr. Stebe's or Mr. Hermann's department can you tell me the country of origin of the items listed here?

A. No sir, some of them, I might have a smattering of an idea where it came from, but that is all.

Q. But take for instance, an item like Amidopyrine, would you know where that came from?

A. No, I don't know what it is.

Q. Could you, or did you ever have occasion to attempt to determine where these drugs came from, from the records available to you at McKesson and Robbins, that is, the drugs that were involved in this W. W. Smith department?

A. Determine where they came from?

Q. That's right.

A. No.

Q. Now, in this inventory, there is an item of Spanish Saffron. According to the exhibits already in evidence, the cost of that as shown on the work sheets of Price, Waterhouse and Company, the cost of that to McKesson was $12 a pound, whereas the Journal of Commerce quoted a market price for that of $23 a pound. Can you account for that discrepancy in price?

A. Well, those two prices given in the Journal of Commerce, I never did know exactly what they meant, but I imagine they meant the range of price from $12 to $23, to be according to the quality, something like that.

Q. I see. In other words, you meant if the Journal of Commerce had two prices in it, you would think that was the range depending on the quality?

A. Yes.

Q. But in this case, the Journal of Commerce price was a straight $23 and the McKesson price was a straight $12. Now, do you know why the Journal of Commerce price would be so much greater than the McKesson and Robbins price?

A. No, I would imagine it was inferior quality some way.

Q. But you don't know?

A. No.

Q. That is just a guess?

A. That's right.

Q. Now, there is an item on the same inventory, Mr. Osterhout, which is listed on McKesson records as Rhodinol, pure from oil of Geranium, Bourbon. In the Journal of Commerce that item is listed simply as Rhodinol. Do you know whether the two items are the same, or what the additional words "Pure from oil of Geranium, Bourbon" means?

A. No.

Q. Now, Mr. Osterhout, the records of McKesson showed that the Balsam of fir, Canada, which was supposedly carried in this department, were in 40 pound cans, and that the price was 60 cents a pound. The Journal of Commerce lists it at $16 a gallon can.

A. There are eight pounds to a gallon.

Q. There are eight pounds in a gallon?

A. Yes sir.

Q. In every product, or just that one?

A. No, not every, but there is in Balsam of fir, Canada; eight pounds constitutes a gallon.

Q. Do you know why the Journal of Commerce would list them as gallons and why you were carrying them as pounds?

A. No.

* * * * * * *

Q. Well, if there are eight pounds in a gallon, and it is 60 cents a pound, then it would be $4.80 a gallon; is that right?

A. Yes.

Q. Well, now, if that price would then come to $4.80 a gallon, and the Journal of Commerce price was $16 a gallon, can you account for that difference in price?

A. Its a big difference but I don't know why. I shouldn't think—I don't know but this is my opinion: I shouldn't think the Journal of Commerce would have given it at $16. I don't know. I imagine it did if it is there, but it seems to me that is a high price for it. We did handle that a little bit—Mr. Hermann, in his department, handled Balsam of fir, Canada.[960]

* * * * * * *

Q. Well, in any event, whatever created that difference in price, you don't know what would account for that?

A. No, I don't. One of those Balsams is handled in pounds and the other is in gallons. I don't know which it is. There is Balsam of fir, Oregon, and Balsam of fir, Canada. One of them is priced by pounds, and the other is priced by gallons. I don't know which is which.[961]

* * * * * * *

Q. Now, I think you testified to Mr. Stewart that the quantity that McKesson bought might affect the price that they paid for it. Do you mean that as a possibility, or as something that you know is a fact?

A. Well, it is a possibility. I wouldn't know for a fact, but I would imagine that the more of an article that a person would buy—they would get a reduction in price, perhaps.

Mr. STEWART. Don't be too modest, Mr. Osterhout. Don't you know that that is a fact; that they always do get more for the money when they buy in large quantities? Don't you know that from your experience?

The WITNESS. Well, I would say yes; I would suspect so.

Q. [By Mr. GALPEER.] Well, now, take this item on the inventory—any item here. Take Musk Pods, for example. Do you know whether what this department was buying would be considered a large quantity or a small quantity?

A. No, I don't know; I wouldn't know what the sale volume of Musk Pods would be.

Q. So that when you are referring to large quantities, which department do you mean—this department or Mr. Stebe's department?

A. Well, I might be referring more to Mr. Hermann's department.

Q. I see. And as far as this department through W. W. Smith was concerned, do you know whether the purchases which went through the McKesson books would be considered large or small in the trade?

A. No, because I wouldn't know what Mr. Coster's sale possibilities of that was, and I wouldn't know whether that was a large purchase for him or a small purchase.

Q. Would you know whether it was a large purchase or a small purchase in the trade as a whole in those particular products?

A. It would be for Mr. Hermann, yes.

* * * * * * *

Q. How about the items here that Mr. Hermann did not carry?

A. I wouldn't know about that, because I don't know—on those turpeneless oils, I don't know what the sale volume of those are liable to be." [962]

In all cases since 1934 the published prices and prices secured from dealers were higher than the McKesson inventory prices and fre-

[960] R. 4516–4520.

[961] R. 4521.

[962] R. 4526–4527.

quently substantially higher than the McKesson selling prices. An example was santonine crystals inventoried at $18, selling price $19.62 and quoted prices $23 and $25 per pound. Hill summed up his reaction to a situation like this and the entire pricing problem as follows:

"I never put too much faith in these market prices. The subsequent sale price was the thing I was chiefly interested in. As long as the price was higher than the price at which it was valued in the inventory and the subsequent sale price was higher than the cost, I was satisfied that the price in the inventory was conservative. It agreed with the vendor's invoice, it was under the market and compared favorably with the price at the end of the preceding year and was under the subsequent sale price.

With these four verifications it looked conservative to me. I wasn't looking for anything off-color. I mean, I wasn't looking for any trouble. I mean, I had no reason to suspicion any one. I was simply trying to confirm the price shown in the inventory. That was the object of the price test, to verify the price shown in the inventory. There was no other object in that price verification." [963]

Two juniors completed the inventory work at Bridgeport in 1937. One junior's work was chiefly checking extensions and footings. He also checked the price test schedules for several classes of goods to the inventory books, which involved a comparison of the descriptions, extensions, quantities, and unit prices. He traced the larger items (which meant all of the crude drugs held in Canada) to stock cards. The item on the program specified stock cards or warehouse receipts but he used the cards and never asked for warehouse receipts.[964] He worked on these cards in Robert Dietrich's office but could not say where the inventory itself, amounting to approximately $9,000,000, was supposed to have been held and never asked anybody.[965]

The other junior also did his work in Robert Dietrich's department in an office where a number of girls worked. What clerical work they did he didn't know. He traced year-end shipments to customers to make sure that they had been posted on inventory cards under the correct date. In this work he compared sales invoices (whether there were any papers attached he could not recall) with the cards which were handled by two girls. He did not know how the filing system worked or whether he could have worked on the files independently for he could see no reason for refusing help.[966]

The inventory work, as Hill pointed out, was subject to review by Ritts who was in charge of the job and who, therefore, was questioned in detail on various phases of the work. According to Ritts' testimony, all items in the inventory valued at $10,000 or more, were given special consideration by him in his review. This would include all of the crude drugs of the type sold through W. W. Smith & Com-

[963] R. 1291–1292.
[964] R. 395–396.
[965] R. 397–398.
[966] R. 1113–1117.

pany, Inc. and, in 1937, only about $200,000 of other merchandise in the Connecticut Division.[967]

In his review Ritts testified that he was not disturbed by wide variations between the McKesson prices and published quotations for it seemed obvious to him that the published prices might be based on transactions in smaller quantities than those handled by McKesson who he had always understood more or less controlled the world market in crude drugs.[968] When pressed as to his specific knowledge and consideration given to the balsam of fir item mentioned above, Ritts was unable to say whether the McKesson quantities dealt in as compared with the total market were large or small, or whether they were large or small as compared with the transactions of other dealers. He said that he did not know how the published price was reached and never had much confidence in such prices. The McKesson selling price he knew was higher than cost and quite reliable for his purpose and indicated that the inventory was not overvalued. The discrepancy in prices of a purchase on December 10, 1937, of 136,000 pounds of balsam of fir, Canada, at 60 cents, a published year-end quotation of $1.60 (if 10 pounds to the gallon is correct, $2 if 8 pounds to the gallon) and a sale of 24,960 pounds at 67 cents on February 2, 1938, to a customer in Brisbane, Australia, did not raise any question in his mind and certainly in his opinion did not require any action on his part, although if the published price had been below McKesson's cost, the Company would have been required to write down the value.[969] Discrepancies between the methods of packing of the McKesson inventory and the methods of packing referred to in the published quotations apparently caused him no concern.[970]

Charles Hermann, who is McKesson's buyer in the sales department of bulk drugs and chemicals conducted at the Cliff Street office in New York City (he started with the old McKesson firm as a boy 36 years before the hearings, had served in his present capacity over 20 years, and therefore had had a long experience in the crude drug trade) was not on hand at the plant at Bridgeport and was never

[967] R. 481–482.

[968] "It was always my understanding that that was the biggest contribution that Coster and Dietrich made to McKesson & Robbins, Inc., their knowledge of this crude drug business, contacts that they had with people throughout the world, selling crude drug stocks." R. 491. But see footnote 1026 *infra* for what appears to be some uneasiness as to prices expressed in Ritts, first memorandum on the Connecticut accounts. Compare also the action taken by Jaureguy in obtaining prices for pepper as reported in his memorandum on the 1931 accounts of the Connecticut Company: "In attempting to obtain market prices as at December 31, 1931, it became apparent that the spice department of McKesson & Robbins was the principal factor in the pepper trade and we were, for this reason, inclined to be skeptical of the market quotations obtainable in New York. A great deal of the spice trade centers in London and Rotterdam. We therefore cabled our London office for quotations, which compared fairly closely with those we have secured in New York. The company's inventories have been written down about $40,000 to a cost or market basis.

"The importance of this department is evidenced by the fact that its gross long position at December 31, 1931 (mostly in pepper), was more than $1,500,000." Ex. 82.

[969] R. 487–494.

[970] R. 495–498.

consulted by the auditors concerning the foreign crude drug business. It is interesting, however, to contrast Hermann's testimony with Osterhout's set forth above.

In Hermann's opinion the quantities of practically all the items in the inventory were greater than would be traded in the United States either domestically or for export in the course of a year. Likewise, from an inspection of the list he indicated that eight of the 40 items were carried in sizes or types of containers not found in the trade. Santonine crystals is a good example of both conditions. This product, he stated, is packed in 25 one-kilo cans, rather than in 17-pound cases as the inventory stated. The United States, in Hermann's opinion, is the largest consumer and uses not over 5,000 pounds per year. The inventory listed 13,260 pounds on hand at December 31, 1937. 18,000 pounds of castor fibre powder, a product used in very small quantities in making perfume, was to him another highly improbable quantity.[971]

Four of the commodities were subject to cartel or other types of control and in Hermann's experience could not have been regularly brought to Canada and reshipped to other parts of the British Empire at a profit. These were crude iodine (controlled by a syndicate in Chile and one manufacturer in the United States), quinine (controlled by the Dutch), natural camphor (controlled by Japan) and santonine (controlled by Russia).[972] In this connection, it is significant that Hermann stated that the importing and exporting of many of the items on the inventory was abandoned by the old McKesson Company about 1924 because they could not make any money at it.[973] Hermann, a vice-president of the Canadian, Connecticut, and Maryland Companies for many years, testified that his activities were limited to the Cliff Street office and that he had not known that Coster and George Dietrich were operating in bulk drugs, chemicals, and essential oils in either the Connecticut Division or the Canadian Company, and that he had never seen the inventories of these items nor a list of them.[974] He also testified that Coster, although reputed to be a drug expert, never exercised any control over the real trading in drugs which he conducted at the Cliff Street office.[975]

While Osterhout "* * * wondered about it, because—well, they made $100,000 a month profit, and had big sales * * *" he had confidence that Coster knew what he was doing and, therefore, was not suspicious that there was anything wrong.[976] Hermann's

---

971 R. 2600–2603.
972 R. 2605–2609.
973 R. 2626.
974 R. 2612–2613, 2633.
975 R. 2616, 2628–2629.
976 R. 4524–4525.

testimony may be summed up by saying that he would have been suspicious of the physical existence of the inventory in any particular warehouses.[977]

Ritts in his appraisal of the inventory quantities and prices never consulted any public records reporting statistics of the drug trade.[978] It will be recalled that all of the fictitious business was supposed to have been carried on through Canada since early in 1935 and largely in products not native to Canada. Canadian statistics of imports easily available in a Dominion Government publication, like Hermann's testimony, also show the quantities in the McKesson crude drug inventories to have been impossible.[979]

Two items of the 40 in the inventory can be identified definitely as products of Canada. One of these mentioned previously, castor fibre powder, is not exported in sufficient quantities to give it a separate listing in a rather detailed report of exports; the other, balsam of fir, Canada, listed in the inventory at December 31, 1936 at $225,600 and a year later at $168,000 with no old stock carried, may be compared with Canadian exports of $14,184 in 1937, about equally divided between the United Kingdom, Germany, and the United States. A copy of the portion of the foreign crude drug sales book included in the Price, Waterhouse & Co. working papers in connection with the price testing showed a single shipment of this product under date of January 2, 1937 in the amount of $13,363.20 destined for London, England, and another 5 days later for $10,612.80 to another customer at the same place. Six other shipments averaging over $10,000 were made the same month, two to Scotland, two to England, and one each to Ireland and Australia.[980]

Fifteen of the 40 items on the list in 1937 as being carried in Canada appear to fall in the group reported in the Canadian statistics as essential oils. The 15, all acquired for the most part in the last 6 months of 1937 and none carried over from previous inventories, weighed 398,670 pounds and were valued at $3,680,230. The Canadian statistics, however, show that the aggregate of all essential oils imported for that year weighed 650,985 pounds and had a value of $927,699. There were no exports reported in this group. In addition, oil of peppermint is accorded a separate listing. Canada for the year imported for consumption 31,075 pounds of this commodity valued at $69,547 while McKesson was supposed to have held 189,000 pounds valued at $330,750, all acquired during the year.

Musk pods is another item not native to Canada of which she imported 147 ounces valued at $2,600 during 1937. No exports were

977 R. 2633–2635.

978 R. 655.

979 R. 2610–2611; Ex. 191. Trade of Canada (Imports for Consumption and Exports) calendar year 1937, Department of Trade and Commerce, Ottawa.

980 Ex. 40.

reported. McKesson claimed to be carrying in Canada 12,800 ounces of this product valued at $153,600 at that year end. McKesson also reported a brisk business in Mexican vanilla beans for the inventory of 100,000 pounds carried in Canada at December 31, 1936 was entirely sold during 1937 to foreign customers, but Canada did not report any exports of the beans. This recital seems adequate to indicate the impossible character of the so-called crude drug inventories, most of which do not come under that definition as used in the drug trade;[981] but in addition we mention one product with an easily identifiable odor—camphor. Canadian imports of natural and synthetic camphor for 1937 totaled 121,865 pounds valued at $51,260. McKesson had purchased during the year and was supposedly carrying in Canada an inventory of 764,000 pounds of gum camphor slabs valued at $313,240.

As in the case of the Canadian Company, letters attesting the existence and ownership of these goods were obtained directly from the same five Canadian vendors, who were supposed to have been storing them at December 31, 1935, 1936, and 1937.[982] They were attested also by an over-all certificate which Price, Waterhouse & Co. secured from the responsible officers of the McKesson & Robbins organization.

Letters requesting confirmation of inventories were prepared by R. J. Dietrich under date of December 31, 1935, and were mailed under date of January 13, 1936 to Price, Waterhouse & Co., who in turn mailed them to the suppliers. These elicited replies from the five Canadian vendors under dates of January 20, 21, and 22, 1936. The copies of the requests in the auditors' working papers were uniform in wording and asked for a statement of merchandise held in storage for the McKesson account and the name of the state in which the merchandise was warehoused as the latter information was

---

[981] R. 2624; Ex. 191. See footnote 110 *supra*.

[982] At December 31, 1937, the five Canadian vendors were supposedly carrying the following inventories for the Connecticut Division (Ex. 85, 255):

B. Miller & Company	$2,079,480.00
H. Monroe & Company	1,530,520.00
P. Pierson & Company	3,078,215.00
A. H. Raymond & Company	653,750.00
D. C. Reynolds & Company	1,755,150.00
Total Connecticut Division	$9,097,115.00
In addition, the same vendors were supposedly carrying in the aggregate for the Canadian Company	990,585.00
Total, five Canadian vendors	$10,087,700.00

needed for tax purposes.[983] As in the case of the Canadian Company, the replies were all slightly different in wording and referred to carrying or holding the merchandise but without stating the location of the goods.[984]

A similar exchange of letters took place on the audits of 1936 and 1937. The 1936 working papers contained a list of 50 warehouses to which requests were sent, and a supplemental list for the spice department on which 10 names not common to the other list appeared.[985] The replies received from the five Canadian vendors in January 1938 were dated January 11, 12, and 13. The replies received in January 1937 revealed a slight variation from those of January 1936 and 1938. The address of B. Miller & Company on their letterhead was 45 Queen Street, Ottawa, Canada, but on the list sent to Price, Waterhouse & Co. by E. A. Johnson, Jr., office manager at McKesson & Robbins, the address was given as 48 Queen Street. The reply from this firm was dated January 25, while the other responses that year were dated on January 11 and 12. Johnson explained that on this occasion the letter addressed to 48 rather than 45 Queen Street came back undelivered to Price, Waterhouse & Co. and was returned to him for correction.[986]

The inventory certificate obtained from the responsible officials listed several classes of inventories on hand and included paragraphs covering quantities, ownership, valuation, and sundry other matters such as the cut-off and purchase commitments. This was signed by

---

983 Ex. 41 (D 86).

"C-O-P-Y

R. J. DIETRICH: AP;
December 31, 1935.

D. C. REYNOLDS & COMPANY,
192 Bank St.,
Ottawa, Canada.

GENTELEMEN:

In connection with our annual closing of our books and inventory, we shall be obliged if you will furnish our auditors, Price, Waterhouse and Company, of 56 Pine Street, New York City, with a statement certifying to the amount of merchandise you hold in storage for our account as of the close of business December 31, 1935.

As this will also serve for our checking of cards and for tax purpose, please state in what state this merchandise is warehoused, and we will appreciate if you will send this inventory in duplicate, one copy direct to our auditors and the carbon to us for our records.

For your convenience we are enclosing self-addressed stamped envelopes for both replies.

Very truly yours,
MCKESSON & ROBBINS, INC.

ENC.

Production-Planning Manager"

984 See pages 102–103, 253–254 *supra*.

985 Ex. 40.

986 R. 1366. Ritts' testimony at R. 505–506 concerning the securing of a second confirmation from a Canadian supplier apparently has reference to this incident. B. Miller & Company at December 31, 1936 were supposed to have held for the McKesson Companies crude drugs valued in excess of $2,000,000. Ex. 40.

F. D. Coster, J. H. McGloon, Geo. E. Dietrich, E. A. Johnson and, as to quantities only, by Robert J. Dietrich.[987]

[987] R. 795–796; Ex. 62:

"McKESSON & ROBBINS
Incorporated

Bridgeport, Conn., U. S. A.

CONNECTICUT DIVISION

MEMORANDUM TO PRICE, WATERHOUSE & CO., REGARDING INVENTORIES AS AT DECEMBER 31, 1937

SUMMARY OF INVENTORIES

(Including Kobe, Japan—$3,286.49)

Drums and containers	$ 654. 50
Raw materials	9, 744, 659. 71
Finishing supplies	196, 076. 00
Merchandise in process	8, 157. 88
Finished stock	712, 145. 44
Miscellaneous	27, 721. 03
	$10, 689, 414. 56
Less: General inventory reserve	91, 500. 00
	$10, 597, 914. 56

1. QUANTITIES:

All quantities were ascertained by actual count, weight or measurement by an inventory crew of competent employees, and such quantities were independently checked throughout by a second inventory crew.

Certain sections of the inventory were taken from December 20, 1937 to December 31, 1937 and were adjusted to December 31, 1937 by giving effect to all changes between the time of stock taking and December 31, 1937, as shown by the sales, receiving and consignment records, etc.

All inventories stored in outside warehouses at December 31, 1937 were confirmed by certificates received direct from the custodians thereof.

All stocks of any substantial value belonging to the company were included in the inventories, including stocks on consignment with customers, agents, etc.

2. OWNERSHIP:

The foregoing inventories were the unpledged and unencumbered property of the branch and did not include:

Stocks on consignment from others or stored for others
Unshipped stocks billed to customers at or prior to the above date
Advance payments on account of purchase contracts for future delivery

The stocks on hand that were covered by postdated sales invoices were included in the inventories and excluded from sales.

3. VALUATION:

Each item in the inventories was priced at the lower of cost or market, explained as follows:

Cost is understood to exclude trade or quantity discounts and administrative, selling or financial expenses

Market is understood to mean either replacement cost or realizable value, but in no event, in excess of realizable value

Obsolete, defective, unsalable or slow-moving items and items the manufacture of which has been discontinued, were not priced in excess of realizable values

The inventory was carefully compiled and checked in accordance with the procedure outlined in the company's closing instructions.

The inventories were valued on the same basis as the inventories as at December 31, 1936.

4. OTHER MATTERS:

The inventories included all substantial incoming shipments in transit at December 31, 1937 which were ordered F. O. B. shipping point.

Liabilities for all items included in the inventories were recorded in the general books of accounts as at or prior to December 31, 1937

The inventories did not include equipment, miscellaneous investments or other assets that were charged on the general books to other than inventory accounts as at or prior to December 31, 1937

The memoranda covering the work on the Canadian Company for 1931 and 1934 stated unequivocally that the Company's inventory was in Bridgeport but beginning in 1935 the memoranda stated positively that the goods were held by the Canadian suppliers.[988] Although Ritts prepared both memoranda for 1935, that on the Connecticut Division does not mention the fact that inventories of foreign crude drugs at the end of that year were in Canada.[989] The section on inventories was similar in form to that of 1933 and 1934 memoranda which do not state the location of the merchandise though Ritts testified that in those years they were held at the plant at Bridgeport.[990] In 1936, however, Ritts adopted in the Connecticut Division memorandum the form he had used in the Canadian Company memorandum of 1935 and said that the goods were held by the various suppliers and although the confirmation did not state the location of the stocks, company officials assured him that the merchandise was shipped promptly from the vendors' warehouses upon advices submitted to them from the Bridgeport office. A similar comment was made at the close of the 1937 audit.[991]

This situation raised some question in Ritts' mind as to whether the suppliers might not be dealing in futures. On the 1935 audit he questioned George Dietrich as to this matter. His approach was to ask for financial statements of the suppliers so that he could see if they were responsible people. Dietrich pointed out to him that he had evidence of shipment by the suppliers which Ritts agreed was proof that the goods were on hand. In this connection, also, Ritts inquired about the expenses of carrying the goods in Canada, warehousing charges, taxes, insurance, and so forth, which he was told were borne by the suppliers. The explanations he received satisfied

---

The branch's purchase commitments at December 31, 1937 were neither for quantities in excess of normal requirements nor at prices in excess of present current market prices.

Furthermore, at the time of signing this memorandum we have no knowledge of any other information relating to the inventories which would have a substantial effect on the branch's accounts that is not referred to herein or that was not fully disclosed in the general books of account of the branch as at or before December 31, 1937.

(s) F. D. Coster
President

(s) J. H. McGloon
Comptroller

(s) Geo. E. Dietrich
Assistant Treasurer

(s) E. A. Johnson
Office Manager

As to quantities: (s) Robert J. Dietrich.

Date: February 23, 1938.

(s) A. B. Ritts,

Representative of Price, Waterhouse & Co."

988 Quoted at page 256 *supra*.

989 Ex. 73, 79. Cf. also footnote 991*a* *infra*.

990 R. 639, 4475; Ex. 80, 268, 57, 58, 59, 60.

991 Ex. 49, 78; R. 593.

him for he referred to his discussion with Dietrich as a casual inquiry which he had no recollection of reporting to Thorn.[991a] Thorn, however, testified that he probably had a telephone call from Ritts on the subject of futures and financial responsibility of the suppliers during which he pointed out that these drugs were sold in "bunches" and it was entirely unlikely that the suppliers could fill orders on short notice if they were short of the commodities since most of them came from long distances. Apparently Ritts also had considered the difficulty of filling orders on demand if the suppliers did not have the merchandise. In any event Thorn thought that Ritts undoubtedly agreed with him after that discussion and dropped the matter.[992] The fact remains, however, that Ritts agreed that he never knew the exact address of the vendors' warehouses, which he understood were in Canada, where approximately $10,000,000 in inventories were supposedly held,[993] and never asked for credit reports on the suppliers.

"Mr. Stewart. If you had thought it necessary to get any further credit reports on those companies, how would you have gone about it, Mr. Ritts?

The Witness. I presume I would have followed the same procedure we did with respect to W. W. Smith & Co. to obtain a credit report from Dun & Bradstreet had we thought it necessary.

[991a] "A. [By Ritts.] I recall discussing the question of warehousing charges, insurance and other expenses in connection with these stocks stored in Canada.

Q. [By Mr. Galpeer.] But there is no notation in your papers, no physical evidence of anything of that sort?

A. Nothing at all.

Q. On this question of insurance, this conversation where you were told—have you any idea approximately what year that was?

A. No, sir, it may be 1935. I believe it was because I think 1935 was the first time that we found all of these stocks in Canada and in my 1935 working papers I did find a notation on the rough work sheet filed on top of the working papers to the effect that all stocks were stored in Canada, meaning that there is a point I must clear with some one.

Q. Whom did you clear it with?

A. When I say clear with someone I wanted to know more about it.

Q. What more did you find out?

A. Just what I told you, that in discussing the question of warehouse expenses and other expense incidental to the storing of these goods, we were informed that all such expenses were borne by the custodian of the stock.

Q. Did you make any inquiry if they did, do you think?

A. We may have, yes.

Q. Do you know whether in 1936, 1937 or any of the subsequent years you made any inquiry?

A. I don't recall at the moment any specific date. It seems that I questioned George Dietrich at one date with regard to these actual stocks in this respect; I think I asked him whether he had financial reports or a file of these reports of these various suppliers.

Q. And what did he say?

A. His answer as nearly as I can recall it is, 'No, what do you want with them, Mr. Ritts?' I said, 'I just wondered if you had them in the files, I was wondering if these people were really responsible.' He said, 'Well, that is quite evident from the shipments they have made.' I said, 'Yes, but I thought you may have had them in your files.' I said, 'I thought it might be a question of these people dealing in futures.' He said, 'That is quite evident to you, isn't it, that they are not. We are quite satisfied they have these stocks and are shipping them. You have seen evidence in our records to prove that.'

Q. Did you discuss that with Mr. Thorn subsequently?

A. I don't recall. I don't have any recollection of it in my mind.

Q. You just took his answer and were satisfied with it?

A. Yes, it was a casual inquiry with regard to financial statements and his question as to what I wanted with them and why I asked for them." R. 518–520.

[992] R. 605–606, 1059–1060.

[993] R. 597–599.

Mr. STEWART. And of whom would you have asked that?
The WITNESS. Mr. Dietrich." [994]

As stated above, the auditors understood that since some time in 1935 the stock was supposed to have been in Canada. As of April 3, 1935, the Canadian Company qualified to do business in the State of Connecticut and filed a state tax return for the remainder of 1935. Taxable income allocable to Connecticut was determined on the average of three bases: average monthly fair value of tangible property in Connecticut; total salaries, wages, and other compensations paid in Connecticut; and gross receipts from business operations conducted in Connecticut. This return reported 5% of the first two items in Connecticut and 100% of the third. The return was supported in McKesson's tax files by letters from the five Canadian vendors (which Ritts testified Price, Waterhouse & Co. representatives had never seen) [995] in which they stated, under dates varying from the 3rd to the 10th of June 1936, that as of March 31, 1935 and December 31, 1935, the inventories were held by them in various warehouses in Jersey City, Perth Amboy, Hoboken, and in one case just New Jersey without naming a city. Two replies gave the warehouses' names, and three referred to "our warehouse." None of the replies gave a street location for the warehouses.[996]

Connecticut State tax returns were also filed for the Maryland Company. A copy of the return for the year 1934 when all the foreign crude drugs amounting to over $6,000,000 were supposed to be at Bridgeport stated that the fair cash value of real estate and tangible personal property in each town in Connecticut during the period was for Bridgeport and Fairfield $566,343.02 and for New Haven $123,-354.66 and that which was located outside of Connecticut in "Various locations throughout the United States and in foreign countries" amounted to $10,302,539.09. A schedule in McKesson's tax files indicated that $8,719,073.28 of this latter total represented average value of inventories. Another schedule showed that this was the average at three dates, January 1, June 30, and December 31, 1934, with the amounts at the first two dates (being prior to the date the Maryland Company took over directly the business of its subsidiary companies) zero.[997] Supporting this were two further schedules (again, Ritts testified, not seen by Price, Waterhouse & Co. representatives) [998] giving the details of the portion arising from the Con-

[994] R. 520–522A.
[995] R. 4474.
[996] Ex. 234.
[997] Ex. 235: Inventories as at December 31, 1934, as shown on the schedule for various locations outside Connecticut, were $26,157,219.83.
[998] R. 4474.

necticut Division inventories. The first of these dated March 8, 1935 showed the location of all of this Division's inventories at December 31, 1934 to have been as follows:

Connecticut	$ 666, 915. 17
Massachusetts	725. 02
New York	63, 317. 75
New Jersey	3, 191. 39
Pennsylvania	10, 036. 19
Missouri	364. 99
Montreal—Canada	427. 45
In Transit and Afloat	293, 418. 81
Kobe	853. 04
Miscellaneous—New Jersey [a]	6, 389, 125. 00
Total Connecticut	$7, 428, 374. 81

[a] "Miscellaneous" was in type—"New Jersey" was written in. Also written in but below the total was: "Cod Liver Oil Department (Merchandise inside Connecticut), $26, 873.86."

The item "Miscellaneous—New Jersey" was in turn supported by the second schedule set forth below which consisted of a list of 50 items of crude drugs and essential oils of the kind carried in connection with the Smith foreign crude drug business in this and later years, signed by Robert J. Dietrich, stating that the merchandise as listed was held in the firm's New Jersey warehouse at December 31, 1934.[999]

[999] Ex. 235:

"STATEMENT OF MERCHANDISE DECEMBER 31, 1934 IN WAREHOUSES LOCATED IN NEW JERSEY

This is to state that we are holding in our New Jersey Warehouse the following merchandise as of December 31, 1934.

ITEM	PACKING	QUANTITY	EXTENSION
Aloin U. S. P.	140 lbs. to a barrel	147,000 lbs.	$132,300.00
Amidopyrine	50 lbs. net to a drum	60,500 lbs.	205,700.00
Antipyrine Crystals U. S. P.	100 lbs. net to a case	95,000 lbs.	161,500.00
Balsam of Fir Canada	2-40 lb. cans to a case	160,000 lbs.	115,200.00
Balsam of Peru	2-60 lb. cans to a case	156,000 lbs.	132,600.00
Benzoin Siam Large Tears	25 lbs. to a box	50,000 lbs.	70,000.00
Bismuth Metal	100 lbs. to a case	70,000 lbs.	73,500.00
Bismuth Subcarbonate	25 lbs. to a box	150,000 lbs.	187,500.00
Bismuth Subnitrate	50 lbs. to a box	125,000 lbs.	118,750.00
Gum Camphor, Slabs	100 lbs. to a case	200,000 lbs.	82,000.00
Carmine Powder #40	100 lbs. net to a keg	40,000 lbs.	106,000.00
Castor Fibre Powder	100-1 lb. tins to a case	6,000 lbs.	81,000.00
Coumarin	100 lbs. to a tin	58,000 lbs.	153,120.00
Dragon's Blood Powder Bright	25 lbs to a box	125,000 lbs.	68,750.00
Hexylresorcinol	50 lbs. to a can	10,000 lbs.	140,000.00
Crude Iodine	100 lbs. to a keg	50,000 lbs.	57,500.00
Iodine Resublimed	4-25 lb. jars to a case	50,000 lbs.	80,000.00
Iodoform U. S. P.	4-25 lb. jars to a case	40,000 lbs.	118,000.00
Menthol	60 lbs. to a case	66,000 lbs.	145,860.00
Artificial Ketone Musk	100-1 lb. tins to a case	15,000 lbs.	76,500.00
Musk Pods	20 ozs. net to a cady	11,500 ozs.	138,000.00
Virgin Mercury	Flasks	3,100 flasks	197,625.00
Oil of Cardamon	100-1 lb. bottles to a case	18,000 lbs.	198,000.00
Oil of Cinnamon Ceylon Pure	50-1 lb. bottles to a case	15,000 lbs.	75,000.00
Oil of Coriander Terpeneless	100-1 lb. bottles to acase	30,000 lbs.	210,000.00
Oil of Cumin	100-1 lb. bottles to a case	30,000 lbs.	191,400.00
Oil of Dill Seed	100-1 lb. bottles to a case	70,000 lbs.	210,000.00
Oil of Geranium Rose Algerian	25 lbs. net to a case	25,000 lbs.	122,250.00
Oil of Ginger Terpeneless	100-1 lb. bottles to a case	4,000 lbs.	112,000.00
Oil of Juniper Berries Terpeneless	100-1 lb. bottles to a case	10,500 lbs.	99,750.00
Oil of Lemon Sequiterpeneless	100-1 lb. bottles to a case	20,000 lbs.	160,000.00
Oil of Limes Distilled Terpeneless	10-1 lb. bottles to a case	3,000 lbs.	126,000.00
Oil of Limes Expressed Terpeneless	10-1 lb. bottles to a case	1,200 lbs.	162,000.00
Oil of Lovage	10-1 lb. bottles to a case	3,100 lbs.	139,500.00
Oil of Neroli Artificial	100-1 lb. bottles to a case	28,500 lbs.	213,750.00
Oil of Orange Sweet Terpeneless	10-1 lb. bottles to a case	2,810 lb.	174,220.00
Oil of Patchouli Finest	100-1 lb. bottles to a case	20,000 lbs.	58,000.00
Oil of Pepper Black	100-1 lb. bottles to a case	20,000 lbs.	132,000.00
Oil of Peppermint Natural	100-1 lb. bottles to a case	72,000 lbs.	151,200.00
Potassium Iodide	100 lbs. net to a case	60,000 lbs.	63,000.00
Procain	25-1 lb. tins to a case	5,750 lbs.	103,500.00
Pyrogallic Acid Resublimed Crystals	100 lbs. net to a tin	70,000 lbs.	113,400.00
Quindine Alkaloid Crystals	10-100 oz. tins to a case	185,000 ozs.	138,750.00
Quinine Sulphate	10-100 oz. tins to a case	320,000 ozs.	115,200.00
Sacharine Powder U. S. P.	4-25 lb. tins to a case	110.000 lbs.	148,500.00
Salol Powder U. S. P.	200 lbs. to a keg	180,000 lbs.	138,600.00
Santonine Crystals	17 lbs. to a case	5,610 lbs.	112,200.00
Spanish Saffron	50-1 lb. tins to a case	15,000 lbs.	121,500.00
Mexican Vanilla Beans	200 lbs. to a bag	40,000 lbs.	96,000.00
Pure White Vanillin	100 lbs. net to a case	20,000 lbs.	62,000.00
		TOTAL	$6,389,125.00

(s) ROBERT J. DIETRICH.

R. J. DIETRICH"

Prior to the time these tax returns were introduced, Thorn had testified:

"* * * if some merchandise was stored in New York and some was stored in Connecticut, that made a difference in their Connecticut State tax return and their New York State tax return which had given us some interest in where these goods were located * * *."[1000]

and Ritts had testified:

"Q. [By Mr. GALPEER.] Now, Mr. Ritts, just to illustrate what you have in mind, what would you do in reference to, let us say, the various state taxes that might have to be paid, or reserves set up for? What sort of schedule would you prepare, and what sort of check would you make?

A. Well, the company, in the last number of years, prepared an over-all tax schedule, setting forth the particulars of the various taxes, the nature of the tax, and the period covered, the amount chargeable to the current period, the amount deferred, the amount accrued; and that summary schedule would be supported by schedules—say, as an illustration, Connecticut State income tax: There would be a supporting schedule covering that item, setting forth the computations of the tax itself, based upon the book figures. There would be similar supporting schedules to the various other taxes where it would be necessary.

Q. And you would examine those supporting schedules?

A. Yes sir. I should have mentioned that tax payments, the tax receipts were examined by us for the payments they made.

Q. Did you ever look at the tax returns themselves?

A. Yes, we would look at the tax returns for the preceding period particularly those which were still open * * *."[1001]

When these tax returns were introduced the following record was made:

"Q. [By Mr. STEWART.] Mr. Ritts, you have examined the schedules and letters attached to the last two exhibits which have just been introduced; that is, you did examine them just now, since they have been introduced.

A. Yes, I have.

Q. Did you ever see them before?

A. I haven't any recollection of seeing the State returns. If we did, we would have a transcript of it, or summary, which would be in our working papers. I think I stated previously that we did examine tax returns.

Well, I had in mind specifically the United States Federal tax returns which we would examine, and I think I said at the time that the State taxes that we would look into would be set forth on the schedule showing the computation of the tax; so I haven't any recollection of seeing that—I haven't any present recollection of seeing a return, and I know definitely we never saw the supporting papers or letters to the returns.

Q. Did you ever ask any questions of anybody at McKesson & Robbins as to where the merchandise confirmed by the Canadian suppliers was stored?

A. Yes, frequently.

Q. And were you ever told that any of it was stored in New Jersey?

A. No, sir, we were not. * * *"

Ritts concluded by stating that he thought of one exception in 1932 when McKesson "* * * had a certain amount of merchandise

---

1000 R. 941.

1001 R. 4445–4446.

stored in British American Storage Warehouse * * *" in Jersey City but that thereafter and through December 31, 1934, the merchandise was located at Bridgeport and from 1935 it was always represented as being in Canada.[1002]

The foregoing tax papers should be compared with the inventory situation, as Price, Waterhouse & Co.'s representatives understood it, at December 31, 1934, the last year end that the inventories in question were believed to have been at the Bridgeport plant.[1003] Documentary evidence relied upon for this belief began with the inventory books, in which in book 7 at pages 6, 7, and 8 were listed the items covered by the certificate attached to the 1934 Connecticut tax return set forth in a previous footnote. Each of the three pages expressly stated the location of the inventory to be on the first floor of building No. 2, which is a unit of the plant at Fairfield (Bridgeport).[1004]

The original materials from which the inventory book was prepared were count sheets of which a set of six copies were made, two retained in the office for checking purposes and four sent to the plant. Of these, three were used for independent counts and the fourth was used as a control sheet by the supervisor.[1005] Count sheets for 1934 indicated that this system was applied in counting merchandise actually on hand in the plant at December 31, 1934.[1006] Three sheets covering counts of the same stock, each bearing different pairs of names and written in different handwriting, were accompanied by a fourth, the control sheet, which listed the three pairs of names but no figures indicating the count. The names as written by the supervisor, John White, were Hackett, Millar, Perry, Cocozza, Mull, and Takacs, each succeeding pair being a count team. The original sheet in each group was kept by the supervisor and did not show quantities, while the carbons were used by the counters.[1007] Each sheet under the caption crude drug inventory carried the location, as: "BLDG #2—1st FLOOR CENTER LEFT," "BUILDING #2—FIRST FLOOR—RIGHT CENTER," "BUILDING #2—1st FLOOR FRONT," "BLDG. #2—1st FLOOR—RIGHT SECTION," "BUILDING #2—FIRST FLOOR—LEFT."[1008]

Count sheets prepared in the foregoing manner were available except for the foreign crude drug stock. The two sets of count sheets covering these false items which were listed on pages 6, 7, and 8 of book 7 were supposed to have been in Bridgeport at this time showed counts on the original sheets and two carbons of each set with the remaining four carbons of each set blank except for the typed description of items and sizes and top captions common to all in the set. None of

1002 R. 4473-4475. Cf. R. 598-599.

1003 R. 204, 639.

1004 Ex. 59; footnote 999 *supra*.

1005 Ex. 42, "Notes on Inventory" from Price, Waterhouse & Co. 1934 work papers.

1006 However, an original and six carbons were found in each set of count sheets. Ex. 57, 58, 60.

1007 R. 1495-1497; Ex. 57.

1008 Ex. 57.

these count sheets carried the counters' names or initials nor did the fourth sheet list names of crews. As in the case of the Canadian Company count sheets previously described, the location of the stock appeared in original typewriting on all the carbon sheets and read "BUILDING #2—1st FLOOR" without giving the location on the floor as was done on the sheets for stock actually on hand.[1009]

Ritts testified that he had never done a complete inventory examination on this engagement and that "* * * It has been my practice to take the man who is going to work on the inventories to the office manager and the various people that you come in contact with and discuss with those people, at that time, the method of taking the inventory, who all was involved in actually counting the stock and particularly the people that supervised this job." He testified that Robert J. Dietrich would have been the supervisor in charge of the inventory in book 7.[1010] Dietrich's name appeared on the general certificate covering the entire inventory.

The inventory certificate signed by the officers of McKesson & Robbins at the request of Price, Waterhouse & Co. was in the same general form as the one for 1937 reproduced above[1011] and, therefore, was not conclusive support for any statements in respect to location of the stock for it covered without segregation both goods in the plant and in outside warehouses. This earlier certificate carried the same signatures as the later ones except for George Dietrich's name which was added when the change in location of the merchandise was made in 1935.[1012]

As stated above, Hill, the last junior in charge of inventory work, gained his knowledge of the McKesson inventory procedures from Johnson, Geiger, and Osterhout, all of the accounting office, and there is no testimony that John White, who directed the actual count in 1934 and subsequent years under Robert Dietrich's supervision, was consulted about crude drugs. Referring to the 1934 count when the goods in question were supposed to have been in Bridgeport, White testified that since he supervised the stock taking on the first floor of building number two (his count sheets showed all the goods that in fact were there) and the floor was full with that alone, it appeared impossible to him that approximately 1300 tons of the foreign crude drugs also could have been in the same place.[1013] White also testified that original copies of the count sheets supposed to support pages 6, 7, and 8 of book 7, the fictitious merchandise in question, were given to him by Robert Dietrich, who asked him to make up the sheets from the inventory cards kept in Dietrich's office. The number of

1009 Ex. 58.
1010 R. 660–662.
1011 Ex. 62; footnote 987 *supra*.
1012 Ex. 63; R. 795, 658–665.
1013 R. 1521; Ex. 108 and testimony quoted at pages 110–111 *supra*.

containers was determined by dividing the quantity on the inventory card by the size of the container as typed on the count sheet.[1014] This procedure was followed in exactly the same way in prior years.[1015] White, who was first employed as a shipping clerk by McKesson in December 1926, and hence had worked under Robert Dietrich for almost the entire life of the business since Coster merged Girard & Co., Inc. with it, first learned of the export business about 1928 to 1930 when he happened to notice some orders on Robert Dietrich's desk. He was told that this covered direct shipments of merchandise which did not have to be handled physically by McKesson. Soon after this he was given the job of preparing the inventory count sheets and continued to do so in the manner described.[1016] He testified " * * * that it has always been driven in to us that all transactions had to conform to the same procedure irrespective of whether it was direct shipping or not." [1017] White could not recall that he ever had any occasion to tell the accounting department how these count sheets were made up and never told any representative of Price, Waterhouse & Co. because he was never questioned by them as to the methods used in taking inventory.[1018] He said he never suspected anything wrong in what he was instructed to do or in what he did.[1019]

McGloon testified that he thought the crude drug inventories in question had been in Bridgeport and that he had seen inventory sheets initialed by White and another shipping clerk, Howard Cone, showing that the merchandise had been counted by the first and recounted by the second and that these sheets indicated that the merchandise was in the Company's Bridgeport warehouse. It was his understanding that the inventories were carried in the warehouse in Bridgeport until 1935, and his department relied on the inventory sheets to that effect.[1020] The inventory sheets to which McGloon referred were the inventory book sheets for December 31, 1931. The pages, introduced in evidence, are 51 and 52 of book 7, which total $4,982,898.95 for items similar to those of the 1934 inventory. The sheets are labelled "Warehouse Crude Drugs." [1021] White explained the presence of his initials on such sheets by the fact that he and another employee were instructed by Robert Dietrich to initial them before they were sent in to the main office.[1022]

It has been noted earlier that Ritts had never inspected the plant at Bridgeport, but that in leaving the building after closing time he

[1014] R. 1478–1480, quoted at pages 108–110 *supra.*
[1015] R. 1501.
[1016] R. 1500–1501, 1523.
[1017] R. 1561.
[1018] R. 1518–1519.
[1019] R. 1541–1542.
[1020] R. 1677–1682.
[1021] Ex. E.
[1022] R. 1512–1514; quoted in part at page 112 *supra.*

and his staff left by the employees' exit which required walking through part of one floor of the plant. Ritts testified that he did not know the identity of this building but that he did see merchandise stored in it, although in the audit work neither he nor his staff would go into the plant for the purpose of identifying or counting any of the merchandise. Since he did not know that the building he had passed through on floor one was building No. 2, the purported location of the foreign crude drug stocks, he could not say whether the stock he saw was that merchandise or whether the approximately 1,300 tons of it could have been stored there.[1023]

The auditors' verification was limited to an inquiry as to the methods employed in taking the physical inventory (the "Notes on Inventory" in the 1934 work papers clearly sets forth the method supposed to have been followed by the company and apparently actually followed for the real goods) [1024] and accounting tests to see that the results corresponded to the book records. Occasionally adjustments in quantities between the physical count and the inventory cards were necessary in some of the stock but no discrepancies of this kind were ever found in the foreign crude drugs, and adjustments to reduce from cost to market were rare on this class of merchandise.[1025] The only occasion Ritts remembered when the latter problem arose was in 1932 when he had some difficulty in convincing the two Dietrichs, Johnson, Geiger, Osterhout, and McGloon that a reserve of $18,000 to $20,000 was necessary on two items.[1026]

Ritts testified that he was convinced that in this case if he had attempted a physical examination or a test count of inventories he would have been delayed in one way or another until some kind of merchandise could have been produced with the proper labels to represent the crude stocks. Furthermore, he did not consider himself qualified to

---

1023 R. 640, 646–649.

1024 Ex. 42, M–21.

1025 Compare testimony of E. A. Johnson, Jr. at R. 1418–1421 and that of Ritts at R. 651–652 and R. 726–729. Ex. 42 (D 35).

1026 "The inventory of crude stocks are all carried at cost and in the case of two specific items, viz., iodine resublimed and potassium iodide, specific reserves were provided to reduce them to market. These were the only items which appeared to be carried above the market quotations as shown by the Journal of Commerce and the Oil, Paint & Drug Reporter, but it appears from a review of these journals for the periods at which time these stocks were purchased that the prices quoted are invariably above the company's costs and are not entirely satisfactory for our purposes, but they are the only sources available from which published quotations may be obtained. We requested the company to have W. W. Smith & Co. (from whom the bulk of their crude stocks are purchased) furnish us with market quotations at December 31, 1932 of the principal items appearing in the inventory but they (the company) preferred to have the prices confirmed through several outside brokers. The quotations they obtained by letter from these brokers conformed with the prices quoted in the above named journals but we are inclined to be somewhat skeptical of their reliability. We feel that a possible loss, due to a market decline, may have existed in these stocks at December 31, 1932 but we are at a disadvantage in trying to show that any of the prices, apart from the two specific items mentioned above, are wrong, due to the fact that there are several grades of most raw materials and due to the limited trading done in these commodities. It was noted, however, that approximately 50% of the company's December 31, 1932 inventory of crude stocks had been sold prior to the date of completion of our examination at a small margin of profit." Ex. 81 (Ritts' memorandum on the 1932 accounts of the Connecticut Company); R. 520–521. See also footnote 942 *supra*.

identify any of the stock and did not consider it an accountant's duty to employ chemists to make tests.[1027] As an example of the problem on this audit Mr. Stewart asked Ritts:

> "Q. Do you think it is a part of the duties of an independent accountant to be able to recognize Aloin when he sees it?
>
> A. I think any accountant that attempts to say he does is only trying to kid the public." [1028]

Prior to carrying inventories supposedly at vendors' warehouses, receiving tickets were prepared indicating delivery of the merchandise at the Bridgeport plant by "Our Truck." Afterward the same form was used but with it a rubber stamp stating "Held at Suppliers, No other Charges." The line reading "Received at McK. & R. Receiving Department at" was filled in by crossing out "at" and adding "as Bpt. Plant." The next line "Received by" carried an initial and "at their Warehouse."[1029] Ritts was unable to account for the use of such a ticket after 1934[1030] except to venture an opinion after one was introduced in evidence that it indicated that the goods had been set aside at the suppliers for McKesson. This was a conjectural explanation by Ritts for he said he did not recall that he had ever seen such tickets. These tickets, Ritts thought, would not have been examined by the auditors because the goods were not received at the Company's own plant and the invoices from the suppliers, together with the year-end confirmations from the same source, were ample support for the purchases and remaining balances.[1031]

Another possible test of the presence of inventories among the real assets of the Company was suggested for Ritts' opinion. The Maryland Company carried two blanket insurance policies, one for $21,000,000 and the other for $3,300,000 but Ritts did not know whether these covered the Canadian Company assets or not.[1032] In fact he had been informed that the foreign crude drug stocks in the hands of vendors were insured by them.[1033] Even if this had not been the case he felt that if the client had a competent insurance man it would not be customary for the auditors to make any test of the ade-

---

[1027] R. 775–776, 835–837, 841–843.

[1028] R. 836.

[1029] Ex. F, 20; page 76 *supra;* R. 1709–1711.

[1030] "Q. [By Mr. Galpeer.] Is it likely that there would be documents in the plant such as that receiving ticket that you would not examine as part of your audit, as part of your check of the internal control or otherwise?

A. [By Ritts.] We would examine receiving tickets for merchandise actually received at the plant, yes, particularly that copy that was attached to the invoice, but if the company was buying merchandise and storing it in Canada, certainly we would not be foolish enough to ask for a receiving ticket on something that had never been received by the company at their own plant.

Q. Well, now, if I told you that such receiving tickets were prepared, wouldn't that seem foolish to you, as you state?

A. Yes, certainly." R. 284.

[1031] R. 709–712, 283–287.

[1032] R. 549–550. See also Ex. M–28.

[1033] R. 429.

quacy of the insurance coverage, except perhaps in a general way.[1034]

Thorn's testimony on inventories supported Ritts in most particulars. Points in common were that he never made any count or other physical test of inventory quantities[1035] and never estimated warehouse capacity in respect to inventory quantities.[1036] He also considered the McKesson selling prices the best test of market in judging the correctness of the inventory prices because of the difficulty of identification and large volume handled by McKesson, although he never made any independent inquiry to establish this fact.[1037] If he had considered it desirable to establish the financial stability of the Canadian vendors he would have asked Dietrich for Dun & Bradstreet reports, and also would have asked him to get financial statements from the suppliers themselves.[1038] Thorn could not throw any new light on the purpose or manner of preparation of receiving tickets after the change in location of inventories in 1935.[1039] Thorn was also in agreement with Ritts that at least two independent counts of the inventory of merchandise actually on hand were taken, as White explained was the case—three counts in some instances. It may be noted, however, that the procedure laid down in McGloon's printed instructions for taking the inventory merely provided for signatures of two counters on the same count tag or sheet, so that the second crew would have knowledge of the first count. In this case, therefore, the practice was stronger than the instructions.[1040]

On two occasions major changes were made in the supposed location of the foreign crude drug stocks. In the Canadian Company the stocks were supposed to have been in Montreal until 1931. From 1931 to 1935 they supposedly were held in Bridgeport. Thereafter the five Canadian suppliers were supposed to have retained them in their control. In the Connecticut Division substantial stocks were supposed to have been kept in the warehouse of the British-American Stores, Inc. in Jersey City, N. J., until sometime in 1933, after which all the stock was supposed to have been in Bridgeport until sometime in 1935. After that time vendors were supposed to have retained possession of the goods in Canada. Thorn says it would not be part of the audit to trace these changes to the extent of discovering whether the merchandise in fact was moved, or, as he assumed, that the goods were sold out at the one location and built up again in the next.[1041]

1034 R. 839.

1035 R. 865.

1036 R. 870, 1225–1226.

1037 R. 1009-1012, 1027–1038.

1038 R. 1062–1063.

1039 R. 1241.

1040 R. 1006–1007, 475–478; Ex. 16.

1041 R. 1222–1225; Ex. 104A, 104B; R. 938–940.

"Q. [By GALPEER.] And do you know in what year those inventories were supposedly shifted from Bridgeport to Canada, that is, foreign crude drug inventories we are speaking of?

A. [By THORN.] At December 31, 1934, the inventories were all held in Bridgeport, that is, say, Fairfield. At December 31, 1935, they were all held in Canada." R. 938–939.

The question of the location of the merchandise was important for the Canadian Company in connection with taxes. Prior to April 3, 1935, as a Canadian corporation, taxes on income were paid to the Canadian government. During part of the period from organization in 1928 to April 3, 1935, inventories were supposed to have been in Bridgeport and during all of the period the books and records were kept in Bridgeport. This situation led Thorn in 1930 to refer the matter to Price, Waterhouse & Co.'s tax department, whose representative, Ashbaugh, advised Coster that as long as the Canadian "* * * Company was operating in the United States, or maintained inventories in the United States, it was probably liable for Federal income taxes." Thorn commented on this opinion in strong language in his memoranda on the 1931 and 1932 audits,[1042] but no reserve was provided and no tax returns were filed except in Canada. In 1933 a two-page memorandum of Ashbaugh's addressed to Rowbotham emphasized the same point again, and the fact that the bulk of the transactions of the company seemed to be handled through Bridgeport. This resulted in a provision of a $50,000 reserve from surplus but no United States tax return.[1043]

There was no change in the situation in 1934.[1044] As previously stated, in 1935 the inventories were supposedly shifted from Bridgeport to Canada. Beginning with April 3, 1935, the company filed United States tax returns and also filed in Connecticut as a foreign corporation, and according to the memorandum of accounts intended to claim exemption from Canadian income taxes "* * * under Section 4K, Part II, of the Dominion Income War Tax Act on all profits arising since the latter date * * *." Memoranda for 1936 and 1937 reported the settlement of all claims with both the United States and Canada, but with no United States tax due for periods prior to 1935 and no Canadian tax due after that date.[1045] The only change in the supposed physical operations of the business which took place during the year 1935 was the shifting of the inventories from Bridgeport to Canada. Cummings of Sullivan & Cromwell, a director and counsel for McKesson, testified:

> "* * * I thought probably if they were kept in Canada, it was more likely liable to double taxation." [1046]

And Section 4 (k) of the Canadian Income War Tax Act referred to in the Price, Waterhouse & Co. 1935 memorandum on the Canadian Company, as quoted above, in fact provided exemption for:

> "(k) the income of incorporated companies (except personal corporations), whose business is not only carried on but *whose assets, also, are situate entirely outside of*

[1042] Ex. 76, 205.
[1043] Ex. 75.
[1044] Ex. 74.
[1045] Ex. 72, 73, 26.
[1046] R. 2444.

Canada, provided that such companies file annually a fully completed return, on the form prescribed, and pay a filing fee of one hundred dollars, in each case within four months from the close of their fiscal period. * * *"[1047] [Italics supplied.]

Thorn, it appears, relied on the fact that Ritts had discussed these questions with the Canadian tax authorities when they were in Bridgeport, as Thorn was unable to say how the decision had been reached and was not familiar with the Canadian law.[1048]

As partner in charge of the engagement, Rowbotham's opinion was sought in the hearings on the various matters dealt with in the testimony of his staff. As in the case of cash and accounts receivable, he found by detailed comparison that his firm's work program on inventories was substantially in accord with the suggested procedure of the American Institute of Accountant's Bulletin—no material differences were noted.[1049]

More specifically, following the Bulletin's suggestion to "Make reasonable inquiries and tests to ascertain that quantities have been carefully determined and that quality and condition have received due consideration", Rowbotham stated that he would get the Company's inventory instructions and talk to the actual supervisors on the job. On quality and condition he would make a study of the perpetual inventory cards to determine rapidity of movement. The supervisors in this case he would assume to be Robert Dietrich and possibly Johnson and McGloon. He would not talk to those who had actually done the counting.[1050]

The tests referred to, Rowbotham thought, would be accounting tests of the records and not actual physical sampling or counting. Nor would it include estimates of warehouse capacities or reference to public sources of statistical information on trade and manufacturers.[1051] In one instance in connection with the McKesson work, Price, Waterhouse & Co. representatives served as umpire between McKesson and the sellers of a wholesale house in taking the inventory. This was merely a matter of acting as arbitrator between a willing buyer and a willing seller for the purpose of settling differences at once. Let Rowbotham explain further:

"Now, in those circumstances, our partner who looked at this thing while I was away did not see any objection to handling that and I should not have seen any objection, either, had I been there, but I do not think it has any bearing on the question of taking stock as between, let us say, ourselves and the publc, in an opinion that we would sign on an annual balance sheet. A lot of this was package

[1047] As amended by 24 & 25 Geo. V, c. 55, §2 (1934). Also amended by 1 Edw. VIII, c. 38, §4 (1936).

[1048] R. 946–948.

[1049] R. 1858, 1863–1864.

[1050] "I think you would speak to Dietrich himself, you might talk to Johnson or McGloon—I don't know how far down the line you would go on this thing. I don't think you want me to answer what I think is the specific question in your mind—I don't think you would go out and talk to the men who had actually done the counting." R. 1869–1870.

[1051] R. 187.

goods, of course, and if one side was willing to accept a package without opening it and the other side was willing too, it made little difference." [1052]

In Rowbotham's opinion the client practically never requested the auditor to supervise the inventory taking and he was convinced that in many lines of business, such as textiles, lumber, hides, furs, crude drugs, and steel such supervision would not be worth anything if undertaken. However, although he felt that in these cases the books were often more reliable than the physical inventory, he was not ready to say that the future might not bring auditor participation in inventory taking.[1053]

This, he said, might have a good moral effect but at the same time create an illusory safeguard.[1054] In the case of McKesson he estimated that to supervise the inventory at December 31 would have required 300 men a week's time on the job. In Rowbotham's opinion this would be an impossible task on a calendar year closing in view of the number of companies which keep their books on a calendar year basis.[1055]

[1052] R. 1872–1873; Ex. 101-A.

[1053] "Q. [By the EXAMINER.] You do actually supervise taking inventories, don't you, in other audits if the client requests it?

A. [By ROWBOTHAM.] Well, the client practically, sir, never requests it nowadays. What he is going to request in the future I don't know, but right now the client is usually content with his own method, and when he gets out his own inventory instructions he takes the inventory in a way he thinks is satisfactory and he does not ask us to supervise that inventory, I should say, in almost every case that we have. What might happen in the future, I don't know.

Q. [By Mr. STEWART.] Let me just ask one question on that point, if I may. Regardless of whatever supervision you might be able to make on the count of merchandise, recognition of which involves a technical or specialized knowledge, Mr. Rowbotham, do you think it would be possible by reason of such supervision to give an unqualified certificate as to the quantity, quality and condition of inventories without placing substantially the same reliance on the client in your statement which you now place and have placed in the McKesson & Robbins certificate?

A. No, sir, I do not, because you can take quite a lot of commodities almost without thinking. I mean, you can—stuff like textiles and lumber and hides and furs and crude drugs here, I mean, the client—an accountant can go out and supervise that and I do not think his supervision would be worth anything. Take carpets, for instance, what does he know about carpets? I mean, there are quite a lot of things that the accountant simply cannot supervise on. Now, then, take the case of—the obvious case of an ore pile in a steel company. I have gone out to steel companies and looked at ore piles and it looked to me like a huge mountain of earth; he has to rely, in a case like that, on his book records and it has been pretty well proved, I think, in the steel companies that the book records are more reliable than the physical counts. There have been steel companies who have gotten a sudden rush to the head of what they thought were modern methods and they sent out an engineer to look at those things and the books have been right and the engineer has ultimately been wrong.

Q. [By Mr. GALPEER.] Do you think, then, that your participation in inventory taking would not add significantly to the value or the correctness or the accuracy, or authenticity of that inventory?

A. I do not go as far as that, sir. I think, perhaps, our present inventory practice may be extended to go further and do what you call supervising. I mean, I think that is a step that perhaps might come; it has not been done so far, but it might come, but all I am trying to say is this, sir, that even if you did supervise, even if the accountant does supervise, if I went out and saw a huge yard filled with lumber covered with a tarpaulin and was told it was hardwood and was supervising the taking of that hardwood, I am sure I would still end up by relying on the book figures and the representations of the company's officials." R. 1873–1876. Cf. footnote 1369 *infra*.

[1054] "Q. [By the EXAMINER.] Have you formed any conclusions as to the possible psychological or moral effect on such supervision?

A. [By ROWBOTHAM.] I have, sir. It may have some psychological or moral effect for the good, but I am deadly afraid, to be quite frank about it, that you would be creating a safeguard or having people rely on it that would not really represent it. I am giving you my personal opinion now and not the opinion of the American Institute or anybody else." R. 1876.

[1055] R. 1876–1881.

Rowbotham was positive about the inefficacy of an attempt by accountants to spot test inventories physically. His views are stated best in his own words:

"Q. [By Mr. Galpeer.] Well, under the system as you have described it, what would be the purposes of having what I have referred to as test checks of inventory or spot tests or something to that effect?

A. Well, if by test checks or spot checks you mean the accountant going out and taking hold of a physical part of the inventory and looking at it himself, frankly I am talking personally now, I don't think they are any good at all. I just can't see them, because you could go into this plant here and they could show you a barrel of something or a bottle of something and you could even take samples and they could palm the samples upon you. I think it just gives a false impression of security if you take test checks.

Q. Now, take the comparison of a building. Assuming a building is carried on the books of a corporation, assuming an accountant cannot determine the exact value of that building, in an appraiser's sense, he could nevertheless by seeing the building know that at least such a building existed. Don't you think that is so, and I am just trying to establish the thought here—don't you think that by at least looking at the inventory he could establish whether such inventory existed.

A. To take your example of the building, he might see a building was there but if it was part of a steel plant, he wouldn't know if it was modern, if the machinery was up to date, whether it was fit for what it was supposed to be fit for, and looking at the building I don't think would tell the accountant anything except the very bare fact which I don't think has any meaning, that there is a building there; now, if you look at the material out here, you might see that something is there but what that something is I think is practically meaningless.

Q. Well, take the situation here: Don't you think that to have determined the bare fact as to whether the inventory existed would have been helpful?

A. I don't regard it so. You are talking about the goods in Bridgeport or in Canada or both.

Q. I am talking about the crude drugs. Let us speak of the time they were supposed to be in Bridgeport.

A. If we had gone there, I am certain, and I am sorry to say this is hindsight, I am certain if we had gone to Coster and said, 'We want to look at this stuff,' they would have shown us something, and then we would be in a worse position than today because we would have had to say that we had test checked that inventory and I am quite certain it wouldn't have been what we probably thought it was.

* * * * * * *

Q. [By the Examiner.] Do you feel that the extent of your inventory investigation will be identical in a detailed audit as with a balance sheet examination?

A. Yes, I don't think in a detailed audit we would go into the quantities, quality or condition of the inventories at all. I don't think the accountant has any concern with it.

Q. Whether the McKesson & Robbins audit or any other audit was a detailed audit or balance sheet examination you would treat the inventory question identical in both circumstances?

A. Yes, in my opinion they should be so treated."[1056]

Rowbotham's opinions were asked on sundry other matters which were raised during the testimony of his staff. For example, he could

[1056] R. 1893-1895.

not recall any occasion in his experience when he had called upon another office of his firm to make an inquiry as to the existence of merchandise or warehouses in another city unless a subsidiary of the client being audited was involved.[1057]

If insurance policies had been requested on the crude drug stocks, Rowbotham agreed with Ritts that Coster would have produced something that looked authentic. With a competent insurance department it was his judgment that a study of insurance coverage was unnecessary.[1058]

The arrangement by which the vendors of crude drugs held the inventories in Canada and shipped on Coster's orders seemed entirely reliable to Rowbotham because the same vendors had seemed to establish themselves as responsible people through several years' business relations while the inventories were supposed to have been in Bridgeport. The idea that Ritts brought to Thorn's attention that the vendors might have been dealing in futures did not come to Rowbotham's attention until recently and for reasons just stated he thought that independent credit reports on the companies were unnecessary.[1059] If doubt had arisen as to the inventories, Rowbotham thought that Price, Waterhouse & Co. would have consulted Coster who would have sent Robert Dietrich to take an inventory with which Rowbotham would have been thoroughly satisfied.[1060]

Rowbotham's testimony on prices was largely a reiteration of the points brought out with Ritts and Thorn, leading to the conclusion that the client's records of purchases and sales were more reliable than published quotations.[1061]

To summarize very briefly at this point, the Price, Waterhouse & Co. verification of inventories in the Connecticut Division and Canadian Company was confined to an accounting test of the records supported by what appeared to be authentic confirmations of a substantial part of the stock in the warehouses of vendors whose financial standing was never questioned due to years of satisfactory business relations prior to the time when they became responsible for warehousing of the

---

1057 "Q. [By Mr. GALPEER.] Mr. Rowbotham, not referring to this McKesson situation, but speaking generally has the occasion ever arisen wherein doing any examination work you make independent inquiry through one of your other offices to establish certain facts? In other words, to be specific, would the occasion ever arise where you would want to check the existence of merchandise or the validity of a warehouse, or anything like that, where you would write to some one of your other offices near that spot to check it for you?

A. No, I can't recall any occasion of that kind where we would call in another office unless there was an actual subcompany in that town as there was, of course, in many of these towns covered by this McKesson set-up.

Q. [By Mr. STEWART.] And when you said subcompany, you mean a subsidiary of the company under examination and not merely a company with which it was doing business?

A. Yes, I mean what we call nowadays divisions." R. 1980–1981.

1058 R. 1881–1885.

1059 R. 1885–1888.

1060 R. 1888–1890.

1061 R. 1955–1956.

merchandise. The Price, Waterhouse & Co. procedure at Bridgeport did not include physical contact of any kind with the inventory.[1062]

H. OTHER BALANCE SHEET ACCOUNTS

1. Unexpired Insurance

Unexpired insurance as an asset on the balance sheet was, by comparison, a trifling amount, being only a part of $554,245.36 which included taxes and other prepaid expenses, out of the total of $87,182,765.74 assets on the consolidated balance sheet at December 31, 1937. At that date only $2,627.76 of unexpired premiums applied to policies on the books of the Connecticut Division, as most of the insurance was taken up on the books of what was known as the Central Division of the Maryland Company.[1063] As previously stated in connection with the discussion of inventories, the auditors did not consider it to be a part of their duty to check on the adequacy of insurance coverage under the circumstances of this case because the client had an expert insurance man (Robinson) in its employ.[1064] Furthermore, the fact that the blanket insurance policies were reduced a substantial amount in 1935 was deemed confirmation of the explanation received that the custodians who commenced storing the goods in that year assumed such responsibility.[1065] Insurance protection Ritts thought was an operating problem while the accountants' primary purpose in examining insurance policies was to compute the prepaid insurance or to establish the premium liability that should appear on the Company's books.[1066] Rowbotham summarized this idea completely in answer to a question by Mr. Galpeer:

"Q. Would you say, then, sir, that as far as your work had to do with insurance, it was for the purpose of analyzing premiums to determine which of them were paid in advance and to be sure that all premiums paid were included as operating expense?

A. And to see that a proper charge had gone into the income account for insurance." [1067]

2. Fixed Assets

Fixed assets, less reserves, constituted less than 8 percent of total consolidated assets of McKesson & Robbins, Incorporated, at December 31, 1937, and have only small place in this inquiry for that reason, as well as because there is no evidence that these accounts were

---

1062 For variations in inventory practice in other divisions of the Company see page 318 *infra*.

1063 Ex. 48; R. 547–549.

1064 Pages 284–285 and 290 *supra*.

1065 The record on this subject is found as follows: Ritts, R. 417–429, 547–549, 838–839, 843–844; Thorn, R. 1207–1208; Rowbotham, R. 1881–1885. See also Thompson, R. 2096–2098, quoted in part at pages 127–128 *supra*. The record does not indicate, however, whether the date of the reduction in insurance coincided with the time of change in the location of the inventory.

1066 R. 420.

1067 R. 1882. Cf. Ex. M–28 for the auditors' comments on the adequacy of the Company's insurance records.

involved in the fraud. However, to complete the record there is included the brief audit work program on this topic for the Connecticut Division in 1937 as carried out by a junior (item 6 by Ritts):

"FIXED ASSETS AND RESERVES

1 Obtain summary from Co. of changes; check from ledger & foot.

2 Vouch additions of $75, or over on list of additions prepared for us by Company.

3 Check larger deductions into detail property records to see that asset & reserve have been relieved in the proper amounts.

4 Schedule profit & loss on the disposal of fixed assets. Check the consideration received on the larger items.

5 Test check calculation of 1937 depreciation provided against individual items & calculate effective depreciation rate by classification for year.

6 Trace transfers to and from other divisions and companies to see that they will eliminate in consolidation.

7 Obtain list of depreciation rates applicable to purchases since date of appraisal. Test check large items for monthly depreciation set up on books. Should take same life as similar assets shown in American Appraisal Co. report."[106]

As in the case of the inventories this program was confined to an examination of the records and as has been pointed out previously no inspection of the plant was included as a step in the audit program. "The accountant does not go out and actually touch or see the plant." [1069] Rowbotham has explained why in his opinion this comment of his must be so:

"* * * the accountant is not an engineer. He very often does not know the actual existence, to be quite blunt about it, of the capital assets. He may know that there are buildings there. He does not know the buildings are suitable for the purpose. He does not know the machinery is suitable to the purpose He is not a lawyer. He does not know that the titles rest in the company."[107]

However, in relying on the books, the auditors seem to have had some trouble in getting at the facts from the accounts, as extracts from successive years' working papers indicate. A note by Ritts on Schedule K–3, Connecticut Company papers for 1933 stated:

"The company has capitalized a number of items during 1933 which appear questionable but due to the small amounts involved we have not attempted to adjust their accounts. We have, however, discussed the matter with Mr. Cairns[1071] and he informed us that it was not their intentions to capitalize any expenditures under $50 but because of certain changes in the personnel these additions were made without his knowledge. Mr. Shoemacher is now handling the property ledger and he has been given definite instructions regarding these matters. We have prepared skeleton schedules for his use during the coming year and it is expected that the property accounts will be handled more satisfactory in the future." [1072]

[1068] Ex. 44; R. 538.

[1069] R. 1749.

[1070] R. 2019. See also R. 1894.

[1071] Assistant to McGloon—also formerly with Price, Waterhouse & Co.

[1072] Ex. M–14.

Ritts was too optimistic for on the 1934 audit a junior wrote as follows in regard to his work on fixed assets:

"The summary schedules were in such form that we were unable to use them and drew up schedules of our own. The supporting schedules were likewise very unintelligible and practically useless. However, we tried to salvage them as well as possible. Mr. McGloon and Mr. Johnson have been informed of the deplorable state of the property accounts. They have informed us that this situation will be rectified and that adequate plant ledgers will be kept in the future." [1073]

The poor condition of the Company's books reported above is given added interest when it is realized that the properties had been appraised by the American Appraisal Company as at October 31, 1934, and the asset and reserve accounts adjusted to conform as at that date.[1074]

3. Liabilities

a. ACCOUNTS PAYABLE

The following work program on accounts payable used on the 1937 audit at Bridgeport for the Connecticut Division and Canadian Company was the same form of mimeographed work program used on all divisions handled out of the New York office of Price, Waterhouse & Co.:

"ACCOUNTS PAYABLE—WORK PROGRAM

(1) Obtain a trial balance of accounts payable at December 31st and make arrangements with client to withhold invoices paid subsequent to the period under review from the files until they are examined.

(2) Verify footings and agree total with general ledger control.

(3) Check accounts payable ledger, or open items in voucher register, to trial balance.

(4) Test check larger items to ascertain (1) nature of liability, (2) whether invoices were properly approved, (3) whether particulars, i. e., price, extension, and footings, were verified, (4) whether merchandise receipts, etc. were verified by reference to receiving tickets, and (5) whether vouchers or invoices were properly recorded.

(5) Test check open balances at December 31st by reference to creditors' monthly statements.

(6) Transfer debit balances in accounts payable to miscellaneous accounts receivable, and inquire into collectibility.

(7) Scrutinize liabilities for intercompany or interdivision payables.

(8) Examine all invoices and statements entered subsequent to December 31st and those not yet entered, for liabilities applicable to the period under review.

(9) Examine cash disbursements record, journal entries, and all other records of original entry subsequent to December 31st for liabilities applicable to the period under review.

(10) Examine receiving records for the last five days of the period to see that corresponding liabilities were properly recorded.

(11) Examine cash-book to see if disbursements are charged to any accounts other than accounts payable.

[1073] Ex. M-20.

[1074] Ex. 160 (p. 14).

(12) Ascertain whether any differences existed between the accounts payable records and the general ledger control during the period; state what disposition was made of these differences, if any, and whether they were brought to the attention of the client.

(13) Prepare liability certificate, exercising due precaution to see that all points are covered, and obtain the signatures of responsible officials.

(14) The foregoing is a general program outlining the minimum work to be done on accounts payable. This program should, of course, be modified and added to in order to meet the requirements of each particular examination. The additional work done should be described below." [1075]

Accounts payable of the Canadian Company at December 31, 1937 consisted of two invoices, one of $750 for the December installment of the "W. W. Smith & Company" service charge and the other for $2,221.42 being ¾ of 1% on December sales of $296,189. There were no liabilities on the same date for merchandise purchased of the five vendors. The only work required in connection with these two items was to verify the calculations and since it was his first work at Bridgeport, Wyman said he related these items to the contract which, as previously pointed out, was thought to be with W. W. Smith & Company, Inc., guaranteed by W. W. Smith & Co. The accounts payable work sheet in the Price, Waterhouse & Co. papers listed only the two Smith items, above referred to, both of which were tick-marked "Invoice seen." [1076]

These two items for December were included when paid with vouchers covering similar charges for January and February 1938. All six invoices were on stationery labelled "Branch Account Statement", of "W. W. Smith & Co. Commission Merchants, Purchasing, Forwarding & Shipping Agents, Liverpool, 3, England", to be paid at " * * * our *New York* [stamped] office in *U.S.* [typed] currency. Address all inquiries there." The six vouchers involved were made out to "W. W. Smith & Co." and "Selling Expense" was charged. They were paid by two checks dated March 14, 1938 drawn on The Bridgeport-City Trust Company to the order of W. W. Smith & Co., Ltd. The first of these two checks covered 3 months' service charge ($2,250) and was endorsed

"FOR DEPOSIT ONLY IN
THE ROYAL BANK OF CANADA
GREENE AVE. BRANCH
TO THE CREDIT OF
W. W. SMITH & CO. LTD."

The other check for the guaranty fee of ¾ of 1% for the 3 months amounted to $6,171.26 and was endorsed

[1075] Ex. 47, 24.

[1076] R. 364–368; Ex. L.

"PAY TO THE ORDER OF
THE CHASE NATIONAL BANK
OF THE CITY OF NEW YORK
HAMILTON TRUST BRANCH
W. W. SMITH & CO., LTD.,
MONTREAL
CANADA" [1077]

Although the foregoing checks were issued after the audit and therefore might not have come to the attention of the auditors, Wyman, who did the work on the Canadian Company for 1937 would at least have seen the checks dated December 31, 1937, covering November 1937 charges, which were similarly drawn to W. W. Smith & Co., Ltd., and so endorsed,[1078] since they appeared as outstanding checks on the December 31, 1937 cash reconciliation.[1079] Item 13 of the cash work program previously referred to required that sometime in January checks paid to date should be secured from the bank and that all paid checks dated December 31 or prior thereto should be traced to the checks outstanding on the reconciliation.[1080] According to endorsements thereon the checks in question cleared through the banks during the first 10 days in January and therefore must have been included in this step which, although not initialed, Wyman testified was done.[1081]

Here is the situation to which reference was made earlier in this report. The contract was thought to be with W. W. Smith & Company, Inc., a New York corporation, and was guaranteed by W. W. Smith & Co., a copartnership of Liverpool, but the checks drawn in settlement of invoices rendered on the partnership stationery were drawn to W. W. Smith & Co., Ltd. and so endorsed.

At December 31, 1936, accounts payable of the Canadian Company consisted of two items, $300 due to Brown, Montgomery & McMichael, lawyers of Montreal; and $1,655.70 listed as payable to "W. W. Smith & Company." [1082] The latter item was paid by a check dated April 15, 1937 drawn for $3,239.58 (this included the January 1937 guaranty fee of $1,583.88) on the Canadian Bank of Commerce, New York, N. Y. to the order of "W. W. Smith & Company Ltd." The invoices supporting the voucher were on the stationery of W. W. Smith & Co. Ltd., 1405 Bishop Street, Montreal, Canada, terms "Net U. S. Cy." [1083] The invoices preceding these last, covered September, October, and November 1936 charges and were on the

---

1077 Ex. 226, 227. Similar W. W. Smith & Co. statements and checks in payment are reproduced at page 101 *supra*.

1078 Ex. 86A, 86B, 224, 225.

1079 Ex. K.

1080 Ex. 21, 29; quoted at pages 259–261 *supra*.

1081 R. 329–330.

1082 Ex. J.

1083 Ex. 223.

same statement form, but the check dated December 31, 1936 covering them was drawn to "W. W. Smith & Co." The check, however, was endorsed like those above by "W. W. Smith & Co., Ltd." [1084]

Although, as above indicated, it was not followed meticulously, particularly as to lists or papers prepared for office use or given to the auditors,[1085] Miss Walsh, bookkeeper for the Canadian Company, testified that in recent years "Ltd." was always added on the checks on instructions from George Dietrich. She could not remember precisely when these instructions were given. Similar checks to the order of W. W. Smith & Co., Ltd. for payments under the contract thought to be with W. W. Smith & Company, Inc., guaranteed by W. W. Smith & Co. were also issued by the Connecticut Division.[1086]

Ritts was asked about these discrepancies between the parties to the contract, and the payee on the checks but he seemed to think the subject was of no significance.[1087]

"Q. [By Mr. GALPEER.] Would you say W. W. Smith & Company, Limited was W. W. Smith, Incorporated or W. W. Smith and Company?

A. I don't know as I would make a distinction.

Q. Would you consider those checks proper payment under the contract referred to?

A. I think so. I do not think it is significant that a check is not made out in the exact name.

Q. That is, you do not think it is significant that under a contract with W. W. Smith & Company, Incorporated, guaranteed by W. W. Smith & Company, the co-partnership, if the checks are made out to W. W. Smith & Company, Limited?

A. I don't think that is significant." [1088]

He had no recollection of having seen the vouchers or the invoices from Smith as he stated he relied on a calculation of the fee in accordance with the terms of the contract in checking the liability.[1089] Prior to being questioned in the instant hearings he had never heard of Smith as a limited company [1090] and did not consider the distinction in names of any more importance than between "McKesson & Robbins, Inc.," as used in the order for this hearing, and "McKesson

---

1084 Ex. 222.

1085 R. 4433–4434; Ex. 222, 223, 224, 225, 226, 227, I, J, K, L.

1086 Ex. 86C, 86D.

1087 R. 822-824.

1088 R. 823.

1089 R. 4467–4468.

1090 "Q. [By the EXAMINER.] Mr. Galpeer mentioned a moment ago W. W. Smith & Co., Ltd. I believe this is the first time that a Limited Company by the name of W. W. Smith & Co. has come into this hearing——

A. [By RITTS.] Yes, sir.

Q. Is that the first time you heard of it?

A. Yes, sir, this is the first time that I recall ever seeing or even hearing of Smith being referred to as a Limited Company.

Q. We have already discussed W. W. Smith, Inc. and W. W. Smith & Co. of Liverpool. You do not know whether this W. W. Smith & Co. Ltd. is a third company or not?

A. No, sir, I do not; I have no knowledge as to that." R. 844.

& Robbins, Incorporated" which he pointed out was the correct legal title.[1091]

Item 5 of the work program on accounts payable: "Test check open balances at December 31st by reference to creditors' monthly statements" provoked some discussion at the hearings. In carrying out this test Ritts stated that it would be his practice to call for all available statements if he got to this step before the statements had been destroyed, but he would not make a request in advance nor ask for confirmations from creditors if the statements were missing. In doing this work he could not recall having seen statements from the five Canadian vendors. He did not think it unusual that no amounts were owing at the year end to this source of all of the Canadian Company's and most of the Connecticut Division's purchases.[1092] The balance of the program was initialed as completed without amendments or additions.

b. ACCEPTANCES PAYABLE

The largest single class of liabilities of the Connecticut Division at December 31, 1937 was acceptances payable although as previously stated, since 1932, these did not include any items relating to the foreign crude drug transactions. The work on this was done by Wyman, who wrote out an audit program describing what he had accomplished. The points covered are listed below:

"WORK PROGRAM—ACCEPTANCES & DRAFTS PAYABLE

Also: Currency engagements,
Unused balances under letters of credit.

1. Obtain company schedule of direct liabilities for trade acceptances and for acceptances under letters of credit issued by bank.

2. Agree items as above scheduled with items in acceptance register shown as not due until 1938.

3. Agree items on schedules or schedule in total with amounts of direct liabilities reported by banks.

4. Further identify the open items by tracing from cashbook. The payment in 1937 of all items showing on register as due from 9/1/37 to 12/31/37.

5. Check on conversion of items stated by cash in sterling or francs by noting that they are restated by company in dollars as covered by future currency engagements or that they are converted at closing cable rates.

6. Re currency engagement a/c commitment. All sterling acceptances covered by engagements to purchase sterling before due date. Currency engagements in excess of direct liability at 12/31/37 as per notation on A-11, Head office papers. Rate of engagement lower than closing cable.

7. Check clerical accuracy of company schedule.

8. Agree company schedule of unused balances under letter of credit with letter of credit register and bank confirmation."[1093]

1091 R. 571. See also R. 172–173.

1092 R. 540–545. See also Ex. M-10, M-15.

1093 Ex. 45.

c. TAXES

In the discussion of inventories, the relationship of their location to the problem of Canadian, Connecticut, and United States income taxes was discussed and it was also brought out that some concern was felt by Price, Waterhouse & Co. in the early thirties as to whether the Canadian Company was liable for United States income taxes.

Ritts explained that the client had a competent tax department which calculated the taxes due to various authorities and caused proper reserves to be provided. As a part of the audit Ritts testified that schedules prepared by this tax department were examined and checked to the books and for the calculation of the tax. After this check the tax problems of the client were reviewed in a general way by the tax department of Price, Waterhouse & Co., as indicated above. The audit working papers would include a reconciliation of the taxable income and the book profit for the year and in this connection the federal tax returns would be examined as would tax receipts for other payments.[1094]

In a letter to Thorn in January 1933, while on the 1932 audit, Ritts raised an interesting point on the Canadian Company's tax payments. In 1931 and 1932 the books showed a profit on Canadian exchange in the payment of the income tax due Canada on income of the Canadian Company, since the books were kept and tax returns computed and filed in United States dollars (not indicated on the returns) but payment was then made in an equal number of, as distinguished from an equivalent amount of, Canadian dollars which were then cheaper than United States dollars.[1095] Miss Walsh's testimony brought out another occasion when settlement of Canadian liabilities raised an exchange question. Rent of $1,000 per month was paid for some time on a leased warehouse in Montreal, usually by checks drawn on Canadian banks.[1096] These and other actual transactions previously mentioned may be contrasted to the transactions with Manning & Company all foreign, from purchase of the merchandise to collection from the customer, and all purported to have been conducted in United States currency.

d. CONTINGENT LIABILITIES

As a final step in the audit of liabilities, as in the case of receivables and inventories, a certificate was obtained from the Company's officials. This covered all liabilities of the Division and paid particular attention to possible losses, contingent liabilities, and various contractual obliga-

---

[1094] See pages 276–280, 286–287 *supra*.

[1095] Ex. M–29.

[1096] R. 4406–4407.

tions of the Company. Coster, McGloon, George Dietrich, and Johnson signed the certificate for 1937.[1097]

I. PROFIT AND LOSS ACCOUNTS

1. Sales, Cost of Sales, and Gross Profit

Much of the audit work having a bearing on the profit and loss accounts is done in connection with the balance sheet accounts so that the operating accounts as such are given relatively much less attention than the asset and liability accounts in a balance sheet examination.

1097 Ex. 66:

"McKESSON & ROBBINS

Incorporated

Bridgeport, Conn., U. S. A.

CONNECTICUT DIVISION

MEMORANDUM TO PRICE, WATERHOUSE & CO., REGARDING LIABILITIES AS AT DECEMBER 31, 1937

(Including Kobe, Japan—$4,313.13)

DIRECT LIABILITIES:	
Acceptances payable	$ 542,883.41
Accounts payable	268,465.69
Wages, taxes and other accrued liabilities	394,477.91
	$1,205,827.01
CONTINGENT LIABILITIES:	
Bankers acceptances discounted	141,358.00

1. All liabilities (both known or established, and contingent) and all claims of any kind against the branch as at December 31, 1937 are included in the foregoing summary.

2. No extraordinary losses or contingent liabilities have been incurred during the period from December 31, 1937, to the time of signing this memorandum.

3. There are no law suits pending against the branch.

4. There were no contractual obligations as at December 31, 1937 for the purchase or extension of plant facilities, for the purchase of any other assets not required in the ordinary course of business or for the purchase or sale of any assets at prices involving substantial losses to the branch.

5. As at December 31, 1937 there were no contingent assets of the branch by reason of which the assets were understated, the liabilities or reserves overstated and the income account and surplus account understated on the general books of account.

Furthermore, at the time of signing this memorandum we have no knowledge of any other information relating to the above, which would have any substantial effect on the branch's accounts, that is not referred to herein or that was not clearly disclosed in the branch's general books of account as at or before December 31, 1937.

(s) F. D. Coster
President

(s) J. H. McGloon
Comptroller

(s) Geo. E. Dietrich
Assistant Treasurer

(s) E. A. Johnson
Office Manager

Date: February 23 1938.

(s) A. B. Ritts,
Representative of Price, Waterhouse & Co."

The only profit and loss work program for the 1937 audit of the Connecticut Division was one for sales, prepared by Wyman as a handwritten copy of the previous year's program. Most of the work required by this program was designed to establish a proper sales cut-off in connection with the verification of inventories and accounts receivable. Consequently, the details involved and documents examined in this connection were discussed in connection with those topics. The program itself follows:

"WORK PROGRAM—SALES

Summarize totals of triplicate sales invoices on adding machine tape for each business day in Dec.

Trace totals for each day to sales register (and accounts receivable control).

Foot sales register to nearest $100—and trace totals to general ledger controls for sales & accts. receivable.

Test check Dec. postings to customer's ledger.

Test-check all invoices billed in last five days of Dec. and first five days in Jan. to shipping advices to see that date of shipment corresponds with billing dates.

Obtain duplicate invoices and shipping advices for larger December shipments of crude drugs and essential oils per dates shown on accounts receivable trial balance and compare dates of shipments with dates of invoices. Trace such shipments to inventory cards to see that stock balances were reduced.

Test check larger shipments in last five days of Dec. to inventory stock cards to see that inventory balances were reduced.

Check shipments on which no stock cards are maintained to "N" book to see that shipment dates correspond with billing dates **(Cliff St. invt. cards.)**

Examine Jan. shipping records and trace orders that were registered in the Acctg Dept prior to Jan. to billing records to see that unshipped orders at Dec. 31 were not taken up." [1098]

There are other auditing tests involving the use of sales figures which are not brought out by this program, but which memoranda on the accounts, schedules in the working papers, and testimony of Ritts, Thorn, and Rowbotham indicated were made to some extent. These tests were directed primarily to establishing the general reliability of the operating accounts rather than of the related balance sheet accounts. The bulletin, "Examination of Financial Statements", for example, suggests that "Whenever the necessary statistics are available it is desirable to reconcile the quantities of the principal products sold with the production or purchases during the period, taking into consideration the inventories at the beginning and end of the period." The Bulletin also suggests that the profit and loss account should be

---

[1098] Ex. 46. A somewhat similar program except for the first item was prepared by Wyman for the Canadian Company:

"1. Prepare summary of sales by commodities and agree with ledger control.

"2. Trace duplicate invoices to December sales register.

"3. Foot sales register for Dec & trace to ledger control.

"4. Examine shipping advices on all Dec. shipments.

"5. Trace quantities shown on invoices & shipping advices in December to perpetual inventory cards.

"6. Examine all shipping advices for first ten days in January to see that charges have been made in proper period.

"7. Check postings for December for duplicate invoices to customer's ledger." Ex. 25.

analyzed in as much detail as is readily available and that comparable figures for prior years should be obtained as an aid in ascertaining and inquiring into unusual items during the year under review. In this work "* * * budgets adopted by the company and monthly financial statements, where available, should be obtained for comparison with the annual results." The gross profit on sales should also be determined and marked variations from previous years investigated. The Bulletin further states that, among other things, the ledger accounts for selling, general, and administrative expenses should be examined to see that the accounts are properly classified; and suggests that a comparison of the net profit on sales with that of previous years is desirable.[1099]

The memorandum on the Canadian Company's accounts for 1937 was almost an exact copy of the 2 previous years, all carrying a one-line reference to a commodity analysis of sales such as that suggested above and all stating that a profit had been made on all transactions throughout the year. A condensed summary of operating results disclosed that sales for 1937 were 10% greater than the year before but yielded a lower rate of gross profit. With the exception of intercompany sales to the Connecticut Division all the sales were of crude drugs and essential oils to customers abroad under the Smith contract.[1100]

While a commodity analysis was not attempted on the Connecticut Division, more detailed material for a part of the year was included in the working papers. These were sheets from a sales register for the latter part of December of the year of the audit and January and part of February for the following year used as an aid in price testing. The sheets involved applied only to sales through W. W. Smith & Company, Inc. and showed the customer's name, invoice number, commodity, quantity, selling price, amount of the invoice, unit cost price, cost of sales, and gross profit for each item. Each transaction listed on this section of the register from December 27, 1937 to February 7, 1938 resulted in a gross profit. Similar sheets were included in the inventory working papers for the prior year's audit. Ritts could not recall any sale in this department that was not made at a gross profit. However, he did not know whether records similar to that just described existed for the entire year of their engagement,[1101] so that this condition could have been determined as a fact.

It seems reasonable to suppose that this sort of information for the Connecticut Company could have been obtained at least for the period since 1930 for Johnson, office manager, in investigating the background of the false transactions, prepared from records regularly kept in the accounting department a table showing by months in 1931 the sales, cost of sales, and gross profit for two classes of merchandise of the

---

1099 Ex. 117 (pp. 30–33, 35–36).

1100 R. 376–380, 800–804. Ex. 25, 26, 71, 72, 73. Page 255 *supra*.

1101 R. 814–820, 798–800. Ex. 84, 40 (D 15, D 16, D 17). See pages 261–263 *supra*.

Special Sales Department: resale stock and finished stock. The former was fictitious foreign crude drugs and the latter included hand lotion and a product known as Dandrofuge, which also appear to have been fictitious for the sales at this time at least were recorded as "* * * made to the same customers and in the same manner as crude drugs sold by Mr. Coster." [1102] Johnson also identified the more recent sales register as a record kept continuously in his department to record only foreign sales of crude drugs in which he never saw a transaction that was not concluded at a gross profit.[1103]

Thorn's attention was directed to sales as reported in 1930. In the memorandum on the Connecticut Company for that year, a table showing foreign sales separate from other sales for each of the last 4 months of the year was presented, in which foreign sales during October, November, and December were more than one-third greater than September. The memorandum also noted that because of a change in account classification, it was difficult to tell what the foreign sales amounted to for the year. Thorn testified that while he thought the December sales were out of line and therefore had the December sales invoices totaled on an adding machine, the only purpose of this work was to make sure that the books were supported by the underlying records for that month. The thought had occurred to him that some January sales might have been included in December and, in addition, the running of the total satisfied him that the transactions as recorded were authentic, because they agreed in total with the duplicate invoices on file.[1104]

Thorn also explained that he usually compared sales in the aggregate, but not by commodities, month by month through the year to pick up any extraordinary changes. His papers for the next year 1931 included a notation of work to be done at Bridgeport which carried the question "Why are December sales higher?" Opposite this question was a mark which indicated that the point had been disposed of to his satisfaction. He had no recollection of anything unusual and found no other reference to the matter in the papers.[1105] He had also noted that the foreign business ran in bunches but made no further inquiry as to the cause.[1106]

Thorn's conclusions may be judged by examining the following table which reproduces in part the table prepared by Johnson (referred to above) showing the sales, cost of sales, and gross profits by months for 1931 of the Special Sales Department, listing separately the "Finished Stock" (hand lotion and Dandrofuge) and "Resale Stock" (foreign crude drugs).[1107]

[1102] R. 1075. Testimony of Thorn.
[1103] R. 1372–1376; Ex. 105.
[1104] R. 911–916.
[1105] R. 1118–1119, 1067–1070.
[1106] R. 1061.
[1107] Ex. 105.

STATEMENT OF SALES, COST OF SALES & GROSS PROFIT—SPECIAL SALES DEPT. 1931

Month	Finished Stock			Resale Stock		
	Sales	Cost of Sales	Gross Profit	Sales	Cost of Sales	Gross Profit
January	$ 139, 000. 00	$ 21, 625. 00	$ 117, 375. 00	$ 53, 000. 50	$ 48, 000. 00	$ 5, 000. 50
February	139, 000. 00	21, 625. 00	117, 375. 00	53, 000. 00	48, 000. 00	5, 000. 00
March	139, 000. 00	21, 625. 00	117, 375. 00	—	—	—
April	139, 000. 00	21, 625. 00	117, 375. 00	28, 125. 00	24, 375. 00	3, 750. 00
May	139, 000. 00	21, 625. 00	117, 375. 00	—	—	—
June	139, 000. 00	21, 625. 00	117, 375. 00	—	—	—
July	139, 000. 00	21, 625. 00	117, 375. 00	29, 988. 00	29, 682. 00	306. 00
August	139, 000. 00	21, 625. 00	117, 375. 00	7, 546. 00	7, 469. 00	77. 00
September	69, 500. 00	10, 812. 50	58, 687. 50	54, 035. 60	52, 615. 80	1, 419. 80
October	139, 000. 00	21, 625. 00	117, 375. 00	49, 135. 60	47, 765. 80	1, 369. 80
November	41, 300. 00	5, 412. 50	35, 887. 50	966, 770. 40	872, 532. 67	94, 237. 73
December	—	—	—	1, 253, 915. 92	1, 081, 009. 38	172, 906. 54
	$1, 361, 800. 00	$210, 850. 00	$1, 150, 950. 00	$2, 495, 517. 02	$2, 211, 449. 65	$284, 067. 37

The situation revealed in the above table was not recognized in any way in the audit working papers except by the question quoted above concerning December sales which Thorn testified must have been answered to his satisfaction.

A somewhat similar heavy concentration of sales toward the end of accounting periods also existed in the records covering the short life of Girard & Co., Inc. A schedule of accounts receivable was prepared from Price, Waterhouse & Co.'s working papers listing accounts with balances at the date of the audits of Girard & Co., Inc., December 31, 1924; December 31, 1925; and March 31, June 30, September 30, and November 30, 1926. At the earliest date, six of 11 accounts (billing date not known) totaled $34,415.88 ($9,305.05 due from W. W. Smith & Co.), while the other five totaled $276.52. Net sales for the 9 months ended December 31, 1924, totaled $251,977.06. The next year end, six accounts all billed from December 17 to 31 (including J. P. Meyer & Co. billed December 30 for $17,250 and W. W. Smith & Co. billed on December 21 and 23 for a total of $22,750) totaled $155,972.00, while 212 others totaled only $14,145.56. Sales for 1925 were $1,129,302.38. The four reports in 1926 show still larger balances due from a very small proportion of the accounts, which included the names of Chas. Manning Chem. Co., J. P. Meyer & Co., W. W. Smith & Co., and Geo. Vernard & Co. indicating the same concentration of billing (as compared with prior sales) in the last 15 days before the audit date.[1108]

Another instance of heavy concentration of sales in a short period was noted in Ritts' memorandum (dated February 18, 1933) on the Connecticut accounts for 1932. In connection with difficulties of establishing inventory prices, Ritts called attention to the fact "* * * that approximately 50% of the company's December 31, 1932, inventory of crude drug stocks had been sold prior to the date of completion of our examination at a small margin of profit." [1109] The inventory corresponding to the sales referred to here was turned 1.67 times in 1932 and 2.38 times in 1933,[1110] whereas the indicated annual rate for 1933 based on the period to February 18 was approximately 4 times.

Returning to the 1931 memorandum on the Connecticut Company accounts, Jaureguy, on information supplied by Thorn who was in charge at Bridgeport, stated "The net sales during 1931, which include $2,000,000 from the new spice department, amounted to $14,007,607.94 compared to $13,890,246.55 for 1930." [1111] There followed a full page explanation of the spice department which, on the

[1108] Ex. 170.

[1109] Ex. 81. See footnote 1026 *supra*.

[1110] Based upon Ex. 43 which for the periods involved included figures relating to crude drug transactions other than those of the fictitious foreign crude drug business. The figures based upon the fictitious foreign crude drug business alone were 1.21 times in 1932 and 2.12 times in 1933. Ex. Q, 267.

[1111] Ex. 82.

volume quoted above, made approximately $10,000 on what was claimed to be a virtual corner in pepper. The memorandum set forth the following summary of gross profit on the several classes of sales:

"Manufactured products (the McKesson line)	$1, 485, 530. 12	35. 41%
Resale departments—crude drugs, China wood oil, spices, etc.	379, 761. 80	6. 16
Export sales of crude drugs and finished stock through W. W. Smith & Co.	1, 413, 889. 25	37. 20
Essential oil department [1112]	13, 774. 58	5. 47
	$3, 292, 955. 75	
Less—Cash discounts, transportation on sales and adjustments	438, 726. 68	
Total gross profit on sales	$2, 854, 229. 07	20. 52"

But there was no mention in connection with the export sales of crude drugs and finished stock through W. W. Smith & Company, Inc. of the cutting down of the "Finished Stock" line and the sudden expansion of the "Resale Stock" sales in November and December of 1931 as indicated on Johnson's table previously set forth.[1113] Specifically, there was no indication that in 1931, the Dandrofuge and hand lotion line (finished stock) produced 84.5% gross profit on sales; or that sales of crude drugs (resale stock) also sold through W. W. Smith & Company, Inc. surged up in November and December to replace it in dollars of gross profit although producing only 11.4% gross profit on sales. A combination of approximately one-third Dandrofuge and hand lotion sales and two-thirds crude drug sales accounted for the 37.2% rate of gross profit on combined sales for the year of $3,857,317.02.

The memorandum for the following year 1932 also contained a summary of gross profits on the several classes of sales in which comparative figures were shown for the preceding year but without including the percentages of profit.[1114] Again much space was devoted to a discussion of the troubles of the spice department (in which a loss of $250,438.93 was suffered in pepper) but no explanation was given for the drop from $1,413,889.25 to $996,319.27 in the gross profit in the export sales of crude drugs and finished stock through "W. W. Smith & Co." [1115] The sales figures were not reported in this memorandum for either year, so it was impossible to discover from a comparison of the figures or from the text of the 1932 memorandum that the change in profit was due principally to a reduction in the rate of profit resulting from the elimination of the hand lotion and Dandrofuge line.

[1112] Real and not to be confused with the essential oils included with crude drugs as part of the fictitious foreign business supposedly conducted through W. W. Smith & Company, Inc.

[1113] Page 303 *supra*.

[1114] The real essential oil department was included with the other resale departments.

[1115] Ex. 81.

A reconciliation of the gross profit of $996,319.27 from "Export sales of crude drugs and finished stock through W. W. Smith & Co." reported in the 1932 memorandum with a schedule of sales, cost of sales, and gross profits for 1932 included in Price, Waterhouse & Co.'s working papers discloses that in addition to the two items supposed to have been handled in that manner, seven other items were also included in the gross profit figure on transactions through Smith. The sales of the two fictitious items supposed to have been handled through Smith were "Special Finished Stock" (hand lotion and Dandrofuge) $438,000.00 and "Special Resale Stock" (foreign crude drugs) $6,508,510.53. Profits of $368,305.00 (84.1% of sales) were recorded on the former and $576,238.78 (8.9% of sales) on the latter. The principal items incorrectly classified with the Smith transactions in the 1932 memorandum were from Hermann's domestic department, "General Crude" sales of $1,035,266.29 and "General Camphor" sales of $122,785.87, and from Stebe's export sales of $229,603.43. Total net sales of the items incorrectly included were $1,436,715.12 and gross profits incorrectly included as applicable to sales through Smith amounted to $51,775.49. The profit reported in the memorandum therefore applied to $8,383,225.65 of sales or at the rate of 11.9%.[1116]

In 1933 the spice department loss was separately reported and commented upon in the memorandum for that year but the profit from all other Bridgeport operations was reported in one figure.[1117] The memorandum on the Connecticut Division for 1934 included, in addition to a brief analysis of the increase in net profit, a comparative summary of the Division's gross profit for 1933 and 1934, showing the results for the spice department, four classes of manufactured products, general-export and import (included real items mentioned above in connection with the 1932 memorandum as well as the fictitious foreign business), and miscellaneous (sundry small categories of sales and unallocated adjustments). The spice department was again the only one commented upon separately. Neither sales nor rates of gross profit were given for any department.[1118]

Beginning in 1935 the division in the statement of gross profits was made between all crude drugs on the one hand and sales of manufactured products on the other. In that year Thorn in his memorandum noted the interesting fact that approximately $15,000,000 of the former produced 10% gross profit while "only $3,800,000" of the the latter produced 35% gross profit.[1119] Sales of manufactured products gradually increased in proportion to crude sales but the

[1116] Ex. 81, N, Q.
[1117] Ex. 80.
[1118] Ex. 268.
[1119] Ex. 79.

relationship in rate of profit remained about the same. Sales of non-manufactured items increased until in 1937 the total was approximately $18,000,000 in the Connecticut Division. Combining this Division and the Canadian Company, the sales increased from about $12,000,000 in 1932 to $21,365,000 in 1937. The increase in the Connecticut Division was attended by a fairly uniform rate of gross profit—9% in 1934, 10% in 1935, 10.18% in 1936, with a drop to 8.89% in 1937.[1120] Ritts explained the drop in the crude sales gross profit percentage in 1937 as being due to a change in proportion of sales of crude drugs and essential oils.[1121] The rate of gross profit in the Canadian Company was 13.05% of net sales in 1928, 12.97% in 1929 and from 1932 to 1937 fluctuated from approximately 8½% to 9%.[1122] These figures for non-manufactured products since 1932 included in addition to the fictitious Smith business, real business amounting to approximately 10% and 15% of the total sales in the Canadian Company and Connecticut Division respectively.

The figures quoted from the memoranda were not developed by Price, Waterhouse & Co. during the audit but were taken by them from schedules similar to the one for 1932 referred to above, which were supplied to them by the Company. Such schedules in Price, Waterhouse & Co.'s papers for 1934 through 1937 show 10 to 13 classes of manufactured goods; five items under general sales, including "Special Resale Crude" (the fictitious business),[1123] "General Crude," and "General Camphor" as the principal ones; and two other minor categories of sales. In 1934 and 1935 Stebe's exports were included under general sales but in 1936 and 1937 were shown separately. Gross profit and rate of gross profit were developed for each item and for the total.[1124]

Although the results of the foreign crude drug business were thus separately set forth, both Ritts and Thorn at the hearings stated that there was no record by which they could separately state the gross profits for the various years. The contradiction apparently arises from the fact that they never treated this business as being departmentalized and never checked the various detailed classifications to determine what they included.[1125]

A rather extended discussion was had with Thorn over the study the accountant should make of these departmental sales and gross profit figures. He explained that the memoranda were written for internal office use and were designed to save the time of the partner.

1120 Ex. 79, 78, 49.

1121 Ex. 49.

1122 Ex. 150, 162, 163, 164, 73, 72, 26.

1123 Exact correspondence of the amount of sales shown for "Special Resale Crude" for 1936 on the schedule in Price, Waterhouse & Co.'s working papers with the amount reported by S. D. Leidesdorf & Co. as fictitious sales for the same year indicates this to be the false department. Ex. 120, 255.

1124 R. 1072–1073; Ex. 120, 124, N.

1125 R. 526–533, 1072–1073, 1081–1082, 1901–1902. Cf: Ex. 43 and Q.

He agreed that a change in rate of gross profit on Smith transactions from 37.2% to approximately 10% was a very large one and due to the elimination of the Dandrofuge line but that this fact could not be discovered from the memoranda of 1931 and 1932, even if compared, for no percentages were given in the latter nor were the base figures of sales readily available. Thorn said that if the partner happened to ask for the figures, the man who prepared the memorandum could make the calculation.[1126]

On another phase of this question, Thorn explained that the only purpose of making the gross profit percentage calculation was to indicate any possible errors in the basis of valuation of the inventories and for this purpose he would approach the question from the standpoint of the Company as a whole.[1127] Thorn explained that the only departmental analysis he would want would be to separate McKesson products from their other business. Dandrofuge, he thought, was an exception to that rule because, while it was supposed to have been made in Bridgeport, it was not a part of the McKesson line sold to the subsidiary houses but instead was sold largely in Australia to the same customers as the crude drugs and through the same agency, "W. W. Smith & Co.", and hence was more properly grouped with foreign sales, even though this did merge lines of business with widely different profit characteristics. He explained further that a change in rate of gross profit would indicate, perhaps, that inventories at the end of the year had been valued on a different basis than at the beginning, or that some stock had not been properly accounted for, but he did not think a change might suggest the possibility of fictitious transactions. The review of the profit and loss account, Thorn thought, was only incidental to determining the financial position of

1126 R. 1077-1078, 1086-1094, especially:

"Q. [By Mr. GALPEER.] There is nothing in the memoranda, exhibit 81, itself, on which the partner could make any calculation of gross profit for that year, is there?

A. [By THORN.] No, sir. The partner, I might say, would not make any calculations of gross profit in any case, he would ask the man that was taking the accounts up with him to do that.

Q. Let me ask you one more thing; why wasn't this change shown in the exhibit 81 in the first instance?

A. That is on the 1932 memoranda?

Q. Right.

A. I can't answer that, I don't know.

Q. Let me ask you just one more thing. What was there in the 1932 memorandum which would have focused the partner's eye to the fact that there might be some question here, or might be some reason for considering the percentage of gross profit which may have been far out of line and instead of 37 percent is 10 percent?

A. I don't think there is anything in the memorandum calling particular attention to that. It is a matter of his general review of the accounts that would cover that." R. 1092-1093.

1127 "Q. [By Mr. GALPEER.] Do you know, as a matter of fact, in this gross percentage figure of 37.2 how much represented Dandrofuge and how much of their resales, not based upon facts which happened subsequently?

A. No, sir, I do not, and I doubt if I can tell from our papers. We would approach that question, really, from the standpoint of the company as a whole and we always, of course, have the gross profit test there, and if there is any substantial change we require an explanation because of the fact that it may mean there is a difference in the basis of valuation of the inventories from the beginning of the year to the end of the year; that is the only value of the so-called gross profit test." R. 1076-1077.

the Company so the auditor would not be concerned with departmental operations.[1128]

However, the partial analyses of profits referred to in the foregoing discussion indicate that *over-all* gross profit percentages were inadequate to disclose important changes in the business. And the record also shows that the changes in rate of profit resulting from irregularities were not the reflection of changes in method or errors in taking the year-end inventories as Thorn suggested would be a principal reason for examining a change in rate.

Rowbotham was asked for his opinion on the foregoing subjects discussed with Ritts and Thorn. On the first point concerning the consistent realization of gross profit on foreign crude drug sales and record of every sale at a gross profit, Rowbotham was not disturbed for Coster was supposed to have been the leading crude drug expert of this country and was in a position to wait for his market.[1129]

Although, as previously stated, the memoranda on their face gave no clew to the hand lotion and Dandrofuge line with their high rate of gross profit, as compared to the crude drugs purportedly sold through W. W. Smith & Company, Inc. and although the questionnaire filled out for 1932 carried the answer "No" after "Has the company abandoned any line of manufacture, and if so, for what reason?"; [1130] Rowbotham testified that he thought that the drop in over-all gross profits was noted at the time and that it was explained by the fact that these products were abandoned.[1131]

On the question of analyzing sales by departments, Rowbotham stated that the purpose of the examination was to express an opinion on the annual accounts of the Company which did not require going into departmental or operating questions. He cited the bulletin, "Examination of Financial Statements," as authority (because no ref-

---

1128 R. 1077–1082:

" * * * Could I add a little information here which I have been thinking might be pertinent in connection with these questions. As you know, we are making a balance sheet examination with only a review of the profit-and-loss accounts, that is, we don't make an examination of all their various departments as such separately. We are not particularly concerned with the gross profit that one department might have made or might not have made.

We are concerned with the financial position at a certain moment and all of these things which you have mentioned probably have been discussed when these accounts were taken up with the partner but I think we would not consider them points of any particular importance.

We are only concerned, in other words, with the profit-and-loss accounts as they have relationship to the assets and liabilities of the company.

In these particular items which we are discussing, that gross profit which the company makes on all its transactions is of interest to us because it has a bearing on the inventories of the company. That is why we do give that consideration." R. 1078.

1129 " * * * I don't think, in a case like this, where Coster was supposed to be the leading crude drug expert of this country, and I think that is proved by the confidence in him of his own directors who were also practical drug men, and I do not think in view of the volume of business he was doing that this last thing would have caused me any disquiet because I think he was in a position to wait for his market if he wanted to." R. 1950–1951.

1130 Sales of hand lotion and Dandrofuge ("Special Finished Stock") after 1932 were less than $50,000. Ex. 267.

1131 R. 1808–1812.

erence to the subject appeared therein) for the statement that the accountant has no "* * * control or right of criticism of the company's operating policies." [1132]

Rowbotham's testimony on concentration of sales in short periods appeared in connection with three exhibits referred to earlier.[1133] As a part of the audit program for checking the year-end sales cut-off, he stated that the auditor should see that the client "* * * does not pile up sales in the first 10 days of January and take them into December." The important point here was to see that the cut-off was clean and the sales were not deliberately piled up. For example, if he saw a disproportionate number of sales at the year end he would wonder what was being done.[1134] He thought that the situation disclosed in the Girard & Co., Inc., accounts must have been explained to the man in charge of the audit perhaps as the natural result of an expanding business.[1135]

Rowbotham seemed more concerned about the sale of approximately half the December 31, 1932 inventory of crude drugs prior to February 18, 1933, for he thought that the sentence in the memorandum reporting this fact meant that the client had firm contracts for future delivery for that amount but had not actually billed customers for half the year-end inventory in a month and a half. Ritts, however, stated that actual sales were meant. With this point clear Rowbotham felt that these figures did represent a substantial increase in activity from the previous year's annual inventory turnover of 1.67 times. The 1933 rate was 2.38, the highest of the last 6 years but still much under the rate for the period in question.[1136]

2. Other Profit and Loss Accounts

Memoranda on the Connecticut Company through 1933 indicated that the profit and loss accounts were reviewed in some detail. In 1930, for example, it was reported that over $1,000,000 of various classes of advertising expenses were charged to the Maryland Company with the approval of the operating committee and Coster.[1137] In 1931, 1932, and 1933, an analysis of deferred charges, budgeted

---

[1132] R. 1896–1897.

[1133] Ex. 43, 81, 170; pages 246 ff., 304 *supra*.

[1134] R. 1868.

[1135] R. 2032–2033. "* * * it would come to us as an increase in the month and not in the 15 days." R. 2033.

[1136] R. 1957–1960; Ex. 43. Later more accurate schedules (Ex. Q, 267) show the annual turnover of foreign crude drug inventories to have been as follows:

Year:	*Connecticut Division*	*Canadian Company*
1932	1.21	1.57
1933	2.12	1.98
1934	1.82	2.23
1935	1.75	2.58
1936	1.79	2.72
1937	1.60	3.01

[1137] Ex. 83.

expenses, and changes in net profit were set out.[1138] Beginning in 1934 a sufficient analysis of expenses was made to meet the requirements of Forms 10 and 10–K filed with the Securities and Exchange Commission.[1139] In recent years comparison of profit and loss accounts in the memoranda was ended at gross profit except in the Canadian Company where complete condensed profit and loss statements were given showing percentages of all items to sales.[1140] The accounts for the Connecticut Division, as submitted to Coster without comment by the auditors, included a two-year comparative statement of profit and loss in which the percentage of major categories of expenses to sales was set out. The principal expense item in this statement "other selling, distributing, administrative and general expenses" was supported by a detailed statement of these expenses. No departmental analysis of the operations of the Connecticut Division was reflected in these statements.[1140a]

The monthly reports prepared by the comptroller and submitted to the directors and operating heads of the Company in addition to sales and net profits for each of the wholesale houses, included a statement of profit and loss in five categories for the Connecticut Division. The categories were: general sales (which merged real domestic and fictitious foreign crude drugs in one figure), cosmetics, McKesson products (manufactured goods), Spanish-American (exports of Stebe's department), Angostura bitters, and spice department. Selling, distributing, administrative, and fixed expenses, as well as other income (interest, dividends, cash discounts, etc.) and other charges (interest, provision for doubtful notes and accounts, etc.) were reported separately for each category. Income tax was charged to the profitable ones.[1141] This means that Thorn was correct in his views that net results for what has been found to be the fictitious business were not determined separately from real transactions, but he was unaware, when questioned at the hearings, that net results on resale transactions were reported separately from net profits on manufactured goods.[1142]

Keeping in mind that Company schedules in Price, Waterhouse & Co.'s working papers in recent years showed sales, returns and allowances, and gross profits for what have been discovered to have been fictitious crude drug sales separately from the real business but that McGloon's profit and loss statements combined these classes of sales in the department "General Sales", a comparison of the statements with the schedules may be of interest. In 1937, for example, fictitious gross sales (shown on the Company's schedule in the working papers

1138 Ex. 82, 81, 80.

1139 R. 406–412; Ex. 27.

1140 Ex. 79, 78, 49, 73, 72, 26.

1140a Ex. 261.

1141 The reports, however, did not give such breakdown of assets, only of operating accounts.

1142 R. 1897–1902, 901–904.

as "Special Resale Crude") were \$15,126,825.20 and real general crude gross sales (shown as "General Crude") were \$2,711,150.89 for the same period.[1143] There were no returns and allowances charged to the former but \$38,327.20 to the latter. The real crude sales produced 6.45% gross profit while the fictitious gross profit reported was 10.02%. The comptroller's report for the same period, as presented to the directors, combined these classes of sales and included "General Camphor" and "Drums and Containers" to make a total for general gross sales of \$18,136,180.77.[1144] Applicable to the total, the profit and loss statement shows merchandise returned \$39,318.72, cash discounts allowed \$34,228.63, transportation on sales of \$4,234.94, and cash discounts received of \$103,935.35. Among the detailed selling and distributing expenses are salesmen's salaries and commissions, salesmen's traveling expense, miscellaneous selling expense (the largest item, 0.69% of net sales, apparently included the Smith guaranty premium and fee), warehouse payroll, drayage and cartage, outside storage charges, and miscellaneous distributing expenses. In accordance with explanations given by the auditors and the terms of the W. W. Smith & Company, Inc. contract, *none* of the expenses mentioned in this paragraph, with the one exception of the guaranty premium and fee, apply to the foreign resale crude drug business conducted through Smith. Therefore, as indicated in the table below, prepared from the comptroller's report, comparison of percentages to sales of the various items in the statements was futile and misleading because of the distortion in the general sales figure caused by combining the domestic resales with the foreign resale business to which many of the expense and adjustment accounts did not apply.

1143 Ex. N. In addition to the two categories mentioned General Camphor sales were \$271,132.28, less returns of \$991.52.

1144 Ex. 262 reconciled with details in Ex. N.

McKESSON & ROBBINS, INCORPORATED (CONNECTICUT DIVISION),

Statement of Profit and Loss by Departments

Twelve Months Ending December 31, 1937

(Expressed in Percent to Net Sales)

	General Sales	Cosmetics	Manufactured Goods	Spanish American	Spice Department	Total
Gross Sales (000's omitted)	$18, 136	$343	$6, 357	$446	$168	$25, 451
Percent to Net Sales	100. 22	110. 92	103. 66	102. 48	100. 00	101. 23
Merchandise Returned	. 22	10. 92	3. 66	2. 48	—	1. 23
Sales, less Returns	100. 00	100. 00	100. 00	100. 00	100. 00	100. 00
Cost of Sales	90. 63	87. 92	52. 09	80. 37	92. 78	81. 03
Gross Profit before Discounts	9. 37	12. 08	47. 91	19. 63	7. 22	18. 97
Deduct:						
Cash Discounts	. 19	. 46	1. 33	—	. 32	. 47
Transportation on Sales	. 02	1. 26	4. 72	—	—	1. 18
Samples and Free Goods	—	2. 33	6. 67	—	—	1. 66
Total Discounts and Transportation	. 21	4. 05	12. 72	—	. 32	3. 31
Gross Profit after Discounts	9. 16	8. 03	35. 19	19. 63	6. 90	15. 66
Selling Expenses	. 87	8. 89	17. 20	5. 06	1. 08	5. 03
Distributing Expenses	. 33	. 65	1. 65	5. 97	1. 45	. 76
Administrative Expenses	. 48	. 84	2. 63	8. 45	4. 47	1. 17
Fixed Expenses	. 11	. 05	. 29	1. 58	. 57	. 19
Total Operating Expenses	1. 79	10. 43	21. 77	21. 06	7. 57	7. 15
Profit from Operations	7. 37	(2. 40)	13. 42	(1. 43)	(. 67)	8. 51
Balance of Statement Selected Items Only:						
Cash Discounts Received	. 58	. 32	. 44	. 49	—	. 53
Provision for Doubtful Notes and Accounts	. 03	(. 32)	. 04	. 48	—	. 04
Net Profit after Federal Income Tax [a]	6. 87	(2. 17)	11. 29	(1. 25)	(. 67)	7. 72

[a] Ex. 262. Bedsole testified that a report in this form was given to the directors beginning in 1932. Ex, 185; R. 2517–2519, 4254. McGloon testified that the foreign resale and domestic resale business were always merged in all the profit and loss statements prepared by his department and that no one ever suggested separating the two. R. 1708. See also testimony of Murray, R. 2157–2158; Weinberg, R. 2423; Michaels, R. 4265–4266.

Nevertheless Thorn did not consider it the duty of the auditors to make or suggest a proper segregation of the departments of the business.[1145] Rowbotham considered it to be an auditor's duty to review the operating accounts sufficiently to uncover any abnormal variations but insisted that this did not extend to a criticism of the client's operating policies.[1146]

In connection with the subject of profit and loss analysis Ritts and Thorn were asked to what extent they used statements prepared by the client's accounting department. Thorn testified that while he may have seen copies of internal profit and loss accounts prepared by McGloon's department and thought some of them were included in his working papers with extracts from directors' minutes, he did

---

1145 "A. [By THORN.] When I say crude drugs I mean all of their resale transactions. In examining those accounts, I don't care whether the crude drugs are sold by Mr. Coster or by Mr. Hermann or by Mr. Jackson. It is all the same type of business." R. 1082.

"By Mr. GALPEER:

Q. But the two types of business, I am now looking at it as a business, are distinguishable?

A. As I say, from an accounting standpoint there is a distinction between the manufacturing business and goods which are simply resold without processing, which require a different type of verification work.

Q. Didn't you think it was your duty as an accountant to suggest, if anybody wanted to study this picture, in order to get a clearer concept of exactly what the Connecticut Division consisted of, that those two things, those two businesses which were different in nature be set up separately so that the results of each could be definitely determined?

A. No, I did not feel that was my duty as an accountant. I think from an accounting standpoint I was interested in an examination of this kind so that I could give an opinion on them, and from an operating standpoint, if that was of importance to the operating heads of the business, that they could develop that information for themselves internally, but for me, as an outside accountant, I feel that I might even have been presumptuous to have told them to divide up their business into several different baskets there.

* * * * * * *

* * * I believe that the monthly reports furnished to the operating heads,—that is the internal report prepared by the companies themselves, showed some breakdown of those operations. To sum up, I feel that is an internal matter with which I am not concerned.

* * * * * * *

I might say that the only work we have done has been on the annual year end examination so that when we talk about any monthly report or anything of that kind, it is something that we have had nothing to do with, but in these monthly reports—I don't know that I have ever seen a copy of those, but I have seen copies of reports made to the directors by Mr. Coster; I would see those in reviewing the minutes. As I recall it, there is a break down of figures there. I do not recall how extensive it is, but I think they do show, at least, the gross results of operations as between the manufacturing and the raw material transactions, but I am very hazy on that.

* * * * * * *

Q. And you felt here that there was no duty on you as an auditor or as an accountant, in preparing your report for the directors, to take a division like the Connecticut Division where you have two different types of operations and to work your report up so that it would disclose each type of operation separately?

A. Yes, that is true. As I say, from reading the extract of the minutes, I gained the impression that the directors were being fully informed by the internal report which they received as to operations." R. 899–903.

1146 "Q. [By Mr. GALPEER.] Coming back now, Mr. Rowbotham, to something you stated, I believe your final statement was that you were not concerned with operating results. My question is whether it is necessary as part of an auditing job, part of an examination, in order to verify the balance sheet, to observe the operating details, to determine whether there are variations from normal and if such variations appear to trace down those variations to see whether there were legitimate reasons for their existence or whether there is something illegitimate or unauthentic about them.

A. [By ROWBOTHAM.] Well, I think the auditor ought to observe variation in the sense that if he sees anything that needs explanation, he ought to ask for an explanation of it, but the point I was trying to make is what I thought your question was, was whether the accountant was concerned with controlling or criticizing the operating policies of the company as such, and I don't think he is.

Q. Well, my question was not directed to that. My question is, whether it should be part of an accountant's job to look for variations, as a test of authenticity.

A. I think you should look for those variations, yes, sir." R. 1899–1900.

not remember what they were.[1147] Ritts, who was questioned on this point after the hearings had progressed for nearly 4 months and he had had more time than Thorn to review the working papers, explained that he made a practice of getting all of these reports and that he reviewed them for variations in sales during the year. As part of this review he made test checks with the sales registers. He also reviewed schedules of cost of sales and factory burden accounts with special reference to year-end adjustments of these accounts, but he could not recall for how long these reports had been available.[1148]

J. THE WHOLESALE HOUSES

1. Number of Houses

The head office, wholesale houses, and other divisions and subsidiaries of McKesson & Robbins, Incorporated, exclusive of the Connecticut Division and Canadian Company, varied slightly in number during the last few years but approximated 80 different units each year. These units accounted for about 70% of the total assets and about 85% of the total volume of business. The net income of these units fluctuated widely, presenting a sharp contrast to the two units we have examined in detail which were engaged in an entirely different type of business and were apparently consistently profitable during periods of prosperity and depression.

2. Control of the Audit

The entire audit since the organization of the Maryland Company was controlled by Price, Waterhouse & Co. from its New York office under Rowbotham's direction, with Jaureguy as manager for the years 1928 to 1932, inclusive, and Thorn from 1933 to the end. All of the United States offices of Price, Waterhouse & Co. were called upon to do one or more of the branch audits, while two foreign subsidiaries were handled by the English and Continental firms of Price, Waterhouse & Co. and several small houses were examined by other independent accountants.

All of this work was coordinated by means of the closing instructions issued from Bridgeport by McGloon and "Private and Confidential * * * Instructions to Representatives of Price, Waterhouse & Co. in Charge of Examinations * * *" [1149] issued from the latter's New York office. The first of these documents it will be recalled contained detailed instructions to McKesson accountants for preparing the accounts for closing and for preparing schedules required by the auditors to expedite their work. The second document included instructions to Price, Waterhouse & Co. representatives as to the form in which work-

[1147] R. 904.
[1148] R. 4447–4449; Ex. 185.
[1149] Ex. 15, 13; pages 165–166 *supra*.

ing papers were to be prepared and the papers to be sent to the New York office. There followed a general description of the work to be done on the various accounts, and finally a list of the divisions and subsidiary companies to be examined. Audit steps to be omitted, as specified in the letters of engagement, were mentioned.

For work done out of the New York office directly, work programs and questionnaires were prepared in mimeographed form. For work done by other Price, Waterhouse & Co. offices, responsibility for detailed work meeting the requirements of the instructions issued from the New York office rested with the Price, Waterhouse & Co. branches involved. Only noted deviations from the programs used at Bridgeport will be considered in connection with the wholesale houses.[1150]

3. Special Features of the Work in the Wholesale Houses

a. CASH

Two significant differences appeared on the cash program. As drawn up for general use this required the checking of "* * * the details of the last three deposits in December and first three deposits in January from the cash receipts book to the company's duplicate deposit tickets." It will be recalled that this was not done at Bridgeport because there were no duplicate deposit tickets.[1151] A second bank reconciliation at July 31st, as required by the program, was carried out for the branches but "That work was not done at Bridgeport. It was a special step inserted for the purpose of the satisfaction of the officials at Bridgeport as to the handling of cash at the branches, I understand."[1152]

b. ACCOUNTS RECEIVABLE AND BAD DEBT RESERVES

One of the major problems, perhaps recognized as the most troublesome problem especially in the depression years, was the proper determination of bad debt reserves for receivables due from thousands of retail druggists. The adequate control of cash collections from these customers also gave the auditors some concern which, from time to time, led to the suggestion that test circularization of receivables should be made. Circularization of the accounts was not a part of the regular examination procedure.[1153] However, the possible desirability of circularizing accounts was noted in a letter dated January 27, 1930, from Price, Waterhouse & Co.'s representative at work on a McKesson branch in New Orleans, to his office in St. Louis. The letter reported an unsatisfactory condition found in that branch which led to calling

1150 R. 354, 879.

1151 Ex. 21, 29; R. 439-441.

1152 R. 328 (testimony of Wyman); see also page 197 *supra*.

1153 Pages 145 ff. *supra*.

for original deposit slips at the bank and an agreement by the house to make a circularization of receivables as at January 31, 1930.[1154] The general condition of the accounts in the wholesale houses led finally to the letter which is quoted earlier in this report,[1155] wherein Jaureguy, with Rowbotham's approval, urged the surprise circularization of the larger notes and accounts receivable. More recently a similar situation developed in one of the liquor subsidiaries after discovery that salesmen were witholding collections from customers. The Price, Waterhouse & Co. office handling this engagement suggested to the New York office that a circularization of the accounts should be made at December 31, 1937, in connection with their audit, even though the client had done so in November but with unsatisfactory results. After consultation with McGloon it was decided that the losses involved were not sufficient to warrant a test circularization by the auditors.[1156]

A number of the directors were questioned on their views as to the circularization of accounts with retail drug stores. All made the statement that conditions in the trade were such that circularization would tend to destroy confidence in the wholesale houses, as the druggists were not bookkeepers and accepted the creditor's statement as correct. They all feared that such customers would not understand a request to confirm a balance, but that in the case of manufacturers and other large customers, this argument would not hold and circularization might be desirable.[1157]

The question of bad debt reserves was not so easily solved and led to much discussion between the auditors and officers of the client.[1158] A dispute about reserves at the time of the bank holiday in 1933, during which the auditors insisted upon very much larger reserves than had been provided, set George V. Doerr, a vice-president, director, and, at that time, chairman of the Sub-committee on Accounting, to thinking about the problem. He worked out a plan for setting up reserves which he thought might avoid the inevitable dispute that would arise if the credit manager thought an account was good but the auditors' representative thought it was not. Doerr felt that Company employees were better judges than the auditors. The results of this plan, when put in operation, ultimately led to excess reserves.[1159]

1154 Ex. 113.

1155 Ex. 88; footnote 544 *supra*.

1156 Ex. C 1, C 2, C 3.

1157 Bedsole, R. 2498, 2505; Doerr, R. 2579–2582; Faxon, R. 2530; Michaels, R. 4296–4297.

1158 R. 2193; Ex. 247 (p. 2); Ex. 243 (p. 1); Ex. 246 (pp. 5, 7–11).

1159 R. 2570–2571; Ex. 188–A and B, 189–A and B. The plan is described as follows in the audit report for 1935:

> "Prior to 1935, the amount of the provision for bad debt losses was based on an appraisal of the notes and accounts receivable, and on the bad debt experience of the particular division or company. Beginning January 1, 1935, the policy was adopted of providing reserves against balances arising since January 1, 1934 according to the age of the balance. Under this plan, a reserve of one-half of one percent. is provided for balances arising during the current month and the percentage is increased each month until a full reserve is provided against balances one year old. The amount of the provision for balances arising prior to January 1, 1934 was determined as heretofore by an appraisal of the balances." Ex. 158 (pp. 11–12).

c. INVENTORIES

The inventory program followed at Bridgeport was also used for the branches, at least those done by the New York office, which meant that the auditors' representatives had no specific instructions to make any physical tests by inspection or counting of stock to establish the quantities on hand. In some houses the auditors seem to have gone beyond this to some extent, for directors who were heads of wholesale houses testified that they personally accompanied the auditors to the warehouse to inspect certain items of merchandise, or that their house managers had reported to them, in response to direct inquiries on the subject, that such tests had been made, at least prior to the 1937 audit. Murray, for example, said the auditors asked to see particularly large items;[1160] Bedsole recalled that they checked on slow moving stock;[1161] Faxon [1162] and Doerr [1163] had been informed recently that some physical inspection of inventories was a part of the auditors' procedure. On at least one occasion the examination included extensive spot checking:

> "We have conferred with you a number of times recently regarding the tampering with the inventory stock sheets by employees of the company which was discovered by our representative in charge of the audit. As a result of this a second inventory was taken on January 23, 1932, after which it appeared that the inventory had been overstated to the extent of some $7,000 in the stock sheets originally given to us. The second inventory taken, which was worked back to December 31,1931, showed a total shrinkage of $8,371.55 as compared with the book inventory. While we are not, of course, in a position to be held responsible for the correctness of the quantities in the second inventory, our representatives made extensive spot checks the following day and found a few discrepancies, all of which were of a minor nature." [1164]

d. INTERNAL CHECK AND CONTROL

The perennial problem in the wholesale houses was the difficulty encountered because of faulty bookkeeping and the inadequacy of internal control primarily due to the small staffs in the houses. Price, Waterhouse & Co., in accordance with Coster's request, reported to him each year on the condition of each house. These reports were brief letters transmitting financial statements and giving a summary of significant financial changes during the year, accounting for changes in profit, and closing with special reference to weaknesses in internal check and control. These letters were reviewed by McGloon and copies or extracts[1165] were sent to the divisional vice-presidents in charge of the houses involved for remedial action.

[1160] R. 2168–2169, 2193–2195, 2204–2205.

[1161] R. 2514–2516.

[1162] R. 2534, 2537.

[1163] R. 2577–2579.

[1164] Ex. 242. Price, Waterhouse & Co.'s letter to F. D. Coster, February 19, 1932, re McKesson-Peter-Neat-Richardson Company.

[1165] Ex. 246.

A summary of the comments in these letters for the years 1931, 1934, and 1937, gives a birdseye view of the nature and persistence of the weaknesses reported. Criticisms were most frequent in 1931, which might have been expected because of the short time since the organization of the Company. The 1934 letters were relatively free from criticism although some chronic cases seemed to persist. In 1937 there was a recurrence of rather wide criticism, especially on the score that accounting staffs were too small to permit of adequate internal control. Specific topics covered in the several years included general cash control, handling of petty cash, control of cash and c. o. d. sales, payrolls, inventories, bad debts and allowances, consignments in, charge sales, purchases, claims, and the handling of customers' and creditors' accounts. The most frequent criticisms, in addition to inadequate staff, were on the handling of cash and cash sales. The criticisms, in one year or another, were reported by every Price, Waterhouse & Co. office in this country and judging from letters available were lodged against all but seven of the 57 wholesale houses acquired prior to 1934. Of 20 units organized after 1931 (mostly liquor units) eight escaped specific criticism, while nine had inadequate accounting staffs to afford effective control (as well as other specified weaknesses in five cases—in one of these cases weaknesses reported in 1934 had not been corrected by 1937).[1166]

Some of these comments and criticisms are quoted below from letters covering the 1931 audit. Except for the first letter which was addressed to the New York office of Price, Waterhouse & Co. by their Chicago office, all of the remaining quotations are from letters addressed to F. D. Coster, president of McKesson & Robbins, by the New York office of Price, Waterhouse & Co.[1167]

Letter dated February 27, 1932, referring to:

"McKesson-Churchill Drug Company
Burlington, Iowa

"During the recent examination of the books and accounts of the above named Company for the year 1931, our representatives made a brief review of the system of internal check and the following comments set forth the principal weaknesses which came to our attention:

"(1) The Treasurer also serves in the capacity of chief accountant and Credit Manager.

"(2) The Treasurer, as Credit Manager, authorizes credits to customers and also authorizes bad debt write offs, which are not approved by any other official of the Company.

"(3) Checks are not countersigned.

"(4) Payrolls are not checked or otherwise approved and while wages are paid in cash, receipts are not obtained therefor.

1166 Ex. 253.

1167 Ex. (in order quoted) 126, 127, 240, 241, 243, 244, 245.

"(5) The procedure with respect to cash sales is unsatisfactory and it would appear that misappropriation of merchandise could only be detected by observations of officers and employees.

"(6) Vouchers in respect of disbursements from office cash fund are not marked 'paid' or otherwise cancelled so as to preclude their use in support of irregular disbursements.

"(7) Vouchers and supporting documents, such as vendors' invoices, are not always scrutinized by the officers when checks are signed.

"The foregoing observations cover the more important weaknesses noted in the system of internal check and so far as we were able to determine, no apparent improvements or changes were made during the year 1931 in the routine office procedure."

Letter dated March 22, 1932, quoting from letter from Price, Waterhouse & Co., Chicago:

" 'So far as we were able to determine, there has been no substantial improvement during the year 1931 in the system of internal check at any of the points visited by us and it would appear that the companies are not generally safeguarded against misappropriation of merchandise excepting as to such special stocks as liquors, narcotics, etc.

'We realize that the organization of most of the subsidiary companies does not permit the arranging of the office duties in such a manner as to provide an adequate system of internal check and it is not unlikely that in most of the smaller companies, the chief source of protection must be in obtaining suitable and sufficient amount of fidelity insurance.' "

Letter dated February 20, 1932, in regard to McKesson-More & Porterfield, a division covered by the above general comment:

"With reference to the company's accounting records and the system of internal check, our representatives have offered the following comments:

'(1) The cashier is in charge of all accounting records including the general ledger, which is posted by the cashier.

(2) Checks are not countersigned.

(3) Vouchers and supporting documents have not been presented to officials simultaneously with checks presented for signature.

(4) Petty cash vouchers have not been cancelled so as to preclude their use a second time.

(5) Cashier reconciles bank accounts.

(6) Cash funds are not audited by an official or a responsible employee.

(7) Cash sales are not adequately safeguarded.

(8) Checks are issued payable to currency.

(9) Treasurer at times opens the mail and an independent record of incoming remittances is not prepared.

(10) Cashier prepares payrolls and generally distributes salaries and wages. Temporary employees are paid in cash and receipts are not obtained for cash payments.

(11) Accounts receivable ledger clerks also check extensions on sales invoices.

(12) Secretary and Treasurer is also credit manager and authorizes bad debt write offs, which are not otherwise approved.

(13) Notes on hand are not regularly balanced with relative control account.

(14) Excepting in the case of liquors, narcotics and a few other items, there is no satisfactory check against misappropriation of merchandise by employees.

(15) The procedure with respect of city orders does not afford a check as to whether all such orders are properly charged on books.

The books were found to have been carefully kept and so far as the examination extended there is no reason to question the general accuracy of the accounts for the year.' "

Letter dated Febuary 17, 1932, re McKesson-Pacific Drug Company:

"With reference to the company's system of internal check, our Portland representatives have written us as follows:

'In connection with our examination for the prior year, various weaknesses were found in the company's accounting methods which were fully discussed with Mr. Woodruff and Mr. Fry and our recommendations were set forth in our letter to the company under date of February 20, 1931. While certain changes have been made in the company's routine, it is found for the most part, that our suggestions have not been adopted and the condition at present is still subject to criticism. It does not appear that the local officials are willing to accept our recommendations as they feel that the present practice is satisfactory. The absence of internal check in certain respects appears to us to be sufficiently important to require the serious consideration of the officials of the parent company.' " (Detailed criticism omitted to avoid repetition.)

Letter dated February 20, 1932, re McKesson-Schuh Drug Company:

" 'Certain matters concerning the system of accounting and internal check are discussed in the memorandum. *Mr. Schuh does not appear disposed to adopt our suggestions.* In considering the system of internal check, it should be borne in mind that the organization is very small.' " [Italics supplied.] (Compare with letter in 1934 and 1937 to follow.)

Letter dated February 20, 1932 re McKesson-Springfield Drug Company:

"Our representatives have written as follows regarding the company's system of internal check:

'We made a study of the system of internal check at this company and found it to be weak, mainly because of the numerous duties handled by one comparatively low-salaried employee, Mr. Jones, the accountant at this office. He is in charge of all books of account, is also credit manager, assistant treasurer, office manager and secretary of the corporation. Although he claims that he would discuss any bad accounts with the treasurer before charging them off, he evidently has authority to charge them off without doing so. A few small accounts were charged off during the period without being taken up with the treasurer. All mail pertaining to the accounts is opened by Mr. Jones.' "

Letter dated February 6, 1932, re McKesson-Whittlesey Company:

"In connection with our audit, we made it a point to look into this company's system of internal check. We consider the system of internal check inadequate to provide the necessary safeguard against malpractices, relative to the following matters:

(a) Cash in bank and on hand:

1. Checks may be signed by any one of five people, including the bookkeeper but they are not countersigned.

2. Vouchers and supporting documents are not presented to officials for inspection simultaneously with the checks presented for signature.

3. Supporting documents to vouchers are not impressed with paid stamp or other distinctive mark so as to prevent the presentation thereof for duplicate payment.

4. Bank accounts are reconciled by the same employee keeping cash records and preparing checks.

5. An independent record of incoming remittances is not prepared for comparison later with the collections recorded by the cashier.

6. No maximum figure has been established for payments out of imprest fund.

7. Receipts or other documentary evidence supporting disbursements from imprest fund are not cancelled to preclude the use thereof in support of fictitious disbursements.

8. Payrolls are not checked or approved; authorizations for increases are not kept on file.

(b) Accounts receivable:

1. No control is exercised over customers' accounts; charges are posted to accounts receivable cards and the totals of postings for the day are recorded in the general ledger.

2. No control is exercised over bad debts after they are written off.

(c) Sales:

1. Sales orders are not registered before being sent to stockroom for shipment.

2. No control is exercised over shipping orders and/or invoices to ensure proper charge to accounts."

The following are extracts from Price, Waterhouse & Co. letters compiled by McGloon and sent to divisional vice-presidents for consideration and action following the 1934 audit.[1168]

"*Eastern Wine & Spirits, Inc.:*

* * * * * * *

'The internal check of the company was reviewed by us and found to be very unsatisfactory. The principal weaknesses are, briefly, as follows:

1. Inadequate inventory control.
2. Many checks are drawn to the order of "cash" and are not endorsed.
3. Cash receipts have not regularly been deposited daily intact.
4. There were no written approvals of payroll, either as to amount or rates.
5. There are no written approvals of write-offs of customers' accounts and salesmen's balances.

In general, we found an extreme laxity in many features of the accounting procedure. Disbursements in many cases were not supported by adequate evidence as to the propriety of the payment. The organization is small and no effective system of check of the work of individual employees by other employees has yet been developed.'

* * * * * * *

"*McKesson-Berry-Martin:*

* * * * * * *

' "Regarding the system of internal check, we are pleased to report that the majority of our recommendations have been adopted by the company, and it is hoped that further improvements will be made in the near future. However, as previously explained, the organization is too small to permit of a very satisfactory system of internal control." '

* * * * * * *

"*McKesson-Peter-Neat:*

* * * * * * *

[1168] Ex. 246.

'Our representatives state that the office force is too small to provide an adequate system of internal control, but they have suggested that the practice of officials signing blank checks should be discontinued.'

* * * * * * *

"*McKesson-Fuller-Morrisson:*

* * * * * * *

'Our representatives understand that the accounts of the branch are examined from time to time by a representative of the head office, and they believe that these examinations should be fairly extensive in view of the fact that the responsibilities of the local officials are not divided sufficiently to provide the usual accounting safeguards.'

* * * * * * *

"*McKesson-Schuh:*

'Our representatives have advised us that the branch's system of internal check, which was mentioned in our letter to you of February 16, 1934, has been changed very little during the year. Our representatives have again this year written a letter to Mr. Schuh on this subject.' "

The following comments are from letters addressed to F. D. Coster, president of McKesson & Robbins, by the New York office of Price, Waterhouse & Co. following completion of the 1937 examinations: [1169]

Billings Division:

"Since one employee does a large part of the office work, there is no effective system of internal check."

McKesson Liquor Co. (Boston):

"Our Boston office made the following comments regarding the system of internal check:

'During November 1937 the office and warehouse of the Boston division of the company was moved from 14 Fulton Street, the location of the Boston division of McKesson & Robbins, Incorporated, to 481 Summer Street. The separation of the two organizations necessitated many changes in the system of accounting and control, and rearrangement of duties of the office personnel of this company. We feel that there now are several weaknesses in the system of internal check at the Boston division of this company, the more important of which are as follows:

(1) The cashier, who receives incoming mail remittances and makes up the daily deposit, also assists the credit manager and, in this capacity, necessarily has access to the accounts receivable ledger cards.

(2) The division accountant keeps the cash records and the general books, reconciles the bank account, vouches the invoices previously approved by the purchasing department, and draws and countersigns the checks.

(3) The checks are signed by the division manager, but we understand that the voucher jackets only, without the supporting documents, are presented to him at the time the checks are presented for signature.

(4) Individual invoices are not invariably stamped "paid" or otherwise cancelled to prevent duplicate payment, although the voucher jacket attached to one or more invoices is always so stamped.

(5) From our discussion, it appears that the company does not invariably account for sales invoices by number each day to be sure that all invoices are listed on the daily sales summary and are posted to the control and to the customers' accounts. There may be some further weakness in the fact that sales invoices are not prenumbered but are numbered consecutively by a numbering machine after the invoice has been made out.

[1169] Ex. (in order quoted) 248, 249, 250, 251, 247.

'We have discussed the above weaknesses with the division accountant and have made such suggestions for strengthening the system as seemed to us to be practicable. To some extent the weaknesses are inherent in an organization of this relatively small size, because of the limited number of office employees to whom the various duties and functions may be assigned.

'For several years we have recommended a perpetual stock record for this company, which we feel could be maintained with relatively little additional expense. The principal advantages seem to us to be:

(1) Better accounting control and protection.

(2) Better control over purchasing.

(3) Possible elimination of the present procedure of taking physical inventories once a month.

(4) Possible savings of time in

(a) Preparing the required monthly state tax reports.

(b) Pricing the inventories each month or every six months.

(c) Listing stocks of intercompany merchandise.

'The system of internal check of the Springfield division appears to be reasonably satisfactory.' "

Milwaukee Drug Division:

"Our Milwaukee office made the following comments with regard to weaknesses in the system of internal check:

'(A) The cashier has access to the customers' ledgers; he assists in preparing customers' statements and investigates differences reported by customers.

'(B) The general ledger bookkeeper (1) reconciles the bank accounts (including payroll accounts); (2) prepares and countersigns checks drawn on the general bank account; and (3) prepares, signs and distributes the payroll checks.

'(C) No independent record of remittances received through the mail is maintained for comparison later with recorded cash collections.

'(D) Receipts and other evidence supporting petty cash disbursements are not cancelled or impressed with a 'paid' stamp. (We were advised that this would be done in the future).

'(E) The payroll is not checked or approved before payment thereof (See (B) above).' "

Rochester Division

"With reference to the system of internal check, our Buffalo office has reported the following weaknesses which came to their attention:

(1) No independent record of incoming remittances is prepared for comparison later with the collections recorded by the Cashier.

(2) Pay envelopes are distributed by Mr. Nelson who also checks payroll. Occasionally envelopes are distributed by Mr. Fairchild, Assistant to Mr. Nelson, who prepares payroll.

(3) Differences in accounts receivable reported by customers are investigated by General Cashier who also keeps cash receipts book wherein collections on accounts receivable are recorded for posting to customers' accounts."

Schuh Drug Division:

"The comments of our St. Louis office regarding the system of internal check are quoted below:

'1. Preparation of request for petty cash reimbursement, compiling and approving of supporting data, and cashing of reimbursing cheque all done by same man, who also signs cheques, reconciles bank accounts, distributes payroll, and keeps general ledger.

'2. It was observed that certain disbursements from petty cash during November and December had no supporting data attached.

'3. Receipts evidencing petty cash disbursements are not approved until reimbursed.

'4. Petty cash receipts are usually written in pencil, and the amounts appear to be frequently changed.

'5. There is no adequate check on cash sales, and no independent record is made of incoming receipts.

'6. Receipts are not deposited intact, due to sundry cheques cashed and expenditures made therefrom.

'7. Payroll is paid in cash; employees sign for pay received, but sheet does not show amount paid.

'8. Accounts receivable records are kept by the cashier.

'9. It was noted that merchandise stock is accessible to sundry persons during and after regular business hours.

'10. During December, 1937, and January, 1938, * * *, vice-president, and * * *, office manager, drew their salaries in advance. On January 14, * * * drew $150 against his February salary.' "

These letters are an effective demonstration of the conditions under which the audit of the wholesale houses was carried out. The situation in the McKesson-Schuh Division is an outstanding example of the lack of understanding on the part of the vice-presidents in charge of the houses as to auditing methods and the necessity for observing, in so far as personnel permits, of sound methods of internal control. With the weaknesses set forth in the last quotation in mind one series of three letters and a memorandum is of special interest. The first letter dated January 24, 1938, from Price, Waterhouse & Co.'s St. Louis office to the New York office enclosed a schedule of discrepancies uncovered in an examination of petty cash vouchers. The list included an exceptionally wide range of methods of falsification in this limited sphere of action. A copy of this schedule had been given to Schuh when unsatisfactory explanations were obtained from the cashier, who complained to the auditors that they were spending an unreasonable time on a petty cash fund of $300. The New York office passed the schedule on to McGloon by letter dated January 28, 1938. The following letter from Price, Waterhouse & Co.'s New York office to their St. Louis office on March 16, 1938, closed the matter:

"McKesson & Robbins, Incorporated,
Schuh Drug Division

"You may be interested to know that, as a result of the information and recommendations in your memorandum and letter of January 24, 1938, the comptroller at Bridgeport made an investigation of the accounts of the above-named division which disclosed a defalcation of at least several hundred dollars.

"Before the investigation was completed, the office manager, * * * confessed that he had been misappropriating funds over a period of several months. We understand that most of the money was taken from the petty cash fund in the manner suggested in your letter, but we have not been furnished with full particulars." [1170]

[1170] Ex. 252.

e. INTERNAL AUDIT—TRAVELING AUDITORS

One is entitled to ask what McKesson & Robbins did after 1928 by way of improving accounting methods in the wholesale houses to prevent such occurrences as the above. The answer must be—very little consistently [1171] other than to rely on their independent auditors, even though the engagement was not for a detailed audit such as might be expected to review sufficient transactions to uncover such minor defalcations as occurred repeatedly at one place or another in the organization.

It should be said, however, that McGloon undertook at the outset to bring order out of chaos by designing a uniform system of accounts for all the houses with uniform financial statements and reports to be supplied to the home office. This was to be made effective January 1, 1929. McGloon held meetings of the wholesale house accountants to instruct them in the new procedures.[1172] He also attempted from the beginning to establish a corps of travelling auditors. For a short period in 1929 he had four or five but these were discharged because the other officials thought they were too expensive. In 1932 he worked on a program for such auditors and invited Price, Waterhouse & Co. to prepare an outline of procedure for such a staff. This was submitted under date of September 22, 1932. A few years after that, one auditor was employed but was immediately assigned to divisional vice-presidents for special work and never carried out the duties of a travelling auditor under the jurisdiction of the comptroller's office. The point was raised repeatedly, and as recently as October 1938. At that time McGloon wrote a memorandum to Coster suggesting three travelling auditors. The result was a decision that the estimated cost of $30,000 per year was too expensive, so the less costly procedure of increasing the fidelity insurance from $100,000 to $250,000 was adopted, although losses sustained in a case then pending in one branch house were in excess of the amount that could be proven to the satisfaction of the insurance company.[1173]

Not all of McGloon's difficulty in this regard can be charged to Coster's ideas. Some of the directors who were heads of wholesale houses had a mistaken idea of the duties and services that could be rendered by a permanent staff of travelling auditors. Bedsole of Mobile, for example, thought that after the auditors had aided in

[1171] R. 1596; Ex. 14 (p. 13).

[1172] R. 1570, 1573–1574.

[1173] R. 1579-1583, 1674–1676; Ex. 91, 125.

establishing a good system, their services were no longer required.[1174] Doerr, at one time chairman of the Sub-committee on Accounting, seemed to think that the travelling auditors were a crew of trouble shooters rather than a regular preventative measure. In his opinion the Bridgeport office control of accounting methods ended with letters from McGloon, after that it was the duty of the divisional vice-presidents to see that the houses complied with instructions.[1175] Michaels, who succeeded Coster as president, was very vague on this subject.[1176] Faxon, secretary of the Corporation as well as vice-president and director, testified that the methods in the 60 houses were different and that McGloon tried to control them by issuing bulletins from Bridgeport. He thought travelling auditors went around looking for trouble but were hired primarily to bring the accounting system into better shape.[1177] Of the directors examined on this point, Murray seemed to have the best conception of the duty of travelling auditors. He agreed with McGloon that insurance was not an adequate substitute.[1178]

Rowbotham's appraisal of travelling auditors and fidelity insurance and their relation to the audit is appropriate here. He felt that in a situation such as this in which it was impossible to have adequate internal control in each house that both travelling auditors and fidelity insurance were necessary—the two were not mutually exclusive but as an accountant he thought that the travelling auditors should come first, although in his experience, their work was never as satisfactory in practice as it seemed to promise in theory. The reason for this weakness in most companies was that the travelling auditors felt that they had no opportunity to advance in such work. Rowbotham cited

---

1174 "Q. [By Mr. GALPEER] Now, Mr. Bedsole, was it customary for McKesson to employ travelling auditors of their own in addition to the annual audits?

A. They did, at times.

Q. But it was not a regular habit?

A. I think maybe they had some up until recently, but there have been no travelling auditors in our division for some years.

Q. What is your view on that, Mr. Bedsole? Do you think it is advisable, inadvisable? Why did you have it at one time, and why not at others?

A. Well, the committee voted at one time that we would have some travelling auditors, principally, as I remember it, to check the internal methods of operation, and to throw up certain safeguards, or throw out certain weaknesses. There was an auditor that came down in my division and worked all the houses, but that was the greatest good that I got from him—revealing certain weaknesses, maybe, and handling certain C. O. D. sales, and things of that kind—credit memoranda, for instance.

Q. Why was it abolished, then, if it did a certain amount of good?

A. You couldn't keep on, you know. If you have the thing going good, you have a good system set up, why change again?

Q. So that these men just came in principally to check the system, you might say, and then they would make their reports to you, would they?

A. Well, they made their reports to Mr. McGloon and to me. That is, the gentlemen who worked in my division did.

Q. Who put the reforms into operation?

A. I did." R. 2496-2497.

1175 R. 2555-2557.

1176 R. 4284-4288.

1177 R. 2526-2528.

1178 R. 2164-2166.

one example, however, where this difficulty was overcome by the president of a corporation who happened to be a certified public accountant. This man employed certified public accountants for his travelling auditors and promised them that promotion to comptrollers of the subsidiary companies would be made from their group.[1179]

The auditors' appraisal of conditions in respect to internal check and control in the wholesale houses as they affected the audit work in contrast with those in the crude drug operations at Bridgeport are significant. In the wholesale houses more extensive cash work was done because the transactions in the houses were large in number but relatively small in unit dollar values and involved the handling of numerous receipts in money rather than in checks. Furthermore, Thorn emphasized the division of control in the wholesale houses where he felt that there was no one executive with sufficient knowledge of all operations to serve as an effective check on the bookkeeper in the absence of an adequate mechanical system of internal check. At Bridgeport, however, although several operating functions were controlled by George E. Dietrich, less auditing work was believed necessary than in the other branches because very little cash was handled. It will be recalled that all receipts and disbursements arising from sales and purchases of foreign crude drug stocks were large in dollar value and relatively few in number of transactions and, since 1932, were cleared directly through what was considered to be a bank (Manning & Company) and were reported by it on debit and credit forms. In addition there was the fact that Coster was supposed to have had detailed knowledge of all of these operations and to have exercised close supervision over them.[1180]

McGloon, the comptroller of the Corporation, had a somewhat different conception of the effect of the differences in organization at Bridgeport and the wholesale houses. He testified that the greater separation of duties in the houses would have required more widespread collusion among the Company's operating executives than was necessary at Bridgeport for concealment of a fraud such as was carried on by the Musica brothers disguised as: president, Coster; assistant treasurer, buying and sales manager, George E. Dietrich; and Robert J. Dietrich, head of the shipping, receiving and stockkeeping departments.[1181]

As has been seen more auditing work was done in the branches on the cash program because of weaknesses in internal check and control

---

1179 R. 1963–1973.

1180 "Q. [By Mr. STEWART.] And is it also true that in the wholesale houses, for the most part, there was no one executive who had sufficient knowledge of the transactions to operate as a check upon the bookkeeper, in the absence of an adequate system of internal check on the bookkeeper?

A. [By THORN] Yes, that is true. Even in the smaller wholesale houses there are usually three or four operating heads.

Q. As contrasted, for example, with the unity of operating head in the crude drug division at Bridgeport?

A. Yes, that's right." R. 4544.

1181 R. 1653–1658.

than was considered necessary at Bridgeport [1182] even though in Rowbotham's opinion Coster exercised a very salutary influence on the divisional vice-presidents and the accounting in these units.[1183] The additional work was done despite the fact that in the larger units of the wholesale houses there was a greater subdivision of functions among the executive staffs than in the crude drug operations.

K. REVIEW PROCEDURE

Review procedure and the mechanical preparation of the report are so inseparable that these phases must be considered together. However, the content of the finished product and the uses to which it was put are reserved for separate consideration in the next subsection. A very brief preview of the review procedure was obtained from Rowbotham on the first day of the hearings. The work of juniors as has been observed in foregoing sections was controlled and reviewed by the seniors. The managers of the various offices engaged on the audit reviewed the work of the seniors working out of their offices, and after this review, the papers with a covering memorandum and the accounts on each unit were mailed to New York (except on units handled directly by the New York office) where the manager of the entire engagement reviewed the papers preliminary to preparing the consolidated accounts. The partner in charge did not go over the individual working papers but kept himself posted generally during the progress of the job and finally reviewed all accounting points that arose.[1184] Working in this way Rowbotham, the partner in charge of McKesson, handled at least 20 engagements during the year.[1185]

The first reports to be completed were those covering individual units of the Company. The manager in charge in New York (in recent years Thorn) wrote a letter to Coster on each one based on the memorandum accompanying the working papers when mailed in or brought in to the New York office.[1186] The nature of these letters was discussed in some detail in the preceding subsection of this report. They were all read and signed by Rowbotham for the firm.[1187] Two copies of the accounts were supplied, one for McGloon's files and one for the head of each house in question, but these letters and accounts were not sent to the directors as such, except as they might head particular houses.

On work done under his direct supervision, Thorn sat down with the senior in charge who would have with him the working papers, a draft of the financial statements, and usually a brief memorandum on

[1182] Footnotes 679, 686 *supra*.
[1183] R. 1836–1837; footnote 552 *supra*.
[1184] R. 24–25, 74–75, 83–85, 879–880, 1915–1916.
[1185] R. 33.
[1186] R. 95, 880–881.
[1187] R. 883, 1929–1931.

the accounts. Similar memoranda have been referred to repeatedly in telling the story of the work done at Bridgeport. The first step was to check the figures on the draft financial statements to the principal schedules in the working papers and from these to the underlying schedules. The papers then were reviewed in detail and any questions raised were discussed until the work was "pretty well covered." Such a review consumed several hours, after which the draft statements were approved for typing.[1188] In most years Thorn made a preliminary review of the Bridgeport papers at the client's office.[1189]

Rowbotham's review of the work was a more or less continuous affair as the letters mentioned above were completed on each division but was most thorough when the accounts of the Connecticut Division, Canadian Company, and lastly the consolidated accounts for the entire organization were ready.[1190] The accounts on the Bridgeport units were accompanied by memoranda referred to above but were submitted to Coster usually without comment, because any comment necessary was conveyed directly while the work was in progress; "* * * In other words we would be reporting to them on their own houses in that case." [1191] The consolidated accounts were part of a long form report the contents of which are described in the next subsection.

This review by Rowbotham was confined to what he termed the points of the job and did not involve a review of the questionnaires on internal check and control or of the working papers except for occasional reference purposes. The internal check and control at Bridgeport, it will be recalled, Thorn, who was considered competent to judge, told him was good.[1192] The principal points of the job, however, were: the possibility of exchange restrictions on the foreign accounts; the increase in accounts receivable; the relationship of W. W. Smith & Co. to McKesson and the ability of Smith to make good on the guaranty; whether circularization of receivables was necessary; reserves for doubtful accounts; increase in inventories and their basis of valuation; the method of confirming inventories held by suppliers; purchase and sales commitments; the spice department; foreign exchange problems; and a comparison of the current accounts with the previous year. In addition, the manner of presenting the accounts was given a great deal of consideration and finally there was the question of whether exceptions should be taken in drafting the opinion on the accounts. In recent years the relationship of the accounts to the annual reports filed with the Securities and Exchange Commission was an added problem. This recital, it was testified, was

---

1188 R. 881-882.

1189 R. 878.

1190 R. 1921-1932.

1191 Testimony of Thorn, R. 882.

1192 R. 1921, 1932-1934.

illustrative of the kind of questions raised but neither Rowbotham nor Thorn had a formal list or review program.[1193]

To make this story complete as to mechanical details reference must be made to the firm's Office Manual and to the booklet written by Berger. This booklet states that only after the reports and statements have been reviewed by the partner and approved by him are they ready for typing.[1194] The Office Manual required that the office copy of the typed report and accounts be submitted to one of the assistants who worked on the engagement for checking of all footings, cross footings, and references. Corrections made in the office copy must be called back to all the other copies as corrected, after which the partner, manager, or senior responsible for the work must initial the office copy before any of the other copies may be released. "The senior assistants in charge of the work must themselves read through * * *" the finished report before submitting it to the partner for final approval.[1195]

Advice on review procedure is also contained in Berger's dissertation on "Organization Ethics and Team Work." [1196] He counsels all staff men to write the best report of which they are capable before submitting it to the principal with whom they should have had a preliminary discussion on exceptional points before starting to write. The extent of the principal's review will then depend upon the importance of the engagement, the accounting difficulties involved in the business, the ability of the staff man in charge, and the knowledge of the engagement possessed by the principal.

> "Regardless of the extent of the review, the man in charge should be fully prepared to make all necessary explanations and to submit evidence therefor when called for and generally to show a complete mastery of the work, as nothing is so convincing in inspiring confidence as a ready and decisive answer to all pertinent questions regarding the work." [1197]

The paragraph following the above quotation is a fitting conclusion for this section:

> "Similar to the requirement previously mentioned that the assistant should draw the attention of the man in charge to any important points developed, so likewise should the latter report to the principal any points of doubt affecting the integrity of the accounts or the sufficiency of the verification without waiting for this information to be elicited by questioning. The responsibilities of the profession are necessarily broad and it would be folly to add to those which are inherent in the work any further dangers resulting from a lack of coordination between the people involved in the various steps needed to submit the findings to the client. Above all the man in charge should not show a spirit of resenting changes or criticism by a principal or of impatience when the review is more extended than was expected."

1193 R. 2034-2040, 879.
1194 Ex. 168 (pp. 26-27.)
1195 Ex. 121 (p. 15).
1196 Ex. 168 (p. 23).
1197 Ex. 168 (p. 23).

L. THE REPORT AND CERTIFICATE

Berger wrote the paper from which we have quoted in the preceding subsection in the same year in which Girard & Co., Inc. was formed, and Price, Waterhouse & Co. published it privately for the benefit of their staff in the year in which their first report was rendered to F. D. Coster, president of Girard & Co., Inc. Since this booklet was adopted as an adjunct to the booklet of office rules, its doctrine, in respect to report writing, may be considered as controlling.[1198] The following extract forms an excellent background for the discussion to follow:

"Where detailed reports are submitted for the use of the management little need be added to what has already been said except that there should be intelligent discussion of the figures and points of interest and of the basis upon which the accounts have been prepared, and attention should be drawn to any shortcomings in the company's accounting practices and questions affecting the integrity of the accounts. With such full comments, the accountant should be fully protected against a charge of making insufficient disclosure of material points.

"A much greater responsibility, however, attaches to the giving of certificates in condensed form wherein the accountant declares within a few words or sentences that in his opinion the accounts set forth the true financial position or the correct results from operation. Among the more important purposes for which such brief certificates are issued may be mentioned:

Annual reports to stockholders,

Submission to Banks and Note Brokers for credit purposes,

Submission to Banks and Investment Houses contemplating the underwriting of securities,

Submission to the public when inviting investment in such securities,

Submission to Trustees of bond issues or other agent acting for the protection of security holders,

Settlement of dispute between parties,

Confirmation of figures called for under the provisions of a Contract.

"As a rule the recipients of such certificates are not furnished with the detailed report to the management and have not the time or inclination, or perhaps even the technical ability, to go into the details but form their judgment on the information contained in the bare certificates and the statements which accompany them. This makes it necessary to determine whether the accounts read in conjunction with the certificate make the facts sufficiently clear to set forth all material points, which immediately brings up the question whether the client is entitled to a 'clean' certificate or whether a qualification is necessary to put the stockholders, creditors, prospective investors or other interested party on guard as to any point of doubtful propriety.

"In considering the form of the certificate it is necessary to take a detached view and reason out carefully the rights and interests of all people involved and then reach a decision which is fair to the client and the public and yet protects the firm in its responsibilities to both. When a qualification seems desirable the client should be given the opportunity of stating his side of the case and where his information and views are not convincing as a rule he will be prepared to cure the defect so as to remove the qualification. On the other hand the principal in

[1198] R. O. Berger signed the booklet in Chicago, May 1, 1923, and the cover carries the date 1925.

representing the firm should show a combination of reasonableness and firmness and have the courage to resist undue pressure and be prepared to withdraw from the work and give up the connection rather than submit a certificate more favorable than the client is entitled to." [1199]

The detailed or long-form reports to management during the entire history of the engagement were addressed to F. D. Coster, president of the successive corporations. Such long-form reports were rendered on Girard & Co., Inc., on the Connecticut and Canadian Companies through 1929 and thereafter only on the Maryland Company. The certificates, beginning with the first balance sheet for Girard & Co., Inc. at December 31, 1924, carried no salutation until the certificate on the Maryland Company accounts for 1930, which was addressed to the directors, setting a style to be followed thereafter. The Canadian Company certificates in the published reports were addressed to the shareholders in accordance with the requirements of the Dominion's Companies Act.

The content of the detailed reports to Coster on the Girard & Co., Inc. and Connecticut Company examinations through 1929 was uniform in style and followed this general outline:

1. Paragraph transmitting the report and listing exhibits included as follows:
   I. Balance sheet.
   II. Statement of profit and loss.
   III. Statement of cost of sales (Girard & Co., Inc. only).
   IV. Statement of factory burden (beginning with first quarter 1926).
   V. Statement of administrative, selling, and general expenses.
   VI. Statement of paid in surplus (Connecticut Company eight months ended December 31, 1928, only).
   VII. Statement of earned surplus (1928 and 1929).
   VIII. Intercompany accounts receivable December 31, 1929.
   IX. Intercompany accounts payable December 31, 1929.
2. Paragraph on history (1924 and 1926 only).
3. Paragraph on scope of the audit.
4. Paragraph on results of operations (beginning in 1925).
5. Paragraphs discussing principal balance sheet accounts.
6. Section showing changes in financial position including a statement of sources and application of funds supplemented by a detailed comparative statement of current assets and liabilities.[1200]

For the Canadian Company long-form reports were submitted to cover the audit of the last 8 months of 1928 and the year 1929. Each of these consisted of three pages of comments and three statements—balance sheet, statement of surplus, and statement of profit and loss for the period.[1201] Thereafter only the statements accompanied by a certificate addressed to the shareholders was supplied on this unit.

The first full report on the Maryland Company was written by Jaureguy and set the pattern for those to follow. It included 22

[1199] Ex. 168 (pp. 24—25).
[1200] Ex. 138-148, 151.
[1201] Ex. 149, 150.

pages of text and 13 exhibits bound in a gold stamped leather cover. The exhibits included a consolidated balance sheet, consolidated profit and loss statements for 2 years; analyses of surplus; summaries for 2 years by companies of notes and accounts receivable, inventories, advances to customers and instalment notes and accounts receivable, miscellaneous investments and deposits; and analysis of mortgages payable and other long-term obligations. This list varied somewhat during the years. For 1930 and several years thereafter consolidating statements were included. The number of exhibits reached a maximum for 1932 and 1933 when 19 and 20 exhibits respectively were included. The list was reduced to 10 for the last 2 years 1936 and 1937. Throughout the period 2-year comparisons by divisions and companies of current notes and accounts receivable, inventories, non-current notes and accounts receivable, and trade and miscellaneous investments were presented. These schedules therefore gave totals for these categories for the Connecticut Division and for the Canadian Company, but no departmental analysis for either.[1202]

The review of these long-form reports was an important part of Rowbotham's duties as partner in charge of the engagement. Their texts were devoted primarily to the financing of the Company and to the balance sheet accounts, closing with a statement regarding the legality of dividends. A brief statement of the scope of the audit followed the introductory statement and list of exhibits.[1203] No comments on operating accounts were included. The customary closing paragraph acknowledging the facilities extended, used for 1929 and 1930 only, stated "* * * that all information required by us for the purposes of the examination was readily obtained."[1204] The signature of Price, Waterhouse & Co. was by Rowbotham throughout the period of the Maryland Company. Six copies of these detailed reports were delivered to Coster each year but most of the directors who testified at the Commission's hearings said that they had never seen them before and had never asked to see them but did get the letters and accounts on their own houses and the published stockholders' report.[1205]

There follows a consideration of the text of all of the long-form reports in which there were comments by the auditors dealing directly with the foreign crude drug operations and comments which might

[1202] Ex. 152–160.

[1203] See pages 153–154 *supra*.

[1204] Ex. 152, 153.

[1205] Thompson (treasurer and director) read the full report each year but did not think it ever was submitted to a board meeting, R. 2111; Pettingill (lawyer) saw one of these about 2 weeks prior to December 5, 1938, R. 2226; Phillips (investment banker) did not remember seeing anything but the published report, R. 2352 and 2368; Weinberg (investment banker) had seen the published report only, R. 2399–2401; Cummings (lawyer) had seen the private report recently, R. 2448; Michaels, Murray, Bedsole, and Faxon (wholesalers) had not seen the leather-bound report, R. 4294, 2177, 2498–2499, 2528; but Doerr had seen one several years ago, R. 2588–2589.

have suggested such a business or which might have provoked an inquiry thereon.

Comments on the cash work, from time to time through the reports, mentioned that bank acceptances of varying but substantial amounts arose from export sales of bulk stock, the first such comment being in the report on the Connecticut Company for the 4 months ended March 31, 1927.[1206] Similar references appeared in reports on the Canadian Company for 1928,[1207] in the last separate report on the Connecticut Company (1929)[1208] and in the 1929 report on the Maryland Company in which the item was referred to as arising from export sales by the Connecticut Company and its Canadian subsidiary.[1209] In connection with these comments it may be recalled that, beginning in 1931, the collections from foreign crude drug customers were supposed to have been made through Manning & Company but neither this fact nor the name Manning & Company was mentioned in any of the reports.

The excellent condition of the foreign accounts receivable was the subject of frequent comment in the reports as was noted in the discussion of the receivables phase of the audit program. That the fictitious foreign business was a development from the Girard & Co., Inc. business is suggested, not only by the fact that the accounts receivable at December 31, 1924 seemed to be remarkably good,[1210] the outstanding characteristic of the fictitious accounts, but also by the gradual evolution in the descriptions used in the classification of the receivables in succeeding reports. The second report on the Connecticut Company classified customers' accounts as "Domestic" and "Foreign" and aged each group. "Domestic" was subdivided in another table to show "Retailers, wholesalers and jobbers" separate from "Distributors".[1211] The third report showed the classes of accounts as:

"Wholesalers, distributors, etc:
    Wholesalers and jobbers.
    Distributors.
    Girard division—foreign and domestic.
Export department:
    Spanish.
    Foreign.
    City Export."[1212]

But following this was an aging schedule in which "Wholesalers, jobbers and distributors" were grouped and agreed with the sum of

---

1206 Ex. 145.

1207 Ex. 149.

1208 Ex. 151.

1209 Ex. 152.

1210 "Customers' accounts aggregating $34,692.40 had all been paid at the date of examination with the exception of two accounts amounting to $2,625.18, which were considered good and collectible." Ex. 138, dated March 9, 1925. Reference is also made in a later report to "* * * the insurance company which has insured their collectibility." Ex. 140. Coster, in his President's Report for 1925, says, "We have had no bad debts in 1925." Ex. 176.

1211 Ex. 145 (p. 4).

1212 Ex. 146 (p. 5).

the two groups so named above, as did a separate aging for "Export department", but the amounts under "Special foreign (Girard division)" agreed in total with the amounts shown under "Girard division—foreign and domestic" in the previous list.[1213] The next report for the first 4 months of 1928 used the terms "Distributors", "General" and "Export department" with the amounts involved indicating that "General" [1214] referred to the business previously described as "Special foreign (Girard division)". The term "General" was retained in the final reports submitted for the Connecticut Company [1215] but included some accounts other than those arising from foreign sales of crude drugs. The last report on the Connecticut Company (for the year 1929) contained the following paragraph which is a typical comment as to the collectibility of the Connecticut and Canadian Company foreign accounts receivable:

> "The trade accounts receivable have increased $2,107,191.35 during the year largely as the result of larger balances arising through the export sales of crude drugs. Despite this increase in the balances, no proportionate increase in the reserve for doubtful accounts was considered necessary because past experience has shown these foreign accounts to be safe and liquid. No credit losses have been sustained by the company thus far in this department of the business." [1216]

The increase referred to resulted in over three times the balances due at the close of the preceding year.

Although the Maryland Company reports beginning with 1929 did not present analyses of the customers' accounts receivable, in 1930 the report referred to increased sales of crude drugs and raw materials in the Connecticut and Canadian Companies and in 1932 the report in commenting on a reduction in receivables of approximately $1,900,000 during the year stated: "* * * This reduction is net, the receivables of McKesson & Robbins, Incorporated (Connecticut) and McKesson & Robbins, Limited, principally due from foreign customers, having increased approximately $1,100,000 while the balance of the receivables were reduced by approximately $3,000,000." [1217] Thereafter comparative figures for 2 years were presented in each report showing total accounts receivable for each company or division of the McKesson organization so that such over-all changes as were formerly commented upon in the text could have been observed by scanning the schedules.[1218]

An interesting account of the changes in the inventories may be traced through the audit reports. Figures of some significance appeared in successive reports on Girard & Co., Inc. through 1926, the last rendered on this company. No comment was offered in the reports, however, on the large quantities of raw material in proportion to the other

[1213] Ex. 146 (pp. 5–6).
[1214] Ex. 147 (p. 4).
[1215] Ex. 148 (pp. 7–8), 151 (pp. 2–3)
[1216] Ex. 151 (p. 3).
[1217] Ex. 153 (p. 20), 155 (p. 17).
[1218] Ex. 156–160.

items or on the doubling of the amount in 2 months as revealed in the following table:[1219]

Inventories of Girard & Co., Inc., as at Sept. 30, 1926 and Nov. 30, 1926

	Sept. 30, 1926	Nov. 30, 1926
Raw materials	$244, 144. 56	$558, 731. 59
Containers and supplies	19, 376. 49	22, 334. 02
Manufactured products	30, 590. 77	25, 699. 86
Total	$294, 111. 82	$606, 765. 47

The report on the Connecticut Company for the 4 months ended March 31, 1927 gave more detail than the above as to inventories, the largest category being described as "Raw materials and crude stock", referred to in subsequent reports as "* * * on hand, in transit and in public warehouses." [1220] Advantage was taken of the simplicity of the crude drug transactions beginning in 1928 to present in the Connecticut Company report an analysis by commodities of changes in the inventory of this class of merchandise. For example at April 30, 1928, an increase in raw materials and crude stock of over two-thirds over the value of raw materials and crude stock on hand at December 31, 1927 is accounted for by the following increases:[1221]

"Commodity:	*Approximate increase during period*
Crude iodine	$230, 000. 00
Santonine crystals	149, 000. 00
Camphor	52, 000. 00
Cod liver oil	28, 000. 00
	$459, 000. 00"

And at the close of the same year, 1928, a further net increase of $330,310.04 in all inventories was accounted for in the Connecticut Company report as follows, but as previously, and in the year to follow, without further comment in the report:[1222]

"It will be noted that the inventory of raw materials and crude stock increased approximately $350,000.00 during the period. In examining the inventories we found increases and decreases in the quantities of certain commodities in approximately the following amounts:

[1219] Ex. 142–143.
[1220] Ex. 145–148, 151.
[1221] Ex. 147 (p. 7).
[1222] Ex. 148 (p. 11).

	Increase	Decrease
Menthol	$233, 000. 00	
Mercury	75, 000. 00	
Senega root	52, 000. 00	
Cod liver oil	49, 000. 00	
Potassium iodide	167, 000. 00	
Crude iodine		$192, 000. 00
Camphor		81, 000. 00
Santonine crystals		24, 000. 00
Miscellaneous raw materials	71, 000. 00	
	$647, 000. 00	$297, 000. 00
	297, 000. 00	
Approximate net increase, as above	$350, 000. 00"	

By December 31, 1929, the inventories of the Connecticut Company had increased $1,345,193.07 over the previous year end, principally in "Raw material and crude stock", $472,242.54; "China wood oil," $348,263.01; "Containers and packing supplies", $154,379.23; and "manufactured products" $385,735.98.[1223]

"The larger items making up the increase of approximately $472,000.00 in the amount of raw materials and crude stock are:

	Increase	Decrease
Menthol		$27, 000. 00
Mercury	$146, 000. 00	
Cod liver oil		30, 000. 00
Potassium iodide		27, 000. 00
Crude iodine	122, 000. 00	
Camphor	58, 000. 00	
Santonine crystals	18, 000. 00	
Quinine sulphate	134, 000. 00	
Pyrethrum flowers	29, 000. 00	
Antimony	20, 000. 00	
Miscellaneous raw materials	29, 000. 00	
	$556, 000. 00	$84, 000. 00
	84, 000. 00	
	$472, 000. 00"	

Comments in the Canadian Company reports for 1928 and 1929 were very brief—merely noting that the merchandise was all in a public warehouse from which the auditors had received a certificate as to quantities which agreed with the books. In 1928 the inventory amounting to $456,112.95 was reported to have consisted solely of mercury and senega root.[1224]

[1223] Ex. 151 (p. 6).
[1224] Ex. 149, 150.

Reports of the Maryland Company beginning with that for 1929 contained schedules showing the inventories by companies or divisions of McKesson compared with the preceding year. The first of these comparisons included 3 years, December 31, 1927, 1928, and 1929. The text of the 1929 report merely noted a total increase of approximately $2,400,000.[1225]

The reports for 1930, 1931, and 1932 included comments stating the increase or decrease in the Connecticut and Canadian Company inventories combined compared with the change for the Maryland Company as a whole consolidated. The approximate changes reported, closing with total inventories at December 31, 1932 of approximately $23,850,000, were: [1226]

	1930	1931	1932
Net increase (decrease) in total inventories	($ 970,000)	$ 700,000	($4,500,000)
(Decrease) in wholesale house inventories	(2,910,000)	(2,900,000)	(2,900,000)
Increase (decrease) in Canadian and Connecticut Companies' combined inventories	1,940,000	3,600,000	(1,600,000)

The increases in Canadian and Connecticut Companies were attributed largely to the purchase of crude drugs and raw materials in the primary markets in 1930 and 1931, and to the carrying of somewhat larger stocks of finished products in 1930, with the sales of crude drugs and raw materials in that year in excess of 1929 sales.[1227]

In addition to the separate treatment given to the principal current assets discussed above, all of the reports rendered on quarterly and annual audits of Girard & Co., Inc. and the Connecticut Company included a summary of the Company's change in financial position during the period under review. These statements were prepared in a manner which emphasized the increases and decreases in the accounts covered in the above discussion and related the net change in working capital to the profit for the period. As an example of the form in which these statements appeared each year the one from the report on the Connecticut Company for 1929 is reproduced here: [1228]

1225 Ex. 152 (p. 12).

1226 Ex. 153 (p. 20); 154 (p. 19); 155 (pp. 20–21).

1227 Ex. 153 (p. 20), 154 (p. 19).

1228 Ex. 151 (p. 15), used because it is the last included in a report to the client, although, as noted at pages 244–245 *supra*, the auditors prepared such statements subsequently for their own use.

"Disposition of Profits and Change in Financial Position

The change in financial position of the company during the period under review is summarized in the following statement:

Net profit for the year ending December 31, 1929 (per exhibit C)		$1, 271, 647. 75
Provision for depreciation not representing cash outlay, less charges thereto		68, 889. 06
Increase in reserve for contingencies		4, 833. 07
		$1, 345, 369. 88
Investments and notes receivable of affiliated companies disposed of, etc.		1, 359, 686. 79
		$2, 705, 056. 67
Deduct:		
Additions to properties (net)	$592, 577. 90	
Reduction of mortgage on property	10, 000. 00	
Reduction of liability for sprinkler system	3, 942. 00	
Reduction of liability for manufacturing rights	6, 666. 66	
Cash dividends paid	733, 125. 00	1, 346, 311. 56
Balance of funds retained in the business as additional working capital as shown in the following comparative statement		$1, 358, 745. 11

	As at December 31, 1928	As at December 31, 1929	Increase or Decrease* in funds
Cash in banks and on hand	$ 368, 744. 31	$ 267, 416. 17	$ 101, 328. 14*
Bankers' acceptances	282, 950. 00	280, 110. 18	2, 839. 82*
Notes and accounts receivable, less reserves	1, 475, 072. 34	3, 325, 554. 55	1, 850, 482. 21
Inventories, less reserves	1, 936, 756. 98	3, 270, 950. 05	1, 334, 193. 07
	$4, 063, 523. 63	$7, 144, 030. 95	$3, 080, 507. 32
Current liabilities	1, 953, 102. 45	4, 302, 278. 08	2, 349, 175. 63
	$2, 110, 421. 18	$2, 841, 752. 87	$ 731, 331. 69
Intercompany accounts receivable (net)	732, 400. 00	1, 204, 275. 08	471, 875. 08
Prepaid expenses and sundry supplies	73, 178. 74	228, 717. 08	155, 538. 34
Net totals	$2, 915, 999. 92	$4, 274, 745. 03	$1, 358, 745. 11"

It was noted above that these long-form reports dealt with financing and the propriety of dividend payments and Thorn testified that one of the copies of the report was for the use of the trustee of the "indenture" issue.[1229] The 1930 report referred to the issuance of $22,000,000 of debentures in April of that year and stated:

[1229] R. 887. Article Two, Section 11 of the indenture dated as of May 1, 1930 covering $25,000,000 20-year

"The indenture relating to the issue contains certain restrictions: among other things the Maryland Company has agreed not to borrow money, or permit the subsidiary companies to borrow money, unless a consolidated current ratio of 2½ to 1 can be maintained; and has also consented to the following restrictions on the payment of dividends or the investment of current assets in fixed assets:

"(a) Consolidated net current assets to be equivalent to 1¾ times the sum of the outstanding debentures plus mortgages and other long-term obligations.

"(b) Consolidated current assets not to be reduced to less than 3½ times the consolidated current liabilities.

"(c) Consolidated current assets not to be reduced to less than 1¼ times the sum of the consolidated current liabilities plus the sum of the outstanding debentures, mortgages and other long-term obligations.

"The disposition of the proceeds received from the sale of subsidiary companies is also restricted under the indenture." [1230]

Reports for 1931, 1932, and 1933 referred to the 1930 report for the details quoted above, concluding a one paragraph summary with the phrase "* * * and it would appear that these terms have been complied with as at December 31 * * * ." [1231] In reports for the succeeding 4 years, 1934–1937, a shortened paragraph was used concluding with the sentence "* * * The terms of the indenture in respect of such ratios were complied with as at December 31, * * * ." [1232]

Section 14 of Article Two of the indenture provides that for the purposes mentioned above "Consolidated current assets" shall be defined to include among other things the following:

"Inventories of merchandise, materials and supplies taken at cost or market value, whichever shall be lower *exclusive of goods purchased abroad which are either in foreign warehouses or in transit at the date of such determination and* exclusive of plants and equipment." [Italics supplied.] [1233]

If, at December 31, 1936 and 1937, the foreign crude drug inventories, which the representatives of Price, Waterhouse & Co. testified they believed were purchased from the Canadian vendors and were at that time stored in warehouses located in Canada, had been ex-

---

5½% convertible debentures provides that:

"At all times the Company will, and it will cause each subsidiary company at all times to, keep proper books of record and account, in which full, true and correct entry will be made of all dealings, business and affairs of the Company and its subsidiary companies, all in accordance with good accounting practice. The Company further agrees to deliver to the Trustee, as soon as available after the close of each fiscal half-year, Consolidated Balance Sheets and Combined Earnings Statements certified to by the Treasurer or an Assistant Treasurer of the Company, setting forth in reasonable detail the condition and operation of the business of the Company and its subsidiary companies, for and as of the close of such fiscal half-year, and as soon as available after the close of each fiscal year, it will deliver to the Trustee, Consolidated Balance Sheets and Combined Earnings Statements certified to by public accountants satisfactory to the Trustee, setting forth in reasonable detail the condition and operation of the business of the Company and its subsidiary companies for and as of the close of such fiscal year." McKesson & Robbins, Incorporated, Securities Registration, Form 10, File No. 1–1435, Exhibit B (p. 37).

1230 Ex. 153 (pp. 3–4).

1231 Ex. 154, 155, 156.

1232 157, 158, 159, 160.

1233 McKesson & Robbins, Incorporated, Securities Registration, Form 10, File No. 1–1435, Exhibit B (p. 41).

cluded from consolidated current assets, the ratio specified in "(b)" above would not have been complied with as at December 31 of those years, although the Price, Waterhouse & Co. reports stated that the terms of the indenture in respect to the ratios had been complied with at the year ends.[1234]

The portion of the indenture italicized above was inserted after Jaureguy of Price, Waterhouse & Co. had read the draft and suggested that provision be made to cover the practice which McKesson then followed of not including in their asset *or liability* totals on the balance sheet "Goods purchased abroad, in foreign warehouses or in transit * * *."[1235] Despite the language of the indenture, the auditors' position is that the provision was not meant to apply to inventories such as the Canadian merchandise in question which had been paid for or for which a liability had been set up. And in any event the auditors claim that Canada, where the goods were purchased and warehoused, is not "abroad."

The purpose and content of the reports we have reviewed were discussed at the hearings with some of the Price, Waterhouse & Co. representatives responsible for their preparation. The problem was

[1234] McGloon in his comptroller's report for 1937 noted that "The balance sheet ratios of current assets to current liabilities * * *" were 3.56 and 3.46 respectively at December 31, 1936 and 1937 and commented as follows, Ex. 266 (pp. 17–18):

"RATIOS REQUIRED UNDER INDENTURE:

All of the ratio requirements under the indenture governing our debentures were met at December 31, 1937, with the exception of the ratio of current assets to current liabilities governing the declaration of dividends, etc. (which ratio has since been corrected in 1938 to meet with terms of our indenture) as is shown in the following summary. It might again be mentioned that various adjustments are made to the balance sheet figures when computing the ratios required under the indenture.

Otherwise, the fulfillment of the terms of our indenture relating to our debentures was observed, and no notice from the Trustees of any default during the year 1937 on the part of the Company has been received.

	Required Ratio	Actual Ratios as at December 31, 1937	June 30, 1937	December 31, 1936
Governing the declaration of dividends and the conversion of current into fixed assets:				
1. Net current assets to debentures, plus other non-current indebtedness and mortgages not assumed	1.75	3.02	3.02	2.89
2. Current assets to current liabilities	3.50	3.49	3.61	3.56
3. Current assets to current liabilities, plus debentures and other non-current indebtedness, including mortgages not assumed	1.25	1.91	1.94	1.88
Governing the borrowing of money:				
Current assets to current liabilities	2.50	3.49	3.61	3.55"

A comparison of the balance sheet current ratios and the adjusted ratios as presented by McGloon indicates that such adjustments as were made at December 31, 1937 strengthened the ratio slightly while those at December 31, 1936 (if any), made no difference in the result. If, however, the inventories understood to have been in warehouses in Canada on those dates had been eliminated from current assets, the balance sheet current ratios would have been less than 3.2 at December 31, 1936, and less than 3.1 at December 31, 1937.

[1235] The Annual Report for 1929, the one current at the time the indenture was drawn, carried the following note under inventories:

"NOTE.—Goods purchased abroad, in foreign warehouses or in transit at December 31, 1929, not included above, amounted to approximately $1,085,000." Ex. 130.

first raised and discussed with Thorn who explained that the details covered in the letters on the audits of the wholesale houses and discussions he may have had with Coster in respect to the Connecticut Division and Canadian Company were not covered in the consolidated long-form report "* * * because that is for the use of the directors and the trustee of the indenture issue [and certain banks which extend credit] and they were not concerned with those minor matters we would mention of an individual house." [1236] Coster and the divisional vice-presidents, Thorn felt, would be more concerned with the operating details included in the individual letters than they would be in the accounting problems covered in the overall report which also described the scope of the examination and what was or was not done in respect to important accounts.[1237] Thorn felt that he would have been presumptuous if he had suggested breaking up the Connecticut Division accounts to show crude drugs and manufacturing separately so that the separate operations could be seen and commented on in the auditors' report as the purpose of the annual examination was to enable the auditors to give an opinion as to whether "accounts * * * prepared * * * by the company * * * do or do not fairly present the financial position and results of the operations for the year and whether accepted accounting practices have been consistently followed." [1238] There was no place in any of the Price, Waterhouse & Co. reports where the results of the crude drug transactions standing separately could be seen.[1239]

Thorn's testimony referred to above, used language stating that the accounts were "prepared by the Company." He testified, however, that it was his practice to draft a report and send it to McGloon so that all statements of fact could be checked before completion in final form. Thorn also understood that Coster read the report as well as McGloon. Drafts of the 1935, 1936, and 1937 reports obtained from McKesson's files carry notes by McGloon to the effect that Coster had reviewed the report.[1240] In this connection it may be noted that Thorn stated that the financial statements and attached footnotes included in McKesson's annual reports to the Securities and Exchange Commission were typed in the office of Price, Waterhouse & Co.[1241]

Rowbotham, who signed the report for Price, Waterhouse & Co., stated that although negotiations in respect to the engagement were

---

1236 R. 887.

1237 R. 891, 897.

1238 R. 903, see also R. 900.

"Q. [By Mr. GALPEER.] And it is not your duty to comment upon such operating conclusions as might be drawn from the figures or to point out various conclusions that might be drawn by a study or breaking up of the figures just from an operating point of view?

A. [By THORN.] No, sir, I personally should, as I said a while ago, I would feel presumptuous if I attempted to get very far into the operating end of the business." R. 903.

1239 R. 909.

1240 Ex. 93, 94, 95; R. 991-995.

1241 R. 1026.

conducted by Coster—at times through McGloon—he thought he was reporting to the Corporation through Coster, its president. The crude drug department was not reported upon because he thought it was the best run department of the business, conditions were satisfactory and required no comment.[1242] He understood that the letters on the wholesale houses were used by Coster and McGloon to prod the heads of those houses into corrective measures where conditions were criticized but he did not suppose that they would be referred to in directors' meetings, although the directors would have a right to see them. This last opinion was qualified to some extent for Rowbotham thought that if a director who was head of one of the wholesale houses called upon him for permission to see a letter covering another house, he would probably not have released the letter if the contents were a serious matter or if the director's inquiry was based on suspicion. Rowbotham thought that the inquirer should be refused the information and directed to seek it of Coster, the executive head of the corporation.[1243] This seems to be along the same line as the idea expressed by Ritts, in response to a question based on a statement that the check on operations effected by the president himself was an important element of internal control in this case:

> "Well, our first duty, of course, is to the president or the Board of Directors, the people that hire us. I assume we do have a responsibility, though, to the stockholders in certifying accounts that we know are going to be published." [1244]

This responsibility to stockholders was called upon in several ways from 1924 through 1937 for the client's financial statements carrying Price, Waterhouse & Co.'s certificate were used in reports submitted to stockholders, to prospective stockholders in prospectuses issued in connection with the sale of securities, and in listing applications filed with the New York Stock Exchange; and, more recently, in reports filed with the Securities and Exchange Commission.

The form and content of the published stockholders' reports have shown a gradual change through the years in conformity with pre-

---

1242 R. 1981–1983.

1243 "Q. [By Mr. STEWART.] Perhaps you misunderstood Mr. Galpeer and me both—I didn't mean we were talking about working papers. I am talking about letters sent to Coster and then to the divisional vice president in charge of a particular company, commenting on weaknesses in that company. Now, if another director should come in and ask for a copy of such a letter, and give you an explanation that he was suspicious about something in that company, is that a letter which you would release to him?—it has nothing to do with the working papers now.

A. [By ROWBOTHAM.] Probably not, because it wouldn't seem to me that that was any of his business. If he had suspicions in that connection, I think his job in that case would be to take it up with Coster, who is the executive head of the corporation. I am assuming that his suspicions related to the divisional point and not to Coster himself.

Q. Suppose he expressed some suspicions as to Coster himself, then what would your reaction be?

A. Then the question would have been what his suspicions were, and I really can't answer that question any better than this, that I would have given it the most serious consideration and probably, I think, if it was sufficiently serious, we would have taken it up with our attorneys and simply wanted to know what we should do next.

Q. That occasion never arose.

A. That occasion never did arise." R. 1987–1988.

1244 R. 667.

vailing accounting practice, the most marked change being in the increase in information given in the profit and loss statement. Rowbotham was asked whether this tendency should be carried further by reporting profit and loss accounts for major lines of business conducted by large corporations such as McKesson & Robbins, Incorporated, had grown to be. His opinion was that "* * * the simpler and more compact you can make the documents you offer to the public, the more likely they are to understand them." He pointed out that corporations were required to report sales in many cases against their will and he thought that they would have good reasons for not wanting to split up this figure in published reports.[1245]

It seems unnecessary to discuss in detail the changes in reporting through the years but a brief comparison of the material in the long-form reports addressed to Coster with the reports to the stockholders and to the Securities and Exchange Commission may be of interest. With the exception of the balance sheets and surplus accounts the statements in the long-form report are in comparative form for 2 years with the current year outside. In the stockholders' report the consolidated balance sheet and surplus accounts are reproduced without change but the consolidated profit and loss statement condenses some detail (opening with "net sales" instead of gross sales for example) and the current year's figures are brought inside the prior year's (a suggestion marked by McGloon on the draft report submitted to him). None of the supporting schedules were published, nor financial statements for the parent company only. The only notes that appear on the stockholders' reports are those on the face of the balance sheet as parenthetical expressions, and statements as to contingent liabilities, and some detail in respect to preferred stock which are reported at the foot of the right-hand side. The annual report filed with the Commission substitutes required schedules for those in the long-form report and makes certain changes in the profit and loss statement as required by the form. The balance sheets refer to three pages of footnotes for each and the profit and loss statements to one.[1246]

1245 R. 1977–1980.

"Q. [By Mr. GALPEER.] Do you think that any distinction might be made in your answer between a company, let us say, as an oil company, where you refer to their having one product and take it through various stages and a firm like McKesson & Robbins, where in addition to their own products, as I understand it, they job and wholesale the products of others as well?

A. [By ROWBOTHAM.] I don't think so, in any case where you believe as we believed here, that this business was genuine and that those profits were genuine. If you believed that this business, as we did and as I did, was a genuine business and those profits were made, I don't think that you would want to make the split-up. I think you would meet some objections from the company which I think would have seemed to you or would have seemed to me reasonable from the directors, that they didn't want to disclose the amount of profit in this specialty business to possible competitors. We have had that objection on other companies." R. 1979–80.

1246 Ex. 160, 106, and McKesson & Robbins, Incorporated, Securities Registration and Annual Reports, Forms 10 and 10-K, File No. 1-1435.

It was noted earlier in this account that the financial statements for the annual report to the Commission were typed by Price, Waterhouse & Co. It may be noted here that Thorn wrote the footnotes. This point was established in connection with the note in regard to inventories. The following quotation will make the accountant's position clear in this regard:

"Q. [By Mr. STEWART.] Now, as I understand it, this footnote with regard to the quantities of goods on hand being counted was not a part of your certificate, but a footnote to the company's balance sheet?

A. [By THORN.] That is correct. I wrote that note.

Q. You wrote it for the company?

A. For the company.

Q. And expressed an opinion with regard to it?

A. I am writing what I think the company should say. Then, of course, this is sent to the company and they change it any way they want. This is their statement, you understand (indicating [Form 10-K])." [1247]

A statement of Rowbotham's is also in point here on the subject as to whether the financial statements are the accountants' or the clients'. He said that on an earlier balance sheet he put a note on himself in the most conspicuous place he could find to draw "* * * to the stockholders' attention that as to quantity, quality and condition of the inventories we relied on responsible officials * * *." [1248] A note "* * * as certified by responsible officials" or "* * * certified as to quantity and condition by responsible officials * * *" appeared on every certified balance sheet prepared for McKesson by Price, Waterhouse & Co. except the first one for Girard & Co., Inc., for December 31, 1924.[1249]

The certificate attached to the statements rendered throughout the engagement were the usual short form without qualifications and conformed to the changing manner of expression of the period. All of the certificates supplied to Girard & Co., Inc., were substantially the same as the first which stated:

[1247] R. 1046-1047, see also R. 1014. The testimony quoted in the text arose in connection with a discussion of the footnote to inventories on the balance sheet filed with this Commission as part of the Annual Reports for 1935 and 1936, which, after listing the entire inventories in four commodity groupings, stated "The quantities of goods on hand at December 31 * * * were determined by actual count, weight or measurement by officers and employees of the companies, and were priced on the basis of cost or market, whichever was lower." The corresponding footnote for 1937 added: "* * * and the quantities of goods stored in outside warehouses were confirmed by the warehouses. * * *" Although there was no mention in this connection in the 1935 and 1936 reports of the goods not in McKesson's own warehouses, Thorn testified that, like "cash on hand" as distinguished from "in banks", only goods held in the Company's warehouses were "on hand" and that such statements, therefore, did not apply to goods held in outside warehouses. R. 995-1000, 1046-1057.

[1248] R. 2005. See also:

"Q. [By Mr. STEWART.] It is simply designed for the purpose of making it clear to anybody who reads the balance sheet that on that point they must accept the word of the company officials rather than the word of the accountants?

A. [By ROWBOTHAM.] Yes, sir." R. 2043.

[1249] R. 1992; Ex. 128-137, 161-167, 106.

"We have examined the books and accounts of Girard & Co., Inc. as of December 31, 1924 and we certify that, in our opinion, the above balance sheet fairly sets forth the financial position of the company at that date." [1250]

The style adopted for the first published report for McKesson & Robbins, Incorporated, of Connecticut, served without substantial change for the Maryland Company as well through 1932. To avoid minor variations arising from special circumstances existing through the formative period of the Maryland Company, the certificate from the report for that company for 1929 is used as an example:

"We have examined the books and accounts of McKesson & Robbins, Incorporated (Maryland), and subsidiary companies for the year ending December 31, 1929, and we certify that the attached consolidated balance sheet and relative statements of profit and loss and earned surplus have been correctly prepared from the books and, in our opinion, set forth the financial position of the combined companies as at December 31, 1929, and the result of operations for the year ending on that date." [1251]

Reference to correct preparation from the books was omitted for 1932.[1252] With the 1933 report the form recommended by the American Institute of Accountants, in cooperation with the New York Stock Exchange, became standard. To complete the series, the last certificate is reproduced:

"PRICE, WATERHOUSE & CO.

56 Pine Street
New York March 7, 1938

"To the Board of Directors of
McKesson & Robbins, Incorporated

"We have made an examination of the consolidated balance sheet of McKesson & Robbins, Incorporated and subsidiary companies as at December 31, 1937, and of the consolidated statements of profit and loss and surplus for the year 1937. In connection therewith, we examined or tested accounting records of the companies and other supporting evidence and obtained information and explanations from officers and employees of the companies; we also made a general review of the accounting methods and of the operating and income accounts for the year, but we did not make a detailed audit of the transactions.

"In our opinion, based upon such examination, the accompanying consolidated balance sheet and related statements of profit and loss and surplus fairly present, in accordance with accepted principles of accounting consistently maintained by the companies during the year under review, the position of the combined companies at December 31, 1937, and the result of their operations for the year.

PRICE, WATERHOUSE & CO."[1253]

The certificate filed with this Commission was altered only to include a reference to the index to financial statements and to the footnotes. It was signed for the firm by Rowbotham.[1254]

[1250] Ex. 2.
[1251] Ex. 130.
[1252] Ex. 133.
[1253] Ex. 106.
[1254] R. 2014-2015, 2058-2059. See pages 358-359 *infra*.

The certificates for the Canadian Company revealed a similar transition with a blending in recent years of the requirements of the Canadian Companies Act and the style of the United States form of report. The differences in form in the two countries may be observed by comparing the last certificate for the Maryland Company quoted above with the last for the Canadian Company which is shown below:

"PRICE, WATERHOUSE & CO.

56 Pine Street
New York
February 11, 1938.

"To the Shareholders of
McKesson & Robbins, Limited

"We have made an examination of the consolidated balance sheet of McKesson & Robbins, Limited and its subsidiary company in England as at December 31, 1937, and of the consolidated statement of profit and loss and surplus for the year 1937. In connection therewith, we examined or tested accounting records of the companies and other supporting evidence and we have obtained from officers and employees of the companies all the information and explanations we have required; we have also made a general review of the accounting methods and of the operating and income accounts for the year, but we did not make a detailed audit of the transactions.

"In our opinion, based upon such examination, the accompanying consolidated balance sheet and related statement of profit and loss and surplus are properly drawn up so as to exhibit a true and correct view of the state of the companies' affairs according to the best of our information and the explanations given to us, and as shown by the books of the companies.

PRICE, WATERHOUSE & CO."[1255]

Rowbotham explained that all of these certificates covered the same type of work and that therefore the language used could be interpreted merely as a changing preference in the manner of reporting. Rowbotham thought the earlier style was too laconic so the changes were made in an effort to give more explanation to the stockholder of what an accountant does when he examines accounts.[1256]

Rowbotham's interpretation of the last American certificate and a reconciliation of it with the requirements of the "Instruction Book for Form 10-K for Corporations, Annual Report", was requested. The second sentence of the certificate he understood to be compliance with the requirement that the certificate should be reasonably comprehensive as to the scope of the audit made.[1257] The certificate was not as informative as to scope as the long-form report for in the latter a statement was made that debtors and creditors were not circular-

[1255] Ex. 167.
[1256] R. 1994-1997, 2014.
[1257] R. 1998.

ized.[1258] Rowbotham thought that this information should not go in the report to stockholders or in a footnote on the balance sheet because it is the accountants' duty to decide whether circularization is necessary and, if it is not, a statement that it was not done would give the stockholders the impression that there was something wrong with the debtors. He felt that if the auditor thinks circularization is necessary he should insist upon it—a sentence in the report would not be a substitute.[1259] This situation Rowbotham thought was different from the note in respect to inventories because it was common practice for ac-

---

1258 The comparison here is betwen the certificate and the paragraph in the long-form report entitled "Scope of Examination." It should be observed, however, that in the discussion of the principal balance sheet accounts the long-form report commented briefly on the audit procedures followed in verifying certain of the items. The following excerpts from the report on the 1937 examination illustrate this practice:

> "The cash in banks as at December 31, 1937 was reconciled with certificates received direct from the banks, and the cash on hand was counted at the time of our examination. In accordance with instructions, we did not request the banks to confirm the details of deposits made near the end of the year.
>
> * * * * * * *
>
> "The notes receivable as at December 31, 1937 which were on hand at the time of our examination were inspected by us and those held by others were confirmed by correspondence. Trial balances of the accounts receivable were checked to the detailed ledger accounts and the totals were agreed with the general ledger controlling accounts. In accordance with instructions, we did not circularize the debtors for confirmations of their balances.
>
> * * * * * * *
>
> "The amounts of the reserves for doubtful notes and accounts and for sales discounts, returns and allowances as at December 31, 1937 were adequate, in our opinion. In considering the collectibility of the receivables, we reviewed such credit information as was available relating to balances that were past due or relatively large in amount, and discussed such balances with local officials. Because retail druggists, in general, appear to be unable or unwilling to furnish satisfactory financial statements, our conclusions as to the adequacy of the reserves were necessarily based, to a large extent, on the discussions with local officials and the paying records of the respective debtors. In the case of each house, consideration was also given to the bad debt experience of that particular house during recent years.
>
> * * * * * * *
>
> "The quantities of merchandise, materials and supplies on hand at December 31, 1937 were determined by actual count, weight or measurement by employees of the companies and the quantities stored in outside warehouses were confirmed direct to us.
>
> "We made a comprehensive check of the arithmetical accuracy and of the prices used which indicated that the inventories were carefully compiled and properly priced on the basis of cost or market, whichever was lower, and that sufficient allowance had been made for slow-moving and unsalable stock.
>
> * * * * * * *
>
> "Responsible officials of the companies have certified to the quantities, condition and ownership of the goods included in the inventories, as well as to the prices used and the adequacy of the allowances for obsolete, damaged and slow-moving stock.
>
> * * * * * * *
>
> "So far as our examination extended, it appeared that all known liabilities as of December 31, 1937 had been taken up on the books of the respective companies as at that date, and we secured certificates from responsible officials stating that, to the best of their knowledge and belief, all liabilities had been taken up.
>
> * * * * * * *
>
> "We received a certificate from the Manufacturers Trust Company, successor trustee under the indenture, confirming the amount of twenty-year 5½% convertible debentures outstanding at December 31, 1937.
>
> * * * * * * *
>
> "With reference to the capital stock of McKesson & Robbins, Incorporated, we received certificates from the transfer agent and from the registrar confirming the number of shares of preference stock and common stock outstanding at December 31, 1937. * * *" Ex. 160.

1259 "In other words, it seems to me that if an accountant wishes to say in his report that he has not circularized the debtors, that he is implying that there is something wrong with those debtors and I think then the point is for him having that idea not to try to get away with it by simply making a sentence in his report but by going and having a row with the company." R. 2004.

countants to refer to certificates of officials in respect to inventories but that was not true of circularization of accounts.[1260] Reliance on the books he considered was feasible for receivables because collection subsequent to the balance sheet date and prior to completion of the audit was proof of their authenticity but in the case of inventories collections on receivables arising from sales of stocks on hand at the balance sheet date, because of the long credit terms, would not be made until after the audit was concluded and hence collections during the audit would not be satisfactory proof of the existence of such inventories. Matters such as these were descriptive of the work done on the audit and in Rowbotham's opinion were beyond the intent of the term "* * * comprehensive * * * description of the scope of the audit." [1261]

Continuing a study of the certificate, Rowbotham explained that a general review of the operating and income accounts, referred to therein, contemplated a search for extraordinary or non-recurring items rather than a criticism of the client's classification of accounts provided the classification seemed reasonable. The certificate was signed with the requirements of the American Institute Bulletin in mind that the form should be modified, if necessary, to embody any qualifications, reservations, or supplementary explanations and in the belief that the examination made was adequate and in conformity with the principles outlined in the Bulletin.[1262]

In respect to the permissive sentence in the Commission's instructions to the effect that independent accountants "* * * may give due weight to an internal system of audit regularly maintained by means of auditors employed on the registrant's own staff",[1263] Rowbotham said that he had always interpreted internal audit to mean internal control and the meaning of the entire sentence to be that in the case of large companies where a detailed audit is practically humanly impossible the accountants should "* * * review the internal control and satisfy themselves that proper accounting procedures are being followed" which does not mean that internal auditors are a necessary part of the procedure.[1264] The certificate, as used by accountants, in Rowbotham's opinion means that the accounts are honestly and consistently presented in accordance with accepted principles

---

[1260] R. 2005–2006.

[1261] R. 2007–2011, 2044–2045.

[1262] R. 2015. Assurance of compliance with the requirements of the predecessor Federal Reserve Bulletin was given to Coster for transmission to the New York Stock Exchange in a letter dated April 11, 1933. Ex. 118. See also footnotes 550, 590 *supra*.

[1263] Instruction Book for Form 10-K (pp. 11–12).

[1264] R. 2026–2028.

of accounting and that there are documents to prove that they represent an actual business.[1265]

M. THE FEE

The professional services rendered by Price, Waterhouse & Co. to McKesson & Robbins, Incorporated, of Maryland, and affiliated and predecessor companies controlled by F. D. Coster from the early part of 1925 to the latter part of 1938 comprised balance sheet audits throughout the period, purchase audits of wholesale drug houses during 1928 and 1929, tax work during part of the earlier years, work in connection with statements filed with the Securities and Exchange Commission since its creation, special examinations, and other special services from time to time during the period. The following table

---

1265 "Q. [By Mr. GALPEER.] Summing up, Mr. Rowbotham, can you tell me specifically what impression you mean to give the shareholders through your certificate on the McKesson & Robbins consolidated report, for example, which I understand is a standard form—what reliance are they entitled to place upon the authenticity and accuracy of the report to which the certificate has been attached?

The EXAMINER. Do you refer specifically to any one, for example, the 1937 report for example?

Mr. GALPEER. No, I just mean what that certificate form intends to convey in general.

A. Well, I think that we accountants try to embody that in this opinion itself. For instance, in the first paragraph here we state that we examined or tested accounting records of the company and have obtained information and explanation from officers and employees of the company; in other words, that we have made an examination of books and had interviews with individuals, that we have made a general review of the accounting methods.

In other words, that we have there a definite set of records of what has every appearance of being genuine and full business. Now, in our opinion section here we state that as a result of having made this examination in the first paragraph that the accounts are presented in accordance with accepted principles of accounting, in other words, the accounts are fairly presented in accordance with the accepted principles of accounting; in other words, that there is no, to our belief, no misleading of the public in the manner in which these accounts are shown. I think I testified, I don't know whether it was yesterday or on Friday that most of our quarrels with clients and most of the rows we have with them come on what we call purely accounting points as to whether or not accounts should be stated this way or that and this statement here of accepted principles is three-fold: That we believe this is a fair presentation, that it is in accordance with accepted principles and that they have been consistently maintained by the company during the period. I think I said in answer to some question you asked yesterday perhaps, that the accountant is not an engineer. He very often does not know the actual existence, to be quite blunt about it, of the capital assets. He may know that there are buildings there. He does not know the buildings are suitable for the purpose He does not know the machinery is suitable to the purpose. He is not a lawyer. He does not know that the titles rest in the company. And when the S. E. C. started out, I don't know that you remember it, we accountants tried to put all these things in our certificates—I mean to state much more bluntly and much more compactly than this what our position was and what our position was not.

In short, that we were accountants here trying to present accounts fairly and honestly. Now, the S. E. C. came along and told us, which was true, that we accountants were trying to get lawyers to write our certificates for us. That happened to be said by Mr. Commissioner Landis to one of my partners and it happened to be true at the time and we swung away, perhaps, from explaining these things in certificates as to the things we do not do, but forgetting for the moment these negative things what I do want to say is this: That as a result of our work on the accounts and our interviews with the officials, that this is a statement of our opinion that these accounts are honestly presented.

Q. [By Mr. GALPEER.] * * * what would you summarize as being your position in regard to the authenticity of the account?

A. The authenticity of the account. If the accounts exist, if there are documents to prove them, if there is every evidence shown to the accountant that such accounts are the accounts of an actual business, I mean, I think, that is the proof of the authenticity that you speak of.

Q. And just one more question, Mr. Rowbotham. You state here in the opinion: 'We examined or tested accounting records of the company and other supporting evidence'. What is meant by the words 'and other supporting evidence'?

A. I would say, sir, that my understanding here was that the accounting records had more direct reference to the books themselves and other supporting evidence would refer, let us say, to the invoices and vouchers and various other documents that you would naturally see in the course of your work." R. 2017-2021.

gives a fair conception of the growth of the McKesson organization and of its importance as a fee-producing client for Price, Waterhouse & Co. The fees and out-of-pocket expenses are charges for annual audits, except as noted, performed by United States offices of Price, Waterhouse & Co. Fees for other services are excluded as they are not directly related to the audit work which is the subject of this investigation.

McKesson & Robbins, Incorporated
(and Predecessor Companies)

	Charges of Price, Waterhouse & Co.			Consolidated Accounts	
Year	Fee	Expenses	Total	Total Assets at December 31 (000's omitted)	Sales for Year (000's omitted)
1924 [a]	$ 550.00	$ —	$ 550.00	$ 295	$ [a] 252
1925 [b]	[f] 2, 137.50	316.06	2, 453.56	584	1, 134
1926 [c]	3, 900.00	247.04	4, 147.04	[c] 1, 306	[c] 2, 227
1927 [d]	5, 350.00	767.46	6, 117.46	4, 134	[d] 6, 250
1928 [e]	43, 250.00	5, 767.01	49, 017.01	43, 090	88, 721
1929	118, 300.00	20, 068.11	138, 368.11	77, 071	140, 635
1930	80, 147.41	12, 824.37	93, 071.78	82, 048	143, 908
1931	70, 000.00	11, 998.73	81, 998.73	79, 967	127, 963
1932	62, 500.00	10, 800.67	73, 300.67	65, 422	111, 241
1933	62, 500.00	11, 197.68	73, 697.68	65, 801	111, 608
1934	70, 000.00	11, 295.68	81, 295.68	69, 251	131, 778
1935	70, 000.00	11, 408.15	81, 408.15	71, 410	140, 163
1936	70, 000.00	11, 545.14	81, 545.14	82, 672	162, 960
1937	72, 500.00	11, 351.95	83, 851.95	87, 183	184, 981

[a] Girard & Co., Inc., 9 months ended Dec. 31, 1924.
[b] Girard & Co., Inc., 4 quarterly audits.
[c] Girard & Co., Inc., sales for 11 months ended Nov. 30, assets at Nov. 30, 1926.
[d] McKesson & Robbins, Incorporated (Connecticut), sales for 13 months ended Dec. 31, 1927, audits for 4 months to Mar. 31, 1927, and 9 months to Dec. 31, 1927.
[e] McKesson & Robbins, Incorporated (Maryland), consolidated, beginning with this date.
[f] $2,387.50 reported in Ex. 169 less $250.00 described by Jaureguy as for special work. R. 58. The rest of the table is based on Ex. 1, 169.

In addition to the regular audit fees listed above, the English and Continental firms of Price, Waterhouse & Co. made examinations of the London subsidiary of McKesson & Robbins, Limited, and Isdahl & Co., A/S, respectively, since 1931 for the former, and since 1928 for the latter. It may be observed that the total of fees and expenses charged by Price, Waterhouse & Co., of London, for the London subsidiary have averaged more than double the fee for its parent, the Canadian Company (no expenses were allotted to the parent from the total expenses incurred at Bridgeport).[1266] Four of the smaller

[1266] It should be noted in this connection in respect to the Canadian Company that its London subsidiary is comparable to the wholesale houses in character of business, and that it was examined quarterly in 1931, 1932, first 2 quarters of 1933, and semi-annually thereafter, whereas the parent was examined annually. Ex. 1.

divisions have been audited regularly by other accountants whose reports have been accepted by Price, Waterhouse & Co. for consolidation purposes.[1267]

To judge the adequacy of the fees charged by the United States firm, two methods of calculation must be known. One calculation is based upon per diem charges for time employed on the engagement. For this purpose partners' time is charged for at the rate of $100 per day, managers' $50 to $75 per day, seniors' $30 to $35, and juniors' $20 to $25. A supplementary calculation is then made by doubling the *actual* direct salary cost on the engagement and adding 35%. This formula may be stated another way as 50 parts direct cost based on time spent, 50 parts to cover overhead and the 35 parts for profit. The results based on the per diem charges and the formula are compared and a proper fee reached after discussion with the client.[1268]

The following tables give pertinent information for an appraisal of the fee in relation to time charged to the client in the last 5 years.

[1267] Billings, El Paso, and Honolulu wholesale houses, and Hollister Drug Co., Ltd. in all years and, in addition, the Kansas City wholesale house in 1933.

[1268] R. 26–28, 81. In recent years a staff man has averaged 1600 hours chargeable time and seven hours has been considered a day's work for billing purposes. In applying the formula, overhead or burden is not computed on partners' time.

McKESSON & ROBBINS, INCORPORATED

Comparative Statement of Annual Audit Fees and Expenses of United States Offices of Price, Waterhouse & Co.—for the Years 1933 to 1937, Inclusive, and Corresponding Time Charges of Price, Waterhouse & Co. Staff

	1933	1934	1935	1936	1937
Fees:					
Wholesale houses	$48, 725	$57, 800	$54, 775	$56, 425	$58, 800
(Number of houses)	(50)	(57)	(59)	(64)	(64)
Connecticut Division	1, 750	1, 675	1, 650	1, 575	1, 625
McKesson & Robbins, Limited (Canada)	250	250	225	250	275
Liquor production divisions	1, 300	975	3, 650	4, 100	3, 800
All other units, including home office	1, 875	1, 800	2, 725	1, 800	1, 600
Consolidation and miscellaneous services	8, 600	7, 500	6, 975	5, 850	6, 400
Total as per Ex. 1 (details from Ex. 220)	$62, 500	$70, 000	$70, 000	$70, 000	$72, 500
Hours by Classes of Staff:					
Partners	180	131	105	71	86
Managers	1, 453	1, 032	1, 241	1, 244	1, 769
Seniors	4, 579	4, 556	5, 130	3, 813	3, 714
Assistants	16, 333	16, 267	15, 068	16, 812	16, 051
Total as per Ex. 123A	22, 545	21, 986	21, 544	21, 940	21, 620
Expenses:					
Wholesale houses	$ 9, 914	$10, 187	$10, 279	$10, 512	$10, 130
(Number of houses to which charges were made)	(50)	(54)	(54)	(55)	(60)
Connecticut Division	444	424	422	511	504
Liquor production divisions	34	—	113	212	306
All other units, including home office	260	227	235	5	7
Consolidation and miscellaneous services	545	458	360	309	385
Total as per Ex. 1 (details from Ex. 220)	$11, 198	$11, 296	$11, 408	$11, 545	$11, 352

A test calculation of the fee may be made in the following manner, using 1937 for the experiment:

Class of Staff	Hours Charged	Days at 7 Hours Per Day	Rate Per Day	Total Charge
Partners	86	12. 3	$100	$ 1, 230
Managers	1, 769	252. 7	[a] 50	12, 635
Seniors	3, 714	530. 6	[a] 30	15, 918
Assistants	16, 051	2, 293. 0	[a] 20	45, 860
Total	21, 620	3, 088. 6	—	$75, 643

[a] Minimum rates stated by Rowbotham. These are the same as rates quoted Girard & Co., Inc. in letter dated Dec. 18, 1924. Ex. 116.

The following figures are supplied for comparison with the above tables:

Assets at December 31:	1933	1934	1935	1936	1937
			(000's omitted)		
McKesson & Robbins, Limited (Canada)[a]	$ 2, 817	$ 2, 852	$ 2, 925	$ 3, 027	$ 3, 067
Connecticut Division [b]	15, 481	16, 466	17, 531	19, 379	21, 686
McKesson & Robbins, Incorporated, and subsidiary companies consolidated	65, 801	69, 251	71, 410	82, 672	87, 183
Sales For the Year:					
McKesson & Robbins, Limited (Canada)[a]	$ 2, 885	$ 3, 187	$ 3, 207	$ 3, 345	$ 3, 811
Connecticut Division [b]	19, 576	19, 019	20, 153	22, 820	25, 326
McKesson & Robbins, Incorporated, and subsidiary companies consolidated	111, 608	131, 778	140, 163	162, 960	184, 981

[a] Amounts as in annual reports for McKesson & Robbins, Limited and London, England branch consolidated. Ex. 163-167. The London branch adds less than $50,000 to the asset totals at the dates shown, and approximately $300,000 to $450,000 to sales in the several years. The Canadian Company assets include Goodwill, Trade Names, Franchises, etc., as valued by directors, $420,000. Sales in 1937 include approximately $245,000 to the Connecticut Division. Ex. 255.

[b] Amounts are combined totals from Ex. 169 less Canadian Company consolidated. Assets include investment in Canadian Company stated at $420,000.

It can be seen from the above figures that after the Maryland Company had more or less shaken down into an operating organization the time required for the work and consequently the cost and the fee became fairly stable figures. The most difficulty was experienced in 1929 when 34,086 hours of staff time (including 295 hours for partners) were required for the engagement. The following year the time dropped to 22,303 hours and remained fairly uniform thereafter.[1269] The individual fees for each wholesale house during the last 5 years averaged less than $1,000 per year except in 1934, when the average

[1269] Ex. 123A.

slightly exceeded this figure. Out-of-pocket expenses chargeable to the client averaged approximately $200 per house per year during the same period. The Connecticut Division and Canadian Company combined,[1270] representing as they do about 30% of consolidated assets and approximately one-sixth of sales for the entire organization, were handled at a cost of an average fee of $1,900 and average out-of-pocket expenses of $450 during the same period. The range in fees for the wholesale houses in these recent years has been from $25 for Sioux Falls to $3,375 at Los Angeles, both for 1937. Expenses charged to the houses have ranged from nothing to amounts in excess of $700.[1271]

In our discussion of arrangements for conducting the audits reference was made to objections of various directors and wholesale house heads to the expense and scope of the work.[1272] This was a continuous problem with the expense apparently the outstanding factor in the minds of many of the directors. McGloon explained that the executive vice-presidents required him to prepare and submit to them comparative tables of fees and expenses in connection with the audit. The most recent of these [1273] is the basis of the foregoing discussion. Five years earlier, following the 1932 audit, he was instructed to advise Price, Waterhouse & Co. that some of their charges for the wholesale houses seemed "* * * out of line and inconsistent with the volume of business * * * ." He found this to be the case in 14 houses and desired to know if the cause was inefficiency on the part of McKesson's staff in the houses or that too much work was being done by the auditors. His letter closed:

> "Please do not construe this letter as criticism on the part of the Management. We are of the opinion that if we can find ways and means of reducing the audit fee that it will tend to make us both happy. Moreover, on the basis of efficiency I think we are both interested in keeping the annual audit charge down to a minimum." [1274]

Price, Waterhouse & Co.'s reply pointed out the error in the McKesson argument, in a two-page letter in which one paragraph stated their case:

> "The principal reason why the fees charged to your various companies do not vary in proportion to the net sales is that in a balance sheet examination, such as we have made of your subsidiary companies, the volume of sales has very little direct effect on the amount of work required, although in many cases the amount of the sales do give some indication of the size of the balance sheet items. As you know, the major portion of our work on your companies has been devoted to the current assets and the non-current notes and accounts receivable. It follows

[1270] Financial statements in the record do not show a separate consolidation of the Connecticut and Canadian Companies. As the comparison used here is only a rough approximation it was not considered necessary to make the consolidation. The principal factors are indicated, however, in notes (a) and (b) in the table on the preceding page.

[1271] Ex. 220.

[1272] See Ex. 112, 119, 186, 187; pages 171–172 *supra*.

[1273] Ex. 220.

[1274] R. 1583–1584; Ex. 109A, 109B.

therefore, that the amount of work required for the examination and, consequently, the size of the fee, depends much more on the amount of these assets than on the volume of sales, which require a relatively small amount of our time." [1275]

Testimony of three of the directors who were questioned about the expense of the audit was uniformly in support of their primary object—a reduction of the expense. Murray, for example, stated that the scope of the audit "* * * was usually decided by Mr. Coster in Bridgeport" while discussions of the audit in meetings of the Board of Directors, or of the Operating or Executive Committees were devoted to the expense of the work.[1276] Bedsole had nothing to say as to the scope but was impressed by the fact that he had to pay the auditors.[1277] One of Doerr's objectives, as a member of the Sub-Committee on Accounting was to improve conditions so that the auditing would require less time.[1278] Faxon, however, thought the satisfaction arising from an audit was worth what it cost.[1279] Michaels and Cummings expressed the opinion that the audit program must be a compromise between thoroughness in detail, the results to be accomplished, and the expense involved.[1280]

George O. May, senior partner of Price, Waterhouse & Co., expressed the same ideas, at about the time the Girard & Co., Inc. engagement was accepted by his firm, in the following language:

> "In any such work we must be practical; it is no use laying down counsels of perfection or attempting to extend the scope of the audit unduly. An audit is a safeguard; the maintenance of this safeguard entails an expense; and this expense can be justified only if the value of the safeguard is found to be fully commensurate with its cost. The cost of an audit so extensive as to be a complete safeguard would be enormous and far beyond any value to be derived from it. A superficial audit is dangerous because of the sense of false security which it creates. Between the two extremes there lies a mean, at which the audit abundantly justifies its cost." [1281]

N. PRICE, WATERHOUSE & CO.'S APPRAISAL OF THEIR AUDIT

A general appraisal of the work that has been described in considerable detail in the foregoing pages was made by the two representatives

---

1275 R. 1583–1584; Ex. 109A, 109B. But compare the relation of the Connecticut Division fee to total fees with the proportion of that Division's assets to the total. A factor not specifically mentioned in either letter, but important in a proper comparison of audit fees, is the character of the business as reflected in the number of transactions involved in a given volume of business.

1276 R. 2167–2168.

1277 R. 2501.

1278 R. 2565–2572.

1279 "Well, we got in my houses in the middle west what I considered a most careful checking and overhauling, so that if I had qualms about the way things were going, they were eased off after the annual audit. That is what I got out of it, and I think it is well worth the money." R. 2531–2532.

1280 R. 2453. 4296.

1281 An address delivered to the Society of Certified Public Accountants of the State of New Jersey, Newark, N. J., October 19, 1926; reprinted in May, George Oliver, Twenty-five Years of Accounting Responsibility, 1911–1936; American Institute Publishing Co., Inc., New York, 1936. Quoted in Ex. 118.

of Price, Waterhouse & Co. who were primarily responsible for its direction during the last 5 years of the engagement.

Ralph E. Thorn, manager of the engagement, stated his opinion in the following passage of testimony:

"Q. [By Mr. STEWART.] From what you know of the jobs that were done for McKesson & Robbins during the period that you were connected with them and considering them in the light of all the things that Mr. Galpeer has called to your attention and to Mr. Ritts' attention during the course of this hearing, are you or are you not satisfied that the jobs done by Price, Waterhouse & Company were conducted in accordance with good audit procedure?

A. I am satisfied that we have made a good balance sheet examination in accordance with accepted accounting procedures.

Q. [By Mr. GALPEER.] Would you say that what you did followed the outline set forth in the booklet entitled 'Examination of Financial Statements' published by the Institute?

A. Yes, I would say that generally speaking. As I have tried to bring out once or twice, this work is entirely on a professional basis. By the time a man becomes a senior he has to use his own judgment and his own experience in exactly how to proceed with a particular examination. I think I hardly need to elaborate on that, we all understand that. There is no such thing as taking a pamphlet like the one you mentioned and starting out and making an examination on a set of accounts than there is in a doctor going out on a sick call with a fixed list of what he is going to do when he reaches the patient. It is entirely on a professional basis, and I may be elaborating too much, but I just want to make it clear that that is, I think, a fair statement of a balance sheet examination. The work which we have done is a balance sheet examination and—

Q. In other words, you would fit the particular undertaking to the needs of what you discovered on the particular job but in general the procedure you would follow is the outline as set forth in the pamphlet I have stated; in other words, you would start off with a generalization and then fit the job to the particular need?

A. I think it is a fair outline of a balance sheet examination, yes sir." [1282]

Geoffrey G. Rowbotham, partner in charge of the engagement, closed his testimony in the hearings as follows:

"Q. [By Mr. STEWART.] Mr. Rowbotham, in the light of what you know about the system of internal control which existed at McKesson & Robbins during the period under examination by Price, Waterhouse, and in the light of the testimony brought out in this proceeding, is it, in your opinion, fair to say that under that system it would have been impossible for the fraud now indicated in this situation to have been carried out without collusion between the president of the corporation, the assistant treasurer of the corporation, the head of the stock department of the corporation, and somebody on the outside to take care of sending in invoices from suppliers, bank statements, bank debit advices and other papers?

A. No, sir, it had to be carried out with the collusion of these men.

Q. And when you say that, am I correct in understanding you to mean that even if there had been collusion between the assistant treasurer and the head of the stock department and somebody on the outside, to take care of sending in papers, the fraud would necessarily have been discovered in short order by the president, had the president not been also in collusion?

A. Yes, sir. You have to know Coster. He was a man of ability. And he worked extremely hard. He attended to his business. This thing could not have happened if Coster had not been in it himself. If either George Dietrich

[1282] R. 1252–1254.

or Robert Dietrich had tried to do anything and Coster had been honest, they couldn't have gotten away with it for 30 days.

Q. And did you, prior to the disclosure of December 5th and subsequently, have any suspicion or any suggestion to you by anybody that there was a possibility of the nonexistence of the crude drug department?

A. No, sir, I certainly did not. This thing broke in my face like a bombshell on the night of December 5th.

Q. Now, Mr. Galpeer has called to your attention specifically notes No. 1 and No. 6 on page 41 of Commission's Exhibit 117, which is the bulletin on examination of financial statements. Those notes read, 'It is contemplated that before signing a report of the type suggested, the accountant will be satisfied that his examination has been adequate and in conformity with the principles outlined in this bulletin.'

And note 6 reads: 'It is contemplated that the form of report would be modified when and as necessary to embody any qualifications, reservations or supplementary explanations.' With those notes in front of you now and with what you know about the manner in which the examination of the McKesson & Robbins accounts was conducted by Price, Waterhouse & Co., and in the light of all the points which have been raised during the course of the testimony in this proceeding, do you still think that you were justified in signing the accounts?

A. Yes, sir, I certainly do. I signed those accounts in good faith in the belief that those accounts were thoroughly true. I thoroughly think I was justified in signing them." [1283]

[1283] R. 2056-2059.

Section V

CONCLUSIONS AS TO THE PRICE, WATERHOUSE & CO. AUDIT OF McKESSON & ROBBINS, INCORPORATED, AND AS TO THE ADEQUACY OF THE SAFEGUARDS INHERING IN GENERALLY ACCEPTED AUDITING PRACTICES

In section II of this report the circumstances surrounding the exposure of the Musica brothers and in section III a description of the manner by which they accomplished the manipulation of the accounts of the McKesson Companies were set forth as fully as the facts were developed. In section IV a detailed description of the manner in which Price, Waterhouse & Co. performed the audit for the McKesson Companies was presented with special emphasis on the work done on the divisions in which the manipulation of the accounts was carried out. In this section, the work of Price, Waterhouse & Co. will be evaluated in the light of available published material on auditing theory and practice and of the testimony of witnesses called by the Commission to give their expert opinions on auditing procedures.[1284] The purpose of this appraisal will be to reach a conclusion as to whether Price, Waterhouse & Co. in their work followed auditing procedures generally accepted at that time and, if so, whether those procedures are adequate to assure to investors the reliability of financial statements certified by independent public accountants. Where weaknesses appear to exist it will be our purpose to indicate the defects and, in a general way, the manner in which we believe they may be overcome.

In developing our conclusions we find it necessary to recognize a distinction between auditing procedures as such and the manner in which they are applied in a given case. In the pages to follow, after an introductory consideration of the material available for judging existing standards, we examine the various procedures involved and comment upon the manner of their application by Price, Waterhouse & Co. However, in arriving at our conclusions under each topic we limit ourselves to an opinion as to whether the procedures as outlined for this engagement equalled those accepted by the profession generally and whether the latter are adequate for the purpose

[1284] Since this section of the report generally follows the same order as section IV, specific cross references thereto will be omitted except for references to material not contained in the corresponding subsection.

intended. Although the manner in which Price, Waterhouse & Co. applied particular procedures is to some extent also discussed under each of the topics, a conclusion as to whether, within the procedures followed, there was sufficient evidence to have led properly alert and inquisitive auditors to the discovery of the fraud must be reserved for discussion to the end of this section where it seems to us the matter can be better considered in a subsection devoted exclusively to that topic.[1285]

A. MATERIAL FOR JUDGING STANDARDS PREVAILING DURING THE PERIOD OF THE GIRARD-McKESSON ENGAGEMENT

1. Published Materials

Authoritative published material on auditing principles and procedures is not as extensive as that on accounting principles and procedures nor as voluminous as the growth in the profession might suggest.[1286] This may be attributed, possibly, to a reluctance on the part of professional accountants to write in specific terms about practices they follow in the profession or, possibly, to the thorough character of the first important contribution to the literature of auditing.[1287] The great demand for auditing instruction in this country in the last twenty-five years, however, has brought a few textbooks into the field.

The most useful material for our purpose, however, is the series of bulletins referred to in section IV of this report,[1288] which culminated in the one entitled, "Examination of Financial Statements by Independent Public Accountants," a 41 page pamphlet prepared and published by the American Institute of Accountants in January 1936. A

1285 Subsection N, pages 438 ff. *infra*.

1286 Broadly speaking, accounting principles and procedures govern the manner in which the accounts are kept and the results presented in financial statements; e. g. whether inventories should be stated at cost, market, or cost or market whichever is lower. Auditing principles and procedures relate to the manner in which the accounting records are reviewed and the resulting financial statements are verified by persons who had no part in making the original record; e. g., an independent review of the accounts and supporting evidence to determine that the inventory has been accurately stated on whatever basis selected.

1287 The first important contribution to the literature appears to have been "Auditing: A Practical Manual for Auditors" by Lawrence R. Dicksee, F. C. A., of the firm of Price & Dicksee, Formerly Lecturer on Bookkeeping at the Technical Schools of the County Borough of Cardiff, London, Gee and Co., 34 Moorgate Street, E. C., 1892; viii and 305 pages. One thousand copies of this edition were printed, followed by the same number of the second, third, and fourth editions in 1895, 1898, and 1900; 1500 copies each of the fifth through the ninth editions in 1902, 1904, 1907, 1909, and 1912; 2500 copies of the tenth, eleventh, and twelfth editions in 1915, 1919, and 1922; and 3000 copies of the thirteenth and fourteenth editions in 1924 and 1928. In 1905 the first authorized American edition of this work, edited by Robert H. Montgomery and containing an introduction by Arthur Lowes Dickinson, a volume of 385 pages, was published in a printing of 1000 copies. Reprintings of this edition were 500 copies in May 1907, 2000 copies in January 1908, and 750 copies in April 1908. A second American edition, edited by Montgomery, appeared in a printing of 3500 copies in 1909. This was followed by five editions of Montgomery's Auditing Theory and Practice in 1912, 1915, 1921, 1927, and 1934; the fifth printing of the last edition being dated October 1938, a volume of viii and 772 pages. 84,000 copies of this book had been sold prior to December 31, 1938, and 18,000 copies of the abridged edition, Montgomery and Staub, Auditing Principles. Ritts named Robert H. Montgomery's Auditing Theory and Practice as the recognized book on auditing procedure. R. 852–854.

1288 Page 141 *supra*.

partner of Price, Waterhouse & Co. participated in the preparation of this Bulletin, and members of their staff wrote interpretations of this Bulletin and its immediate predecessor. Forty-one and twenty-six page bulletins cannot be considered exhaustive treatises on the subject of auditing, yet by virtue of their sponsorship and wide acceptance among the profession and their avowed purpose of making known to bankers and business men the nature of the work done by an accountant in the performance of an examination of financial statements, they have been the most acceptable general guide to the requirements of such work. In the preceding section it was observed that the Price, Waterhouse & Co. questionnaire on internal check and control [1289] referred to the first of this series of Bulletins, and that Thorn and Rowbotham accepted the latest edition as a fair general statement of the procedure to be followed in an examination of financial statements.[1290] As will be seen in the next subsection, partners of other public accounting firms also expressed similar opinions.

2. Testimony of Expert Witnesses

As an addition to available published material, the importance of the conclusions to be drawn from the facts developed in this proceeding warranted calling upon a number of public accountants of broad experience in the profession to aid in developing a clear impression of what was considered generally accepted auditing procedure as practiced by representative firms. On the morning of January 4, 1939, (the day before hearings opened) representatives of the American Institute of Accountants called upon the Chairman and other representatives of the Commission and offered to cooperate with the Commission in any way possible. Further discussions were held in the office of the Regional Administrator in New York, during which it was determined that the Institute could be of assistance in arranging for the appearance of representative accountants to testify as to the authoritative character of the Bulletin referred to above, and in some detail as to the interpretation they placed upon some of its more important provisions.

In the hearings twelve accountants were asked to testify, three of these on the suggestion of the Institute. The list included eleven partners of public accounting firms and one representative of the teaching profession.

In the order of their appearance, they were:

Samuel J. Broad—Peat, Marwick, Mitchell & Co., New York.
Charles Oliver Wellington—Scovell, Wellington & Co., New York.
William H. Bell—Haskins & Sells, New York.
Victor H. Stempf—Touche, Niven & Co., New York.

[1289] Ex. 17.
[1290] See pages 155-157, 358 *supra*.

Norman J. Lenhart—Lybrand, Ross Bros. & Montgomery, New York.
John K. Mathieson—Mathieson, Aitken & Co., Philadelphia.
Henry A. Horne—Webster, Horne & Blanchard, New York.
Charles B. Couchman—Barrow, Wade, Guthrie & Co., New York.
Hiram T. Scovill—professor of accountancy and head of the Department of Business Organization and Operation, University of Illinois, Urbana.
Joseph J. Klein—Klein, Hinds & Finke, New York.
George D. Bailey—Ernst & Ernst, Detroit.
Charles W. Jones—Arthur Andersen & Co., Chicago. [1291]

Testimony of these witnesses upon uniform questions based upon the Bulletin occupied one day for each witness during the period February 20, 1939 to March 14, 1939, a time of intense activity in the accounting profession, during which, nevertheless, the witnesses devoted considerable time to the preparation for their appearance. [1292]

All of the witnesses were thoroughly familiar with the bulletin, "Examination of Financial Statements by Independent Public Accountants." Broad served as chairman and Lenhart as an active member of the Committee which drafted it. Six others of the group were represented in its preparation, either in criticizing the draft, or as members of firms which were represented on the Committee by another partner. The prevailing opinion of the group was that the Bulletin was designed to provide the public, as well as the profession, with an up-to-date outline of accepted procedures followed by independent auditors in examining financial statements for credit purposes and for annual reports to stockholders and to describe the functions of auditors and the limitations inhering in their work.[1293]

[1291] The activity of the profession during the season of the year when the testimony was taken dictated that the majority of the witnesses be called from the city in which the hearings were held. The experience of the partners of public accounting firms averaged twenty-six years in public practice of which an average of approximately eighteen years was as a partner. With four exceptions, substantially all of the business life of the witnesses had been devoted to public accounting. Scovill, following five years in public accounting practice, became professor of accountancy and then head of his department in which he had served twenty-five years at the time of the hearings. A schedule showing the size of the firms represented is given at page 137 *supra*.

[1292] *In the Matter of McKesson & Robbins, Inc.*, Testimony of Expert Witnesses, Government Printing Office, Washington, D. C., 638 pp., price 65 cents. This testimony will be referred to repeatedly in the pages to follow. However, since that volume contains a comprehensive table of contents, page references to it will be omitted in those cases in which the basis for a general statement may be found by consulting the table of contents. In this report P. followed by a numeral refers to pages in this printed testimony. See footnote 1 *supra*.

[1293] As an introduction to their testimony these witnesses were asked to define the classes of accountancy services rendered by independent public accountants as a basis for the issuance of a certificate. Three witnesses stated that occasionally an examination confined only to the balance sheet would lead to a certificate. (Broad, Lenhart, Bailey, P. 3, 223, 538.) Four other witnesses stated that special examinations could lead to a certificate but rarely did. (Wellington, Stempf, Mathieson, Klein, P. 64, 121, 272, 479.) The witnesses agreed that a detailed audit could lead to a certificate, but it was pointed out that such audits for large corporations were out of the question and that such work usually was confined to special features of an examination and therefore rarely led to a certificate. *There was, therefore, a general and complete concurrence in the view that a balance sheet examination which included a review of the profit and loss account was the type of service generally resulting in the certification of financial statements. It is this type of work which is contemplated when, in this report, we use the terms financial or balance sheet examination or audit.* This type of work supplemented by additional analyses required to complete schedules included in registration statements and annual reports was considered by all of the witnesses in public practice to be the type contemplated by the rules and regulations of the Commission.

Except for variations based on the extent of internal check and control and special circumstances of each individual case, there was a general agreement among the accountants that the principles laid down in the Bulletin were of general application to all types and sizes of companies, and most witnesses stated that the Bulletin was used as a general guide in their practice. This was to be construed broadly, however, as audit programs were developed for each individual engagement and the majority considered the procedures outlined to be a minimum for most examinations. Six of the twelve witnesses stated that they generally went beyond the requirements of the Bulletin, and the other six stated that their work was generally about the same as prescribed but that limiting the work to this minimum depended upon the circumstances of each case. The consensus was that the Bulletin represented a codification of existing accepted practice and probably resulted in a re-examination of procedures followed by individual firms but that the publication of the work did not lead to any material changes in auditing procedures. With one exception, the witnesses stated that all members of their staffs were required to be familiar with the Bulletin and in some instances were supplied with copies.[1294]

B. APPOINTMENT OF AUDITORS, ORGANIZATION OF STAFF, AND BEGINNING THE EXAMINATION

1. Appointment and Responsibility of Auditors; Determination of the Scope of the Engagement

All appointments of Price, Waterhouse & Co. as auditors for Girard & Co., Inc. and the successor McKesson Companies were made by letter from Coster or McGloon near the close of the year to be audited. Likewise, all of the long-form reports were addressed to Coster as president of the several Companies. The certificates published in the Corporations' reports to stockholders in the early years contained no salutation but from 1930 on the Maryland Company reports were addressed to the directors, and the Canadian Company reports to the shareholders as required by Canadian law.[1295] Of these, as noted above, only the printed reports to stockholders, as distinguished from the typewritten long-form reports addressed to Coster, reached the hands of all of the directors.

The tenor of the testimony of Rowbotham, Thorn, and Ritts, as previously referred to, especially in connection with the auditors' report, leaves the distinct impression that they all regarded Coster

[1294] Klein stated that his firm had no precise requirement but that as a matter of fact all of his firm's staff were familiar with the Bulletin. P. 480. Scovill requires all of his instruction staff to be familiar with it and uses it himself as a basis for lectures but pointed out that it is inadequate as a textbook. However, his advanced students are urged to get it. P. 434.

[1295] Page 333 *supra*.

as their firm's employer. Ritts, as will be recalled, stated that the first duty of the auditors was to "* * * the President or the Board of Directors, the people that hired us. * * *"[1296] Thorn in explaining the omission of comments in submitting the accounts of the units whose books were kept at Bridgeport stated that while matters would be brought to their attention during the examination, written comment was unnecessary for the auditors "* * * would be reporting to them on their own houses in that case."[1297] Rowbotham, although stating that he thought the report was to the Corporation through Coster, would, with the possible exception in the case of serious suspicions as to Coster himself, have first referred an individual director to Coster in all cases before disclosing information requested on any Division except his own.[1298]

The manner of appointing the auditors in this case was the same as that described by the expert witnesses as perhaps the typical American situation. They testified that an executive officer, ordinarily the president but sometimes the treasurer or comptroller, appoints the auditors usually with no affirmative action by the board of directors, especially in the case of renewals. In rare cases the stockholders elect, but in the usual case under the proxy system, this usually means, in practical effect, indirect appointment by the officers. In respect to the responsibility of the auditors, most of the accountant witnesses stated that they felt that their primary responsibility ran to the Corporation or to the directors as representing the stockholders. While all admitted responsibility to stockholders through some chain, only one stated a primary responsibility directly to them.

The manner in which the auditors are appointed raises an interesting question of public policy and may also directly affect the approach and responsibility which the auditors and their staffs take toward

1296 Page 344 *supra*.

1297 Page 330 *supra*.

1298 Page 344 *supra*. While there is no evidence that the majority of other accountants would have acted differently, we cannot help but commend the procedure suggested in the following quotation from Montgomery, Robert H., Auditing Theory and Practice, 5th Ed., Ronald Press, New York, 1934 (hereinafter referred to as Montgomery, 5th Ed.), p. 743:

> "As the persons responsible for the corporation's affairs, the directors are legally entitled to see any and all accounts and records of the corporation and cannot properly be refused access thereto by officers or employees. This is a very important right. Knowledge of it and action under it may enable representatives of minority interests on a board to protect the interests they represent from illegal discrimination against them by the majority. Auditors should feel free to invite any and all of the directors to have the benefit, individually, of such information as the auditor can give from his examination."

their work.[1299] A much discussed proposal has been that American corporations should adopt the English and Canadian practice of requiring appointment of auditors by the stockholders. The efficacy of this proposal as a panacea for all the weaknesses in the procedures most commonly followed in this country is challenged at once by some who state that in practice appointment would be controlled by those who solicit the proxies, most often the officer-directors of the company.

An alternative proposal is that in the larger corporations, appointment of the auditors by a non-officer committee of the board of directors would have the merit of placing the appointment in a group of men familiar with the corporation's affairs but at the same time removed from the daily routine of the business. Appointment by such a group should emphasize the necessity for including the entire operating organization within the scope of the auditors' examination.

A third proposal is a blend of the first two and it is claimed secures advantages attributed to each of them. This plan contemplates the election of the auditors by vote of the stockholders, with the company or management nomination to be made by a committee of the board selected from the non-officer members.

For an adequate consideration of the foregoing problem, two collateral questions must be treated at the same time. The first is the time of the appointment and the second is who, under any one of the three options, will be delegated to confer with the auditors as to the details of the engagement.

The importance of these aspects of the question is illustrated very well by the history of the Girard-McKesson engagement. It will be recalled that all of the work was done after the closing date, under constant pressure by Coster for early completion of the work and submission of the final report. The scope of the engagement was set forth in the letters exchanged between Coster or McGloon and the auditors as related in an earlier part of this report. These letters indicated that Price, Waterhouse & Co. performed a balance sheet audit apparently without limitations being imposed by the client until 1930,

1299 Cf. the position of lawyers as stated in Securities and Exchange Commission, Report on the Study and Investigation of the Work, Activities, Personnel and Functions of Protective and Reorganization Committees, Part VII, Management Plans without Aid of Committees, p. 13:

> "In many respects the conflicts which attach to a management which promulgates a voluntary plan [of reorganization] likewise attach to the company's counsel. These plans are often involved and complex; counsel necessarily must play a large part in their preparation and in their presentation to security holders. Moreover counsel frequently must solve difficult legal problems involving the validity of the proposed corporate action. In brief the company's counsel in these voluntary situations often assumes as important a role as in reorganizations consummated in judicial proceedings. But these voluntary plans frequently place counsel in an equivocal position. To the extent that the management's duty to security holders is attenuated by the existence of conflicts of interest of the nature described above, the same will hold true of company's counsel because of the relations between them. Ostensibly they are retained by the corporation and paid by it; actually their loyalties run to the management which was responsible for the creation and continuance of their employment. Consciously or otherwise their point of view is likely to be identical with the management's. And where the management's interests clash with those of security holders, the company's counsel often will be found supporting and furthering the manaement's objectives."

when Coster instructed Jaureguy not to carry out the auditors' proposal that a few days' original bank deposit slips be checked to the cash receipts book.[1300] In subsequent years this limitation was retained and an understanding that receivables, and later accounts payable, would not be circularized, was incorporated in letters acknowledging the engagement. The testimony of the directors is that with rare exceptions, members of the board had no part in arranging for the audit and did not know the content either of the letters of engagement or of the long-form report addressed to Coster, in which the character of the work was set forth. The principal contact the directors had with the audit was by observation in their own wholesale houses which led them to infer that the work at Bridgeport was of the same nature.

Returning to the main question of the method of appointing auditors, a study of the various proposals which have been communicated to the Commission and of the testimony of the expert witnesses who were asked their opinion on the various aspects of the question leads to the conclusion that the general adoption of changes in respect to the appointment of auditors would have a salutary effect upon auditing practice in the United States. The following program appears to us to have some advantages over others:[1301]

1. Election of the auditors for the current year by a vote of the stockholders at the annual meeting followed immediately by notice to the auditors of their appointment.

2. Establishment of a committee to be selected from non-officer members of the board of directors which shall make all company or management nominations of auditors and shall be charged with the duty of arranging the details of the engagement.

3. The certificate (sometimes called short-form report or opinion) should be addressed to the stockholders. All other reports should be addressed to the board of directors and copies delivered by the auditors to each member of the board.

4. The auditors should be required to attend meetings of the stockholders at which their report is presented to answer questions thereon, to state whether or not they have been given all the information and access to all the books and records which they have required, and to have the right to make any statement or explanation they desire with respect to the accounts.

5. If for any reason the auditors do not complete the engagement and render a report thereon, they shall nevertheless render a report

[1300] See pages 196–197 and footnote 682 *supra*.

[1301] Cf. recommendations of the American Institute of Accountants and of the New York Stock Exchange, Appendix A; and provisions of the English Companies Act, 1929 and Horace B. Samuel's proposed amendments to that Act, Appendix B. See also Samuel's discussion in Shareholders' Money, Sir Isaac Pitman & Sons, Ltd., London, 1933, at pp. 231–235, 315–321. For a recent adoption in the United States of the essential features of a program substantially in accord with that proposed in the text, see Section 32 (a) of the Investment Company Act of 1940.

on the amount of work they have done and the reasons for non-completion, which report should be sent by the company to all stockholders.

Election by the stockholders should carry with it unquestioned direct responsibility of the auditors to them. In the event of a disagreement over procedures, the knowledge that the cause of a breach in relations would have to be reported to the stockholders should strengthen the position of the auditor. Respecting determination of the scope of the audit Montgomery states:

"The auditor should insist that he be permitted to make such an examination of the books and records of the undertaking as will enable him to fulfill the purpose for which the audit is to be made. He must make it clear that the object cannot be attained unless he alone defines the extent of the work to be done. Only harm can result from any departure from this rule." [1302]

The quotation above raises a distinction which was emphasized by several of the witnesses, namely that the client may specify the class of work desired or in the words of the quotation, the "object" desired to be attained but the auditor must reserve to himself the decision as to the scope or extent of the work to be done. Whether the purpose of the engagement is to be more comprehensive than merely securing certified financial statements is usually determined by discussion between a partner of the accounting firm and an officer of the client (to be determined by the committee on auditing in the above program), but in any case determination of the scope of the examination necessary to achieve the purpose or object of the engagement must be reserved to a partner or supervisor of the accounting firm.[1303]

Election of the auditors at the annual meeting early in the year to be audited is desirable as an aid to efficient work for such election should carry with it the opportunity for the auditors to do part of their work during the year. This will not only alleviate the burden at the year end, but will also permit a more deliberate review and check of the accounting procedures of the company.

Copies of all reports rendered by the auditors should be sent to all of the directors to insure that their contents are not confined to certain officers or to a minority of the board as was the case with McKesson & Robbins. The short report or certificate under the program should be addressed to the stockholders. With the auditors also available for questioning when the report is presented at stockholders' meetings, a greater feeling of direct responsibility to others than the officers of the company should be engendered and since the certificate not only usually forms a part of the corporation's annual

---

1302 Montgomery, 5th Ed., p. 33.

1303 The materiality of the limitations in the McKesson case will be discussed in connection with the various topics which they concern.

report to stockholders but also is included in the annual report filed with this Commission under the Securities Exchange Act of 1934, this inclusion must recognize also the auditors' responsibility to all classes of investors whom the Act seeks to protect.

In short, while the appointment of Price, Waterhouse & Co. and the determination of the scope of the engagement in this case was made in the manner followed by generally accepted practice, we do not feel that it affords sufficient safeguards to investors. While, as we have previously said,[1304] the primary responsibility for the accuracy of information filed with us and disseminated among investors rests upon management, it is the duty of auditors to check the purported results of operation of that management and to report thereon to investors. Therefore we think that the appointment and absolute control of the selection of auditors by management or by any program short of that suggested above would not sufficiently mark the lines of responsibility to investors or give the auditors sufficient freedom of action to insure to them that independence which we deem necessary for the purpose of certifying financial statements to be filed with us and to be rendered to stockholders.

2. Organization and Training of Staff

An important problem which this case presents is whether the composition of the Price, Waterhouse & Co. staff was materially different from that of contemporary public accounting organizations and whether the character and training of the staff and its supervision were contributing factors in the failure of the auditing procedures to reveal the fraud perpetrated over a period of fourteen years in a business subject to the auditors' scrutiny at least annually during that time.

The subject is necessarily intangible and because of the human factors involved does not lend itself to absolute appraisal, but some analysis must be attempted as a background for estimating the adequacy of the audit as a whole. Staff organization in an accountant's office varies with the size of the office, but all follow substantially the same pattern. Almost all public accounting firms are partnerships of varying size. Excluding stenographic and other office employees, the professional staff in a large organization consists of managers of offices, supervising or managing accountants, senior accountants, semi-senior accountants, and junior accountants The smaller firms do not have managers or supervisors as the partners fulfill those functions, and some of the firms do not use the classification of semi-senior.

The size of staff employed by firms represented by partners who testified in the hearings was presented in section IV of this report.

1304 *In the Matter of Interstate Hosiery Mills, Inc.*, 4 S. E. C. 706 (1939).

An indication of the seasonal nature of public accounting work and the responsibilities devolving upon partners of the firms is given below:

Firm [a]	Number of Partners	Number of Staff Per Partner [b]		Peak Season Increase – Per Cent of Permanent
		Permanent	Peak	
Price, Waterhouse & Co.	24	31.3	61.0	95
Peat, Marwick, Mitchell & Co.	25	(c)	(c)	(c)
Scovell, Wellington & Co.	11	11.4	15.9	39
Touche, Niven & Co.	17	8.8	13.5	54
Haskins & Sells	57	12.6	19.7	56
Lybrand, Ross Bros. & Montgomery	32	18.4	25.5	39
Mathieson, Aitken & Co.	4	10.0	10.0	0
Webster, Horne & Blanchard	4	6.3	6.3	0
Barrow, Wade, Guthrie & Co.	17	15.3	20.6	35
Klein, Hinds & Finke	6	8.3	16.7	100
Ernst & Ernst	27	24.1	35.2	46
Arthur Andersen & Co.	15	(c)	(c)	54

[a] Arranged in the order of the partner's appearance in the hearings.
[b] Partner load is calculated from data shown in the table at page 137 *supra*.
[c] Information sufficiently accurate for this purpose not supplied.

The table shows clearly that Price, Waterhouse & Co., with the exception of one much smaller firm, expanded its staff in the peak season to a much greater extent than the other firms represented and that this expansion was added to a staff which in the slack season was much larger in relation to the number of partners than was the case for any of the other firms listed. It seems inevitable that the burden on the partners, managers, and permanent staff seniors must have been greater with an increase of ninety-five per cent in the staff during the peak season (over sixty per cent of these serving for the first time) than with the increase of fifty-six per cent or less shown for the other large firms.[1305] And although it is claimed by Price, Waterhouse & Co. that their managers, by virtue of their long service and of their contracts giving them a share in the profits

[1305] Thornton, F. W., Duties of the Senior Accountant, Published for The American Institute of Accountants by the American Institute Publishing Co., Inc., New York, 1932, (hereinafter referred to as Duties of the Senior Accountant), pp. 88–89:

"In all the better accounting organizations even reasonably good seniors are kept employed through good business and bad; it is the juniors and mediocre seniors that are employed only during the busy season. For this reason the senior is more distinctly a part of the firm organization and has the stronger obligation to support his firm's standards of work. Seniors are the hardest worked of all the men in any accounting organization. The junior does his day's work, under direction, somewhat mechanically, perhaps, and forgets it when the whistle blows. The manager and partner have worries enough, but they do not have a great amount of actual clerical calculation to do. The senior must do quite as much actual computing as any of his juniors and must also bear some of the same kind of worry that besets the manager. The responsibility is good for him if he is ever to become a managing accountant or partner."

of the firm, are exceptionally qualified to take over the important responsibilities that are delegated to them by the partners, nevertheless the conclusion seems inescapable that, based upon figures supplied to the Commission in this investigation, Price, Waterhouse & Co. partners could not have given adequate attention to the training, development, and supervision of their staff.

In the assignments of the staff, Price, Waterhouse & Co.'s practice as revealed in this case was supported uniformly by all of the expert witnesses. Partners and top staff men are usually permanently assigned to a client, seniors below those in charge are shifted to some extent, while juniors are generally rotated. This practice has both advantages and disadvantages. Permanent assignment of top men is frequently, if not generally, requested by the client and tends to keep down the cost of the engagement and increase its efficiency because of the familiarity with the client's problems gained through consecutive years on the work. Danger from staleness and intimacy is present in this arrangement but is avoided, to some extent at least, by the rotation of seniors and juniors who provide a new point of view. Rotation in these lower classes is provided by normal progress in the ranks and by a desire on the part of the firms to provide a broad experience for permanent staff members. Assignments in all cases are made on the basis of availability and adaptability for the work in hand.

It will be recalled that prior to Rowbotham's assignment in 1928 as partner in charge, the Girard-McKesson engagement was a relatively small one and the men employed on the work were mostly from the permanent staff. With the corporate expansion of the client, the group assigned to the work at Bridgeport included a high percentage of new and temporary employees, higher in fact than the average for the firm as a whole, for of the thirty-seven different staff men who were engaged on the audits at Bridgeport for 1928 to 1937 inclusive, twenty-eight were temporary juniors and three others who later became permanent members of the staff served there in the first year of their employment. Moreover, during this period from 1928 through 1937, seventeen juniors were assigned to Bridgeport in the first or only year of their employment with Price, Waterhouse & Co. and except for the New York manager in charge of the entire engagement, in only two years (1928 and 1937) did the staff assigned to the Bridgeport work include any one who had received a certified public accountant's certificate or was a chartered accountant.

Judging from the testimony of the partners of other firms, partiality for apprenticeship training, as expressed by Rowbotham, has now been abandoned by those firms, for the majority of them in the present selection of juniors for the permanent staff seemed to favor college graduates who had concentrated in accounting and had had some business experience. This does not mean that actual auditing experience is not also necessary before a staffman is ready to assume important responsibilities or that in the past capable auditors have not been developed through such training, but it does mean that in accord with the trend in other professions broader academic training as a present and future prerequisite to ultimate professional standing is now recognized. However, in the selection of men for the temporary staff, who are employed sometimes for a few days and seldom for more than a few months during the peak season, all agreed that the emphasis was on prior public accounting experience so that time would not be lost in training. We cannot state too strongly that such short periods of employment are inherently unfair not only to the men but also, in view of the nature of the professional services that might reasonably be expected under such conditions of employment, to the firms themselves in their efforts to maintain high standards of professional responsibility.

The general practice of all the firms, including Price, Waterhouse & Co., seems to be to require the permanent staff to study for and obtain the certified public accountant certificate to qualify for advancement to the higher ranks. In addition to actual work on engagements, various methods of training are followed, such as staff meetings and prescribed reading. The trend seems to be to urge attendance at night schools, if available, since the instruction to be obtained in that way was considered by the witnesses to be more effective than office classes. In line with this policy the status of staff senior is attained in most cases through promotion within the firm.

The rapid rise of Thorn and Ritts under the sponsorship of Rowbotham requires consideration. Rowbotham, the partner in charge of the McKesson work since 1928, was apprentice trained. Of his principal assistants, Jaureguy was college trained. Thorn and Ritts had never taken any college courses in accountancy,[1306] but were trained in the apprenticeship fashion, the former by Jaureguy and the latter, for the period on the McKesson job, by Thorn. Thorn had never been on an audit before he joined Jaureguy at Bridgeport in January 1928. A substantial part of that year and much of the next he worked on the mechanics of the merger, and early in 1930 became senior in charge of the work at Bridgeport. This record seems to indicate relatively little experience or training in the basic principles of auditing. Ritts in turn had had two years of junior experience before coming under Thorn's tutelage early in 1931 and became senior

[1306] It is interesting to note that Hartzell and McGloon who carried out most of the work for Girard & Co., Inc. had much less business experience and very little more formal education than Ritts prior to their employment by Price, Waterhouse & Co.

in charge at Bridgeport early in 1933 about the time Thorn was appointed manager of the entire engagement. In this connection it is interesting to recall that Ritts passed his C. P. A. examination in 1936, nearly four years after attaining the status of senior in charge at Bridgeport and Thorn passed the examination in 1931, two years after attaining a senior rating. Neither of these men could be called well-seasoned auditors with a broad training at the time they were placed in charge of the examination of the home office divisions of McKesson which were under the direct supervision of Coster, a man recognized as having a powerful personality.

These then were the men upon whom Rowbotham relied during a major part of the life of the McKesson work. Rowbotham's control of the work was exercised through formal approval of the audit program, consultation with the manager in charge at New York, and review of the accounts and reports. On the whole McKesson engagement for 1937, comprising approximately 84 separate units, total partners' time in all offices was 86 hours against 21,534 hours spent by the staff.[1306a] While there was no consistent testimony that other accountants would necessarily have done more, this procedure would certainly appear to be a minimum of partner participation in conducting the audit.

An appraisal of the character of the work done on the various phases of the job by the several juniors engaged on the 1937 audit will be the subject of subsequent comment. It seems desirable here to make only a few general comments on the training and supervision of the juniors while on the job. The record indicates that guidance of the juniors on the work was of two types—reference to the papers used on the prior year's engagement, which were followed meticulously, and instruction from the senior in charge. It appears that Ritts' emphasis throughout was on dispatch in completing the mechanical work rather than in making sure that his staff had a proper understanding of the work they did. This impression is gained, for example, from one junior's inability to explain the purpose of certain steps he performed in his cash work; another's acceptance of and work on the foreign crude drug sales register believing it covered all crude drugs and his refusal to comment upon phases of inventory work not done by him; a third's insistence upon short answers to questions on the questionnaires and his apparent lack of interest in his surroundings; a fourth junior's mechanical approach to the inventory work; Wyman's unquestioning following of the prior year's papers on the Canadian Company work; and Ritts' failure to insist that correct explanations be obtained for accounting procedures.[1307] Ritts' own difficulty in

[1306a] Time spent by the staff was as follows: managers 1,769 hours, seniors 3,714 hours, and assistants 16,051 hours. See page 355 *supra*.

[1307] See pages 199–200; 260–261, 262–263; 178, 267; 267; 217, 218, 222; 178–179, 231–232 *supra*.

identifying documents and in explaining the client's methods seem to indicate that his supervision of his staff was not sufficiently detailed to keep these matters fresh in his own mind. If he had followed Thornton's advice more closely his testimony in this proceeding should have been clearer.[1308] Not all of the accountant witnesses would go as far as Thornton suggests though some indicated as much.[1309]

The entire Price, Waterhouse & Co. staff on the Bridgeport unit of the engagement from Rowbotham down indicated a surprising lack of interest in the nature of the documents used in carrying on what they understood to be the leading crude drug business in this country. They also failed to make any independent inquiry as to the nature of the products and the characteristics of the crude drug trade. It is not surprising that the juniors on the work did no more than they were told when their superiors had so little interest in learning what they could about the crude drug business over a period of fourteen years. Rowbotham testified that he had no other experience in that field. Ritts and Thorn likewise had no other experience in the field but accepted Coster as the leading crude drug expert in the country. After the exposure of the fraud an encyclopedia was consulted for enlightenment as to the nature of the products which were supposed to have been bought and sold in such quantities. It apparently never occurred to anyone while on this engagement to study any public sources of information about the drug business in general or the crude drug trade in particular.[1310]

1308 Duties of the Senior Accountant, pp. 15–17:

"A senior should work with his staff on the detailed vouching until the character of the vouchers is established, after which the assistants may be instructed which they are to accept and which are to be questioned.

* * * * * * *

"Only by taking some part in the detail work of each section can the senior be reasonably sure that the assistants, however conscientious they be, are doing their work as it should be done.

"Systematically inadequate vouchers and questionable entries will have a far better chance of passing without notice if they are scrutinized only by relatively inexperienced assistants.

"Upon the whole, the senior will find the trouble of doing some of the routine work highly recompensed by the lively understanding of the accounts that it gives.

"After the assistants have been fairly started on their work, attention may be given to the work to be done personally by the senior. This is to be interrupted at intervals so that the senior may inspect the work being done by his subordinates."

1309 Another evidence of weakness of supervision and training of the staff is found in the condition of some of the working papers. Although Ritts, himself, seems to have been careful to write legibly and to date and initial all papers he prepared, he does not seem to have required this of his juniors for there are numerous papers in the record which are illegible or with no evidence on them to indicate the year of the audit or who prepared them. Perfection in these matters is not just an end in itself, for Cipriani includes these points in a list of six "* * * important, though apparently trivial points to which the junior accountant should pay particular attention in preparing working papers." Cipriani, Alfred B., Duties of the Junior Accountant, American Institute Publishing Co., Inc., New York, 1933 (hereinafter referred to as Cipriani) pp. 34–35. See also Montgomery, 5th Ed., p. 47; Jackson, J. Hugh, Audit Working Papers, American Institute of Accountants Foundation, New York, 1923, (hereinafter referred to as Jackson) pp. 11, 19 and model set of working papers in the appendix; Palmer, Leslie E., and Bell, William H., Accountants' Working Papers, Rev. Ed., The Ronald Press Company, New York, 1929, pp. 7–8; and Wildman, John R., Principles of Auditing, The William G. Hewitt Press, Brooklyn, 1920, pp. 54–55.

1310 In the wholesale houses, to some extent at least, each of the 60 odd houses acted as a source of information for and comparative check on the other. But the crude drug business, particularly the foreign which was considered by the auditors as a specialty business operated by a specialist in that field (Coster), was in the absence of any independent knowledge, a blind spot.

Without exception, all of the expert witnesses testified generally that they expected their staffs to become familiar with the trade or industry of the client before going on the job or at least before finishing it the first time. Many of the witnesses merely answered "Yes" or "We do" without further explanation.[1311] While the evidence before us is not conclusive that most other accountants would have done more, it does not seem unreasonable to us to expect an accountant to have sufficient interest in his client's business to learn enough independently about that trade or industry to give him a background for his work and a basis for appraising the operations of his client.[1312] Failure to do this in this case was an omission of the first magnitude. On the first point made in the preceding paragraph, all of the experts expected the seniors on their staffs to instruct juniors in the determination of the authenticity of documentary evidence of transactions, and all were quite positive in their assertion that staff members were expected to be alert to detect significant irregularities. The answers indicated full support of the old idea that an audit should reveal evidence of fraud if reflected by significant irregularities in the documents under review.[1313]

In general the witnesses stated paradoxically that while fraud accomplished by means of widespread collusion would not necessarily be uncovered by methods followed in a balance sheet audit, such methods should ordinarily lead to a reliable conclusion as to the general accuracy and integrity of the records.[1314] We can only interpret this as meaning that the discovery of fraud is a matter of alertness and not of simple mathematical precision and that, therefore, an inadequately trained staff unaware of the purpose of steps pursued by them and not fully supervised, especially when accentuated by a large number

---

1311 But see Scovill's answer at P. 442 for an excellent statement of the means by which such information may be acquired.

1312 Cf. P. 488. See also Montgomery, 5th Ed., p. 184 at which it is stated in respect to inventories:

> "A general familiarity with the normal stock which any well-conducted concern in the same business should carry is desirable."

1313 Even though the examination of samples of the records arouses no suspicion it is not necessarily to be assumed that the remaining records are also free from irregularities, which might be contrary to the fact. To this extent a detailed audit brings more transactions under review than a balance sheet examination based on tests and samples. However, where, as in the instant case, a detailed audit would have merely brought under review more of the same kind of records as were examined in the course of the balance sheet examination, it does not appear that the broader scope of the detailed audit would thus have necessarily assisted in the disclosure of the fraud.

1314 Cf. testimony of Victor H. Stempf:

> "I think the public interest requires a continuance of a type of examination which provides reasonable protection under normal circumstances as has been demonstrated adequately in the past. This precludes detailed examinations and advocates the use of sampling and testing.
>
> "On the other hand, it follows that the auditor's work does not follow the continuous path of recorded transactions, but on the contrary the auditor's course crosses and recrosses the path of recorded transactions. If the path be irregular, suspicion may be aroused. If the path be muddy, the inferences to be drawn become rather obvious, but if the path be scientifically built and particularly if its irregularities be screened with shrubbery and flowers, it is still likely that some of the irregularities will be found by the auditor who crosses and recrosses the path. But it is also probable that in so doing he may overlook or fail to encounter some of these irregularities which may in fact be the most vital." P. 168.

of temporary employees in the busy season, seems a dangerous basis for a conclusion that the records are reliable.[1315] In short, we feel that the increasing complexities of modern business require the highest type of trained personnel combined with adequate supervision if the auditors' signatures to the accounts are not to be misleading.

3. Investigation of New Clients

Public accountants are in an unusual position as compared with other professional and business men when it comes to the question of determining the precise nature of the business, financial standing, and reputation of the firm with which they are dealing. This unique position, however, arises only after the accountant has entered upon the first engagement and has had an opportunity to inspect the books of the client. The question is raised, therefore, as to whether it is good professional practice for public accountants to make an outside investigation of the reputation or credit rating of prospective clients, either before accepting an engagement or during the course of the first audit.

Price, Waterhouse & Co. accepted the Girard & Co., Inc. engagement without making any inquiry as to the nature of the business or the character of the men engaged in it. Coster was an acquaintance of a friend of a member of the Price, Waterhouse & Co. staff. Whether mere acquaintanceship constitutes a relationship such as to bring Coster into the category of a recommended client seems doubtful, although it may fairly be assumed that a friend of the firm would not knowingly send to them, as a prospect, a man with a record for manipulation of accounts and fraud of other descriptions.

Four of the eleven practicing accountant witnesses stated that new clients came to them through sources upon which they could rely so that no further investigation of the new client would be made. Seven of the eleven reported that if a prospective client came to them unrecommended, appropriate inquiries would be made before accepting the engagement. These inquiries were in some cases made of banks and in rare cases credit reports were obtained from investigating agencies. One witness stated, however, that it was a routine requirement of his organization to obtain credit ratings on all new clients.[1316] No advice to this effect in a treatise on auditing has come to our attention.

[1315] Kohler, Eric L., and Pettengill, Paul W., Principles of Auditing, McGraw-Hill Book Company, Inc., New York, 1932, (hereinafter referred to as Kohler and Pettengill) p. 39:

> ". . . a mere inspection of accounts by an intelligent and seasoned auditor may be of much greater significance than the most detailed examination by a person less competent."

See also Bacas, P. E., Madden, J. T., and Rosenkampff, A. H., Auditing Procedure, Ronald Press, New York, 1937, (hereinafter referred to as Bacas, Madden, and Rosenkampff) pp. 180–181:

> "There is really no special procedure which should be followed to bring fraud to light where there is no surface indication that something is not in order. It is necessary that the public accountant should do his work thoroughly so that nothing may escape him. Naturally, any peculiarities must be investigated, and, if suspicions are aroused, they should be the cause of a more concentrated effort. Fraud will usually be brought to light by capable public accountants if their work is done in an efficient manner."

[1316] Bailey, P. 640.

From the record, therefore, it appears that on the basis of general practice Price, Waterhouse & Co. were justified in accepting the engagement under the conditions recited and in not supplementing their own investigation of records by independent inquiry as to the reputation and past associations of the management of the business unless the fact that the firm of Girard & Co., Inc., described by its letterhead as "manufacturing chemists",[1317] was a newcomer during prohibition and a large user of alcohol for the preparation of hair tonics might be considered as taking the case out of the general rule. While there is no indication that an investigation by an independent agency would have, in this case, disclosed the fraud we feel that for the future the small expense involved in making some check of the reputation of the management of the client would be well warranted for even if such reports on their face do not disclose clear irregularities they may condition the approach to certain phases of the work or the acceptance of explanations given by officers of the client.

C. REVIEW OF THE CLIENT'S SYSTEM OF INTERNAL CHECK AND CONTROL

On a balance sheet audit, the examination of the client's system of internal check and control has a twofold purpose. A correct appraisal of the client's system is needed not only to ascertain the proportion of transactions necessary to be examined but also the type of tests necessary to be made in order to determine the reliability of the records specifically examined and by inference (though not conclusive) of those not specifically examined. In other words, to reach his conclusion as to the reliability of the figures contained on the financial statements, the auditor will examine certain records and will make various tests not only based on the company's records but independent of them. The proportion of the records to be examined and the type of the tests to be made will depend upon how much confidence as to reliability of the records can, in the first instance, be placed in the company's own system—whether because of internal check and control arising automatically from division of functions of personnel or from physical and mechanical checks, or as the result of internal audits.

The review of internal control is then a most important step on balance sheet audits or examinations.[1318] In our opinion that review would also be pertinent even though a detailed audit of all transactions were made. To assume that on a detailed audit an appraisal

[1317] Ex. 116.

[1318] "* * * the ordinary procedure of a balance sheet audit is adequate only when the auditor can satisfy himself of the sufficiency of the system of internal check—which in combination with a balance sheet audit and reasonable tests will afford substantial protection to the client against the risk of defalcations." Jackson, p. 8.

of internal control is superfluous is to assume that the auditor's concern with internal control is solely an attempt to assure himself that transactions not specifically reviewed are as reliable as those examined. Just as important however is a full knowledge of the company's system of internal control in order to appraise properly records specifically examined and to determine the procedures which should be followed to assure the reliability of those records. This latter point involving the relationship between the examination of internal control and the type of tests to be made as distinguished from the mere number of transactions to be examined has, it seems to us, not been properly emphasized in the past. Thornton's discussion of the subject is illustrative:

> "There arises the question, important to the auditor, as to how far internal check can be used as an auxiliary to the auditor's own examination. It will not do to accept internal check as a substitute for audit; a certificate must not be based upon figures verified only by the client's internal check or even by the client's auditing staff, if there be one; but the amount of detailed checking may well be reduced where the internal checking system is good and the observation of the senior leads to the firm belief that the check is properly carried out. For example, if the customer's ledger be kept by a clerk who does not handle money, if monthly statements are compared with the trial balance and mailed by another clerk who also does not handle money, if the control account is in order, less detailed checking of the customers' ledger will be needed than would be proper if the ledger clerk handled collections and mailed the statements himself." [1319]

Finally it seems to us that an examination of the system of internal check is not to be limited to particular accounting functions but should lead to a full knowledge of the manner in which, persons by whom, and place where the transactions are handled. In this subsection we will consider first the method of examination of the system of internal check and control and then the appraisal of the system.

1. Examination of the System

a. INSPECTION OF THE PLANT

In the work at Bridgeport it has been noted that Thorn in his first year as a senior in charge thought a knowledge of the manufacturing operations would be helpful to him in his work on the audit and that he did go through the plant. However, he did not take any of his staff through the plant. And Ritts neither inspected the plant himself nor took any of his staff through it. Contact was limited to that gained incidentally in going from the board room where most of the work was done to other offices on the same floor to do particular audit steps which could not conveniently be done elsewhere.

This lack of interest in making physical contact with the assets and operations of the business under examination is not supported by the

[1319] Duties of a Senior Accountant, pp. 80–81.

authorities. All of the expert witnesses testified that the men in charge of the examination were expected to become familiar, as accountants but not as engineering experts, with the nature of the plant, its products, and operating methods. Such knowledge was considered by the witnesses to be necessary as a background for appraising the adequacy of the system of internal check and as an aid in understanding the book records. Trouant sums up the advantages of a plant inspection very well:

> "A tour of the plant may assist the accountant in many ways, viz:
>
> "A look at the buildings and machinery may afford greater insight into the depreciation provisions required and the policy of the company with regard to maintenance; it may also help in reviewing the current capital expenditures and the charges for dismantled or abandoned equipment.
>
> "A general knowledge of the processes is essential to an understanding of the cost-accounting records.
>
> "Seeing the materials and supplies, processes and products assists in reviewing the methods of taking and pricing the inventory.
>
> "It is not expected that the accountant will be able to understand all that he sees or to exercise the function of an engineer, efficiency expert or appraiser, but he may obtain much helpful information and his client is usually glad to afford him the opportunity." [1320]

Thornton although warning that "While the senior may and should use knowledge so gained to guide him in his accounting work, he must not permit the client to lead him into the position of one who approves the accounts on the basis of physical inspection of the assets" nevertheless notes similar advantages from such inspection and suggests that "* * * The visit should be made after the examination has progressed so far that the senior has a rather comprehensive idea of the assets as shown by the books." [1321] Thus it appears that Thornton and Trouant of Price, Waterhouse & Co. advocate a procedure of plant inspection that Ritts would have done well to follow and which while it may have greater pertinency to manufacturing operations need not be so restricted but can well be extended to non-processing operations as well.

[1320] Trouant, D. L., Financial Audits, American Institute Publishing Co., Inc., New York, 1937, (hereinafter referred to as Trouant) p. 17. A similar opinion is expressed in Kohler and Pettengill, p. 29; also in Dicksee, Lawrence R., Auditing, First American Edition, Edited by Robert H. Montgomery, with an introduction by Arthur Lowes Dickinson, 1905, p. 106:

> "Even the Auditor experienced in Colliery Accounts will probably find that the thorough inspection of a new mine is really a wise economy of time; *in fact, whatever the nature of the business may be*, the Auditor who acquaints himself with the manner in which it is carried on does wisely." [Italics supplied.]

[1321] Duties of a Senior Accountant, p. 18. Cf. Thornton, F. W., Financial Examination, American Institute Publishing Co., Inc., New York, 1933 (hereinafter referred to as Financial Examinations), p. 50:

> "If the auditor has been consulted before the stocktaking it will be to his advantage to review the book records and to determine how frequently stock on hand has been wholly or partly checked physically and ascertain what differences were found when physical counts were made. Then, after a visit to the warehouse, factory or storerooms in which the merchandise is kept, he may make such suggestions as he thinks will be in the interest of better arrangement of the stock and of more effective stocktaking."

b. DETERMINATION OF DUTIES OF CLIENT'S PERSONNEL

Closely related to the physical properties of the client are the officers and employees who operate them and who record the transactions relating to them. All of the expert witnesses stated that a knowledge of the client's personnel and their respective duties was essential to the auditor and the majority stated that such knowledge was to be gained either by preparing charts of the organization or by listing the divisions of the business and the names of the persons working in the divisions having a bearing on the accounting work.[1322] These memoranda in whatever form were usually preserved in the permanent working paper file and brought up to date each year. A similar requirement, it will be recalled, appears on the Price, Waterhouse & Co. questionnaire on internal check and control but, except for occasional notes in the papers, was not fulfilled on this engagement at least for the Bridgeport office and plant. This failure may be attributed directly to Rowbotham for in his opinion, while the senior on the job should have such knowledge in his head and keep the manager posted, the partner would not be concerned with it and the firm's printed instruction he characterized as "* * * a text book requirement; it is not done in real life."

However, it seems probable that the text books reflected the actual audit programs of practicing accountants. Dicksee's first edition published in 1892, reproduced an audit program of one "Mr. David Chadwick, F. C. A.", an accountant of fifty years' experience. The first three items in a list of twenty-two on this program were:

"1. In commencing a new audit you should obtain a list of all the books kept, and of all persons authorized to receive or pay money and order goods.

"2. In the case of a joint stock company, examine the articles and board minutes respecting the receipt and payment of money, and the drawing of cheques, acceptances, etc.

"3. Ascertain and take note of the general system upon which the books are constructed, and the plan of checking the correctness of the accounts paid, and whether exclusively or generally by cheques." [1323]

In any event the idea was good in 1892, possibly as early as 1842, and is still good. A requirement for a record of observations not only forces clearer analysis but makes possible a proper review of the facts by superiors.

c. QUESTIONNAIRES

The questionnaire method of developing information in respect to the client's system of internal check and control as employed by Price, Waterhouse & Co. is one of several methods in general use among accountants today. Two of the expert witnesses stated that

---

1322 See also Trouant, p. 17; Bacas, Madden, and Rosenkampff, p. 178; Kohler and Pettengill, p. 29; Montgomery, 5th Ed., p. 62; Jackson, pp. 13–14.

1323 Dicksee, Lawrence R., Auditing, 1st Ed., Gee & Co., London, 1892, p. 3. The same program is reproduced in the 1928 edition of this book.

their firms used the questionnaire method, three provided their staff men with an outline to be followed in developing such information while the remaining seven had no formal program of this character but expected a permanent record to be made of important points. All stated that they relied upon inquiry and observation during the audit to determine that the system as explained to them was in fact being followed. Quite clearly the testimony of the several witnesses, including those from Price, Waterhouse & Co., indicates that this problem of reviewing the system of internal check and control is treated in entirely too casual a manner by many accountants.

On paper the Price, Waterhouse & Co. procedures would appear to be designed to produce a comprehensive review of the client's accounting procedures and the relationship of the various members of the office staff affected by the audit. However, the results obtained were weakened by two factors. The failure to carry out the item of the questionnaire which called for an outline of the company's organization showing each department and to whom it is responsible left undisclosed, at least in writing, that George Dietrich, the assistant treasurer, who, according to the 1932 questionnaire, controlled the cashiers, signed checks, supervised the cashiers who reconciled the bank accounts, held the petty cash fund, opened the mail, held unclaimed wages, mailed regular monthly statements to customers, passed on credits, held securities, authorized capital expenditures, signed notes payable and acceptances, and authorized loans to officials and employees, *also*, under Coster, ran the foreign crude drug business (which comprised over 65% of all business done at Bridgeport) at least to the extent that his initials or verbal clearance furnished the internal authority respecting all foreign crude drug purchase and sales transactions. The other factor concerns the failure, particularly in connection with the supplementary questionnaires and notes on individual phases of the system, to observe distinctions in the manner of handling foreign crude drug transactions which would have brought out more clearly the specific control of the Dietrich brothers over this business.[1324] This is particularly noticeable from Ritts' inability after eight years on the job to describe accurately the manner in which the foreign crude drug transactions were handled at the Bridgeport office and from his testimony stating that he did not know that since 1932 all foreign crude drug transactions throughout the year were purportedly collected by Manning & Company thus indicating that he could not have made the careful and thorough verification of the system of internal check required by his firm's printed instructions. This latter point is also illustrated by Ritts'

[1324] Answers to many of the questions were obtained from McGloon, the comptroller, and Johnson, the office manager, whose testimony shows that they themselves, in many particulars, did not know the exact manner in which the foreign crude drug transactions were handled.

failure to discover, in subsequent years, at any rate, after McGloon's initial answer "Yes" in 1932 to the question "Do employees in position of trust take regular annual vacations?" that George Dietrich never took a vacation and that when he did leave his desk, even for a few hours, his brother Robert Dietrich (who himself was never away for more than two or three days) would move up and occupy George's office (next to Coster's) but not do any of his work.

It follows that if the use of samples and tests on an audit is governed by the adequacy of the company's system of internal check, the latter should be the subject of a careful examination each year, not only to determine where safeguards are provided and where not, but also as stated at the beginning of the Price, Waterhouse & Co. questionnaire to establish "* * * from observation, inquiry and tests during the course of the examination that the prescribed procedure is being observed."[1325] Entirely aside from the appraisal of the system of internal check and control, alert observation of the system in operation, whether weak or strong, affords one of the best opportunities for the detection of fraud. Nor can this requirement for observation of the procedures be satisfied without a full knowledge and careful testing of the procedures and this in turn cannot be accomplished by a mere interrogation of officials without independent observation of the basic facts.

2. Appraisal of the System

Ritts' report to Thorn and Thorn's to Rowbotham were to the effect that the system of internal check at Bridgeport was good but Rowbotham's review of the questionnaires on the witness stand (apparently the first time he had seen them) resulted in his opinion that numerous points did not indicate strength in the system. On two points at least sharp divergence would appear between the treatment of the situation at Bridgeport and in other divisions. Letters of Price, Waterhouse & Co. criticising the failure of some houses to make independent records of remittances [1326] and the procedure whereby all the books were kept by one bookkeeper [1327] were common. However, at Bridgeport, George Dietrich, who opened the mail, did not make such lists and all the books of the Canadian Company were kept at first by George Dietrich and later by one bookkeeper under his direction.

Some distinction arises from the fact that at Bridgeport, as distinguished from the other houses, little currency was handled. However, the difference in treatment can not be explained solely on this ground. Price, Waterhouse & Co. also place emphasis on the fact that in the wholesale houses, as distinguished from Bridgeport, the

[1325] Ex. 17. See also Instruction Book to Form 10-K, pp. 11–12 quoted at pages 429–430 *infra*.

[1326] See pages 320, 322, 324, 325 *supra*.

[1327] See pages 319 ff. *supra*, especially McKesson-Fuller-Morrison letter at page 323.

executive functions were so divided that no single executive had the necessary information which would enable him to act as an effective check upon the bookkeeper and on the fact that remittances were not received and opened in the first instance by a fiscal officer of the Company. In Bridgeport, George Dietrich and Coster were deemed to have the necessary knowledge and Dietrich, assistant treasurer, handled the mail. In our opinion criticisms leveled at the other houses were equally applicable to the Bridgeport office irrespective of the status of the persons involved.

While lack of segregation of executive functions may increase control over bookkeepers and cashiers, the price, with this case as an illustration, would seem to be a heavy one.[1328] To us it appears that a lack of segregation of operating or executive functions especially when, as here, it is coupled with control over cash and other functions shows a weakness which should call forth more detailed investigation or testing, in the same way as though there had been a lack of segregation of accounting functions.

True, George Dietrich was subject to some internal checks on the foreign crude drug transactions. But the shipping, receiving, and warehousing were centered in his brother Robert and after 1934 when the goods were supposedly kept in Canada, fraud could have originated without Robert's assistance. On the accounting work, the check exercised by McGloon's department was based on documents, external and internal, which in every instance emanated from and were returned to George Dietrich with the single exception of inventory records prior to 1935 which came from George's brother Robert.[1329] As to the control exercised by Coster himself, while it seems to us that George Dietrich could have committed some frauds without the former's immediate cognizance, it is clear that a fraud in the amount and for the period indicated must have been within Coster's ken or conducted for him.

However, while these checks did exist, it nevertheless seems to us that the complete control assembled in George Dietrich's hands did

[1328] A feature of this case is that instead of using control of cash and mailing of statements to cover up misappropriations of collections from customers, these measures were used to conceal the fictitious nature of the accounts themselves and the falsity of the purported receipts. See also, *In the Matter of Monroe Loan Society*, 3 S. E. C. 407 (1938).

[1329] Cf. Bell's warning in Bell, William H. and Powelson, John A., Auditing, Prentice-Hall, Inc., New York, 1924 (hereinafter referred to as Bell and Powelson), p. 39:

> "The auditor should be careful not to be misled by indications of internal control when in fact it may be non-existent or purely perfunctory. The office personnel may include an 'auditor' but it does not follow that there is any effectual control over even the disbursement of cash. * * *"

indicate a possible point of weakness in the system [1330] whether to be used alone or in conjunction with Coster, particularly since this was supposedly a specialty business of which others, especially the auditors, had no independent knowledge. And the mere fact that George Dietrich could have committed some fraud should have caused a more detailed investigation which might well have led to the discovery of the larger fraud. And the further fact that, in addition, George Dietrich did not take any vacations, Price, Waterhouse & Co. apparently never discovered. The relative indifference to this latter point, as indicated in the testimony of Rowbotham and Ritts, is not supported by the authorities.[1331]

Whether other accountants would have broken through the mask of Coster-Dietrich explanations in their examination of the system of internal check and control or in their appraisal of it is difficult to say. One important conclusion, however, to be drawn from this case, which is of general applicability in auditing practice and with which those witnesses who were asked agreed, is that although the great majority of corporation officers may be assumed to be honest and statements

---

[1330] Cf.

"Typical of some of the basic features of a system of internal control, it is rudimentary that the functions of cashiering and the maintenance of accounts receivable ledgers should be separate functional divisions of the accounting department.

"Bookkeepers engaged on such ledgers should have no connection with the cashier's work and, on the other hand, cashiers should have no access to ledgers nor to statements sent to customers.

* * * * * * *

"Ideally, a responsible employee not associated with the cashier's department should supervise the opening of the mail and prepare for subsequent review by the accounting department an independent list of cash received in this manner.

* * * * * * *

"We do consider the mailing of statements at least partial assurance that the accounts are authentic, particularly if such statements are prepared and mailed by an accounts receivable section which is clearly independent of the cashier's department or even better, if such statements, although prepared in the accounts receivable department are checked by a representative of the comptroller's department before being actually mailed." P. 130, 143 (Testimony of Stempf).

In addition to being head of the cashier's department and conducting some of the other functions mentioned above, George Dietrich's activities in the handling of foreign crude drug purchase and sales transactions should also be remembered.

[1331] Dicksee, Auditing, First American Edition, 1905, p. 55:

"Every member of the [client's] staff should be required to take a holiday at least once a year."

Montgomery, 5th Ed., 1934, p. 70:

"Every member of the office staff should be required to take a vacation at least once a year. It is advisable to transfer employees from one position to another more or less frequently, depending upon the class of work which they perform. Changing persons from one position to another often increases efficiency by relieving part of the monotony of routine work. Fraud is sometimes brought to light by an enforced vacation or by rotation of work."

Bell and Powelson, p. 82:

"* * * As a matter of fact, nearly all frauds are committed by 'trusted' officers or employees; their opportunities for fraud arise through their being trusted.

"All officers and employees who are concerned with the handling of cash and securities and with keeping the accounts should be required to take vacations and should, whenever at all practicable, be assigned to different duties occasionally."

Bennett, George E., Fraud, Its Control Through Accounts (Published under the auspices of the American Institute of Accountants), The Century Co., New York, 1930, p. 39:

"Annual holidays should be enforced. No one should be considered so indispensable as to be given absolute and complete control over any one part of the work for more than fifty weeks each year; in fact, such control at all times should be subject to check by some other person * * *."

made by them may be accepted as free from deliberate misrepresentation, facts susceptible of independent verification by the auditor in a reasonable and practicable manner should be so verified. The history of financial fraud indicates that the officers should not be exempted from the operation of the checks provided to prevent manipulation by employees. Adherence to such a rule may well cut short many manipulations of accounts by trusted officers.[1332]

D. CASH

1. Adequacy of the Program

Testimony of Ritts, Thorn, and Rowbotham and exhibits introduced in evidence indicate that the apparent collection of cash was considered the best evidence of the authenticity of the transactions and that therefore great emphasis was placed on the results of the cash work.[1333] The comparison of the Price, Waterhouse & Co. cash program with the bulletin "Examination of Financial Statements" revealed that the Price, Waterhouse & Co. program was more extensive. The Price, Waterhouse & Co. methods compared favorably also with the testimony of the expert witnesses for while the majority of the witnesses recommended more extensive work on cash than that laid down in the Bulletin in only a few instances did they describe work of a stronger nature than that prescribed by Price, Waterhouse & Co. for the McKesson audit.

2. Confirmation of Deposits

Three witnesses testified that it was their usual practice to obtain from banks original or authenticated copies of deposit slips for a few days before and a few days after the close of the fiscal year.[1334] A fourth stated that his firm required this in cases where there were undeposited receipts at the year end.[1335] The other witnesses stated that this step would be taken only when there was suspicion of a defalcation or when other checks were lacking. Two of the witnesses

---

1332 See Bacas, Madden, and Rosenkampff, p. 17:

> "The large business organizations, as a rule, can afford the services of competent chief accountants who, in many respects, may be as well qualified as the average public accountant. * * * Even in these organizations it is usually considered advisable to have an audit by a public accountant as a means of protecting the concern so that losses of substantial amounts may not occur from fraudulent practices on the part of its officers or employees."

See also, Duties of the Senior Accountant, pp. 77–78:

> "Assuming that a good system exists, there will still be danger if those employees who are supposed to be a check one upon another be especially intimate or if the head of an office have established himself as an unreasoning dictator, his subordinates compelled to follow his orders with or without explanation. If the outside auditor ask questions of subordinate bookkeepers and find them afraid to answer reasonable enquiries, referring the auditor always to the head of the office, the internal check is untrustworthy."

1333 See pages 226–228, 231, 274–276 *supra*.

1334 "In the usual case, however, we do make some of these tests and we generally find enough in the way of defalcation in that way to make it a continued practice." Lenhart, P. 238. See also Bell, P. 187–188; Klein, P. 497–498.

1335 Jones, P. 600.

who made it their usual procedure (Lenhart and Klein) pointed out that there was a tendency, in recent years, for this test to be less reliable than formerly because of a change in practice in the larger banks in checking deposits. In view of the growth of this practice we strongly suggest that accountants reconsider this matter with the banks in question and adopt revised or substitute procedures to secure the necessary check since the authentication now rendered by such banks may be of little value and, in fact, may be misleading.

It will be recalled that Jaureguy on the 1930 audit requested Coster to consider whether the auditors should secure copies of original deposit slips from the banks but that after a few days Coster instructed them not to do this and this agreement was incorporated in subsequent letters of engagement and applied to the other branches as well as to Bridgeport. Insistence upon seeing original deposit slips at Bridgeport for the last few days of 1930 would have revealed the deposit of single checks covering collections from two or more customers. While Dietrich and Coster would doubtless have attempted some explanation, it seems to us that such a discovery should have led to a more thorough investigation of the method of handling the foreign accounts. Price, Waterhouse & Co. point out, however, that the situation at Bridgeport was not one where the obtaining of copies of original deposit slips was indicated to be a mandatory procedure and that, in their judgment, it was quite proper for them to forego this test even though duplicate deposit slips were not available in the client's Bridgeport office. Duplicate deposit slips were available and were inspected in the other offices. The test is used primarily (and the expert witnesses agreed) to detect kiting and lapping. Other methods of checking kiting are available and were used. Also, the danger from lapping was minimized at Bridgeport by the fact that substantially all receipts were in checks or drafts. Hence, the non-inspection at Bridgeport is upheld by a majority of at least two to one of the expert witnesses. None of the textbooks examined make the confirmation of deposits with the bank a mandatory feature of a balance sheet audit but some suggest rather strongly that it be done.[1336] The American Institute Bulletin mentions the procedure

[1336] Montgomery, 5th Ed., p. 118:

"The requests for confirmation of bank balances should include a request for confirmation of deposits made during the week immediately following the date of the balance confirmed."

Kohler and Pettengill, pp. 59–60:

"The detection of such fraud ('lapping') can usually be ascertained by checking the detailed deposit slips to the entries in the cash-receipts book by days. In making this check the auditor must be positive that the detailed deposit slips are copies of those actually used in making the deposit; this can be verified at the bank. While most banks file deposit slips by days, their officials have become accustomed to requests of auditors, and the auditor need not be afraid of imposing on any bank's good will by asking to see a reasonable number of deposit slips."

Bacas, Madden, and Rosenkampff, p. 208:

"This process should be used when a detailed audit is being made. It should also be used if a balance sheet audit is being made and there is no good system of automatic internal audit and the cash is of such a nature that it might be manipulated easily. The deposit for three to seven days just before the close of the period might be verified in this manner." (Continued on next page.)

only as an optional step: "In certain instances such comparison may be extended to include a check of original deposit slips or authenticated copies thereof." [1337]

While the character of the cash receipts was different in the wholesale houses and in view of the generally weak internal check and control created more justification for an examination of original deposit slips yet even here in view of such checks as were made and, more important, the dispersion of the risk, we conclude that normal audit procedure did not require Price, Waterhouse & Co. to secure original deposit slips from the banks as a part of their balance sheet examination. Having called the procedure to the attention of the client as a desirable step to take if the audit was expected to reveal defalcation by cashiers, they violated no professional responsibility when they acquiesed in Coster's instructions to omit the procedure. However, they did examine duplicate deposit slips kept in offices other than Bridgeport, and securing authenticated copies from the banks themselves would have entailèd little, if any, extra work.[1338] Foregoing this additional step prompts an obvious reminder that if auditors in their judgment consider an audit procedure to be necessary under a given set of circumstances in order to provide a proper basis for their certification of financial statements, the omission of such a procedure at the request of the client would constitute an abdication of their professional responsibility if they nevertheless issued an unqualified certificate.

3. Manning & Company

Should Price, Waterhouse & Co. have discovered that Manning & Company was a bookkeeping fiction and not a bank? Of the many

---

Trouant, p. 37:

"* * * copies of deposit slips may be made for confirmation by the bank."

Financial Examinations, p. 19:

"Then, total deposits shown on the bank statement should be reconciled with the total receipts entered in the cashbook, and for the last few days the bank deposit should be compared in detail with the entries of daily receipts as shown in the cashbook and with the duplicate deposit slips. If irregularities are suspected, the original slips may be inspected at the bank."

Cipriani, pp. 49–53:

"Cash in Banks:

"An acceptable program of work to be done, in the typical case, follows:

* * * * * * *

"19—Make out copies of bank deposit slips for the last few days in December and the first few days in January, and ask banks to certify the slips and to return them direct to the auditor's office."

That Cipriani does not conceive this to be a mandatory procedure may be deduced from the following paragraph from p. 6:

"The procedure to be mentioned hereafter is applicable in the examination of the accounts of nonspecialized types of medium-sized businesses. The work required is discussed in detail. It must be remembered, however, that in no specific case should it be necessary to do everything mentioned. What to do and what to leave undone are matters that experience alone can decide. In fact, it is not too much to say that the development of the accountant can be gauged by his increasing competence in knowing what to omit and when to omit it."

[1337] Ex. 117 (p. 12).

[1338] Except where request is made for copies of exceptionally numerous and lengthy deposit slips from the same bank, such copies are generally readily mailed by the bank direct to the auditor. In the other cases they are made easily available for inspection.

questions which will arise in the minds of those who read of this fraud, this should rank with the failure to discover that receivables and inventories were fictitious. Discovery that cash, or inventories, or receivables were fictitious would necessarily have exposed the entire fraud. The very acceptance of Manning & Company as real supported the acceptance of the cash transactions as authentic and thus helped support the entire fiction from 1931 to the day of its revelation.

No text examined suggests the necessity for making sure that accounts purporting to be with banks actually represent transactions with a real bank. Only one of the twelve expert witnesses stated that his firm had ever had occasion to inquire as to the character of a bank to determine its existence. This witness said that in certain cases inquiry as to the character of a particular depositary was made from banks known to them and that reference had been made to a bank directory.[1339] All of the witnesses mentioned one or more of the following points as satisfactory evidence of the existence of a bank:

1. Common knowledge.
2. Resolutions of the board of directors authorizing the establishment of bank accounts and designating officers to sign checks.
3. Letterheads, statements, checks, and other stationery of the bank in customary form.
4. A confirmation of the balance with the bank signed by an officer of the bank.
5. Apparent regularity of the transactions.

In this case the auditors' acceptance of Manning & Company as represented was originally made by Thorn who testified that he would not discuss such a subject with a partner. Whether Thorn was justified in accepting Manning & Company on the evidence before him will be tested under the five points above:

1. Events have shown that common knowledge played no part in the decision, for the auditors had never heard of the name Manning & Company except in connection with the McKesson engagement.

2. At meetings held practically at the same time on September 3, 1931, the directors of the Canadian and Connecticut Companies who, with the exception of one member, were identical, approved "* * * a contract with Manning & Co., a co-partnership of Montreal, Canada, and of a subsidiary contract with W. W. Smith, Inc., a New York corporation, dated as of the first day of August 1931 * * *."[1340] Although the minutes stated that both contracts were exhibited, neither the resolutions nor the minutes mentioned banks or banking functions in any way—merely referring to foreign buying commissionaires and brokers.[1341] The auditors never saw the contract with

[1339] Jones, P. 614. Klein stated that exceptionally large deposits in small country banks would be investigated. P. 500.

[1340] Footnote 177 *supra*.

[1341] Ex. 179, 180. Quoted at page 60 *supra*.

Manning & Company. The contract with W. W. Smith & Company, Inc., which they did see, recited that Charles Manning & Company, Limited, with whom the McKesson companies had in 1930 entered a contract to render certain services in connection with foreign trade, had been acquired by Manning & Company which had transferred the buying and selling agency business formerly conducted by Charles Manning & Company, Limited to W. W. Smith & Company, Inc. which Manning & Company had caused to be organized for that purpose and of which it owned one hundred per cent of the stock. However, the auditors were told, what certain other documents which they did examine indicated, that the one hundred per cent ownership of W. W. Smith & Company, Inc. was in W. W. Smith & Co. of Liverpool which by contract guaranteed performance of the foregoing contract of W. W. Smith & Company, Inc. The auditors were also informed that, as stated in the Manning & Company contract which they did not see, Manning & Company had acquired all of the foreign exchange and banking business formerly conducted by Charles Manning & Company, Limited and that it was thereafter going to continue such business under its own name, but there was no evidence that Charles Manning & Company, Limited had in fact ever conducted a banking business. Concerning the directors' meetings, a director testified that the names in the resolutions "* * * meant nothing * * *. However, in voting to appoint them as agents and so forth, I undoubtedly would have done it on the recommendation of the president." [1342] The only other record of directors' approval produced by the auditors at the hearings was a copy of a minute of a meeting of the Canadian Company board held on April 4, 1935 (abstracted by Ritts for the working papers), which approved Manning & Company as a bank depositary for the Canadian Company.[1343]

3. Checks were not drawn on the Manning & Company account. The debit and credit memos, of which the Company received only one copy, an original, when considered from the point of view of form, lack of supporting documents, and the absence of entries for service charges were clearly different from those of ordinary commercial banks.

4. The confirmations mailed directly to the auditors each year end conformed in every respect with what they should have expected to find about the account except that in some years no qualification appeared after the request "state if balance is not subject to withdrawal by check."

[1342] R. 2330. Testimony of Phillips. Quoted at page 125 *supra*.

[1343] R. 694–695. Quoted at page 68 *supra*. A search of the minutes of the several Companies disclosed that Manning & Company was also included in a long list of banking depositaries approved by the Executive Committee of the Maryland Company in October 1934 when the assets of the subsidiary companies were taken over and the Connecticut Company thereupon became the Connecticut Division of the Maryland Company.

5. It was noted above that Coster contrived to give an appearance of reality to the Manning account by starting business with the firm with a letter of credit in precisely the same manner in which he handled millions of dollars of business through New York banks and thereafter for several years, while using the debit and credit memo method of operation, purported to transfer funds from Manning & Company to New York banks. S. D. Leidesdorf & Co.'s investigation showed that cash transfers actually were made to bank accounts of the McKesson Companies and were recorded as coming from Manning & Company. From December 31, 1931 to December 18, 1933, $1,013,000 was transferred on the Connecticut Company books and from December 24, 1931 to December 31, 1936, $902,800 was transferred on the Canadian Company books. In addition, from November 25, 1932 to January 27, 1933, $345,000 was deposited in the Connecticut Company's account with the Guaranty Trust Company of New York and recorded as coming from the Canadian Company's account with Manning & Company. These transactions would naturally tend to allay rather than to raise any suspicion. Thorn's acceptance of Coster's explanation that the purpose of the account was to generate goodwill with the British Empire customers by collecting and holding the funds in Canada seems in conflict with his further understanding that the money had to be paid in United States currency and that Manning kept it on deposit in New York. This conflict coupled with the absence of any evidence of charges by or income to Manning & Company from handling this business and the fact that neither Ritts nor Thorn was certain as to how customers were advised to pay Manning and how Manning was authorized to pay vendors, must in some degree undermine their conclusion that the transactions with Manning & Company appeared regular in every way. Both witnesses waived aside the advices and authorizations as unimportant mechanical details in the face of the confirmation letters which they accepted as authentic, and the other apparently conclusive evidence as to the reality of Manning & Company. Of interest also is the fact that the supposed balance carried with Manning & Company was not included in the cashier's daily cash report. While examination of such internal reports has not heretofore been regarded as necessary audit procedure, the many instances in which such somewhat informal reports on cash, sales, receivables, and so forth have for the necessities of actual business operation reflected the real situation while the more formal reports have been falsified [1344] indicates to us the usefulness of comparing such reports with the book records and of the thorough investigation of any discrepancies.

1344 E. g. *In the Matter of Interstate Hosiery Mills, Inc.*, 4 S. E. C. 706, at 718–19 (1939); and *National Surety Corporation* v. *Lybrand et al.*, 9 N. Y. S. (2d) 554 at 558.

4. Conclusion

To sum up, the annual confirmations and the record of transfers of funds during a large part of the period under review were strong support for accepting Manning & Company as real. However, it is equally clear that Manning & Company was not acting as a regular commercial bank and although the auditors made no claim of accepting it as such, this fact, when coupled with the idea that in apparent collection of cash from customers lies one of the best proofs of the authenticity of the entire set of transactions, might well have prompted further inquiry here especially in view of the direct dealing of both the vendors and the customers with that one fiscal agent, and in view of some of the other points mentioned above. This situation was further accentuated during the last three years of the engagement by the fact that the inventories were supposedly held by the vendors and shipped directly to the customers by the independent sales agency of W. W. Smith & Company, Inc. with the result that throughout this period neither the goods themselves nor the actual remittances from customers were available for anyone's inspection at the client's premises.

However, fictitious banks have been so rare that it must be conceded that in the presence of convincing evidence of a normal banking relationship, special inquiry as to the authenticity of the bank would not have been considered normal audit procedure. To us it appears that a most salutary lesson to be drawn from this case is that since transactions through a bank, as apparent collection and payment of cash, are regarded as evidence of the authenticity of the transactions underlying them, greater care should be exercised in determining the reality of such banking transactions both in establishing the authenticity of unknown banks and in establishing that the actual transactions going through a bank are what they purport to be; that is, for example, that the cash, although received by the bank, does emanate from the customers and in the manner as indicated by the client's records. But in any event it seems to us that the cash work even at its best cannot sustain the burden which it appears to us is placed upon it by most auditors as the keystone of the entire audit program and that other audit steps should be strengthened to share the load as will be more fully developed hereinafter.

E. ACCOUNTS RECEIVABLE

1. The Audit Program in General

Viewed as a whole the program on accounts receivable used by Price, Waterhouse & Co. followed generally accepted outlines for an examination of financial statements. Failure of that program to yield a warning to the auditors that the accounts of the foreign crude drug department were fictitious resulted from lack of proper observation and appreciation of the evidence in hand and the omission of direct confirmation, an audit step which at the time was generally considered optional except when there was cause for suspicion. The details as to receivables have been related in a preceding section and the principal points there raised will be appraised in the following paragraphs.

2. Character of the Accounts

The outstanding features of the customers' accounts of Girard & Co., Inc., the Canadian Company, Connecticut Company, and Connecticut Division of the Maryland Company were the concentration of the bulk of the business in a relatively small number of accounts with large balances on long credit terms and, since the merger of Girard with McKesson, with customers in foreign countries gradually restricted to addresses within units of the British Empire. The accounts were also unique in that they purportedly resulted from sales through first, Charles Manning & Company, Limited and then W. W. Smith & Company, Inc. under a contract by which the accounts were understood to be guaranteed against loss up to a certain amount and by which all expenses in connection with the sales were to have been paid by W. W. Smith & Company, Inc. and passed on to the customer. The latter, wherever he was, purportedly invariably paid when due, in full, in United States currency, through years of prosperity and depression and foreign exchange restrictions and depreciations, with no deductions for claims or adjustments. Business with these customers grew practically without interruption even in periods when other departments of the business were experiencing the difficulties of the depression years.

The phenomenal regularity of the transactions either was not noticed or was not appreciated by the auditors. The absence of claims for adjustments was thought explainable on the ground that Smith and/or the Canadian vendors might absorb them, although the auditors saw no evidence that there were any claims or that they were so absorbed. The complete absence of bad debt losses or claims therefor was attributed principally to the contract of guaranty with Smith although the interpretation thereof accepted by the auditors did not fully agree with its provisions.

While it seems incredible to us that these characteristics could have prevailed with respect to real accounts over such a long period, the accounts were accepted by the auditors as authentic because the documentary evidence seemed regular to them and the records indicated that the accounts were duly collected. On the first point it appears that Ritts and the men who worked under him never discovered the differences in the routine handling of the foreign crude drug transactions (which comprised over 65% of the business done at

Bridgeport) from other transactions nor really understood the purported flow of the documents involved. The second point was looked upon as one of the best evidences that the accounts were genuine and the business therefore real. Prior to 1931 this support for the accounts receivable rested upon actual cash receipts but the cash came from accounts controlled by Coster out of McKesson's own funds previously disbursed in purported payment of foreign crude drug purchases. Beginning in 1931, proof of collection rested on the acceptance of Manning & Company as a bank or at least as a legitimate collection and disbursement agency. Since in no event did the money really emanate from the customers as indicated on the books of McKesson, the appearance of collection proved to be a mirage.[1344a]

3. Confirmation of Accounts

Price, Waterhouse & Co. maintain that the circularization of receivables proposed by them from time to time but not accepted by Coster was intended only for the wholesale drug and liquor divisions in which it was felt that the accounts were bad and internal control non-existent or poor.[1345] While this step was suggested for the benefit of the client, the risk was so distributed over the 84 units that it was not considered mandatory in order to express an opinion as to the accounts. Furthermore circularization of the foreign crude drug accounts was never considered necessary because of the guaranty of accounts, the apparent regularity of the transactions, the documentary evidence thereof, and the close supervision over the accounts by Coster and George Dietrich, and because a large portion of the accounts was always collected before the conclusion of the audit. The majority of authoritative opinion at the time of the hearings supported the view that circularization of receivables was not an essential in cases in which substantial collection of the accounts prior to the conclusion of the audit is proven. This appeared to Price, Waterhouse & Co. to have been the situation at Bridgeport. Judged by the practice in vogue when the audits were performed we believe that, under these circumstances, the failure to consider this step in connection with the foreign crude drug receivables or the failure to place any significance on Coster's rejection of this step for the wholesale houses can not be questioned.[1346] However, if circularization of receivables, even on a selective test basis, had been accepted practice under all conditions it is clear that such a test at any time in the life of the Canadian and Connecticut Companies and possibly as early as the first audit of Girard & Co., Inc. would have revealed the fictitious character of the receivables.

[1344a] See footnote 407 *supra*.

[1345] Pages 316–317 *supra*.

[1346] P. 29, 142, 191, 241, 289, 400, 504, 557, 602. See also Bacas, Madden, and Rosenkampff, p. 96; Kohler and Pettengill, p. 68.

The importance of this subject warrants its general discussion at this point. The bulletin, "Examination of Financial Statements by Independent Public Accountants", says in respect to this matter that

"the best verification of accounts receivable is to communicate directly with the debtor regarding the existence of the debt, and this course may be taken after arrangement with the client. While such confirmation is frequently considered unnecessary in the case of companies having an adequate system of internal check, it is one of the most effective means of disclosing irregularities. If it is to be undertaken, mail personally the requests for confirmation, after comparing them with the lists of outstanding accounts, in envelopes bearing the accountant's return address and enclose return envelopes addressed to the accountant."[1347]

The expert witnesses understood that this language was a suggestion to confirm but not that confirmation of accounts was ordinary practice. The chairman of the committee which drafted the Bulletin testified that the sentence was intended to encourage confirmation but did not imply that accounts usually were confirmed.[1348] Despite their interpretation of the Bulletin, the majority of these witnesses stated that they confirmed accounts in a great many cases, especially when internal control was weak or when the nature or condition of the accounts indicated that such a test was desirable. Situations mentioned were large balances apparently in controversy, concentration of balances in a few accounts resulting from charges late in the year, and customers of stock brokers.

There are three methods of carrying out the suggestion to confirm customers' accounts. A positive confirmation of all balances, by which all customers are asked to respond to an inquiry, is the most expensive and therefore practically prohibitive in some kinds of business. Seven witnesses considered this the best test but recognized its practical limitations. All of these witnesses recommended a judicious sampling of the accounts as a substitute and three other witnesses considered this to be the best approach to the problem. Two witnesses considered a negative confirmation to be the most satisfactory. By this latter method all customers are asked to respond directly to the auditors only if they find an error in the account as rendered.

Circularization of accounts has been recommended by writers for some years. Thornton, Cipriani, and Trouant of Price, Waterhouse & Co.'s staff, recommended the practice.[1349] Bacas, Madden, and Rosenkampff state that:

"It is a basic principle of the work of the public accountant that if an item is of sufficient importance, wherever possible, its verification is made through in-

---

1347 Ex. 117 (pp. 14–15).

1348 Scovill, however, interpreted the language, since it was stronger than in the predecessor Bulletin of 1929, as indicating that the authors were recommending confirmation as normal procedure. P. 453–454.

1349 Financial Examinations, p. 33; Cipriani, p. 71; Trouant, p. 45:

"A test circularization of larger and older accounts (and of some of the larger accounts written off) selected by the accountant may support the balances and has a psychological advantage with regard to internal check. It may also reduce the amount of checking of detailed transactions and trial balances usually considered necessary."

formation obtained from an outside source. Wherever such information may be obtained verbal explanations should not be accepted." [1350]

The opening and closing paragraphs of Montgomery's discussion of confirmation of customers' accounts constitute a good close for this consideration of the subject, as they are not only accurately prophetic in nature, but also give sound reasons for advocating the practice.[1351]

"*Confirmations of Outstanding Accounts.*—The auditor can best verify the balances of outstanding customers' accounts and detect defalcations arising out of the manipulation of such accounts by sending statements to all customers, requesting them to confirm the accuracy of the balance and other details such as due date, etc., preferably on a form inclosed for the purpose, which is to be returned directly to the auditor's office. This practice is followed by many leading auditors. The matter should be thoroughly discussed with the client and the advantages of the affirmative and negative methods pointed out. If all of the accounts cannot be confirmed, the auditor should suggest that a test be made by confirming all of one or more letters of the alphabet. If the client does not or will not consent to such a course, the responsibility for the integrity of the customers' balances is squarely up to him and such refusal should be mentioned in the auditor's report. The objections to this practice become fewer each year. No doubt within a few years the verification of customers' outstanding balances by correspondence with the auditor will be the rule rather than the exception.

* * * * * * *

"*Value of Confirmations.*—This independent check is of value not only in the disclosure of fraud, but also because of the information which it gives as to the condition of the accounts with respect to unadjusted items, allowances, etc. It is needless to say that some bookkeepers are careless and others lazy. When this is so, it is important for the auditor to find it out. In all classes of business various claims and errors crop out from time to time. When these affect customers' accounts, adjusting entries should be made at once, otherwise the outstanding balances do not reflect the true state of the accounts. If a bookkeeper *is* lazy or careless, it will soon develop in the replies from customers to the requests for confirmations. In several instances this inquiry has demonstrated a very unsatisfactory condition, the cause of which was carelessness rather than fraud. In many instances, however, carelessness leads to fraud. Whenever the auditor can check loose methods, he may really be preventing fraud. The auditor who prevents fraud is doing a greater service than in discovering it."

A judicious confirmation of customers' accounts, while it has not been considered mandatory in all cases, is good practice and in our opinion should be a normal audit procedure. We, therefore, commend the recent action of the American Institute of Accountants in requiring this procedure "* * * wherever practicable and reasonable, and where the aggregate amount of notes and accounts receivable

---

[1350] Bacas, Madden, and Rosenkampff, p. 90. For situations in which circularization of customers is inadvisable, see p. 90 ff.

[1351] Montgomery, 5th Ed., pp. 153 and 156. For a dissenting vote see Kohler and Pettengill, p. 67 (following a discussion in which the negative method was favored):

> "But the verification of accounts receivable through correspondence, or **circularization** as it is sometimes called, is not to be recommended for most balance sheet audits. Its only purpose lies in the detection and prevention of fraud by employees, though it serves occasionally to aid in the collection of old accounts. Other proof is available; besides, the method may be objectionable to the client. Generally speaking, it should be made use of only where other tests are unsatisfactory."

represents a significant proportion of the current assets or of the total assets of a concern * * *."[1352]

4. Reliance Upon Credit Reports

The record in this case reveals a reliance upon reports of credit agencies taken from the files of, or supplied by, the client. A number of these reports on the foreign accounts receivable were examined even though the accounts were understood to be guaranteed by W. W. Smith & Company, Inc. Also a special request was made of the client for a credit report on W. W. Smith & Co., the partnership which guaranteed the guaranty by W. W. Smith & Company, Inc. The reports covering the foreign customers were apparently authentic although the accounts receivable represented false entries. The reports on W. W. Smith & Co. were forgeries.

Reference to the use of credit reports in connection with an audit are meager in the literature of auditing that has come to our attention. In discussing the scrutiny of the accounts receivable for doubtful items, Kohler and Pettengill say:

> "The financial stability of a debtor may be determined to a certain degree by reference to Dun's or Bradstreet's, but the experience within the business relating to its customers is, if available, the best test."[1353]

This comment seems to refer to the credit-rating books rather than to special reports. Bacas, Madden, and Rosenkampff in a general discussion of confirmations imply that some types of material may be obtained in the client's office.[1354] As a test of the nature of credit information secured by the client, a review of reports in the files, in the absence of any suspicion of irregularity, seems reasonable and proper.

However, when the accountants deem it necessary, as in this case, to make a special request for a credit report covering a major element in the situation under review, it would appear only prudent to apply the customary rules of obtaining independent confirmations by having the person requested therefor reply directly to the office of the auditors rather than to accept a report of this importance from the hands of the client.

F. INTERCOMPANY ACCOUNTS

Except for intercompany items, after 1932 all payments and collections on account of the purchase and sale transactions of the Canadian Company were recorded as passing through Manning & Company by means of the debit and credit memo device. Since Manning was not

---

1352 See Appendix A for the full text of "Extensions of Auditing Procedure" as approved at the Annual Meeting of the Institute, September 19, 1939.

1353 Kohler and Pettengill, p. 67.

1354 BacasMadden, and Rosenkampff, p. 90: "* * * for instance, monthly statements from vendors." Perhaps the authors would include credit reports on vendees.

a checking account, dividends and other necessary actual cash disbursements were made by checks drawn on other bank accounts. Neither Ritts nor Thorn were certain as to how the cash was made available in these other bank accounts for such purposes. However, it has been shown that if the intercompany accounts had been analyzed, they would have revealed that while prior to 1937 funds were received and recorded as transferred by Manning & Company and as loans from the parent Company, in 1937 these funds were supplied to the Canadian Company by the Connecticut Division in payment for purported transfers of foreign crude drugs.[1355]

A study of the comptroller's reports would also have shown that of the major divisions of the Corporation, the Connecticut Division, although the most uniformly profitable, was exceptional in that it did not contribute funds to the head office for the payment of interest and dividends and reduction of debt. Statements of application of funds, analyses of the branch control account, and schedules of accounts receivable and inventories prepared from year to year by the auditors revealed that profits of the Connecticut Division, formerly Company, were being plowed back into these two items, but Ritts testified that, even if he had noted that all the earnings were plowed back, this would have been an operating question for the Company rather than an accounting question. Thorn and Rowbotham testified that they were only concerned with whether the increases in accounts receivable and inventories reflected on the collectibility of the accounts and the salability of the merchandise. The plowing back of profits in a profitable business was considered commendable rather than cause for suspicion.

There is no question but that a reconciliation of year-end balances of all intercompany accounts and of intercompany sales and services is necessary if the accounts of the affiliated branches and companies are to be eliminated properly in preparing the consolidated financial statements. The real question here is as to whether an analysis of the interim transactions sufficient to reveal the movement of funds between the affiliates is a necessary part of an examination of financial statements.

The authorities vary in their opinion as to the amount of work that should be done in connection with these accounts. Montgomery and Bacas, Madden, and Rosenkampff emphasize the reconciliation problem. Kohler and Pettengill go a little further and suggest an analysis to disclose the reason for advances. Thornton says that:

> "Intercompany advances and other transactions between parent and subsidiary and between subsidiaries should be reviewed * * *,"

while Trouant says that:

> "A review of the entries in accounts with affiliated companies is of assistance in determining intercompany transactions which may have resulted in unrealized

[1355] Also in 1938 subsequent to the last Price, Waterhouse & Co. audit and to some extent in 1935.

profits or losses or which may require special authorizations because of the relationship between the parties." [1356]

Three of these five books suggest a review of the intercompany accounts more extensive than would be necessary to reconcile differences between affiliated companies which would seem to have been the limit of examination of the transactions between the Canadian Company and the Connecticut Division in this case.

In our opinion a general review of the intercompany accounts is a necessary procedure. Such a review in the case of the Canadian Company transactions with its affiliates during the last year audited by Price, Waterhouse & Co. would have revealed that the cash it used for payment of expenses and dividends did not come from its own trading with customers which was consistently recorded as profitable but from transfers of merchandise to its parent. Likewise, a less complacent acceptance of the observed plowing back of profits in the Connecticut Division might well have instigated some examination by the auditors for, as we have seen, it was this very point which led to Thompson's activities that resulted in the exposure of the fraud.

G. INVENTORIES

1. The Audit Program in General

"1. The accountant's examination of inventories falls naturally into three main divisions:

"(a) Accuracy of computations, footings and recapitulations.

"(b) Basis of pricing.

"(c) Quantities, quality and condition.

"2. The responsibility of the accountant in the first two cases is clear; check the inventories sufficiently to be satisfied as to the substantial accuracy of the clerical work performed and that the goods are valued in accordance with the usual commercial practice—that is, at cost or market, whichever is lower or on some other reasonable basis which is accepted as sound accounting practice in the particular trade or business.

"3. The duties and responsibilities of the accountant in the case of quantities, quality and condition of stock vary with the circumstances; but he must rely principally for information as to quantities, quality and condition upon the responsible officers and employees of the company. In the case of a business which does not call for technical knowledge and presents no substantial difficulties, the accountant, by special arrangement with his client, may be justified in assuming a greater degree of responsibility than in cases where expert knowledge is essential. Make reasonable inquiries and tests to ascertain that quantities have been carefully determined and that quality and condition have received due consideration." [1357]

The material above quoted from the Institute's Bulletin introduces an audit program essentially the same as that followed by Price, Waterhouse & Co. and which the testimony of all expert witnesses

[1356] Montgomery, p. 593; Bacas, Madden, and Rosenkampff, p. 409; Kohler and Pettengill, p. 71; Financial Examinations, p. 86; Trouant, p. 104.

[1357] Ex. 117 (pp. 17–18).

and published material indicates is generally accepted auditing practice today. However, in one important particular—the extent of the auditor's duties and responsibilities in connection with physical verification of quantities, quality, and condition—there has been a sharp difference of opinion for many years. This point will be discussed more fully after disposing of the other two in order.

2. Accuracy of Computations, Footings, and Recapitulations

The time spent on the mathematical features of inventory checking was cause for complaint from time to time by various officers of McKesson & Robbins and at one time led to a suggestion from the client that Price, Waterhouse & Co. have the work done by comptometer operators. This suggestion, however, was not accepted by Price, Waterhouse & Co. The expert witnesses testified that when the engagement required a substantial amount of such checking they employed machine operators to do this work.[1358] With proper control it would appear that machine operators can do this work more quickly and cheaply than the average junior accountant.[1359] If this is done, however, the inventories must still be carefully scrutinized by an experienced accountant to detect evidence of deliberate irregularity, a task on which the auditor must be alert to pick up various devices used by the unscrupulous to accomplish an overstatement in inventories, or even an understatement, as part of a manipulation of accounts to conceal fraud. The employment of comptometer operators on a large engagement to do the purely mechanical parts of the work rather than lessening the opportunities for such observation, should, by relieving the accountant of the pressure of himself completing this purely mathematical work, provide more time for intelligent scrutiny and consideration of the accounts.

3. Pricing

This is not the place to debate the propriety of methods of inventory valuation. All accountants recognize their duty to determine that the pricing has been done in accordance with generally accepted principles, consistently maintained. The question which arises in this case is whether the Price, Waterhouse & Co. staff determined in a competent manner that the inventories were priced at cost or market whichever was lower, which, for inventories such as McKesson's, was a generally accepted method.

[1358] It may be that McKesson's suggestion was to have calculating bureaus take over and certify the work themselves. R. 1713–1714. Cf. Ex. 112. This procedure would probably not have been acceptable to the experts who testified that they hired the operators directly and assumed responsibility for the work. See also item "b", page 169 *supra*.

[1359] "* * * I think it is a waste of money to have a junior accountant, who doesn't know how to add anyway, most of them, spend their time on adding up inventory sheets and multiplying them." Testimony of Bell, p. 197.

In making their tests Price, Waterhouse & Co. compared inventory prices with the previous year's inventory prices, with the current year's purchase prices, with the client's sales prices for a period subsequent to the inventory date, and also with quoted market prices. All of these tests have authoritative support.

A blending of phrases from Trouant and Thornton provides a fair summary of opinion on market prices not only for Price, Waterhouse & Co. but also for other accountants.

> "Market" is susceptible to many interpretations. In using published quotations for purposes of application to inventory amounts it is necessary to employ quoted prices for quantities comparable with those usually bought at one time by the client; if there be no such market, prices in the company's sales market may be used after making proper deductions for selling and other expenses and for normal profit.[1360]

In this case, however, the comparison of the foreign crude drug prices with quoted prices revealed that some items could not be properly matched with quoted prices as to quality and method of packing and that wide discrepancies appeared between the quoted prices and both purchase and sale prices, quoted prices with rare exceptions being higher but much more so in some cases than others. The auditors accepted the explanation offered at the plant that this was due to the quantity traded but made no attempt to verify the quantities to which the quoted prices applied. The Price, Waterhouse & Co. staff responsible for this work assumed instead that the quoted prices were not satisfactory and that prices of sales after the inventory date but while the audit was still in progress (not, however, covering all of the items carried) were their best reliance. By relying principally upon sales and purchase invoices in connection with price testing, the auditors must necessarily have depended upon the authenticity of the cycle of business transactions ending with apparent collection from the customer, which it will be remembered they deemed the best evidence of the reality of the cycle. Thus in effect, as previously mentioned, they again relied upon the cash work, instead of making independent inquiry concerning the business in which Coster was supposedly engaged. Knowledge gained from such an inquiry might well have led to the disclosure of the falsity of the entire cycle.

We do not mean by this to say that sales and purchase invoices should not be examined. Such work is important not only for a check of prices contained thereon, but if alertly considered may disclose evidences of fraud. In the instant case, for example, the price test schedules over several years revealed no transaction that was not concluded at a gross profit, no uneven quantities, and an unnatural

---

[1360] Trouant, p. 66; Financial Examinations, p. 66.

regularity of transactions as more fully summarized in the table on page 105 *supra*.

4. Quantities, Quality, and Condition

a. TESTS BASED ON RECORDS

Accounting tests of quantity of the inventory that may be made from the records include examination of documents covering the purchasing and receiving and the selling and shipping of merchandise, primarily at the close of one accounting period and the opening of the next, to make certain that goods taken into inventory and the liabilities therefor are recorded in the same accounting period and that the inventory does not include merchandise for which a charge has been made to a customer. Expert witnesses, accounting texts, and Price, Waterhouse & Co. are in agreement as to the general auditing procedures to be followed. In their application to the McKesson work the principal question raised was as to whether the W. W. Smith & Co. orders and advices of shipment and subsequent receipt of payment through Manning & Company were sufficient evidence of shipment or whether the auditors should have seen other evidence covering these shipments such as duplicates of bills of lading. The texts consulted and some of the expert witnesses used the ambiguous term "shipping records" to cover the documents which should be examined in support of the sales cut-off. Several of the witnesses, however, mentioned bills of lading as the documents that would be referred to in proof of shipment. While events have shown that a careful examination of the so-called McKesson bills of lading should have aroused suspicion, the Price, Waterhouse & Co. view, that the examination of the notice of shipment from the shipping agent, W. W. Smith & Company, Inc., if regular in itself, was sufficient, seems to have support.[1361] However, as previously pointed out, there were several features of these notices which if observed might well have called forth further inquiry.

Another phase of the accounting check of inventories requires the investigation of the methods of inventory taking and the examination of the perpetual inventory records. The general conception of the requirements of this work was met by Price, Waterhouse & Co. except in one important respect. The testimony and the results obtained show that inquiries made of the client's employees as to the inventory procedure were not extended to the employees who

[1361] But see Kohler and Pettengill, pp. 67–68:

"A comparison of the sales invoices and shipping records should be made for the last few weeks of the fiscal year for the purpose of determining that all accounts are actual receivables rather than finished stock inventory. This will eliminate the possibility of the predating of invoices and serve as a test check to a certain extent in ascertaining that the billing has been made to bona fide customers rather than fictitious ones. This latter check can, of course, be carried out quite extensively as the various freight bills, packing records, and so forth, may be checked."

did, or had direct supervision of, the work under Robert Dietrich. Several of the expert witnesses testified that a proper inquiry of the client's inventory methods must extend to the men who actually did the work to make certain that prescribed methods were followed.[1362] If inquiry had been made of White, the McKesson & Robbins employee, who, on the 1934 examination for example, filled in the original count sheets on the foreign crude drugs and supervised the taking of the inventory that was actually in the space at the Fairfield plant designated on the count sheets for the foreign crude drug stocks, his testimony is conclusive that he could not have even pointed out the latter merchandise.

Of the various book tests of reasonableness of the inventory quantities, none would have revealed the fantastic character of the foreign crude drug inventories unless in this connection comparisons had been made with independent sources of information, since the rates of turnover and gross profit as shown by McKesson's books varied slightly from year to year so that it is not surprising that no suspicion was aroused. This general statement is subject to one exception in the years 1931 and 1932 when the Dandrofuge line which produced approximately 85% gross profit on sales was dropped and the foreign crude drug operations which yielded only approximately 10% gross profit on sales were expanded enormously to take the former's place in total gross profit produced. Thorn's conception of the gross profit test as merely an over-all test of inventory valuation is erroneous for variations in the rate of gross profit may also indicate errors or manipulations in purchases and sales. Moreover, as he applied it to a combination of lines the results were quite uninformative even as a check on inventories.[1363] There was general agreement among the expert witnesses that the gross profits test was of very little value unless departmental figures were available. This seems so fundamental that it requires no further discussion.

In a previous section it was brought out that an independent inquiry of anyone familiar with the trade or a reference to applicable trade statistics would have revealed the improbability of accumulating and storing such large stocks in the normal course of business or of disposing of them in regular channels of trade. When the goods were supposed to have been in Bridgeport, an inquiry of persons who were supposed to have actually handled the merchandise or a test of the designated storage space would have revealed that the goods were not at the location designated on the inventory sheets.[1364] Most of the expert witnesses testified that such over-all tests as they made were confined to the client's own records, the most common test

---

1362 P. 93, 249, 297, 349, 407, 563, 607; see also Kohler and Pettengill, p. 78.

1363 Pages 307–309 *supra*.

1364 See also discussion in respect to the location of inventories under taxes at pages 417–418 *infra*.

being the one employed by Price, Waterhouse & Co. for the Canadian Company of proving the ending inventory by accounting for purchases and sales since the opening of the fiscal year. Here again the value of this test has been shown to depend basically on the validity of the assumption that if the cash records are proved to be reliable other accounts related to those records may be relied upon.

The same witnesses testified that they would expect their top men to be generally familiar with the trade of the client under examination. It would seem unfair, therefore, to conclude from their answers to the question on over-all tests that no accountant would have a basis for testing the reasonableness of inventory quantities except by the records of the client. Two of the twelve witnesses cited examples in their experience where a quick calculation of storage capacity revealed the falsity of the inventories,[1365] and one witness said that trade statistics of production and consumption would be used to some extent.[1366] While such procedures have not been regular practice in the past, the situations in which their use would have disclosed fraud have not been uncommon [1367] and we believe they may with profit be judiciously employed in the future.

b. PHYSICAL TESTS

One of the important and controversial subjects in auditing practice has been the extent to which accountants should make physical tests of clients' inventories and whether such tests should lead the accountant to accept responsibility for inventory quantities, quality, and condition. While resolutions similar to that adopted by the New York State Society of Certified Public Accountants have attempted to limit the auditors' responsibility,[1368] opinion and practice,

1365 Lenhart, P. 251; Scovill, P. 461.

1366 Jones, P. 608.

1367 See P. 514–515.

1368 Monthly Bulletin, New York State Society of Certified Public Accountants, June 1934, p. 5:

"Resolved: That it is the sense of The New York State Society of Certified Public Accountants that, if a certified public accountant reports on a balance sheet of a concern over his signature without qualification or special explanation as to the item of merchandise inventories contained therein, it shall imply that he has exercised care in his examination by making accounting tests and checks of the concern's books of account and other available records pertaining to merchandise inventories, that he has received all information and explanations he has required from the officers and employees responsible for the taking and valuation of the merchandise inventories, and so far as accounting methods permit, has satisfied himself as to their substantial correctness, but that, as regards the information and explanations he has required and as to ownership, physical quantities, description, quality, condition, marketability and valuation of the merchandise, he has relied upon the representations of the concern's management, subject to such checks as may have been obtainable from the records in respect thereto; and be it

"Further Resolved: That it is the sense of this Society, that while the certified public accountant, through his experience in various lines of industry, may be of value in assisting and cooperating with the management of a concern in the supervision of a physical inventory taking, it should be clearly understood that in undertaking this work the certified public accountant does so only in his capacity as an accountant and does not assume responsibility as an appraiser or valuer for the physical quantities, description, quality, condition, marketability and valuation of the merchandise."

See also the New York State Society of Certified Public Accountants, Report of the Committee on Co-as revealed by auditing texts and the testimony of expert witnesses, have been sharply divided on this question during the period of the Girard-McKesson engagement.

One extreme view is that held by Rowbotham that the accountant has no concern with physical quantities, quality, or condition of the inventories.[1369] Representations of management are accepted and that fact reported on the balance sheet. The opposite view is that accountants are obliged to do such work as they consider necessary to establish to their own satisfaction that the inventories are as represented.[1370] The former group maintain that the latter cannot do enough work to assure themselves, and representation that they can is misleading and likely to have more disastrous consequences than reliance upon management. Those who rely upon management and refuse to make physical tests apparently follow the opinion in the English case of *In re Kingston Cotton Mill Company*[1371] as ample defense for their position if it should develop that their reliance on certificates by management proved to have been misplaced. Those who uphold the opposite view maintain that an accountant should not avoid his responsibility in so important a matter even though there is some legal precedent for so doing. In the Kingston case the court held that the auditors were not negligent in relying on a manager's certificate even though a bookkeeping calculation such as Price, Waterhouse & Co. employed in the McKesson work would have revealed that the inventory quantities could not have been correct. Montgomery's comment on this case, in which a mathematical test would have disclosed the fraud, is, "* * * Most prominent American auditors would now, however, probably agree that such failure to discover the true state of affairs when the means for doing so were available would be inexcusable."[1372]

---

operation with Bankers and Other Credit Grantors on Results of Meetings Held with Officials and Members of the New York Credit Men's Association, dated October 31, 1938, which stated that:

> "Before giving the results of the discussions * * * it may be well to call attention to the fact that the members of the credit fraternity attending the annual meetings referred to were largely those serving the textile and related industries in the mid-town area of the City"

and after repeating the resolutions quoted above continued:

> "The credit men present at the meetings expressed their full satisfaction with the provisions of the foregoing resolution. It was recognized that the inventory resolution adopted by the Society represented a rule or guide for the membership of the Society and that any member going beyond its scope and intent did so at his own risk and could not look to the Society for support in the event that he becomes embarrassed by reason of the adoption by him of a different or extended procedure." The New York Certified Public Accountant, December 1938, pp. 109-113.

1369 See Audit Procedure in America, Journal of Accountancy, LXVIII (August 1939), 101-103, reprinted from "The Accountant, London" in support of Rowbotham's position; but see Correspondence, idem 103-104.

1370 Bacas, Madden, and Rosenkampff, p. 246:

> "There are certain types of merchandise where it is inadvisable or practically impossible for the public accountant to endeavor to make a physical count of the items. . . .
>
> "However, there are other types of merchandise where the public accountant can easily make verification. If such an item was in question and it was found at a later date that the quantities had been overstated, it would be difficult for the public accountant to justify his omission to make the count."

1371 2 Ch. Div. 279 (Court of Appeal, May 19, 1896).

1372 Montgomery, 5th Ed., p. 184.

The question may now be raised as to what extent a physical inspection of inventory quantities is also one of the means available to auditors which, if omitted, would be inexcusable. Even in a case such as this in which there was no assumption of responsibility for quantities, quality, and condition of inventory, some actual inspection was made, as for example, at the wholesale houses where inspection of slow moving items of large quantity and test counts when the inventory as taken was suspected of being inaccurate apparently were deemed by the seniors there in charge to be reasonable steps for a prudent auditor to take.[1373] Thus, tests of the physical existence of inventories are clearly not forbidden in the Price, Waterhouse & Co. organization. Thornton says:

"* * * If, however, the auditor cannot satisfy himself that the inventory has been properly taken or that the permanent inventory records are correct, it may be necessary to have substantial tests made of the physical quantities. * * *" [1374]

and Trouant in 1937 wrote:

"Usually the accountant accepts as his starting point the original count records signed by the employees taking the inventory. Counting bales of cotton or wool, bags of cement, flour or fertilizer, rolls of cloth or paper, or other relatively large units may serve to satisfy the accountant that the total recorded quantities are actually on hand, and such tests are occasionally made." [1375]

Professional curiosity as to the business being audited might well have prompted a request to see merchandise of the character supposedly carried in the McKesson foreign crude drug inventories when it was recorded as on hand in Bridgeport. A wide awake tour through the plant with the preposterous foreign crude drug quantities in mind (for example 5,000 25-pound boxes of Dragon's Blood Powder Bright, 500 100-pound kegs of Crude Iodine, 3,100 flasks of Virgin Mercury, 2,000 100-pound cases of Gum Camphor slabs, and 200 200-pound bags of perishable Vanilla Beans) would have been quite sufficient to have revealed the fraud that was being perpetrated. Such a trip might well have been suggested by the following paragraph from Thornton:

"If the auditor have not been consulted in advance he should ascertain how the quantities were determined, the nature of the goods, their location and the way in which they are handled, physically and on the books. If he is dissatisfied with the method of stocktaking he must consider the advisability and practicability of again taking the stock in whole or in part." [1376]

[1373] Page 318 *supra*.

[1374] Financial Examinations, p. 53.

[1375] Trouant, p. 59. See also Duties of a Senior Accountant, pp. 20–21:

"It is quite permissible for the senior to consult with the client as to methods of taking and valuing inventory. On proper instructions he may even supervise the actual work of taking inventory, provided that he does not take responsibility for either quantities or values, except as to their agreement with the records."

[1376] Financial Examinations, p. 51. See also p. 50 referring to procedure recommended when the auditor is consulted prior to inventory taking, quoted in part in footnote 1321 *supra*.

In our opinion the complete omission of any attempt at physical contact with the inventory while it was supposed to have been at Bridgeport cannot be justified even on the theory of nonassumption of responsibility by the auditors for inventory quantities. While in view of the size of this fraud such inquiry, if boldly attempted, might well have disclosed the inflation, a mere cursory inspection cannot, of course, be relied upon in place of a regular test of and assumption of reasonable responsibility for inventory quantities.

There are two generally recognized methods for making such tests. The auditor may arrange with the client to be present as an observer while the inventory is being taken and make or supervise such test counts as he deems necessary during the course of the work. Or the auditor may go in at some other date and make sample counts (spot-tests) of stock for comparison with permanent inventory records or for reconciliation with the physical inventory by taking purchases and sales in the interim into account.

All of the expert witnesses testified that spot testing of inventories was feasible in many lines of business and that such testing or observation of inventory taking was by no means an uncommon procedure, although none of the witnesses required that either be done as an invariable rule in their auditing procedure. There is considerable difference in manner of expression among the witnesses but a general summary of the opinions expressed must recognize the following points:

1. The accountant in undertaking inventory tests should have a general knowledge of the client's products but does not profess to have a technical knowledge of all items in the inventory or to exercise the functions of an appraiser as to quality and condition.

2. The tests are considered to be based upon ordinary business judgment and are collateral and circumstantial support for the primary accounting tests based upon the records.

3. Reliance may be placed upon the manner in which the business is conducted in judging whether packages contain material described on the labels.

4. There are occasional industries and lines of business in which the nature of the product or character of the merchandise makes physical testing practically impossible in which case spot testing would not be a reasonable or practicable requirement.

Those who oppose physical tests of the inventory fear that if such testing is considered good and generally accepted practice, the uninformed will consider auditors to be guarantors or insurers of the inventories. Even the possibility of this erroneous impression by laymen, if it does exist, does not seem to us to be an adequate excuse for refusal to make such reasonable and practical tests as are within the four points stated above. The importance of this subject warrants

205078—40——27

quotations from three of the witnesses who in their opinions indicate various views on the question. George D. Bailey of Ernst & Ernst testified:

"Q. [By Mr. WERNTZ.] * * * looking to the future, what procedures do you think auditors should use in verifying quantity, quality, and condition of inventory?

A. Well, I think the tests that they have been using in the past do not need to be changed except as to degree. My experience with quantity tests has led me to believe that auditors in the future can more frequently supervise or oversee the process of inventory taking or that they can more frequently test the inventory quantities.

However, I think we will need to be careful not to be too dogmatic about the whole question of inventory tests, because, as I said once before, there are some situations where a satisfactory physical test may not be practicable.

I think perhaps there may be something to be said for an acceptance of greater participation in inventory with a definite statement as to the extent of that participation and not just a negative statement when such participation does not exist.

Certainly we should strive for greater clarification as to whether we are reasonably satisfied with our test. And I think we should strive also to bring out more clearly that our examination as to grade, quality, and things of that kind has to be made largely from the evidence that is available from the records, because the number of cases in which inspection might show the error in grade or classification is not very large.

Q. You mention in the first part of that statement that in some situations verification of quantity was not practicable. Would you characterize that more fully?

A. I am thinking again of department stores, chain stores, and things of that kind where the number of items is so large and the total of each individual item so small that the tests of quantities would not be practically satisfactory. We could move forward on those, of course, to be present at the inventory, when it was taken, but we rely in that kind of situation upon checking the departments against one another and against prior years and against turn-over figures and many other things, so that I hesitate to be so definite as to say we should in all cases participate in inventory.

I personally have a feeling that if we say flatly what we do and have it understood what we mean by that wording, that we will find we work out to a pretty definite position for the accountant in connection with the accuracy of the inventory item." [1377]

William H. Bell of Haskins & Sells answered Mr. Werntz' first question:

"A. * * * I don't see why accountants should not serve the useful purpose of making an independent, reasonable, physical substantiation of inventory quantities.

In any case, where quality and condition may be a matter of unusually great importance, it may be desirable to have an expert in the particular industry make an investigation.

Q. * * * again looking to the future, what do you think of the auditor participating in the taking of inventory, in a supervisory capacity?

A. The ideal method of substantiating inventory quantities is to supervise, or observe the process of inventory taking by the company.

[1377] P. 567.

As I have previously stated, I think this is entirely practical.

It is subject, however, as far as general observance is concerned, to lessening the congestion of auditing work at the end of the year by the wider adoption of the natural business year for corporations.

In this connection, the case of companies which maintain well kept and controlled perpetual inventory records, and which take annual physical inventories at the time when their business activities have reached the lowest point of their business cycle, that is the close of the natural business date, or at other dates not coinciding with the balance sheet, physical tests could be made by accountants at such other dates supplemented by such review of the records of intervening transactions to the balance sheet date and such supplementary physical tests as they consider appropriate." [1378]

Charles W. Jones of Arthur Andersen & Co. gave the following opinion on the same subject:

"A. The complete verification of the quantity, quality, and condition of inventory, in my mind, by auditors, is wholly impractical. The procedure of observing the taking of physical inventory and spot-testing quantities, I think, might be applied to a greater extent than it has been in the past, but I am not prepared to say to what extent such procedure should be extended because I am not convinced that from a practical point of view any material or substantial extension of those procedures would, in the last analysis, be worth their cost to industry.

Q. How do you feel about participation in and supervision of the inventory taking?

A. I think that is important.

Q. And would be a desirable thing?

A. Not so much from a point of view of supervision as to observe the steps in the procedure.

Also it is important, I think, to ascertain in advance of the inventory, just what a company plans to do in connection with taking inventory." [1379]

Perhaps the reluctance of some accountants to assume greater responsibility for inventories is based upon the common knowledge that this asset is easy to falsify and is frequently used in manipulations of accounts intended to distort profits, one of the principal bases for valuing securities. To us these two facts make it all the more necessary that accountants should do all that their training and experience qualifies them to do in ascertaining that the inventories are fairly stated. Many of the tests of the records, generally considered mandatory, aid materially in determining that quantities, quality, and condition are as represented, and, as has been noted, some accountants consider these tests more reliable than inspection under certain circumstances. However, it seems consistent and desirable to us for the accountant, in addition, to make any reasonable and practicable test that will reassure him of the actual existence of an inventory.

Montgomery in twenty-two pages discusses the problems of inventory verification and presents a twenty-two point program for the

[1378] P. 202, see also longer discussion at P. 200.

[1379] P. 609.

purpose. He supports the proposition, in no uncertain terms, that auditors can assume a reasonable degree of responsibility for most inventories and should make physical tests in the process of verifying them.

"The author is of the opinion that in the majority of cases the auditor can make, at reasonable cost to his client, such an examination as will enable him to certify to the balance sheet without qualification and to accept a reasonable degree of responsibility with respect to the inventory. To what extent this may involve independent verification of quantities and other factors will depend upon the kind and size of the business, the adequacy of the perpetual inventory records, the opportunities for proving quantities by independent checks, and the efficiency of the organization that is responsibile for the custody and inventorying of the merchandise and materials." [1380]

The following excerpts from Montgomery's rules for verifying inventories indicate his positive views on physical tests and require no further comment:

"The rules suggested below rest upon the assumption that, as an auditor is not a valuer, he is not charged with a special or technical knowledge of the elements constituting stock in trade. If he exercises due care and skill, he may feel that he has conscientiously discharged the duties imposed upon him.

* * * * * * *

"2. * * * If the inventory has not been taken under supervision by the auditor, he should look over the stock before dealing with the inventory sheets.

"There are such things as 'bonds' representing debts, and 'bonds' which are used in track construction. Familiarity with terms in use is most rapidly gained by object lessons.

* * * * * * *

"8. * * * Physical tests should then be made of a sufficient number of items to test the accuracy of the records. [Refers to perpetual inventory records.]

* * * * * * *

"Large thefts of goods have been discovered by tests.

* * * * * * *

"21. When the audit is being made, during the taking of the inventory or immediately thereafter, select some items from the inventory sheets and verify by inspection of the goods on hand.

* * * * * * *

"22. In the case of inventories stored in the client's plant or own warehouses the auditor must make a good physical test even when book quantities have not substantially changed, as fraud has been concealed by overstating the quantity of stored goods."[1381]

In our opinion, the time has come when auditors must, as part of their examination whenever reasonable and practicable, make physical contact with the inventory and assume reasonable responsibility therefor as had already become the practice in many cases before the

---

[1380] Montgomery, 5th Ed., p. 180.

[1381] Idem. pp 181–187.

present hearings.[1382] By this we do not mean that auditors should be, or by making such tests become, the guarantors of inventories any more than of any of the other items in the financial statements but we do mean that they should make all reasonable tests and inquiries, and not merely those limited to the books, in order to state their professional opinion, as auditors, as to the truthfulness of that item in the same way as they do for the other items in the statements. As in the case of confirmation of receivables we approve the action of the American Institute of Accountants in prescribing the use of physical tests of inventories or observation of the inventory taking by independent public accountants as regular audit procedure.[1383]

5. Ownership

a. MERCHANDISE ON THE CLIENT'S PREMISES

The difficulty of assuring himself that the merchandise he sees is the client's is one of the strongest arguments brought to bear by auditors against the proposition that inventories should be tested by physical count. The accounting tests, however, that are relied upon for pricing and for quantity supply substantial evidence of ownership if they are reliable for the first two purposes. And if, under the tests suggested above, these records are supported by actual possession and there appears a proper relationship between observed quantity and payment, the test would appear fairly reliable and certainly is stronger than if the records only are relied upon for evidence of ownership.

All of the authorities are in agreement that, in addition to the usual tests, inquiries must also be made to establish that goods on hand and included in the inventory are the property of the client. It is also

---

1382 That this is far from impossible is clearly illustrated by the following certificate dated after the disclosure of the fraud in the present case:

"OPINION OF INDEPENDENT PUBLIC ACCOUNTANTS

To the BOARD OF DIRECTORS OF
EMSCO DERRICK & EQUIPMENT COMPANY,
Los Angeles, California.

We have made an examination of the financial statements and schedules of Emsco Derrick & Equipment Company that are listed on the accompanying index. In connection therewith we examined or tested accounting records of the company and other supporting evidence and obtained information and explanations from officers and employees of the company; we made extensive tests of the inventory quantities by inspection of the physical stocks, in which we were assisted by persons who were not employees of the company but who were qualified to identify its products to us; we also made a general review of the accounting methods and of the operating and income accounts for the year, but we did not make a detailed audit of the transactions.

In our opinion, based upon such examination, the accompanying financial statements with the notes appended thereto fairly present, in accordance with accepted principles of accounting consistently maintained by the company during the year under review, its position at December 31 1938 and the results of its operations for the year ending on that date.

[s] PRICE, WATERHOUSE & CO.
(Price, Waterhouse & Co.)

LOS ANGELES, CALIFORNIA,
April 25 1939."

1383 Appendix A contains the full text of "Extensions of Auditing Procedure" as approved at the Annual Meeting of the American Institute of Accountants, September 19, 1939.

general practice, as was done in this case, to request the client to sign a certificate covering this and all other phases of the inventory question.

The purpose of the certificate is clearly stated by Montgomery:

> "An inventory certificate is not to be regarded as a substitute for, but merely as a complement to, a proper examination of the inventory by the auditor, and it is important for several reasons. Banks and others interested in financial statements often raise a question regarding the confidence expressed by the management in inventory quantities and valuations. Furthermore, it often occurs that there is not an exact meeting of minds between the auditor and the management as to the general basis of inventory count and value. The signing of an inventory certificate on the part of the management brings clearly to the latter's attention the general basis used in arriving at inventory count and valuation. A request for an inventory certificate is, in no sense, any reflection upon the integrity of the management, but the obtaining of such a certificate does satisfy the auditor of the management's own conviction with respect to the inventory." [1384]

All of the expert witnesses agree with Montgomery that the inventory certificate from responsible officials does not relieve them of making the usual tests and inquiries in regard to inventories.

b. MERCHANDISE NOT ON THE CLIENT'S PREMISES

A novel question raised by this case is whether an auditor should investigate custodians of the client's merchandise. The storing of merchandise in public warehouses is a common practice and the holding of customers' merchandise by vendors was not unknown before this case. Price, Waterhouse & Co. confirmed merchandise held off the client's premises in both public and vendors' warehouses by direct correspondence which in the case of the foreign crude drugs resulted in receipt of documents from the five dummy Canadian vendors.

All of the authorities examined are in substantial agreement that goods stored off the premises should be confirmed by correspondence if material in amount. All of the expert witnesses are in agreement that confirmations would not disclose a misappropriation of the merchandise by the holder, but only one testified that he had ever required evidence of financial responsibility of the holder. In this case the witness had had an experience which indicated the desirability for this precaution where goods had been paid for and left in the vendor's warehouse.[1385] This witness and another stated that a situation in which vendors held goods that had been paid for, as was pretended in the instant case, was rare in their experience.

It should be recalled at this point that Ritts suggested securing financial statements on the five Canadian vendors, who at that time supposedly held McKesson inventories valued in excess of $7,000,000, because of the possibility that they might not have all of the goods,

[1384] Montgomery, 5th Ed., pp. 188–190.

[1385] P. 39.

but that George Dietrich convinced him that since the goods came from distant countries their prompt shipment of sales orders was evidence that the goods must be on hand. Thorn testified that he thought he had approved Ritts' acceptance of Dietrich's explanation. Here again reliance was placed on the cycle of transactions which ended with apparent cash collection.

If Ritts had insisted upon securing financial reports from Dietrich, it is not unlikely that falsified ones would have been produced. If it had occurred to any of the auditors' representatives to question or investigate independently the legitimacy of these concerns by requesting the Canadian firm of Price, Waterhouse & Co. to make an inquiry on the scene, or otherwise, it is hardly conceivable that an exposure would not have resulted. The situation here was so unique that it is difficult to say exactly what established practice was in this respect, but it is probable that for some time to come public accountants will be more cautious in a situation of this kind. In any event we believe that supplementary independent inquiry should be added as a normal audit procedure if the amounts of inventory represented as being held in outside warehouses are significant, particularly if the purchase price for such goods has been paid.[1386]

H. OTHER BALANCE SHEET ACCOUNTS

1. Unexpired Insurance

The discussion of insurance brings out more clearly than any other topic in this report the differences in practice due to the size of the business under examination. It will be recalled that Ritts, with Rowbotham endorsing the idea, testified that the examination of insurance policies was limited to a verification of the unexpired portion of the premiums thereby determining the amount of the remaining asset and the amount chargeable to expense. It was not considered necessary to review coverage, for the client had an insurance expert in its employ in charge of the insurance department.[1387]

The expert witnesses were in substantial accord with the position taken by Price, Waterhouse & Co. The point was made by some of the witnesses, however, that the question of coverage was considered in the audit of small and medium-sized businesses and one witness testified that the policies should be examined in order to detect liens against property.[1388] This latter point is made in some of the textbooks.

1386 The American Institute of Accountants' "Extensions of Auditing Procedure" adopted September 19, 1939 recommends this procedure. See Appendix A.

1387 As previously pointed out the fact that the blanket insurance policies were reduced a substantial amount in 1935 was deemed confirmation of the auditors' understanding that the merchandise was insured by the custodians who commenced storing the goods in that year. But see footnote 1065 *supra*.

1388 Klein, P. 519.

All of the texts examined state that the auditor at least should know the amount of insurance coverage in relation to the book value of the assets of the client and, under certain circumstances, should comment upon it in his report. The character of the discussion in some of the books indicates that the small or medium-sized business without an insurance department is in the minds of the authors. However, it is clear that all deem it necessary for the auditor to be reassured in one way or another that the client has made proper provision for the various kinds of business risks which may be insured against.[1389] The most clear-cut statement of the reasons for this position is found in Bacas, Madden, and Rosenkampff, who sum up their conclusions as to the auditor's duty in this regard as follows:

"It would seem, however, that the public accountant should have the responsibility to see that, at the very least, the client is fully protected as to the risks incidental to fire, workmen's compensation, public liability and automobile insurance."

2. Fixed Assets

Fixed assets were a minor factor in the McKesson examination and warrant discussion here only because of the additional light that is thrown on Rowbotham's philosophy of complete reliance upon book records without reference to the physical properties represented. It will be recalled that he stated that the accountant did not actually see or touch the plant and that if he did do so, he would be no wiser.

All of the expert witnesses support this position, to some extent, on the grounds that the records are adequate and better evidence of detailed changes in plant assets than a superficial inspection. However, seven of the twelve witnesses stated that the plant was sometimes inspected for major additions. One of these stated that such an inspection would be quite detailed under these conditions.[1390]

The prevailing opinion is clearly and briefly stated by Montgomery:

"The duty of the auditor with reference to fixed assets differs from his duty relative to current assets. He must verify, upon his own responsibility, both existence and value of current assets or specify in his certificate the extent to which he has relied on the statements of others. It is good practice to depend largely on the information to be obtained from others with respect to fixed assets." [1391]

That Montgomery does not intend that the auditor should stay out of the plant is clear from his advice that "* * * The auditor should personally inspect the plant and note whether it appears to be in good condition or not," and in connection with discovery of undisclosed liabilities, "Inspection of the plant may disclose the

[1389] Montgomery, 5th Ed., pp. 292, 353, 521–523; Kohler and Pettengill, pp. 91–93; Trouant, pp. 92–93; Financial Examinations, p. 127; Cipriani, p. 121; Bacas, Madden, and Rosenkampff, pp. 356–359; Bell and Powelson, pp. 251–252; and Jackson, pp. 106–108.

[1390] Jones, P. 610.

[1391] Montgomery, 5th Ed., p. 247.

existence of major items of equipment not dentified on the books. * * *" [1392] Reference has already been made to Trouant's advice that a tour of the plant aids in the audit of additions and abandonments.[1393] Kohler and Pettengill suggest that if the equipment records are in good shape"* * * and good accounting practice has been followed, the auditor's examination may be limited to a test check of some of the individual cards against the machines themselves." [1394]

While reliance must be placed on the records for the precise details of fixed asset changes, it may be observed that in those cases where the auditors do their work, or some of it, at the client's plant, the staff on the engagement must become aware of the principal physical changes that take place from year to year and that whether consciously or not this must lend reality to the work done on the records. As previously stated in the case of inventories we believe that whatever physical inspection of fixed assets can reasonably be made should be undertaken as a supplement to the examination of the book records and that this can only enhance the value of such examination.

3. Liabilities

a. THE AUDIT PROGRAM IN GENERAL

The work done by Price, Waterhouse & Co. on liabilities was substantially in accord with the suggestions of the bulletin "Examination of Financial Statements by Independent Public Accountants" and with those of other publications examined. Some special points raised in connection with the McKesson work will be reviewed in the following paragraphs.

b. ACCOUNTS PAYABLE

Price, Waterhouse & Co.'s appraisal of McKesson's internal check on purchasing procedure may be responsible for the failure of the audit of accounts payable to reveal a clue to the fraud. George Dietrich it will be recalled authorized all purchase orders and approved the vouchers authorizing payments for foreign crude drugs and at the same time occupied the office of assistant treasurer which controlled the daily cash routine including the Manning & Company account through which payment was supposed to have been made. Prior to the Manning period Dietrich signed the checks without countersignature. Every expert called to testify stated that such a combination of duties was prohibited by sound principles of internal check and control, yet Ritts and Thorn were not disturbed by this for in their opinion Coster

---

[1392] Idem., pp. 260 and 352.

[1393] Page 380 *supra*.

[1394] Kohler and Pettengill, p. 108. The same authors state that horses may be counted. It is even possible that some auditors could judge of their condition.

was supposed to have exercised complete and detailed supervision over Dietrich's handling of the purchase orders; and the accounting department, relying on what appeared to be genuine documents from outside sources, exercised proper control over disbursements. It seems clear to us that even if the vendors had been real the accounting department would not have been an adequate check on Dietrich for he approved the vouchers and signed the checks to cover purchases which he had authorized.[1395] With the acceptance of this situation, it seems improbable that Price, Waterhouse & Co.'s suspicions would have been aroused in carrying out the mechanics of this phase of the audit.

The conclusion stated in the foregoing paragraph is supported by the same result growing out of another step of this program—the examination of creditors' statements. The authorities vary as to the extent of this test and as to whether balances should be confirmed.[1396] Some maintain that large balances on creditors' accounts should be confirmed but if not confirmed, the statements should be examined.[1397] As previously discussed in connection with accounts receivable, it was stated in the letters of engagement that such confirmations would not be made in this case. However, examination of available statements was part of the Price, Waterhouse & Co. program. This step, however, would not have involved an examination of statements from the five Canadian vendors because no amounts were owing to them at the audit dates, all purchases prior to that time having purportedly been regularly paid through Manning & Company. Here again, therefore, reliance goes back to the cash work.

If confirmation of these accounts payable had been attempted as of any date, it is certain that the auditors would have received documents which confirmed the book records as they did on the inventories supposed to have been in the possession of these dummy concerns. These two situations are of course distinguishable from the accounts receivable of the McKesson Companies in which the customers were real and would not have confirmed that they owed the sums indicated on the

[1395] The importance of this point is clearly brought out in the following paragraph from Trouant, p. 101:

"Accounts Payable

"Probably no other single account presents so great an opportunity for latitude in the accountant's examination as does 'accounts payable.' From the balance-sheet point of view, the book amount may sometimes be accepted as a fact and the review limited to a search for liabilities not included. On the other hand, the details relative to accounts payable may be of the greatest importance from the point of view of internal check. Disbursements of cash may follow almost automatically upon the presentation of invoices for payment, and, hence, the control over the approval and entry of the invoices may be the crux of the whole system. Not only the propriety of the amounts is important, but the distribution of the charges directly affects the accuracy of the records and particularly the classification of expenses. Since the accountant ordinarily analyzes relatively few of the expense accounts in detail, it is essential that he should satisfy himself by other means that the book classification is sufficiently accurate for purposes of determining production costs and for the review of statements of profit and loss."

[1396] Montgomery, 5th Ed., p. 336; Cipriani, p. 136; Financial Examinations, p. 135; Bacas, Madden, and Rosenkampff, pp. 285–287; Trouant, p. 102.

[1397] Kohler and Pettengill, p. 119.

books. In the former situation five concerns purportedly held more than $10,000,000 worth of merchandise. In the latter case over $9,000,000 worth of receivables were divided among approximately 750 customers.[1398] The facts here illustrate that where accounts are particularly large and the risk is not divided, mail confirmations cannot be solely relied upon to establish the reality of the account but other independent knowledge or investigation is necessary.[1399]

c. TAX LIABILITIES

A situation very similar to that discussed in connection with insurance prevailed in respect to taxes, for McKesson & Robbins was assumed to have a competent tax department. The problems surrounding the United States taxation of the Canadian Company, however, were reviewed quite thoroughly by the auditors and referred to their own tax department. That senior accountants should be able to recognize these problems is expected. The record raises a serious question however as to the adequacy of the investigation of the Canadian tax law under which it was thought that since 1935 the Canadian Company was exempt from the Dominion income tax. As we read the section of the law referred to by Ritts in his memorandum of the accounts such exemption was in conflict with Price, Waterhouse & Co.'s belief that after 1934 the foreign crude drug inventories were held in Canada for the law states that the exemption is granted if the business is carried on, and the *assets are also situated*, entirely outside of Canada.[1400]

Another important question of procedure, which arises in this case, is whether it was proper for Ritts to accept schedules prepared by the client's tax department showing the computation of all state taxes, or whether he should have examined the tax returns themselves in his verification of the computation of the tax liability. All of the authorities examined require a review of the tax situation of the client, but of those examined only the three Price, Waterhouse & Co. authors answer the specific question here involved.

The comment of these three authors in order of publication follows: Cipriani, January 1933:

> "Vouchers and tax returns must be examined to substantiate all payments that have been made. The accountant must see that all taxes have been paid or otherwise are recorded as liabilities." [1401]

[1398] The five concerns purportedly sold McKesson over $16,000,000 worth of merchandise during 1937 while McKesson's sales of over $18,000,000 went to more than 750 customers.

[1399] Ritts testified that independent credit reports on W. W. Smith & Co. and the five Canadian vendors would have exposed the fraud. R. 774. Thorn agreed but said ". . . I never heard of any accountant doing that, however." R. 1245-1246.

[1400] See pages 286-287 *supra*.

[1401] Cipriani, p. 125.

Thornton, September 1933:

"It is worthwhile to compare inventories as prepared by the client for his balance-sheet with the corresponding inventories shown on federal, state and other tax returns. It usually happens that it is to the interest of a taxpayer to state his inventory at as low a figure as possible in his return, while an inclination to over-value it for balance-sheet purposes may at times exist." [1402]

Trouant, January 1937:

"Substantiation of amounts of accrued taxes should include reference to expense accounts, to state and local tax laws and to copies of tax notices and tax returns." [1403]

Complete compliance with any of the three suggestions would have turned up the fact that the foreign crude drug inventories shown on inventory books as in the Fairfield (Bridgeport) plant as at December 31, 1934 were shown on the Maryland Company's Connecticut tax return for the period ended that date as outside Connecticut. A similar disparity between the supposed location of the inventories and the location assigned for tax purposes was disclosed on the Connecticut Company's state tax return for 1934 and resulted in a lower tax payable to Connecticut.[1403a] Examination of the tax receipts during the 1935 audit should have disclosed a substantial discrepancy between the amount of tax actually paid in 1935 and the amount accrued at the time of the previous year's audit based on the assumption that the merchandise was in Connecticut during the year 1934. The discrepancy should have been sufficient to have warranted investigation as to its cause. Similarly, a review of the Canadian Company's Connecticut tax return and supporting papers for 1935 would have revealed inventory certificates from the Canadian vendors giving the location of the merchandise as New Jersey rather than Canada as understood by the auditors.[1404]

d. CONTINGENT LIABILITIES

All accountants are aware of the difficulties involved in assuring themselves that they have done everything a prudent accountant should do to uncover contingent liabilities. Much of the work done on other phases of the audit contributes information as to various contingencies that exist. In addition, the reading of contracts and minutes of various governing bodies of the client is generally accepted practice and was done by Price, Waterhouse & Co.

As an added precaution in connection with all liabilities, it is customary for the auditor to secure a certificate from responsible officers

1402 Financial Examinations, pp. 56–57.

1403 Trouant, p. 105.

1403a The Connecticut Company's return, introduced at the trial of *U. S. of America* v. *George Musica et al.*, footnote 23 *supra*, covered the operations of that Company to the date when the Maryland Company took over its business on or about October 31, 1934, and was filed under its subsequently changed name, McK & R Manufacturing Company, Incorporated.

1404 See pages 276–280 *supra*.

of the client to the effect that all liabilities of every description have been disclosed. The customary certificate was secured in this case.

In connection with the reading of contracts and minutes it may be recalled with respect to the Smith-Manning arrangement which governed the conduct of substantially all of the Canadian Company's business and approximately sixty-five percent of that of the Connecticut Company, later Division, that although the minutes of September 3, 1931, referred to a contract with Manning & Company and one with W. W. Smith & Company, Inc. the auditors were unaware of the former and that in abstracting the latter no reference was made to the 100% ownership of W. W. Smith & Company, Inc. by Manning & Company, a fact at variance with other evidence relied on by the auditors. One way of avoiding such errors is suggested by Bacas, Madden, and Rosenkampff when they point out the necessity of verbatim copies of important documents having a bearing on the accounts. They suggest that photostating provides the method of producing such copies in many cases. This method has the advantage of preserving in the working papers a document which may be reviewed by a manager or a partner without raising doubts as to the accuracy of the copy.

I. PROFIT AND LOSS ACCOUNTS

1. Sales, Cost of Sales, and Gross Profit

As previously pointed out, the working papers on Girard & Co., Inc. indicate that the billings during the last fifteen days prior to audit dates were disproportionately heavy as compared with prior sales. Also, the auditors' papers on the Connecticut Company for 1931 carried the notation, "Why are December sales higher?" Opposite this there was a red vertical line indicating that the step had been disposed of, apparently with satisfactory results, for no comment was made concerning this point in the memorandum on accounts submitted to the partner. In view of the length of time since the events and lack of more definite information in the working papers, the auditors were unable to say precisely how these things were disposed of at the time. Rowbotham thought that they might have been explained as the natural result of an expanding business. In any event, the testimony of Rowbotham and Thorn is clear that the primary purpose of any check they might have made in this connection was to see that the cut-off was proper, and that they would not have gone behind the factory orders or duplicate invoices to see that the transactions were real.[1405]

Their work in this respect was subject to another weakness—their failure to use proper departmentalized figures for such tests or com-

[1405] For discussion of this point see page 402 *supra*.

parisons as might have been made with sales or gross profit figures. Such widely dissimilar products as hand lotion and Dandrofuge (manufactured items) were combined with crude drugs and essential oils (resale items) because supposedly exported to the same type of customers. The gross profit on the former was over 80% and on the latter under 15%, yet the memoranda on accounts listed only the combined sales and gross profit figures. And since 1932 it was maintained that no separate consideration could have been given to foreign crude drug sales as distinguished from the domestic because the Company did not classify its accounts separately. Yet sales and gross profit schedules obtained from the client and contained in the auditors' working papers gave the necessary departmental breakdown.[1406] Obviously comparison of sales and of gross profit percentages in which different departments are lumped together defeats the purpose of these tests in disclosing and locating variations. Employing these tests only for the Company as a whole and using the gross profit test with the sole purpose in mind of checking the valuation of inventories, as Thorn's testimony would indicate he did, falls far short we feel of the full utilization of these tests to discover variations which if not properly explained may indicate possibilities of fraud. That the possibility of uncovering fraud is one object of this study should be clear from the following quotations:

> Cipriani: "Some test must be made of the accuracy of sales records to be sure that only genuine sales have been included" [1407]
>
> Thornton: "Abnormal fluctuations should be examined and explained. The officers of the client company should be consulted as to such fluctuations and their opinions should be given due but not conclusive weight. The auditor would not be held free of blame if, accepting without verification the opinions expressed by officers, those opinions were found to be in error. Independent investigation of wide variations from normal are necessary." [1408]
>
> Trouant: "Changes in sales volume and prices, the withdrawal of old products and the introduction of new products are all of interest to the accountant and may have a direct bearing upon the tests of inventories and sales expenses. A comparison of unfilled sales orders with amounts at the close of previous periods may throw additional light on the company's condition and prospects. Comparison of the company's sales volume with published information as to volume for the trade as a whole and comparison of monthly sales figures for the current and prior years may be helpful. If abnormally large billings are recorded for the closing months of the period, they should be investigated." [1409]

And finally in this connection it should be noted that while a sales and gross profit schedule would not on its face disclose such fact, greater consideration of departmental records should have revealed what the inventory work papers clearly indicated, that every trans-

---

[1406] Ex. N. The auditors claim that they used these schedules but solely as a basis for eliminating unrealized profits on inter-company sales of manufactured products from the consolidated accounts.

[1407] Cipriani, p. 155.

[1408] Financial Examinations, p. 186.

[1409] Trouant, p. 140.

action in foreign crude drugs was concluded at a gross profit and so recorded in a separate sales register. While Coster's alleged expertness in this trading might explain over-all good results, it seems to us that some question might well have been raised when year after year the many hundreds of transactions were concluded, every one at a gross profit. Further inquiry would then have revealed that all these foreign sales were allegedly paid when due in United States currency with never a deduction for allowances of any kind.

2. Other Profit and Loss Accounts

Examination of the comptroller's monthly reports of operations of McKesson & Robbins would not disclose the amount of foreign and domestic crude drug sales separately. As a result these reports left the directors uninformed as to the proportion of these two classes of business and, therefore, as to the significance of the expenses charged to the combined departments. That foreign business and domestic business have marked differences in many respects is widely recognized. How Thorn could believe, as he testified he did, that the directors and operating heads were properly informed of the Company's operations by these statements from McGloon's department is not clear. Perhaps general auditing practice did not dictate that he should have urged improvement in this respect. However, it seems to us that one of the services that independent auditors should render to clients is to make suggestions looking toward improvement in the client's accounting and internal auditing procedure so that the results obtained will be truly informative and reliable. And in any event with the separate figures available,[1410] Ritts' use of the combined figures from these reports for such review as he claims to have made does not seem logical.

J. THE WHOLESALE HOUSES

In judging the work of Price, Waterhouse & Co. it must not be forgotten that since the formation of the Maryland Company in 1928 the work at Bridgeport on the Canadian Company and the Connecticut Company, later Division, represented only a small portion of the auditors' entire engagement. In the last year (1937) sixty-four wholesale houses and eighteen other units in addition to the Canadian Company and Connecticut Division made up the work for which Price, Waterhouse & Co. were engaged. On these last two units the auditors spent less than three per cent of their time on the last five audits.

The work in the other units was criticized by some of the directors and managers of those units as too thorough. Such criticism came especially from employees who themselves were criticized for unsatis-

---

[1410] See footnote 1406 *supra*.

factory bookkeeping and who in some cases subsequently were caught in defalcations. Although the bulk of the testimony and evidence produced in this case deals with the situation at Bridgeport, enough material bearing on the work in the other units was introduced at the hearings to indicate that the work there was carried out in a thorough fashion and in accordance with generally accepted auditing practice prevailing during the periods involved. This important fact must not be overlooked in arriving at an opinion of the work of over two hundred men in any single year who represented Price, Waterhouse & Co. on this engagement throughout the country and which required the attention of every branch office of the firm in the United States.

The success of the work in the branches as contrasted with that done in Bridgeport may possibly be found in a difference in approach toward management. All of the branches were subjected to a thorough audit when merged with McKesson & Robbins and under instructions from the New York office of Price, Waterhouse & Co. the auditors of the branches were on the alert to report annually any defects in internal check and control.[1411] These instructions seem to have been interpreted quite literally, judging from the mass of criticism registered each year and passed on by Rowbotham to Coster in the individual reports on each house. This criticism, it may be observed, did not exempt the highest officers in the various branches if it appeared to the auditors that such officers were responsible for the conditions reported.

At Bridgeport, on the other hand, the audit work grew out of an engagement for a small corporation, all of whose stock was held by officers. With the development of the business the work at Bridgeport became an audit of units of a large organization, but these units had the distinction of having the president in residence and in charge of a major portion of the operations. This president and his chief aid, George Dietrich, had apparently won the confidence of successive Price, Waterhouse & Co. representatives and at the same time kept the other branches on the defensive because the Bridgeport operations apparently were always profitable, while those in the field were not uniformly successful. It may be recalled in this connection that Thorn and Ritts did not consider the instructions for work at the branches to be applicable to the Bridgeport units and never considered it necessary to report in detail on the system of internal check and control in these units.[1412]

The conditions in the wholesale houses which Price, Waterhouse & Co. did report in detail year after year were not their responsibility to correct. Their obligation was met when they adjusted their audit work to fit the situation and warned the client that the system of

[1411] Page 165 *supra*.

[1412] Page 187 *supra*.

internal check and control was inadequate in most of the units of the Company. If the registrant is to take full advantage of the economy of an audit based upon tests and samples under which, by our rules, the auditor "* * * may give due weight to an internal system of audit regularly maintained by means of auditors employed on the registrant's own staff * * *",[1413] it would appear to be a duty of the registrant to cooperate with the independent auditors by improving accounting procedures wherever practicable and more particularly to correct weaknesses brought to their attention by the auditors.

The general principle which we observed in our opinion in the *Interstate Hosiery* case appears to be applicable here. In that opinion we said:

> "* * * The fundamental and primary responsibility for accuracy of information filed with the Commission and disseminated among the investors rests upon management. Management does not discharge its obligations in this respect by the employment of independent public accountants, however reputable. Accountants' certificates are required not as a substitute for management's accounting of its stewardship, but as a check upon that accounting * * *."[1414]

Failure of the client to provide an adequate system of internal check and control can only be overcome by the auditors, if at all, by making a more comprehensive audit than would otherwise be necessary. Under existing standards the auditors appear to have done more than the minimum necessary in order to overcome this situation at the wholesale houses and would have done still more, as for example, in confirming receivables and securing original deposit slips from the bank if these steps had been acceptable to the management.

The facts of this case impel us to observe that the auditors should not be looked upon as the only defense against collusive fraud committed by dishonest corporate officials. In the corporate organization the directors presumably represent the stockholders in the management of the company's affairs and they in turn entrust active operation of the business to certain of their number or to others who are elected to serve as administrative officers. It seems to us that the directors have a duty to the stockholders to inform themselves concerning the nature of the business conducted and to see that proper internal safeguards are provided to protect the assets committed to their care. Among the safeguards suggested by this record are appropriate subdivision of operating and accounting functions consistent with available personnel and reasonable economy, and the strengthening of the position of the comptroller by making him responsible to the board of directors rather than subservient to operating officials whose operations he is expected to report upon in a

[1413] Instruction Book for Form 10 for Corporations, p. 15; Instruction Book for Form 10-K for Corporations, pp. 11-12; and Regulations S-X, Rule 2-02 (*b*). Interpreted in practice as including an adequate system of internal check and control.

[1414] *In the Matter of Interstate Hosiery Mills, Inc.*, 4 S. E. C. 706 (1939).

candid manner. To fulfill his protective function the comptroller needs the sympathetic support of the board in providing him with assistance to perform his many duties in an effective manner.

K. REVIEW PROCEDURE

Adequate and competent supervision of the audit seems to be taken for granted by most writers on auditing for very little attention is given in the texts to the problems of staff management and review procedure. On this latter point, the testimony of Ritts, Thorn, and Rowbotham as to the part played by senior, manager, and partner parallels quite closely Thornton's book on the "Duties of the Senior Accountant". This pocket-size book of ninety-one pages appears to be a fair summary of the Price, Waterhouse & Co. conception of staff management and control and review of the work.

The procedure laid down contemplates a continuous process of review, for the senior is expected to check all schedules turned in by juniors and to apply various tests to determine the reliability of the results obtained.

"Small errors and inflations are not to be detected in this way; the object is to make certain that the accounts are not grossly wrong. The detail work of the staff must be depended upon for detection of smaller errors.

"Briefly, the statement of what a company claims to have should be met with the question: Where did the company get it? Conversely, the claim that profits have been made should be met by the question: Where are the proceeds? If the auditor can satisfy himself that the records answer these questions satisfactorily he is not likely to be seriously deceived." [1415]

Work on McKesson units audited by branch offices of Price, Waterhouse & Co. was subjected to a double check—once in the branch and again by the manager in the New York office before the reports were submitted to the partner. Responsibility for making a final review of all work in the McKesson case rested on the partner, Rowbotham. On an engagement of this size the detailed review of the working papers ended with the manager, and the partner's time was saved by the preparation of a memorandum covering the important points on the job. As to this stage in the procedure Thornton observes:

"A senior who is once detected in the act of smoothing over defects in order that the partner who reviews the work may not know of them is forever barred from complete trust and will find promotion limited.

"Partners' time is valuable; the senior should try to present his work and explain his ideas about it as briefly as possible consistent with a clear exposition of the facts. At the same time, if there be any questionable matter involved in the work he must, if necessary, force it upon the attention of the reviewer. If trouble should come later because of such a matter, the excuse that the partner was too busy to listen would not be accepted.

[1415] Duties of a Senior Accountant, p. 27.

"When accounts have been made up correctly in accordance with the records, the senior's work is not completed. If the work has been done properly the senior should have formed definite opinions as to the amount of faith that may be put in the records and the system of accounting, the faults and weaknesses of methods in use and the possibilities of improvement. These conclusions should be laid concisely before the reviewing partner." [1416]

This review program, which in addition included the checking by staff members of extensions, footings, and references in the typed report, is fairly representative of current practice. However, the question remains as to how well it was executed by Rowbotham in his review of Jaureguy's and Thorn's work over a period of ten years.

Judging from Rowbotham's testimony, reported elsewhere in this volume, his primary interest was in assuring himself that sound accounting principles were employed and that proper inquiry had been made in connection with certain features which he called "points of the job." Except to ask whether the matter had been looked into, he did not concern himself directly with the question of internal check and control.

Under the regular procedure established by Price, Waterhouse & Co., important points, worthy of Rowbotham's mature reflection (he had been with the firm twenty years when he took over the McKesson assignment), were reported to him in writing in two ways—in the memoranda prepared by the senior or manager to bring out important points in the work and in the detailed report on the consolidated accounts and shorter letters on the other accounts prepared for submission to Coster. As previously stated, however, the letters on the Canadian Company and Connecticut Company, later Division, usually contained no comment.

While the memoranda pointed out many of the significant features of the business purportedly carried on through W. W. Smith & Company, Inc., particularly the remarkable record of collections, something would appear to have been lacking either in their preparation or review for Rowbotham remained uninformed on some vital points. For example, the 1932 memorandum on the Connecticut Company [1417] mentioned on one page that the bulk of the crude stocks were purchased from W. W. Smith & Co., and on the next that McKesson's sales to a large class of foreign trade were made through this concern.[1418] In connection with a discussion of the difficulty of getting satisfactory price quotations on the foreign crude drug inventory and in considering whether because of falling market prices the inventory should have been marked down at the year end, the memorandum also noted that approximately 50% of the Connecticut Company's December 31, 1932 inventory was sold at a small margin of profit

[1416] Idem, pp. 35–36.

[1417] Ex. 81.

[1418] Pages 225–226 *supra*.

prior to the completion of the examination, indicating an annual rate of turnover for 1933 based on the period to February 18, 1933 (the date of the memorandum) of approximately 4 times. The annual rate of turnover for 1933 was only slightly over 2 times and for 1932 had been below 2.[1419] Rowbotham when questioned at the hearings concerning this disproportion testified that he thought the sentence in the memorandum referred to firm contracts for future billings, thus not indicating recorded sales; but Ritts then stated that actual sales were meant.[1420] It thus appears that the manner in which the business was purportedly conducted through Smith was not clear to Rowbotham.

Again the 1935 memorandum on the Canadian Company reported that the Company intended to claim exemption "* * * under Section 4K, Part II, of the Dominion Income War Tax Act on all profits arising since * * *" April 3, 1935 as of which date it was authori ed to carry on business as a foreign corporation in the State of Connecticut.[1421] Also, on top of the 1935 working papers, Ritts had made a notation to the effect that at December 31, 1935 all stocks were stored in Canada "* * * meaning that there is a point I must clear with someone."[1422] (The inventories were supposed to have been in Bridgeport at December 31, 1934.) As previously pointed out, the 4 (k) exemption applied only to companies whose assets were situated entirely outside of Canada.[1423]

Finally there was only one reference in any of the memoranda to Manning & Company as a bank. The 1931 memorandum on the Connecticut Company [1424] reported that "* * * Prior to 1931, McKesson & Robbins did this class of business through Manning & Co., Montreal, but during the year the latter went into the private banking business exclusively and sold its export business to W. W. Smith & Co. * * *."[1425] But no further mention was ever made of Manning & Company or that since 1932 all payments on account of foreign crude drug sales throughout the year were purportedly made by the customers directly to Manning & Company who in recent years also purportedly made all payments on account of foreign crude drug purchases. Since even Ritts and Thorn testified that they were unaware of this prior to the hearings,[1426] Rowbotham must also have

---

1419 Page 304 *supra*.

1420 Page 310 *supra*.

1421 Ex. 73.

1422 R. 518 quoted at page 275 *supra*. See also R. 599, 4471. The 1935 memorandum on the Canadian Company and the 1936 and 1937 memoranda on the Connecticut Division point out that the confirmations received from the Canadian vendor-custodians did not state the exact location of the stocks. Page 274 *supra*.

1423 Pages 286-287 *supra*. Cf. also indenture provision "* * * exclusive of goods purchased abroad which are either in foreign warehouses or in transit * * *" The inventories in question were not so considered and treated by the auditors. Pages 341-342 *supra*.

1424 Ex. 82.

1425 Pages 201-202 *supra*.

1426 Footnote 642 *supra*.

been uninformed on this. It follows that Rowbotham must also have been unaware of, and thus could not have reviewed the work with respect to, the fact that for the last three years of the engagement the actual remittances from customers were not available for anyone's inspection at the client's premises and since the goods themselves were supposedly held by the suppliers and shipped to the customers by Smith, the transactions were conducted entirely "offstage".[1427]

Turning now to a consideration of the detailed audit reports on the consolidated accounts, it seems to us that such figures as were set forth concerning particulars of the foreign crude drug business and indicating its remarkable growth with all profits going back into increased inventories and receivables [1428] should have suggested the desirability of independent inquiry to a person with some knowledge of the drug trade. If review by a partner is to prevent less experienced staff men from being too easily satisfied by explanations of clients and to keep them from erroneous conclusions as to the satisfactory state of the clients' affairs, it would appear necessary that the partner have had experience with other companies in the same line of business or else undertake to inform himself in respect to the industry as a basis for a sound judgment.[1429]

A paragraph in Montgomery's Auditing is so directly in point here that it is quoted:

> "There is available a constantly increasing quantity of informative business statistics compiled by government bureaus, chambers of commerce, bureaus of research, financial institutions, trade associations, and manufacturing groups. Many large audit firms have available statistical information relative to clients in the same line of business which they can ethically use without divulging confidential information. The auditor should take advantage of the comparisons which these sources of information afford. He may be enabled to make valuable comparisons of the client's production costs with those of the industry as a whole or of ratios based on the client's records with ratios for the industry as a whole. The knowledge thus gained should be of great aid in reviewing the client's operations." [1430]

The mechanics of the review procedure as carried out by Price, Waterhouse & Co. on the McKesson & Robbins engagement were substantially the same as that of the majority of accounting firms. A review of the record convinces us that the seniors' reports to the partner in charge were intended to be fully informative of important points of the engagement, and that any omissions now noted were due to a failure to perceive their significance at the time. It is equally clear that in Rowbotham's mind Thornton's two questions: "Where

---

[1427] Cf. page 392 *supra*.

[1428] Pages 334 ff. *supra*.

[1429] R. 1945–1946 (Rowbotham): "No, I have not had any other experience in a business like this except this."

[1430] Montgomery, 5th Ed., p. 685. See also Thornton and Trouant quoted at page 420 *supra*. Cf. footnote 1311 *supra*.

did the company get what it had?" and "Where are the proceeds of profitable operations?" were answered to his satisfaction before he approved the report. However, the review of the work did not result in a searching analysis of the ultimate facts developed in the course of the actual audit, because, although performed by a partner of many years' experience,[1431] it was not done by a person sufficiently familiar with the business practices of the client's industry, or with a sufficient interest in the basic questions of internal check and control to comprehend the significance of the facts reported.[1432]

L. THE REPORT AND CERTIFICATE

Our conclusions concerning the use of the auditors' detailed report submitted to Coster have already been discussed [1433] and therefore present consideration of this subject may be limited to the certificate which is attached to the financial statements which are filed with this Commission and the various stock exchanges, which are submitted to stockholders, and which are otherwise made available to investors. As to the form of the certificate, Price, Waterhouse & Co. followed generally accepted practice during the period of the Girard-McKesson engagement and hence the facts in this case may be used as a point of departure for a discussion of the general problem.

For five years prior to the McKesson hearings the form of certificate below, developed by the American Institute of Accountants in collab-

---

1431 See page 374 *supra*.

1432 "We think it is self-evident that the review upon which an accounting firm assumes responsibility for work done by subordinates must be more than a series of perfunctory questions as to the performance of particular items in an audit program. Nor should explanations of unusual items be accepted by a reviewer without support in detail from the working papers. As a matter of principle, a review should, it seems to us, be designed with two objectives in mind: first, to insure the integration of the original work papers with the financial statements; second, a searching analysis of the ultimate facts developed in the course of the actual audit. An adequate review with the first purpose in mind should serve not only to disclose intentional or accidental misstatements but should also serve as a method of internal check and control on the work of the firm's subordinates. This branch of the review, it seems to us, need not necessarily be carried out by a partner but should at least be done by one well versed in the procedures adopted by the firm and in the general principles and terminology of auditing and accounting. If not a partner of the firm, such review should, in our opinion, be made by persons who are independent of those actually performing or supervising the audit work as well as of those who prepared the draft of the financial statements. The second branch of the review is designed to enable the accounting firm to interpret intelligently the figures it has obtained and to which it is to certify. This part of the review should, it seems to us, be made by a person, preferably a partner, qualified by his knowledge of sound accounting principles and his familiarity with the accounting phases of the industry and the more important problems of the particular company. In this manner the facts ascertained by competent employees can be subjected to the independent and broader judgment of a more experienced person who can by searching inquiry of the supervisor or senior and by examination of significant items in the work papers and schedules reach an informed judgment both as to the adequacy of the audit work done and as to the integrity and clarity of the financial statements themselves. We are satisfied that a review along these lines would have exposed the irregularities in this case." *In the Matter of Interstate Hosiery Mills, Inc.*, 4 S. E. C. 706 (1939).

Of the testimony of the expert witnesses, at least that of Horne, P. 362-363; Couchman, P. 415-417; Bailey, P. 573-575; and Jones, P. 614-615, indicates that their practice is fully as strong as that contemplated in the opinion quoted. It should be noted in this regard that this testimony was given before the opinion referred to was published.

In respect to the importance of a thorough inquiry into the client's system of internal audit and control in relation to the audit by independent public accountants, see *In the Matter of Monroe Loan Society*, 3 S. E. C. 407 (1938).

1433 Pages 368 ff., 427 *supra*.

oration with the New York Stock Exchange, had been in common use:

"To the XYZ COMPANY:

"We have made an examination of the balance sheet of the XYZ Company as at December 31, 1935, and of the statement of income and surplus for the year 1935. In connection therewith, we examined or tested accounting records of the Company and other supporting evidence and obtained information and explanations from officers and employees of the Company; we also made a general review of the accounting methods and of the operating and income accounts for the year, but we did not make a detailed audit of the transactions.

"In our opinion, based upon such examination, the accompanying balance sheet and related statement of income and surplus fairly present, in accordance with accepted principles of accounting consistently maintained by the XYZ Company during the year under review, its position at December 31, 1935, and the results of its operations for the year."

This form of certificate is set out in the bulletin, "Examination of Financial Statements by Independent Public Accountants," but it is there stated that its use is appropriate only if the terms laid down in the following notes, which are published immediately below the form, have been observed:

"1. It is contemplated that, before signing a report of the type suggested, the accountant will be satisfied that his examination has been adequate and in conformity with the principles outlined in this bulletin.

"2. The report should be addressed to the directors of the company or to the stockholders, if the appointment is made by them.

"3. The statement of what has been examined would, of course, conform to the titles of the accounts or statements reported upon.

"4. In the second sentence, any special forms of confirmation could be mentioned: e. g., 'including confirmation of cash and securities by inspection or certificates from depositaries.'

"5. This certificate is appropriate only if the accounting for the year is consistent in basis with that for the preceding year. If there has been any material change either in accounting principles or in the manner of their application, the nature of the change should be indicated.

"6. It is contemplated that the form of report would be modified when and as necessary to embody any qualifications, reservations or supplementary explanations." [1434]

The essential features of the foregoing certificate have also been used by independent public accountants as complying with the requirements of this Commission as expressed in the Instruction Book for Form 10-K for Corporations:

"ACCOUNTANTS' CERTIFICATE

The financial statements required shall be accompanied by a certificate of an independent public or independent certified public accountant or accountants. This certificate shall be dated, shall be reasonably comprehensive as to the scope of the audit made, and shall state clearly the opinion of the accountant or accountants in respect of the financial statements of, and the accounting principles and procedures followed by, the registrant and its subsidiaries. In certifying to the

[1434] Ex. 117 (p. 41).

financial statements, independent public or independent certified public accountants may give due weight to an internal system of audit regularly maintained by means of auditors employed on the registrant's own staff. In such case the independent accountants shall review the accounting procedures followed by the registrant and its subsidiaries and by appropriate measures shall satisfy themselves that such accounting procedures are in fact being followed. Nothing in these instructions shall be construed to imply authority for the omission of any procedure which independent public accountants would ordinarily employ in the course of a regular annual audit." [1435]

All of the witnesses interpreted the last three sentences so as to permit and not to forbid the certifying accountant to give due weight to the client's system of internal check and control, whether or not this system included a staff of internal auditors.[1436] That the accountant must determine as a part of his audit the effectiveness of this system and adjust his audit program thereto should be recognized as the cornerstone of any examination of financial statements. In our opinion, the determination of the effectiveness of control requires the attention of an auditor of experience and sound judgment as many of the factors involved are of an intangible nature and not capable of reduction to precise rules. Final appraisal of the extent to which the audit program may be affected by the system of internal control is a problem worthy of consideration by the person who signs the certificate and should be the subject of searching review by him before the conclusion of the engagement.

On another point opinion among the accountants was also substantially uniform. The second sentence of the standard certificate was understood to be in full compliance with that part of the Commission's rule which requires that the certificate "* * * shall be reasonably comprehensive as to the scope of the audit made * * *." [1437] This general opinion was based on the fact that accountants understood that the certificate in this form should not be used unless the examination has been substantially that outlined in the Bulletin. Although the Bulletin has had a fairly wide distribution in financial circles, it may be safely assumed that the majority of corporation stockholders have either never heard of it or are unfamiliar with its contents. This raises a puzzling problem therefore as to whether the second sentence in the certificate, as respects the average investor, actually amounts to a reasonably comprehensive description of the audit made and if not, how the defect can be cured. In expressing their opinion on the sentence, two witnesses extended their answers to suggest possible solutions to the problem just raised.

1435 Pp. 11–12. Similar requirements appear in other forms adopted by the Commission under the Securities Exchange Act of 1934 and in Rule 651 under the Securities Act of 1933. See Regulation S-X, Rule 2-02 adopted in 1940, for a restatement of the requirements.

1436 E. g. Rowbotham, pages 348–350 *supra;* Bell, P. 212; Lenhart, P. 264; Bailey, P. 577.

1437 Rowbotham, page 348 *supra*; P. 50, 107, 161, 212, 261, 308, 364, 417, 469, 526 (taking exception), 616.

The question asked of all the expert witnesses was:

"Q. [By Mr. WERNTZ.] * * * is it your understanding that the second sentence of the first paragraph [of the standard certificate] is intended to be a reasonably comprehensive statement of the scope of the audit?

* * * * * * *

A. [By STEMPF.] Yes. Here it is a question of deciding where to draw the line. Full details of all audit steps are obviously impossible, because they are so voluminous. The so-called long form of certificate goes only slightly further than the second sentence. The second sentence points out the general scope of the examination in conformity with the bulletin and indicates its limitations.

I should like to add there that the standard form of accountant's report cannot be read and cannot be understood unless the reader knows that it is directly related to the bulletin. And I am sorry to say that it is my distinct impression that there are relatively few investors who have any knowledge of that fact and perhaps to some degree a reasonable number of informed men who do not realize the relationship between the standard form of report and the pamphlet, and that in spite of the issuance of, I think, about 50,000 copies of the pamphlet.

Q. Have you any thought there as to how a better mutual understanding could be reached?

A. I think all of us should try to emphasize that fact whenever the discussion of accountant's reports, particularly in the standard form, arises, regardless of who may raise the question. I think if we can continue to reiterate the fact that the two must be read to be understood, that we'll do everyone a real service.[1438]

* * * * * * *

A. [By BAILEY.] I don't think it is particularly comprehensive or definite. I think it is a conventional wording intended to be used for such an examination as is contemplated by the bulletin, but before the wording can be really useful I think there must be a wider appreciation of that particular convention.

I think we accountants may find that the difficulty of a common understanding on that sentence is great, so great that we may find it advisable to make the scope paragraph more definite.[1439]

The issue is clearly drawn in these two views. Before the agreement on the standard form of certificate in 1934, accountants had used a rather wide variety of language in which to couch their certificate. Samples of three methods of attacking the problem are presented by Montgomery with his opinion of each. Two of his examples demonstrate methods of complying with Bailey's suggestion so that a somewhat extended quotation provides a suitable means of illustrating the differences of opinion on a question which has been debated extensively in recent years.

"*Types of Certificates.*—In the author's opinion the certificate should be as short and concise as possible. Extended statements of the steps taken by the auditor in his verification are of little interest to the reader and do not belong in the formal certification. The auditor is expected to take responsibility for judging what constitutes a reasonable program of verification for any particular examination and based on such verification, to be prepared to express a positive opinion. Of course if he has been restricted in his examination but still feels justified in making

[1438] P. 161.

[1439] P. 576.

some formal statement, such limitation will have to be expressed as a qualification in the certificate.

"Likewise the author believes it is generally better to exclude from the certificate comments regarding items in the financial statements, except when explanations of material significance are required to make the statements complete. It is preferable that the financial statements be complete in themselves so that the auditor's certificate may conform as nearly as possible to the unqualified short type.

"*Short Form.*—When asked their preference, most bankers and clients ask for short certificates. In support of the argument for a short certificate, the president of a large bank wrote the author, 'We frequently observe certificates which require as close an analysis as the figures themselves. Some standardized form of audit which would carry with it all that the word implies would be most acceptable, I think, to bankers generally.'

"The ideal certificate is brief, to the point and embodies conclusions based solely on the auditor's investigations.

* * * * * * *

"When an income account is submitted in addition to a balance sheet, the following form of certificate (drawn also to cover the case of consolidated statements) may be used:

"D. E. F. COMPANY,
New York, N. Y.

"We have examined the accounts of D. E. F. Company and its subsidiary companies as at December 31, 1933, and we certify that, in our opinion, the above consolidated balance sheet and the accompanying consolidated income and surplus accounts set forth the financial position of the company and its subsidiaries at that date and the results of their operations for the year then ended.

X. Y. Z.

"NEW YORK, *March 10, 1934.*

* * * * * * *

"*Long Form.*—Some auditing firms frequently use the so-called long form or amplified certificate in which comments are made regarding the inventories, depreciation, plant additions, etc. A form of this type, subject to variations to suit particular situations, is as follows:

"THE BOARD OF DIRECTORS, A. B. C. COMPANY.

"We have made an examination of the books of account of A. B. C. Company and its subsidiaries as at December 31, 193—, and have made a general review of the accounting methods and of the operating and income accounts for the year.

"We have confirmed the cash and securities by count and inspection, or by certificates which we obtained from the depositaries. The investments in wholly owned and majority owned companies not consolidated, but included as 'investments' in the accompanying consolidated balance sheet, are carried at valuations which in our opinion are conservative.

"We have scrutinized the accounts and notes receivable and believe that full provision has been made for probable losses through bad and doubtful debts.

"Certified inventories of merchandise, work in progress and materials and supplies, have been submitted to us and, in our opinion, these inventories have been taken in a careful manner with ample allowance for old or inactive stocks and are conservatively stated on the basis of cost or market, whichever is lower.

"We examined the charges to capital accounts and believe them to represent additions or improvements to the company's property. In our opinion, adequate allowance has been made in the operating accounts for repairs, renewals and depreciation, and all ascertained liabilities at December 31, 193—, have been included in the accounts.

"In our opinion, based upon such examination, the accompanying consolidated balance sheet and statements of income and surplus, fairly present the consolidated financial position of the companies as at December 31, 193—, and the consolidated results of their operations for the year ended that date.

X. Y. Z.

"NEW YORK, *February 10, 193—*.

"The weakness of the long form of certificate illustrated above is that while certain specific aspects of the scope of verification are set forth, the phrase 'based upon such examination' in the last paragraph places the burden on the reader of judging whether the scope was adequate, a responsibility which, as has been pointed out, the auditor himself should assume.

"In the following portion of a certificate, which might replace all but the first paragraph of the preceding example, a brief statement of opinion on certain major matters is combined with the auditor's opinion regarding the statements as a whole in a manner which is not objectionable:

"In our opinion, based upon such examination, the charges to property accounts cover only actual additions and extensions, the allowances for depreciation and depletion are reasonable, the valuations of stocks of material and supplies on hand (as shown by inventories certified by the responsible officials) have been made at the lower of cost or market prices, proper allowance has been made for doubtful accounts receivable and for all ascertained liabilities, and the accompanying con olidated balance sheet and related consolidated income and surplus accounts fairly present, in accordance with acceptable principles of accounting consistently followed by the companies during the year under review, the consolidated financial position of * * * Corporation and its subsidiary companies as at * * *, 193—, and the consolidated results of their operations for the year then ended." [1440]

Another problem in this field is illustrated in the present case by the fact that although the certificate was in the usual standard form without mentioning any limitations on the work, certain audit steps were specifically noted in the letters of engagement as points which were not to be done.

"In accordance with your instructions, our work will be conducted, as heretofore, along the lines of a financial or balance sheet examination consisting of an examination of the balance sheets of McKesson & Robbins, Incorporated and its subsidiary companies as at December 31, 1937 and a general review of the profit and loss accounts for the year ending on that date, but will not include a detailed check of the cash and other bookkeeping transactions such as might disclose a misappropriation of funds or manipulation of the accounts, should any exist. It is our understanding that the examination will not include an inspection of bank deposit slips or any circularization of debtors or creditors in verification of receivables and payables." [1441]

[1440] Montgomery, 5th Ed. pp. 697-700.

[1441] Ex. 116. See also pages 151-152 *supra*. Cf. also Ex. 100, letter transmitting accounts of Canadian Company:

> "In accordance with your instructions, our examination was conducted along the lines of a financial or balance sheet examination, and the debtors and creditors were not circularized for verifications of the receivables and payables. The merchandise carried in the inventories of McKesson & Robbins, Limited at December 31, 1937 was confirmed to us by the vendors who held this merchandise at that date but we have not attempted to otherwise verify the amount of merchandise so held."

The certificate on the Canadian Company accounts was addressed to the shareholders but was otherwise similar to the one on the accounts of the Maryland Company and subsidiaries consolidated. Page 348 *supra*.

And as previously pointed out the auditors placed a note on the balance sheet after inventories, "(certified as to quantity and condition by responsible officials)" "* * * for the purpose of making it clear to anybody who reads the balance sheet that on that point they must accept the word of the company officials rather than the word of the accountants." [1442] At the time of the audits in question the observation of inventory taking or the making of systematic physical tests of inventories and the performance of other audit steps mentioned in the letters of engagement above quoted were not considered mandatory procedures for auditors. Construing the certificate as referring to the type of examination set forth in the Bulletin, no qualification or exception would therefore have been necessary in the auditors' opinion on account of such omissions.

The disclaimer by the auditors as expressed in their letters must, therefore, be construed as merely applying to possible steps which might have been done in excess of what was necessary in order to certify to the financial statements and which, not having been accepted by the client, the auditors specified in their letters in order to relieve themselves from liability for the non-detection of what might have been disclosed thereby. It is generally proper, for example, to certify financial statements without exception although auditing procedures have not been so extensively applied as to disclose every minor defalcation or manipulation, and to avoid any misunderstanding which may arise from subsequent events, for the accountant to state in writing to the client the steps omitted. Obviously, however, if the certificate attached to McKesson accounts is not to be construed as a misrepresentation, it must be interpreted as not limited by the letters of engagement or the note on the balance sheet in stating the full performance of a regular balance sheet examination sufficient in scope for the unqualified expression of opinion as to the authenticity of the accounts.[1443]

From all of the foregoing it appears to us that the following principles should be adopted respecting the form and content of accountants' certificates in order to avoid possibility of confusion in the future.

The work done should be described as the auditor sees fit and any desired information concerning the accounts may be stated. While we do not think that each audit step should necessarily be set forth, it is to be hoped that really descriptive language will be used as distinguished from a standard form based upon procedures set forth in

---

1442 Testimony of Rowbotham, page 346 *supra*.

1443 The most conservative free translation of the meaning of an accountant's certificate was given by the last to appear of the twelve expert witnesses:

> "We mean to imply in our certificate that we have made such tests and examinations of the client's accounts and records and supplementary documents and have made such inquiry that we have reason to believe and no reason for disbelief that the statements which we are certifying fairly reflect the condition of the company and the results of its operations." P. 620 (Jones).

(purportedly a Canadian firm) as agent to carry on this business was to promote goodwill within the British Empire. Pages 67, 205–208, 391.

3. Foreign Crude Drug Receivables

17. Remarkable collection experience—prompt payment in U. S. currency and complete absence of bad debts, allowances, or adjustments of any kind. Pages 93, 97, 98, 217–220, 222–224, 335–336, 393.

18. Goods bought f. o. b. New York and sold f. o. b. New York were purportedly shipped directly from Canada to foreign countries with no adjustments made on this account. Page 86.

19. Nature of the basic guaranty provisions of the W. W. Smith & Company, Inc., contracts as interpreted and applied by McKesson and accepted by the auditors. Pages 218, 220–225.

20. Use of United States domestic bill of lading forms made out to foreign crude drug customers beyond the seas showing "Route THEIR TRUCK" and shipping dates inconsistent with the time that would have been required after receipt of order to make shipments from Canada to overseas customers and without indication on this or other shipping documents as to which vendor was supposedly supplying the merchandise. Pages 77–80, 87–89, 234–238, 402.

21. "Pet" orders were handled in bunches and followed a different office routine from the other orders. Pages 80–86, 239, 302.

4. Intercompany Accounts

22. Sales of foreign crude drugs by Canadian Company to Connecticut Division providing funds for Canadian Company's dividend payments in 1937. Pages 98–99, 242, 397–399.

5. Foreign Crude Drug Inventories

23. Confirmations secured by Price, Waterhouse & Co. from the vendors did not state where the merchandise was held nor did they give any identifying markings of the items supposedly held. Pages 104, 107, 253–254, 256, 271–272, 276.

24. Lack of correspondence between market quotations and price, quality, packing, and description of items in McKesson's foreign crude drug inventory. Pages 106, 255, 263–270, 400–402.

25. Establishment of Canadian Company with the announced purpose to manufacture and distribute McKesson products in Canada and the British Empire, purchase of goodwill and rights thereto from the Connecticut Company, renting of a warehouse in Canada but failure to use it or to engage in such activities. Pages 28–30, 256–257.

26. Small number of commodities and large quantity of each in the inventory. Pages 105–106, 254, 256–257, 268–271, 337–338.

27. Appearance of the foreign crude drug inventory count sheets of December 31 1934 when compared with other inventory count sheets of the same date, especially the absence of names or initials of inventory crews on the foreign crude drug count sheets. Pages 108–110, 111–112, 257–258, 280–281.

28. Space noted on December 31, 1934 inventory count sheets as the location of the foreign crude drug stocks was inadequate to hold the quantities listed and was designated on other count sheets as, and in fact was, occupied by other goods. Pages 110–111, 280–282, 403–404.

29. Perpetual inventory records never had to be adjusted for discrepancies with the physical count and very rarely to reduce cost to market at the inventory dates. Page 111–112, 283.

30. Slow inventory turn-over but with no goods held over from one year end to the next. Pages 261, 304, 310.

31. Although sales were in smaller quantities than purchases, year-end inventories with rare exceptions corresponded exactly with individual purchases. Pages 104–105 257, 261–262.

32. Lack of knowledge respecting foreign crude items on the part of the clerk to whom the auditors were referred and upon whom they relied for information and assistance in pricing. Pages 264–267.

33. Complete operating isolation of the foreign crude drug business from Hermann's department, although combined in the comptroller's reports to officials. Pages 107–108, 191, 262–263, 269, 301, 310–314.

34. Regular importing of foreign crude drug items for export in conflict with existing cartel restrictions or for shipment in bulk to countries nearer the source of supply. Pages 105–106, 269.

35. Auditors' request for confirmation of over $2,000,000 in foreign crude drugs addressed to B. Miller & Company, 48 Queen Street, Ottawa, Canada, instead of to 45 Queen Street, was returned because of incorrect address. Pages 104, 272.

36. At December 31, 1934 when count sheets placed the stock in the Bridgeport plant, the Maryland Company's Connecticut tax return for 1934 placed the foreign crude drug inventories outside the state of Connecticut and was supported in McKesson's files with schedules showing this inventory in New Jersey at December 31, 1934. Pages 276–283, 418.

37. The auditors' acceptance of a representation of exemption from Canadian income taxes after 1934 based upon a law exempting corporations doing no business in and holding no assets in Canada although the auditors understood that the inventories were held in Canada after 1934. Pages 274–276, 285–287, 417, 426.

6. Other Balance Sheet Accounts

38. Lack of differentiation between W. W. Smith & Company, Inc., W. W. Smith & Co., and W. W. Smith & Co., Ltd. Pages 101, 129, 294–297.

39. Multiple relationships with the Smith Companies as vendee, vendor, sales agency, and guarantor of accounts. Pages 53–67, 99–101, 129, 294–297.

40. Problems encountered on foreign exchange in small matters as contrasted with the absence of such problems in the foreign crude drug business. Pages 205–208, 228, 298.

7. Profit and Loss Accounts

41. Classification of sales and cost of sales in comptroller's report to management so that the amount of the foreign crude drug business was not revealed. Pages 107–108, 120–127, 310–315, 421.

42. Every foreign crude drug sale was made at a gross profit. Pages 89–91, 301.

43. Discontinuance of the high profit Dandrofuge and hand lotion line coincident with a compensating spurt in the low profit crude drug business in 1931 and 1932 to the same class of customers in Australia and New Zealand. Pages 301–306.

44. Sale of half the inventory prior to completion of the 1932 audit of the Connecticut Company as compared to an inventory turn-over of less than two times for the period under review. Pages 304, 310, 425–426.

45. Relation between the growth of foreign crude drug inventories and receivables and the gross profits of the Connecticut Division (and of the Connecticut Division and the Canadian Company combined) and the failure of the Connecticut Division to produce cash for the Maryland Company. Pages 241–249, 339–340, 427.

O. SUMMARY

Our conclusion based upon the facts revealed by the record, the testimony of the expert witnesses, and the writings of recognized authorities is that the audits performed by Price, Waterhouse & Co. substantially conformed, in form, as to the scope and procedures employed, to what was generally considered mandatory during the period of the Girard-McKesson engagements. Their failure to discover the gross overstatement of assets and of earnings is attributable to the manner in which the audit work was done. In carrying out the work they failed to employ that degree of vigilance, inquisitiveness, and analysis of the evidence available that is necessary in a professional undertaking and is recommended in all well-known and authoritative works on auditing. In addition, the overstatement should have been disclosed if the auditors had corroborated the Company's records by actual observation and independent confirmation through procedures involving regular inspection of inventories and confirmation of accounts receivable, audit steps which, although considered better practice and used by many accountants, were not considered mandatory by the profession prior to our hearings.

Price, Waterhouse & Co. maintain that a balance sheet examination is not intended and cannot be expected to detect a falsification of records concealing an inflation of assets and of earnings if accomplished by a widespread conspiracy carried on by the president of a corporation, aided by others within and without the recognized ranks of a corporation's operating personnel, and that no practical system of internal check can be devised the effectiveness of which cannot be nullified by criminal collusion on the part of a chief executive and key employees. Such cases are so rare, in their opinion, that there is no economic justification for the amount of auditing work which would be required to increase materially the protection against it.

The inference to be drawn from this position and from statements made by others in connection with this case is that a detailed audit of all transactions as distinguished from an examination based on tests and samples would have been necessary to reveal the falsification. However, as we view the situation in this case, a detailed audit of all transactions carried out by the same staff would merely have covered a larger volume of the same kinds of fictitious documents and transactions. While this might have brought under review more instances of what we have listed as circumstances suggesting further investigations, there is little ground for believing that this alone would have raised any greater question as to the authenticity of the transactions.

Moreover, we believe that, even in balance sheet examinations for corporations whose securities are held by the public, accountants can be expected to detect gross overstatements of assets and profits whether resulting from collusive fraud or otherwise. We believe that alertness on the part of the entire staff, coupled with intelligent analysis by experienced accountants of the manner of doing business, should detect overstatements in the accounts, regardless of their cause, long before they assume the magnitude reached in this case. Furthermore, an examination of this kind should not, in our opinion, exclude the highest officers of the corporation from its appraisal of the manner in which the business under review is conducted. Without underestimating the important service rendered by independent public accountants in their review of the accounting principles employed in the preparation of financial statements filed with us and issued to stockholders, we feel that the discovery of gross overstatements in the accounts is a major purpose of such an audit even though it be conceded that it might not disclose every minor defalcation. In short, Price, Waterhouse & Co.'s failure to uncover the gross overstatement of assets and of earnings in this case should not, in our opinion, lead to general condemnation of recognized procedures for the examination of financial statements by means of tests and samples.

We do feel, however, that there should be a material advance in the development of auditing procedures whereby the facts disclosed by the records and documents of the firm being examined are to a greater extent checked by the auditors through physical inspection or independent confirmation. The time has long passed, if it ever existed, when the basis of an audit was restricted to the material appearing in the books and records. For many years accountants have in regularly applied procedures gone outside the records to establish the actual existence of assets and liabilities by physical inspection or independent confirmation. As pointed out repeatedly in this report, there are many ways in which this can be extended. Particularly, it is our opinion that auditing procedures relating to the inspection of inventories and confirmation of receivables, which, prior to our hearings, had been considered optional steps, should, in accordance with the resolutions already adopted by the various accounting societies, be accepted as normal auditing procedures in connection with the presentation of comprehensive and dependable financial statements to investors.

We have carefully considered the desirability of specific rules and regulations governing the auditing steps to be performed by accountants in certifying financial statements to be filed with us. Action has already been taken by the accounting profession adopting certain of the auditing procedures considered in this case. We have no reason to believe at this time that these extensions will not be maintained or that further extensions of auditing procedures along the lines suggested in this report will not be made. Further, the adoption of the specific recommendations made in this report as to the type of disclosure to be made in the accountant's certificate and as to the election of accountants by stockholders should insure that acceptable standards of auditing procedure will be observed, that specific deviations therefrom may be considered in the particular instances in which they arise, and that accountants will be more independent of management. Until experience should prove the contrary, we feel that this program is preferable to its alternative—the detailed prescription of the scope of and procedures to be followed in the audit for the various types of issuers of securities who file statements with us—and will allow for further consideration of varying audit procedures and for the development of different treatment for specific types of issuers.

APPENDIX A

Action Taken Since the McKesson & Robbins Disclosures With Respect to Auditing Procedures by Professional Accounting and Other Interested Organizations

There is presented herein a brief summary of the activities of the public accounting profession and of certain other organizations relative to questions of auditing procedure and practice that arose as a result of the disclosures made in the McKesson & Robbins case.

The summary includes the activities of the American Institute of Accountants, the national organization of certified public accountants, as well as the activities of state organizations or societies of public accountants to the extent of information available. Included also is a brief reference to the activities of a group of organizations outside the public accounting field. These organizations, although not directly concerned with the formulation of auditing procedures and practices for the guidance of public accountants, are nevertheless interested in the results which such procedures are intended to accomplish. This group is composed of the Controllers Institute of America, National Association of Cost Accountants, National Association of Credit Men, National Association of Manufacturers, New York Stock Exchange, and the Robert Morris Associates. The summary is based upon information reported in official organs or bulletins issued by the foregoing organizations or obtained directly from such organizations through correspondence.

The sensational disclosures in the McKesson & Robbins case received immediate widespread publicity through newspapers and other publications. The magnitude of the sums involved, the prominence of the Company in its field of industry, and the extraordinary and unusual circumstances attending the conception and long continuation of the inflations disclosed were features that heightened public interest in the case. It was a matter of general information that the books and records of the Company had been audited and the financial statements certified for many years by a well-known firm of public accountants, Price, Waterhouse & Co. Under such circumstances, it was to be expected that the accounting profession would be subjected to critical comment in regard to auditing procedures.

A short time after the overstatements in the financial statements of the Company were disclosed in early December 1938, the Attorney

General of the State of New York invited, among others, the American Institute of Accountants and the New York State Society of Certified Public Accountants to send representatives to an open meeting to be held, January 6, 1939, for the purpose of discussing "certain fundamental weaknesses in the preparation of financial statements of large corporations" which the Attorney General stated had been revealed by recent investigations conducted by his office into certain matters.[1]

The American Institute of Accountants and the New York State Society of Certified Public Accountants each appointed a special committee of three members, who prepared a joint statement which was presented at the Attorney General's meeting. This statement gave a brief description of the two organizations, including number of members, requirements for admission, and character of activities; it reviewed the development of present standards of auditing and accounting procedure; discussed the responsibility of auditors and possible improvements in auditing and in auditing procedures relating to inventories and accounts receivable; and commented on methods of appointment of auditors, the natural business year, and internal check and control.[2]

A report making certain observations and recommendations regarding auditing practices was submitted to the Attorney General by members of his staff in charge of the meeting.[3] The principal recommendations were that physical testing of inventory quantities and verification of accounts receivable by direct communication with the debtors should be adopted as general auditing procedures and if omitted on any audit the balance sheet should state that the assets in question were not verified by these methods.

The position of the American Institute of Accountants [4] on questions raised by the disclosures in the McKesson & Robbins case was stated in an editorial appearing in the Journal of Accountancy (official organ of the Institute), February 1939, in the following language:

"In the light of circumstances so unusual, one might predict that such a case could never occur again. Yet the fact remains that auditors had been misled and that a published balance sheet had contained substantial overstatements of assets. The need for a critical review of audit procedure was evident. Members of the Institute from all parts of the country were demanding some public statement by the executive committee to clarify the position of the profession as a whole. After extensive deliberation, the executive committee issued a short statement to the press on December 28,[5] simply saying that in the interest of the

[1] For complete text of Attorney General's letter, see The Certified Public Accountant, January 1939.

[2] For complete text of this statement see Statement to Attorney General Bennett, New York Certified Public Accountant, January 1939. See also editorial in Journal of Accountancy, February 1939, for comment on the statement.

[3] For the text of the report, see The Certified Public Accountant, February 1939.

[4] The American Institute of Accountants reported that it had 5118 members at May 1, 1939. The Certified Public Accountant, June 1939, p. 5.

[5] For the text of this statement see The Certified Public Accountant, January 1939, p. 2.

public and the accounting profession the Institute would review customary auditing procedure in the light of the McKesson & Robbins case to determine what, if any, changes should be adopted; that a standard of accounting procedure had been in existence for many years in written form in the bulletin, Examination of Financial Statements by Independent Public Accountants (a copy of which was sent to every newspaper which received the release); that the McKesson & Robbins case was an extraordinary one in which there was testimony indicating collusive fraud on the part of high officers and the forging of accounting records, and therefore should not be emphasized unduly in consideration of proper auditing procedure in the great majority of cases; that the problem of auditing was to find means of affording adequate protection at a cost which would not constitute an undue burden on honestly administered companies.

"The principal purposes of this statement were to inform the public that certified public accountants are members of a well organized profession which recognizes its responsibilities in this case, and that the profession had not neglected its duty to set up standards of procedure and to publish them for the information of the financial community. At the same time it was made clear that the profession was ready and willing to reexamine those procedures and to change them if they could be strengthened."

A special committee on auditing procedure was appointed by the American Institute of Accountants and in due course it reported to the Council of the Institute that,

"Pursuant to its appointment the special committee on auditing procedure has reviewed certain phases of auditing procedures and related matters. It has taken cognizance of recent discussions regarding such procedures, both within and without the profession, and now submits its report and recommendations relating to the following:

Examination of inventories.
Examination of receivables.
Appointment of independent certified public accountants.
Form of independent certified public accountant's report."

This report was submitted under the title, "Extensions of Auditing Procedure" and was formally adopted by the Council of the American Institute of Accountants on May 9, 1939. Publication and widespread distribution of this report [6] led to extensive discussion of its proposals culminating in the drafting of a modified report which was approved on September 19, 1939 at the annual meeting of the Institute. Both of these reports prescribe as normal audit procedure attendance of the independent accountant at the inventory taking or the observing of or making of physical test checks of inventory quantities and the confirmation of receivables by direct communication with debtors. The principal modifications in the September report were changes in the language of the proposed short-form report (or certificate) and the elimination of the requirement for an explanation in the auditor's report, when he has not confirmed accounts receivable or made a physical verification of inventories in those cases where doing so was

[6] The Institute reported that at June 30, 1939, 23,319 copies of this report had been distributed. The Certified Public Accountant, July 1939, p. 6.

not reasonable or practicable. The modified report is reproduced at the end of this appendix.

An editorial in the Journal of Accountancy, June 1939, referring to the report of May 9, 1939 read in part as follows:

"The adoption of this report fulfills the promise made publicly by the executive committee of the Institute last December that auditing procedure would be carefully reviewed by the Institute in the light of current public discussion. The fact that recommendations on important aspects of auditing procedure have been suggested, considered, and adopted in so short a space of time has led observers to ask whether the proposals were 'hasty and ill considered'. This question could not arise in the mind of anyone who had had the privilege of observing the intensive study which the proposals received before adoption. It is estimated that 1500 man-days of time were spent by the committees of the Institute and the New York State Society of Certified Public Accountants which collaborated in drafting the report. More than 300 persons outside the committees, including representatives of business organizations and regulatory bodies, as well as state societies of certified public accountants, controllers and others were provided with successive drafts, and their numerous and frank criticisms were studied in the greatest detail * * *."

In respect to the modified report The Journal of Accountancy stated editorially [7] (in part):

"Another point of immediate interest and importance is the elimination by the council at its September meeting of the recommendation in the May 9th report that an explanation be included in the auditor's report where the additional procedures with regard to inventories and receivables have not been undertaken because it was not practicable and reasonable to do so, even though the auditor had satisfied himself by other means. Discussion and criticism of this feature of the original report convinced the council that it was unwise and that no useful purpose would be served by requiring a negative explanation in the auditor's report, but rather that it would tend to convey unwarranted implications of reservations or exceptions when none was intended. The revised report will place the responsibility squarely upon the accountant to determine the scope of the examination which he should make before giving his opinion on the statements under review. The council reiterated, however, that if the additional procedures recommended in the May 9th report are practicable and reasonable and the auditor has omitted them he should make a clear-cut exception in his opinion."

In the early part of July 1939, a letter was addressed by the Chief Accountant of the Securities and Exchange Commission to all state societies or organizations of public accountants inquiring whether any rules, resolutions, or other materials relating to auditing theory or practice had been promulgated or approved during 1939, whether any such matters were pending, and whether any accounting forums, conferences, or other similar meetings which included a discussion of auditing theory and practice had been sponsored or participated in during 1939. The purpose of this inquiry was to secure information as to activities these organizations had undertaken with respect to the foregoing matters.

[7] November 1939, p. 290.

The replies [8] to this inquiry indicate that generally the state societies expected the American Institute of Accountants to take the initiative in dealing with questions of auditing procedure and that they should await the final action of that body before taking decisive action themselves on such questions.

The New York State Society of Certified Public Accountants was an exception in that respect. A special committee of this Society cooperated with the Committee of the American Institute of Accountants and prepared a report on auditing practice and procedure which was adopted by the Society at a special meeting, May 22, 1939. This report is identical in all essential respects to that submitted in the same month by the special committee on auditing procedure of the American Institute of Accountants.[9] This report was reconsidered at a special meeting of the Society held on December 5, 1939 and modifications similar to those of the American Institute of Accountants' modified report were adopted.

A number of state societies of public accountants formally adopted by resolution the May report of the special committee of the American Institute of Accountants and others delayed action and adopted the revised report. Falling in one category or the other are the societies of the states of Connecticut, Florida, Idaho, Illinois, Iowa, Kansas, Massachusetts, Missouri, Nebraska, North Carolina, Oklahoma, Oregon, Pennsylvania, Rhode Island, South Carolina, Texas, Utah, Washington, and of the District of Columbia.[10]

Soon after the May 1939 report was published, each of three separate groups of state societies held joint conferences at which resolutions were adopted, recommending to the several state societies represented at the conference that they support the report of the American Institute of Accountants by giving it their approval. The three conferences referred to and the societies represented are as follows:

East Four States Conference, embracing the Societies of Connecticut, New York, New Jersey, and Pennsylvania.

Central States Conference, embracing the Societies of Illinois, Iowa, Kansas, Minnesota, Missouri, Nebraska, South Dakota, and Wisconsin.

Middle Atlantic States Conference,[11] embracing the District of Columbia Institute of Certified Public Accountants, Kanawha Valley (W. Va.) Accountants Association, Maryland Association of Certified Public Accountants, North Carolina Association of Certified Public Accountants, South Carolina Association

8 As of July 1, 1940 all but five state societies had responded.

9 Printed report available from New York State Society of Certified Public Accountants.

10 Missouri approved "in substance" and Rhode Island "in principle," the latter society taking exception to the form of the certificate which they felt could not be used in all cases. The District of Columbia Society approved the revised report as minimum requirements. The Illinois Society favors a positive statement in the certificate as to the nature and extent of the auditor's tests of quantities "in all cases where inventories are a material factor." Washington refers to the Seattle chapter which includes about seventy-five percent of that State's members.

11 Papers presented at this conference have been published in a volume which includes some of the papers presented at the Central States conference.

of Certified Public Accountants, Virginia Society of Public Accountants, West Virginia Society of Certified Public Accountants.

As to matters pending relative to auditing procedure and practice, many of the state societies indicated that the report of the American Institute of Accountants was under consideration. In a number of instances it was stated that the report was not completed in time to be considered and acted upon at meetings of Societies held early in the year, 1939, but that action on the report would probably be taken at meetings to be held in the latter part of the year. In a few instances the probability of approval of the report was indicated.[12]

Thirty-five state societies were reported to have devoted considerable time and attention during the year 1939 to consideration of auditing procedures and practices. Numerous open forum or round-table discussions were held at which these matters were discussed. In addition, many papers dealing with various aspects of auditing procedure and practice were presented and discussed at state conventions and interstate group conferences. Procedures relating to the verification of inventories and accounts receivable, including the report of the American Institute of Accountants on these matters, were the subject of extended discussion at these conventions and conferences. In addition, a substantial part of the program of the 1939 annual meeting of the American Institute of Accountants was devoted to these questions.[13]

In addition to the "Extensions of Auditing Procedure" two additional formal statements of the American Institute of Accountants Special Committee on Auditing Procedure should be mentioned. The first, "The Auditor's Opinion on the Basis of a Restricted Examination" was published in the Journal of Accountancy for December 1939. The statement constitutes an opinion of the Committee in respect to an audit in which a large proportion of the assets were receivables and inventories in branch offices of the client and the audit had been restricted to head office records and omitted confirmation of receivables and generally accepted auditing procedures with regard to physical quantities of inventories. The opinion given was that under the circumstances the exceptions with regard to the scope of the examination would have been so material as to negative the expression of an opinion and that, consequently, the auditors should refrain from expressing one. The second, "Inventories and Receivables of Department Stores, Instalment Houses, Chain Stores, and Other Retailers"[14] takes the position that the extensions of auditing proce-

[12] As of July 1, 1940 the following societies had not advised us of final action but had stated previously that such action was pending: Alabama, California, Colorado, Georgia, Indiana, Michigan, Minnesota, Montana, New Jersey, Ohio, Virginia, West Virginia, and Wyoming.

[13] Papers on Auditing Procedure and other Accounting Subjects, American Institute of Accountants, New York, 1939, 295 pages.

[14] 69 Journal of Accountancy 88 (1940).

dures in respect to receivables and inventories are reasonable and practicable in these lines of business in which some accountants had expressed some doubt as to their applicability. The prompt publication of these statements and of the "Extensions of Auditing Procedures" may be considered an emergency measure pending the incorporation of these ideas in a thorough revision of the bulletin, "Examination of Financial Statements by Independent Public Accountants", a project with which the Committee on Auditing Procedure plans to proceed.[15]

Those organizations, referred to hereinabove as being outside the public accounting field but interested in its objectives, reported that their activities during 1939 relating to auditing procedures and practices consisted principally in cooperating and consulting with organizations of public accountants directly concerned with these matters. Relations of this character were cited by the National Association of Credit Men, National Association of Cost Accountants, National Association of Manufacturers, New York Stock Exchange, and Robert Morris Associates. It is quite possible that organizations other than these had similar relationships with the public accounting profession. Other activities in the field of auditing procedures and practice which were mentioned specifically by certain organizations in this group follow.

The National Association of Manufacturers reported that its Committee on Industrial Practices made a study during 1939 of the auditing practices of business. The Committee made a report [16] which was subsequently approved by the Association's Board of Directors recommending, among other things, selection of the auditors by a committee of the board of directors with approval by the full board and if feasible by the stockholders, spot checking of inventories on interim dates as a test of perpetual inventories, clarification of the auditors' report and "that business should attempt to adopt its natural business year as its fiscal year."

The National Association of Cost Accountants carried out a survey during 1939 on "The Place of Internal Auditing in Industrial Companies." [17] The report is based on questionnaire replies from 285 N. A. C. A. members and is an illuminating document on the function of the controller and the purpose of internal auditing. It also covers important points in the internal control procedures intended to safeguard the company from losses in connection with cash, receivables, inventories, and capital expenditures.

The New York Stock Exchange on August 23, 1939, adopted a report of the Sub-Committee on Independent Audits and Audit Procedure of Committee on Stock List in which the McKesson &

---

[15] The Certified Public Accountant, June 1940, p. 4.

[16] See N. A. M. News Letter, June 23, 1939.

[17] For text of report see N. A. C. A. Bulletin, June 1, 1939, Section III.

Robbins case was considered and the scope of independent audits was discussed. The report endorses the extensions of audit procedure adopted by the American Institute of Accountants and states that the Sub-Committee "believes that the primary responsibility for establishing standards of the scope of the independent auditor's examination must rest with the accounting profession." A section of the report dealing with the manner and time of appointment of auditors; increasing the responsibility, authority, and facilities of the controller or internal auditor; and the adoption of the natural business year in lieu of the calendar year is reproduced at the end of this appendix.

The Sub-Committee favored a short certificate but recognized the need for further education of the public in a concise summary of efforts in this direction:

> "It is generally conceded that a program of general education of the public in the significance and necessary limitations of financial statements and audits is highly desirable. In recent accountants' speeches and reports, widely quoted in newspapers and periodicals, very explicit statements are made of the meaning, value and inevitable limitation of independent audits. Your Sub-Committee urges more widespread familiarity with the Institute's Bulletin, 'Examination of Financial Statements'; the 'Report on Independent Audits', made to the Board of Governors of the Exchange in 1933; 'Extensions of Auditing Procedure', the most recent report of the Institute; and the April, May, and June, 1939, issues of 'The Journal of Accountancy', which include enlightening summaries of parts of the recent S. E. C. hearings following the McKesson & Robbins case, at which the views of twelve leading members of the accounting profession were given on numerous questions of auditing procedure. These summaries are not long, and the views expressed are worded so that even those with little technical knowledge may get a broad view of present day auditing problems and experience."

This brief survey of the activity of organizations interested in the work of professional accountants indicates that they have confidence in the accountants' ability to cope with the problems presented to the profession as a result of the McKesson & Robbins case. The American Institute of Accountants' "Extensions of Auditing Procedure" and an extract from the Report of the New York Stock Exchange's Sub-Committee on Independent Audits and Audit Procedure of Committee on Stock List are reproduced in the following pages.

EXTENSIONS
OF
AUDITING PROCEDURE

Report of May 9, 1939, as Modified and Approved

at the Annual Meeting, September 19, 1939

October 18, 1939

American Institute of Accountants

EXTENSIONS OF AUDITING PROCEDURE

To the Members of the American Institute of Accountants:

GENTLEMEN: Under date of May 9, 1939, the council of the American Institute of Accountants adopted a report submitted by the special committee on auditing procedure entitled "Extensions of Auditing Procedure," and at the same time it was anticipated that the committee would make a supplemental report at the September meeting. The report of May 9th emphasized that it was the ultimate responsibility of the independent certified public accountant to adopt such procedures as in his professional judgment he deemed appropriate, but recommended that certain additional procedures regarding inventories and accounts receivable should be considered as generally accepted practice. It further recommended that, where these additional procedures regarding inventories and accounts receivable had not been undertaken, that fact should be disclosed in the auditors' report or opinion.

The action of the council received widespread support of state organizations of certified public accountants, and the recommendations evoked the hearty approval of investors, credit grantors, the press, and the public.

During the four months which elapsed between the issuance of the report and the September meeting, the committee had considerable discussion and correspondence with informed people, both within and without the profession, and held a number of meetings. While the recommended additional procedures had the united support of independent accountants, it was evident that there was some misconception as to the meaning intended to be conveyed by the term "physical tests" as applied to inventory quantities, that considerable misunderstanding had arisen as to the responsibility which the auditor might be assuming, and that the recommended reference in the auditors' report of opinion to the omission of such procedures has been misconstrued.

In its supplemental report presented to council under date of September 18th, the committee explained the term "physical tests" and indicated that in his capacity as auditor the independent certified public accountant could properly attend at the inventory-taking and observe the methods of taking the inventory, making in conjunction therewith such suitable inquiries or requiring such test checks under his observation as he deemed advisable, and that such a program was within the meaning of the term "physical tests."

The auditor's duty was increased in that the additional procedures were adopted as generally accepted practice wherever they are practicable and reasonable, but beyond this the auditor's responsibility remained unchanged. The responsibility of the management for taking proper inventories was again emphasized.

The committee reiterated its recommendation of May 9th that, where exceptions were required, such exceptions should be expressed clearly and unequivocally. However, where exception was not called for under the terms of the report, it was felt that no good purpose would be served by requiring negative explanations, because discussion and experience in the meantime had demonstrated that negative references in the auditors' report gave rise to misconception in that they tended to convey implications of reservations or exceptions where none existed or was intended. In other words, they had the effect of casting an unwarranted cloud on the statements.

The council at its meeting on September 18, 1939, adopted the supplemental report of the committee which, after discussion at the meeting of the Institute on September 19th, was approved. The executive committee was authorized and instructed by council to coordinate the two reports into one document and to distribute it to the membership. This document is submitted herewith; it supersedes the report of May 9, 1939.

Respectfully submitted.

EXECUTIVE COMMITTEE,
By JOHN L. CAREY, *Secretary*.

OCTOBER 18, 1939.

EXTENSIONS OF AUDITING PROCEDURE

Report of May 9, 1939, as Modified and Approved at the Annual Meeting, September 19, 1939

Following the adoption by council on May 9, 1939, of the report of the special committee on auditing procedure entitled "Extensions of Auditing Procedure" and the approval at the annual meeting of the supplementing and interpreting report of the same committee dated September 18, 1939, the executive committee was instructed by council to coördinate the two reports into one document and to distribute it. There is presented herewith the modified report which deals with the following matters:

Examination of inventories
Examination of receivables
Appointment of independent certified public accountants
Form of independent certified public accountants' report

Auditing procedures and related matters dealt with herein relate to those cases in which financial statements are accompanied by a report and opinion of an independent certified public accountant. Accordingly, that which follows should be read in the light of this limitation.

At the outset it is pertinent to state that, since the late disclosure of conditions existing in exceptional cases, certified public accountants have been considering possible implications which may arise therefrom in relation to their practice. The committee desires to state its opinion that auditing procedure has kept, and continues to keep, pace with the growth and development of industry and that the well established custom of making test checks of accounting records and related data and, beyond that, reliance upon the system of internal check and control after investigation of its adequacy and effectiveness has with very few exceptions proved sufficient for its purpose. Because of public interest and discussion in the press, there is a question now before the profession as to whether its procedures shall be extended. In order to consider the question intelligently there must first be some general understanding of certain fundamentals.

In the performance of his duties as auditor, the independent certified public accountant holds himself out as one who is proficient in accounting practice and auditing procedure. The function of the independent certified public accountant is to examine a concern's accounting records and supporting data, in certain matters to obtain outside confirmations, and to require and consider supplementary explanations and information from the management and employees, to the extent necessary to enable him to form an opinion as to whether or not the financial statements as submitted present fairly the position and the results of periodic operations. Generally speaking, his function is limited to reporting upon situations arising out of business transactions that have taken place in the past. In no sense is he an insurer or guarantor. In offering his opinion, the independent certified public accountant assumes heavy responsibilities. He must be skilled in his professional work and must have made a reasonable examination of the accounts in order to warrant his expression of an opinion. He must state his opinion clearly and unequivocally.

Management itself has the direct responsibility for the maintenance of an adequate and effective system of accounts, for the proper recording of transactions in the books of account, and for the safeguarding of the assets of a concern. It is also charged with the primary responsibility to stockholders and to creditors for the substantial accuracy and adequacy of statements of position and operations.

In order to qualify himself to carry out his function, the independent certified public accountant has completed a rigorous course of professional study and training as a background to the essential practical experience he must obtain, for it is only by study, training, and practical experience that the independent auditor acquires skill in accounting and related matters. In the ordinary course of his day-to-day practice, he encounters a wide range of judgment on the part of management, varying from true objective judgment to the occasional extreme of deliberate misstatement. He is retained to examine and report upon the affairs of a concern because, through his training and experience, he has become not only skilled in accounting and auditing but has acquired the ability and habit of considering dispassionately and independently the facts recorded in books of account or otherwise disclosed by his examination and because, as a result, his opinion provides reasonable assurance that a fair and adequate presentation of pertinent information has been made in the financial statements.

The independent auditor must also exercise his best judgment in determining the scope of his examination and in deciding whether the interests of stockholders and creditors justify the time and expense involved in the extension of any particular line of inquiry. Experience shows that, with few exceptions, the personnel of business organizations is honest. The ordinary examination incident to the issuance of financial statements accompanied by a report and opinion of an independent certified public accountant is not designed to discover all defalcations, because that is not its primary objective, although discovery of defalcation frequently results. In a well organized concern the principal reliance for the detection of such irregularities is placed upon the maintenance of an adequate system of accounting records with appropriate internal check and control. It is the duty of the independent auditor to review the system of internal check and accounting control so as to determine the extent to which he considers that he is entitled to rely upon it. To exhaust the possibility of exposure of all cases of dishonesty or fraud, the independent auditor would have to examine in detail all transactions. This would entail a prohibitive cost to the great majority of business enterprises—a cost which would pass all bounds of reasonable expectation of benefit or safeguard therefrom, and place an undue burden on industry.

In carrying out his work the independent certified public accountant must always be on his guard against collusive fraud and be alert in detecting any sign of such collusion. However, on the basis of his examination by tests and checks, he relies upon the integrity of the client's organization unless circumstances are such as to arouse suspicion, in which case he must extend his procedures to determine whether or not such suspicions are justified.

The independent certified public accountant should not express the opinion that financial statements present fairly the position of the company and the results of its operations, in conformity with generally accepted accounting principles, when his exceptions are such as to negative the opinion, or when the examination has been less in scope than he considers necessary. In such circumstances, the independent certified public accountant should limit his report to a statement of his findings and, if appropriate, his reasons for omitting an expression of opinion.

Turning now to consideration of the specific matters referred to at the beginning of this report, it may be noted in passing that in some cases independent certified public accountants have attended at the inventory taking or observed physical test checks of inventories and have confirmed receivables by direct communication with debtors. Such steps, however, have usually been undertaken as additional procedures under arrangement with the client, or where the accountant thought them essential or desirable in a particular case.

It is believed that recognition should be given to the widespread demand for an extension of auditing procedures with regard to inventories and receivables. However, it should be noted that additional expense to business will be involved in the added procedures.

Inventories

Added steps may well be taken to give greater assurance with regard to inventories. The extent of such additional procedures will necessarily vary with the circumstances, because the independent auditor is justified in giving consideration to the effectiveness of the internal check and control as applied not only to book records, but also to the procedure of taking physical inventories. But, however extensive these may be, the training and experience of an independent certified public accountant do not qualify him as a general appraiser, valuer, or expert in materials. The public should understand that, while he can in his capacity as an auditor undertake additional procedures as to inventories, such procedures do not invest his opinion with a degree of authority which he does not claim for it or impose upon him a measure of responsibility which the nature of his work does not justify. Such procedures are only for the purpose of satisfying himself as to the credibility of the representations of the management regarding quantity and condition.

Taken in consideration with the foregoing discussion of auditing procedures, the following recommendations are made concerning inventories:

(A) That hereafter, where the independent certified public accountant intends to report over his signature on the financial statements of a concern in which inventories are a material factor, it should be generally accepted auditing procedure that, in addition to making auditing tests and checks of the inventory accounts and records, he shall, wherever practicable and reasonable, be present, either in person or by his representatives, at the inventory taking and by suitable observation and inquiry satisfy himself as to the effectiveness of the methods of inventory taking and as to the measure of reliance which may be placed upon the client's representations as to inventories and upon the records thereof. In this connection the independent certified public accountant may require physical tests of inventories to be made under his observation.

In cases where the inventory is determined solely by means of a physical inventory at the end of the accounting period (or at a date prior or subsequent thereto but within a reasonable time thereof, with adequate records supporting the interim changes), it will ordinarily be necessary for the foregoing procedures to be followed at that time.

In cases where the concern maintains well kept and controlled perpetual inventory records supported by (1) a complete physical inventory at a date not coincident with the balance-sheet date, or (2) physical inventories of individual items taken from time to time so that the quantity of each item on hand is compared with the inventory record for that item at least once in each year, it will be satisfactory to undertake the procedure outlined at any interim date or dates selected by the auditor, his purpose being to satisfy himself as to the credibility of the perpetual inventory records and whether they may be relied upon to support the inventory totals as shown on the balance-sheet.[18]

[18] See page 436 *supra* for paragraphs of the May 9, 1939 version omitted in this revision.

(B) That hereafter, in the case of inventories which in the ordinary course of business are in the hands of public warehouses or other outside custodians, direct confirmation in writing from such custodians is acceptable procedure; except that, where the amount involved represents a significant proportion of the current assets or of the total assets of a concern, the independent certified public accountant shall make supplementary inquiries.

It should be clearly understood that in undertaking these auditing procedures regarding inventories, the independent certified public accountant does so for the purpose of satisfying himself as to the credibility of the representations of the management regarding quantity and condition and does not hold himself out as a general appraiser, valuer, or expert in materials.

The general adoption of such added procedures regarding inventories may necessitate procedural changes on the part of clients. So many corporations close their books upon a calendar-year basis that it is doubtful whether the profession as at present organized can undertake the additional work adequately and satisfactorily on the last day of each year. Many corporations do not have adequate perpetual inventory records and greater use of them should be encouraged.

The extension of procedures regarding inventories would be greatly facilitated if each concern adopted its natural business year instead of the calendar year as its fiscal year, and introduced continuous well kept perpetual inventory records.

The proposed changes will take time to bring about, and in the meantime the profession may well be faced with the necessity of submitting qualified reports in those cases in which it has been impracticable to carry out the added procedures.

Receivables

In regard to the question of confirming receivables by direct communication with the debtor, the following recommendation is made:

That hereafter, wherever practicable and reasonable, and where the aggregate amount of notes and accounts receivable represents a significant proportion of the current assets or of the total assets of a concern, confirmation of notes and accounts receivable by direct communication with the debtors shall be regarded as generally accepted auditing procedure in the examination of the accounts of a concern whose financial statements are accompanied by an independent certified public accountant's report; and that the method, extent, and time of confirming receivables in each engagement, and whether of all receivables or a part thereof, be determined by the independent certified public accountant as in other phases of procedure requiring the exercise of his judgment.[18]

[18] See page 436 *supra* for paragraphs of the May 9, 1939 version omitted in this revision.

Appointment of Independent Certified Public Accountants

Apart from the specific phases of auditing procedure which have been the subject of consideration, the method of appointment of the independent auditor and his status in relation to the client are believed to be subjects of great importance to stockholders and creditors.

To emphasize the auditor's independence of the management, some corporations affected by public interest have adopted the practice of having the independent auditor engaged or nominated by the board of directors or elected annually by the stockholders. Other corporations have provided that the stockholders be given an opportunity to ratify the selection made by the directors.

It is suggested that the auditor should be appointed early in each fiscal year so that he may carry out part of his work during the year.

Form of Independent Certified Public Accountant's Report or Opinion

The services which independent auditors render usually culminate in a report, which may take varying forms. In some cases a detailed report is rendered, accompanied by statements and supporting schedules; in other cases the report is limited to a concise statement of the scope of the examination and the related opinion of the independent auditor concerning the accompanying financial statements of the client. For present purposes the discussion is confined to the short form of auditor's report, which is sometimes described as a certificate. The terms "report," "opinion," "report and opinion," and "certificate" have been used interchangeably. As uniformity is desirable, either of the words "report" or "opinion" is recommended for general use. The word "report" has been adopted in the following comments.

In January, 1934, the Institute issued a pamphlet entitled *Audits of Corporate Accounts,* dealing with a standard form of auditor's report. The short form of report then recommended, and since widely adopted by the profession, met a long-felt need.

Developments during the five years in which the standard form of report has been used indicate the need of revision in the interest of clarity. The revised short form of report consists of two paragraphs. The first contains a brief statement of the scope of the examination, and the second deals with the auditor's opinion on the financial statements of the client as a result of his examination.

The major changes recommended pertain to the description of the scope of the examination, specifically to include reference to the system of internal control. The phrase "obtained information and explanations from officers and employees of the company" has been omitted because it is inherent in all auditing procedure to obtain information and explanations from officers and employees concerning the accounts, either as supplementing information obtained from other sources or as constituting the only available information on the subject. In the latter case, the auditor must decide, in view of all the circumstances, whether he should rely upon such information without disclosure of the source. The phrase in question has led to serious misconception as to the degree of reliance on such information and explanations. The sense of the statement "but we did not make a detailed audit of the transactions" has been retained in a revised form. It will be recalled that this clause was included in the standard form of 1934 in order to make clear that the auditor's usual procedure consisted of testing and sampling rather than a detailed audit. It is believed that the business and financial public now fully understand that, in a well organized concern, the detection of irregularities is primarily a matter of internal procedure, and that testing and sampling to determine whether such procedure is adequate in scope and effective in operation is the usual practice of the independent auditor. Nevertheless, it is considered advisable for the purpose of emphasis to include the phrase, "without making a detailed audit of the transactions." There has been excluded the phrase "based upon such examination," as it is obvious that the independent certified public accountant can express an opinion only after he has completed the work set forth in the first paragraph of the report.

The independent certified public accountant should recognize that in some cases the revised short form recommended may not be altogether appropriate. For instance, there may be cases where the auditor may prefer to alter the first sentence of the standard short form, substituting some words to the effect that the accounting records (instead of the financial statements) have been examined. Obviously, also, it would be erroneous to mention internal control if none existed. Accordingly, while the proposed form is submitted as a standard, it is not prescribed or recommended for invariable use, but should be adapted to the needs of the particular case. For example, the report may be used in connection with an examination covering a period of years, in which case a modification of language would be necessary. Also, in new engagements appropriate investigations relating to prior years will have to be made to justify the use of the short-form report. However, in the interest of reasonable uniformity it is recommended that the substance of phrases in the standard form be used unless inappropriate.

In considering the independent certified public accountant's opinion, the reader should bear in mind one of the most important underlying concepts of financial statements, viz., that normally many of the assets of a concern are not realizable in cash, but are commonly stated at their historical cost or going-concern basis at amounts which are usually greater than the realizable value in forced liquidation. Again, the true profit or loss of a concern can be determined with accuracy only over its entire existence. Therefore, in any attempt to allocate to specific periods profit or loss applicable thereto, it must be recognized among other considerations that, as many transactions are not fully completed within such periods, the result as shown must contain many estimates and approximations in the endeavor to present fairly the operating results of a period in conformity with generally accepted accounting principles.

Assuming that normal procedures have been carried out, it is not considered necessary to describe the details of the examination in this form of report. Any such details as are given should be included in separate paragraphs of the report. For example, reference may be made to procedures which the accountant has adopted regarding the examination of inventories and receivables; also, it may be pertinent to mention the fact that certain portions of the auditor's work have been carried out at different times during the course of the year. This may be indicated by inserting the words "at times" in the first paragraph of the short form of report immediately after the words "by methods."

It should be borne in mind that the financial statements, with all supplemental descriptive and explanatory data, including footnotes, are regarded as representations of the client. It is upon all these representations that the independent certified public accountant renders his opinion. If he considers explanations essential or desirable, and they have not been made in the financial statements, it will be necessary for him to make such explanations in a separate paragraph of his report.

In explanation of the general principles governing the auditor's opinion, with particular regard to explanations and exceptions, it is pertinent to state that the auditor satisfies himself as to the fairness of the statements "by methods and to the extent he deems appropriate," in general conformity with the auditing procedures recommended in the Institute's bulletin *Examination of Financial Statements*. Ordinarily, if he has so satisfied himself, he is in a position to express an unqualified opinion. However, if he considers it in the interest of clear disclosure of material fact to include explanations of procedures followed, he is free to do so. If, on the other hand, such disclosures are made by reason of any reservation or desire to qualify the opinion, they become exceptions and should be expressly stated as such in the opinion paragraph of the auditor's report. As previously stated, if such exceptions are sufficiently material to negative the expression of an opinion, the auditor should refrain from giving any opinion at all, although he may render an informative report in which he states that the limitations or exceptions relating to the examination are such as to make it impossible for him to express an opinion as to the fairness of the financial statements as a whole.

It is desirable as a general rule that exceptions by the independent certified public accountant be included in a paragraph separate from all others in the report and be referred to specifically in the final paragraph in which the opinion is stated. Any exception should be expressed clearly and unequivocally as to whether it affects the scope of the work, any particular item of the financial statements, the soundness of the company's procedures (as regards either the books or the financial statements) or the consistency of accounting practices where lack of consistency calls for exception.

It is the responsibility of the accountant—and one which he cannot escape—to determine the scope of the examination which he should make before giving his opinion on the statements under review. If in his judgment it is not practicable and reasonable in the circumstances of a given engagement to undertake the auditing procedures regarding inventories and/or receivables set forth in this report as generally accepted procedure and he has satisfied himself by other methods regarding such inventories and/or receivables no useful purpose will be served by requiring an explanation in his report. If physical tests of inventories and/or confirmation of receivables are practicable and reasonable and the auditor has omitted such generally accepted auditing procedure, he should make a clear-cut exception in his report.

It is worthy of repetition that the extent of sampling and testing should be based upon the independent auditor's judgment as to the effectiveness of internal control, arrived at as the result of investigations, tests, and inquiries. Depending upon his conclusions in this respect, the independent certified public accountant should extend or may restrict the degree of detailed examination. Consequently in some cases it may be necessary to modify or omit reference to reliance upon the system of internal control. Clearly also where a detailed examination is made, the phrase "without making a detailed audit of the transactions" would be inappropriate.

It is contemplated that, before signing a report of the short-form type suggested, the independent certified public accountant will be satisfied that his examination is in conformity with the procedures and practices outlined in *Examination of Financial Statements*, a bulletin published by the American Institute of Accountants in January, 1936, or in any subsequent revision thereof.

The report should be addressed to the board of directors or the stockholders if the appointment is made by them.

The description of the financial statements in both paragraphs should, of course, conform to the titles of the accompanying statements.

In consideration of the foregoing remarks the following short form of report is recommended:

Short Form of Independent Certified Public Accountant's Report or Opinion

To the Board of Directors (or Stockholders) of the XYZ Company:

We have examined the balance-sheet of the XYZ Company as of April 30, 1939, and the statements of income and surplus for the fiscal year then ended, have reviewed the system of internal control and the accounting procedures of the company and, without making a detailed audit of the transactions, have examined or tested accounting records of the company and other supporting evidence, by methods and to the extent we deemed appropriate.

In our opinion, the accompanying balance-sheet and related statements of income and surplus present fairly the position of the XYZ Company at April 30, 1939, and the results of its operations for the fiscal year, in conformity with generally accepted accounting principles applied on a basis consistent with that of the preceding year.

It is worthy of repetition and emphasis that while the proposed form is submitted as a standard, it is not prescribed or recommended for invariable use but should be adapted to the needs of the particular case.

RECOMMENDATIONS AS TO CORPORATE PROCEDURES

An Extract from New York Stock Exchange—Report of Sub-Committee on Independent Audits and Audit Procedure of Committee on Stock List

"Your Sub-Committee regards the responsibilities of corporations in auditing matters as two-fold: to institute such corporate procedures as will make its system of bookkeeping, and of internal control and audit, as efficient as possible; and to facilitate in every reasonable way the work of the independent auditor. Of a large number of proposals considered in these connections, your Sub-Committee has selected four as sufficiently important and practicable to warrant endorsement by the New York Stock Exchange. These recommendations are made subject to consideration of applicability in the particular case, and in the knowledge that their usefulness in connection with audits might have to be weighed against other disadvantages.

1. Strengthening the Position of the Independent Public Accountant.

This might best be accomplished through the general assumption by Boards of Directors of direct responsibility for either the appointment of the auditors or for their selection and recommendation to the stockholders for approval. Where practicable, the selection of the auditors by a Special Committee of the Board composed of Directors who are not officers of the Company appears desirable.

The results of the auditor's examination should always be available to the Board of Directors, his report should be addressed to the stockholders, and he should be afforded the opportunity to appear at any stockholders meeting.

2. Increasing the Responsibility, Authority, and Facilities of the Controller or Internal Auditor.

More emphasis should be placed on the responsibility of the Controller and the assurance to him of adequate authority and facilities. The scope of his responsibilities should be fixed by the Board of Directors, and he should report periodically to them, in addition to making his customary reports to the operating management.

The Controller or chief financial officer should sign the published financial statements of his company, even in those cases where the statements are accompanied by the report of the independent public accountant.

Independent and efficient accounting and internal auditing departments are a vital factor in assuring the accuracy of the books and published reports. The importance of the Controller or internal auditor in these connections is paramount and the Board of Directors should take an active interest in his selection.

3. Adoption of Natural Business Year in Lieu of Calendar Year.

The Natural Business Year of the industry in which a company is engaged is recommended, unless impracticable for special reasons, as the fiscal year of the company instead of the Calendar Year. The more general adoption of the natural business year by companies in each industry would to a large extent smooth out the huge peaks of audit work which now occur in the early part of each calendar year. By adopting a Natural Business Year which conforms to the true business cycle of the particular industry, corporations may simplify their problems of year end adjustment and reduce the cost of stock-taking, besides permitting a more efficient and more economical audit. The income account of a company based on a completed cycle of a normal year's operations would give the investor a fairer picture of the operations of his company. Reports of companies in the same field of business would be directly comparable, as almost all industries have their own clearly defined natural business years.

4. Appointment of the Independent Public Accountants Early in the Fiscal Year.

The appointment of the independent auditor early in the fiscal year appears eminently desirable, so that part of his work may be done during the year and he may be free to make an examination of any phase of the company's operations at any time."

APPENDIX B

Comparison of Those Sections of the English Companies Act, 1929 Dealing with Appointment of Auditors and Horace B. Samuel's Suggested Amendments to Those Sections of that Act.

COMPANIES ACT, 1929

"132.—(1) Every company shall at each annual general meeting appoint an auditor or auditors to hold office until the next annual general meeting.

(2) If an appointment of auditors is not made at an annual general meeting, the Board of Trade may, on the application of any member of the company, appoint an auditor of the company for the current year.

(3) A person, other than a retiring auditor, shall not be capable of being appointed auditor at an annual general meeting unless notice of an intention to nominate that person to the office of auditor has been given by a member to the company not less than fourteen days before the annual general meeting, and the company shall send a copy of any such notice to the retiring auditor, and shall give notice thereof to the members, either by advertisement or in any other mode allowed by the articles, not less than seven days before the annual general meeting:

Provided that if, after notice of the intention to nominate an auditor has been so given, an annual general meeting is called for a date fourteen days or less after the notice has been given, the notice, though not given within the time required by this subsection, shall be deemed to have been properly given for the purposes thereof, and the notice to be sent or given by the company may, instead of being sent or given within the time required by this subsection, be sent or given at the same time as the notice of the annual general meeting.

SAMUEL'S PROPOSED AMENDMENTS[19]

"47. Subsection (1) of section 132 of the Principal Act shall be repealed and the following subsection substituted therefor—

(1) (a) Every company shall at its first general meeting appoint an auditor or auditors who shall hold office until removed by an extraordinary resolution of the company, or by the Court, or until he or they resign or die or become otherwise incapable of acting as auditors.

(b) In the event of an auditor resigning, he shall attend personally the next general meeting of the company and explain his reasons for resignation, or, if prevented by illness or other reasonable cause, send a letter to the company explaining his reasons, which letter shall be read to the meeting by the secretary of the company."

[19] Samuel, Horace B., Shareholders' Money, Sir Isaac Pitman & Sons, Ltd., London, 1933, pp. 360, 361-362.

205078—40——31

(4) Subject as hereinafter provided, the first auditors of the company may be appointed by the directors at any time before the first annual general meeting, and auditors so appointed shall hold office until that meeting:

Provided that—

(a) the company may at a general meeting of which notice has been served on the auditors in the same manner as on members of the company remove any such auditors and appoint in their place any other persons being persons who have been nominated for appointment by any member of the company and of whose nomination notice has been given to the members of the company not less than seven days before the date of the meeting; and

(b) if the directors fail to exercise their powers under this subsection, the company in general meeting may appoint the first auditors, and thereupon the said powers of the directors shall cease.

(5) The directors may fill any casual vacancy in the office of auditor, but while any such vacancy continues the surviving or continuing auditor or auditors, if any, may act.

(6) The remuneration of the auditors of a company shall be fixed by the company in general meeting, except that the remuneration of an auditor appointed before the first annual general meeting, or of an auditor appointed to fill a casual vacancy, may be fixed by the directors, and that the remuneration of an auditor appointed by the Board of Trade may be fixed by the Board."

"134.—(1) The auditors shall make a report to the members on the accounts examined by them, and on every balance sheet laid before the company in general meeting during their tenure of office, and the report shall state—

(a) whether or not they have obtained all the information and explanations they have required; and

(b) whether, in their opinion, the balance sheet referred to in the report is properly drawn up so as to exhibit a true and correct view of the state of the company's affairs according to the

"49. Section 134 of the Principal Act shall be repealed and the following section substituted therefor—

(1) The auditors shall make a report to the members on the accounts examined by them, and on every balance sheet and profit and loss account including documents and statements appended thereto laid before the company in general meeting during their tenure of office, and the report shall state

(a) whether or not they have obtained all the information and explanations they have required,

best of their information and the explanations given to them, and as shown by the books of the company.

(2) Every auditor of a company shall have a right of access at all times to the books and accounts and vouchers of the company, and shall be entitled to require from the directors and officers of the company such information and explanation as may be necessary for the performance of the duties of the auditors:

Provided that, in the case of a banking company which was registered after the fifteenth day of August, eighteen hundred and seventy-nine, and which has branch banks beyond the limits of Europe, it shall be sufficient if the auditor is allowed access to such copies and extracts from such books and accounts of any such branch as have been transmitted to the head office of the company in Great Britain.

(b) whether in their opinion the said balance sheet, and the said profit and loss account and the said documents and statements are properly drawn up so as to exhibit a full and fair and true view of the state of the company's affairs in relation to existing conditions.

(2) Every auditor of a company shall have a right of access at all times to the books and accounts and documents and property of the company, and shall exercise all due diligence and vigilance in examining them and in requiring from the directors and officers of the company such facilities, information and explanations as is within the power of such directors and officers to give, and as may be reasonably necessary in order that the auditor shall be satisfied that the balance sheet and profit and loss account and the documents and statements appended thereto exhibit a full and fair and true view of the state of the company's affairs having regard to existing conditions.

(3) In the event of any director or other officer of a company not giving an auditor the facilities, information and explanations required by this section, such director or officer shall be deemed to have committed an offence under the Principal Act and shall also, on application in a summary way by the auditor by summons to the Judge of the Chancery Division of the High Court of Justice to whom companies business is assigned, be compellable to give such facilities, explanations, or information.

(4) In the event of an auditor apprehending that the books and documents shown to him and the information and explanations given to him are inadequate to enable him to form an opinion as to the financial situation of the company in regard to existing conditions, such auditor shall, if of opinion that it is reasonably practicable so to do, endeavour to obtain such information and explanations elsewhere, and the reasonable expenses involved in so doing shall be payable by the company.

(3) The auditors of a company shall be entitled to attend any general meeting of the company at which any accounts which have been examined or reported on by them are to be laid before the company and to make any statement or explanation they desire with respect to the accounts."

(5) It shall be the duty of the auditors to draw attention in their report to any item or fact either appearing in the accounts, or directly or indirectly reflected therein, which is in their opinion of an artificial or window-dressing character.

(6) (a) It shall be the duty of the auditors of a company to attend any general meeting of the company at which any accounts which have been examined or reported on by them are to be laid before the company.

(b) The auditors at such meeting shall—

(i) be entitled to make any statement or explanation they desire with regard to the said accounts, including the documents and statements annexed thereto;

(ii) be under a duty to make such statements or explanations as they may think reasonable or desirable, in the event of their being of opinion that any statement made by any director or officer of the company may be calculated to mislead the shareholders with regard to the affairs of the company."

APPENDIX C

UNITED STATES OF AMERICA
BEFORE THE SECURITIES AND EXCHANGE COMMISSION

At a regular session of the Securities and Exchange Commission, held at its office in the City of Washington, D. C., on the 29th day of December, A. D., 1938.

In the Matter of McKESSON & ROBBINS, INC.

ORDER FOR PUBLIC HEARING DESIGNATING OFFICER FOR TAKING TESTIMONY

It appearing to the Commission that McKesson & Robbins, Inc., an issuer of securities registered pursuant to Section 12 of the Securities Exchange Act of 1934, as amended, on the New York Stock Exchange, a national securities exchange, did on or about the 21st day of May, 1935, file with this Commission pursuant to the provisions of said section a registration statement covering the said securities and did on or about the 29th day of June, 1936, the 19th day of May, 1937, and the 29th day of April, 1938, file with this Commission pursuant to Section 13 of the said Act, annual reports covering the said securities, all of which registration statement and reports contain financial statements and schedules prepared and certified by Price, Waterhouse & Co.; and

It further appearing to the Commission that the information set forth in said registration statement, annual reports and in the financial statements included therein, was materially false and misleading in that, among other things, there was included in the item "inventories" merchandise purportedly carried for the account of McKesson & Robbins by certain Canadian firms, which firms except as mailing addresses and which merchandise were non-existent and in that there were included in the item "customers' accounts receivable" large sums purportedly owing by reputable foreign firms, which firms did not in fact have any transactions with or owe any moneys to McKesson & Robbins, and in that there was included in the item "cash on hand and demand deposits in banks" a sum owing by Manning & Co., which purported to be a private banking firm but which firm was non-existent except as a mailing address, and in that there was included in the item "sales" a large sum representing the proceeds of purported sales to said foreign firms out of the inventories carried by the said Canadian firms above referred to, made through the purported sales agency of W. W. Smith & Co., all of which were never effected and were mere book entries, and in that there was included, in the item "expense" as an actual current charge of operations, a large sum paid to the said W. W. Smith & Co. purportedly as guarantee and service charges on the said sales, which were never in fact effected, and in that there were included in the item "profits" large sums purportedly arising out of said sales which were never in fact realized; and

It further appearing to the Commission necessary and proper and in the public interest to determine (1) the character, detail and scope of the audit procedure followed by Price, Waterhouse & Co. in the preparation of the financial statements included in the said registration statement and reports; (2) the extent to which prevailing and generally accepted standards and requirements of audit procedure were adhered to and applied by Price, Waterhouse & Co. in the preparation of the said financial statements; and (3) the adequacy of the safeguards inhering in the said generally accepted practices and principles of audit procedure to assure reliability and accuracy of financial statements.

It is ordered, pursuant to Section 21(a) of the Securities Exchange Act of 1934, as amended, that a public hearing be held to determine the facts, conditions, practices and matters above referred to to aid (1) in the enforcement of the provisions of the Securities Exchange Act of 1934, as amended; (2) in the prescribing of rules and regulations pursuant to Sections 12(a) and (b) and 13(a) and (b) and other pertinent provisions of such Act, as amended; and (3) in securing information to serve as a basis for recommending further legislation concerning any matters to which such Act, as amended, relates as may appear to the Commission to be necessary or appropriate; and

It is further ordered, pursuant to Section 21(b) of the Securities Exchange Act of 1934, as amended, for the purposes of such public hearing that Adrian C. Humphreys, an officer of the Commission, is hereby designated to administer oaths and affirmations, subpoena witnesses, compel their attendance, take evidence, require the production of any books, papers, correspondence, memoranda, or other records deemed relevant or material to the inquiry, and to perform all other duties in connection therewith authorized by law; and

It is further ordered that a public hearing for the taking of testimony begin on the 5th day of January, 1939, at 10:30 A. M., or as soon thereafter as counsel can be heard, at the office of the Securities and Exchange Commission, Room 2006, 120 Broadway, New York, N. Y., and continue thereafter at such times and places as said officer may determine.

By the Commission.

Francis P. Brassor, *Secretary.*

[seal]

APPENDIX D

Index to Testimony of Witnesses

[18] R. refers to mimeographed transcript of testimony. P. refers to printed transcript of testimony. To obtain copies see footnote 1, page 2 *supra*.

Transcript Page No.

Arthur Seal .... R. 4558–4587

(Senior Accountant for S. D. Leidesdorf & Co. on McKesson & Robbins fraud audit for Trustee in Reorganization.)

Victor H. Stempf .... R. 2989–3119; P. 119–170

(Member of accounting firm of Touche, Niven & Co.)

Julian F. Thompson .... R. 2060–2142

(Formerly Treasurer and Director of McKesson & Robbins.)

Ralph E. Thorn .... R. 87–103, 857–978, 981–1016, 1025–1038, 1041–1103, 1118–1184, 1187–1255, 1898–1902, 4455–4457, 4542–4544

(Manager for Price, Waterhouse & Co., in charge of McKesson & Robbins audit.)

Arthur R. Tucker .... R. 4480–4481; P. 623–630

(Managing Director of Controllers Institute of America.)

Margaret Walsh .... R. 4380–4437

(Bookkeeper for McKesson & Robbins, Limited.)

Sidney J. Weinberg .... R. 2377–2434

(Member of investment banking firm of Goldman, Sachs & Co., New York; Director of McKesson & Robbins.)

Charles Oliver Wellington .... R. 2851–2986; P. 63–118

(Member of accounting firm of Scovell, Wellington & Co.)

John White .... R. 1471–1565

(Clerk in Shipping and Receiving Department of McKesson & Robbins at Bridgeport.)

George F. Wyman .... R. 304–386

(Senior Accountant for Price, Waterhouse & Co. on McKesson & Robbins audit at Bridgeport.)

APPENDIX E

Commission Exhibits

No.	Description	Received in Evidence Transcript Page No.[19]	Referred to in Report at Page No.[20]	Number of Pages in the Exhibit
1	Schedule of Bills rendered by P. W. & Co. to McKesson & Robbins, Incorporated, from Dec. 6, 1926, through Dec. 5, 1938.	R. 68	117, 352, 354	4
2	Girard & Co., Inc. Balance Sheet Dec. 31, 1924, certified by P. W. & Co.	R. 69	24, 26, 40, 347	1
3	McKesson & Robbins, Incorporated and Subsidiary Companies, Composition of Consolidated Inventory Total showing amount of inventory by divisions and companies as at Dec. 31, 1937.	R. 98	251	3
4	Same, for Cash in Banks and on Hand, as at Dec. 31, 1937.	R. 100	251	2
5	Same, for Current Notes and Accounts Receivable less reserves as at Dec. 31, 1937 with comparable amounts as at Dec. 31, 1936.	R. 100	251	2
6	P. W. & Co., summary by classes, Inventories Connecticut Division, as at Dec. 31, 1937.	R. 115	251	1
7	Sale by McKesson & Robbins, Incorporated (Connecticut Division) to African Soap & Chemical Works, Johannesburg, South Africa, of 15 cases of Oil of Lemon sequiterpeneless:	R. 153		
	(a) McKesson Factory Order No. 3926, Mar. 7, 1938.		80, 85, 89	1
	(b) W. W. Smith & Co. Purchase Order No. 17983, Mar. 4, 1938.		77, 101	1
	(c) McKesson duplicate Invoice No. 31149, Mar. 7, 1938.		80, 89	1
8	Sale by McKesson & Robbins, Incorporated (Connecticut Division) to Briggs, William & Sons, Ltd., Dundee, Scotland, of 17 cases of Quinine Sulphate.	R. 175		
	A McKesson Factory Order No. 2994, Jan. 31, 1938.		80, 84, 85, 117	1
	B W. W. Smith & Co. Purchase Order No. 17740, Jan. 28, 1938.		77, 84, 101, 117, 222	1
	C W. W. Smith & Co. Notice of Shipment, Jan. 31, 1938.		77, 80, 84, 117, 238	1
	D McKesson duplicate Invoice Number 131240, Jan. 31, 1938.		80, 118, 207	1
9	Sale by McKesson & Robbins, Incorporated (Connecticut Division) to Silverton Tannery, Ltd., Pretoria, So. Africa, of 331 cases of Gum Camphor, Slabs.	R. 180		
	(a) Copies 1, 3 & 4 of McKesson Bill of Lading No. 2993, Jan. 31, 1938.		87, 88, 89, 118, 237, 238.	3
	(b) McKesson Factory Order and Duplicate No. 2993, Jan. 31, 1938.		80, 85, 86, 89	2

[19] Id. following record reference indicates that the exhibit was marked for identification at page cited.

[20] Page numbers in **bold face** type indicate that the exhibit or a substantial part of it is reproduced at that point in the report.

Commission Exhibits—Continued

No.	Description	Received in Evidence Transcript Page No.	Referred to in Report at Page No.	Number of Pages in the Exhibit
10	Same, 114 other shipments Foreign Crude Drugs, Jan. 1938.	R. 189 Id., R. 1382.	80, 85, 86, 87, 89	570
11	Sale by McKesson & Robbins, Incorporated (Connecticut Division) to Silverton Tannery, Ltd., Pretoria, So. Africa, of 331 cases Gum Camphor, Slabs.	R. 199		
	A McKesson Factory Order No. 2993, Jan. 31, 1938.		80, 83, 85, 86, 89, 117	1
	B W. W. Smith & Co. Notice of Shipment, Jan. 31, 1938.		77, 79, 80, 89, 101, 117, 235.	1
	C W. W. Smith & Co. Purchase Order No. 17738, Jan. 28, 1938.		77, 78, 101, 117, 235	1
	D McKesson duplicate Invoice No. 131239, Jan. 31, 1938.		80, 81, 89, 118	1
12	Purchase by McKesson & Robbins, Incorporated (Connecticut Division) from D. C. Reynolds & Company, Ottawa, Canada, of 310 Cadys Musk Pods:	R. 224		
	A D. C. Reynolds & Company, Invoice, Dec. 29, 1937.		72, 75, 86, 117	1
	B McKesson Purchase Order, Acctg. Dept. Copy, No. 5634, Dec. 27, 1937.		71, 86, 117	1
	C McKesson voucher, Dec. 29, 1937		75	1
13	Instructions to Representatives of P. W. & Co. in Charge of Examinations of McKesson & Robbins, Incorporated as at Dec. 31, 1937.	R. 232	165, 166, 315	16
13-A	Same (from McKesson files)	R. 682		16
14	Special Executive Bulletin A-163 (re Master Organization Chart of McKesson & Robbins, Incorporated, Ex. 97), Instructions Effective Sept. 1, 1937.	R. 240 Id., R. 1385.	190, 326, 440	18
15	McKesson & Robbins, Incorporated, Closing Instructions, Dec. 31, 1937.	R. 247	166, 315	69
16	Same, June 30, 1934	R. 248	285	49
17	P. W. & Co. Questionnaire on Internal Check, Connecticut Company, dated Jan. 1933. Memorandum Regarding Verification of Cash and Bank Balances.	R. 257	50, 76, 99, 115, 177, 179, 193, 363, 383.	19
18	P. W. & Co. questionnaires as at Dec. 31, 1936	R. 259		
	A-3—Cash, Canadian Company			1
	A-3, 4—Cash, Connecticut Division		99	2
	C-3—Receivables, Canadian Company			1
	C-9—Receivables, Connecticut Division			1
	D-8, 9, 10—Inventories—Connecticut Division		178	3
19	Same as at Dec. 31, 1937	R. 259		
	A-4, 5—Cash, Connecticut Division		179	2
	A-3, 3a—Cash, Canadian Company		51, 93	2
	C-4—Receivables, Connecticut Division		232	1
	C-4—Receivables, Canadian Company		98	1
	D-8, 9, 10—Inventories, Connecticut Division		178, 259	3
	DD-2—Note on Accounts Payable, Connecticut Division.			1
20	15 McKesson & Robbins, Incorporated (Connecticut Division) Receiving Tickets on Foreign Crude Drugs Dec. 1937 (including Receiving Ticket No. 22237 on Purchase Order 5634 D. C. Reynolds & Co., Ottawa, Canada, 310 Cadys Musk Pods, Dec. 31, 1937).	R. 285 Id., R. 711, R. 1386.	76, 77, 97, 284	15
21	P. W. & Co. work program, Cash—Canadian Company, as at Dec. 31, 1937.	R. 311	194, 195-196, 198, 295, 316.	2

Commission Exhibits—Continued

No.	Description	Received in Evidence Transcript Page No.	Referred to in Report at Page No.	Number of Pages in the Exhibit
22	P. W. & Co. work program, Accounts Receivable—Canadian Company, as at Dec. 31, 1937.	R. 332	216	2
23	P. W. & Co. work program, Inventories—Canadian Company, as at Dec. 31, 1937.	R. 357	252-253	2
24	P. W. & Co. work program, Accounts Payable—Canadian Company, as at Dec. 31, 1937.	R. 365	293-294	1
25	P. W. & Co. work program, Sales—Canadian Company, as at Dec. 31, 1937.	R. 376	233, 300, 301	1
26	P. W. & Co. Memorandum on Consolidated Accounts—Canadian Company, as at Dec. 31, 1937.	R. 383	66, 98, 101, 105, 217, 218, 229, 241, 242, 253, 255, 286, 301, 307, 311.	6
27	P. W. & Co. Supplementary Profit and Loss Information—Connecticut Division, 1937.	R. 407	311	1
28	Schedule of Percentages, Cash, Receivables and Investories to Total Assets, Connecticut Division, Canadian Company and McKesson & Robbins, Incorporated, Consolidated, as at Dec. 31, 1937.	R. 429	45, 250	1
29	P. W. & Co. work program, Cash—Connecticut Division, as at Dec. 31, 1937.	R. 431	194, 195-196, 198, 295, 316.	2
29-A	P. W. & Co. work program, Factory Payroll Account, Connecticut Division, as at Dec. 31, 1937.	R. 444	198	1
30	Manning & Company statements	R. 448	99, 118, 205, 220	
	(a) Connecticut Division, Nov. 30, 1938		68, 212	2
	(b) Connecticut Division, Jan. 31, 1938		212	2
	(c) Canadian Company, Dec. 31, 1937		99, 100, 200	1
31	Manning & Company Confirmations to P. W. & Co. as at Dec. 31, 1937.	R. 452		
	A Connecticut Division		212	1
	B Canadian Company		212	1
32	P. W. & Co. work program, Accounts Receivable—Connecticut Division, as at Dec. 31, 1937.	R. 456	216	2
33	Manning & Company Advice of Debit, May 5, 1938	R. 456	76, 117, 205, 207, 212.	1
34	Manning & Company Advice of Credit, Nov. 26, 1938.	R. 457	91, 118, 205, 207	1
35	Manning & Company Business Declaration filed June 30, 1931.	R. 458 Id		1
36	McKesson & Robbins, Incorporated, Connecticut Division, Schedule of Returns, Allowances, Discounts, etc. by months for the year 1937 (from P. W. & Co. work papers).	R. 465	220	1
37	P. W. & Co. work program, Inventories—Connecticut Division, as at Dec. 31, 1937.	R. 475	251, 259, 260	1
38	P. W. & Co., "Inventory Price Test—Book 7—General Crude" (including foreign) Connecticut Division, as at Dec. 31, 1937.	R. 485	91, 105, 261, 262	5
39	P. W. & Co., Schedule of Inventory by Classes, Connecticut Division, as at Dec. 31, 1937.	R. 499		1
40	P. W. & Co., selected work papers re Inventories, Connecticut Division, as at Dec. 31, 1936.	R. 523		
	D 7 Work Program		251, 260	1
	D 13, 14 Summary of Foreign Crude Drug Sales by Commodities, Jan. 1937.		89, 105, 220, 262, 263.	2
	D 15, 16, 17—Photocopies of Sales Journal sheets, Foreign Crude Drugs, Jan. 1937.		262, 270, 301	3
	D 21 Inventory Adjustments			1
	D 55, 56, 57 Inventory price test schedules, book 7, general crude (including foreign).		91, 105, 262	3

Commission Exhibits—Continued

No.	Description	Received in Evidence Transcript Page No.	Referred to in Report at Page No.	Number of Pages in the Exhibit
	P. W. & Co. selected work papers re Inventors. Connecticut Division, as at Dec. 31, 1936—Con.			
	1, 2, 3 Letter from McKesson & Robbins, Incorporated to P. W. & Co. enclosing copies of letters requesting confirmations of merchandise and list of warehouses, etc., Dec. 29, 1936.		104, 272	3
	4 Schedule of confirmations mailed		272	1
	5, 16, 18, 20, 22, 23 Confirmations to P. W. & Co. from five Canadian vendors re foreign crude drugs.		104	6
41	P. W. & Co. selected work papers re Inventories, Connecticut Division, as at Dec. 31, 1935.	R. 524		
	D 5 Work program		251, 258, 260	1
	D 8c Recapitulation by product of crude drug sales (including foreign) Jan. 1936.		105, 262	1
	D 5b Schedule of inventory differences			1
	D 8, 8a, 8b Summary of crude drug sales by commodities (including foreign) Jan. 1936.		105, 262	3
	D 41, 42, 43, 44 Inventory price test schedules, book 7, general crude (including foreign).		91, 105, 262	4
	D 45 Miscellaneous notes on book 7, general crude.			1
	D 8d Schedule of inventory by classes			1
	D 71 Miscellaneous notes			1
	D 85 Letter from McKesson & Robbins, Incorporated to P. W. & Co. enclosing copies of letters requesting confirmations of merchandise, Jan. 13, 1936.		104	1
	D 86, 87, 88, 89, 90 Copies of requests to five Canadian vendors.		104, 272	5
	D 91, 92, 93, 94, 95, 96 Confirmations to P. W. & Co. from five Canadian vendors re foreign crude drugs.		102–104	6
42	P. W. & Co., selected work papers re Inventories, Connecticut Division, as at Dec. 31, 1934:	R. 525		
	D 1 Summary of inventories, less reserves			1
	D 2 Summary of inventory reserves			1
	Notes on physical count of inventory		280, 283	1
	D 3 Inventory reconciliation			1
	D 4 Work program			1
	D 5 Recapitulation of physical inventories by books and accounts.			1
	D 6, 7 Summary of larger inventory items			2
	D 8 Recapitulation by product of foreign crude drug sales Jan. 1935.		105, 262	1
	D 9, 10 Summary of foreign crude drug sales by commodities, Jan. 1935.		105, 262	2
	D 15, 16 Inventory price test schedules, book 3, production crude.			2
	D 17, 18 Miscellaneous notes on book 3			2
	D 33, 34, 35, 36, 37, 38 Inventory price test schedules, book 7, general crude (including foreign).		66, 91, 105, 262, 283	6
	D 39 Miscellaneous notes on book 7			1
	D 40, 41, 42 Letters to McKesson & Robbins, Incorporated, giving market quotations.			3
43	Schedule showing Crude Drug Sales, Gross Profits, Inventories and Accounts Receiveable of Connecticut (later Division) and Canadian Companies, 1932 to 1937, inclusive. (Includes some non-foreign figures—see Ex. Q.)	R. 526	45, 46, 108, 248, 304, 307, 310.	1

Commission Exhibits—Continued

No.	Description	Received in Evidence Transcript Page No.	Referred to in Report at Page No.	Number of Pages in the Exhibit
44	P. W. & Co. work program, Fixed Assets and Reserves—Connecticut Division, as at Dec. 31, 1937.	R. 538	292	1
45	P. W. & Co. work program, Acceptances and Drafts Payable—Connecticut Division, as at Dec. 31, 1937.	R. 539	297	1
46	P. W. & Co. work program, Sales—Connecticut Division, as at Dec. 31, 1937.	R. 539	300	1
47	P. W. & Co. work program, Accounts Payable—Connecticut Division, as at Dec. 31, 1937.	R. 540	177, 293–294	1
48	Schedule Unexpired Insurance—Connecticut Division, as at Dec. 31, 1937 (from P. W. & Co. work papers).	R. 547	291	1
49	P. W. & Co., Memorandum on Accounts, Connecticut Division, as at Dec. 31, 1937.	R. 560	86, 91, 93, 101, 104, 105, 229, 274, 307, 311.	5
50	"Agreement between McKesson & Robbins, Incorporated, and McKesson & Robbins, Limited, and W. W. Smith & Company, Inc.—Guarantee of W. W. Smith & Co.—Both Dated as of August 1, 1935."	R. 563	64, 65, 66, 86, 99, 101, 205, 224.	13
51	Purported report of Dun and Bradstreet of Canada, Limited, on W. W. Smith & Co., Jan. 29, 1938.	R. 565	61	1
52	Same, Jan. 28, 1937	R. 567	61	1
53	Confirmations to P. W. & Co., from five Canadian vendors re foreign crude drugs, Connecticut Division, as at Dec. 31, 1937.	R. 597	102–103, 104, 118	6
54	Same, Canadian Company	R. 597	104, 118, 254	6
55	P. W. & Co. "Abstract of Agreement with Smith & Co., Inc." dated Aug. 1, 1931.	R. 634	201, 204	2
56	P. W. & Co. "Abstract of Extension Agreement between W. W. Smith & Co., Inc. (N. Y.) and McKesson & Robbins, Inc. (Conn.) and McKesson & Robbins, Ltd. (Canada)" July 1 [31], 1933 and "Abstract of Guaranty Agreement by W. W. Smith & Co. (Co-Partnership) to McKesson Robbins, Inc., et al.".	R. 635	63, 66, 205, 223	2
57	McKesson & Robbins, Incorporated, Inventory Count Sheets, Crude Drug Inventory, Connecticut Division, Dec. 31, 1934. (Non-foreign).	R. 642 Id., R. 1475.	108, 109, 110, 274, 280.	[21] 42
58	Same (Foreign)	R. 642 Id., R. 1475.	109, 110, 111, 274, 280, 281.	[22] 14
59	McKesson & Robbins, Incorporated, Inventory Book Sheets, Book No. 7 (including foreign crude drugs), Connecticut Division, as at Dec. 31, 1934.	R. 646	111, 274, 280	14
60	McKesson & Robbins, Limited, Inventory Count Sheets, Dec. 31, 1934.	R. 653 Id., R. 1534.	110, 257, 274, 280	[23] 7
61	P. W. & Co., Inventory Price Test schedules, Canadian Company, as at Dec. 31, 1934.	R. 654	105, 257, 258	2
62	Certification of Inventories, Connecticut Division, by McKesson officials to P. W. & Co., as at Dec. 31, 1937.	R. 659	273–274, 281	3
63	Same, as at Dec. 31, 1934	R. 669	281	2
64	Same, Spice Department, as at Dec. 31, 1937	R. 671		2
65	Certification of Inventories, Canadian Company, by McKesson officials to P. W. & Co., as at Dec. 31, 1937.	R. 671	251	3

[21] 6 sets of 7 sheets each.
[22] 2 sets of 7 sheets each.
[23] 1 Set.

Commission Exhibits—Continued

No.	Description	Received in Evidence Transcript Page No.	Referred to in Report at Page No.	Number of Pages in the Exhibit
66	Certification of Liabilities, Connecticut Division, by McKesson officials to P. W. & Co., as at Dec. 31, 1937.	R. 672	299	2
67	Certification of Receivables, Connecticut Division, by McKesson officials to P. W. & Co., as at Dec. 31, 1937.	R. 672	229, 230	3
68	Schedule of Compensation received by A. B. Ritts from P. W. & Co.	R. 730		1
69	P. W. & Co. Schedule of Inventory Adjustments, Connecticut Division, as at Dec. 31, 1934.	R. 733		1
70	Certification of Inventories, Connecticut Division, by McKesson officials to P. W. & Co., as at Dec. 31, 1935.	R. 796		3
71	P. W. & Co. Summary of Cost of Sales and Gross Profit by Commodities, Canadian Company, 1936.	R. 802	301	1
72	P. W. & Co. Memorandum on Accounts, Canadian Company, as at Dec. 31, 1936.	R. 804	98, 229, 254, 255, 286, 301, 307, 311.	5
73	Same, as at Dec. 31, 1935	R. 804	98, 104, 229, 254, 255, 256, 274, 286, 301, 307, 311, 420.	5
74	Same, as at Dec. 31, 1934	R. 805	30, 98, 229, 254, 256, 286.	4
75	Same, as at Dec. 31, 1933	R. 806	66, 98, 226, 229, 254, 256, 286.	5
76	Same, as at Dec. 31, 1931	R. 807	66, 98, 108, 225, 254, 256, 286.	3
77	Same, as at Dec. 31, 1930	R. 808	98, 227	1
78	P. W. & Co. Memorandum on Accounts, Connecticut Division, as at Dec. 31, 1936.	R. 809	86, 93, 104, 229, 274, 307, 311.	4
79	Same, as at Dec. 31, 1935	R. 809	86, 93, 229, 262, 274, 311, 306, 307.	3
80	Same, as at Dec. 31, 1933	R. 810	86, 93, 229, 262, 274, 306, 311.	6
81	Same, as at Dec. 31, 1932	R. 810	45, 66, 93, 211, 226, 283, 304, 306, 308, 310, 311, 425.	8
82	Same, as at Dec. 31, 1931	R. 811	45, 46, 67, 91, 93, 201, 202, 225, 228, 268, 305, 311, 426.	11
83	Same, as at Dec. 31, 1930	R. 812	46, 50, 55, 93, 108, 154, 197, 201, 227, 310.	7
84	McKesson & Robbins, Incorporated, Connecticut Division, Sales Journal Sheets, Foreign Crude Drugs, Dec. 24, 1937 through Feb. 7, 1938. (From P. W. & Co. work papers.)	R. 815	89, 105, 262, 263, 301.	5
85	McKesson & Robbins, Incorporated, Inventory Book Sheets, Book No. 7 (including foreign crude drugs) Connecticut Division, as at Dec. 31, 1937.	R. 820	259, 261, 271	13

Commission Exhibits—Continued

No.	Description	Received in Evidence Transcript Page No.	Referred to in Report at Page No.	Number of Pages in the Exhibit
86	Four checks, payable to W. W. Smith & Co., Ltd.	R. 824	101	
	A Canadian Company check No. B-620, Dec. 31, 1937, $750.		101, 295	1
	B Canadian Company check No. B-621, Dec. 31, 1937, $1,811.91.		101, 295	1
	C Connecticut Division check No. GC-6449, Jan. 17, 1938, $11,994.75.		296	1
	D Connecticut Division check No. GC-6450, Jan. 17, 1938, $750.		296	1
87	Letter to P. W. & Co. from H. W. Henning & Son, Jan. 25, 1936, giving market quotations on certain crude drugs and essential oils as of Dec. 31, 1935.	R. 826		1
88	Letter from P. W. & Co. to F. Donald Coster, Feb. 13, 1933, re 1932 audit.	R. 930	154-155, 229, 317	1
89	P. W. & Co. Abstract of Agreement between Charles Manning & Company, Limited and McKesson & Robbins, Incorporated (Connecticut) and McKesson & Robbins, Limited, Mar. 12, 1930.	R. 956	55, 66, 201	1
90	Excerpt from the Minutes of Special Meeting of Board of Directors of McKesson & Robbins, Incorporated (Connecticut) held Sept. 3, 1931, re approval of "contract with Manning & Co." and "subsidiary contract with W. W. Smith, Inc." dated Aug. 1, 1931. (See Ex. 179.)	R. 961 Id.		1
91	Letter from P. W. & Co. to J. H. McGloon, Comptroller, McKesson & Robbins, Incorporated, re traveling auditors, Sept. 22, 1932. (See Ex. 125.)	R. 972	326	2
92	Text of Draft Nov. 22, 1938, P. W. & Co. Memorandum on Examination of Accounts of Branch Offices of McKesson & Robbins, Incorporated, as at Dec. 31, 1938 (from McKesson files).	R. 991	165, 166	17
93	Text of Draft Apr. 14, 1936, P. W. & Co. Report on McKesson & Robbins, Incorporated, (Maryland and subsidiary companies) year ended Dec. 31, 1935 (from McKesson files).	R. 992	343	26
94	Text of Draft Apr. 17, 1937, P. W. & Co. Report on McKesson & Robbins, Incorporated, (Maryland and subsidiary companies) year ended Dec. 31, 1936 (from McKesson files).	R. 993	343	14
95	Text of Draft Apr. 28, 1938, P. W. & Co. Report on McKesson & Robbins, Incorporated, (Maryland and subsidiary companies.) Year ended Dec. 31, 1937 (from McKesson files).	R. 994	343	20
96	Certification of Inventories, Canadian Company, by McKesson officials to P. W. & Co., as at Dec. 31, 1935.	R. 1045		2
97	Master Organization Chart of McKesson & Robbins, Incorporated, effective Sept. 1, 1937.	R. 1157 Id., R. 1385.	50, 52, 190	1
98	P. W. & Co. Statement of Application of Funds, McKesson & Robbins, Incorporated, Manufacturing Division (Connecticut), year ended Dec. 31, 1934.	R. 1192		3
99	Schedule of Apportionment of P. W. & Co. Fees and Expenses by branches and subsidiary companies, Dec. 31, 1937 examination of McKesson & Robbins, Incorporated.	R. 1202		2
100	Letter from P. W. & Co. to F. D. Coster, Feb. 11, 1938 re 1937 audit of Canadian Company.	R. 1214	152, 154, 433	1

Commission Exhibits—Continued

No.	Description	Received in Evidence Transcript Page No.	Referred to in Report at Page No.	Number of Pages in the Exhibit
101	Correspondence between P. W. & Co. and McKesson & Robbins, Incorporated, re acquisition of Blumauer Frank Drug Company:	R. 1215		
	A Letter from P. W. & Co. to F. D. Coster, Sept. 17, 1937.		288	1
	B Letter from P. W. & Co. to J. H. McGloon, Sept. 24, 1937, and memorandum of conference between McGloon and Brundage of P. W. & Co.			4
	C Letter from P. W. & Co. to F. D. Coster, Sept. 25, 1937.			1
102	Schedule of Compensation received by R. E. Thorn from P. W. & Co.	R. 1217		1
103	P. W. & Co. report on McKesson & Robbins, Limited, (Consolidated) year ended Dec. 31, 1937.	R. 1218		5
104	Confirmation on Inventories McKesson & Robbins, Incorporated, from British-American Stores, Inc., to P. W. & Co., as at Dec. 31, 1932.	R. 1223	108.	
	A Stock Report		285	1
	B Letter of Transmittal		285	1
105	Statement of Sales, Cost of Sales, and Gross Profit of Connecticut Company, Special Sales Dept. (foreign), by months, 1931.	R. 1375	46, 302, 303	1
106	McKesson & Robbins, Incorporated, (Maryland) Annual Report to Stockholders, 1937.	R. 1388	39, 40, 41, 43, 44, 154, 345, 346, 347.	54
107	Connecticut Division perpetual inventory card	R. 1478	77	1
108	Floor plan, first floor, Building No. 2, Fairfield plant, showing location of stocks as at Dec. 31, 1934.	R. 1559	281	1
109	Correspondence between P. W. & Co. and McKesson & Robbins, Incorporated, re audit fees, 1932 examination:	R. 1584.		
	A J. H. McGloon, to P. W. & Co., July 12, 1933		356, 357	1
	B P. W. & Co. to J. H. McGloon, July 20, 1933, and supporting schedules.		356, 357	4
110	Memorandum from F. D. Coster to J. H. McGloon, June 7, 1938, re title of accounts.	R. 1708	107	1
111	McKesson & Robbins, Incorporated, memorandum dated October 27, 1930 re Points to be discussed with P. W. & Co. in connection with 1930 audit.	R. 1718 Id., R. 1727.	167–171	6
112	Memorandum from J. H. Parks, V. P., McKesson & Robbins, Incorporated, to C. F. Michaels, V. P., McKesson & Robbins, Incorporated, February 15, 1933, re auditing expense.	R. 1734	171, 356, 400	3
113	Letter from P. W. & Co. representative, New Orleans to P. W. & Co., St. Louis, January 27, 1930, re weaknesses of system at McKesson-Parker Blake Corp.	R. 1735	317	4
114	Memorandum from J. F. Thompson to F. D. Coster, C. F. Michaels and W. J. Murray, Jr., April 18, 1938, re reduction in inventories.	R. 1738	46, 244	9
115	Report of J. H. McGloon to F. D. Coster, C. F. Michaels, W. J. Murray, Jr., J. F. Thompson and Divisional Vice Presidents, March 10, 1938, showing analysis of changes in Branch Control or Corporation's Capital Employed and Net profits during the year 1937.	R. 1741	46, 243	9
116	Correspondence between P. W. & Co. and Girard & Co., Inc., and McKesson & Robbins, Incorporated, from December 17, 1924 to December 17, 1937, re engagements of P. W. & Co. (43 letters).	R. 1747	147, 148, 149, 150, 151, 152, 155, 355, 378, 433	68

Commission Exhibits—Continued

No.	Description	Received in Evidence Transcript Page No.	Referred to in Report at Page No.	Number of Pages in the Exhibit
117	"Examination of Financial Statements by Independent Public Accountants, a Bulletin prepared and published by the American Institute of Accountants January, 1936."	R. 1766	141, 156, 173, 174, 196, 231, 301, 359, 388, 395, 399, 429	47
118	Letter from P. W. & Co. to F. D. Coster, April 11, 1933, on scope of examination and copy of letter from a group of public accountants to the New York Stock Exchange, Feb. 24, 1933.	R. 1833	156, 350, 357	6
119	Letter from P. W. & Co., New York to P. W. & Co., Seattle, October 3, 1929, re complaint of time on audit, Stewart & Holmes Drug Company.	R. 1834	172, 356	2
120	Photocopy of McKesson & Robbins, Incorporated, Statement of Gross Sales, Returns and Allowances, Cost of Sales, and Gross Profit for the month of December, 1937 by classes of merchandise for the Connecticut Division. (From P. W. & Co. work papers).	R. 1902	93, 108, 220, 307	1
121	P. W. & Co. Office Manual (1931)	R. 1906	145, 156, 165, 331	23
122	P. W. & Co., all offices, staff by months, for year ending June 30, 1938.	R. 1908	143	1
123	P. W. & Co. Schedule showing hours worked by partners, managers, seniors, and assistants.	R. 1909.		
	A McKesson & Robbins, Incorporated, (Maryland) and subsidiary companies 1928 through 1937.		354	1
	B Examinations of wholesale houses before acquisition.			1
	C Girard & Co., Inc., McKesson & Robbins, Incorporated (New York), and McKesson & Robbins, Incorporated (Connecticut) 1924 through 1927.			1
124	Photocopy of McKesson & Robbins, Incorporated, Statement of Gross Sales, Returns and Allowances, Cost of Sales, and Gross Profit for the 12-month period ending Dec. 31, 1936 by classes of merchandise for the Connecticut Division. (From P. W. & Co. work papers).	R. 1943	45, 93, 108, 220, 244, 307	1
125	P. W. & Co. preliminary outline of suggested procedure to be followed by McKesson & Robbins, Incorporated's internal auditing staff. Sept. 22, 1932. (See Ex. 91.)	R. 1966	326	6
126	Letter from P. W. & Co., Chicago, to P. W. & Co., New York, Feb. 27, 1932, re weaknesses in system McKesson-Churchill Drug Company, Burlington, Iowa.	R. 1967	319–320	2
127	Letter from P. W. & Co. to F. D. Coster, Mar. 22, 1932, re weaknesses in system in four wholesale houses.	R. 1967	320	1
128	McKesson & Robbins, Incorporated (Connecticut) Annual Report to stockholders, 1927.	R. 1992	28, 154, 346	11
129	McKesson & Robbins, Incorporated (Maryland) Annual Report to Stockholders, 1928.	R. 1992	35, 346	11
130	Same, 1929	R. 1992	35, 342, 346, 347	13
131	Same, 1930	R. 1992	36, 40, 346	26
132	Same, 1931	R. 1992	346	12
133	Same, 1932	R. 1992	37, 346, 347	12
134	Same, 1933	R. 1992	37, 38, 346	12
135	Same, 1934	R. 1992	39, 346	33
136	Same, 1935	R. 1992	39, 346	29
137	Same, 1936	R. 1992	39, 40, 346	24

Commission Exhibits—Continued

No.	Description	Received in Evidence Transcript Page No.	Referred to in Report at Page No.	Number of Pages in the Exhibit
138	P. W. & Co. Text of report on Girard & Co., Inc., 9 Months Ended Dec. 31, 1924. (Does not include financial statements.)	R. 2001	24, 25, 153, 245, 333	5
139	Same, Year Ended Dec. 31, 1925	R. 2001	25, 153, 245, 333	5
140	Same, 3 Months Ended Mar. 31, 1926	R. 2001	25, 153, 224, 245, 333	5
141	Same, 3 Months Ended June 30, 1926	R. 2001	26, 153, 224, 245, 333	9
142	Same, 3 Months Ended Sept. 30, 1926	R. 2001	26, 153, 224, 245, 333. 337,	7
143	Same, 2 Months Ended Nov. 30, 1926	R. 2001	153, 245, 333, 337	6
144	P. W. & Co. Text of Report on McKesson & Robbins, Incorporated (Connecticut) Oct. 28, 1926 to Nov. 30, 1926. (Does not include financial statements.)	R. 2001	27, 245, 333	6
145	Same, 4 Months Ended Mar. 30, 1927	R. 2001	54, 245, 333, 335, 337	9
146	Same, 9 Months and 13 Months Ended Dec. 31, 1927	R. 2001	28, 29, 48, 149, 333, 153, 245, 335, 336, 337.	10
147	Same, 4 Months Ended Apr. 30, 1928	R. 2001	46, 117, 150, 153, 245, 333, 336, 337.	11
148	Same, 8 Months Ended Dec. 31, 1928	R. 2001	32, 33, 46, 153, 245, 333, 336, 337.	16
149	P. W. & Co. Report on McKesson & Robbins, Limited, 8 Months Ended Dec. 31, 1928. (Complete.)	R. 2001	46, 153, 254, 333, 335, 338.	6
150	Same, Year Ended December 31, 1929	R. 2001	46, 153, 307, 333, 338	6
151	P. W. & Co. Text of Report on McKesson & Robbins, Incorporated (Connecticut) Year Ended Dec. 31, 1929. (Does not include financial statements.)	R. 2001	46, 93, 153, 245, 249, 333, 335, 336, 337, 338, 339.	16
152	P. W. & Co. Text of Report on McKesson & Robbins, Incorporated (Maryland and subsidiary companies), Year Ended Dec. 31, 1929. (Does not include Financial statements.)	R. 2001	32, 33, 34, 35, 153, 229, 334, 335, 339.	23
153	Same, Year Ended Dec. 31, 1930	R. 2001	35, 36, 46, 153, 334, 336, 339, 341.	32
154	Same, Year Ended Dec. 31, 1931	R. 2001	30, 36, 46, 334, 339, 341.	31
155	Same, Year Ended Dec. 31, 1932	R. 2001	37, 334, 336, 339, 341	33
156	Same, Year Ended Dec. 31, 1933	R. 2001	334, 336, 341	20
157	Same, Year Ended Dec. 31, 1934	R. 2001	38, 153, 334, 336, 341	17
158	Same, Year Ended Dec. 31, 1935	R. 2001	38, 39, 154, 317, 334, 336, 341.	24
159	Same, Year Ended Dec. 31, 1936	R. 2001	38, 39, 154, 334, 336, 341.	15
160	P. W. & Co. Report on McKesson & Robbins, Incorporated (Maryland and subsidiary companies) Year Ended Dec. 31, 1937. (Complete.)	R. 2001	38, 154, 293, 334, 336, 341, 345, 349.	34
161	McKesson & Robbins, Ltd., Annual Report to Stockholders, 1931.	R. 2012	30, 46, 346	9
162	Same, 1932	R. 2012	30, 307, 346	7
163	Same, 1933	R. 2012	30, 307, 346, 355	7
164	Same, 1934	R. 2012	30, 38, 307, 346, 355.	7
165	Same, 1935	R. 2012	30, 346, 355	6
166	Same, 1936	R. 2012	30, 346, 355	6
167	Same, 1937	R. 2012	30, 43, 44, 346, 348, 355.	6

Commission Exhibits—Continued

No.	Description	Received in Evidence Transcript Page No.	Referred to in Report at Page No.	Number of Pages in the Exhibit
168	"Organization, Ethics and Team Work", by R. O. Berger, partner, P. W. & Co., 1925.	R. 2029	142, 143, 145, 174, 331, 333.	33
169	Schedule showing charges by years made by P. W. & Co. to McKesson & Robbins, Incorporated and Predecessor Companies, 1924 through 1938 and related assets, sales, and profits.	R. 2030	25, 352, 355	1
170	Analysis of Accounts Receivable of Girard & Co., Inc. as at audit dates from Dec. 31, 1924 through Nov. 30, 1926, prepared from work papers of P. W. & Co.	R. 2032	26, 46, 48, 54, 66, 256, 304, 310.	1
171	Letter from J. H. McGloon to Sullivan & Cromwell, Apr. 12, 1938, re reporting on Form 10-K fees paid under contract with W. W. Smith & Company, Inc.	R. 2232	127	1
172	Letter from Sullivan & Cromwell to McKesson & Robbins, Incorporated Apr. 14, 1938, replying to above.	R. 2233	127	2
173	Letter from Marsh, Stoddard & Day to Sullivan & Cromwell, Dec. 17, 1934, re merger of the Connecticut and Maryland Companies.	R. 2233	63, 127	2
174	Letter from F. D. Coster to Horace B. Merwin, January 18, 1926, re proposal to acquire McKesson & Robbins, Incorporated (New York).	R. 2251	26	3
175	Letter from Horace B. Merwin to F. D. Coster, Jan. 27, 1926, replying to above.	R. 2251	26	2
176	President's Report to Stockholders and Directors of Girard & Co., Inc., 1925.	R. 2252	26, 66, 158, 224, 256, 335.	15
177	Report of Julian F. Thompson on "Girard & Company, Inc." (1925).	R. 2252	24, 25, 53, 54, 140, 146, 147.	18
178	Prospectus on 193,907 Shares 7% Convertible Preference Stock of McKesson & Robbins, Incorporated (Maryland), offered in 1928.	R. 2266	32, 33	4
179	Minutes of Meeting of Board of Directors of McKesson & Robbins, Limited, Sept. 3, 1931, including approval of "contract with Manning & Co." and "subsidiary contract with W. W. Smith, Inc." dated Aug. 1, 1931.	R. 2333	60, 125, 202, 389	4
180	Minutes of Special Meeting of Board of Directors of McKesson & Robbins, Incorporated (Connecticut). Sept. 3, 1931, including approval of "contract with Manning & Co." and "subsidiary contract with W. W. Smith, Inc." dated Aug. 1, 1931.	R. 2333	60, 125, 202, 389	10
181	Letter from Sidney J. Weinberg to F. D. Coster, Apr. 4, 1934, re becoming director of McKesson & Robbins, Incorporated, and memorandum of Weinberg's re responsibility of Directors and an Outline of the Program suggested as the basis of Cooperation between Officers and Directors of a Corporation, and Coster's reply Apr. 5, 1934.	R. 2386	126	6
182	Letter from Sidney J. Weinberg to F. D. Coster, Nov. 23, 1938, and acceptance of contract on sale of $3,000,000 debentures.	R. 2411	40	3
183	Letter from F. D. Coster to Committee on Stock List of New York Stock Exchange Dec. 2, 1938, re listing of $3,000,000 debentures	R. 2415 Id.	40	1
184	Prospectus on $22,000,000, 5½% Convertible Debentures of McKesson & Robbins, Incorporated (Maryland), offered in 1930.	R. 2430	36	4

Commission Exhibits—Continued

No.	Description	Received in Evidence Transcript Page No.	Referred to in Report at Page No.	Number of Pages in the Exhibit
185	Sept. 1938 Financial Report of J. H. McGloon to F. D. Coster, C. F. Michaels, W. J. Murray, Jr., J. F. Thompson, Divisional Vice Presidents and Assistants to Divisional Vice Presidents, dated Oct. 28, 1938, consisting of the following:	R. 2519, R. 4254.	315	
	Letter of transmittal			1
	Cover Sheet			1
	Form 1000:			
	Consolidated Balance Sheets as at Sept. 30, 1938 and 1937.			3
	Consolidated Profit and Loss Statements for the nine months ending Sept. 30, 1938 and 1937.			1
	Form 1001:			
	Summary of Net Sales and Estimated Net Profits for Sept. 1938 and 1937.			2
	Form 1002: Summary of Net Sales and Estimated Net Profits for the nine months ending Sept. 30, 1938 and 1937, together with Summary of Net Sales of Wines and Liquors and Gross Profit thereon.		107	4
	Form 1003: Summary of Net Sales and Estimated Net Profits of Wholesale Houses and Retail Stores for the month of September 1938 and the nine months ending Sept. 30, 1938 and 1937.			14
	Form 1004: Statement of Central Office and Home Office Expenses for the month of September 1938 and for the nine months ending Sept. 30, 1938 and 1937.			9
	Connecticut Division:			
	Statement of Factory Burden for Sept. 1938 and 1937.			1
	Statement of Profit and Loss and Operating Expenses (by departments) for the month of Sept. 1938 and for the nine months ending Sept. 30, 1938.		107, 222, 313, 315	4
186	Letter from J. H. McGloon to P. W. & Co., Mar. 2, 1933, quoting from George V. Doerr's letter re Akron and Cleveland 1932 examinations.	R. 2567	171, 356	2
187	Letter from P. W. & Co. to J. H. McGloon Mar. 14, 1933, replying to above.	R. 2567	171, 356	2
188	Correspondence re reserves for bad debts at McKesson-Minneapolis Drug Company.	R. 2568		
	A Letter from P. W. & Co., Chicago, to George V. Doerr, V. P. McKesson & Robbins, Incorporated, Feb. 9, 1934.		317	1
	B Memo from George V. Doerr to J. H. McGloon.		317	1
189	Correspondence re test plan for reserves for bad debts	R. 2569		
	A Letter from P. W. & Co. to George V. Doerr, V. P. McKesson & Robbins, Incorporated, Mar. 22, 1935.		317	2
	B Letter of P. W. & Co. to J. H. McGloon, Mar. 23, 1935.		317	1
190	Extracts from inventories (foreign crude drugs), Connecticut Division and Canadian Company, Dec. 31, 1937.	R. 2595 Id	106, 264, 269	2

Commission Exhibits—Continued

No.	Description	Received in Evidence Transcript Page No.	Referred to in Report at Page No.	Number of Pages in the Exhibit
191	"Trade of Canada (Imports for Consumption and Exports) Calendar Year 1937", Department of Trade and Commerce, Dominion Bureau of Statistics, External Trade Branch, Ottawa, Canada.	R. 2609a	106, 270, 271	534
192	McKesson & Robbins, Incorporated (Connecticut) Cash Received Record, Dec. 27, 1930.	R. 2643		1
193	Same, Dec. 30, 1930	R. 2644	115	1
194	McKesson & Robbins, Incorporated (Connecticut) 5 Cash Tickets, Dec. 30, 1930 (Non-foreign).	R. 2645		1
195	McKesson & Robbins, Incorporated (Connecticut) 7 Cash Tickets, Dec. 27 and 30, 1930 (Foreign).	R. 2648	113, 115	1
196	Deposit slip, Connecticut Company, Bridgeport City Trust Company, Dec. 30, 1930, $18,077.23 (Non-foreign).	R. 2652		1
197	Deposit slip, Connecticut Company, Bridgeport City Trust Company, Dec. 30, 1930, $34,224 (Foreign).	R. 2654	115, 116	1
198	Statement, Bridgeport City Trust Company, Connecticut Company, Dec. 27-31, 1930.	R. 2658	200	2
199	Statement, Guaranty Trust Company, Connecticut Company, Dec. 27-31, 1930.	R. 2658	200	1
200	McKesson & Robbins, Limited, Cash Received Record, Dec. 18-31, 1930.	R. 2662		1
201	2 Deposit slips, Canadian Company, Bridgeport City Trust Company, Dec. 29, 1930, $30,000, and Dec. 30, 1930, $33,279.75.	R. 2664	115, 116	1
202	McKesson & Robbins, Incorporated, 7 Duplicate Invoices Corresponding to Cash Tickets, Ex. 195.	R. 2669		7
203	Memorandum from C. F. Michaels to F. D. Coster, Nov. 17, 1933, re status of Comptroller.	R. 4280	190	1
204	Letter from Rowley W. Phillips, Feb. 9, 1939, and copies of letters to him from Jonathan Grout, Sept. 16 and 23, 1931, re changes in minutes of meeting of board of directors, Canadian Company, held on Sept. 3, 1931.	R. 4347	60, 125	4
205	P. W. & Co. Memorandum on Accounts, Canadian Company, as at Dec. 31, 1932.	R. 4347	98, 206, 211, 227, 254, 286.	4
206	"Agreement, W. W. Smith & Co., Inc. and McKesson & Robbins, Incorporated (of Connecticut) and McKesson & Robbins, Limited (of Canada)", Aug. 1, 1931.	R. 4348	55, 56, 57-59, 61, 66, 67, 202.	10
207	Purported report of Bradstreet's on W. W. Smith & Co., Oct. 14, 1931.	R. 4349	61, 62, 202, 204, 205.	1
208	P. W. & Co. Condensed Examination Summary, Canadian Company, 1937.	R. 4451	187	2
209	Same, 1935	R. 4451	187	2
210	P. W. & Co. Condensed Examination Summary, Maryland Company, 1937.	R. 4452	187	2
211	Same, 1934	R. 4453	186	2
212	Statement of Business and Educational Background of P. W. & Co. staff on Girard & Co., Inc. and McKesson & Robbins, Incorporated examinations at Bridgeport.	R. 4458	158, 159, 162, 163, 198, 251.	6
212-A	Supplemental Statement to above	R. 4545		2
212-B	Supplemental Statement to above	R. 4545		1
213	Letter from Waddill Catchings to J. L. Bedsole, March 24, 1934.	R. 4458		3

Commission Exhibits—Continued

No.	Description	Received in Evidence Transcript Page No.	Referred to in Report at Page No.	Number of Pages in the Exhibit
214	Report of Waddill Catchings, Chairman of the Operating Committee to Board of Directors McKesson & Robbins, Incorporated (Maryland), March 31, 1934.	R. 4459		7
215	McKesson & Robbins, Incorporated, Digest of contract of guarantee between W. W. Smith & Co. and McKesson & Robbins, Incorporated (Connecticut) and/or McKesson & Robbins, Limited, Aug. 1, 1931.	R. 4460	55, 56, 59-60, 66, 202, 204.	1
216	"Agreement,—Manning & Company and McKesson & Robbins, Incorporated (of Connecticut), and McKesson & Robbins, Limited (of Canada)", Aug. 1, 1931, to which is attached copy of agreement between W. W. Smith & Company, Inc. and McKesson & Robbins, Incorporated (Connecticut) and McKesson & Robbins, Limited (Canada), Aug. 1, 1931 (unsigned copies from McKesson files).	R. 4461	55, 56-57, 61, 66, 67, 203, 204.	19
217	Purported report of Dun and Bradstreet, Inc. on W. W. Smith & Co., Jan. 30, 1934.	R. 4461	61	1
218	Same, Jan. 31, 1935	R. 4461	61	1
219	Same, Jan 30, 1936	R. 4461	61	1
220	Report of J. H. McGloon to F. Donald Coster, C. F. Michaels, W. J. Murray, Jr., J. F. Thompson, Divisional Vice Presidents and Assistants to Divisional Vice Presidents, May 6, 1938, re 1937 audit fees.	R. 4463	354, 356	7
221	Time schedule of Julian F. Thompson's activities in investigating Foreign Crude Drug Department, Dec. 28, 1938.	R. 4464	128	4
222	Canadian Company check to W. W. Smith & Co., Dec. 31, 1936, \$6,055.33, with vouchers and statements of W. W. Smith & Co., Ltd., attached.	R. 4465	118, 296	7
223	Canadian Company check to W. W. Smith & Company, Ltd., Apr. 15, 1937, \$3,239.58, with vouchers and statements of W. W. Smith & Co., Ltd. attached.	R. 4466	295, 296	5
224	Canadian Company check to W. W. Smith & Co., Ltd., Dec. 31, 1937, \$750, with voucher and statement of W. W. Smith & Co. attached.	R. 4466	101, 118, 295, 296	3
225	Canadian Company check to W. W. Smith & Co., Ltd., Dec. 31, 1937, \$1,811.91, with voucher and statement of W. W. Smith & Co. attached.	R. 4466	101, 118, 295, 296	3
226	Canadian Company check to W. W. Smith & Co., Ltd., Mar. 14, 1938, \$2,250, with vouchers and statements of W. W. Smith & Co. attached.	R. 4467	101, 295, 296	7
227	Canadian Company check to W. W. Smith & Co., Ltd., Mar. 14, 1938, \$6.171.26, with vouchers and statements of W. W. Smith & Co. attached.	R. 4467	101, 295, 296	7
228	McKesson & Robbins, Incorporated, Cash Report for Mar. 7, 1938.	R. 4469	68, 206	1
229	Imprint of rubber stamp reading "Payment for this invoice must be made in U. S. Currency" used on invoices of foreign crude drug sales.	R. 4469	80, 207	1
230	Copy McKesson & Robbins, Incorporated letter transmitting purchase order for 310 cadys of Musk Pods and authorizing D. C. Reynolds & Company, Ottawa, Canada, to draw on Manning & Company for same, Dec. 27, 1937.	R. 4470	72, 73, 214	1

Commission Exhibits—Continued

No.	Description	Received in Evidence Transcript Page No.	Referred to in Report at Page No.	Number of Pages in the Exhibit
231	Copy of McKesson & Robbins, Incorporated letter to Manning & Company, authorizing the honoring of above, Dec. 27, 1937.	R. 4471	72, 74, 214	1
232	McKesson & Robbins, Incorporated letter to Briggs, William & Sons, Lim., Dundee, Scotland, Feb. 4, 1938, re shipment 17 Cases Quinine Sulphate.	R. 4472	89, 117	1
233	McKesson & Robbins, Incorporated letter to African Soap & Chemical Works, Johannesburg, South Africa, Mar. 11, 1938, re shipment 15 Cases Oil of Lemon Sequiterpeneless.	R. 4472	89, 90, 117	1
234	McKesson & Robbins, Limited, Income Tax Return to the State of Connecticut, Apr. 3, 1935 to Dec. 31, 1935, with confirmations from five Canadian vendors stating inventories (foreign crude drugs) held in New Jersey as at Mar. 31, 1935 and Dec. 31, 1935.	R. 4473	107, 276	18
235	McKesson & Robbins, Incorporated (Maryland) Income Tax Return to the State of Connecticut, for calendar year 1934 with supporting work papers including allocation of invento.ies (foreign crude drug) as at Dec. 31, 1934 to New Jersey.	R. 4473	112, 276, 278	8
236	Memorandum of Arthur R. Tucker, Managing Director, Controllers Institute of America re duties and responsibilities of a controller.	R. 4481		6
237	Statement of George W. Burpee, American Institute of Consulting Engineers, in the matter of Engineering Verification of Inventories.	R. 4483		11
238	McKesson & Robbins, Incorporated requests for quotations on foreign crude drugs Apr. 26, 1938, with replying offers by Canadian vendors.	R. 4497	68, 118	
	A B. Miller & Company		69, 70	2
	B H. Monroe & Company			2
	C D. C. Reynolds & Company			2
	D A. H. Raymond & Company			2
	E P. Pierson & Company			2
	F Summary of offers		68, 70	1
239	Statement, Royal Bank of Canada, Canadian Company, Jan. 1936.	R. 4537	200	1
240	Letter from P. W. & Co. to F. D. Coster, Feb. 20, 1932, re audit of accounts at McKesson-Moore & Porterfield as at Dec. 31, 1931.	R. 4539	320	3
241	Letter from P. W. & Co. to F. D. Coster, Feb. 17, 1932, re audit of accounts at McKesson-Pacific Drug Company as at Dec. 31, 1931.	R. 4539	321	2
242	Letter from P. W. & Co. to F. D. Coster, Feb. 19, 1932, re audit of accounts at McKesson-Peter-Neat-Richardson Company as at Dec. 31, 1931.	R. 4539	318	3
243	Letter from P. W. & Co. to F. D. Coster, Feb. 20, 1932, re audit of accounts at McKesson-Schuh Drug Company as at Dec. 31, 1931.	R. 4539	317, 321	2
244	Letter from P. W. & Co. to F. D. Coster, Feb. 20, 1932, re audit of accounts at McKesson-Springfield Drug Company as at Dec. 31, 1931.	R. 4539	321	2
245	Letter from P. W. & Co. to F. D. Coster, Feb. 6, 1932, re audit of accounts at McKesson-Whittlesey Company as at Dec. 31, 1931.	R. 4539	321	3
246	Summary by J. H. McGloon of comments offered by P. W. & Co. on examinations at branches as at Dec. 31, 1934.	R. 4540	317, 318, 322	24

Commission Exhibits—Continued

No.	Description	Received in Evidence Transcript Page No.	Referred to in Report at Page No.	Number of Pages in the Exhibit
247	Letter from P. W. & Co. to F. D. Coster, Jan. 27, 1938, re audit of accounts at Schuh Drug Division as at Dec. 31, 1937.	R. 4541	317, 324	3
248	Letter from P. W. & Co. to F. D. Coster, Feb. 11, 1938, re audit of accounts at Billings Division as at Dec. 31, 1937.	R. 4541	323	2
249	Letter from P. W. & Co. to F. D. Coster, Feb. 18, 1938, re audit of accounts at McKesson Liquor Company, Boston, as at Dec. 31, 1937.	R. 4541	323	4
250	Letter from P. W. & Co. to F. D. Coster, Feb. 4, 1938, re audit of accounts at Milwaukee Drug Division as at Dec. 31, 1937.	R. 4541	324	2
251	Letter from P. W. & Co. to F. D. Coster, Feb. 3, 1938, re audit of accounts at Rochester Division as at Dec. 31, 1937.	R. 4541	324	2
252	Letter from P. W. & Co., St. Louis, to P. W. & Co., New York, Jan. 24, 1938, re defalcation at McKesson-Schuh Division and letter of P. W. & Co., New York, to J. H. McGloon, Jan. 28, 1938, and letter of P. W. & Co., New York, to P. W. & Co., St. Louis, Mar. 16, 1938, re above.	R. 4541	325	6
253	Summary of comments by P. W. & Co. on adequacy of internal check and control in units of McKesson & Robbins, Incorporated, following audits for 1931, 1934, and 1937.	R. 4542	319	2
254	Partial list of public offerings of securities of Girard & Co., Inc., McKesson & Robbins, Incorporated (Connecticut), McKesson & Robbins, Limited, and McKesson & Robbins, Incorporated (Maryland).	R. 4545		1
255	Schedule of Fictitious Transactions and Fictitious Assets, McKesson & Robbins, Incorporated, and McKesson & Robbins, Limited, Jan. 1, 1936, to Dec. 7, 1938, prepared by S. D. Leidesdorf & Co.	R. 4547	43, 44, 87, 98, 101, 221, 307, 355, 271.	1
256	Memorandum of S. D. Leidesdorf & Co. with supporting documents tracing the source of McKesson & Robbins, Incorporated's deposit in Bridgeport-City Trust Company on Dec. 30, 1930, of $34,224.00 and McKesson & Robbins, Limited's deposit of $33,279.75 in payment of foreign crude drug receivables to funds disbursed by McKesson & Robbins, Limited, in purchase of foreign crude drugs.	R. 4565	116	10
257	Exhibit prepared by S. D. Leidesdorf & Co. to illustrate "The Steps Gone through in the Tracing of Cash Going Out and Coming In to McKesson & Robbins, Incorporated" in settlement of foreign crude drug transactions.	R. 4573		1
258	Exhibit prepared by S. D. Leidesdorf & Co. showing fictitious inter-company sales as related to the payment of dividends by McKesson & Robbins, Limited.	R. 4586	99, 242	1
259	Prospectus on $1,650,000 7% Cumulative Participating Preferred Stock, McKesson & Robbins, Incorporated (Connecticut), offered in 1926.	Stipulation	27	1
260	Prospectus on $1,000,000 7% Cumulative Convertible Preference Stock, McKesson & Robbins, Limited offered in 1927.	Stipulation	28, 29, 30	1
261	P. W. & Co. financial statements, McKesson & Robbins, Incorporated (Connecticut Division), as of Dec. 31, 1937.	Stipulation	43, 44, 245, 311	5

Commission Exhibits—Continued

No.	Description	Received in Evidence Transcript Page No.	Referred to in Report at Page No.	Number of Pages in the Exhibit
262	Dec. 1937 Financial Report of J. H. McGloon to F. D. Coster, C. F. Michaels, W. J. Murray, Jr., J. F. Thompson and Divisional Vice Presidents dated Mar. 8, 1938, consisting of the following:	Stipulation		
	Letter of Transmittal			1
	Cover Sheet			1
	Form 1000:			
	Consolidated Balance Sheets as at Dec. 31, 1937 and 1936.			4
	Consolidated Profit and Loss Statements for the twelve months ending December 31, 1937 and 1936.			1
	Form 1001: Summary of Net Sales and Net Profits for Dec. 1937 and 1936.			2
	Form 1002: Summary of Net Sales and Net Profits for the twelve months ending Dec. 31, 1937 and 1936, together with Summary of Net Sales of Wines and Liquors and Gross Profit thereon.			3
	Form 1003: Summary of Net Sales and Net Profits of Wholesale Houses and Retail Stores for the month of Dec. 1937 and the twelve months ending Dec. 31, 1937 and 1936.			8
	Form 1004: Statement of Central Office and Home Office Expenses for the month of Dec. 1937 and the twelve months ending Dec. 31, 1937 and 1936.			9
	Connecticut Division:			
	Statement of Factory Burden for Dec. 1937 and 1936.			1
	Statements of Profit and Loss and Operating Expenses for the month of Dec. 1937 and the twelve months ending Dec. 1937.		312, 313	4
263	Dec. 1936 Report of J. H. McGloon to the President, Executive Vice President, Treasurer and Divisional Vice Presidents of McKesson & Robbins, Incorporated, dated Mar. 9, 1937, consisting of the following:	Stipulation		
	Letter of Transmittal			1
	Cover Sheet			1
	Form 1000:			
	Consolidated Balance Sheets as at Dec. 31, 1936 and 1935.			4
	Consolidated Profit and Loss Statements for the twelve months ending Dec. 31, 1936 and 1935.			1
	Form 1001: Summary of Net Sales and Net Profits for Dec. 1936 and 1935.			2
	Form 1002: Summary of Net Sales and Net Profits for the twelve months ending Dec. 31, 1936 and 1935, together with Summary of Net Sales of Wines and Liquors and Gross Profit thereon.			3
	Form 1003: Summary of Net Sales and Net Profits of Wholesale Houses and Retail stores for the month of Dec. 1936 and the twelve months ending Dec. 31, 1936 and 1935.			6

Commission Exhibits—Continued

No.	Description	Received in Evidence Transcript Page No.	Referred to in Report at Page No.	Number of Pages in the Exhibit
263	Dec. 1936 Report of J. H. McGloon, etc—Con.			
	Form 1004: Statement of Central Office and Home Office Expenses for the month of Dec. 1936 and for the twelve months ending Dec. 31, 1936 and 1935.	----------	----------	10
	Form 1005: Particulars regarding certain investments in securities of other companies as at Dec. 31, 1936.	----------	----------	1
	Statement of Factory Burden of the Connecticut Division for Dec. 1936 and 1935.	----------	----------	1
	Statements of Profit and Loss and Operating Expenses of the Connecticut Division for the month of December 1936 and the twelve months ending Dec. 31, 1936.	----------	----------	4
264	McKesson & Robbins, Incorporated (Connecticut Division) Cash Ticket, Nov. 30, 1938 (Foreign).	Stipulation..	92	1
265	13 McKesson & Robbins, Incorporated (Connecticut Division) Purchase Orders, Acctg. Dept. Copies, on Foreign Crude Drugs, Dec. 1937.	Stipulation..	76	13
266	McKesson & Robbins, Incorporated, (Maryland and Subsidiary Companies) Comptroller's Report Covering Operations for the year 1937, dated April 25, 1938, with supporting schedules.	Stipulation..	342	63
267	McKesson & Robins, Incorporated, Statement of Gross Sales, Returns and Allowances, Cost of Sales and Gross Profit for the Twelve Months ending Dec. 31, 1933 by classes of merchandise for the Connecticut Division.	Stipulation..	45, 93, 108, 247, 304, 309, 310.	2
268	P. W. & Co. Memorandum on Accounts, Connecticut Division, as at Dec. 31, 1934.	Stipulation..	86, 93, 229, 262, 274, 306.	6

Price, Waterhouse & Co. Exhibits

No.	Description	Received in Evidence Transcript Page No.	Referred to in Report at Page No.	Number of Pages in the Exhibit
A	Connecticut Division, perpetual inventory card	R. 724 Id., R. 1508.	16, 77	1
B	Journal entries adjusting inventories, Connecticut Division, as at Dec. 31, 1934.	R. 728	341	2
C	Correspondence re circularization of Receivables at McKesson Liquor Company, Boston, Mass.	R. 1608		
	(1) P. W. & Co., Boston to P. W. & Co., New York, Jan. 22, 1938.		317	1
	(2) P. W. & Co., New York, to P. W. & Co., Boston, Jan. 25, 1938.		317	1
	(3) P. W. & Co., New York, to J. H. McGloon, Jan. 25, 1938.		317	1
D	Copy of McKesson & Robbins, Incorporated request to D. C. Reynolds & Company to confirm to P. W. & Co. inventories held as at Dec. 31, 1935.	R. 1663	104	1
E	McKesson & Robbins, Incorporated Inventory Book Sheets, Book 7, Warehouse Crude Drugs (including foreign), Connecticut Company, as at Dec. 31, 1931.	R. 1678	91, 111, 282	2
F	McKesson & Robbins, Incorporated (Connecticut) Receiving Ticket, Apr. 30, 1932, on shipment from J. P. Meyer & Company, Brooklyn, New York.	R. 1710	66, 113, 284	1
G	Schedule of Directors' fees paid by Connecticut Company, 1932. (From P. W. & Co. work papers)	R. 2675 Id		1
H	Schedule of past-due customers accounts receivable, Canadian Company, as at Dec. 31, 1930. (From P. W. & Co. work papers)	R. 2678 Id	98	1
I	Cash reconciliation, Canadian Bank of Commerce, New York, Canadian Company, as at Dec. 31, 1936. (From P. W. & Co. work papers)	R. 4428	296	1
J	Schedule of Accounts Payable, Canadian Company, as at Dec. 31, 1936. (From P. W. & Co. work papers)	R. 4429	295, 296	1
K	Cash reconciliation, Bridgeport City Trust Company, Canadian Company, as at Dec. 31, 1937. (From P. W. & Co. work papers)	R. 4430	295, 296	1
L	Schedule of Accounts Payable, Canadian Company, as at Dec. 31, 1937. (From P. W. & Co. work papers)	R. 4430	101, 294, 296	1
M	Description of attached photocopies of documents in P. W. & Co. work papers and extracts from certain other documents in such work papers. (Items 1-27 from Connecticut Company (later Division) papers. Item 28 from Wholesalers Division and Item 29 from Canadian Company. See below for details.)	R. 4455		3

Price, Waterhouse & Co. Exhibits—Continued

No.	Work papers for examination as of December 31	Description	Referred to in Report at Page No.	Number of Pages in the Exhibit
M-1	1931	Abstracts from credit reports of crude drug customers purchasing through W. W. Smith & Co.	219, 221	2
M-2	1932	Source and application of funds statement	245	2
M-3	1932	Notes re internal control of cash	178, 180, 181	3
M-4	1932	Schedule of McKesson & Robbins, Incorporated checks discussed by Ritts with McGloon.		2
M-5	1932	Notes re receivables from United Drug & Chemical Corporation and balance sheet of United Drug & Chemical Corporation as of December 31, 1932 (from the 1933 Connecticut Division work papers).		2
M-6	1932	Notes on receivables from employees		1
M-7	1932	Notes on loan to F. D. Coster and photostat copy of letter obtained by McKesson & Robbins, Incorporated from their counsel dated April 27, 1932 re the legality of the loan.		3
M-8	1932	Schedule regarding work done in stock department		1
M-9	1932	Summary of slow moving stock		1
M-10	1932	Schedule regarding unrecorded liabilities	297	1
M-11	1933	Source and application of funds statement	245	3
M-12	1933	Schedule of McKesson & Robbins, Incorporated checks discussed by Ritts with McGloon.		1
M-13	1933	Notes regarding receivables from United Drug & Chemical Corporation and balance sheet of United Drug & Chemical Corporation as of December 31, 1933.		2
M-14	1933	Notes regarding fixed asset records	292	1
M-15	1933	Schedule of larger merchandise receipts during period Dec. 15 to 31, and a similar schedule for period subsequent to Jan. 1, 1934.	297	2
M-16	1933	Notes regarding payroll system of McKesson & Robbins, Incorporated.	178	1
M-17	1934	Manning & Co. confirmation showing that McKesson's balance was subject to withdrawal "by draft."	212	1
M-18	1934	Schedule of McKesson & Robbins, Incorporated checks discussed by Ritts with McGloon.		1
M-19	1934	United Drug & Chemical Corporation balance sheet as of December 31, 1934. (See comment in descriptive pages).		1
M-20	1934	A note regarding work done on fixed assets records. (See descriptive pages.)	293	0
M-21	1934	Notes on physical count of inventories	178, 283	1
M-22	1935	Notes regarding crude drug stock cards		1
M-23	1935	Schedule of McKesson & Robbins, Incorporated, checks discussed by Ritts with McGloon.		1
M-24	1936	Schedule of McKesson & Robbins, Incorporated, checks discussed by Ritts with McGloon.		1
M-25	1936	Notes on inventory books 1, 3, 6 and 10, regarding absence of initials on physical inventory summary sheets, and notarized certificate regarding the taking of inventory shown in book 10 (which contained the inventories at 79 Cliff Street, New York) dated Feb. 5, 1937.		5
M-26	1937	Notes on cash receipts	178	2
M-27	1937	Notes on accounts payable	76	2
M-28	1934, 1935 and 1936	Insurance schedules and and notes on insurance records	284, 291	8
M-29	1932	Letter from Ritts of P. W. & Co. to R. E. Thorn of P. W. & Co., dated January 27, 1933 regarding the accounts of the Limited Company.	298	2

Price, Waterhouse & Co. Exhibits—Continued

No.	Description	Received in Evidence Transcript Page No.	Referred to in Report at Page No.	Number of Pages in the Exhibit
N	Photocopies of schedules from files of P. W. & Co. furnished to them by McKesson & Robbins, Incorporated for the Connecticut Company (later Division). Note re source and use of schedules by P. W. & Co.	Stipulation	45, 93, 108, 220	1
	1. Statement of Sales, Cost of Sales and Gross Profit for the Twelve Months ending Dec. 1932 by classes of merchandise.		306	1
	2. Statement of Sales, less Returns, etc. Cost of Sales & Gross Profit for the year ending Dec. 31, 1933 by classes of merchandise.			1
	3. Statement of Gross Sales, Returns & Allowances, Cost of Sales, and Gross Profit for the Twelve Months ending Dec. 31, 1934 by classes of merchandise.		307	2
	4. Statement of Gross Sales, Returns and Allowances, Cost of Sales and Gross Profit for the 12 months Period ending Dec. 31, 1935 by classes of merchandise.		244, 307	1
	5. Statement of Gross Sales, Returns and Allowances, Cost of Sales and Gross Profit for the 12 month period ending Dec. 31, 1937, by classes of merchandise.		244, 307, 312	1
O	Manning & Company Confirmation to P. W. & Co. on Connecticut Company as at Dec. 31, 1931.	Stipulation	67, 204, 206, 212.	1
P	Same on Canadian Company as at Dec. 31, 1931	Stipulation	67, 204, 206, 212.	1
Q	Schedule of Crude Drug Inventories, Sales, Cost of Sales, and Gross Profit; and Accounts Receivable Resulting therefrom (as amended) for the Connecticut (later Division) and Canadian Companies, 1932 to 1937, inclusive, with notes re source of figures and reconciliation of figures shown on original Ex. 43 (includes some non-foreign figures for 1933, see footnote 892 *supra* and excludes some foreign for 1932, see footnote 119 *supra*).	stipulation	45, 46, 104, 108, 247, 261, 304, 306, 307, 310.	4